The Implementation of the EU Services Directive

Ulrich Stelkens · Wolfgang Weiß
Michael Mirschberger
Editors

The Implementation of the EU Services Directive

Transposition, Problems and Strategies

T·M·C·ASSER PRESS

Springer

Ulrich Stelkens
German Research Institute for Public Administration Speyer
German University of Administrative Sciences Speyer
Freiherr-vom-Stein-Straße 2
67324 Speyer
Germany

Michael Mirschberger
German Research Institute for Public Administration Speyer
Freiherr-vom-Stein-Straße 2
67324 Speyer
Germany

Wolfgang Weiß
German Research Institute for Public Administration Speyer
German University of Administrative Sciences Speyer
Freiherr-vom-Stein-Straße 2
67324 Speyer
Germany

ISBN 978-90-6704-839-2
e-ISBN 978-90-6704-840-8
DOI 10.1007/978-90-6704-840-8

Library of Congress Control Number: 2011946236

Published by T.M.C. ASSER PRESS, The Hague, The Netherlands www.asserpress.nl
Produced and distributed for T.M.C. ASSER PRESS by Springer-Verlag Berlin Heidelberg

Printed on acid-free paper

Springer is part of Springer Science+Business Media (www.springer.com)

Preface

The Services Directive is one of the most recent cornerstones in the realisation of the internal market and has attracted a lot of attention both from the general public and from economic and legal experts, in part due to the considerable share services contribute to the GDP of the Member States. The Services Directive was one of the subjects of the 2008 FIDE congress. After quite a long period of deliberation and legislation and heated debates, including between and within European institutions, it was finally adopted in 2006 and was to be transposed into domestic law by the end of 2009. This book presented here is an attempt to take stock of the impact the Services Directive had on the national administrative regulations of the Member States now that the transposition period is over and the Member States have for the most part transposed the exigencies of the directive into their domestic rules.

This volume on the legal implementation of the Services Directive is the result of the collective endeavour of the participants of a Europe-wide legal research project conducted by the editors under the umbrella of the German Research Institute for Public Administration Speyer (Deutsches Forschungsinstitut für Öffentliche Verwaltung Speyer; [http://www.foev-speyer.de/EU-DLR]). It will first of all explain and analyse in detail the different steps taken by each individual Member State in the implementation process of the directive, thus not only providing information about the changes in national law adopted by the Member States (which is good to have for anyone interested in doing business within the EU), but also allowing for a comparison of the different implementation strategies applied by the Member States. Beyond that, it will allow certain basic conclusions to be drawn from this comparison as regards the heterogeneity or homogeneity of implementation concepts and the varying impact that the Services Directive has had on national services regulations, in particular the relevant administrative rules. One can observe, for example, that some Member States used the transposition to implement far reaching alterations of domestic administrative law and intensely modernise the citizen-state/public administration relationship, whereas others made reforms only where absolutely demanded by the Services Directive. The Services Directive shows how European legislation touches even those fields of legislation originally nationally dominated, such as the law of national administration. The volume will also illustrate, by taking the Services Directive as an example, which basic problems arise when European law interferes with established domestic administrative structures and national legislative/dogmatic concepts and traditions in administrative law as well as how deep the impact of the European legislation can be in different administrative traditions in Europe. Thus, this implementation study hopes to raise the awareness of European institutions regarding the specific conditions and problems in the different national transposition contexts, all the more so since EU law after the Lisbon Treaty is often seen as demanding greater respect for fundamental national structures and different legal traditions (allegedly derived from Art. 4 (2) TEU). Analysing and comparing the national transpositions of the EU Member States also allow verifying whether the expectations of the European Commission for cooperation between the Member States in their implementation endeavours and for the development of common examples of best practice have finally been met. If so, this implementation study could form a starting point for further research with regard to the question of which administrative tradition and conception could drive European institutions in their legislative processes, at least as regards the Services Directive.

The aforementioned project started in August/September 2009 with the establishment of the expert network and ended in September 2010. Most reports, therefore, reflect the national situation regarding the implementation process around July 2010 in the respective Member State, though some have been updated since then. The research project was inspired by the difficulties in the transposition process in Germany and by the approach finally adopted by German legislators, which saw the transposition used to initiate ground breaking reforms of core administrative laws in Germany, driven by an awareness of the need for modernisation that went well beyond the requirements of the directive. In order to ensure a common research focus and that the same questions were addressed the participants were provided with a detailed questionnaire to guide their enquiry. This questionnaire and the associated explanations are included as an annex to the general comparative report.

Initially the volume intended to gather the national reports on the implementation results of the Services Directive in all 27 EU Member States and then draw comparative conclusions on the research questions alluded to above. However, during the project period there were some changes as regards the participation of legal experts from some countries. In the end, the only Member State of the European Union that is unfortunately missing in this volume is Greece. Due to the current crises in Greece there are several problems in its public administration/ sector, hence our participants could not provide a final version of the implementation of the Services Directive for this publication. This is very disappointing for us, but we still can provide an overview of the other 26 Member States. The volume profits not only from the expertise of each contributor about his/her national jurisdiction but also from an intensive exchange of views and common analysis of the similarities and differences in the implementation processes which took place at a symposium in Speyer in April 2010. This symposium was kindly supported by the Fritz Thyssen Foundation (http://www.fritz-thyssen-stiftung.de), for which we would like to extend our thanks once again.

We finally would like to thank all the participants for their willingness to take part in this research and to redraft their reports several times due to new developments in the implementation process. Furthermore, we thank the German Research Institute for Public Administration Speyer for their contribution to the funding of the research. Moreover, we thank Hanna Schröder, LL.M. and Olivia Seifert, Ass. Jur., for their excellent help at the symposium. Furthermore, we would like to thank Marion Pfundstein for her valuable support at the symposium and during the whole book project.

July 2011 The Editors

Contents

Part I
Comparative Perspective

General Comparative Report on the Research Project 'The Implementation of the Services Directive in the EU Member States' of the German Research Institute for Public Administration Speyer

Ulrich Stelkens, Wolfgang Weiß and Michael Mirschberger

1 Introduction

Function of the General Report

This general and comparative report demonstrates the main guidelines of the implementation of the Services Directive (SD) in the Member States of the European Union (EU). This overview serves as a general summary and analysis of the implementation and, therefore, cannot substitute for the national reports in this book. Hence, for more details the reader is referred to the reports or references given.

This general report is based on the results and assessments of the national reports enclosed in this book, which were drafted according to a common questionnaire (see the Annex to this chapter) during the end of 2009 through September

Univ.-Prof. Dr. Ulrich Stelkens is Professor of Public Law and German and European Administrative Law at the German University of Administrative Sciences Speyer; Univ.-Prof. Dr. Wolfgang Weiß is Professor of Public Law, European Law and Public International Law at the German University of Administrative Sciences Speyer and Professor of International law at Oxford Brookes University, UK. Both Professors are also fellows of the German Research Institute for Public Administration Speyer. Ass. Jur. Michael Mirschberger is a research assistant at the German Research Institute for Public Administration Speyer.

U. Stelkens (✉) · W. Weiß · M. Mirschberger
German Research Institute for Public Administration Speyer,
German University of Administrative Sciences Speyer, Speyer, Germany

W. Weiß
Oxford Brookes University, Oxford, UK

U. Stelkens et al. (eds.), *The Implementation of the EU Services Directive*,
DOI: 10.1007/978-90-6704-840-8_1,

2010 (and partially updated later on). Therefore, statements with regard to certain Member States and implementation of the SD therein are based not only on information provided in these reports, but have also been slightly amended by official documents of the European Commission. Due to the length of time the implementation of the SD took, even beyond the expiry of the transposition period, certain legislation and data given in the survey may have changed again. Furthermore, it may well be the case that the specifics of certain Member States in the transposition of the SD highlighted in this general report are shared by other legal systems not being explicitly mentioned here, due to the fact that these specifics are not or cannot be reported in the national reports.

Research Motivation

The motivation for this research was the German method of implementation, since the implementation process was discussed in Germany very intensively, for various reasons: first, and in particular, because of its federal system and, second, because the implementation process was assessed as an opportunity to modernise administrative law in general terms. Every single provision of the SD was diligently examined as to its need for transposition both by legal scholars and in the course of the political process of transposition. The huge legal and political effort in transposing the SD is evidenced by the very existence of a legal commentary[1] solely dedicated to the SD[2] that comments on every single article and analyses how each can be interpreted and applied. It is quite unusual to have a standalone commentary that reflects all the provisions of a piece of secondary EU legislation in Germany. Furthermore, there have been several monographs primarily on the SD itself, and not just on the implementation of its requirements. Because of the intense discussion and observance of the SD itself and its implementation into the German administrative legal system, the German method of implementation could, in our point of view, engender criteria for implementation concepts and strategies in other Member States as well.

Research Method

Based on the discussions among German scholars and administrative and political bodies, we elaborated a questionnaire containing questions primarily pertaining to the implementation's strategy, the inducement of changes by the SD in the national legal order, and possible spillover effects to other areas of (administrative) law.

---

[1] There is a long and widespread tradition of commentaries on statutes in the German legal literature written by both judicial practitioners and legal scholars. Every piece of main legislation has been the subject of at least one but usually several commentaries. The commentaries include interpretations of the legal text combined with analyses of and references to related jurisprudence of the courts, as well as references to monographs, journal articles, and so forth. Hence, commentaries are a cornerstone of the German scholarly system, at least regarding daily legal practice. Usually only important pieces of legislation are subject to such commentaries.

[2] Schlachter and Ohler (2008).

Furthermore, questions on the implementation of certain articles of the SD in concreto were provided. This questionnaire was sent to colleagues and practitioners in administrations who are experts in the administrative and European law. They prepared their corresponding country reports on the implementation of the SD according to the issues covered in the questionnaire. As already mentioned in the preface, we initially managed to find reporters from all 27 Member States. Unfortunately, in the end, the current problems in Greece did not allow an up-to-date full report from Greece, so the published research now covers 26 Member States.

Several participants of the research network thus created met in Speyer at the end of April 2010 for a symposium that was kindly supported by the Fritz Thyssen Foundation to specify the questionnaire in more detail and have comparative discussions of the initial research results. Discussing problems of the implementation process and crucial requirements of the SD itself was a vital and important step forward to a comparative perspective on the implementation of the SD in the EU. The symposium also served to identify further specific issues to be highlighted more explicitly in the national reports to elucidate more clearly communalities and differences in the implementation strategy.

The reports of the experts from each Member State can be found in the following chapters and comprises the basis of this general comparative report.

Additional Benefits and Amendments of European Commission Reports

The European Commission published a broad and detailed report on the results of the so-called mutual evaluation process with SEC(2011) 102_final.[3] This process derives from the procedure imposed on the Member States in Article 39 SD. All Member States had to report to the European Commission the measures they had taken to fulfil the requirements of Articles 9, 15, 16, and 25 SD to the European Commission until 28 December 2009 (the so-called "self-assessment reports"). After that there was a period of mutual evaluation based on these reports by working groups of several Member States, meeting in plenary sessions with all Member States to discuss the implementation of the above-mentioned articles of the SD in the Member States. The European Commission document presents the results of this process.

For this book's research topic, these EU documents (as well as others; see the References) can be seen as a marvellous amendment. The report(s) of the European Commission concentrate(s) on a 'negative' transposition approach, whereas the research covered in this book concentrates on a 'positive' approach. This means that the EU documents deliver detailed information from the perspective where national administrative regulations pertaining to providing services within the scope of the SD have been maintained and how this maintenance is justified by the Member States, by recourse to justifications and exceptions

[3] This report is available at http://eur-lex.europa.eu/LexUriServ/LexUriServ.do?uri=SEC:2011:0102:FIN:EN:PDF and builds the basis for COM (2011) 20_final.

(allegedly) stated in the SD. In contrast, our research focuses more on the positive aspects of change caused by the actual transposition and the improvements and alterations induced by the implementation of the SD. As a consequence, legal and political stakeholders gain from two assessments of the transposition process made from two different but complementary perspectives: On the one hand, there is the EU documentation on what has been maintained despite the requirements of the SD and, on the other hand, our research, which focuses on the way national administrative law systems have adapted to the new requirements. Our research also analyses which general improvements of national administrative law were adopted in the course of the transposition of the SD and which consequences and political agenda settings create the blueprint of the national transposition. In a nutshell, the European Commission's view assesses the SD implementation from the view of lowering hurdles on the Internal Market (a transnational perspective),[4] whereas our perspective looks closer at the Member States and their adaptation efforts within their national administrative law tradition, trying to find commonalities (a national perspective, in comparison).

2 Comparison

1. General Remarks on the Transposition Strategy and General Comprehension of the Implementation

1.1 Main References Used in this Research

Please indicate the main references of your research (e.g., parliamentary documents and laws implementing the SD or adopted for the occasion of transposition…). We would be very pleased if you could indicate the place of publication, particularly if available online.

In general, the main references for the research of all participants have been—as might be expected—the documents accompanying the implementation process, including, first of all, the passed legislation itself, in conjunction with the corresponding parliamentary documents issued by the legislative bodies of each Member State. Usually the Member States adopted both a horizontal law (which provided for specific rules on the provision of services) and a vertical law, which contained the necessary amendments to specific administrative laws and regulations. This applies even to federal states or states with strong autonomous regions, such as Spain, which adopted a horizontal 'umbrella law', and Austria, which plans to transpose the SD at the federal level through a federal law (in addition to bills already passed by the Austrian states) whose adoption, however, requires a

[4] See SEC (2011) 102_final, pp. 4 ff.

still-pending amendment to the Austrian constitution (for most recent developments and changes on this issue see the comment of the authors of the Austrian report on page 65). In Ireland, the transposition of the SD was achieved merely by adopting a statutory instrument (European Communities Regulations 2010). In Italy, as well as in Portugal, the transposition was—besides single amendments—accomplished by legislative decree. It is worth mentioning that in Italy's case, initially amendments on special single issues were adopted before the legislative decree was passed by the government. This seems to be unique, since usually the transposition took place the other way round. In Romania a horizontal government decree was approved by parliament to implement the SD. Those Member States with a federal system had to pass laws and regulations at diverse levels of government. Germany did so without introducing a specific services law: It transposed the procedural stipulations of the SD by amending its General Administrative Procedure Acts.[5] In addition, France did not choose a horizontal implementation but, rather, a sectoral one.

Particularly remarkable seems to be the documentation of the implementation in the Netherlands. As far as we can assess, no other Member State published such an intensive discussion process regarding the implementation of the SD.

Some Member States initiated the implementation process only quite recently, and it usually took a long time for transposition legislation to be passed. Although there may be different reasons for the delays, it must be stated that the given deadline for transposition in Article 44 (1) SD, 28 December 2009, was not met by several countries. Several countries already implemented the main parts of the SD but have yet to finalise certain amendments.[6] Thus, it does not come as surprise that the European Commission had to initiate proceedings against seven Member States for failure to comply with EU law under Article 258 Treaty on the Functioning of the European Union (TFEU) due to lack of complete transposition of the SD.

1.2 Impact of the Services Directive

Did the transposition of the SD give a profound cause to the national legislator to alter—beyond the minimum requirements and a one-to-one transposition of the SD—administrative laws in general?

Concerning the impact of the SD to induce fundamental changes or reforms in public administration or to alter national codifications of administrative law or administrative legislation, the survey highlights that, apparently, in general, there has been only very limited impetus in this regard. Most participants report that there was no cause or only little cause to alter pre-existing administrative laws

[5] The German Federation and states do—with some exceptions—have own general administrative procedure acts.

[6] See the notice from the Council of the European Union of 26 February 2010 on the state of implementation of the SD, available at http://ec.europa.eu/internal_market/services/docs/services-dir/implementation/20100301_council_en.pdf. In addition, still recognising the yet to be finalised implementation, SEC (2011) 102_final, p. 9; see also COM (2011) 20_final, pp. 8 and 12.

in general. In Bulgaria, Denmark, Estonia, Finland, Ireland, Italy, Latvia, Romania, Slovakia, and the United Kingdom, more or less no cause for further general changes was perceived. As far as the partially still pending implementation in Luxembourg is concerned, probably the final implementation will not lead to a profound change in the existing system of administrative law in general either; the restrictive scope of the tacit authorisation especially indicates this. In Austria, Belgium, Cyprus, the Czech Republic, France, Lithuania, the Netherlands, Portugal (seeing impact only in certain parts of administrative law), Slovenia, and Sweden, the national rapporteurs see a certain impetus for the national legislator, but usually not beyond the SD's requirements and not in a profound way but, instead, usually limited to selective aspects. Generally speaking, in these countries the SD did release changes in administrative laws (and, partly, there were many of them), but these changes were not seen as a profound change in administrative law in general. Regarding Malta, the SD was used as an impetus for the general liberalisation of services markets and engendered general and universal standards beyond a mere minimum transposition. Besides Germany, only in Spain did the rapporteurs recognise a considerable and profound impact of the SD, since it gave profound cause for altering administrative laws *in general*.[7] In Poland, at least, a profound change in the system of administrative economic law in general can be observed.

All in all, one can conclude that Germany was the only country in Europe that used the implementation of the SD to implement new and potentially generally applicable administrative procedures beyond the scope of the SD, given the restriction in altering the General Administrative Procedure Act in Spain by introducing tacit authorisation only and the still existing uncertainties about the extension of SD standards to economic stakeholders and citizens in Ireland.

The reports also evidence that the establishment of Points of Single Contact (POSCs), procedural simplifications, particularly the introduction/considerable extension of a tacit (fictitious) authorisation, and the establishment of a system of administrative assistance appears to be the most important features of the SD-stipulated changes for national administrative law.

Furthermore, it seems quite peculiar that in Lithuania, and to some extent Ireland (where the importance of the transposition of the SD has been primarily viewed through the prism of its importance to further liberalise the services sector) and Poland, the SD is primarily perceived in light of economic matters, and not in regard to administration. This seems to relocate the focus of the implementation and has, of course, consequences for the implementation process. In addition, in other Member States, the implementation was carried out and/or coordinated by those ministries competent in economics, of course, but nevertheless the discussion and focus of the implementation in these other Member States seem to pertain more to legal questions in the context of administration than to pure economic views. Hence, in all Member States economic growth through lowering hurdles for

[7] See also SEC (2011) 102_final, p. 9: most requirements have been reported to the EU by Germany, the Netherlands, Spain and Austria.

transnational service provision was seen as the *reason* for the SD and its implementation, but the *implementation itself* was seen in most cases from an administrative law perspective, and not from an economic one.

Which authorities and partners were involved in the transposition process? Did close cooperation and coordination with the several levels of administration take place?

First of all, there is a commonality in that in all Member States those ministries competent in economics take a decisive role in the implementation process (although in different contexts and with divergences in detail). In Austria, Belgium, Bulgaria, the Czech Republic, Denmark, Estonia, Finland, France, Germany, Ireland, Lithuania, Luxembourg (with the Ministry of State), Malta, the Netherlands, Poland, Portugal, Slovakia, and the United Kingdom, the ministry responsible for the economy took over the supervising and coordinating role in the transposition process, partly together with other (state) institutions and ministries.

In the case of Denmark, the so-called Danish Internal Market Centre took leadership over the implementation, but this centre is organised by the ministry competent in economics together with the Danish Enterprise and Construction Authority. In Latvia the coordination was conducted by the Cabinet of Ministers, with the Ministry of Economics also taking a decisive role in this regard.

Interestingly Lithuania hired a private law firm to assist in identifying legal areas to be changed or amended due to the provisions of the SD. Moreover, a working group installed by the prime minister was established to prepare the horizontal legislative transposition in Lithuania (alongside the competence of the Ministry of Economy). Since the transposition was seen more from an economic point of view in Lithuania, subsequently the Ministry of Interior Affairs has not been part of this working group.

In Cyprus the already existing Planning Bureau, a public office under the auspices of the Ministry of Finance and competent in matters of economic and social growth, took the lead in the transposition process.

In Hungary and Sweden, the coordinative role was surprisingly (for us) assigned to the Ministry for Foreign Affairs. Romania delegated the overall coordinative role in the transposition process to the Department for European Affairs, which is subordinate to the prime minister's office, while special working groups of representatives of different ministries worked on certain parts of the transposition.

In Spain, inter-ministerial cooperation in coordinating the implementation of the SD was established since the beginning.

In Italy it appears that the government in general was mandated by parliament to conduct the implementation process by legislative decree. Despite this mandate, several governmental departments and levels of government have been involved. The screening process was coordinated by the Department for EU Policies. In Ireland as well, implementation was assigned to the government that adopted a statutory instrument.

In addition to the general supervising institutions, further ministries, representatives of municipalities, non-governmental organisations, trade organisations, chambers, and so forth (including stakeholders in general) have been involved in the legislative process in nearly every Member State. It is not clear whether this involvement is the standard procedure for passing bills in all Member States; probably it is. The Polish report explicitly states that the usual legislative procedure took place. Furthermore, the Czech report explains the usual way of preparing legislative drafts for parliament.

Member States with a federal organisation had to involve further state authorities. This was accomplished by establishing or, if already existing, using certain inter-level groups to coordinate the implementation throughout the whole country (e.g., Austria and Germany). In addition, certain non-federal states such as Denmark or Finland set up inter-organisational working groups to cover all facets of the SD in the implementation process.

In sum, intensive cooperation took place within each Member State. This may be linked to the fact that the SD affects one of the most important branches of the national economy, one with a lot of stakeholder interest. Furthermore, one should bear in mind the very controversial debate and genesis of the SD and the public's and stakeholder's reactions in the Member States. Thus accurate preparation of the transposition appears necessary to ensure that all relevant economic and social groups go along with the implementation. There is only one Member State in which at least a *close* cooperation on all levels of government has been reported as not perceptible: In Estonia, the municipalities were not identified as involved partners, but only as units that have to be informed about the process without being part of it.

1.3 (National) Scope of Application

What is, according to the (prevailing) opinion in your Member State, the directive's scope of application? Are the requirements of the SD perceived as binding only for providing transnational services/for transnational establishment, or are at least Articles 5-15 SD also seen as compulsory for the Member States with regard to purely domestic services/establishment?

Regarding the scope of the SD, there are two different positions among the Member States.[8] Irrespective of the application of the transposing instruments to domestic service providers, many of Member States perceive the SD to be binding for transnational services only.

In Cyprus, Denmark, (probably) Hungary, Ireland, Latvia, Luxembourg, Malta, (partially) Poland, Slovakia, (partially) Slovenia, (probably) Spain, and the United Kingdom, the scope of the SD was not seen as limited to transnational service providers, but was perceived as encompassing also domestic service providers.

[8] This reflects the different positions in the legal literature. See, for example, Barnard (2008), pp. 351–352, 389; Hessel (2009), pp. 84–85.

Several rapporteurs could not answer this question, since there has been no debate or even a prevailing opinion about this issue in their countries.

A different question is whether the national rules transposing the SD are applicable to domestic service providers as well. This problem is dealt with in the following paragraph.

Can only transnational service providers refer to the laws/regulations implementing the SD? Or are the implementing laws/regulations applicable also to domestic service providers and, if so, to what extent?

According to the present reports, in transposing the requirements of the SD, a great majority of Member States extended (sometimes only partly, e.g., with regard to procedural rights only) the scope of application to domestic service providers as well. This was mainly based on the assessment that national service providers would otherwise suffer from discrimination and thus be weakened in competition. It is, however, not always clear whether the Member States extended the rules to domestic services for domestic and particularly constitutional reasons alone (as was done in Slovenia) or because they perceived the SD to be binding with regard to national services as well.

Only two Member States[9] do not grant the equal treatment of domestic service providers: In Austria, the new transposing rules do not apply to domestic service providers at all. In the Czech Republic, the transposition was limited to transnational service providers, at least to a great extent; daily practice regarding POSCs in the Czech Republic seems to be different, in any case. In Finland, the general perception is that the SD regulates transnational activities, but since this perception has not been explicitly spelled out anywhere in the transposing legal rules, these rules may very well be applied to domestic service providers too. Similarly, in Estonia now, the transposing rules can be applied to domestic services and even beyond, to providers of goods. In the Netherlands, basically there is no equal treatment either, but as regards the POSCs, tacit authorisation and Internal Market Information System (IMI) equal treatment are granted to domestic service providers. The situation in Sweden, where only partially equal treatment applies, is comparable.

Are the laws/regulations implementing the SD also applicable (fully or partly) to everybody, that is, do they engender general and universal standards for the way authorities deal with all citizens or all economic stakeholders, so that these laws/regulations can be claimed by everybody?

---

[9] This is true for Member States as a whole. In Germany, for instance, the Free State of Bavaria did not grant equal treatment to their domestic service providers, arguing that they would be familiar with the existing system of public economic law anyway.

Regarding the question of whether the newly implemented laws are applicable to other economic stakeholders, besides domestic service providers, or even beyond, in relation to every citizen, the results are much more heterogeneous.

Only in the Czech Republic (as regards the daily practice of POSCs), Estonia, (potentially) Germany (but not yet in use, as far as perceptible), Latvia, Italy, Poland, Portugal, Slovakia, Slovenia, and Sweden (as regards POSCs) are the transposing rules also (potentially) applicable to businesspersons besides service providers. This may not be very surprising. Considering, however, that most Member States extended their implementation legislation (though sometimes only partially) to domestic services providers and surpass the SD′s minimum requirements in their implementation (assuming that the SD does not require the extension to domestic service providers), the additional step to an even more encompassing scope of application could not have been too far away. Obviously this step was too ambitious.

The application of the newly introduced implementation legislation in relations between citizens and authority, in all potential ways, has been established in Estonia, Germany, Latvia, Portugal, Slovenia, and probably, as regards the POSC, in Sweden. In Finland, it is assumed that the new rules could analogously be applied to the relation between citizens and authority. Similarly, the Irish rapporteurs assume that citizens might finally benefit from the implementation in Ireland as well, even though there is currently no legal source for such extension, but judicial clarification on that matter is expected in the future.

In Bulgaria, the new implementing rules are seen as applicable erga omnes; hence we assume that the rules are applicable even to other businesspersons and citizens.

It is interesting that, for example, in Portugal the implementing decree is also partially applicable to the service providers of third countries, that is, countries outside the European Economic Area.

In case your Member State did not treat transnational and domestic service providers equally, what was the intention for this? Was there at least a discussion about equal treatment?

As indicated above, Austria does not treat transnational and domestic service providers alike since Austria did not want to go beyond a mere minimum transposition. In Austria this is a consequence of the requirement of a (still pending) amendment to the Austrian Constitution.

In the case of the Czech Republic, equal treatment was not directly provided, but, besides applying to the practice of the POSCs, the implementing law also repealed temporal limitations of licences for domestic service providers. Nevertheless, it is stated that the implementing law only refers to transnational situations.

The fact that certain Member States did not grant equal treatment to the full extent can obviously be explained by the argument that, in their view, equal treatment does not call for more.

As far as Finland and Estonia, however, this question appears not to have been discussed during transposition.

1.4 Incorporation of Transposing Legislation

How and to what extent were the requirements of the SD relating to administrative proceedings implemented in your Member State?

Most Member States implemented (as far as the laws that were already passed) requirements via a so-called horizontal approach. Usually there was one horizontal law in the national administrative laws implementing basic provisions or giving certain basic definitions. Additionally, there have been sectoral changes and amendments.[10]

Germany and France did not choose the horizontal approach; Germany could not do so due to its federal system. Spain explicitly divided the implementation legislation into an umbrella law and an omnibus law. In Belgium, the German-speaking community chose not to opt for a horizontal law for implementation, whereas the other regions obviously did.

Did your Member State incorporate the new rules/regulations into existing statutes or was a new codification passed?

Most Member States established both new codifications and amendments and changes to existing statutes. A considerable number of Member States codified new laws for the implementation of the SD, which is supposed to be the paramount source of law for (transnational) service provision (i.e., lex specialis), such that the general rules on administrative law do not apply. Austria and Slovakia, for example, adopted this approach.

1.5 Relationship of the Services Directive to Primary EU Law

How is the relation of the SD to Articles 43 and 49 EC Treaty (now Articles 49 and 56 TFEU) assessed?

Have any problems been identified in this context?

With the exception of Slovenia, the relation of the SD to primary EU law (now Articles 49 and 56 TFEU) was not been intensely discussed by the Member States in general, if there was any discussion at all (e.g., there was none at all in Estonia). It does not come as a surprise that the SD was assessed as a clarification and specification of primary EU law and that the SD must be interpreted in light of primary EU law.

---

[10] Also in accordance with the results in the recent notice from the Council of the European Union of 26 February 2010; see footnote 6.

Accordingly, only a few problems were identified concerning the relation of the SD to primary EU law. Many countries, such as the United Kingdom and Spain, did not identify any problems. One particular point mentioned, for example, in the reports from Denmark, the Netherlands, Lithuania, Germany, and Sweden, was the limitation of justifications (in the parlance of the Court of Justice of the EU, 'imperative requirements in the general interest'[11]) in Article 16 (1), (3) SD to the narrow grounds listed there ('reasons of public policy, public security, public health or the protection of the environment'). Apparently this wording was seen as exhaustive, and no recourse to primary EU law was deemed possible.[12] This is assessed differently in the Romanian report.

A rather intensive discussion took place in the Netherlands regarding the question of whether there should be a direct transposition of Article 16 SD. Finally, a direct transposition was assessed as not being necessary, since it is assumed that the de facto behaviour of the authorities sufficiently safeguards the requirements. There were also discussions on whether services of general economic interest are included in the SD or not. The Austrian report complains about the poor wording in parts of the SD and about several gaps that can result in future problems.

Some reports address the question of which consequences the SD engenders with regard to services outside its scope. All reports dealing with this question agree in that, at least in this regard, primary EU law or other specific directives apply.

The Czech report discusses the influence of the SD on jurisprudence in the Czech Republic, but concludes that there will be no real change. Furthermore, the report states that the freedom to provide services deriving from primary EU law has been 'neglected' in the last years and that therefore the SD is viewed as a sort of 'new' perspective in this regard.

The question of whether the SD can have a direct effect (within its scope) has been treated by some of the reports. The Estonian report, for instance, sees room for a direct effect in some areas, whereas, for instance, the Portuguese report does not. Thus, there is no detectable prevailing opinion as far as this aspect is addressed in the reports.

---

[11] Court of Justice of the European Union, Case C-55/94 (1995), ECR, I-4165, para 37, Gebhard.

[12] Even though the Court of Justice of the European Union (ECJ) holds that primary EU law exceptions to fundamental freedoms cannot justify national derogations from EU secondary law (see van de Gronden and de Waele (2010), pp. 397, 410), the question remains as to whether the SD as a secondary legal instrument conforms to primary EU law (cf. Barnard (2008), p. 367; van de Gronden and de Waele, ibid., pp. 411–415, who expect the ECJ to interpret the SD́s justification clauses more broadly to bring them in line with its jurisprudence on exceptions to the fundamental freedoms).

1.6 Screening

How did your Member State accomplish the 'screening' in concreto (e.g., authorities concerned, committees, division of tasks), and what were the results?

The screening of national law for its conformity with the SD's requirements has been a great challenge to the Member States. Although there are huge differences in detail with regard to screening in the Member States, the process has been driven in a rather complex and challenging way.[13] Basically, the screening took place in a sectoral approach, which means that every ministry and, particularly in federal systems, every level of government had to screen its regulations as a matter of its own responsibility and competence. Some rapporteurs mention assistance specifically provided by the central government or other institutions or expert opinions in the screening process (e.g., Austria and Lithuania). Most often the ministry competent in economics took over the leading and coordinative role in the screening process (except, e.g., in Italy, Hungary, Romania, and Sweden).

In Austria, Salzburg University conducted a study to identify demands for legislative amendments. In Belgium, the Agency for Administrative Simplification supervised and supported the screening process. In the Netherlands, as in many other Member States, leaflets, courses, and information in form of 'Frequently Asked Questions' were provided for the screening process to help the screening authorities. Many countries established specific task forces, working groups, or committees (e.g., Cyprus, France, Germany, Ireland, Malta, Romania, Spain, Sweden, and the United Kingdom). In Germany, a complex screening raster containing many questions to identify the needs of adaptation (about 50 A4 paper pages) was elaborated by a special task force. This raster was transformed into an electronic raster available to all authorities competent for the screening. Thus not only the data of the screening but also the data for the report to the European Commission could be electronic way. In addition, Lithuania provided an electronic information system for the screening, called TAPIS, and involved more than 100 state institutions and municipalities in the screening process.

Besides the aforementioned study of the University of Salzburg in Austria, in Finland, Lithuania, and Poland external agencies and experts were involved in the screening process.

Some of the rapporteurs describe the individual steps of the screening process. The basic steps should be the same for every country (although, of course, there are always country-specific differences): first, identifying those areas affected because they fall under the scope of the SD; second, identifying certain provisions in these areas needing amendments or alterations; and, finally, decision framing/ drafting the necessary amendments or alterations of the single provisions.

Furthermore it should be noted that Spain established 'collaboration lines' for the municipalities, where big municipalities acted as role models for the

---

13 Not all Member States conducted their screening in comparably complex ways (see SEC (2011) 102_final, p. 9).

implementation and passed on their experience to smaller municipalities. Additionally, the Spanish government established a special application and control mechanism to monitor municipal screening.

As for the results of the screening, due to the complexity of the task, only some specifics could be given in the reports.[14] In France, the screening was not transparent enough to provide further information. The following presents some of the remarkable points of these reports.

In Belgium, at the federal level more acts were maintained than amended, and in the French-speaking community the pre-screening did not indicate that further action was necessary at all. In Bulgaria, as a result of the screening, seven acts are to be amended. In addition, in Denmark, only a few adjustments were identified as compulsory. In Italy more than 300 administrative procedures were screened. At the Italian regional level, most regulations were kept on the assumption that they do not contradict the SD. In Latvia, 69 legal acts were identified as requiring amendments and changes. In the Netherlands, the screening started at the national level as early as in 2006 and led, together with subsequent regional/local screenings, to the perception that there was only a very limited need for adaptation, which was justified by the active role deregulation has played in recent years. In contrast, Portugal identified a huge range of areas that needed to be changed. In Romania, 52 acts had to be amended. In Slovakia, 36 acts had to be amended, besides the passing of a new horizontal law. The overall finding from the Slovenian screening was that there is no direct discrimination in the national legislation of the service providers of other Member States, but some indirect discrimination can be identified. In Sweden, at the national level, changes were identified in 20 acts, and at the municipal level only a few changes were identified as well.

It is interesting and surprising that the duty of the screening described by Articles 5, 9, 15, and 25 SD in combination with Article 39 SD was assessed as a great challenge, whereas in none of the Member States[15] was the cross-sectoral screening of all national legal norms, with regard to their compatibility with the administrative simplification requirements of the SD—together with the duty to report these results to the European Commission and to give reasons why certain national provisions were maintained[16]—perceived as an exchange of the active role at the European level. For, now it is the Member States that must deliver information to the European Commission that can be used by it to impose infringement proceedings upon the Member States. Hence a change in the roles of the Member States and the European Commission has taken place: The burden of proving the national law′s compatibility with European law—here the SD—has

[14] Further details can be found in SEC (2011) 102_final, at least regarding the targets of the reporting duties of the Member States. An elaborate overview is given for the relevant service sectors in SEC (2011) 102_final, pp. 62–110.

[15] At least regarding official statements and documents.

[16] See Cornils in Schlachter and Ohler (2008), Article 39 SD, mn. 6 ff.; J. van de Gronden and H. de Waele (2010), pp. 417 ff.; Klamert (2008), pp. 829 ff.; Lemor and Haake (2009), pp. 65, 68 ff.

been shifted away from the European Commission to the Member States themselves. It is the Member States themselves that must now determine and deliver the necessary proof for infringement proceedings.[17] This fact has obviously not been treated in an extensive way by the Member States; the enormous efforts to accomplish the screening itself appear to have primarily captured the attention of the national administrations and the political agendas.

Moreover, one must assume that the SD has been a large but only a single step further towards achieving a real Single Market. Therefore, reported obstacles to free service provision in the EU that can still be maintained in accordance with the requirements of the SD may be subject to further and even stricter secondary legislation in the future.[18]

2. Individual Articles of the Services Directive

2.1 Article 6 SD[19]: Point of Single Contact (POSC)

How were 'points of single contact' (POSCs) in concreto introduced in your Member State?

Does your legislator agree with a subjective understanding of the POSC? Or did your national legislator introduce only a few or even only one POSC in your Member State? How many POSCs will be introduced in your country (approximately)? Did your national legislator reallocate administrative competences (despite Article 6 (2) SD) with the introduction of the POSC(s)?

Were the POSCs introduced in your country as new and independent authorities/ offices or were the tasks of the POSCs assigned to already existing authorities? Were private partners involved in the introduction of POSCs? If so, in what way (e.g., by licence, accreditation)?

Who is liable for the mistakes of the POSCs? According to which principles?

One cornerstone of the implementation of the SD regarding procedural rights and simplification is, without doubt, the introduction of POSCs throughout the internal market of the EU.

---

[17] Calliess and Korte (2009), pp. 65, 91 f.; Lemor and Haake (2009), p. 70.

[18] See COM (2011) 20_final, pp.6 ff., 8 ff.

[19] For further information on this very prominent topic of the implementation of the SD, see also the following studies: RKW Kompetenzzentrum, Umsetzung der Europäischen Dienstleistungsrichtlinie: Analyse der Einrichtung der Einheitlichen Ansprechpartner in den europäischen Staaten, 2010, available at: http://www.rkw-kompetenzzentrum.de/fileadmin/media/Dokumente/Publikationen/2010_Doku_Einheitlicher-Ansprechpartner.pdf; SPOCS, Points of Single Contact Research Study, 2011, available at http://ec.europa.eu/internal_market/services/docs/services-dir/studies/spocs_en.pdf.

although contact by phone and e-mail is possible), as well as Finland, Hungary, Ireland, Latvia (expanding an already established web portal operated by the State Regional Development Agency), Lithuania (although the tasks were assigned to Enterprise Lithuania), Malta, the Netherlands, Poland, Slovenia, Spain, Sweden, and the United Kingdom. At least in Estonia, Hungary, Latvia, Poland, Malta, and Slovenia, a physical POSC should be introduced later on.[23]

Every Member State has at least established a virtual platform for POSCs or expanded already existing websites.[24] The federal states established several POSCs, but non-federal states also established more than one POSC in their countries. Hence, the implementation was very heterogeneous, and it is difficult to group the different ways of introducing POSCs. This may be due to the different administrative traditions and institutions among the Member States. Many POSCs are established by having POSC tasks assigned to pre-existing institutions/ authorities. With the one exception in Germany, no new authorities were established in the EU. As, for example, in Italy, new offices have only been established within pre-existing authorities.[25]

In some Member States, for example, Austria, there have been discussions about whether different chambers should be exclusively entrusted with the tasks of the POSC. These considerations partially resulted in the chambers bearing the task of representing, organising, and helping the local economy. By taking over the tasks of the POSC, the chambers would have to fulfil tasks outside their given framework; moreover, the chambers would even work to the benefit of their members' potential competitors. Furthermore, an entrustment of the chambers would give rise to a new legal framework for chambers. Obviously, this was assessed differently in, for example, Luxembourg, where the Chamber of Commerce and the Chamber of Professional Trades are the physical POSCs for companies.

With regard to the question as to whether an objective or a subjective understanding operates in a Member State, the question has explicitly only been dealt with by a few reports that agree on a subjective understanding. Austria and Germany, by establishing more than one POSC for their country, of course, by necessity had to present the subjective view. The Netherlands, perceiving the SD as allowing more POSCs, did not follow this approach when establishing only one POSC. The Irish rapporteurs mention that, even though unlikely, further POSCs could be established for special service sectors. Those states that established only one POSC may have done so because of an objective perception of the SD′s conception about POSC. But this is mere speculation, since no answers have been provided in this regard.

Regarding the reallocation of competences when the POSC is introduced, the picture is homogeneous. Although in three reports (Ireland, Portugal, Sweden) such reallocations are perceived as not impossible in the further process of

---

[23] Council document 17470/10, p. 4.

[24] An assessment of the POSCs and their individual functions can be found in both studies mentioned in footnote 19.

[25] According to the SPOCS study (footnote 19), there are 500 physical POSCs in Italy.

implementation, all other rapporteurs report that the reallocation of competences was not and is not planned in their Member State. One peculiar exception is Italy, where the law provides that, in case local administrations do not create a POSC, the competence can be transferred to the Chamber of Commerce.[26]

Private partners have not been involved in establishing the functions and work of POSCs in most Member States, but they have been partially involved in infrastructural and predefining work (e.g., Lithuania). In Finland, for instance, private involvement only concerned information technology consultants. Similarly, in Hungary, contractors were involved in the establishment of the procurement procedure of virtual POSCs. In France, the health protection offices, which build one of the seven networks of the Centres for Business and Administrative Proceedings, are a private legal body. Thus, one can assume that private partners are involved in France's POSC system. In Germany, the state of Bremen assigned the POSC tasks to entities run as in a private law firm. In Italy, private partners may be involved in verifying the existence of legal conditions to start, modify, transfer, or close an undertaking, and this verification is equivalent to authorisation if no discretionary power is to be exercised in the course of the verification. Private partners therefore need accreditation, but regulations for this have not yet passed. In Luxembourg, the accreditation of private partners is possible by law but has not yet been established. As mentioned above, in Romania, a private consortium was involved in establishing the POSC infrastructure. Other Member States assume the possibility of involving private partners but have not yet done so.

Finally, with regard to the liability of POSCs, the Member States basically have not established any new rules but have maintained general rules on (state) liability. Only Hungary seems to have drafted a special decree concerning the liability of POSCs. In some other Member States, liability is provided for in specific rules about the division of liability between POSCs and the competent authorities (e.g., Austria, Latvia, and Sweden). In Belgium, insurance against professional liability for POSCs is needed, but besides the usual principles of Belgian administrative law apply. In several cases, the liability is subject to civil law, which is partially the case in France, depending on the network's legal identity, and in Lithuania, where however the administrative courts decide upon state liability issues.

From the inexistence of any *special* remarks in the national reports, one can conclude that, *basically,* there are either no fees for the use of a POSC or only those that usually apply in the national legal systems.

One problem that has not really been solved is whether the POSC portals must be presented in different languages or whether the domestic language suffices. Besides many other topics, this issue was discussed with the participants of this research in a symposium supported by the Fritz Thyssen Foundation[27] in April 2010. The SD itself does not contain any provision on language requirements;

[26] The SPOCS study (see footnote 19) indicates decisional powers in the Czech Republic and Slovakia. However, the country reports do not hint at this assumption.

[27] See http://www.fritz-thyssen-stiftung.de.

it only encourages the Member States to take certain measures to have multilingual POSCs (Article 7 (5) SD). Nevertheless, one can conclude that the aim of lowering hurdles to service provision within the Internal Market indirectly requires a POSC in at least one of the working languages at the European level in addition to the domestic language.[28] After a screening of the POSC websites[29] of the Member States, it is obvious that many of them did offer a POSC website in at least an English version besides their domestic language version, even if not to the same extent as in the domestic language. Only Austria, Bulgaria, France, Germany (not at the federal level, but partially for the federal states), Hungary, and Slovenia have a purely monolingual POSC website at the moment (with the exception of Member States that have English as domestic language). In Italy and Slovakia, it seems that a POSC website has not yet been completely established. For Romania, no Internet platform could be found at all.

Additionally, some unique features should be highlighted regarding the POSC systems of the Member States: In the Czech Republic, the Chamber of Commerce, although not entrusted with the tasks of the POSC, established a system of comparable 'points of contact for entrepreneurs' for administrative business consultation. These unofficial non-state points of contact have led to discussions with the competent ministry about their acceptability. For the Netherlands, the POSC is one of three exceptions to a mere one-to-one minimum implementation of the SD, since it operates for purely domestic service providers as well.

2.2 Article 7 SD: Right to Information

Were the 'rights to information' extended in your national legislation during the transposition process?

For which fields have the 'rights to information' been implemented? Only within the scope of the SD or beyond?

Regarding the extension of information rights, the tenor of the reports appears to be unitary. In all Member States, the rights to information provided for in the SD have been transposed more or less without any extension, subject, of course, to some deviations. Only a few peculiarities seem to be remarkable in this regard: In France, such rights to information pre-existed und were been extended to transnational cases. In Finland, the rights to information were not mentioned at all in the implementing legislation; therefore, one assumes that the SD is directly applicable with regard to these rights. Comparably, in Sweden, the rights have been seen as already existing in the Swedish legal system, so no legislative measures were taken in this regard.

One remark should also be made regarding Article 21 of the SD concerning the Irish implementation. In Ireland, the rights of service recipients provided in Article

28 See the Commission Handbook (2007) 5.3.3, p. 21.

29 Last reviewed on 25 August 2011 at http://www.eu-go.eu.

21 SD were slightly extended in the transposing legislation. Irish service recipients also receive support from the information officers responsible for the information mentioned in Article 21 SD as regards a domestic service, whereas Article 21 SD concerns only the provision of transnational services. However, in other respects, the transposition of Article 21 SD does not appear to have occurred correctly in the Irish case. Pursuant to Article 21 (1) SD, there is an obligation to ensure that advice from competent authorities regarding services provided in other Member States shall, where appropriate, include a simple step-by-step guide; while information and assistance shall be provided in a clear and unambiguous manner, shall be easily accessible at a distance, including by electronic means and shall be kept up to date. By contrast, the Irish Statutory Instrument appears only to specifically apply this obligation to information furnished in respect of services provided in Ireland and it is seemingly not applied to information furnished in respect of services in other Member States.

Regarding the scope of the rights to information, one can again observe great differences between the Member States. The transposition of the SD′s requirements' application of the rights to information is more or less divided between those Member States that implemented the rights to information beyond the scope of the SD (be it also for national service providers or be it for other fields of services/businesses, as in, e.g., Estonia, Belgium, Italy, Lithuania, the Netherlands, and Portugal) and those who adhered to the SD′s scope (e.g., Finland, Cyprus, Latvia, Slovakia, Slovenia, and Sweden). In the Member States that provide more information than required by the SD on their web portals (e.g., in Belgium or the Czech Republic, where information beyond the scope of the SD's application is provided) the provision of information usually does not bestow the service provider with 'rights', since the information is given by the authorities only on a voluntary basis and, in most cases, using pre-existing portals the POSC has clung to. Estonia also falls under this category, because more information is offered, not as a consequence of the requirements of the SD, but as a consequence of determining that in certain areas more information is reasonable.

2.3 Article 8 SD: Procedures by Electronic Means

How did your Member State establish electronic procedures in concreto?

Electronic procedures appear to be quite popular in the EU of the 21st century. Nevertheless, Article 8 of the SD and its stipulations had to be transposed into national law. According to the reports, one perceives the tendency that the SD required an extension of pre-existing, though usually rather limited, e-government possibilities for conducting administrative procedures electronically. Countries such as Estonia, Latvia, Malta, and the United Kingdom had rather well-developed e-governments before the SD. In other countries, however, such as Ireland and Sweden, e-government faced new challenges as it adopted—compared to pre-existing structures in that Member State—a novel role due to the SD. In still other countries, such as Cyprus, the transposition of the SD was an incentive to broaden

more than 30 authorisation schemes were abolished and replaced by mere declaration requirements.[32]

From the reports, one can conclude that there was no need to completely eliminate a specific type of authorisation scheme. Instead, only amendments to certain single provisions, or their elimination, took place in the Member States. But one can also learn that there is great diversity among the Member States regarding the concept of authorisation.[33] Some Member States took great efforts to change their service sector from an 'authorisation sector' to a less restrictive sector for service provision, while there are other Member States where authorisations are still the prevailing instrument of administrative work.

Italy is remarkable in this regard: Since 1990 simple notifications predominate in its legal system, allowing economic activities to start either immediately or after a waiting period of 30 days. The need for prior authorisations was thus already eliminated to a very considerable extent. The Italian implementation of the SD has developed further in this direction, changing the general law of administrative procedure such that this approach has become applicable to all economic activities.[34]

Altogether, and unsurprisingly, one can assume that the Member States especially maintained authorisation schemes in combination with service activities in the fields of safety and security, as well as consumer protection.

Which types of authorisation schemes/authorisation procedures exist in your Member State and which one usually applies? Which types had to be abolished or altered due to the requirements of the SD?

Many Member States have a common approach regarding the types of authorisation schemes. In Member States such as Austria, Germany, Italy, Lithuania, and Spain, one can basically find a triad of authorisations or notifications. First, there are authorisations that demand ex ante control before starting a business. Second, there are notifications/registrations that allow the business to be run while the authority has time to examine the documents provided and assess whether the legal conditions for providing services are met. In case the examination leads to a negative result, the applicant must cease providing services. Finally, there are simple notifications that only require communication with the authorities.

Even though the schemes in the Member States are named differently and may contain some divergences in details, and even though further classifications may exist in many countries, this triad seems to be the blueprint of the authorisation systems in use in the EU.

In Malta, licences were needed for all economic activities before the SD, whereas, for example, in Poland and Slovenia economic activities are basically

32 SEC (2011) 102_final, p. 115.

33 See also conclusion in SEC (2011) 102_final, p. 13.

34 See also SEC (2011) 102_final, pp. 12, 115.

free from authorisation requirements, at least with respect to services in Slovenia. Nevertheless, Malta has abolished some authorisations and replaced them with declaration requirements.[35] In Slovakia, all authorisations under the Trade Licensing Act have been replaced by declarations.[36] Some rapporteurs also refer to some kind of admissions in this regard.

According to your national understanding, are simple notification requirements included in Article 9 ff. SD that had to be abolished?

As far as the rapporteurs refer to the question of whether simple notifications are included in Articles 9 ff. SD that had to be abolished, no report, apart from the Swedish and, depending on the interpretation of the implementing regulation, British reports (if any debates on this topic were conducted at all in the Member State), sees simple notifications as being included in Article 9 SD (with possible exceptions for Slovenia and the Netherlands), although a broad definition of the SD could be interpreted that way.[37] Many authors refer to Article 16 SD for further comments on and the implementation of simple notifications.

2.5 Article 10 SD: Conditions for the Granting of Authorisation

Article 10 (3) SD implies the recognition of authorisations/requirements granted by other Member States. Where and how was this requirement implemented? Did problems occur in this context?

Regarding the transposition of mutual recognition requirements, the results appear to be heterogeneous. Many countries transposed the requirements of Article 10 (3) SD in their horizontal framework law (e.g., Belgium, the Netherlands, Portugal, and Spain). In other countries, such as Germany and Slovenia, the transposition of the recognition requirement is dealt with in specific administrative laws.

Austria, however, did not deal with this topic at either the federal or the state level. Austria identifies two ways of complying with Article 10 (3) SD: either by way of 'interpreting in' the requirements of Article 10 (3) in the application of existing provisions of national law or by assigning direct effects of the SD to this rule.

Most Member States had no problems with the transposition of Article 10 (3) SD. Only Portugal and Spain identified problems or will address them in the future. Portugal identified problems with regard to public contractors, service providers, vendors, and the leasing of goods in public contracts, even before the SD, in light of case law of the Court of Justice of the EU. In Spain, problems with the practical application of the mutual recognition clause were discussed. In Italy,

---

[35] SEC (2011) 102_final, p. 12.

[36] SEC (2011) 102_final, p. 12.

[37] The European Commission does not include simple notification in the definition of authorisation schemes (see SEC (2011) 102_final, p. 10).

unlimited authorisations. Nevertheless, overriding reasons could create exceptions. In Poland, only time-limited authorisations were granted in the field of services. Only if the legislator did not provide for a limited duration was the authorisation granted for an indefinite period. In Ireland, time-limited authorisation is the more usual way of granting authorisation so far; therefore a significant impact of the implementation of the SD has been assessed as possible.

Some countries explicitly prohibited temporal authorisations until now: In Lithuania, the Civil Code stated a principle of temporarily unlimited licences. Slovakia, comparable to Estonia now, applied time limits only if the applicant asked for it, and in Slovenia some licences are subject to periodic renewal.

In some Member States, for instance Malta, the Netherlands, and Lithuania, implementation of Article 11 SD goes along with an incorporation and extension of the wording of Article 12 (1) SD. This means that in the case of scarcity of natural resources or limited technical capacity, limited authorisations should also be allowed.

2.7 Article 12 SD: Selection from Among Several Candidates

To what extent did the requirements of Article 12 SD (regarding selection from among several applicants) change your legal system? Was there any need for the transposition of these requirements (since these requirements had previously been stated in the case law of the ECJ)?

A transposition of Article 12 SD was not seen as necessary at all in some countries (e.g., Denmark, Germany, Finland, Austria, and Slovakia). In the other countries, a more or less literal transposition took place in the horizontal law or by amending procedural law (e.g., Belgium, Bulgaria, Cyprus, Estonia, Hungary, Ireland, Italy, Latvia, Lithuania, the Netherlands, Slovenia, Spain, and the United Kingdom). As for Ireland, the legislator expects only a slight impact from the transposition of the SD.

In a considerable number of countries, the principles laid down in Article 12 SD were already familiar, if not explicitly pre-existing, especially regarding concessions/licences and public procurement. The same seems to apply to Malta and France (with reference to ECJ case law). In Bulgaria, Slovenia, Portugal, Hungary, Germany, Lithuania, and probably Finland, some areas of law (especially public procurement law) already incorporated principles comparable to Article 12 SD. In Austria, the legislators did not deal with this issue and have not made any amendments in this regard. For this reason, it is assumed that, from the legislators' perspective, there has been no need for implementation, since the requirements are already met by Austrian law.

In Estonia, the implementing law introduced the procedural requirement of a competition, as has been demanded in Germany too.

The reported assessment of the Dutch legislator is quite interesting in this regard. The Dutch legislator assumes that most cases to which Article 12 SD would apply are outside the scope of the SD. Hence, during the screening only few constellations could be detected at the national level, and none at the local level. Thus, the mere verbatim transposition of Article 12 SD was basically seen as sufficient.

In Portugal, there is no legislation corresponding to Article 12 SD, but the implementing law decree declares the Code of Public Contracts to be applicable in this regard.

For Romania, the implementation of a general principle in accordance with Article 12 SD is new. Nevertheless, there are still areas of administrative law where these principles do not apply without further notice (e.g., taxi licences).

2.8 Article 13 SD: Authorisation Procedures

Which authority determines* a priori *the duration of an administrative procedure? The legislator by law or the responsible authority by decision?

The prevailing answer to this question is that (basically) the legislator determines the duration of an administrative procedure (e.g., in Austria, Belgium, the Czech Republic, Estonia, Hungary, Latvia, Lithuania, Malta, the Netherlands, Poland, Romania, Slovakia, Slovenia, Spain, and Sweden). Additionally, in some countries, the authorities can decide on the duration too. Whether the authorities really use this competence cannot be assessed from the data provided.

Countries where the authorities can decide, in addition to the legislator, are, for instance, Bulgaria, Cyprus, Denmark, and Portugal. In Bulgaria and Denmark, for instance, the legislator gives certain general time limits, but it is up to the authorities to determine the duration according to the complexity of the case (except for a few cases of legal determination). In Ireland, the legislator only lays down the concept of 'reasonable time'; this term is further specified, as seen below. In the United Kingdom, it is the other way round: Usually it is the authority that determines the duration, and only in specific cases does the legislator decide. In France, besides the legislator (in few cases), the courts decide on the duration by case law.

In contrast, in Finland, Ireland (usually), Italy (usually), and Luxembourg, the competence to decide on the duration of an administrative procedure is basically assigned solely to the authorities. In Italy, the legislator provided for a generally applicable time limit, which applies in case the authority does not establish a specific duration. The same generally applies to Ireland, though the competences to decide the duration of administrative procedures may, in some cases, fall to the legislator. In Ireland, the question of whose responsibility it is to determine the duration of an administrative procedure ultimately depends on the specific sector and the particular governing legislation.

Did your national legislator establish a general rule on the duration of the procedures? Is this general rule applicable only within the scope of application of the SD or does it apply even beyond? If there is a generally fixed duration,

how long is it? If not, did your legislator prescribe different durations in different, specific administrative laws?

Is it possible to differ from the prescribed durations of procedures? If so, is this possibility used?

In Austria, there was already a provision in the general administrative procedures law that after six months the applicant is entitled to sue the authority to decide on his/her application. The transposition of the SD within its scope now obliges the authority to decide within three months. Prolongation by the competent authority is possible once, and deviations from the general duration are possible if provided for in specific administrative laws.

A general duration of three months with the option of one prolongation and possible deviations from the general duration were also implemented in Cyprus, Germany, and Slovenia (with some specialities). In Slovenia, the duration of three months enshrined in the general horizontal law transposing the SD deviates from the two-month duration that is provided in the general Law of Administrative Procedures. Hence there is a peculiar deterioration for service providers. This may provoke the question as to its conformity with EU rules on the equality of procedural standards compared to national cases. But one has to consider here that the general Law of Administrative Procedures provides for a negative 'decision' after inaction by the administration, whereas in the case of services under the scope of the law implementing the SD, the authorisation is deemed granted.

In Belgium, the duration is generally fixed at 30 working days, except in Flanders, where it is 60 working days.

A general duration of 30 days is fixed also in Estonia, Hungary, Italy (if the authority did not set another specific time), Romania, and Lithuania. Prolongations of up to 30 days are possible in Hungary and Lithuania, and up to 15 days in Romania. In Hungary, a shorter time limit can be established by any sort of legislation, but a longer one can only be established by an act or a government decree. In Estonia as well, the duration is applicable beyond the scope of the SD.

The Netherlands determined a duration of eight weeks by Article 31 Service Act; prolongation is possible in reasoned cases. The duration was established as lex specialis by the General Administrative Law Act, the legal effect of an expired deadline applying three days after expiration. The provisions implementing tacit authorisation were transposed beyond the scope of the SD in the Netherlands, and thus also for domestic service providers. Therefore, the implementation took place in the general administrative law in the Netherlands.

The Slovakian report gives a remarkable set of durations. In simple cases, the authority should decide 'immediately'; in other cases, within 30 days; and in difficult cases, within 60 days. Legal effects apply the day after expiration.

In Ireland, ultimately the legislator fixed 60 days as a 'reasonable time' in the implementing statutory instrument, which can be extended for a maximum of another 28 days. The Irish rapporteurs assume that the competent authorities could also apply these time limits outside the scope of the SD, but this would be up to their discretion. Further exceptions to the time limits can be made by the authorities in case of overriding reasons, which have not been further specified in Ireland.

In Latvia, the general duration is one month, but the time limit can be extended up to four months due to 'objective reasons', or up to one year if a 'lengthy determination of facts is necessary'. In Portugal the time limit is determined to be 90 days.

In Spain, the general maximum length (with deviations by law or EU law possible) of administrative procedures in general is six months. If a specific law does not set a different time frame for the specific authorisation, the duration will be three months.

Some Member States did not establish a general rule for the duration of administrative procedures (e.g., Denmark). In Finland, France, Luxembourg, Malta, Sweden, and the United Kingdom, there are no fixed durations and no general rules for a determination. This is partly the case because specific laws or authorities determine the duration in every particular area (Malta and Sweden); because the legislator simply used broadly drafted wording without further substantiation (e.g., 'as fast as possible'), as in Finland and France (except in specific administrative laws), Luxembourg (but a maximum of three months is given), Malta, and the United Kingdom; or because the transposition process is still pending in this regard (the French report even mentions there is no plan to implement a general time limit for the duration of administrative procedures in France).

Is a tacit (fictitious) authorisation already usual in your legal system? Is it usual in general administrative procedures law or only in specific administrative laws?

Concerning the existence of prior tacit authorisations in the Member States, one can again construct three categories. First, there appear to be only four Member States that already used tacit authorisation as a general rule in the (general) administrative procedures law: Hungary, Italy, and to some extent Romania and Spain. In Spain, there was a general rule on tacit authorisation, but it was circumvented by the fact that 'exceptions' in the form of tacit denial of this rule by specific law were possible. Through this loophole the general principle was actually changed to become the true exception, since specific laws made frequent use of the exception clause. The implementation of the SD was taken as motivation to rearrange the intended rule exception system in the formerly intended way by changing the respective articles in the general administrative procedures law.

Most Member States, however, were already familiar with the system of tacit authorisation but had not established it in a general rule and had used it only in specific administrative laws. Regarding these countries, one can therefore not really speak of a 'usual' application. The countries in this category are Austria, Denmark, Germany, Ireland, Portugal, and the United Kingdom, as far as is reported in the country reports.

Finally, the third category consists of those Member States that did not previously have the legal system of tacit authorisation. Hence, this concept was

are expected. With regard to Luxembourg, it appears unclear whether there is a direct implementation: The national report speaks more in favour of an indirect implementation, whereas the European Commission document lists Luxembourg as a Member State with a horizontal implementation in this regard.

In Spain, these articles are perceived as a severe change to Spanish administrative law. In some countries, a transposition is not considered necessary at all or only to a limited extent (e.g., Austria, Latvia, and the Netherlands). At the time of the drafting of the reports, only minor amendments were provided for.[44] Remarkably, in Italy, Article 29 of the implementing law (implementing Article 15 SD) provides that any discriminatory requirement contained in any provision is considered automatically abolished. Although one might assess this rule in a positive way, it lacks legal certainty, since it remains unclear which provision is deemed invalid. In Sweden, in the course of the implementation of the mentioned articles, some delegated legislative powers of the municipalities were withdrawn by the national level.

Is there discussion about the self-screening of the Member States? Are there further problems or discourses regarding these articles in your Member State?

A discussion about the self-screening did not take place in the Member States. Portugal reports some discussions by the civil society on the self-screening. The same holds true regarding further discourses or problems. In Finland, a discussion took place about the adoption of the so-called UK model, which means that the criteria for providing services are extended to cases of establishment to reduce the capacities of a Member State to interfere with this freedom. Finally, this approach was not adopted in Finland. Comparably, in the Netherlands problems and discussions emerged about these articles because Dutch law does not differentiate between 'temporary' and 'permanent' service provision (i.e., establishment; see also Sweden in the next section).

The Romanian report, however doubts that there really is a complete self-screening but expresses fears that it will be the service providers themselves who carry the burden of screening the legislation: The administration may be relying on the fact that as soon as service providers apply for authorisations, the administration responsible will, in the course of the administrative procedures, identify further needs for the transposition of the requirements of the SD.

2.10 Articles 14–19 SD

Are there any discussions with regard to prohibited requirements/restrictions (Articles 14, 15, 16, and 19 SD) and further exemptions (Articles 16 (3), 17, and 18 SD) in your Member State?

---

[44] Regarding Article 16 SD, however, see SEC (2011) 102_final, pp. 48 ff.

Concerning the transposition of Articles 14–19 SD, the reports do not reflect any common approaches or problems. The only topic that has been treated in many Member States is the restricted enumeration of justifying reasons in Article 16 (3) SD, when compared to the existing case law of the Court of Justice of the EU. Such a discussion took place, for instance, in Austria (regarding whether Article 16 (3) SD has to be directly implemented at all), Finland, Germany, Lithuania, and Slovenia. In some countries, such as Lithuania and the Netherlands, the question was discussed of whether Article 16 (2) SD should be regarded as a black list.

In Cyprus, the methodology to be followed regarding the screening exercise was discussed. Sweden raised the issue of how the freedom to provide services relates to the freedom of establishment. Even though a clear solution to this problem could not really be developed, some starting points for a solution were offered, such as the proposal that a service activity lasting more than one year usually must be seen as permanent. Nevertheless, case-by-case decisions are necessary. In Germany, there were discussions about the relations between these articles.

Regarding the Romanian report, Recital 17 and Article 17 SD were discussed regarding 'services of general economic interest'.

In Austria, only Article 18 SD was transposed. Spain implemented all of these articles, apart from certain nuances of Article 17 SD. Spain did not refer to Article 17 SD in its horizontal umbrella law because there is no Europe-wide definition for services of general economic interest. In the Netherlands, none of these articles were transposed directly. Comparably, Slovenia refused to transpose the requirements of some of these SD articles in its general horizontal law and preferred a sector-specific implementation.

2.11 Articles 22–27 SD[45]

Regarding the transposition of Articles 22–27 SD, have there been discussions? Do any issues of the SD transposition process impact on the modernisation of administrative law and administrative procedures law? How is the role of the Member State as an initiator of private regulation (Article 26 SD re certification schemes and quality charters) assessed?

The Member States usually transposed Articles 22–27 SD, but some exceptions were made with regard to specific articles, with the following examples: In Austria, explicit transposition was held to be necessary only with regard to Article 22. Belgium did not transpose Articles 24–26 SD on the federal or regional level. The Netherlands transposed only Articles 22, 26 (2), and 27 SD, whereas Articles 22 and 27 SD were implemented in the Dutch Civil Code. By contrast, Lithuania, for example, transposed all of the above articles. In Slovenia, the transposition of these articles was seen as part of the horizontal implementation. The United

[45] For details regarding Article 25 SD, see also SEC (2011) 102_final, pp. 40–44, and p. 113 for the outcome of the consultation process.

Kingdom implemented all the articles except Article 26 SD. In Germany, transposition was carried out by passing a new statutory instrument. The same applies in Denmark, with the adoption of Regulation 1372/2009.

Interestingly, Germany and Slovenia, for example, clearly identified these articles as a substitute for requirements prohibited by the SD or for the lack of recourse to certain overriding reasons in the general interest not provided for in the SD (such as consumer protection). Sweden, in contrast, states that at least Article 22 SD does not appear to be a substitute for banned requirements.

Finland[46] underlines that the government or the legislator must be very careful when initiating private regulation, because too intense an impact would question the soft law character of private regulations. Regarding the public inducement of private quality measures, many rapporteurs—if this question was addressed—opine that there was no such duty for the Member States and assess quality control to be the duty of private parties where state implementation may be misleading.

The Czech legislator reproduced the requirement of Czech law to have liability insurance with regard also to customer information. The Czech rapporteur explicitly states that these articles constitute ‘recommendations’ rather, so that there was no need for implementation.

In addition, in Ireland, liability insurance can now be imposed on the service provider. Furthermore, the question of commercial communications was, in particular, discussed during the implementation process in Ireland.

In Poland, a comparably wide range of information for customers already existed.

The Romanian report states that the implementing regulations impose fines of €250 to €2500 in case of non-compliance with Articles 22 and 27 SD.

2.12 Articles 28 ff. SD: Administrative Cooperation

Were there provisions on transnational administrative assistance in your Member State prior to the transposition of the SD? If so, were these provisions congruent with the rules on domestic administrative assistance (if any in your country)?

Apart from international agreements or European regulations on transnational administrative cooperation, the national law of most Member States had basically no provisions for transnational administrative assistance prior to the transposition of the SD. In Hungary, a system of transnational assistance already existed and was just amended for services in the implementing law (as a lex specialis). Ireland seems to be another exception in this regard, as there were already regulations on administrative assistance for service providers in Northern Ireland wishing to establish themselves in the Republic of Ireland, and vice versa. Domestic administrative assistance is not usually congruent with the system of transnational

[46] The Finnish report gives a short statement to Article 20 and 21 SD as excursus.

administrative assistance. Before the transposition of the SD, the Law on State Registers of Lithuania stated that register data shall be provided to legal and natural persons of Member States in accordance with the same procedures that apply to legal and natural persons of Lithuania.

Malta did not have any rules at all for administrative assistance before the transposition of the SD.

Did the requirements of the SD give cause to (re)arrange the provisions for administrative assistance in a general, maybe uniform way?

Since most countries did not have domestic provisions on transnational administrative assistance prior to the SD transposition, there was no need for (re)arrangements. In Finland (re)arrangements took place insofar as the coordination of the assistance was transferred to a 'Consumer Agency'. The competent Finnish authorities are included in a network connected to the IMI system.

In the Netherlands, a system with four different procedures was established (general information request, requests to foreign authorities concerning the 'good reputation' of service providers, measures regarding the safety of services, alert mechanism). Generally, the IMI system is also applied to domestic cases.

In the United Kingdom a general regime for transnational assistance was established through the implementation of the SD, but without impacting domestic administrative assistance.

Are there provisions on financial compensation for the wide range of assistance?

Only a few Member States foresee financial compensations. In Hungary, there seems not to be any real difference between domestic and transnational assistance in this regard. In Germany, a new section in the Administrative Procedures Law provides that financial compensation must be given if demanded by legal acts of the EU. In Sweden, fees may be installed, at least with regard to certain information. In all other cases, the principle of reciprocity applies to transnational administrative assistance.

Was there a need to change rules on data protection and professional secrets due to the wide range of information obligations? Have such rules only been adapted or did a profound change take place?

Generally speaking, changes in this regard were not deemed necessary. The transposing legislation of some countries referred to these issues and declared national data protection provisions to be applicable (e.g., Belgium, Denmark, Ireland, Malta, Romania, and Slovenia). In Slovenia, besides the applicable general rules on data protection, there is a detailed list of transferable information in the horizontal implementing law.

Changes with regard to the circulation of criminal data took place in France. The Swedish report identifies future problems regarding professional secrets.

2.13 Article 29 SD: Mutual Assistance—General Obligations for the Member State of Establishment

To what extent is this article seen as problematic? Have there been discussions regarding the confirmation of not unlawful business conduct enshrined in Article 29 (1) SD?

Article 29 SD was not perceived as problematic by the Member States. Only the Finnish report indicates that some problems could occur in daily practice. The same applies to discussions about the confirmation of not unlawful business conduct: Only one country, Poland, reports some concerns about the possible interference of public authorities with the functioning of private subjects.

In our view, Bulgaria's non-implementation of the requirement to deliver a confirmation about the lawful business conduct of a service provider to the authority of other Member States appears to be problematic, even though the Bulgarian authorities would verify the business conduct in case of a reasoned request.

2.14 Problems and Discourses on Administrative Cooperation

Were there any problems or discourses regarding Chapter VI (administrative cooperation) worth mentioning?

The Dutch report contains some amendments in this regard. In the Netherlands, there have been discussions about the scope of the SD and data protection with respect to the area of criminal law. The Netherlands perceive criminal law as not affected by the SD (referring to Article 1 (5) SD). For this reason, the Netherlands will not communicate data on criminal records. Furthermore the 'country of origin principle' still present in Articles 30 (2), 18, and 35 SD was subject to debate in the Netherlands.

Given the expiry of the transposition period not too long ago, it may still be too early for an assessment of the transposition of Article 29 SD (e.g., as in the Spanish report).

In the United Kingdom, the four different options as to which authority/ authorities IMI coordination should be assigned/attributed have been quite widely discussed.

2.15 Convergence Programme (Chapter VII of the Services Directive)

Chapter VII on Convergence: Regarding this chapter, did any discussions take place in your Member State that you think are worth mentioning here? How is the role of the Member State as an initiator of private regulation in Article 37 SD (re codes of conduct) assessed?

Generally, with regard to Chapter VII of the SD, no (great) discussions have been reported. Some remarks made by the rapporteurs should be briefly mentioned here. Italy and Lithuania reported that their transposition did not engender an obligation for the service providers to establish codes of conduct. In the case of Lithuania, such codes of conduct were not known in the legal tradition. In Spain, the horizontal law only provides a generally framed encouragement for public authorities to invite professional bodies and organisations to participate in the preparation of codes of conduct at the Community level. In the Netherlands, transposition was limited to the requirement of Article 37 (2) SD for the electronic accessibility of codes of conduct. In Hungary, an 'ethical codex' is elaborated.

3. Assessment of the Impact of the Services Directive

3.1 Extent of the Impact

In Germany, the impact of the SD on administrative procedures law, administrative law for business activities, and even beyond is assessed as severe. From the perspective of your Member State, do you agree?

As already mentioned above, in many Member States implementation is seen as being too recent for any practical assessments (Estonia, Finland, and Sweden especially refer to this fact). In a nutshell, most rapporteurs are of the opinion that the SD had an impact on administrative law and that its transposition engendered many changes therein. The impact, however, is not assessed as severe (e.g., Austria, Belgium, Malta, and the Netherlands). Italy perceives the impact as small.

A very severe and considerable impact was identified by Germany, Spain, Hungary, and Poland. For Portugal, the rapporteur also partly recognised a severe impact, although Portugal confined itself to a minimum transposition only and the SD neither engendered real novelties for Portuguese administrative law (apart from the elimination of authorisation requirements and the increased significance of tacit authorisations) nor caused a profound administrative reform (in contrast to Poland).

In sum, many rapporteurs deplore the lack of academic analysis and debate during the implementation process, which makes assessing the transposition quite difficult. Thus, chances have been wasted.

3.2 Assessment of the Transposing Legislation

How is the transposition of the SD judged in your Member State? Is it perceived as a great success and an improvement or did only a minimum transposition take place? What aspects guide your assessment?

As already alluded to, in many Member States there was no academic debate about the transposition process (in contrast to the German transposition process). In most cases, a minimum implementation took place (e.g., Austria, Finland, France, Ireland, Lithuania, the Netherlands, and Sweden). In Spain, the transposition is assessed as a profound reform of the services industry. In Germany, the SD was implemented beyond the minimum requirements, and the transposition of the procedural requirements of the SD was identified as a success. Cyprus perceives the transposition process as a decisive step towards simpler, faster, and more modern administrative procedures. Hungary also identified the transposition as a big step forward in its system of administrative proceedings.

In Lithuania and maybe Estonia as well, the implementation is seen as just another transposition of EU law, without further discussions.

3.3 Most Important Changes Induced by the Services Directive

In your view, what is the most important and most profound change induced by the transposition of the SD in your Member State, and why?

Generally speaking, three topics were perceived as the most important regarding profound changes induced by the transposition of the SD: first, the establishment of a system of tacit authorisation; second, the establishment of POSCs, which were new in nearly all Member States; and, finally, the establishment of a system of mutual transnational administrative assistance.

Besides this general assessment, some specific details of certain countries in this regard are mentioned. The Estonian, Spanish, and Finnish rapporteurs are convinced that the new impetus of the implementation of the SD will have a decisive effect on the behaviour of the administration towards service providers, or even beyond their 'customers' in general. The Estonian rapporteur expects a spillover effect.

Finland, Germany, and Lithuania stress the impact of the SD on electronic procedures in general in their country.

In Hungary, the administrative procedure rules were completely revised and screened, which is perceived as huge progress in administrative law.

The Italian rapporteur identifies as the most important improvement the fact that notification requirements became the only formal requirement for starting a business.

In Malta the obligation to reason administrative decisions was identified as an important novelty.

For Poland, the elimination of authorisations of limited duration was a fundamental change. The Polish rapporteur also opines that the way is now open for a general 'principle of trust' in administration.

In Ireland, the SD was substantially assessed in the context of its potential importance to the future growth of the domestic services sector. Additionally, it should be emphasised that in Ireland there is no overarching administrative law statute governing all sectors. Instead, each sector is governed by specific legislation; thus rules regarding authorisations, licences, time limits, and so forth may vary between sectors. Irish administrative law is also comprised of principles of common law established by the courts. Accordingly, it has not seemed feasible or desirable to radically overhaul Irish administrative laws and principles generally above and beyond the requirements of the SD. The narrative adopted in relation to the transposition of the SD primarily relates to its importance in economic terms.

In conclusion, the implementation of the SD in general did have considerable impact on the administrative systems of nearly all the Member States. Although some implementation is still to be carried out, one can expect the impact of the SD to become even greater in the future because the practical application of administrative laws will reveal further need for the implementation of the SD,[47] and the future jurisprudence of the Court of Justice of the EU on the SD will place additional weight on its exigencies.[48] Therefore, changes in administrative practice will have to be examined in due time. The legal changes adopted in the transposition process create the opportunity for further improvements, which is likely in at least some countries. The abovementioned changes in public administration attitudes may lead to further developments.

3 Further Research Conclusion

In our point of view, the results of our project go beyond the mere technical aspects of the implementation of the SD. The transposition process shows that it is quite difficult to devise a common approach for the transposition of legal acts of the EU affecting administrative law in the Member States.

First of all, one suspicion—probably already often assumed but rarely explicitly stated—has been confirmed: The commitments of secondary EU legislation for the Member States are not homogeneously understood in the Member States.[49] This can be exemplified by Article 6 SD: There is not just *one* model of the POSC, but many different ones. This development is only understandable by the fact that the impact of the commitment of Article 6 SD is understood totally differently, since there is no indication that the Member States intentionally circumvented the SD.

This leads to the question of a need for and the possibility of an 'European doctrine of methods'[50] that not only reflects the approaches and methods (if any)

[47] Even beyond, one can expect farther-reaching harmonising effects for the sake of avoiding an 'illogical and unbalanced dichotomy in the law' (Hessel) that will go beyond the legal transposition requirement, since they will concern sectors outside the material scope of the SD, and also purely domestic service provision (see Hessel (2009), pp. 83–86).

[48] At the time of this writing, the Court of Justice of the EU had handed down just one judgement on the SD, concerning Article 24 SD, in which the Court opined that total prohibitions of commercial communications violate Article 24 (1) and cannot be subject to justifications under Article 24 (2), in diametrical contrast to the opinion of A. G. Mazak (cf. his opinion in this case, para 65 ff.), see the judgement of 5 April 2011, Case C-119/09, n.y.r., paras. 42 and 45.

[49] See Knill and Winkler (2007), pp. 1 ff., for an analysis of problems of different legal orders, taking as an example the directive on the assessment of the effects of certain public and private projects on the environment. See also Wahl (2008), pp. 869 ff. and 891 ff., and Harlow (2002), pp. 199, 205 f.

[50] Baldus and Vogel (2006), pp. 237 and 251 f., agree that there still is a lot of work to do on this topic. On the European doctrine of methods, see, inter alia, Riesenhuber (2010), (focussing primarily on civil law); Hahn (2003), p. 163; Vogenauer (2005), p. 234.

of interpretation used by the Court of Justice of the EU,[51] but also takes into account the different cultures of methods in the Member States. For there is a difference in whether one only analyses the methods of interpretation by the Court of Justice of the EU, which deals with single acts of secondary legislation only in the context of very specific questions and problems, or whether one researches the concrete implementation practice in the Member States, which must transpose the act of secondary legislation in its full range in a legislative as well as administrative and judicial manner.[52]

Why can this be seen so prominently by taking the SD as an example? The SD does have a horizontal approach and does not engender only minor, specific changes. It is the way of cross-sectoral harmonisation that has been chosen with the SD. Hence, the SD is a good and maybe currently the best example of secondary legislation to induce a study pertaining to the development of an "European doctrine of methods".

Harmonisation in administrative law and constitutional impact

One could conclude that the supervision of the compatibility of national laws with EU law exercised by the European Commission for the first time was actively passed onto the Member States themselves for the service sector. This, of course, induces an immense workload for the Member States. Therefore it is not astonishing, that the transposition process shows different ways to implement the requirements of the SD—also due to the (partly very) different administrative traditions.

Nevertheless, the transposition process also proves that, despite different approaches and different ways of implementation, it is possible to adhere to a common European framework without violating national principles and thus provide a common basis for service provision throughout Europe. Therefore, one could generally ask whether it really does make a significant difference from the perspective of the national administrative legal orders whether a reform concept derives from the initiative of national actors or from European actors. Is there really a need to protect the national administrative legal order and its specifics from European impulses if there is no protection in case the national legislator is inspired by the administrative experiences of foreign states for his reform projects?

The question is more the other way around: What would actually be the use of interpreting national administrative laws in a holistic way that considers them as a whole and tries to save a certain 'intrinsic value' in situations when domestic administrative rules have to be applied by the Member States implementing/ enforcing (indirectly) EU law? To find such an 'intrinsic value' is quite difficult: The traditional structures of national administrative law in the Member States

[51] On the interpretive approach adopted by the Court of Justice of the EU, see Chalmers et al (2006), pp. 1000 and 1047–1048; Craig and de Burca (2008), pp. 73–74; Kaczorowska (2009), pp. 243 ff; Leisner (2007), pp. 689, 694 ff., and Potacs (2009), p. 465.

[52] Compare Wahl (2008), pp. 869 ff., and Vogenauer (2005), pp. 243 ff.

(which must be distinguished from the fundamental legal principles behind them) cannot have an 'intrinsic value' as such in democracies that would require protection from 'foreign' influences[53]: For example, the national legislator can and indeed does change administrative laws within the boundaries of the constitution. The legislator also sticks to (allegedly) foreign role models while changing them. It would be a profound misunderstanding of the concept of 'national identity' of the Member States [Article 4 (2) Treaty on European Union (TEU)] to use it to protect traditional administrative law structures against 'Europeanisation', as these traditional structures most often developed in a rather incidental way and have a purely ordinal function. Only fundamental legal principles behind the administrative law and the mirrored experiences contained in them can constitute an expression of national identity, but not the 'simple', non-constitutional legislation. To assume that the citizens of a state would identify with certain non-constitutional national institutes of administrative law[54] is pure fiction.[55] In addition, respect for the national identity in Article 4 (2) TEU refers to the fundamental political and constitutional structures only, as underscored by the qualifier added by the Lisbon Treaty to the national identity.

A European administrative law role model, or at least unanimity in best practices?

According to our research, there is no real European national administrative law role model for the Member States of the EU on which the SD is based. There are, of course, certain single provisions that require the adaptation of national administrative law in the Member States in general, but which already existed in some Member States. Nevertheless, a blueprint at the European level is not really detectable. None of the Member States' own models or systems are simply mirrored in the SD provisions to the full extent. Amending documents also do not give any hint that during the drafting of the SD, for example, the POSC requirement or tacit authorisation was taken over from one single Member State.

Therefore it seems to be worth concluding that not only should a deep and intensive handling of the outcome of the transposition process be carried out (i.e., the evaluation process of Article 39 SD[56]), but also some sort of coordination should exist before such a cross-sectoral and wide-reaching directive is passed. Hence it appears necessary to bring together scholars from all Member States before such a directive is adopted to have the best practice models before the final text of the secondary legislation is drafted. Furthermore, problems with legal traditions could be discussed on time before in a broad way that may lead to a better and more comprehensive understanding of the administrative legal orders of

[53] Rightly Zuleeg (1994), pp. 154, 176; with nuances Möllers (2002), pp. 483, 501; Hatje (1998), p. 422.

[54] So della Cananea (2003), pp. 563, 572; Neidhardt (2008), pp. 189, 199 ff.

[55] See Stelkens (2011), pp. 30 f.

[56] For detailed information on this process, see SEC (2011) 102_final, pp. 5 ff.

the Member States. Different interpretations of single passages of the draft directive thus could be avoided or at least minimised. Such 'pre-evaluations' could in the end even lead to some kind of change of consciousness of the European Commission and would without doubt contribute to the fulfilment of the European Commission's Better Regulation promise.[57] Once the transposition of a directive in the Member States has taken place, it is quite unlikely that its subsequent evaluation will lead to reforms and renewal of the rather new implementing laws within a short period of time after their initial adoption.

In their handbook, the European Commission expresses several times the hope that the Member States will exchange best practices in their transposition efforts and cooperatively assist each other in finding simpler administrative rules and foreign practices worth adapting domestically.[58] Our analysis of the SD's implementation process in the Member States, however, evidences that such expectations flowing from the use of new governance techniques in the SD in accordance with the European Commission's White Paper on Governance[59] have not been met. There has been hardly any cooperation or exchange of views between Member States. There is no single example of a uniform best practice developed by the Member States while implementing the SD. Thus, one may conclude that the new governance techniques will only lead to the results hoped for if their use is not saved for the transposition phase or even postponed for subsequent evaluations but already influences the drafting technique of EU legislative acts. In case there is a need to identify best practices in the transposition/implementation process to meet the stipulations of a European directive, then this should not be left to the Member State's transposition efforts but be considered already in the content of the directive. Best practices for transposition should preferably be developed in the legislative process itself and hence can be listed as options for national implementation in the directive. As a consequence, if the EU wants to adopt complex legislative acts such as the SD, it is well advised to get in touch early and intensely with the national bodies entrusted with the transposition in the Member States and to pay attention to their administrative knowledge and experience. Otherwise, the provisions of an EU act may suffer from imprecision and new governance techniques may be met with resentment and not produce the desired results.

[57] The SD was criticised in this respect by J. van de Gronden and H. de Waele (2010), p. 408.

[58] See the Commission Handbook (2007), pp. 17, 21, and 50.

[59] See Barnard (2008), p. 381.

Annex 1: Questionnaire[60]

1. General Remarks on the Transposition Strategy and General Comprehension of the Implementation

1.1 Main References Used in this Research

Please indicate the main references of your research (e.g., parliamentary documents and laws implementing the SD or adopted for the occasion of transposition…). We would be very pleased if you could indicate the place of publication, particularly if available online.

1.2 Impact of the Services Directive

1.2.1 Did the transposition of the SD give a profound cause to the national legislator to alter—beyond the minimum requirements and a one-to-one transposition of the SD—administrative laws in general?
1.2.2 Which authorities and partners were involved in the transposition process? Did close cooperation and coordination with the several levels of administration take place?

1.3 Scope of Application and Extension to Other Fields of Administrative Law

1.3.1 What is, according to the (prevailing) opinion in your Member State, the directive's scope of application? Are the requirements of the SD perceived as binding only for providing transnational services/for transnational establishment, or are at least Articles 5-15 SD also seen as compulsory for the Member States with regard to purely domestic services/establishment?
1.3.2 Can only transnational service providers refer to the laws/regulations implementing the SD? Or are the implementing laws/regulations applicable also to domestic service providers and, if so, to what extent?
1.3.3 Are the laws/regulations implementing the SD also applicable (fully or partly) to everybody, that is, do they engender general and universal standards for the way authorities deal with all citizens or all economic stakeholders, so that these laws/regulations can be claimed by everybody?
1.3.4 In case your Member State did not treat transnational and domestic service providers equally, what was the intention for this? Was there at least a discussion about equal treatment?

1.4 Incorporation of the Transposing Legislation

1.4.1 How and to what extent were the requirements of the SD relating to administrative proceedings implemented in your Member State?

[60] The questionnaire has been elaborated in September 2009. It has been slightly revised for the purpose of this publication.

1.4.2 Did your Member State incorporate the new rules/regulations into existing statutes or was a new codification passed?

1.5 Relationship of the Services Directive to Primary EC (Now: EU) Law

1.5.1 How is the relation of the SD to Articles 43 and 49 EC Treaty (now Articles 49 and 56 TFEU) assessed?
1.5.2 Have any problems been identified in this context?

1.6 Screening

How did your Member State accomplish the 'screening' in concreto (e.g., authorities concerned, committees, division of tasks), and what were the results?

2. Individual Articles of the Services Directive

2.1 Article 6 SD: Point of Single Contact (POSC)

2.1.1 How were 'points of single contact' (POSCs) in concreto introduced in your Member State?
2.1.2 Does your legislator agree with a subjective understanding of the POSC? Or did your national legislator introduce only a few or even only one POSC in your Member State? How many POSCs will be introduced in your country (approximately)? Did your national legislator reallocate administrative competences (despite Article 6 (2) SD) with the introduction of the POSC(s)?
2.1.3 Were the POSCs introduced in your country as new and independent authorities/offices or were the tasks of the POSCs assigned to already existing authorities?
2.1.4 Were private partners involved in the introduction of POSCs? If so, in what way (e.g., by licence, accreditation)?
2.1.5 Who is liable for the mistakes of the POSCs? According to which principles?

2.2 Article 7 SD: Right to Information

2.2.1 Were the 'rights to information' extended in your national legislation during the transposition process?
2.2.2 For which fields have the 'rights to information' been implemented? Only within the scope of the SD or beyond?

2.3 Article 8 SD: Procedures by Electronic Means

2.3.1 How did your Member State establish electronic procedures in concreto?
2.3.2 Did the transposition in this context have a great impact or had your Member State already established electronic procedures to a comparable extent?

2.3.3 Did your Member State—in contrast to the intention of the SD (cf. Recital No. 52; Handbook 5.4.1)—remove other means of administrative proceedings?

2.4 Article 9 SD: Authorisation Schemes

2.4.1 In which areas of administrative law is an 'a posteriori inspection' pursuant to Article 9 (1) lit.c SD not seen as sufficient so that the national legislator maintains the 'authorisation scheme'?
2.4.2 Which types of authorisation schemes/authorisation procedures exist in your Member State and which one usually applies? Which types had to be abolished or altered due to the requirements of the SD?
2.4.3 According to your national understanding, are simple notification requirements included in Article 9 ff. SD that had to be abolished?

2.5 Article 10 SD: Conditions for the Granting of Authorisation

2.5.1 Article 10 (3) SD implies the recognition of authorisations/requirements granted by other Member States. Where and how was this requirement implemented? Did problems occur in this context?
2.5.2 Was it difficult for your Member State to grant authorisations that give access to a service activity or grant permission to exercise an activity throughout the whole national territory? If it was difficult, how was this problem solved? If not, why?
2.5.3 Did your Member State identify areas of 'overriding reasons to the public interest' (Article 10 (4) SD) to justify regional authorisation only?
2.5.4 According to Article 10 (5) SD, the applicant is entitled to get an authorisation once all conditions for the authorisations have been met. Is this any different from your existing administrative laws? To what extent will the courts review the decision by the granting of authorisation? Do courts also review the use of discretion by authorities? Did the transposition of Article 10 (5) SD change this in any way?
2.5.5 Was there a need to change national law due to the obligation to fully reason the decision of the authority (Article 10 (6) SD)?
2.5.6 The SD did not alter the reallocation of administrative competences with regard to the granting of authorisations (Article 10 (7) SD), as Article 6 (2) SD did with the POSC. Despite this intention, did your national legislator change the allocation of competences?

2.6 Article 11 SD: Duration of Authorisation

Was the principle of unlimited validity of authorisations implemented in a generally applicable rule/regulation? What exceptions were made according to Article 11 (1) SD in your Member State? Was there previously a prohibition on time-limited authorisations in your national legal system?

2.7 Article 12 SD: Selection from Among Several Candidates

To what extent did the requirements of Article 12 SD (regarding selection from among several applicants) change your legal system? Was there any need for the transposition of these requirements (since these requirements had previously been stated in the case law of the ECJ)?

2.8 Article 13 SD: Authorisation Procedures

2.8.1 Which authority determines a priori the duration of an administrative procedure? The legislator by law or the responsible authority by decision?
2.8.2 Did your national legislator establish a general rule on the duration of the procedures? Is this general rule only applicable within the scope of application of the SD or does it apply even beyond? If there is a generally fixed duration, how long is it? If not, did your legislator prescribe different durations in different, specific administrative laws?

In case the authority does not respond to the filed application within the prescribed time, the authorisation is "deemed to have been granted to the provider" (Handbook 6.1.8.).

2.8.3 Is it possible to differ from the prescribed durations of procedures? If so, is this possibility used?
2.8.4 Is a tacit (fictitious) authorisation already usual in your legal system? Is it usual in general administrative procedures law or only in specific administrative laws?
2.8.5 Does a tacit (fictitious) authorisation have only formal effects or also substantive ones?
2.8.6 Do the same rules apply to tacit (fictitious) authorisations as apply to formally granted administrative authorisations (e.g., nullity, revocability, or as regards imposing collateral/additional conditions later on…)?
2.8.7 Are other aspects concerning tacit (fictitious) authorisations worth mentioning?

2.9 Articles 14, 15, 16 SD

2.9.1 Did your national legislator identify a need to adapt national law to implement these articles? If so, how was this adaptation achieved?
2.9.2 Is there discussion about the self-screening of the Member States?
2.9.3 Are there further problems or discourses regarding these articles in your Member State?

2.10 Articles 14–19 SD

Are there any discussions with regard to prohibited requirements/restrictions (Articles 14, 15, 16, and 19 SD) and further exemptions (Articles 16 (3), 17, and 18 SD) in your Member State?

2.11 Articles 22–27 SD

Regarding the transposition of Articles 22-27 SD, have there been discussions? Do any issues of the SD transposition process impact on the modernisation of administrative law and administrative procedures law? How is the role of the Member State as an initiator of private regulation (Article 26 SD re certification schemes and quality charters) assessed?

2.12 Articles 28 ff. SD: Administrative Cooperation

2.12.1 Were there provisions on transnational administrative assistance in your Member State prior to the transposition of the SD? If so, were these provisions congruent with the rules on domestic administrative assistance (if any in your country)?
2.12.2 Did the requirements of the SD give cause to (re)arrange the provisions for administrative assistance in a general, maybe uniform way?
2.12.3 Are there provisions on financial compensation for the wide range of assistance?
2.12.4 Was there a need to change rules on data protection and professional secrets due to the wide range of information obligations? Have such rules only been adapted or did a profound change take place?

2.13 Article 29 SD: Mutual Assistance—General Obligations for the Member State of Establishment

To what extent is this article seen as problematic? Have there been discussions regarding the confirmation of not unlawful business conduct enshrined in Article 29 (1) SD?

2.14 Problems and Discourses on Administrative Cooperation

Were there any problems or discourses regarding Chapter VI (administrative cooperation) worth mentioning?

2.15 Convergence Programme (Chapter VII of the Services Directive)

Regarding this chapter, did any discussions take place in your Member State that you think are worth mentioning here? How is the role of the Member State as an initiator of private regulation in Article 37 SD (re codes of conduct) assessed?

3. Assessment of the Impact of the Services Directive

3.1 Extent of the Impact

In Germany, the impact of the SD on administrative procedures law, administrative law for business activities, and even beyond is assessed as severe. From the perspective of your Member State, do you agree?

3.2 Assessment of the Transposing Legislation

How is the transposition of the SD judged in your Member State? Is it perceived as a great success and an improvement or did only a minimum transposition take place? What aspects guide your assessment?

3.3 Most Important Changes Induced by the Services Directive

In your view, what is the most important and most profound change induced by the transposition of the SD in your Member State, and why?

Annex 2: Comments on the Services Directive Questionnaire[61]

on 1.2:
In Germany, the implementation of the Services Directive (SD) triggered simplification, modernisation, and acceleration of administration or better administrative proceedings. This process has been ongoing for more than ten years now in Germany; the SD builds an important step in this context. To support the simplification, modernisation, and acceleration of administrative procedures, the SD has been implemented beyond its minimum requirements. The scope of application of the new rules and regulations implementing the SD has been extended, and to some extent novel and rather generally applicable rights and procedures have been introduced in German law that were modelled according to the rules and requirements of the SD. Accordingly, innovations of the general administrative law statues have been the aim of the German legislator. Thus, the implementation of the SD became an occasion and a cause for modernising parts of the statutes on administrative proceedings in Germany.

on 1.3:
Most lawyers/legal scholars in Germany assume that the SD is solely applicable to transnational rather than domestic services and establishments because of the limited competence of the EU. The "Handbook on the implementation of the Services Directive" of the European Commission seems to disagree with that opinion. However, the European Commission does not give any explanation for this opinion (Handbook 5., 6.). Therefore, the opinions of the Member States are of interest.

The German legislator implemented the SD mainly by creating new rights and proceedings in the general administrative law in Germany (Law on Administrative Proceedings = Verwaltungsverfahrensgesetz, VwVfG). The implementation effectively allows transnational service providers, domestic service providers, and

[61] These comments on some of the questions of the questionnaire provided additional information on the questions for the research participants to give them an idea of the intention behind some of the questions. The comments have been elaborated in September 2009 and slightly revised later on.

potentially every citizen to claim these new rights and proceedings (if a specific administrative law statute is referring to the new provisions). We would like to know whether other Member States also implemented the requirements of the SD in such an extensive way—i.e., beyond the direct scope of the SD, thus giving domestic providers/citizens (potentially) the same benefits as service providers from other Member States (and if so, to what extent). In this context, the concepts and aims the national legislator pursued when extending implementation are also interesting. In case your Member State did not extend the implementation of the SD to purely domestic service providers, we would like to know whether there were discussions in that regard, and why the legislator refused an extension.

on 1.4:
In Germany, the SD was implemented mainly by introducing a new section providing for a new procedure with its own procedural rules in the pre-existing general administrative law statutes (Law on Administrative Proceedings). Those specific administrative laws that fall under the scope of the SD (e.g., German Trade, Commerce and Industry Regulation Act) declare the new procedure applicable by reference to the new section in the Law of Administrative Proceedings. All other administrative laws beyond services (such as planning law) may refer to the new section as well. Thus, the new procedure prompted by the implementation of the SD may be applied in relation to citizens even in contexts outside the scope of application of the SD. Therefore, the new administrative procedure inserts well into the previous administrative legislation in Germany, which consists of a general codification on procedures (Law on Administrative Proceedings) and various specific administrative laws regulating special fields of administration by providing for material standards and/or peculiar procedural rules, in addition to the general ones.

on 1.5:
The SD codifies in certain areas case law of the Court of Justice of the European Union (ECJ) regarding the freedom of services and of establishment. Consequently, the question arises (especially in case of divergence between the case law and a partially more restrictive SD) how the relation of the case law to the provisions of the SD is comprehended in the MS and which conclusions can be drawn from this.

The provisions of Article 16 (1) lit. b., (3) sentence 1 SD and their restricted range of justifications are of particular interest in this regard because the SD limits the established principles of ECJ case law regarding "overriding reasons relating to the public interest" (cf. recital No. 40; Article 4 No. 8 SD). From the German point of view, the enumeration in the articles of the SD seem to be conclusive.

on 1.6:
The MS are obliged to "screen" their legislative acts in light of the provisions of the SD and to alter them accordingly (e.g., Articles 5 (1), 9, 10, 14, 15 SD). This requires an enormous amount of administrative work and questions how in concreto the screening has been accomplished and which offices and

administrative levels have been involved. Which duties did they have to carry out? Which methods were used?

Moreover, what is interesting is the implementation of Article 5 (1) SD. When was a domestic rule/regulation assessed as being "not sufficiently simple"? Was there a uniform standard?

on 2.1:
A probable core issue in the implementation of the SD was the introduction of the "Points of Single Contact" (POSC). As indicated above, in Germany, Article 6 SD has been implemented by introducing a new section providing for a general administrative procedure (called a "single point of contact procedure" ["Verfahren über eine einheitliche Stelle" (§§ 71a-71e VwVfG)]) in the German Statute of Administrative Proceedings Law. By naming the procedure differently than the name in the SD, the general character of the procedure was underlined (as it may be applied in all areas of administrative law). The new section does not determine the office name. The individual name of the POSC can be chosen independently from the procedure name. Due to the federal structure, various names for the POSC may come into existence.

Because Germany is a federal system, not only the national (federal) legislator but the sixteen constituent states are obliged to pass legal regulations on administrative proceedings and to perform changes necessary for the implementation of the SD. Because the SD does not touch upon "the allocation of functions and powers among the authorities" within the national system (see Article 6 (2) SD), the establishment of POSCs requires several levels of responsibility. There is no single federal competence in this regard. All sixteen constituent states are implementing their peculiar system for the POSC, leading to several different systems. At least eight models are discussed, and not all federal states have yet chosen their definite system. This broad discussion in Germany might be unique. But based on the broad discussion of the different systems in Germany, the question arises whether there was a comparable discussion in other MS about the setting-up, the allocation of the POSCs at the administrative level, and about to which authorities the tasks should be attributed. Did other Member States also have cause for general modernisation of administration? Discussing different possibilities of establishing the POSCs implies a subjective understanding of POSCs. The subjective understanding means that is it the service provider's point of view that counts; for a service provider, the same POSC is always responsible for his matters. In strict contrast, a completely different understanding allows only one national POSC for every MS (but this interpretation is too strict even for the European Commission; see Handbook 5.2.1.).

In Germany, the SD was not a chance to change administrative competence (in accordance with Article 6 (2) SD). Nevertheless, other Member States might have taken this occasion to re-allocate their administrative responsibilities and transferred responsibilities even to POSCs. In Germany, POSCs serve only as intermediaries between the service provider and the responsible administrative authority. Furthermore, it would be interesting whether your Member State established virtual POSCs (i.e., only on an electronic basis, like Internet portals). The European Commission claims the establishment of at least a hotline or comparable means (cf. Handbook 5.2.1.). By filing an application to a POSC in Germany, prescribed deadlines for filing an application to an authority are observed. The receipt at the responsible administrative authority is deemed as taking place three days after the filing at the POSC. Have similar regulations been installed in other Member States? Another interesting issue is how the Member States pursue smooth cooperation between the POSCs and the responsible administrative authorities.

The Commission Handbook discourages establishing different POSCs for domestic nationals and nationals from other MSs and from different offices for the freedom of services and the freedom of establishment. In principle, however, different offices are conceivable (Handbook 5.2.1.). Furthermore there are questions regarding the financing of the POSCs. Has a fee-system for using POSCs been established? Is there a problem with the strict principle of proportionality of costs outlined in 5.2.1. in the Commission Handbook and your relevant national regulations? (see also recital No. 49 of the SD). Who will be liable for the actions of POSCs? If there is already a legislative and judicial system of state liability in your country, does the liability of POSCs conform to this system, or was any kind of adaptation necessary? The system of liability can be set up exclusively by the Member States (e.g., cf. recital No. 51). A connected question is the supervision of the POSCs. In Germany, one essentially distinguishes between supervisory power and (merely) legal supervision. The model of supervision may differ according to the chosen way of establishing POSCs.

on 2.3:

In Germany, regulations on electronic administrative procedures existed prior to the implementation of the SD. But these previous regulations did not give the applicant an enforceable right of electronic procedure; the electronic procedure was used at the discretion of the authority. Now, the authority is obliged to use electronic procedures if the applicant so requires (new § 71 e VwVfG). Establishing effective software solutions creates a lot of work. Was there cooperation between the MS in establishing their national software system? Quite interesting is also whether an applicant has to purchase special devices for an electronic procedure (e.g., a signature card). In principle, the implementation of electronic procedure should not replace traditional administrative procedure (cf. recital No. 52, Handbook 5.4.1.). Some countries might have taken the occasion of the SD to abolish other means of driving administrative procedures.

Must the choice of electronic procedure be expressed explicitly, or is an implied expression sufficient (e.g., by filing the application in electronic form)? Once electronic procedure is chosen, does that mean that the administrative procedure must be completely electronic (even for communication between the responsible authority and the POSC)? Can the applicant still change his choice once he opts for electronic procedure?

on 2.4:
In Germany, there are three types in this context. First, there are regulations that require prior authorisation for certain activities or projects; to start without an authorisation is prohibited. Second, there are rules that provide for a simple notification to an authority so that except when there is good cause, no material examination of the activities takes place. Third, there are rules that require a qualified notification to an authority; this means that the applicant can start his business or activity/project once notified, but the authority will still materially examine the project and may prohibit the activity/project if legal requirements are not met. Thus, the applicant bears the risk of later interdiction of his/her activity/ project. He/she might even be obliged to restore former conditions at his/her own expense.

In the implementation process of the SD, it has been discussed whether these three types have to be altered or abolished or whether some of them are compatible with the SD. We would like to know whether comparable types of authorisation schemes exist in other Member States as well, and if so, how the impact of the SD was judged and which solutions have been found.

on 2.5:
Due to the allocation of competence in the German constitution, it is the constituent states and local authorities that are responsible for granting authorisation. This could pose problems in implementing the requirement of the SD that authorisations grant access to service provision throughout the entire territory of the Member State. This problem can probably be solved best by rules on recognition on all levels of the administration structure.

on 2.8:
Article 13 (1) and (2) SD contain general criteria reflecting the requirements of the rule of law. In this context, one has to observe—comparable to Article 6 SD—whether and to which extent the regulations on the costs of administrative procedures had to be adapted pursuant to Article 13 (2) S. 2 SD.

Article 13 (3) SD requests an *a priori* determination of the duration of procedures (cf. recital No. 43). In Germany, there is a general rule on the duration of administrative procedures in the Law of Administrative Procedures and is fixed at three months. Specific administrative laws can lay down different time spans according to their specific needs while still sticking to other general rules on administrative procedures contained in the Law on Administrative Procedures. If specific administrative laws do not provide for a different duration, the general rules will apply.

With regard to the prescribed duration, it is interesting to know when it commences. Does it start with the filing of the application at the POSCs, or does it start when the application is sent to the responsible authority?

Germany implemented the general requirement of tacit authorisation in the Law of Administrative Procedures (section 42a VwVfG). Specific administrative laws refer to this rule. In addition, laws outside the scope of the SD may refer to it as well. In German law, tacit authorisations were already known in exceptional cases.

In Germany, the tacit (fictitious) authorisation has no substantive (material) effect, but only a formal one. This means that the legal fiction only indicates that an authorisation was granted, but not that this authorisation is legal. German administrative law provides several rules about the arrangement of authorizations (administrative acts). According to the prevailing view in Germany, these rules also apply to tacit (fictitious) authorisations, so the tacit authorisation does not differ from formally-granted administrative authorisations.

In Germany, authorities are obliged for the sake of legal certainty to confirm when a legal fiction exists (section 42a (3) VwVfG). The applicant as well as others whose rights might be concerned by the authorisation can request such a letter of confirmation (as documentary evidence). Once such a letter is issued, the period for initiating legal action commences.

It is also of interest whether MS defined areas of administrative law to which tacit authorisation does not apply due to Article 13 (4) sentence 2 SD ("overriding reasons relating to the public interest").

The term "Response" in Article 13 (4) SD is read (as usual) in German administrative law as "issued," not as "decided." It is, however, not certain whether all Member States agree with that interpretation. It is interesting as well whether in your view the provisions of the SD on tacit authorization could be applied directly in case of lacking or wrongful implementation.

on 2.10:

In Germany, there is a debate about the scope of application of Articles 14, 15 SD. In one opinion, Articles 14 and 15 SD are also applicable to the freedom of services and not only to the freedom of establishment—as far as the provisions are suitable for the freedom of services.

Furthermore, some think that Article 17 has also to be applied with regard to Article 19 SD, and that the relation of Article 16 to 18 SD is not very clear. In one opinion, Article 18 SD is only an enforcement regulation that does not provide an additional exemption. The Commission Handbook says in 7.1.5. and 7.1.3.1. (para 107) that Article 18 SD is a ground of justification. It is interesting whether similar discussions took place in other MS and which conclusions have been drawn. Have there been problems with the requirements of the SD in this context? How have they been solved?

on 2.11:

The requirements of Chapter V can first of all be seen as a substitute for prohibited requirements for granting authorisations. Such requirements are replaced by obligations on the service providers, whose fulfilment is supervised by public authorities. This is a transition of responsibilities from the authorities to the private sector. In our view, this chapter is not very fruitful regarding whether the SD engendered an impact on the national legislator—except Articles 23, 25 SD. Perhaps you or the discussion in your MS have a different point of view on this chapter. For this reason, the questionnaire creates room for discussion.

on 2.12:
Administrative cooperation is an important topic for the administrative work in the EU. In this context, it is interesting whether there were any regulations for transnational administrative assistance in your MS before, and whether the rules transposing the SD fit in the already existing system of administrative assistance.

Usually there is no charge for administrative assistance due to comity in public international law and to acts of EC Law. This might have changed in the MS because of the considerable work caused by the required administrative assistance (cf. especially Articles 30, 31 SD). Due to several obligations to provide or disclose information to other Member States (cf. Articles 10 (3), 28, 29 (3), 33 SD), the question arises whether there were any national legal problems regarding data protection or professional secrets.

on 3.1:
Since the first draft, legal and administrative experts and politicians in Germany have broadly discussed the SD because of the expectation that the SD enfolds a strong impact on the administration in Germany.

on 3.2:
Assessment of the implementation of the SD is very contentious in Germany. There are many voices that would have preferred a more ambitious approach when looking at the implementation of each single requirement of the SD in concreto. On the other hand, the implementation in Germany goes beyond the minimum requirements of the SD (e.g., by extending the rules of the SD beyond the scope of application of the SD) and released further impulses for modernisation, simplification, and the acceleration of administrative proceedings.

References

Journal Articles

Barnard C (2008) Unravelling the Services Directive. CML Rev 45:323–394

Callies C, Korte S (2009) Die Dienstleistungsrichtlinie und ihre Umsetzung in Deutschland. Europarecht (EuR) Beiheft 2 44:65–92

della Cananea G (2003) Beyond the State: the Europeanization and Globalization of Procedural Administrative Law. Eur Pub Law (EPL) 9:563–578

Hahn H (2003) Nationale Auslegungsmethoden, vergleichend betrachtet—europäische Anforderungen an die Methodenlehre. Zeitschrift für Rechtsvergleichung, Internationales Privatrecht und Europarecht (ZfRV) 44:163–170

Klamert M (2008) Die Notifizierungspflichten der Dienstleistungsrichtlinie: Ein Fall für den EuGH?. Deutsches Verwaltungsblatt (DVBl) 123:829–832.

Knill C, Winkler D (2007) Konvergenz oder Divergenz nationaler Rechts- und Verwaltungsstrukturen? Der Effekt der Europäisierung am Beispiel der Umweltverträglichkeitsprüfung in Deutschland und England. Verwaltungsarchiv (VerwArch) 98:1–29

Leisner WG (2007) Die subjektiv-historische Auslegung des Gemeinschaftsrechts—der "Wille des Gesetzgebers" in der Judikatur des EuGH. Europarecht (EuR) 42:689–706

Lemor F, Haake K (2009) Ausgesuchte Rechtsfragen der Umsetzung der Dienstleistungsrichtlinie. Europäische Zeitschrift für Wirtschaftsrecht (EuZW) 20:65–70
Möllers C (2002) Durchführung des Gemeinschaftsrechts. Vertragliche Dogmatik und theoretische Implikationen. Europarecht (EuR) 37:483–516
Potacs M (2009) Effet utile als Auslegungsgrundsatz. Europarecht (EuR) 44:465–487
Stelkens U (2011) Art. 291 AEUV, das Unionsverwaltungsrecht und die Verwaltungsautonomie der Mitgliedstaaten, FÖV Discussion Papers N°68. Available at http://www.foev-speyer.de/publikationen/pubdb.asp?reihen_id=0&jahr=2011
van de Gronden JW, de Waele H (2010) All's Well That Bends Well? The Constitutional Dimension to the Services Directive. Eur Const Law Rev 6:397–429
Vogenauer S (2005) Eine gemeineuropäische Methodenlehre des Rechts—Plädoyer und Programm. Zeitschrift für Europäisches Privatrecht (ZEuP) 13:234–263

Book Chapters

Baldus C, Vogel F (2006) Gedanken zu einer europäischen Auslegungslehre: Grammatikalisches und historisches Argument. In: Wallerath M (ed) Fiat iustitia—Recht als Aufgabe der Vernunft—Festschrift für Peter Krause. Duncker & Humblot, Berlin pp 237–252
Harlow C (2002) Voices of Difference in a Plural Community. In: Beaumont P, Lyons C, Walker N (eds) Convergence and Divergence in European Public Law. Hart Publishing, Oxford pp 199–224
Hessel B (2009) The Effects of the Services Directive for Local and Regional Authorities. In: van de Gronden JW (ed) The EU and WTO Law on Services. Kluwer Law International, New York/The Netherlands pp 75–96
Wahl R (2008) Europäisierung: Die miteinander verbundenen Entwicklungen von Rechtsordnungen als ganzen. In: Trute H-H, Gross T, Röhl HC, Möllers C (eds) Allgemeines Verwaltungsrecht—Zur Tragfähigkeit eines Konzepts. Mohr Siebeck, Tübingen pp 869–898
Zuleeg M (1994) Deutsches und europäisches Verwaltungsrecht—Wechselseitige Einwirkungen, VVDStRL 53, pp 154–195

Books

Chalmers D, Hadjiemmanuil C, Monti G, Tomkins A (2006) European Union Law. Cambridge University Press, Cambridge
Commission Handbook (2007) Implementation of the Services Directive. Available at: http://ec.europa.eu/internal_market/services/services-dir/handbook_de.htm
Craig P, de Burca G (2008) EU Law. Text, Cases, and Materials, 4th edn, OUP, Oxford
Hatje A (1998) Die gemeinschaftsrechtliche Steuerung der Wirtschaftsverwaltung, Nomos Verlag, Baden–Baden
Kaczorowska A (2009) European Union Law, Routledge-Cavendish, Abingdon/Oxon
Neidhardt S (2008) Nationale Rechtsinstitute als Bausteine europäischen Verwaltungsrechts, Mohr Siebeck, Tübingen
Riesenhuber K (ed) (2010) Europäische Methodenlehre, 2nd edn, de Gruyter, Berlin
Schlachter M, Ohler C (eds) (2008) Europäische Dienstleistungsrichtlinie, Nomos Verlag, Baden–Baden

Part II
Country Reports

The Implementation of the Services Directive in Austria

Georg Adler and Thomas Kröll

1 General Remarks on the Transposition Strategy and General Understanding of the Implementation

1.1 Main References Used in this Research

It should be noted that as of today (8 July 2011), the main implementing bill at the federal level (draft government bill 317dB XXIV GP) has yet not passed the Austrian Parliament. The reason for this delay is entirely unrelated to Directive 2006/123/EC. However, given the horizontal nature of the Directive encompassing competences of the States, implementing this Directive by federal law requires an amendment of the Austrian constitution, namely, the insertion of a new

---

Dr. Georg Adler, Institute for European and International Law, Vienna University of Economics and Business, and Schoenherr Rechtsanwaelte GmbH (Georgadler@gmx.at); Dr. Thomas Kröll, Institute for Austrian and European Public Law, Vienna University of Economics and Business (thomas.kroell@wu.ac.at). This report was completed in July 2011 and is based on the draft government bill (317dB XXIV GP) that has passed the Austrian Parliament by 4 November 2011 and came into force by 22 November 2011. The main difference between the government bill and the finally adopted DLG lies in the competence clause according to § 1 para 1 draft DLG which was eliminated during the final stage of parliamentary procedure. The elimination of the competence clause and the consequences thereof are neither treated in this report nor in the general report. Besides, the statements contained in this report remain also valid for the finally adopted DLG.

G. Adler (✉)
Institute for European and International Law, Vienna University of Economics and Business, and Schoenherr Rechtsanwaelte GmbH, Vienna, Austria
e-mail: Georgadler@gmx.at

T. Kröll
Institute for Austrian and European Public Law, Vienna University of Economics and Business, Vienna, Austria
e-mail: thomas.kroell@wu.ac.at

U. Stelkens et al. (eds.), *The Implementation of the EU Services Directive*,
DOI: 10.1007/978-90-6704-840-8_2,

competence clause. Such a clause requires a two-thirds quorum in Austrian Parliament, which is not available to the current majority in the Austrian government. Consequently, the support of opposition parties would be needed to some extent. Such support, however, is not available independent of the subject matter at stake—and consequently also not for the transposition of the Directive—due to a political dispute between the government and opposition parties, as already mentioned, entirely unrelated to the Directive.

All legislation documents—the draft, the initiative by the Austrian government, and parliamentary procedures—can be accessed at http://www.parlament.gv.at/PG/DE/XXIV/I/I_00317/pmh.shtml. Our work relies mainly on these documents and, above all, the governmental initiative.

The Styrian implementing bill (*Gesetz vom 15. Dezember 2009, mit dem das Steiermärkische Akkreditierungsgesetz, das Steiermärkische Aufzugsgesetz 2002, das Steiermärkische Baugesetz, das Steiermärkische Bauproduktegesetz, das Steiermärkische Berg- und Schiführergesetz 1976, das Steiermärkische Elektrizitätswirtschafts- und -organisationsgesetz 2005, das Steiermärkische Prostitutionsgesetz, das Steiermärkische Schischulgesetz 1997, das Steiermärkische Tanzschulgesetz 2000 und das Steiermärkische Veranstaltungsgesetz geändert werden—DLRL-Anpassungsgesetz*) was announced in the *Styrian Law Gazette* on 2 March 2010 (*Steiermärkisches Landesgesetzblatt* 2010/7; see www.ris.bka.gv.at).

The implementing bill of Upper Austria (*Landesgesetz vom 30. April 2010, mit dem das Oö. Tanzschulgesetz 2010 erlassen und das Oö. Sportgesetz, das Oö. Bautechnikgesetz, das Oö. Leichenbestattungsgesetz, das Oö. Campingplatzgesetz, das Oö. Luftreinhalte- und Energietechnikgesetz 2002, das Oö. Kinderbetreuungsgesetz und das Oö. Natur- und Landschaftsschutzgesetz 2001 geändert werden (Oö. Dienstleistungsrichtlinie-Anpassungsgesetz 2010)*) was announced in the *Law Gazette of Upper Austria* on 30 April 2010 (Landesgesetzblatt von Oberösterreich 2010/30; see www.ris.bka.gv.at).

The implementing bill of Vorarlberg (*Gesetz zur Umsetzung der Dienstleistungsrichtlinie—Sammelnovelle*) was announced in the *Law Gazette of Vorarlberg* on 13 April 2010 (*Landesgesetzblatt von Vorarlberg 2010/12*; see www.ris.bka.gv.at).

The implementing bill of Salzburg (*Gesetz, mit dem das Salzburger Landessicherheitsgesetz, die Salzburger Feuerpolizeiordnung 1973, das Salzburger Kinderbetreuungsgesetz 2007, das Salzburger Tierzuchtgesetz 2009, das Salzburger Landeselektrizitätsgesetz 1999, das Salzburger Schischul- und Snowboardschulgesetz, das Salzburger Bergführergesetz, das Salzburger Tanzschulgesetz, das Gesetz über den Betrieb von Motorschlitten, das Salzburger Campingplatzgesetz, das Salzburger Veranstaltungsgesetz 1997, das Bauproduktegesetz, das Luftreinhaltegesetz für Heizungsanlagen, das Salzburger Baupolizeigesetz 1997, das Gesetz über die Errichtung des Nationalparkes Hohe Tauern im Land Salzburg, das Salzburger Höhlengesetz, das Salzburger Heilvorkommen- und Kurortegesetz 1997 und das Salzburger Leichen- und Bestattungsgesetz 1986 geändert werden (Salzburger Landesgesetz zur Umsetzung der EU-Dienstleistungsrichtlinie)*) was announced in the *Law Gazette of Salzburg* on 26 February 2010 (*Salzburger Landesgesetzblatt 2010/20*; see www.ris.bka.gv.at).

As far as the implementation of the provisions of Directive 2006/123/EC regarding procedures by electronic means is concerned, see http://www.digitales.oesterreich.gv.at/site/6367/default.aspx and http://www.bmwfj.gv.at/Wirtschaftspolitik/Standortpolitik/Seiten/EU-RichtlinieüberDienstleistungenimBinnenmarktundihre UmsetzunginÖsterreich.aspx.

1.2 Impact of the Services Directive

1.2.1 Profound Cause of Changes to National Law?

According to the European Commission, implementation necessitates a differentiating methodical approach requiring the adoption of *new* sectoral and horizontal provisions, as well as the *amendment* of existing (sectoral and horizontal) laws.[1] However, the draft government bill (317dB XXIV GP)[2] rather seeks to comply with horizontal implementation objectives due to the adoption of the horizontal Services Act (*Dienstleistungsgesetz*, henceforth draft DLG) and the Internal Market Information System (IMI) Act. In addition, a few adaptations of the *Allgemeines Verwaltungsverfahrensgesetz*[3] (henceforth AVG), of the *Verwaltungsstrafgesetz*[4] (henceforth VStG), and the 1991 *Verwaltungsvollstreckungsgesetz*[5] (VVG) and of a few substantive laws were carried out; however, these few adaptations are rather of formal nature.

In Austria, the transposition of Directive 2006/123/EC constitutes a minimum transposition (see http://www.bmwfj.gv.at/Wirtschaftspolitik/Standortpolitik/Seiten/EU-RichtlinieüberDienstleistungenimBinnenmarktundihreUmsetzungzunginÖsterreich.aspx) which does not exceed the requirements contained in the Directive. The main innovations in the Austrian substantive administrative law and administrative procedural law are the Points of Single Contact (POSC), the comprehensive introduction of tacit (fictitious) authorisation, and provisions on transnational administrative assistance.

---

[1] See Commission, *Handbook on the Implementation of the Services Directive* (2007), p. 8.

[2] *RV 317 BlgNR XXIV. GP - Regierungsvorlage betreffend Bundesgesetz, mit dem ein Bundes gesetz über die Erbringung von Dienstleistungen (Dienstleistungsgesetz—DLG) und ein Bundes gesetz über das internetgestützte Behördenkooperationssystem IMI (IMI-Gesetz) erlassen, das Preisauszeichnungsgesetz, das Konsumentenschutzgesetz, das Allgemeine Verwaltungsverfahren sgesetz 1991, das Verwaltungsstrafgesetz 1991 und das Verwaltungsvollstreckungsgesetz 1991 geändert und einige Bundesgesetze aufgehoben werden.*

[3] *Allgemeines Verwaltungsverfahrensgesetz BGBl 1991/51 idF BGBl I Nr. 2009/20*, which can be translated as the General Administrative Procedure Act.

[4] *Verwaltungsstrafgesetz BGBl 1991/52 idF BGBl I Nr. 2009/20*, which can be translated as the Regulatory Offence Procedure Act.

[5] *Verwaltungsvollstreckungsgesetz BGBl Nr. 53/1991 idF BGBl I Nr. 3/2008*, which can be translated as the Administrative Execution Act.

1.4 Incorporation of Transposing Legislation

Similar to the German situation, Austrian administrative law consists of a general codification of procedures, on the one hand, and various substantive laws regulating specific fields of administration, on the other. The latter contain material standards and/or peculiar procedural rules, completing the general ones.

The Austrian legislator finally decided to implement the Directive by adopting entirely new legislative acts and to amend existing laws only insofar as they were in contradiction to the provisions of the Directive. The main innovations of Directive 2006/123/EC—POSC, tacit (fictitious) authorisation, transnational administrative cooperation—were implemented by the draft DLG, horizontally, on the federal level. State laws were amended punctually. In fields covered by the new provisions, such as transnational situations, the AVG statutes are not applied. These latter come into use only when the newly adopted provisions do not suffice. In other words, the provisions implementing the Directive are *leges speciales*.

In addition to this, the authorities in charge of the screening procedure sought to eliminate contradictions between administrative laws and the Directive so that service providers may rely upon the entirely new adopted acts, on the one hand, and beyond that on the existing proceedings.

1.5 The Relationship of the Services Directive to Primary EU Law

1.5.1 Relationship to Article 49 and 56 TFEU

Pursuant to Article 3 para 3 Directive 2006/123/EC, Member States are obliged to implement and apply the provisions of the Directive "in compliance with the rules of the Treaty on the right of establishment and the free movement of services". Thus, the Directive must be interpreted in light of the Treaties and the jurisprudence of the ECJ.

1.5.2 Problems in this Context

Problems can arise not only from the partial poor wording and systematic of the Directive, but also from gaps therein, such as the lack of provisions governing the discriminatory requirements of Member States, restricting the freedom to provide services and possibilities for justification.

Article 2 of the Directive clarifies the fields of services that do not fall within the scope of its application. As a consequence of the direct applicability of Articles 49 ff and 56 ff TFEU and the non-applicability of the Directive in these fields, there is no need to amend national legislation.

1.6 Screening

The Austrian administrative law system divides competences between different levels, for example between federal, state, and, local authorities. Thus, the different territorial authorities ("Gebietskörperschaften") are responsible for compliance of the procedural and substantive laws with the requirements of the Services Directive (SD). According to a governmental decision of 12 March 2008, the competent authorities on the federal and state levels had to screen the relevant legislation, under individual responsibility, through 31 August 2008, and amend the respective laws in cases of non-compliance. On the federal level, the ministries had to screen legislation in their enforcement areas according to the *Bundesministeriengesetz*, and on the state level the state governments had to screen legislation falling within the competence of the States. Furthermore, cities and municipalities had to review their local provisions to comply with the Directive's requirements, for example, market regulations and regulations regarding graveyards. As coordinator of the implementation process, the Ministry for Economics, Family, and Youth assigned a study to the University of Salzburg to identify the demand for legislative amendments on all levels and to define the most appropriate uniform approach regarding the reporting duties pursuant to Article 39 of the Directive.

2 Individual Articles of the Services Directive

2.1 Article 6 SD: Point of Single Contact (POSC)

2.1.1 Establishment of the POSC

In Austria, as in many other Member States, a person seeking the transnational provision of services had to face a large number of administrative bodies, for example, tax offices, building authorities, and competent courts, to receive a tax ID, a building permit, or an entry in the register of companies, and thus complete all procedures and formalities. In implementing Article 6 of the Directive, which, without doubt, constitutes one of its core provisions, the Austrian legislator established the POSC.

The question of allocating the POSC *in concreto* has been a topic of lively discussion. Besides the entrustment of existing authorities or institutions to be newly created, the entrustment of chambers (e.g., chambers of commerce, bar associations, and architectural associations) in their function as for the respective profession responsible institutions was discussed. On the one hand, a certain similarity can be gleaned between the procedures to be accomplished through the POSC and the admission and registration procedures with chambers.[11] In addition,

---

[11] For Germany, see Windoffer (2006), pp. 1216 f.

the comprehensive experience of chambers concerning cooperation with administrative authorities would also be advantageous. However, misgivings concerning the entrustment of chambers expressed in Germany[12] are also of relevance for the Austrian legal system. In particular, the assignment of general administrative duties to chambers would necessitate fundamental amendments to the relevant laws. Chambers would no longer exclusively act in the interests of its members but would have to also serve "external" purposes. The Austrian implementation draft (32/ME XXIV GP) foresaw the insertion of § 20a into the AVG.[13] This should ensure the opportunity of using the POSC not only in the scope of the Directive, but also generally, and thus also for purely internal situations. However, this approach triggered the resistance of the States and some ministries.[14] Consequently, the draft was amended so that the POSC are now exclusively covered by the draft DLG and cover only transnational situations.

2.1.2 Subjective Understanding, Competence Structure, Authorities with POSC-Function, Liability, Involvement of Private Partners

In § 6 para 1 draft DLG the creation of nine POSC (one for every State) is provided for, located in its respective *Amt der Landesregierung*,[15] which is an already existing institution at the state level. Administrative competences were not allocated in the course of the introduction of the POSC. The service provider can submit written requests during the proceeding of first instance at the POSC, who must forward them to the competent authority. The qualification as POSC relates to the perspective of the service provider,[16] who must gain the impression to deal with one single institution.

The Austrian concept seeks the establishment of POSC as mere mail-administrating centres that do not decide on the merits. Thus, the establishment of the POSC

[12] See Cremer (2008), p. 655.

[13] ME 32 BlgNR XXIV. GP.

[14] Compare, for example, *SN 17 zu ME 32 XXIV. GP 12. zu § 20, Stellungnahme von: Amt der Salzburger Landesregierung Legislativ- und Verfassungsdienst zu dem Ministerialentwurf betreffend ein Bundesgesetz über die Erbringung von Dienstleistungen (Dienstleistungsgesetz - DLG) und ein Bundesgesetz über das Internal Market Information System (IMI) (Gesetz – IMI-G) erlassen, das Allgemeine Verwaltungsverfahrensgesetz 1991, das Verwaltungsstrafgesetz 1991 und das Verwaltungsvollstreckungsgesetz 1991 geändert und einige Bundesgesetze aufgehoben werden (Sammelgesetz Dienstleistungsrichtlinie); SN 35 ME 32 XXIV. GP 2.1. zu § 20 AVG, Stellungnahme von: Amt der Burgenländischen Landesregierung zu dem Ministerialentwurf betreffend ein Bundesgesetz über die Erbringung von Dienstleistungen (Dienstleistungsgesetz - DLG) und ein Bundesgesetz über das Internal Market Information System (IMI) (Gesetz—IMI-G) erlassen, das Allgemeine Verwaltungsverfahrensgesetz 1991, das Verwaltungsstrafgesetz 1991 und das Verwaltungsvollstreckungsgesetz 1991 geändert und einige Bundesgesetze aufgehoben werden (Sammelgesetz Dienstleistungsrichtlinie).*

[15] Department of the state government.

[16] Schliesky (2005), p. 891.

does not require any reallocation of competences. In any case, amendments would have been covered by the competences clause contained in § 1 para 1 draft DLG.

The POSC acts functionally for the competent authorities. Thus, the responsible administrative units beyond on federal, state, or community level are liable for damages caused by non- or mis-performance of the POSC.[17] Should the POSC act for various governmental units, compensation must be divided between those units proportionally to their competence areas.[18]

However, in our opinion, the mere delivery function of the POSC does not entirely meet the requirements of the Directive. Even if the Directive certainly does not require the POSC to take binding decisions on the merits, the latter is supposed to offer "assistance"[19] to providers.[20] In particular, such a "partner of proceeding" would have the function to work actively towards a correct and prompt completion of the proceeding[21]; However, this is not the case with the Austrian POSC.

No private partners are involved in performing the duties of the POSC.

2.2 *Article 7 SD: Right to Information*

According to Article 7 para 1 of Directive 2006/123/EC, Member States have to ensure that certain information is easily accessible through the POSC. In this connection, the POSC is obliged to provide information itself and does not only serve as an intermediary station. A mere reference or the reproduction of existing legislation will not suffice to meet the Directive's requirements.[22] In implementing this article, § 7 para 1 of draft DLG states that the POSC has to provide, among other things, information concerning admission conditions, competent authorities, remedies, and other supporting institutions not constituting authorities (e.g., the *WKO Gründerservice* at the Austrian Chamber of Commerce).

To fulfil its information duties towards the service provider, the POSC, on its part, depends on information from the competent authorities. The draft DLG thus stipulates an obligation of the respective competent authority to provide any information to the POSC that is necessary for the fulfilment of its duties.[23] As far as information going beyond the information duties of the POSC is concerned, the

---

[17] Cover page and explanations for 32/ME XXIV. GP.

[18] Ibid.

[19] Recital 48.

[20] See also the term *intermediary*, contained in Recital 12 of Recommendation 97/344/EC on improving and simplifying the business environment for business startups.

[21] Windoffer (2006), p. 1213.

[22] Commission, *Handbook on the Implementation of the Services Directive*, 2007, p. 21.

[23] § 6 draft DLG.

POSC may refer the service provider to the competent authority. Rights to information were therefore not extended in the context of the transposition process. However, the POSC must provide information only within the scope of the Directive.

2.3 Article 8 SD: Procedures by Electronic Means

Similarly to the legal situation in Germany, Austrian law did not contain the right of the applicant to use an electronic procedure.

In implementing Article 8 of Directive 2006/123/EC, the implementation draft (32/ME XXIV GP) sought to introduce § 20a para 6 AVG. However, because of the resistance mentioned previously, the government refrained from coverage also of purely internal situations and, instead, proposed § 10 draft DLG. It provides that the POSC and the authorities have to establish the conditions to accomplish the whole procedure in electronic form, as well as electronic notification, for cross-border situations.

Nevertheless, the service provider also has the opportunity to carry out the proceedings by non-electronic means, as far as legal provisions allow for this approach. A compulsory provision of electronic channels would discriminate against applicants who do not possess electronic means.[24] Thus, other means of administrative procedures have not been abolished. The POSC will have to publish technical prerequisites or organisational restrictions of electronic correspondence on the Internet.

According to § 6 para 4 draft DLG, the POSC has to inform the service provider in case a certain form of application is obligatory.

Being competent for e-government in general, the *Bundeskanzleramt* coordinated the technical premises for the transposition of Directive 2006/123/EC to comply with the requirements regarding procedures by electronic means. The Plattform Digitales Österreich is concerned with the electronic provision of information for service providers and recipients, the electronic handling of procedures, and the electronic means of transnational administrative assistance. To define the technical architecture and requirements, a task force has been established in the context of the cooperation of the Federation, the States, the Cities, and Municipalities and the economy (Digitales Österreich). The main starting point for the electronic service for service providers and recipients is the help.gv.at portal (www.help.gv.at) of the *Bundeskanzleramt*, a government agency help site on the Internet offering information necessary for living and working in Austria, but since the POSC are located at the *Ämter der Landesregierungen*, the help.gv.at portal will not have any official role in the implementation of Directive 2006/123/EC. The help.gv.at portal will therefore provide additional navigation and information functions.

---

[24] Cover page and explanations for 32/ME XXIV. GP *Sammelgesetz Dienstleistungsrichtlinie*.

The provision of information for transnational service providers and recipients by the nine POSC started within the time limit on 28 December 2009 (see http://www.eap.gv.at). The electronic handling of procedures, however, will commence with the adoption and entry into force of the relevant legislation, providing a legal basis for establishing the technical facilities for electronic procedures. It should be pointed out, and this seems to be problematic in our view, in light of the requirements of Article 8 of Directive 2006/123/EC, only procedures applied at least five times a year throughout Austria will be handled by electronic means, according to the decision of the *Landesamtsdirektorenkonferenz* in April 2008 (see http://www.bmwfj.gv.at/Wirtschaftspolitik/Standortpolitik/Seiten/EU-Richtlinieü berDienstleistungenimBinnenmarktundihreUmsetzunginÖsterreich.aspx).

2.4 Article 9 SD: Authorisation Schemes

2.4.1 Means of Less Restrictive Measure

It must be re-emphasised that the Austrian legislator decided that laws adopted in implementing Directive 2006/123/EC do not cover purely internal situations. Thus, authorisation schemes are maintained whenever there is no cross-border dimension. As far as transnational service provision is concerned, it should be noted that neither the legislator on the federal level nor the nine legislators on the state level are dealing with the replacement of authorisation schemes by notifications and a posteriori inspections (*Anmeldeverfahren statt Genehmigungsverfahren*) in a general way. Obviously, the screening of authorisation procedures confirmed the necessity and proportionality of these requirements. Only the initiative for the implementing bill of Upper Austria abolishes the authorisation procedure for the opening of dancing schools and replaces this requirement by a simple notification.

2.4.2 Existing Authorisation Schemes/Procedures

Basically, authorisation schemes in Austria differentiate between three modes of authorisation, comparable to the German approach. The first mode of authorisation constitutes in a notification towards the authority. This suffices in order to be allowed to provide the service. This applies, for example, to crafts (*freie Gewerbe*) according to the Gewerbeordnung (GewO). To meet the conditions of the second mode of authorisation, one not only has to notify the authority, but the latter also materially examines whether the conditions for exercising the profession are met. Here, the applicant is allowed to pursue his or her activity during the examination process, but would eventually have to stop later if the authority finds a conflict with the permission conditions. An example would constitute a facility site permission (*Betriebsanlagengenehmigung*) for a normal facility site (*Normalanlage*) according to the GewO. The last group of permission processes concerns examinations processes, where the applicant must not provide services until permission is obtained from the authority. The GewO also contains an example for this group, namely, sensitive crafts (*sensible Gewerbe*).

In our opinion, only the last group of authorisation schemes needs a check of its compatibility with the provisions of Directive 2006/123/EC. Crafts qualified as sensitive are, for example, those dealing with weapons, pyrotechnics, or laboratories. At first sight, it seems that the maintenance of authorisation schemes in this connection could be justified on the basis of public interest and health. The GewO also qualifies travel agencies as sensitive crafts. Here, a justification on the basis of the reasons mentioned above seems rather unlikely. However, a justification on the basis of consumer protection is conceivable, proportionality seems questionable. However, it seems rather unlikely that the requirement for the receipt of a licence as a chimney sweeper complies with the targets of the Directive 2006/123/EC. In our view, no justification exists for making the receipt of a licence for this sensitive craft dependent on residence in Austria.[25]

2.4.3 Simple Notifications

Neither the legislator on the federal level nor the nine legislators on the state level deal with simple notification requirements in a general way. Only the implementing bill of Upper Austria abolishes the authorisation procedure for the opening of dancing schools and replaces this requirement by a simple notification (*Anmeldeverfahren statt Genehmigungsverfahren*). We are of the opinion that simple notification requirements (*Meldepflichten*) are not covered by Chapter III, of Directive 2006/123/EC. This section deals exclusively with authorisation schemes, the conditions for the granting of authorisations, and the duration of authorisations, as well as authorisation procedures (Articles 9–13). Nevertheless, simple notification requirements are to be qualified as requirements in the sense of Article 4 para 7 and have to be screened in the ambit of Article 16 of Directive 2006/123/EC.

2.5 *Article 10 SD: Conditions for the Granting of Authorisation*

2.5.1 Recognition of Requirements

In contrast to the wording of question 5A (the Questionnaire is reprinted as Annex to this book), Article 10 para 3 of Directive 2006/123/EC does not concern the recognition of authorisations granted in the state of (first) establishment of the service provider, but the recognition of already fulfilled requirements for such an authorisation in the state of (first) establishment. The intention of this duty of recognition is for requirements not to be duplicated at the expense of the service

[25] Compare § 121 para 1 section 2 GewO.

provider in the state of (second) establishment. Article 10 para 3 of Directive 2006/123/EC does not affect the recognition of professional qualifications (Article 3 para 1 d of Directive 2006/123/EC). The state duty of the (second) establishment to recognise requirements already fulfilled by the service provider in the state of (first) establishment can be deduced from the standing jurisprudence of the ECJ. Neither the legislator on the federal level nor the nine legislators on the state level are deal with this duty of recognition in a general way, although there would be two possibilities to implement Article 10 para 3. The duty could be anchored in the draft government bill (317dB XXIV GP)—in the draft DLG—or in the specific administrative laws on federal or state level. In the absence of an explicit implementation clause in federal or state law, the relevant laws must be interpreted according to the principle of harmonious interpretation in light of Article 10 para 3 of the Directive. Furthermore, Article 10 para 3 may be regarded as precise and unconditional, and therefore capable of producing a direct effect as a consequence of the poor transposition.

2.5.2 Granting Authorisation Throughout the Whole National Territory and Exceptions

The implementation of Article 10 para 4 of Directive 2006/123/EC could have constituted a veritable challenge for the Austrian legislator, since the Austrian legal system is based on a federal organisation. On the one hand, Article 10 para 4 explicitly requires that an authorisation, once granted, shall be basically valid throughout the national territory. On the other hand, due to a systematic approach, this might be interpreted narrowly, since Article 10 para 7 states that any distortions of the competences of regional and local authorities must be avoided. Thus, the question arose as to which obligations a national legislator had to meet to comply with these requirements.

The Austrian legislator obviously took the line of least resistance and emphasised the aspect of avoidance with the allocation of competences. According to the Austrian legislator, any discussion on the validity of authorisations throughout the national territory is superfluous, and no amendments of the status quo are regarded as necessary. Neither the legislator on the federal level nor the nine legislators on the state level deal with the scope of authorisations granted, especially authorisations granted by single States, in a general way.

However, in our opinion, Article 10 paras 4 and 7 of Directive 2006/123/EC must not be interpreted in a way that authorisations with a scope throughout the national territory are only requested by Article 10 para 4 if the allocation of regional and local competences remains unaltered. To meet the objective in Article 10 para 4, national measures and instruments are conceivable without touching upon the allocation of competences, so for example, the automatic recognition of one State's authorisation in all the other States or the simple notification of the authorisation granted in one State to the authorities in the other States and the subsequent recognition.

Furthermore, one must pay attention to the recent jurisprudence of the ECJ, which states that the application for a licence for each province *separately* constitutes an infringement of EU law.[26] In the light of this recent judgement, the sufficiency of a declarative notification by the provider at the respective authority must be provided not only in the scope of Directive 2006/123/EC, but also in the field of application of the fundamental freedoms under Articles 49 ff and 56 ff TFEU, in general. In consequence, the approach of a declarative notification would be generally preferable for the whole indirect state administration, that are, purely internal situations as well. Exemptions are only allowed insofar as overriding reasons relating to the public interest are applicable, whereas an exemplary enumeration of those reasons as provided for in Directive 2006/123/EC appears to be suggestive. This should be explicitly clarified not only in the draft DLG, but also in the AVG and in substantive laws on the federal and state levels.

Since legislators on the federal and state levels act on the presumption that existing State authorisations are in compliance with the requirements of Article 10 para 7 of the Directive, no efforts have been made to identify overriding reasons relating to the public interest to justify authorisations whose scope is limited to the State's territory.

2.5.3 Entitlement to Grant Authorisation, Court Review of Administrative Decisions

The Austrian legal system already complied with the objective provided in Article 10 para 5 of Directive 2006/123/EC, where an applicant meeting all conditions has a right to receive an authorisation. In the case where the competent authority nevertheless issues a negative decision, the applicant has the opportunity to take remedies. A court concerned with an appeal against the decision of an authority will decide in fact and in law, and will also check how far the discretion of the authority complies with domestic law. In connection with the discretion of the authority, it must be emphasised that the discretion must also comply with national law, which, on its part, has to comply with the objectives of European Union law.

2.5.4 Reasoning of Administrative Decisions

Austrian administrative law and administrative procedural law already provides that every proceeding is executed by a legal decision (*Bescheid*) of which the applicant must be notified. This decision can be carried out orally or in writing, the latter form being the predominant one. Here § 58 para 1 AVG defines the basic

[26] ECJ, C-134/05, *Commission v. Italy* [2007], I-06251, para 64, which in this connection particularly criticises the applicant's additional obligation to have premises in each province in which the applicant intends to pursue activities, unless he or she confers the authority upon an authorised agent in that other province.

conditions a decision has to meet. Among other things, every decision must be reasoned pursuant to § 58 para 2, § 60, and § 67 AVG, except for the case where the authority fully grants the authorisation according to the application and no objections from other parties or participants (*Beteiligter*) exist. Thus, no further implementation obligations were identified in this regard.

2.5.5 Allocation of Competences

Since national legislators act on the presumption that existing State authorisations are in compliance with the requirements of Article 10 para 7 of Directive 2006/123/EC, no amendments of the allocation of competences in the context of Article 10 were deemed necessary.

2.6 Article 11 SD: Duration of Authorisation

Pursuant to Article 11 para 1 of Directive 2006/123/EC, authorisations shall be granted, in principle, for an unlimited period. As a consequence of the principle of unlimited validity of decisions in the Austrian legal system, anchored in the AVG, neither the legislator on the federal level nor the nine legislators on the state level have to take explicit measures in this regard. Limited periods can be determined by the competent legislators in the substantive administrative laws on federal or state level. However, neither the legislator on the federal level nor the nine legislators on the state level amend substantive administrative laws on the federal or state level in the context of the transposition of Directive 2006/123/EC.

2.7 Article 12 SD: Selection from Among Several Candidates

The requirements codified in Article 12 of Directive 2006/123/EC can already be deduced from the jurisprudence of the ECJ. The most prominent examples for services in this respect, gambling and urban transport, are excluded from the scope of application pursuant to Article 2 para 2 (d) and (h). Neither the legislator on the federal level nor the nine legislators on the state level deal with the requirements of Article 12 in a general way, or in the respective substantive administrative laws. Thus, the legislators did not ascertain any need for amendments of the legislation in force.

2.8 Article 13 SD: Authorisation Procedures

2.8.1 A Priori Determination of the Duration of Administrative Procedures

In § 18 AVG, the Austrian legislator provides that authorities must handle matters in an efficient and cost-saving manner towards all parties and participants.

This approach is complemented by § 73 para 1 AVG, which obliges authorities to make their decisions within six months of an application's receipt. In any case, substantive administrative laws may provide for a different time period; otherwise the general rule is applied. If the respective authority does not decide on the application within six months, the concerned party is allowed to submit a devolution application (*Devolutionsantrag*) according to § 73 para 2 AVG, thus allowing the higher federal or state authority to basically decide on the case's merits.

2.8.2 General Rule for the Duration

Under the scope of application of Directive 2006/123/EC, Article 12 paras 2 and 3 draft DLG provides that authorisations must be granted within three months.[27] Corresponding to Article 13 para 3 of Directive 2006/123/EC, § 12 para 2 draft DLG the time limit of three months may be extended by the competent authority for a limited time.

2.8.3 Exceptions of the General Rule for the Duration

However, § 12 draft DLG only constitutes an "opting in"- clause, since the federal or state legislator competent for the respective substantive administrative law can deviate from this provision. A competent legislator for the respective substantive administrative law, though, must examine whether a deviation from the three-month period is justified. This is particularly possible in situations where mandatory requirements exist (e.g., in some multiparty proceedings).[28]

2.8.4 Tacit Authorisation in the National Legal Order So Far

Pursuant to Article 13 paras 3 and 4 of Directive 2006/123/EC, in case the competent authority does not respond to the filed application within the set or extended time period, the authorisation "is deemed to have been granted" to the service provider. The Austrian AVG does not contain a tacit (fictitious) authorisation. However, some substantive administrative laws provide for this opportunity. For example, the Austrian *Vereinsgesetz*[29] provides in § 13 para 2 that the

---

[27] In relation to § 73 AVG, § 12 draft DLG constitutes a *lex specialis*.

[28] RV 317 BlgNR XXIV. GP—*Regierungsvorlage betreffend Bundesgesetz, mit dem ein Bundesgesetz über die Erbringung von Dienstleistungen (Dienstleistungsgesetz—DLG) und ein Bundesgesetz über das internetgestützte Behördenkooperationssystem IMI (IMI-Gesetz) erlassen, das Preisauszeichnungsgesetz, das Konsumentenschutzgesetz, das Allgemeine Verwaltungsverfahrensgesetz 1991, das Verwaltungsstrafgesetz 1991 und das Verwaltungsvollstreckungsgesetz 1991 geändert und einige Bundesgesetze aufgehoben werden, 4.*

[29] *Vereinsgesetz BGBl I Nr. 66/2002 idF BGBl I Nr. 45/2008*, which can be translated as the Voluntary Association Act.

application for the foundation of a voluntary association according to that law is deemed granted if the authority does not prohibit the activity within six weeks after receipt of the application. The voluntary association is deemed to be founded with expiry of the veto period. However, the possibility of tacit (fictitious) authorisation constitutes more the exception than the rule in Austrian law.

In the implementation of the Directive, § 12 para 1 draft DLG provides that in case the competent authority does not respond to the filed application within the set or extended time period, a tacit (fictitious) authorisation is granted to the service provider.

2.8.5 Formal and Substantive Effects of Tacit Authorisation

As far as the effects of a tacit (fictitious) authorisation are concerned, it must be pointed out that the tacit (fictitious) authorisation is a substitute for the authorisation normally granted in the form of a formal decision (*Bescheid*) and settles the filed application in a formal and substantive way. The legal effects of a tacit (fictitious) authorisation and of a formal decision (*Bescheid*) are equivalent. In the case of a tacit (fictitious) authorisation, it is not possible to prescribe conditions or limitations.

2.8.6 Rules of Formally Granted Authorisations Applicable to Tacit Authorisations

The provisions of the AVG about the *ex officio* modification or repeal of formal decisions (*Abänderung und Behebung von Amts wegen*) and about the reopening of the procedure (*Wiederaufnahme des Verfahrens*) (§§ 68–70 AVG) are applicable also to tacit (fictitious) authorisations.

2.8.7 Further Information on the National Implementation of Tacit Authorisation

As mentioned in the "Comments on the Services Directive Questionnaire", it is important to know not only the duration of the procedure but also the commencement of the time period for the decision. The Austrian legislator is setting up the POSC as a mere mail-administrating centre, that is, it is not to decide on an application's merits and solely delivers each application to the competent authority. According to § 13 para 3 AVG, the respective authority is obliged to return any incomplete or faulty applications to the applicants for revision. The POSC is not authorised to check the application. In § 12 para 3 draft DLG, it is explicitly pointed out that the time period of decision starts with the receipt of an application free from defaults. Since only the authority can assess whether an application is complete or not, the decision period can only start with the authority's receipt of the application.

Pursuant to § 12 para 4 draft DLG, in case the competent authority does not respond to the filed application within the set or extended time period and a tacit (fictitious) authorisation is granted to the service provider, the competent authority must confirm the authorisation to the provider as soon as possible. All parties must be notified of this written confirmation of the granted authorisation. All parties are entitled to apply for a formal confirmation of the authorisation granted in the form of a formal decision (*Bescheid*) within a time limit of four weeks. However, § 12 para 4 draft DLG also constitutes an "opting in" clause, since the federal or state legislator competent for the respective substantive administrative law may deviate from this provision.

Similar to the understanding prevailing in Germany, the term "response" in Article 13 para 4 of Directive 2006/123/EC is read as "notified" and not "decided". Thus, the tacit (fictitious) authorisation is not applicable if notification has already been made regarding the formal decision (*Bescheid*). The relevant point in time for issue will in most situations be the delivery in writing, but Austrian law also provides for the opportunity of oral publication and authentication by the authority according to § 62 para 2 AVG.

2.9 *Articles 14, 15, 16 SD*

2.9.1 Need of Adaptation?

The need Austrian legislators have identified to adapt national rules on the federal and state levels to implement Articles 14–16 of Directive 2006/123/EC is very weak (see http://www.bmwfj.gv.at/Wirtschaftspolitik/Standortpolitik/Seiten/EU-RichtlinieüberDienstleistungenimBinnenmarktundihreUmsetzunginÖsterreich.aspx, according to which adaptation requirements are assessed to be rather weak). As a consequence, there have been no amendments of substantive administrative laws on the federal level in the context of the draft government bill (317dB XXIV GP). In addition, the nine legislators on the state level made very few amendments of substantive administrative laws when dealing with Articles 14–16 of Directive 2006/123/EC. For example, the implementing bill of Upper Austria abolishes the authorisation procedure for the opening of dancing schools and replaces this requirement by a simple notification. Furthermore, also following requirements are abolished: the ban on multiple ownership for ski schools, the needs test for burial facilities, etc. (see www.ris.bka.gv.at).

According to a government decision of 12 March 2008, the competent authorities on the federal and state levels had to screen the relevant legislation under individual responsibility through 31 August 2008, and to amend the respective laws in case of non-compliance. On the federal level, the ministries had to screen legislation in their enforcement areas according to the *Bundesministeriengesetz*; on the state level the state governments had to screen legislation falling within the competence of the States. In the function of coordinator of the implementation process, the Ministry for Economics, Family and Youth assigned a study to the University of Salzburg to identify the demand for legislative amendments on all levels.

2.9.2 Discussion on the Self-Screening of the Member States

There were no discussions about the self-screening of Member States.

2.9.3 Discourses on these Articles

All obvious problems or discourses regarding Articles 14–16 of Directive 2006/123/EC are described under "Need of Adaptation?" above.

2.10 Articles 14–19 SD

As far as the provisions of Directive 2006/123/EC regarding prohibited requirements and restrictions (Articles 14–16 and 19 of Directive 2006/123/EC) and exemptions (Article 16 para 3 and Articles 17 and 18 of Directive 2006/123/EC) are concerned, the Austrian legislators on the federal and state level, confronted with the output of the screening process, apparently did not see any need to implement these articles—besides Article 18 of Directive 2006/123/EC—in an explicit way. Article 18 of Directive 2006/123/EC is implemented by § 20 draft DLG. There have been discussions about the most appropriate form and location for the implementation of Article 16 para 3 of Directive 2006/123/EC, but the federal legislator finally decided not to provide for a(n explicit) corresponding free movement clause in the draft DLG.

2.11 Articles 22–27 SD

Also with regard to Chapter V of Directive 2006/123/EC concerning the quality of services, Austrian legislators on the federal and state levels did not see a need to implement these articles—besides Article 22 of Directive 2006/123/EC—in an explicit way. The substantive administrative laws on the federal and state levels have apparently been deemed to be in line with the requirements of Directive 2006/123/EC. Article 22 of Directive 2006/123/EC is implemented explicitly by § 22 draft DLG for the application scope of the draft DLG, namely the transnational provision of services (see §§ 2 und 5 para 4 draft DLG). This is not only problematic from the of view of the discrimination of domestic service provisions, but also interesting insofar as the information duties are also applicable to service providers who are third-country nationals or who are established in a third country.

Neither the legislator on the federal level nor the nine legislators on the state level deal with the role of Member States as initiators of private regulation in a general way. In this context, the question remains as to whether Article 26 of Directive 2006/123/EC is open and suitable for a formal transposition by law.

2.12 *Articles 28 ff. SD: Administrative Cooperation*

2.12.1 Transnational Administrative Cooperation Prior to the Implementation of the Services Directive

Provisions about transnational administrative assistance prior to the transposition to Directive 2006/123/EC can be found in Austrian law insofar as European Union law (regulations, directives) obliges Member States to provide for transnational assistance, for example Directive 2005/36/EC on the recognition of professional qualifications, Directive 96/71/EC concerning the posting of workers in the framework of the provision of services, or Directive 2006/43/EC on statutory audits of annual accounts and consolidated accounts, amending Council Directives 78/660/EEC and 83/349/EEC and repealing Council Directive 84/253/EEC.

As regards domestic administrative assistance Article 22, *Bundes-Verfassungsgesetz*[30] provides that "all authorities of the Federation, the States and the municipalities are bound within the framework of their legal sphere of competence to render each other mutual assistance". According to the jurisprudence of the Austrian Constitutional Court, Article 22, *Bundes-Verfassungsgesetz* is directly applicable but does not grant a subjective right.

2.12.2 Re-arrangement with National Rules on Administrative Cooperation

The provisions of the draft DLG concerning transnational administrative assistance (Articles 14–21) are applicable exclusively in the scope of application of the draft DLG (§ 2) and Directive 2006/123/EC (Article 2), respectively. As a consequence, national provisions for administrative assistance in general have not been touched or rearranged by the competent legislator.

2.12.3 Provisions on Financial Compensation for Transnational Administrative Cooperation

There are no rules on financial compensation for transnational administrative cooperation.

---

[30] *Bundes-Verfassungsesetz BGBl.Nr. 1/1930 idF BGBl. I Nr. 2/2008*, which can be translated as the Federal Constitution.

2.12.4 Adaptation of the Rules on Data Protection and Professional Secrets

National provisions concerning data protection and professional secrets remain untouched in the course of the transposition of Directive 2006/123/EC.

Pursuant to Article 33 para 1 of Directive 2006/123/EC, Member States shall supply information at the request of a competent authority in another Member State, in conformity with their national law, on disciplinary or administrative actions or criminal sanctions and decisions concerning insolvency or bankruptcy involving fraud with respect to the provider that are directly relevant to the provider's competence or professional reliability. Article 33 para 2 stipulates that these sanctions and actions are only to be communicated if a final decision has been taken. Article 33 is implemented by § 17 draft DLG.

Article 2 (IMI-Gesetz) of the draft government bill (317dB XXIV GP) provides a legal basis for the operation and use of the IMI System.

2.13 Article 29 SD: Mutual Assistance—General Obligations for the Member State of Establishment

Pursuant to Article 29 para 1 of Directive 2006/123/EC, the Member State of establishment is to supply information on providers established in its territory when requested to do so by another Member State and, in particular, confirm that a provider is established in its territory and, to its knowledge, not exercising activities in an unlawful manner. Article 29 of Directive 2006/123/EC and its paragraph 1 are implemented by §§ 17 ff draft DLG. In the context of transnational administrative assistance also, data concerning the lawfulness of the service provision can be transmitted by Austrian authorities (§ 17 para 4 and §§ 18 ff draft DLG). The explanatory report accompanying the draft government bill (317dB XXIV GP) does not reveal whether the implementation of Article 29 para 1 of Directive 2006/123/EC has been regarded as problematic.

2.14 Problems and Discourses on Administrative Cooperation

There have been no problems and discourses on Chapter VI of the Services Directive that would be worth mentioning.

2.15 Convergence Programme (Chapter VII of the Services Directive)

There have been no problems and discourses on Chapter VII of the Services Directive that would be worth mentioning.

3 Assessment of the Impact of the Services Directive

3.1 Extent of the Impact

The transposition process of Directive 2006/123/EC was complicated due to the federal structure of the Republic of Austria, the allocation of competences between the Federation and States, and, finally, the differing attitudes and positions of competent authorities on the federal and state levels. The indispensable amendment of the Austrian constitution, namely, the insertion of a new competence clause, was highly controversial. Also controversial was the scope of the implementing draft DLG, particularly, where to locate the POSC and their function—authority or simple mail-administrating centre that does not decide on a case's merit. Federation and States solely agreed on not going beyond a minimum transposition. The question remains open as to whether the implementation measures can be regarded as a minimum transposition at all.

3.2 Assessment of the Transposing Legislation

The draft government bill (317dB XXIV GP) has not been adopted yet; the competent Ministry for Economics, Family, and Youth seems to be of the opinion that the draft meets the requirements of Directive 2006/123/EC.

3.3 Most Important and Profound Changes Induced by the Services Directive

In our view, the main innovations in Austrian substantive administrative laws and administrative procedural law are the POSC, the comprehensive introduction of the tacit (fictitious) authorisation and the provisions on transnational administrative assistance provided by the Directive.

References

For legislation, jurisprudence and websites please refer to 1.1 of the report and footnotes directly.

Böhret C, Grunow D, Ziekow J (2006) Der Vorschlag zu einer Richtlinie des Europäischen Parlamentes und des Rates über Dienstleistungen im Binnenmarkt, Regelungsgehalt—Problemfelder—Akteurspositionen, 2006, Speyerer Forschungsberichte, Nr. 241

Commission Handbook on the Implementation of the Services Directive (2007) Available at: http://ec.europa.eu/internal_market/services/services-dir/handbook_de.htm

Cremer W (2008) Umsetzung der Dienstleistungsrichtlinie in Deutschland—Verfassungsrechtliche Grenzen für die Installierung der Kammern als einheitliche Ansprechpartner. Europäische Zeitschrift für Wirtschaftsrecht (EuZW), pp 655 ff

Schliesky U (2005) Von der Realisierung des Binnenmarktes über die Verwaltungsreform zu einem gemeineuropäischen Verwaltungsrecht? Die Auswirkungen der geplanten EU-Dienstleistungsrichtlinie auf das deutsche Verwaltungsrecht. Deutsches Verwaltungsblatt (DVBl), pp 887 ff

Windoffer A (2006) Einheitliche Ansprechpartner nach der EU-Dienstleistungsrichtlinie—Aufgabenprofil und Ansiedlungsoptionen. Deutsches Verwaltungsblatt (DVBl), pp 1210 ff

Implementation of the Services Directive in Belgium

Alexandre Geulette

1 General Remarks on the Transposition Strategy and General Understanding of the Implementation

1.1 Main References Used in This Research

As a federal state,[1] the transposition of the Directive in Belgium has required steps to be taken at all levels of government, including the federal level, community level (Flemish-speaking Community, French-speaking Community and German-speaking Community), and regional level (the Flemish Region, the Walloon Region, and the Brussels-Capital Region), as well as at the level of the local authorities.[2]

Alexandre Geulette is currently working as a legal secretary at the General Court of the European Union. Any opinion expressed in this research paper is strictly personal.

[1] Further information regarding the division of competences between federal entities in Belgium can be found on the Belgian government's official portal, available at http://www.belgium.be/en/about_belgium/government/federale_staat. In principle, the federal state, the Communities and the Regions have exclusive competences. Therefore, legislation adopted by the federal legislator within its field of competences does not have precedence over legislation adopted at the level of the Communities and the Regions, i.e., each entity is responsible for implementing the Directive within its own field of competences.

[2] Given its large scope, this research does not cover the implementation of the Directive at the level of local authorities (notably provinces and municipalities) and focuses on the main implementing measures adopted at the federal level, at the community level and at the regional level.

A. Geulette (✉)
General Court of the European Union,
Luxembourg, Luxembourg
e-mail: Alexandre.Geulette@curia.europa.eu

U. Stelkens et al. (eds.), *The Implementation of the EU Services Directive*,
DOI: 10.1007/978-90-6704-840-8_3,

The following legal instruments aim to transpose the Directive[3]:

- The order of the Flemish government of 19 July 2007 implementing the decree of 2 March 2007 establishing the status of travel agencies[4];
- The order of the Flemish government of 19 September 2008 modifying the order of the Flemish government of 6 February 1991 establishing the Flemish regulation relating to the ecological authorisation, the order of the Flemish government of 1 June 1995 establishing the general and sector-specific provisions with respect to environmental and soil hygiene, and the order of the Flemish government of 14 December 2007 establishing the Flemish regulation relating to soil decontamination and soil protection for technical actualisation[5];
- The Walloon decree of 3 April 2009 relating to the registration or the authorisation of employment agencies[6];
- The Walloon decree of 30 April 2009 containing provisions with respect to housing and energy[7];
- The decree of the German-speaking Community of 11 May 2009 relating to the authorisation of temporary work agencies and to the surveillance of private employment agencies[8];
- The order of the Flemish government of 15 May 2009 implementing the decree of 10 July 2008 relating to tourist accommodation[9];
- The order of the Walloon government of 27 May 2009 relating to soil management[10];

---

[3] This list, presented in chronological order, is based on the legal instruments published in the Belgian Official Journal at the time of drafting (31 December 2010). All references to the Belgian Official Journal can be found at www.moniteur.be.

[4] *Besluit van de Vlaamse Regering tot uitvoering van het decreet van 2 maart 2007 houdende het statuut van de reisbureaus*, Belgian Official Journal, 4 September 2007, p. 45947.

[5] *Besluit van de Vlaamse Regering tot wijziging van het besluit van de Vlaamse Regering van 6 februari 1991 houdende vaststelling van het Vlaams reglement betreffende de milieuvergunning, van het besluit van de Vlaamse Regering van 1 juni 1995 houdende algemene en sectorale bepalingen inzake milieuhygiëne en van het besluit van de Vlaamse Regering van 14 december 2007 houdende vaststelling van het Vlaams reglement betreffende de bodemsanering en de bodembescherming ter doorvoering van technische actualisering*, Belgian Official Journal, 27 January 2009, p. 4779.

[6] *Décret relatif à l'enregistrement ou à l'agrément des agences de placement*, Belgian Official Journal, 5 May 2009, p. 35038.

[7] *Décret portant des dispositions en matière de logement et d'énergie*, Belgian Official Journal, 18 June 2009, p. 42592.

[8] *Dekret über die Zulassung der Leiharbeitsvermittler und die Uberwachung der privaten Arbeitsvermittler*, Belgian Official Journal, 13 July 2009, p. 48091.

[9] *Besluit van de Vlaamse Regering tot uitvoering van het decreet van 10 juli 2008 betreffende het toeristische logies*, Belgian Official Journal, 12 October 2009, p. 67408.

[10] *Arrêté du Gouvernement wallon relatif à la gestion des sols*, Belgian Official Journal, 31 August 2009, p. 59385.

- The order of the Flemish government of 5 June 2009 organising employment and professional training[11];
- The federal law of 7 December 2009 amending the law of 16 January 2003 setting up a centralised company register[12] (hereinafter referred to as the 'law of 7 December 2009');
- The Walloon decree of 10 December 2009 aiming to transpose the Directive[13] (hereinafter referred to as the 'horizontal Walloon Decree');
- The Walloon decree of 10 December 2009 aiming to transpose the Directive in matters falling within the scope of Article 138 of the Constitution[14] (hereinafter referred to as the 'Article 138 horizontal Walloon Decree')[15];
- The Walloon decree of 10 December 2009 modifying certain pieces of legislation with a view to transpose the Directive[16] (hereinafter referred to as the 'vertical Walloon Decree');
- The Walloon decree of 10 December 2009 modifying certain pieces of legislation with a view to transpose the Directive in matters falling within the scope of Article 138 of the Constitution[17] (hereinafter referred to as the 'Article 138 vertical Walloon Decree');

---

[11] *Besluit van de Vlaamse Regering houdende de organisering van de arbeidsbemiddeling en de beroepsopleiding*, Belgian Official Journal, 23 September 2009, p. 63442.

[12] *Wet tot wijziging van de wet van 16 januari 2003 tot oprichting van een Kruispuntbank van Ondernemingen, tot modernisering van het handelsregister, tot oprichting van erkende ondernemingsloketten en houdende diverse bepalingen, wat de taken van het één-loket betreft/ Loi modifiant la loi du 6 janvier 2003 portant création d'une Banque-Carrefour des Entreprises, modernisation du registre du commerce, création de guichets-entreprises agréés et portant diverses dispositions, en ce qui concerne les tâches du guichet unique*, Belgian Official Journal, 24 December 2009, p. 81360. The law of 7 December 2009 aims to implement Article 6 of the Directive relating to the single point of contact. The parliamentary documents concerning the adoption of the law of 7 December 2009 can be found at www.lachambre.be (Parliamentary documents 52K2212).

[13] *Décret visant à transposer la Directive 2006/123/CE du Parlement européen et du Conseil du 12 décembre 2006 relative aux services dans le marché intérieur*, Belgian Official Journal, 24 December 2009, p. 81535.

[14] *Décret visant à transposer la Directive 2006/123/CE du Parlement européen et du Conseil du 12 décembre 2006 relative aux services dans le marché intérieur dans les matières visées à l'article 138 de la Constitution*, Belgian Official Journal, 24 December 2009, p. 81648. Matters falling within the scope of Article 138 of the Belgian Constitution are matters within the scope of the competences of the Communities, but whose exercise has been transferred to the Regions.

[15] The horizontal Walloon Decree and the Article 138 horizontal Walloon Decree are hereinafter collectively referred to as the 'horizontal Walloon decrees'.

[16] *Décret modifiant diverses législations en vue de transposer la Directive 2006/123/CE du Parlement européen et du Conseil du 12 décembre 2006 relative aux services dans le marché intérieur*, Belgian Official Journal, 24 December 2009, p. 81556.

[17] *Décret modifiant diverses législations relatives aux matières visées à l'article 138 de la Constitution, en vue de transposer la Directive 2006/123/CE du Parlement européen et du Conseil du 12 décembre 2006 relative aux services dans le marché intérieur*, Belgian Official Journal, 24 December 2009, p. 81562.

- The order of the Walloon government of 10 December 2009 implementing the decree of 3 April 2009 relating to the registration or the authorisation of employment agencies[18];
- The order of the Flemish government of 11 December 2009 partly implementing Articles 6–8 of the Directive[19];
- The Flemish decree of 18 December 2009 containing various accompanying measures to the third adjustment for the 2009 budget[20];
- The federal law of 22 December 2009 adapting specific legislation to the Directive[21] (hereinafter referred to as the law of 22 December 2009);
- The royal decree of 13 January 2010 modifying the royal decree of 22 February 2005 specifying the criteria to be taken into consideration in the examination of projects of commercial establishments and the composition of the socioeconomic file[22];
- The Walloon ministerial order of 24 February 2010 determining the conditions for the provision of a subsidy to day and/or evening and/or night care centres[23];
- The royal decree of 26 February 2010 amending the royal decree of 17 February 2005 regulating the registration of persons who are engaged in the non-judicial recovery of debts and the guarantees such persons must provide[24];

---

[18] *Arrêté du gouvernement wallon portant exécution du décret du 3 avril 2009 relatif à l'enregistrement ou à l'agrément des agences de placement*, Belgian Official Journal, 21 December 2009, p. 80116.

[19] *Besluit van de Vlaamse regering tot gedeeltijlike omzetting van artikelen 6 tot en met 8 van Richtlijn 2006/123/EC van het Europees Parlement en de Raad van 12 december 2006 betreffende diensten op de interne markt*, Belgian Official Journal, 15 March 2010, p. 16316.

[20] *Decreet houdende bepalingen tot begeleiding van de derde aanpassing van de begroting 2009*, Belgian Official Journal, 29 January 2010, p. 4023.

[21] *Wet tot aanpassing van sommige wetgevingen aan de Richtlijn 2006/123/EG van het Europees Parlement en de Raad betreffende diensten op de interne markt/Loi adaptant certaines législations à la Directive 2006/123/CE du Parlement européen et du Conseil relative aux services dans le marché intérieur*, Belgian Official Journal, 29 December 2009, p. 82151. The law of 22 December 2009 aims to adapt specific legislation to the provisions of the Directive. The parliamentary documents concerning the adoption of the law of 22 December 2009 can be found at www.lachambre.be (Parliamentary documents 52K2275).

[22] *Koninklijk besluit tot wijziging van het koninklijk besluit van 22 februari 2005 tot verduidelijking van de criteria waarmede rekening moet worden gehouden bij het onderzoek van ontwerpen van handelsvestiging en de samenstelling van het sociaal-economisch dossier/ Arrêté royal modifiant l'arrêté royal du 22 février 2005 précisant les critères à prendre en considération lors de l'examen de projets d'implantation commerciale et de la composition du dossier socio-économique*, Belgian Official Journal, 22 January 2010, p. 2785.

[23] *Arrêté ministériel déterminant les conditions de l'octroi d'une subvention aux centres d'accueil de jour et/ou de soirée et/ou de nuit*, Belgian Official Journal, 24 February 2010, p. 14561.

[24] *Koninklijk besluit tot wijziging van het koninklijk besluit van 17 februari 2005 tot regeling van de inschrijving van de personen die een activiteit van minnelijke invordering van schulden uitoefenen en van de waarborgen waarover deze personen moeten beschikken/Arrêté royal modifiant l'arrêté royal du 17 février 2005 réglementant l'inscription des personnes qui exercent une activité de recouvrement amiable de dettes et les garanties dont ces personnes doivent disposer*, Belgian Official Journal, 12 March 2010, p. 16169.

- The decree of the German-speaking Community of 15 March 2010 on services[25] (hereinafter referred to as the 'German-speaking Community decree');
- The order of the Walloon government of 24 March 2010 aiming to adapt certain regulation, in matters falling within the scope of Article 138 of the Constitution, to the Directive and implementing the decree of 10 December 2009 aiming to transpose the Directive in matters falling within the scope of Article 138 of the Constitution[26];
- The order of the Walloon government of 24 March 2010 aiming to adapt Walloon regulation to the Directive and implementing the decree of 10 December 2009 aiming to transpose the Directive[27];
- The federal law of 26 March 2010 on services[28] (hereinafter referred to as the 'law on services');
- The federal law of 26 March 2010 on services concerning certain legal aspects referred to in Article 77 of the Constitution[29] (hereinafter referred to as the 'law on services concerning certain legal aspects');
- The ministerial order of 22 April 2010 concerning the profession of butcher[30];
- The order of the Walloon government of 27 May 2010 fixing the status of travel agencies[31];

---

[25] *Dienstleitungsdekret*, Belgian Official Journal, 13 April 2010, p. 21012.

[26] *Arrêté du Gouvernement wallon visant à mettre en conformité diverses réglementations, dans des matières visées à l'article 138 de la Constitution, avec la Directive 2006/123/CE du Parlement européen et du Conseil du 12 décembre 2006 relative aux services dans le marché intérieur et portant exécution du décret du 10 décembre 2009 modifiant diverses législations relatives aux matières visées à l'article 138 de la Constitution, en vue de transposer la Directive 2006/123/CE du Parlement européen et du Conseil du 12 décembre 2006 relative aux services dans le marché intérieur*, Belgian Official Journal, 6 April 2010, p. 20109.

[27] *Arrêté du Gouvernement wallon visant à modifier la réglementation wallonne en vue de transposer la Directive 2006/123/CE du Parlement européen et du Conseil du 12 décembre 2006 relative aux services dans le marché intérieur et portant exécution du décret du 10 décembre 2009 modifiant diverses législations en vue de transposer la Directive 2006/123/CE du Parlement européen et du Conseil du 12 décembre 2006 relative aux services dans le marché intérieur*, Belgian Official Journal, 6 April 2010, p. 20103.

[28] *Dienstenwet/Loi sur les services*, Belgian Official Journal, 30 April 2010, p. 24437. The law on services aims to implement a number of provisions of the Directive by means of autonomous horizontal provisions. The parliamentary documents concerning the law on services can be found at www.lachambre.be (Parliamentary documents 52K2338).

[29] *Dienstenwet betreffende bepaalde jurisdische aspecten bedoeld in artikel 77 van de Grondwet/Loi sur les services concernant certains aspects juridiques visés à l'article 77 de la Constitution*, Belgian Official Journal, 30 April 2010, p. 24435. The law on services concerning certain legal aspects contains provisions on cease-and-desist actions in the event of an infringement of the law on services. The parliamentary documents relating to the law on services concerning certain legal aspects can be found at www.lachambre.be (Parliamentary documents 52K2339).

[30] *Ministerieel besluit betreffende het beroep van beenhouwer en spekslager/Arrêté ministériel concernant la profession de boucher et charcutier*, Belgian Official Journal, 5 May 2010, p. 25149.

[31] *Arrêté du gouvernement wallon portant statut des agences de voyages*, Belgian Official Journal, 16 June 2010, p. 37576.

- The order 2010/111 of the College of the French-speaking Community Commission of the Brussels-Capital Region of 27 May 2010 modifying the order of the French-speaking Community executive of 4 March 1999 establishing the procedure for the granting, suspension, and withdrawal of the approval of 'guest rooms' and the technical requirements to be met by housing containing guest rooms for such approval[32];
- The order 2010/113*bis* of the College of the French-speaking Community Commission of the Brussels-Capital Region of 27 May 2010 modifying the order of the French-speaking Community executive of 24 December 1990 determining the modalities and the procedure for the obtaining of the safety certificate for accommodation facilities existing at 1 January 1991 and establishing safety norms specific to these accommodation facilities in respect of fire protection[33];
- The order 2010/117 of the College of the French-speaking Community Commission of the Brussels-Capital Region of 27 May 2010 modifying the order of the French-speaking Community executive of 24 December 1990 determining the operating conditions, the procedure for the obtaining and the withdrawal of the operating licence, the classification, and the model of the crest of hotels[34];
- The order of the government of the German-speaking Community of 24 June 2010 modifying the government order of 13 April 2000 concerning the authorisation and classification of hotels, the government order of 10 June 2004 on camping permits and the classification of campgrounds, the government order of 26 May 2005 on holiday homes, the government order of 18 January 2007 relating to childcare, and the government order of 10 July 2008

[32] *Arrêté 2010/111 du Collège de la Commission communautaire française modifiant l'arrêté de l'Exécutif de la Communauté française du 4 mars 1999 fixant la procédure d'octroi, de suspension et de retrait de l'agrément en qualité de 'chambres d'hôtes' ainsi que les prescriptions techniques auxquelles doivent satisfaire les habitations contenant les chambres d'hôtes en vue de cet agrément*, Belgian Official Journal, 24 November 2010, p. 72572.

[33] *Arrêté 2010/113bis du Collège de la Commission communautaire française modifiant l'arrêté de l'Exécutif de la Communauté française du 24 décembre 1990 déterminant les modalités et la procédure d'obtention de l'attestation de sécurité des établissements d'hébergement existants au 1er janvier 1991 et fixant les normes de sécurité en matière de protection contre l'incendie spécifiques à ces établissements d'hébergement*, Belgian Official Journal, 24 November 2010, p. 72579.

[34] *Arrêté 2010/117 du Collège de la Commission communautaire française modifiant l'arrêté de l'Exécutif de la Communauté française du 24 décembre 1990 déterminant les conditions d'exploitation, la procédure d'obtention et de retrait de l'autorisation d'exploitation, la classification et le modèle de l'écusson des établissements hôteliers*, Belgian Official Journal, 24 November 2010, p. 72581.

implementing, in the fight against doping, the decree of 30 January 2006 aimed at preventing health damage in sports[35];

- The Flemish decree of 25 June 2010 partly implementing the Directive[36] (hereinafter referred to as the 'Flemish decree');
- The order 2010/236 of the College of the French-speaking Community Commission of the Brussels-Capital Region of 1 July 2010 modifying the order of 10 September 1997 implementing the decree of 5 June 1997 establishing the Brussels French-speaking advisory board for the help to persons and health and fixing its entry into force[37];
- The order 2010/237 of the College of the French-speaking Community Commission of the Brussels-Capital Region of 1 July 2010 modifying the order of 2 April 2009 implementing the decree of 22 March 2007 relating to the housing and hosting policy to conduct towards the elderly[38];
- The order of the government of the Brussels-Capital Region of 8 July 2010 modifying the order of the government of the Brussels-Capital Region of 29 March 2007 relating to taxi and limousine services[39];
- The decree of 9 July 2010 of the French-speaking Community Commission of the Brussels-Capital Region aiming to transpose the Directive[40] (hereinafter referred to as the 'Brussels French-speaking Community Commission decree');

---

35 *Erlass der Regierung zur Änderung des Erlasses der Regierung vom 13. April 2000 über die Hotelgenehmigung und die Einstufung von Hotelbetrieben, des Erlasses der Regierung vom 10. Juni 2004 über die Campinggenehmigung und die Einstufung von Campingplätzen, des Erlasses der Regierung vom 26. Mai 2005 über Ferienwohnungen, des Erlasses der Regierung vom 18. Januar 2007 zur Kinderbetreuung und des Erlasses der Regierung vom 10. Juli 2008 zur Ausführung des Dekretes vom 30. Januar 2006 zur Vorbeugung gesundheitlicher Schäden bei sportlicher Betätigung im Bereich der Dopingbekämpfung*, Belgian Official Journal, 20 July 2010, p. 47078.

36 *Decreet tot gedeeltelijke omzetting van Richtlijn 2006/123/EG van het Europees Parlement en de Raad van 12 december 2006 betreffende diensten op de interne markt*, Belgian Official Journal, 2 August 2010, p. 49567. The parliamentary documents concerning the adoption of the Flemish decree are available at http://jsp.vlaamsparlement.be/docs/stukken/2009-2010/g435-1.pdf. Pursuant to its Article 1, the Flemish decree transposes the Directive in the Flemish Region and the Flemish-speaking Community.

37 *Arrêté 2010/236 du Collège de la Commission communautaire française modifiant l'arrêté du 11 septembre 1997 portant exécution du décret du 5 juin 1997 portant création du Conseil consultatif bruxellois francophone de l'Aide aux Personnes et de la Santé et fixant sa date d'entrée en vigueur*, Belgian Official Journal, 9 September 2010, p. 57372.

38 *Arrêté 2010/237 du Collège de la Commission communautaire française modifiant l'arrêté du 2 avril 2009 portant application du décret du 22 mars 2007 relatif à la politique d'hébergement et d'accueil à mener envers les personnes âgées*, Belgian Official Journal, 9 September 2010, p. 57373.

39 *Arrêté du Gouvernement de la Région de Bruxelles-Capitale du 8 juillet 2010 modifiant l'arrêté du Gouvernement de la Région de Bruxelles-Capitale du 29 mars 2007 relatif aux services de taxis et aux services de location de voitures avec chauffeur*, Belgian Official Journal, 26 July 2010, p. 47844.

40 *Décret visant à transposer la Directive 2006/123/CE du Parlement et du Conseil du 12 décembre 2006 relative aux services dans le marché intérieur*, Belgian Official Journal, 30 August 2010, p. 55672. The parliamentary documents concerning the adoption of the Brussels French-speaking Community Commission decree are available at http://www.pfb.irisnet.be/upload/File/comptes_rendus/16%20(2009-2010)%20CR.pdf.

- The order of 9 July 2010 of French-speaking Community Commission of the Brussels-Capital Region modifying the order of 14 January 1999 on the certification of 'guest rooms' and the authorisation to use the title 'guest rooms'[41];
- The order 2010/238 of the College of the French-speaking Community Commission of the Brussels-Capital Region of 16 July 2010 modifying the order of 22 March 2007 relating to the housing and hosting policy to conduct towards the elderly[42];
- The decree of 19 July 2010 relating to services in the French-speaking Community[43] (hereinafter referred to as the 'French-speaking Community decree');
- The order of the Flemish Government of 23 July 2010 amending the order of the Flemish Government of 3 October 2003 determining and organising the classification of carcasses of cattle and the order of the Flemish Government of 23 January 2004 determining and organising the classification of pig carcasses[44];
- The royal decree of 18 August 2010 amending the internships and ethics regulations established by the National Council of the Order of Architects[45];
- The royal decree of 26 August 2010 modifying the royal decree of 30 April 2004 containing measures relating to the surveillance of the diamond sector[46];
- The order of the government of the German-speaking Community of 26 August 2010 on the authorisation procedure, the first registration and the inspection of assisted living facilities[47];

---

41 *Décret modifiant le décret du 14 janvier 1999 relatif à l'agrément des chambres d'hôtes et à l'autorisation de faire usage de la dénomination chambres d'hôtes,* Belgian Official Journal, 30 August 2010, p. 55670.

42 *Décret 2010/238 de la Commission communautaire française modifiant le décret du 22 mars 2007 relatif à la politique d'hébergement et d'accueil à mener envers les personnes âgées,* Belgian Official Journal, 9 August 2010, p. 50870.

43 *Décret relatif aux services en Communauté française,* Belgian Official Journal, 31 August 2010, p. 55832.

44 *Besluit van de Vlaamse Regering tot wijziging van het besluit van de Vlaamse Regering van 3 oktober 2003 houdende vaststelling en organisatie van de indeling van geslachte volwassen runderen en het besluit van de Vlaamse Regering van 23 januari 2004 houdende vaststelling en organisatie van de indeling van geslachte varkens,* Belgian Official Journal, 10 September 2010, p. 57540.

45 *Koninklijk besluit tot wijziging van het stagereglement en het reglement van beroepsplichten vastgesteld door de Nationale Raad van de Orde van Architecten/Arrêté royal modifiant les règlements de stage et de déontologie établis par le Conseil national de l'Ordre des Architectes,* Belgian Official Journal, 25 August 2010, p. 55036.

46 *Koninklijk besluit tot wijziging van het koninklijk besluit van 30 april 2004 houdende maatregelen betreffende het toezicht op de diamantsector/Arrêté royal modifiant l'arrêté royal du 30 avril 2004 portant des mesures relatives à la surveillance du secteur du diamant,* Belgian Official Journal, 6 September 2010, p. 56540.

47 *Erlass der Regierung bezüglich des Verfahrens zur Genehmigung, Anerkennung und Inspektion der betreuten Wohnungen,* Belgian Official Journal, 14 September 2010, p. 57890.

- The order of the Flemish government of 10 September 2010 amending Article 6 of the order of the Flemish Government of 7 September 2007 organising the establishment and control of the composition of raw milk[48];
- The order of the Walloon government of 16 September 2010 modifying Articles 255/3 and 280 of the Walloon Code for Regional Planning, Urban Planning and Heritage[49];
- The order of the Government of the Brussels-Capital Region of 28 October 2010 bringing environmental and energy legislation in compliance with the requirements of the Directive[50];
- The order of the Government of the Brussels-Capital Region of 28 October 2010 bringing environmental and energy legislation in compliance with the requirements of the Directive[51];
- The order of the Government of the Brussels-Capital Region of 28 October 2010 modifying the order of the Government of the Brussels-Capital Region of 18 May 2006 concerning the authorisation of authors of development municipal plans and related reports on environmental impacts[52];
- The order of the Government of the Brussels-Capital Region of 28 October 2010 modifying the order of the Government of the Brussels-Capital Region of 18

---

48 *Besluit van de Vlaamse Regering tot wijziging van artikel 6 van het besluit van de Vlaamse Regering van 7 september 2007 houdende de organisatie van de vaststelling van en de controle op de samenstelling van rauwe koemelk*, Belgian Official Journal, 7 October 2010, p. 60586.

49 *Arrêté du Gouvernement wallon modifiant les articles 255/3 et 280 du Code wallon de l'Aménagement du Territoire, de l'Urbanisme et du Patrimoine*, Belgian Official Journal, 4 October 2010, p. 59776.

50 *Ordonnantie van de Brusselse Hoofdstedelijke Regering die de milieu- en energiewetgeving in vereenstemming brengt met de regels van Richtlijn 2006/123/EG van het Europees Parlement en de Raad van 12 december 2006 betreffende diensten op de interne markt/Ordonnance du Gouvernement de la Région de Bruxelles-Capitale mettant la législation environnementale et énergétique en conformité avec les exigences de la Directive 2006/123/CE du Parlement européen et du Conseil du 12 décembre 2006 relative aux services dans le marché intérieur*, Belgian Official Journal, 25 November 2010, p. 72977.

51 *Besluit van de Brusselse Hoofdstedelijke Regering die de milieu- en energiewetgeving in vereenstemming brengt met de regels van Richtlijn 2006/123/EG van het Europees Parlement en de Raad van 12 december 2006 betreffende diensten op de interne markt/Arrêté du Gouvernement de la Région de Bruxelles-Capitale mettant la législation environnementale et énergétique en conformité avec les exigences de la Directive 2006/123/CE du Parlement européen et du Conseil du 12 décembre 2006 relative aux services dans le marché intérieur*, Belgian Official Journal, 23 November 2010, p. 72411.

52 *Besluit van de Brusselse Hoofdstedelijke Regering tot wijziging van het besluit van de Brusselse Hoofdstedelijke Regering van 7 december 1995 inzake de erkenning van de ontwerpers van de gemeentelijke ontwikkelingsplannen en van de desbetreffende milieueffectenrapporten/ Arrêté du Gouvernement de la Région de Bruxelles-Capitale modifiant l'arrêté du Gouvernement de la Région de Bruxelles-Capitale du 7 décembre 1995 relatif à l'agrément des auteurs de projet de plans communaux de développement et des rapports sur les incidences environnementales y afférentes*, Belgian Official Journal, 10 November 2010, p. 67868.

May 2006 concerning the authorisation of authors of particular plans for the land use and related reports on environmental impacts[53];

- The order of the Government of the Brussels-Capital Region of 28 October 2010 modifying the order of the Government of the Brussels-Capital Region of 9 July 2008 relating to the accreditation of archaeological researchers[54];
- The order of the Government of the Brussels-Capital Region of 28 October 2010 modifying the order of the Government of the Brussels-Capital Region of 3 July 2008 on the authorisation to undertake archaeological excavations or surveys[55];
- The royal decree of 17 November 2010 modifying the royal decree of 23 May 2000 containing specific provisions concerning the acquisition, the warehousing, the prescription, the provision and the administering of medicines for animals by veterinarians and concerning the possession, and administering of medicines for animals by persons responsible for animals[56];
- The order of the Flemish government of 19 November 2010 amending the order of the Flemish government of 8 November 2002 approving timber buyers and operators in accordance with Article 79 of the forestry decree of 13 June 1990[57];

---

[53] *Besluit van de Brusselse Hoofdstedelijke Regering tot wijziging van het besluit van de Brusselse Hoofdstedelijke Regering van 7 december 1995 inzake de erkenning van de ontwerpers van bezondere bestemmingsplannen en van de desbetreffende milieueffectenrapporten/Arrêté du Gouvernement de la Région de Bruxelles-Capitale modifiant l'arrêté du Gouvernement de la Région de Bruxelles-Capitale du 7 décembre 1995 relatif à l'agrément des auteurs de projet de plans particuliers d'affectation du sol et des rapports sur les incidences environnementales y afférentes*, Belgian Official Journal, 10 November 2010, p. 67869.

[54] *Besluit van de Brusselse Hoofdstedelijke Regering tot wijziging van het besluit van de Brusselse Hoofdstedelijke Regering van 3 juli 2008 betreffende de erkenning van archeologische vorsers/Arrêté du Gouvernement de la Région de Bruxelles-Capitale modifiant l'arrêté du Gouvernement de la Région de Bruxelles-Capitale du 3 juillet 2008 relatif à l'agrément des auteurs de recherches archéologiques*, Belgian Official Journal, 8 November 2010, p. 66590.

[55] *Besluit van de Brusselse Hoofdstedelijke Regering tot wijziging van het besluit van de Brusselse Hoofdstedelijke Regering van 3 juli 2008 betreffende de toestemming voor het uitvoeren van archeologische opgravingen en peilingen/Arrêté du Gouvernement de la Région de Bruxelles-Capitale modifiant l'arrêté du Gouvernement de la Région de Bruxelles-Capitale du 3 juillet 2008 relatif à l'autorisation d'entreprendre des fouilles ou sondages archéologiques*, Belgian Official Journal, 10 November 2010, p. 67867.

[56] *Koninklijk besluit tot wijziging van het koninklijk besluit van 23 mei 2000 houdende bijzondere bepalingen inzake het verwerven, het in depot houden, het voorschrijven, het verschaffen en het toedienen van geneesmiddelen bestemd voor dieren door de dierenarts en inzake het bezit en het toedienen van geneesmiddelen bestemd voor dieren door de verantwoordelijke voor de dieren/Arrêté royal modifiant l'arrêté royal du 23 mai 2000 portant des dispositions particulières concernant l'acquisition, la détention d'un dépôt, la prescription, la fourniture et l'administration de médicaments destinés aux animaux par le médecin vétérinaire et concernant la détention et l'administration de médicaments destinés aux animaux par le responsable des animaux*, Belgian Official Journal, 25 November 2010, p. 72942.

[57] *Besluit van de Vlaamse Regering tot wijziging van het besluit van de Vlaamse Regering van 8 november 2002 houdende de erkenning van kopers en exploitanten van hout, overeenkomstig artikel 79 van het Bosdecreet van 13 juni 1990*, Belgian Official Journal, 23 December 2010, p. 81642.

- The royal decree of 23 November 2010 on mills and flour trade[58];
- The royal decree of 29 November 2010 transposing Article 42 of the Directive[59];
- The Flemish decree of 10 December 2010 on private placement[60]; and
- The order of the Flemish government of 10 December 2010 implementing the decree relating to private placement.[61]

1.2 Impact of the Services Directive

The transposition of the Directive did not give a profound reason to the national legislators to alter administrative laws beyond minimum requirements. Notwithstanding Belgium's initial reservations concerning the contents of the Directive,[62] the National Bank of Belgium,[63] and the Federal Planning Bureau,[64] in their ex ante assessment of the economic effects of the Directive in Belgium,[65] indicated that few provisions of Belgian law abusively restricted the freedom of establishment or the free provision of services. Accordingly, in their opinion, the implementation of the Directive in Belgium would mostly entail the setting up of points of single contact (POSCs) and the simplification of administrative formalities.

In this respect, it should be noted that the modernisation and simplification of administrative procedures have already been underway for a number of years in Belgium prior to the adoption of the Directive. In this context, the Agency for Administrative Simplification[66] (hereinafter referred to as the 'ASA') was set up in 1998 to make proposals to reduce administrative complexity and related costs for companies. The ASA has therefore played a significant role in the transposition of Chapter II of the Directive titled 'Administrative Simplification'.

---

[58] *Koninklijk besluit betreffende de maalderijen en de handel in meel/Arrêté royal relatif aux meuneries et au commerce de la farine*, Belgian Official Journal, 30 November 2010, p. 73409.

[59] *Koninklijk besluit tot omzetting van artikel 42 van de Richtlijn 2006/123/EG van het Europees Parlement en de Raad betreffende diensten op de interne markt/Arrêté royal transposant l'article 42 de la Directive 2006/123/CE du Parlement européen et du Conseil relative aux services dans le marché intérieur*, Belgian Officiel Journal, 7 December 2010, p. 74180.

[60] *Decreet betreffende de private arbeidsbemiddeling*, Belgian Official Journal, 29 December 2010, p. 82856.

[61] *Besluit van de Vlaamse Regering tot uitvoering van het decreet betreffende de private arbeidsbemiddeling*, Belgian Official Journal, 29 December 2010, p. 83034.

[62] See, in this regard, Van De Sande (2008), p. 13.

[63] *Nationale Bank van België/Banque Nationale de Belgique* (www.nbb.be).

[64] *Federaal Planbureau/Bureau Fédéral du Plan* (www.plan.be).

[65] This ex ante assessment is available at www.nbb.be/doc/ts/publications/directive_services 091215Fr.pdf.

[66] *Dienst Administratieve Verrenvoudiging/Agence pour la Simplification Administrative* (www.simplification.fgov.be).

The task of coordinating the transposition of the Directive has been entrusted to the Federal Public Service Economy, SMEs, and Independent Professions and Energy (hereinafter referred to as the 'FPS Economy'). Apart from the legislative and governmental bodies at the federal, regional, and community levels, the institutions involved or consulted within the framework of the transposition of the Directive include the Commission for the Protection of Privacy,[67] the Central Council for the Economy,[68] the National Labour Council,[69] the National Bank of Belgium, and the Federal Planning Bureau.

1.3 (National) Scope of Application

The legal instruments implementing the Directive seem to apply not only to the provision of transnational services, but also to the provision of purely domestic services.[70]

1.4 Incorporation of Transposing Legislation

With the exception of implementation at the level of the German-speaking Community,[71] the implementation of the Directive was effectuated by the following process. First, horizontal legal instruments were adopted that partly implemented the Directive by introducing a number of autonomous provisions, that is, provisions not modifying existing laws (such as provisions relating to applicable definitions, the scope of application, rules relating to the freedom of establishment and the provision of services, rules relating to the obligations of service providers and the rights of service recipients, as well as rules relating to administrative cooperation).[72] Second, vertical legal instruments were adopted that aimed to amend or repeal specific pieces of legislation, to ensure compliance with the Directive. Third, additional pieces of legislation were adopted to implement

---

67 *Commissie voor de bescherming van de persoonlijke levenssfeer/Commission de la protection de la vie privée* (www.privacycommission.be).

68 *Centrale Raad voor het Bedrijfsleven/Conseil Central de l'Economie* (www.ccerb.fgov.be).

69 *Nationale Arbeidsraad/Conseil National du Travail* (www.cnt-nar.be).

70 See, in this regard, Pieters (2010), p. 758.

71 The German-speaking Community decree contains four chapters, entitled, respectively, general provisions, horizontal implementation, vertical implementation and final provisions.

72 As noted in the relevant parliamentary documents, the provisions of the laws and decrees implementing the Directive apply in addition to those which already exist and may potentially be applicable to specific situations.

certain provisions of the Directive.[73] Fourth, a number of additional orders were adopted at the executive level. Finally, a number of provisions of the Directive did not require any amendment to existing laws or decrees, either because Belgian law was already compliant with the Directive or because the Directive, in some instances, merely imposed on Member States (MSs) an obligation not to undertake certain actions.

1.5 The Relationship of the Services Directive to Primary EU Law

No particular issues have been identified regarding the relation between the Directive and Articles 43 EC and 49 EC (now Articles 49 and 56 TFEU).

1.6 Screening

The ASA has been charged with coordinating the screening process, within which every federal and local entity was required to verify whether its legislation was compliant with the provisions of the Directive.

The screening process consisted of three phases: First, a pre-screening phase had as its objective to identify the pieces of legislation likely to be affected by the Directive. Second, a screening phase was aimed at identifying those provisions not in compliance with the Directive and that should be repealed, amended, or justified. Third was a post-screening phrase, during which necessary amendments to existing laws or decrees were adopted.

As far as the results of the screening phase are concerned, the available information shows that at the federal level, approximately 40 legislative or regulatory acts have been or need to be amended, while the maintaining of approximately 60 acts would be justified. At the time of this research, the results of the screening at the federal level were not available online. At the regional level, the results of the screening carried out by the Walloon Region can be found at www.cesrw.be/uploads/fichiers_avis/986.pdf, while the results of the screening carried out by the Flemish Region can be found at http://www.vvsg.be/economie_en_werk/europese_dienstenrichtlijn/Docments/VR%202009%200412%20DOC.1398%20Screenings-

---

73 This is the case, for instance, of the law of 7 December 2009, which aims to implement Article 6 of the Directive by modifying the law of 16 January 2003 setting up a centralised company register as well as the law on services concerning certain legal aspects, which contains provisions relating to cease-and-desist actions, for which a specific parliamentary procedure had to be followed.

resultaten%20Vlaamse%20regelgeving.pdf. In the French-speaking Community, the pre-screening phase did not indicate that any further action was necessary.[74]

2 Individual Articles of the Services Directive

2.1 Article 6 SD: Point of Single Contact (POSC)

The POSCs were introduced by means of an amendment, by the law of 7 December 2009, to the existing law of 16 January 2003 setting up a centralised company register.[75] The amendments introduced by the law of 7 December 2009 assign the tasks of the POSCs to company dockets,[76] which had already been set up by the law of 16 January 2003 and were already entrusted with a number of tasks (such as the registration of companies with the centralised company register, the control over mandatory authorisations, and the provision of relevant information to companies). Company dockets therefore have competences that exceed those imposed on POSCs in the Directive.

The Belgian vade-mecum for the implementation of the Directive confirms the subjective understanding of POSCs by the legislator, that is, POSCs are meant to operate as a one-stop shop for service providers, irrespective of the number of POSCs established in Belgium.[77]

In accordance with Article 6 of the Directive, company dockets are responsible for enabling service providers to complete all procedures and formalities needed to undertake service activities, as well as any applications for authorisation needed to exercise such activities. In view of the division of powers between the various levels of government, Regions and Communities will also be involved in the functioning of company dockets.[78] A consultative committee composed of representatives of all federal entities has been set up for this purpose. Furthermore, a

---

[74] See the statement of the Minister-President of the French-speaking Community at the session of 3 March 2010 at the Parliament of the French-speaking Community, available at http://www.veroniquesalvi.be/pdf/cf_03_03_10_transposition.pdf.

[75] *Wet tot oprichting van een Kruispuntbank van Ondernemingen, tot modernisering van het handelsregister, tot oprichting van erkende ondernemingsloketten en houdende diverse bepalingen/Loi portant création d'une Banque-Carrefour des Entreprises, modernisation du registre de commerce, création de guichets-entreprises agréés et portant diverses dispositions*, Belgian Official Journal, 5 February 2003, p. 4778.

[76] *ondernemingsloketten/guichets d'entreprises.*

[77] See the Belgian vade-mecum for the implementation of the Directive, p. 39, available in French at http://www.socialsecurity.fgov.be/docs/fr/publicaties/conferences/140108/vademecum_richtlijn_diensten_080807_fr.pdf and in Dutch at http://www.socialsecurity.fgov.be/docs/nl/publicaties/conferences/140108/vademecum_richtlijn_diensten_080807_nl.pdf).

[78] See also Article 30 of the Flemish decree of 18 December 2009 containing various accompanying measures to the third adjustment for the 2009 budget and the order of the Flemish government of 11 December 2009 partly implementing Articles 6–8 of the Directive.

formal cooperation agreement, to be approved by law, is to be concluded between all federal entities in this regard.

Pursuant to Article 6 of the law of 7 December 2009, an organisation may be registered as a company docket, provided that it has the legal form of a non-profit organisation within the meaning of the federal law of 27 June 1921[79] and that a number of additional conditions, detailed in the said provision, are met. Specific registration requirements already existed prior to the enactment of the law of 7 December 2009. However, these were amended by the law of 7 December 2009 based on past experience on the functioning of company dockets.

The list of company dockets as well as their places of establishment is published on a yearly basis in the *Belgian Official Journal*. In addition, the law of 7 December 2009 codified the existing administrative practice to publish such a list on the website of the FPS Economy (http://economie.fgov.be). According to the information available on that website of the FPS Economy, there are currently nine company dockets with offices all over Belgium.

The liability of company dockets is determined according to the principles of Belgian administrative law and will depend on the decision-making power of the relevant company docket in the matter at stake. Pursuant to the law of 7 December 2009, company dockets have an obligation to provide quality service and to be insured against professional liability.

2.2 Article 7 SD: Right to Information

Article 7 of the Directive was partly transposed into Article 5 of the law of 7 December 2009, which replaced Article 43 (1) 7° of the law of 16 January 2003. Pursuant to this provision, company dockets must ensure that they make the following information easily accessible to providers and recipients: (a) requirements applicable to providers, in particular those requirements concerning the procedures and formalities to be completed to access and exercise service activities; (b) the contact details of the competent authorities enabling the latter to be contacted directly, including the details of those authorities responsible for matters concerning the exercise of service activities; (c) the means of, and conditions for, accessing public registers and databases on providers and services; (d) the means of redress that are generally available in the event of a dispute between the competent authorities and the provider or the recipient, or between a provider and a recipient or between providers; and (e) the contact details of the associations or organisations, other than the competent authorities, from which providers or recipients may obtain practical assistance. Company dockets must respond within

[79] *Wet betreffende de verenigingen zonder winstoogmerk, de internationale verenigingen zonder winstoogmerk en de stichtingen/Loi sur les associations sans but lucratif, les associations internationales sans but lucratif et les fondations*, Belgian Official Journal, 1 July 1921.

a period of five working days as of the moment the information becomes available and, in cases where the request is faulty or unfounded, must inform the applicant accordingly without delay. Pursuant to Article 43 (2) of the law of 16 January 2003, company dockets are allowed to provide advice and assistance services to companies, with the exception of services reserved by law to certain professionals.

Since the provisions of the Directive require the implementation of a number of organisational measures, the federal government, as well as the aforementioned consultative committee, entrusted the ASA with the task of designing a content management system, called a 'product catalogue' or 'guide to procedures', that would be accessible through a common portal to all levels of government.[80] This guide to procedures is searchable on the basis of a number of different criteria, including the locations of service providers and their activities.

The guide to procedures contains detailed information for each procedure or requirement, including the title of the procedure or requirement, the moment at which the procedure must be carried out or the requirement fulfilled, a description of the procedure or requirement (person responsible, fees, duration of validity, etc.), the procedure for filing a request, the competent administrative authority, the sanctions and rights of redress, the evidence to be submitted, and the existence of a public register where the authorisation is listed other than the centralised company register.

The focus of the guide to procedures was initially placed on procedures and requirements, which fall within the scope of the Directive. However, with a view to provide comprehensive information to service providers, and since the information is also aimed at Belgian undertakings, the catalogue contains information that is not limited to the scope of application of the Directive. In all cases, the catalogue indicates whether or not the applicable procedures and requirements fall within the scope of the Directive.

2.3 Article 8 SD: Procedures by Electronic Means

In accordance with Article 8 of the Directive, Article 5 of the law of 7 December 2009 provides that company dockets must be easily accessible at a distance by electronic means[81] in order to carry out all procedures and formalities related to

---

[80] Further details regarding the guide to procedures can be found in the vade-mecum for the filling out of information sheets, designed for federal administrations, which is available at www.simplification.fgov.be/doc/1245155598-6286.pdf. It must be pointed out that, even before the adoption of the Directive, a large number of relevant information was already readily available online. A non-exhaustive list of the relevant websites can be found in the Belgian vade-mecum for the implementation of the Directive. The guide to procedures is available at http://edrl.belgium.be/fr/procedure-guide/http://edrl.belgium.be/nl/procedure-guide.

[81] Article 4 of the decree of the Flemish government of 11 December 2009 partly implementing Articles 6–8 of the Directive also specifies that authorities granting authorisations may not contest the admissibility of documents provided to them by company dockets where these documents have been provided by a service provider by electronic means.

access to a service activity referred to therein, with the exception of local controls of premises where the service is provided, as well as the equipment used by the service provider concerned, and the physical examination of the capability or personal integrity of the service provider or the responsible staff.

In this regard, it should be noted that a number of legal provisions previously existed in order to encourage administrative authorities to enable electronic communications with citizens and companies.[82]

Belgium has not abolished other means of access to company dockets. According to the ASA, administrative formalities carried out at a distance by electronic means will, at first instance, be carried out by electronic mail, to which shall be attached the relevant form to be completed.[83]

2.4 Article 9 SD: Authorisation Schemes

At the federal level, Article 9 of the Directive was transposed into Article 4 of the law on services, which provides that when an authorisation is required for access to service activities and their exercise, such an authorisation regime may not be discriminatory, its necessity must be justified by an overriding reason relating to the public interest, and the objective pursued cannot be attained by means of a less restrictive measure. Similar provisions have been enacted at the level of the Regions and Communities.[84]

The parliamentary record of the laws and decrees transposing the Directive does not indicate that there has been any significant debate regarding the definition of authorisation schemes. The latter is contained in Article 2 (7) of the law on services and is closely modelled on Article 4 (7) of the Directive. In this regard, the only precision that was provided during the parliamentary works concerns the so-called accreditation schemes (such as accreditation schemes for journalists), which are considered not to fall within the scope of Article 2 (7) of the law on services, since such schemes do not impede the free provision of services but, instead, aim to facilitate the exercise of their activities. Mere notification requirements do not appear to fall within the scope of the said provision.

---

[82] E.g. Article 102, 2° of the program-law of 30 December 2001, Belgian Official Journal, 31 December 2001, p. 45732 and Articles 409 and 410 of the program-law of 24 December 2002, Belgian Official Journal, 31 December 2002, p. 58768.

[83] The URL of the form to be completed will usually be mentioned in the product catalogue referred to above.

[84] See Article 4 of the horizontal Walloon decree; Article 4 of the horizontal Article 138 Walloon decree; Article 6 of the German-speaking Community decree. The Flemish decree does not contain a similar provision.

A number of national legal provisions have been amended or repealed due to their non-compliance with Article 9 of the Directive. In this regard, Belgium had reported authorisation schemes to the Commission in several service sectors,[85] some of which have been repealed while others have been maintained. Authorisation schemes were, *inter alia*, repealed in the mill sector as well as in the sectors of matrimonial intermediary activities and time-sharing activities.[86] Authorisation schemes were, *inter alia,* maintained in the retail sector (for the opening of retail outlets[87] and night shops,[88] as well as for the exercise of itinerant and fairground activities[89]), in the tourism sector (for the exercise of the activity as travel agent,[90] for the operation of tourist accommodation,[91] and camping grounds[92]), in the care sector (infants[93] and elderly[94]), in the sector of heritage protection,[95] in the sector

[85] Also see European Commission, Mutual evaluation foreseen by the Directive—Stakeholders' consultation (30 June 2010–13 September 2010), Information on the situation in Belgium, available at http://ec.europa.eu/internal_market/consultations/2010/services_directive_en.htm.

[86] See Articles 2–9 of the law of 22 December 2009.

[87] See the law of 13 August 2004 relating to the authorisation of commercial establishments (*Wet betreffende de vergunning van handelsvestigingen/Loi relative à l'autorisation d'implantations commerciales*, Belgian Official Journal, 5 October 2004, p. 70159), modified by the law of 22 December 2009.

[88] See Article 18 of the law of 10 November 2006 relating to the opening hours in trade, crafts and service activities (*Wet betreffende de openingsuren in handel, ambacht en dienstverlening/ Loi relative aux heures d'ouverture dans le commerce, l'artisanat et les services*, Belgian Official Journal, 19 December 2006, p. 72879), modified by the law of 22 December 2009.

[89] See the law of 25 June 1993 on the exercise and the organisation of itinerant and fairground activities (*Wet betreffende de uitoefening en de organisatie van ambulante en kermisactiviteiten/ Loi sur l'exercice et l'organisation des activités ambulantes et foraines*, Belgian Official Journal, 30 September 1993, p. 21526), modified by the law of 22 December 2009.

[90] See the decree of the Flemish government of 19 July 2007 implementing the decree of 2 March 2007 establishing the status of travel agencies; the decree of the Walloon government of 27 May 2010 fixing the status of travel agencies.

[91] See the decree of the Flemish government of 15 May 2009 implementing the decree of 10 July 2008 relating to tourist accommodation; see also the decree of the Flemish Parliament relating to tourist accommodation (*Decreet betreffende het toeristische logies*, Belgian Official Journal, 26 August 2008, p. 44414) and Article 49 of the German speaking Community decree and the decree of the government of the German-speaking Community of 24 June 2010.

[92] See the decree of the French-speaking Community of 4 March 1991 relating to the conditions of operations of camping grounds (*Décret relatif aux conditions d'exploitation des terrains de camping-caravaning*, Belgian Official Journal, 26 April 1991, p. 8796) and Article 48 of the German-speaking Community decree and the decree of the government of the German-speaking Community of 24 June 2010.

[93] Article 50 of the German-speaking Community decree. See also the decree of the government of the German-speaking Community of 24 June 2010.

[94] See Article 50 of the German-speaking Community decree.

[95] See Article 46 of the German-speaking Community decree.

of employment services,[96] and for the provision of limousine services.[97] Detailed information about the applicable authorisation schemes can be found in the guide to procedures.[98]

2.5 *Article 10 SD: Conditions for the Granting of Authorisation*

At the federal level, Article 10 of the Directive was transposed into various provisions of the law on services, namely, Article 5 (which transposes Article 10 (1) and (2) of the Directive), Article 7 (which transposes Article 10 (3) of the Directive), Article 9 (which transposes Article 10 (4) of the Directive), and Article 11 (which transposes Article 10 (5) of the Directive). It was not deemed necessary to transpose Article 10 (6) of the Directive into the law on services. At the level of the Regions and Communities, Article 10 was transposed into Articles 5, 7, 9, and 11 of the horizontal Walloon decrees, into Articles 5, 7, 9, and 11 of the French-speaking Community decree, into Articles 5, 7, 9, and 11 of the Brussels French-speaking Community Commission decree, into Articles 5, 6, and 8 of the Flemish decree,[99] and into Articles 6, 7, 9, 11, and 13 of the German-speaking Community decree. The aforementioned implementing provisions are closely modelled on Article 10 of the Directive.

The requirement stated in Article 10 (3) of the Directive was implemented into Article 7 of the law on services, Article 7 of the Walloon horizontal decrees, Article 5 of the Flemish decree and Article 9 of the German-speaking Community decree. The provisions contained in the law on services, the Walloon horizontal decrees, and the German-speaking Community decree state that the conditions for granting authorisation for a new establishment may not duplicate requirements and controls that are equivalent or essentially comparable as regards their purpose to which the provider is already subject in Belgium or in another MS of the European

[96] See the Walloon decree of 3 April 2009 relating to the registration or the authorisation of employment agencies; the decree of the German-speaking Community of 11 May 2009 relating to the authorisation of temporary work agencies and to the surveillance of private employment agencies; the decree of the Walloon government of 10 December 2009 implementing the decree of 3 April 2009 relating to the registration or the authorisation of employment agencies.

[97] See, for instance, the decree of the government of the Brussels-Capital Region of 8 July 2010 modifying the decree of the government of the Brussels-Capital Region of 29 March 2007 relating to taxi services and limousine services.

[98] See also, in this regard, the results of the screening carried out in Wallonia (http://www.-cesrw.be/uploads/fichiers_avis/986.pdf) and in Flanders (http://www.vvsg.be/economie_en_werk/europese_dienstenrichtlijn/Documents/VR%202009%200412%20DOC.1398%20Screenings resultaten%20Vlaamse%20regelgeving.pdf).

[99] The Flemish decree does not, as such, contain a provision similar to Article 5 of the law on services, Article 5 of the horizontal Walloon decrees, Article 5 of the French-speaking Community decree, Article 5 of the Brussels French-speaking Community Commission decree and Article 7 of the German-speaking Community decree.

Union. In this regard, the federal coordinator and the provider must assist the competent authority by providing any necessary information regarding those requirements. Article 5 of the Flemish decree provides that where the competent authority verifies if the applicant satisfies the conditions for granting authorisation for a new establishment, it must 'take account' of equivalent conditions that have already been fulfilled in Belgium or another MS.

In accordance with Article 10 (4) of the Directive, Article 9 of the law on services states the principle that an authorisation enables the provider to have access to and exercise an activity throughout the entire Belgian territory, with the exception of cases where an authorisation for each individual establishment or a limitation of the authorisation for each individual establishment or a limitation of the authorisation to a certain part of the territory is justified by an overriding reason relating to the public interest, as well as cases for which the legislator at the federal level is not competent (Article 10 (7) of the Directive). On the one hand, as regards overriding reasons relating to the public interest, the Belgian Council of State has indicated that this concept is an evolving one and that it was advisable that the legislator refer specifically to the case law of the Court of Justice of the European Union.

This opinion was not followed by the legislator at the federal level, the latter considering that it would have implied transferring a competence belonging to national legislators to the Court of Justice. It is noteworthy that, on their part, the Flemish and horizontal Walloon decrees define this concept by reference to the case law of the Court of Justice. On the other hand, as regards cases where the legislator at the federal level is not competent, it must be stressed that territorial constraints affecting the validity of authorisations are rooted in the competences of the relevant federal entities. In this regard, Article 9 of the horizontal Walloon decree, Article 9 of the French-speaking Community decree, Article 9 of the Brussels French-speaking Community Commission decree and Article 6 of the Flemish decree, provide that an authorisation enables the provider to have access to and exercise an activity throughout the entire territory of the Walloon Region, the entire territory of the French-speaking region, the entire territory of the Brussels-Capital Region and the entire territory of the Flemish Region, respectively. Pursuant to Article 11 of the German-speaking Community decree, an authorisation enables a provider to have access to and exercise an activity throughout the entire Belgian territory, provided that a cooperation agreement with the competent authorities concerned has been concluded and that an overriding reason relating to the public interest does not require a limitation of the authorisation to a well-defined part of the national territory. In this regard, it must be stressed that the allocation of competences between federal entities was not amended in the context of the transposition of Article 10 of the Directive.

The National Bank of Belgium and the Federal Planning Bureau, in their ex-ante assessment of the economic effects of the Directive in Belgium, pointed out that most conditions of access to the exercise of certain professions would remain in place after transposition of the Directive, aside from specific pieces of legislation that would have to be amended, since they merely concern the professional qualifications of service providers.

Article 10 (6) of the Directive did not require transposition in Belgium, since the obligation to reason individual administrative decisions is already contained in the law of 20 July 1991 concerning the formal reasoning of administrative acts.[100]

2.6 Article 11 SD: Duration of Authorisation

At the federal level, Article 11 of the Directive was transposed into Article 12 of the law on services. Article 12 provides that the authorisation granted to a provider has an unlimited duration, except where the authorisation is being automatically renewed, where it is subject only to the continued fulfilment of requirements and the number of available authorisations is limited by an overriding reason relating to the public interest or where a limited authorisation period can be justified by an overriding reason relating to the public interest. Similar provisions are contained in Article 12 of the horizontal Walloon decrees, Article 12 of the French-speaking Community decree, Article 12 of the Brussels French-speaking Community Commission decree, Article 9 of the Flemish decree, and Article 14 of the German-speaking Community decree. The parliamentary record does not indicate that implementation of Article 11 of the Directive raised any specific difficulties.

The exception provided for in Article 11 (1) of the Directive was used, for instance, in the sector of the provision of limousine services,[101] where the limited duration of the authorisation (five years) was deemed to be justified by overriding reasons related to the public interest, such as public order, legal certainty, the protection of consumers, service recipients, and workers, and the fight against fraud.

The guide to procedures provides, where applicable, the duration of the validity of authorisations.

2.7 Article 12 SD: Selection from Among Several Candidates

At the federal level, Article 12 of the Directive was transposed into Article 13 of the law on services. Similar provisions are contained in Article 13 of the horizontal Walloon decrees, Article 13 of the French-speaking Community decree, Article 13

---

[100] *Wet betreffende de uitdrukkelijke motivering van de bestuurshandelingen/Loi relative à la motivation formelle des actes administratifs*, Belgian Official Journal, 12 September 1991, p. 19976.

[101] See, for instance, the decree of the government of the Brussels-Capital Region of 8 July 2010 modifying the decree of the government of the Brussels-Capital Region of 29 March 2007 relating to taxi services and limousine services.

of the Brussels French-speaking Community Commission decree and Article 15 of the German-speaking Community decree.[102] These provisions, which were introduced in Belgian law as part of the implementation process of the Directive, are closely modelled on Article 12 of the latter. The parliamentary record does not indicate that implementation of Article 12 of the Directive raised any specific difficulties.

2.8 Article 13 SD: Authorisation Procedures

In case the authority does not respond to the filed application within the prescribed time, the authorisation is "deemed to have been granted to the provider" (Handbook, p. 28)

At the federal level, Article 13 of the Directive was transposed into various provisions of the law on services, namely, Article 6 (which transposes Article 13 (2) of the Directive), Article 10 (which transposes Article 13 (5), (6) and (7) of the Directive), and Article 11 (which transposes Article 13 (3) and (4) of the Directive). At the level of the Regions and Communities, Article 13 of the Directive was transposed into Articles 6, 10, and 11 of the horizontal Walloon decrees, into Articles 6, 10, and 11 of the French-speaking Community decree, into Articles 6, 10 and 11 of the Brussels French-speaking Community Commission decree, into Articles 7 and 8 of the Flemish decree, and into Article 13 of the German-speaking Community decree.

The transposition of Article 13 of the Directive did not raise any specific difficulties, with the exception of its fourth paragraph.[103] The transposition of this paragraph induced a substantial change to the existing legislation, which only provided for tacit authorisations in exceptional cases.[104] In this regard, it should be noted that the Council of State previously expressed reservations regarding tacit

---

[102] The Flemish decree does not, as such, contain a provision similar to Article 12 of the law on services, Article 12 of the horizontal Walloon decrees, Article 13 of the French-speaking Community decree and Article 14 of the German-speaking Community decree.

[103] It should be noted that, pursuant to Article 10 of the law on services, Article 10 of the horizontal Walloon decrees, Article 10 of the French-speaking Community decree and Article 10 of the Brussels French-speaking Community Commission decree, applications for authorisation must be acknowledged within ten working days. Pursuant to Article 7 of the Flemish decree and Article 12 of the German-speaking Community decree, such acknowledgment of receipt must be issued as quickly as possible.

[104] This principle was generally applied in the area of price regulation. Another example of the application of this principle can be found in the law of 13 August 2004 relating to the authorisation of commercial establishments. It should also be noted that, in general administrative law, where no time period is provided for or where the time period provided for is not obligatory, administrative decisions must be taken within a reasonable period of time, i.e., the time necessary for the administrative authority to have in its possession all legal and factual elements to enable it to take a decision.

authorisations. First, the granting of tacit authorisations does not contribute to legal certainty in the absence of a written decision, which could raise issues with regard to the administration of proof. Furthermore, a tacit authorisation is necessarily neither reasoned nor published in the same manner as express decisions. Second, the Council of State considered the granting of tacit authorisations likely to impede on collective interests, to the extent that such a mechanism could lead to certain decisions being taken without careful preparation and without balancing all interests at stake. Nevertheless, Article 13 (4) was duly transposed into Belgian law, since the aforementioned reservations do not qualify as overriding reasons relating to the public interest within the meaning of the Directive and of the case law of the Court of Justice. It would appear that identical rules apply to both formally granted and tacit authorisations, although this issue does not seem to have been discussed during the parliamentary works.

As a general rule, the duration of administrative procedures is determined by particular laws or decrees. Article 11 of the law on services, Article 11 of the horizontal Walloon decrees, Article 11 of the French-speaking Community decree, Article 11 of the Brussels French-speaking Community Commission decree and Article 11 of the German-speaking Community decree provide that, within their scope of application, where no specific provision is contained in the applicable regulation as regards the duration of an authorisation procedure, it must be issued at the latest 30 working days from the date of the acknowledgement of receipt or, where the file is incomplete, from the date on which the applicant provided the required additional documents. This time period is 60 days in Flanders.[105] These provisions also state that a one-time extension may be granted to this time period where justified by the complexity of the file. This extension and its duration must be duly motivated and must be notified to the applicant before the initial period has expired.

2.9 Articles 14, 15, 16 SD

At the federal level, Articles 14 and 16 were transposed, respectively, into Articles 14 and 15 of the law on services. At the level of the Regions and Communities, Articles 14 and 16 of the Directive were transposed into Articles 14 and 15 of the horizontal Walloon decrees, into Articles 14 and 15 of the French-speaking Community decree, into Articles 14 and 15 of the Brussels French-speaking Community Commission decree and into Articles 16 and 17 of the German-speaking Community decree.[106] These provisions did not raise any specific debates during the parliamentary works.

---

[105] Article 8 of the Flemish decree.

[106] The Flemish decree does not, as such, contain a provision similar to Articles 14 and 15 of the law on services, Articles 14 and 15 of the horizontal Walloon decrees and Articles 16 and 17 of the German-speaking Community decree.

Article 14 of the Directive required, *inter alia*, the amendment of the law of 13 August 2004 relating to the authorisation of commercial establishments[107] and its implementing royal decree, and the amendment of the law of 25 June 1993 on the exercise and organisation of itinerant and fairground activities, which both provided for an economic test, contrary to Article 14 (5) of the Directive. Article 15 of the Directive required, *inter alia*, the amendment of legislation that imposed on service providers the obligation to take a specific legal form (e.g., for persons engaged in the non-judicial recovery of debts[108] and for private employment agencies[109]).

2.10 Articles 14–19 SD[110]

At the federal level, Articles 17, 18, and 19 of the Directive were transposed into Articles 16, 17, and 23, respectively, of the law on services. At the level of the Regions and Communities, Articles 17, 18, and 19 of the Directive were transposed into Articles 16, 17, and 23, respectively, of the horizontal Walloon decrees, into Articles 16, 17, and 23, respectively, of the French-speaking Community decree, into Articles 16, 17, and 23, respectively, of the Brussels French-speaking Community Commission decree, into Article 10 of the Flemish decree,[111] and into Articles 18, 19, and 25, respectively, of the German-speaking Community decree.

These general provisions, which are closely modelled on the Directive, did not give rise to any specific debates.

An example of a requirement imposed on service providers established in another MS and providing services in Belgium that has been reported to the Commission[112] is

[107] The amendments were effectuated by Article 18 of the law of 22 December 2009 and by the adoption on 13 January 2010 of a royal decree modifying the royal decree of 22 February 2005 specifying the criteria to be taken into consideration in the examination of projects of commercial establishments and the composition of the socio-economic file.

[108] See the royal decree of 26 February 2010 amending the royal decree of 17 February 2005 regulating the registration of persons who are engaged in the non-judicial recovery of debts and the guarantees such persons must provide.

[109] See e.g., the Walloon decree of 3 April 2009 relating to the registration or the authorisation of employment agencies.

[110] As regards discussions on Articles 14, 15 and 16 of the Directive, please refer to Sect. 2.9.

[111] The Flemish decree does not, as such, contain a provision similar to Articles 16 and 23 of the law on services, Articles 16 and 23 of the horizontal Walloon decrees and Articles 18 and 25 of the German-speaking Community decree.

[112] See European Commission, Mutual evaluation foreseen by the Directive—Stakeholders' consultation (30 June 2010 to 13 September 2010), Information on the situation in Belgium, available at http://ec.europa.eu/internal_market/consultations/2010/services_directive_en.htm.

the general obligation for self-employed service providers to make a prior notification when providing cross-border services in Belgium.[113]

With regard to Article 17 (3) of the Directive, it is worth noting that the law on services initially contained a provision stating that Article 15 thereof does not apply to 'matters covered by the law of 8 December 1992 on the protection of privacy in relation to the processing of personal data'.[114] However, it was decided to suppress this exclusion, following the opinion of the Commission for the Protection of Privacy,[115] which considered the purpose of this provision to be unclear. Finally, it should be noted that Article 16 (13) of the law on services provides that Article 15 thereof does not apply to matters covered by Articles 132–134 of the Belgian Company Code.[116]

2.11 Articles 22–27 SD

At the federal level, Article 22 of the Directive was transposed into Articles 18–22 of the law on services. Article 23 of the Directive was transposed into Article 9 of the law on services. The law on services does not contain provisions transposing Articles 24–26 of the Directive, and the parliamentary record does not indicate that any discussion occurred in this respect. This would appear to indicate that these provisions will require the adoption or amendment of non-legislative measures. Article 27 of the Directive was transposed into Articles 26–28 of the law on services.

At the level of the Regions and Communities, Article 22 of the Directive was transposed into Articles 18–22 of the horizontal Walloon decrees, into Articles 18–22 of the French-speaking Community decree, into Articles 18–22 of the Brussels French-speaking Community Commission decree and into Articles 20–24 of the German-speaking Community decree.[117] Article 23 of the Directive was

---

[113] Articles 153 and 154 of the federal program law of 27 December 2006 (*Programmawet (I)/Loi-programme (I)*, Belgian Official Journal, 28 December 2006, p. 75178). See also the implementing royal decree (*Koninklijk besluit tot uitvoering van het Hoofdstuk 8 van Titel IV van de programmawet (I) van 27 december 2006 tot voorafgaande melding voor gedetacheerde werknemers en zelfstandigen/Arrêté royal pris en exécution du Chapitre 8 du Titre IV de la loi-programme (I) du 27 décembre 2006 instaurant une déclaration préalable pour les travailleurs salariés et indépendants détachés*, Belgian Official Journal, 28 March 2007, p. 16975).

[114] *Wet tot bescherming van de persoonlijke levensfeer ten opzichte van de verwerking van persoonsgegevens/Loi relative à la protection de la vie privée à l'égard des traitements de données à caractère personnel*, Belgian Official Journal, 18 March 1993, p. 5801.

[115] Opinion no 25/2009 of 2 September 2009, p. 16, available at http://www.privacy-commission.be/fr/docs/Commission/2009/avis_25_2009.pdf.

[116] These provisions concern the appointment and remuneration of commissioners (*commissarissen/commissaires*), who are in charge of controlling companies' annual accounts and consolidated accounts. The Belgian Company Code is available at http://www.ejustice.just.fgov.be/loi/loi.htm.

[117] Chapter V of the Directive on the quality of services was not transposed into the Flemish decree. According to the Flemish parliamentary documents, this was decided in order not to exceed the Flemish authority's competences.

transposed into Article 8 of the horizontal Walloon decrees and Article 10 of the German-speaking Community decree.[118] These do not contain any provisions implementing Articles 24–26 of the Directive. Article 27 of the Directive was transposed into Articles 25–28 of the horizontal Walloon decrees and into Articles 27–30 of the German-speaking Community decree.[119]

Belgium reported legal provisions to limit the possibilities of service providers to engage in multidisciplinary activities[120] for the exercise of certain professions, such as architect,[121] accountant and tax advisor,[122] veterinarian,[123] and automobile expert.[124] These provisions did not give rise to specific debates during the parliamentary works.

2.12 Articles 28 ff. SD: Administrative Cooperation

At the federal level, the provisions on administrative cooperation contained in Articles 28–36 of the Directive were transposed into Articles 29–40 of the law on services. At the level of the Regions and Communities, the provisions on administrative cooperation were transposed into Articles 29–40 of the horizontal Walloon decrees, into Articles 29–40 of the French-speaking Community decree, into Articles 29–40 of the Brussels French-speaking Community Commission decree, into Articles 11–22 of the Flemish decree, and into Articles 31–41 of the German-speaking Community decree. These provisions are closely modelled on the Directive.

---

[118] The parliamentary record indicates that the transposition of this provision will also require the adoption of sector-specific legislation.

[119] Article 27 (3) of the Directive is only to be transposed at the federal level, since it concerns the execution of judicial decisions in Belgium, which is a federal competence.

[120] See European Commission, Mutual evaluation foreseen by the Directive—Stakeholders' consultation (30 June 2010 to 13 September 2010), Information on the situation in Belgium, available at http://ec.europa.eu/internal_market/consultations/2010/services_directive_en.htm.

[121] Federal law of 20 February 1939 on the protection of the title and the profession of architect (*Wet op de bescherming van den titel en van het beroep van architect/Loi sur la protection du titre et de la profession d'architecte*, Belgian Official Journal, 25 March 1939).

[122] Federal law of 22 April 1999 concerning the profession of accountant and tax advisor (*Wet betreffende de boekhoudkundige en fiscale beroepen/Loi relative aux professions comptables et fiscales*, Belgian Official Journal, 11 May 1999, p. 16290).

[123] Federal law of 28 August 1991 concerning the exercise of veterinary activities (*Wet op de uitoefening van de diergeneeskunde/Loi sur l'exercice de la médecine vétérinaire*, Belgian Official Journal, 15 October 1991, p. 22981).

[124] Federal law of 15 May 2007 regarding the recognition and the profession of car expert and the setting-up of the Institute of car experts (*Wet tot erkenning en bescherming van het beroep van auto-expert en tot oprichting van een Instituut van de auto-experts/Loi relative à la reconnaissance et à la protection de la profession d'expert en automobiles et créant un Institut des experts en automobiles*, Belgian Official Journal, 2 June 2008, p. 28087).

Prior to the transposition of the Directive, there already existed provisions on administrative cooperation, notably in labour-related, tax-related,[125] and cultural matters.

The following remarks on the implementation of the Directive's provisions on administrative cooperation can be made. First, with regard to the transposition of Article 33 of the Directive, Article 30 of the law on services and the relevant provisions in the decrees submitted or adopted at the level of the Regions and Communities provide that the transmission of information relating to criminal convictions should be made in accordance with the Belgian Code of Criminal Procedure.[126] Second, at the level of the Walloon Region, the transposition of Article 28 (7) of the Directive by means of a general provision was not considered possible due to the large number of specific procedures for access to registers. This issue will therefore be dealt with in specific decrees. Third, at the federal level, following the opinion of the Council of State and the Commission for the Protection of Privacy,[127] a specific chapter of the law on services (Articles 41–49 of the law on services) was dedicated to specifying the requirements (already contained in the law of 8 December 1992) relating to the protection of personal data within the framework of administrative cooperation. Finally, the implementing measures do not contain provisions on financial compensation for administrative assistance.

2.13 *Article 29 SD: Mutual Assistance—General Obligations for the Member State of Establishment*

At the federal level, Article 29 of the Directive was transposed into Articles 29 and 38 of the law on services. At the level of the Regions and Communities, this provision was transposed into Articles 29 and 39 of the horizontal Walloon decrees, Articles 29 and 39 of the French-speaking Community decree, Articles 29 and 39 of the Brussels French-speaking Community Commission decree and into Articles 11 and 20 of the Flemish decree. It appears that the transposition of this provision did not give rise to any specific debates.

---

[125] A list of the international administrative agreements to which Belgium is a party is provided on the website of the Federal Public Service for Finances (http://fiscus.fgov.be/interfafznl/fr/international/cooperation/index.htm).

[126] *Wetboek van Strafvordering/Code d'instruction criminelle*, available at http://www.ejustice.just.fgov.be/loi/loi.htm.

[127] Opinion no 25/2009 of 2 September 2009, available at http://www.privacy-commission.be/fr/docs/Commission/2009/avis_25_2009.pdf.

2.14 *Problems and Discourses on Administrative Cooperation*

Apart from the issues mentioned under Question 2.12, the transposition of Chapter VI did not give rise to specific problems or discussions.

2.15 *Convergence Programme (Chapter VII of the Services Directive)*

There do not appear to have been any specific discussions regarding Chapter VII on convergence. Article 42 of the Directive was transposed in the royal decree of 29 November 2010.

3 Assessment of the Impact of the Services Directive

The impact of the Directive on administrative procedure law and administrative law for business activities in Belgium seems to be rather limited.

From an economic point of view, the National Bank of Belgium and the Federal Planning Bureau, in their ex ante assessment of the economic effects of the Directive in Belgium,[128] estimated that the transposition of the Directive in Belgium would, aside from a decrease in administrative formalities for services providers, lead to a 0.5% growth of the economy (limited growth in exports in sectors relating to real estate, construction, leasing, information technology, and company services; limited effect on direct foreign investments; limited effect on importation of services). In fact, the implementation of the Directive will probably enable sufficiently efficient, very small or small and medium enterprises to seize existing opportunities in other MSs, which may have been discouraged until now because of administrative burdens.

From a legal point of view, despite the adoption of a large number of implementing legal instruments, it appears that only a minimum transposition took place. Parliamentary records do not indicate that extensive discussions about the content of the Directive occurred during the implementation process. This may be related to the late stage at which transposition took place or to Belgium's initial reservations concerning the contents of the Directive.[129] It may be also be due to the fact that even before the implementation of the Directive, there were relatively few rules impeding access of foreign providers to service activities.

[128] See http://www.nbb.be/doc/ts/publications/directive_services091215Nl.pdf; http://www.nbb.be/doc/ts/publications/directive_services091215Fr.pdf.

[129] See, in this regard, Van De Sande (2008), p. 13.

In many instances, the horizontal laws and decrees that have been adopted at the various levels of government merely reproduce the contents of the provisions of the Directive, leaving the necessary amendments of existing legislation to specific laws and decrees adopted on an ad hoc basis. Regarding the implementation process, it is noteworthy that the latter, in some respects, has not been entirely consistent among the Belgian federal entities.

The most important changes induced by the transposition of the Directive appear to be the establishment of a system of tacit authorisations, which was only applicable in Belgium in exceptional circumstances, as well as the assignment of new tasks and responsibilities to company dockets in their new role as POSCs.

References

For legislation, jurisprudence and websites please refer to 1.1 of the report and footnotes directly.

Commission Handbook on the Implementation of the Services Directive (2007) Available at: http://ec.europa.eu/internal_market/services/docs/services-dir/guides/handbook_en.pdf
Pieters E (2010) La loi du 26 mars 2010 sur les services, R.D.C./T.B.H., 2010/8, p 758, no 62
Van De Sande J-M (2008) Belgium national report. In: Koeck HF, Karollus MM (eds) The New Services Directive of the European Union, FIDE XXIII Congress Linz 2008, vol 3. Congress Publications, Vienna, Nomos

Implementation of the Services Directive in the Republic of Bulgaria

Hristo Ilkov Hristev

1 General Remarks on the Transposition Strategy and General Understanding of the Implementation

1.1 Main References Used in this Research

The Services Directive is being transposed in Bulgarian legislation through a Law on the activities for granting services. The process of adoption of the relevant legislation was finished after the Parliament approved the relevant draft law. The law was published in the State Gazette and entered into force on 23 February 2010. The proposed draft law can be found on the internet site of the Bulgarian Parliament—www.parliament.bg. The adopted act is available on the internet site of the Bulgarian State Gazette (State Gazette No 15, 23 February 2010). In addition to the relevant legislation, the current analysis uses also a report of the Ministry of Economy and Energy Industry from March 2008 on the impact of the implementation of the Services Directive. This document can be downloaded from the internet site of the Ministry at the following address: http://www.mi.government.bg/integration/eu/docs.html?id=223898.

Both documents are available only in Bulgarian. Originally, it was envisioned given by the Council of Ministers to give the draft law retroactive force so that it would be legally binding from the 10 November 2009 (excluding the administrative and penal provisions, since the Constitution forbids the use of this

The author is Assistant Professor at the Faculty of Law, Department of International Law and International Relations, Sofia University 'St. Kliment Ohridski'.

H. I. Hristev (✉)
Department of International Law and International Relations,
Sofia University St Kliment Ohridski, Sofia, Bulgaria
e-mail: h.hristev@law.uni-sofia.bg

U. Stelkens et al. (eds.), *The Implementation of the EU Services Directive*,
DOI: 10.1007/978-90-6704-840-8_4,

technique for matters concerned with sanctions). During the debates on the adoption of the law this idea was rejected. However, the law entered into force on the day of its publication in the State Gazette. Thus the usual *vacatio legis* according the Constitution was not used.[1]

1.2 Impact of the Services Directive

In the process of transposing the Services Directive, the national authorities stressed the necessity of altering the legislation in accordance with the law. However, it must be noted that the legal acts that were altered are not many. Most of the amendments include measures which help avoid legislative contradiction between provisions which govern specific regulated professions and the new legislative act.

The legal drafting was carried out by the Ministry of the Economy, Energy and Tourism. The legal draft was approved by the Council of Ministers with Decision 881 on 12 November 2009 and was lodged with the Parliament on the same date (see footnote 1). The final legislative act was, as stated above, published on 23 February 2010 in the State Gazette and entered into force the same day.

1.3 (National) Scope of Application

Though the law aims mainly at those services providers that are established in another Member State, by securing the application of the freedom of establishment and the freedom of movement of services its provisions are legally binding for all of the domestic services/establishments. The legal provisions of the law are intended to be applicable erga *omnes* and anyone who has legal interest can take advantage of it. The law includes several non-discrimination measures, e.g. the prohibition of laying down restrictive conditions on the freedom of establishment and the freedom of movement.

1.4 Incorporation of Transposing Legislation

Some of the requirements of the SD relate to the administrative conditions with which providers from another Member State must be in compliance in order to provide services in Bulgaria. In that vien, such conditions in the existing legal acts were altered in order to ensure equal treatment. No changes were made to the

[1] The usual *vacatio legis* according Article 5 (5) of the Constitution is 3 days after the publication in the State Gazette. However the Parliament has the right to alter this period and set another one.

Administrative Procedure Act, which is a codification of the administrative proceedings in Bulgaria. For the purposes of transposition the Bulgarian government created a new legal act designed to meet the requirements of the directive, i.e. the proposed draft law, which was adopted at the end of February. The existing administrative proceedings will be applied *mutatis mutandis* according to the principles enshrined in the Directive and the implementing act, e.g. non-discrimination, proportionality, necessity (Article 10 (2) of the law).

1.5 The Relationship of the Services Directive to Primary EU Law

The new piece of legislation directs attention towards the primacy of the EU legislation and attaches great importance to the principles of freedom of establishment and freedom of movement found in the Treaties. The subject of the act according to Article 1 (1) is providing regulations for the exercise of rights that derive from the latter mentioned principles. In that regard, there was a necessity to design new non-discrimination provisions, which would give a wide range of rights to the services providers and would prohibit any possibility for discrimination based on nationality, place of establishment or other administrative measures which are more favourable to national entities.

1.6 Screening

During the screening period, the Bulgarian administration made an inquiry into all the public bodies concerned with the application of the future act in order to discover the possible obstacles in the existing national legislation. The result is a proposal for amendments in seven legal acts. Also a seminar on the application of the SD was held on 21 April 2008. A report on the impact of the implementation and application of the Services Directive was written in March 2008. The presentations of the seminar and the report on the impact can be found on the internet site of the Ministry of Economy, Tourism and Energy (link given in 1.1 of the current file).

2 Individual Articles of the Services Directive

2.1 Article 6 SD: Point of Single Contact (POSC)

According to Article 3 (1) of the law, the function of POSC will be provided for by the single portal for access to electronic administrative services created by the Electronic Government Act. The Ministry Council will issue a decree for the enforcement of this provision and how the Point of Single Contact will function. The law does not specify how many Single Points of Contact will be created. The wording of Article 3 speaks of the existence of only one POSC on the national level. The introduction of the POSC does not include re-allocation of administrative competences. Regarding public bodies that possess competences for the provision of services, the statute is clear that these bodies retain their competences, though they have one extra obligation in that they must give detailed information in a timely manner to the POSC (Article 5 of the law). The POSC in Bulgaria was not introduced through the creation of a new administrative body; its functions are attributed to the single portal for access to electronic administrative services. The state will be liable for mistakes made by the POSC in accordance with the provisions for state liability in the Act on the Liability for Damage Incurred by the State and the Municipalities. The state may be held responsible for the actions of public bodies according to the principle of state liability for damage caused to individuals by infringements of Community law.

2.2 Article 7 SD: Right to Information

The rights of information were not extended in the process of transposition, as one may notice in the draft law and the final act adopted. The rights under Article 7 SD are transposed in Article 4 of the law.

2.3 Article 8 SD: Procedures by Electronic Means

Electronic procedures were known in Bulgarian legislation to some extent, though they are not widely used. They were first introduced with the Electronic Government Act in 2007. The administration is obliged to communicate with private persons or other public bodies when they have chosen this type of communication. For this purpose, the private person must obtain an electronic signature from one of the licensed providers. Article 4 of the law implementing the SD obliges the administrator of the POSC to help the providers and the recipients of services with the needed information and even to help them with the filing of documents needed to exercise their rights. The other administrative means of communication were not removed and coexist. The provider has the right to choose what method is most suitable for him/her to deal with the national administration.

2.4 Article 9 SD: Authorisation Schemes

In Bulgarian legislation there are three main types of administrative regimes—(1) license regime, (2) authorisation regime and (3) registration regime. The application of these regimes can be followed through the online Register of administrative structures in Bulgaria.[2] The authorisation and registration regimes are those which are applied in most of the cases. The license regime is used in those fields where the risk of the economic activity is thought to be relatively high, e.g. in the financial sector.

2.5 Article 10 SD: Conditions for the Granting of Authorisation

The requirement for recognition of authorisations given by other Member States is fulfilled through a general obligation for recognition by the competent national bodies. The competent public body may not require the original document that gives the authorisation, authenticated copy of the document or a translation, nor shall they duplicate the requirements and controls to which the provider is already subject in another MS or in Bulgaria. There is no problem for authorisation to be granted on a national level. There was no need to introduce the obligation to provide the reasoning for the decision of the competent body, since it is a fundamental principle in administrative law in Bulgaria. Nevertheless, Article 13 of the law draws the attention to this obligation of the authorities. The judicial review is governed by the provisions of the Administrative Proceedings Code. When an authorisation is granted or denied, the administrative act can be contested following the common procedure laid out in the Administrative Proceedings Code. It follows from Article 169 APC that the court shall verify whether the public body possessed discretion and whether the said authority complied with the requirement for legal conformity of administrative acts. However, the judges may not issue a decision in lieu of the administration when the public body acted with discretion. In this case the court has only the right to revoke or declare the nullity of the administrative acts.

2.6 Article 11 SD: Duration of Authorisation

According to Article 12, section 2 the authorisation has unlimited validity unless it depends on continuous fulfilment of the requirements for the authorisation; or the authorisation is subject to automatic renewal; or the authorisation is time-limited or is limited in respect of the number of the authorisations due to the overriding public interest.

2 http://www1.government.bg/ras/regimes/index.html

2.7 Article 12 SD: Selection from Among Several Candidates

Even before the transposition of the Services Directive, Bulgarian legislation provided for a selection procedure in the public sector in cases where there is no possibility for an unlimited number of authorisations. Nonetheless, all the requirements of Article 12 SD were implemented in Article 18 of the law. Similar procedures can be found in the Law of the Concessions and Law for public procurement. When holding a procedure for the granting of a concession, the criterion for assessment of the offers shall be the most economically favourable one. According to the law, the most economically favourable offer shall be determined on the basis of a complex assessment of predetermined criteria (Article 27 of The Law of the Concessions). Major principles in the procedure for the granting of a concession are the principles of non-discrimination and of free and fair competition. Similar rules govern the procedure for assigning public procurement.

2.8 Article 13 SD: Authorisation Procedures

The competent public body which grants the authorisation shall specify *in concreto* the duration of each administrative procedure according to the relevant statutes in the field. The legislator establishes general time-limits, which must be followed, for every procedure in the statutes. However, it should be noted that it is for the competent administrative body to specify the deadline for pronouncement in every case after it has considered the complexity of the matter. This period cannot exceed the one laid down in the respective legal act. In accordance with the law, the authorisation is deemed to be granted if the administrative body does not give its response in the legally specified time-limit, unless other legal conditions like the prevailing public interest or the legal interest of third parties are concerned. Such exceptions should flow from another law. The idea of tacit consent is contrary to the general rule in Administrative legislation, which instead established that there is a general rule for tacit dissent in Bulgarian legislation. Only in special cases, like those under the law implementing the SD, may the lack of response be considered as tacit consent. Article 58 (4) APC reads "Non-pronouncement in due time shall be considered as a tacit consent in the cases and under the terms provided for in special laws." Tacit consent and tacit refusal can be contested in the same way as ordinary administrative acts can be contested, unless a special law requires something else to be done.

2.9 Articles 14, 15, 16 SD

The requirements of Articles 14, 15, 16 SD have been implemented in Articles 9–21 of the law. Several laws—like Law for Tourism, Law of the Spatial Planning, Law on energy efficiency, Law for the crafts, and Law of protection of the consumers—were adapted due to the implementation of the directive. According to the Supplementary Provisions of the law, all of the competent bodies who act in the scope of the law have a period of one month to send their reports to the Minister of Economy, Tourism and Energy concerning the application of the law and the compatibility of the procedures they use with the law. It is for the competent bodies to inform the Minister of all the new legal acts which introduce new obligations for the providers of services. After the Minister has received the reports he/she summarises them into one compiled document and sends the summary report to the European Commission. The Minister then notifies the European Commission of the changes in Bulgarian legislation, in compliance with the procedures laid down in Directive 98/34/EC.

2.10 Articles 14–19 SD

It is hard to say that during the process of implementation there was a serious public discussion as regards to the prohibitions, restrictions and exemptions in Articles 14–19 SD. Nearly all of the possibilities for derogation listed in Article 17 SD were implemented in Article 20 of the Bulgarian law. Not mentioned in the adopted act are the derogations in paras 9 and 10 of Article 17 SD, which were concerned with the Schengen Agreement and the shipment of waste.

2.11 Articles 22–27 SD

It could hardly be said that in the process of transposition there was a debate about the renewal of the Administrative Procedure Code in Bulgaria. In the adopted law there are a number of provisions with a procedural character concerning the manner for the settlement of disputes. Disputes can be settled through agreement, by extrajudicial (if the providers are subject to a code of conduct or are members of a trade association or professional body) or judicial means.

2.12 Articles 28 ff. SD: Administrative Cooperation

The requirements of the Directive were introduced not through changes in the Administrative Procedure Code, but were instead implemented in the Council of Ministers' draft law, which was adopted by the Bulgarian Parliament. According to the law in force, access to the registries is given on equal conditions to all the corresponding Member States. It can be observed from the adopted legislation for the implementation of the Services Directive (the law and the amendments to other legal acts) that the Parliament did not see any need for adaptation of the legislation regarding data protection. There was no debate about this issue in the procedure of adoption of the legal act and as a consequence the data protection legislation is not subject to any amendments.

2.13 Article 29 SD: Mutual Assistance—General Obligations for the Member State of Establishment

In accordance with Article 34 of the law, the competent bodies supply information to other Member States upon request in order to verify the fact that the provider is established on the territory of Bulgaria. The part in Article 29 SD about the confirmation that a business is not unlawful is not transposed, so *ex lege* the public bodies shall give information only about the fact of whether the provider is established or not. If there is any concern from another Member State about illegal activities of the provider, the national authorities are obliged to investigate the problem and send information to the other MS.

3 Assessment of the Impact of the Services Directive

It is expected that the implementation of the Services Directive will have a positive effect on the economy in times of crisis and will lead to an administrative simplification when it comes to the use of electronic procedures and the way that public administration functions. It must be noted that the electronic procedures were not introduced through the implementation of the Services Directive, as they have existed since the Electronic Government Act came into force. Still, they have not been widely used.

The Implementation of the Services Directive in Cyprus

Chrystalla Neophytou

1 General Remarks on the Transposition Strategy and General Understanding of the Implementation

The necessary mechanisms to manage the implementation arrangements have been put in place by the Council of Ministers Decision, which lays out the following: (a) Overall responsibility for the coordination of the Implementation of the Services Directive in Cyprus has been assigned to the Planning Bureau, which is a body under the Ministry of Finance entrusted inter alia with the coordinating roles for various EU matters, (b) Utilisation will also be made of the existing One Stop Shop for Investors at the Ministry of Commerce, Industry and Tourism.

The Government of Cyprus has decided (Council decision 9 of July 2008) to upgrade and expand the One Stop Shop currently operating within the Ministry of Commerce, Industry and Tourism in order to serve as a Point of Single Contact (POSC). A webportal is under development to support the POSC of Cyprus. It is designed in such a way as to provide the relevant information/procedures, to allow the submission of documents and applications, to receive feedback regarding ongoing procedures, and to receive the decisions and other replies relating to the applications made through them.

A Guide has been prepared by the Planning Bureau and circulated to the Ministries and other relevant authorities to assist them with the screening exercise. Working groups have been established in each Ministry, with Representatives from the Law Office of the Republic, the Planning Bureau, other broad public sector organizations including local authorities, as well as competent bodies from

The author is advocate at Andreas Neocleous & Co LLC and Member of the Cyprus Bar Association.

C. Neophytou (✉)
Andreas Neocleous & Co LLC, Nicosia, Cyprus

U. Stelkens et al. (eds.), *The Implementation of the EU Services Directive*, DOI: 10.1007/978-90-6704-840-8_5,

the private sector. A two-stage approach was followed for screening: first, all relevant provisions in legislative acts and administrative practice were identified. In the second stage, through a structured comparison these provisions were checked against the provisions of the Directive. The results of the screening exercise were discussed in the respective working groups.

The Planning Bureau has assumed the responsibility of IMI Coordinator (DIMIC) for the Services Directive, while the Ministry of Commerce, Industry and Tourism will continue to be the National IMI Coordinator (NIMIC), as in the case of the Directive for the Recognition of the Professional Qualifications. The decentralized model will continue to apply, whereby the Competent Authorities will be exchanging requests directly with their counterparts in other Member States.

The Services Directive has been implemented into Cyprus domestic law by June 2010 by Law 76(I)/2010 which is regulating issues concerning the freedom of establishment of service providers and the free movement of services ("the Law").

1.1 Main References Used in this Research

The answers to this report are based on information provided to us by the Planning Bureau officials. It is also based on information provided by the Law office of the Republic, which took part in the whole consultation process, as well as on information provided by the Parliamentary Commission of Commerce, Industry and Tourism. The information is based either on internal documents that have not been published or on personal interviews with the parties involved in the implementation process. Furthermore this report is based on the Law 76(I)/2010 which has implemented the SD into Cyprus domestic law.

1.2 Impact of the Services Directive

1.2.1 Profound Cause of Changes to National Law?

Cyprus adopted a horizontal law for the implementation of the Services Directive, due to the SD several amendments, as well as modernisation of authorisation schemes found in sector specific legislation, have been introduced, along with more simplified administrative procedures.

In Cyprus, legal persons are generally required to obtain a license from the local authorities (community or municipality council) for exercising any business, trade or profession within its jurisdiction and to pay the yearly corresponding fee.

Cyprus has also specific authorisation schemes in several service sectors.

In addition to the obligation to obtain a general trade licence, there are several service activities that require an application to a specific competent authority and enrolment in a relevant register, for example in sectors like wholesale and retail, construction and real estate.

In the food and beverages sector, a license is required for the supply of alcoholic beverages. Furthermore, Cyprus has reported several authorisation schemes in the tourism sector, such as an authorisation scheme for recreational centres (including bars, clubs, restaurants etc.), licences for hotels and other tourism accommodations, swimming pools and travel agencies. There are several authorisation schemes in the private education sector, such as a licence for private universities and private schools. In addition, authorisations exist in the private social care sector, such as an authorisation for adults care centres, an authorisation for child care at home and child centres, an authorisation for homes for elderly and handicapped people.

Some regulated professions are subject to an obligation to exercise their specific service activity exclusively. This seems to apply, in particular, to real estate agents, lawyers and contractors of buildings or technical works.

The implementation of the SD directive in Cyprus introduced important changes aiming at lifting unjustified barriers to the provision of cross-border services into Cyprus. The inclusion of "free movement clauses" in the new horizontal law or in sector-specific legislations and as a result the situation of business and self employed wanting to provide services across Cyprus, most of the remaining establishment requirements (i.e. requirements obliging the service provider to be established in the country before it can provide the service) have been abolished.

Prior authorisations imposed on those that want to provide cross-border services have also been removed.

1.2.2 Involvement in the Transposition Process

The following institutions/organizations have been involved in the transposition process: Planning Bureau (coordinators), Law Office of the Republic, Competent Authorities/Line Ministries, Office of the Commissioner for the Protection of Personal Data, Local Authorities, Professional Bodies such as the Cyprus Bar Association, the Cyprus Association of Chartered Accountants, the Council of Registration and Control of Constructors, Developing and Technical Projects, the Cyprus Sports Association, Chamber of Commerce and Industry, Employers' Federation, Trade Unions.

1.3 (National) Scope of Application

Articles 5–15 SD were incorporated in the national draft law as horizontal legislation that makes no reference to whether it applies to transnational or domestic service providers and therefore it is thus understood that they apply equally to both transnational and domestic service providers. In the same way the amendments made to the sector specific legislation aim to treat transnational and domestic service providers equally.

Article 3 of the Law provides that the purpose of the Law is the establishment of general principles to facilitate the exercise of the right of the freedom of establishment of service providers in the Republic as well as the freedom of movement of services and simultaneously retaining a high level of provision of services. Neither specific reference nor any distinction is made under the provisions of the Law to a distinction between transnational and domestic service providers.

There is no reference under Cyprus Law regarding to a distinction between transnational and domestic service providers.

1.4 Incorporation of Transposing Legislation

The majority of the articles of the SD were transposed into the relevant national law(s). The ideas, main provision and principles provided by the SD have been replicated in the provisions of national law.

As far as sector specific legislation is concerned, an amendment of existing laws/regulations was preferred over the passing of a new codification.

1.5 The Relationship of the Services Directive to Primary EU Law

There was no specific assessment of Articles 43 and 49 of the Treaty (now: Articles 49 and 56 TFEU) in relation to the SD, given that the principles of Articles 43 and 49 are already reflected in the SD. No problems have been identified in this context.

1.6 Screening

The screening exercise was carried out in working groups with the participation of all relevant competent authorities of the public and private sector, including professional bodies and local authorities under the coordination and guidance of the Planning Bureau and in consultation with the Law Office of the Republic of Cyprus. This process resulted in the submission to the European Commission of 106 Reports (IPM) concerning authorisation schemes and other requirements which could be justified by the provisions of the Directive.

Main changes in legislation as a result of the screening process:
Horizontal requirements

- Amendment of the relevant provisions concerning the licensing of legal entities to exercise any business, trade or profession for a profit, within the limits of local authorities, so that the said entities will no longer be required to obtain a license, though they will continue to be required to pay the fixed fees provided by the Law.

Sectoral requirements include:

Wholesale and retail services

- Abolition of the regulation setting a maximum sale price for newspapers, magazines and printed material.

Construction and property related services

- Amendment of the relevant legislation in order to allow legal—in addition to natural—persons to provide Engineering services.
- Abolition of the authorisation/"special permit" for the provision of cross-border construction services by natural and legal persons.
- Amendment of the obligation that building contractors—natural or legal persons—exclusively provide building services.

Real estate activities

- Abolition of the requirement that real estate agents established in another Member State cooperate with licensed estate agents in Cyprus for the provision of cross-border services.
- Abolition of the requirement that real estate agents established in another Member State take and pass examinations set by the Competent Authority for the provision of cross-border services.
- Abolition of the obligation that real estate agents exclusively provide real estate services.

Tourism and related services

- Abolition of the quantitative restrictions on the issuance of new road licenses for motor vehicles in respect to vehicle rental services.
- Abolition of the authorisation requirement for the provision of motor vehicle rental services.

Services of the regulated professions

- Abolition of the authorisation requirement on driving instructors for the cross-border provision of their services.

2 Individual Articles of the Services Directive

2.1 Article 6 SD: Point of Single Contact (POSC)

The provisions of the Directive related to the Point of Single Contact in Cyprus were transposed into Article 6 of Section II of the Horizontal (Framework) Law. The government of Cyprus has upgraded and expanded the One Stop Shop, already operating under the auspices of the Ministry of Commerce, Industry and Tourism, in order to serve as POSC. The POSC Cyprus is centralised and accessible through a unique web portal.

The Council of Ministers decided on the establishment/operation of only one Point of Single Contact.

For the purpose of the Point of Single Contact, the Council of Ministers' decision provided for the upgrading and expansion of the One Stop Shop already operational under the administrative auspices of the Ministry of Commerce, Industry and Tourism. The Point of Single Contact will continue to provide the services currently offered by the One Stop Shop, such as Registration of Companies, Income Tax Registration, VAT Registration and the issuance of residence and work permits.

The Point of Single Contact has been developed through the close cooperation of all relevant governmental departments (such as Department of Information Technologies of the Ministry of Finance and Department of Electronic Communications of the Ministry of Communications and Works).

According to the national legislation, the Point of Single Contact is liable only for its actions or omissions arising during its operation. The POSC Cyprus has only a coordinating role and the final decisions remain with the existing competent authorities, which are liable for the accuracy and validity of information provided through the POSC.

2.2 *Article 7 SD: Right to Information*

The provisions of the SD concerning the "rights of information" were transposed into the Horizontal (Framework) Law. Specifically according to section 8 of the Law the Single Point of Contact provides to the service providers the following information:

(a) Requirements in relation to service providers residing in the Republic of Cyprus and especially those concerning procedures and statements that have to be completed as to access in the activities of service provision and to the exercise of provision of services
(b) The details of correspondence of the relevant authorities for the direct correspondence with such authorities including the details which are competent for issues of exercise of activities of provision of services
(c) The means and the requirements of access to public registers and data bases regarding service providers and services
(d) The means of application that are generally available in case where a conflict arises between the relevant authorities and the provider and the receiver of services or between the provider and the recipient of services or between service providers.

(e) The details of correspondence of organizations and unions, other than the competent authorities, from which the providers and the recipient may obtain practical assistance.

Upon request by the recipients or the providers, the competent authorities provide information in simple and understandable language, relating to the common way of interpretation and application of the requirements set out in paragraph (a) of subsection 1 of section 8 and where it is appropriate the advise may include a step by step guidance;

Furthermore the Law provides that the obligation of the competent authorities to assist the service providers and recipients does not result to the provision of legal advice in limited cases.

It is also provided by the Law that the Council of Ministers has the discretion to issue regulations that are published in the Official Gazette by which the details of cooperation between the POSC and the competent authorities regarding the provision of information to the providers and the recipients.

The "rights to information" have been implemented only within the scope of the application of the SD.

2.3 Article 8 SD: Procedures by Electronic Means

A portal for the Point of Single Contact has been developed. The portal provides information on procedures and formalities, it allows for the possibility to download forms and applications, to apply online and to track the progress of one's application. Furthermore, the Austrian tools (MOCCA, MOA) for the e-signing of applications and the verification of documents received have been integrated into the developed website.

We consider the integration of the Austrian tools into the website as a step forward since Cyprus had not yet developed an e-signature framework.

2.4 Article 9 SD: Authorisation Schemes

2.4.1 Means of Less Restrictive Measure

The authorisation scheme was maintained in all cases where the competent authorities believed that an "a posteriori inspection" would not serve an overriding purpose related to public interest as recognised in the case law of the court of justice. The discretion of the competent authorities may be challenged by any interested party and examined by the Supreme Court as far as to the reasoning given and the research conducted by the competent authority are concerned and as to the applicable law in any given case.

2.4.2 Existing Authorisation Schemes/Procedures

There is not one particular type of authorisation scheme/procedure. The screening process required the responsible authorities to check the requirements of the authorisation schemes in every piece of legislation in order to establish whether they could be justified by the conditions of section 9 of the SD. The authorisation schemes abolished were those which the "posteriori inspections" considered sufficient.

2.4.3 Simple Notifications

Simple notifications are not seen as included by Articles 9 ff. SD.

2.5 Article 10 SD: Conditions for the Granting of Authorisation

The provisions of Article 10 of the SD were transposed into the Horizontal (Framework) Law without any specific difficulties. Authorisations granted by the competent authorities cover the whole territory of Cyprus with the exception of authorisations granted by local authorities and by District Administration Offices which are valid only within the limits within which they exercise their jurisdiction.

The respective provisions of Article 10 (5) of SD have been transposed into the Horizontal (Framework) Law. The refusal of the competent authorities to grant an authorisation can be appealed to the Supreme Court of Cyprus according to article 146 of the Cyprus Constitution. The use of discretion by the authorities is also subject to examination by the Court.

An obligation to fully reason decisions of the administration existed even before the SD.

Finally, the allocation of administrative competences has not been altered.

2.6 Article 11 SD: Duration of Authorisation

Article 11 of the SD has been transposed as it is into Article 11 of Section III of the Horizontal (Framework) Law.

2.7 Article 12 SD: Selection from Among Several Candidates

Article 12 of the SD has been transposed as it is into Article 12 of Section III of the Horizontal (Framework) Law.

2.8 Article 13 SD: Authorisation Procedures

The Horizontal (Framework) Law provides in principle for a maximum period of three months, though in certain cases the competent authorities are granted the possibility to deviate from this rule and through a special law set a different duration for the administrative procedure. If the authority does not respond within the prescribed time limits, the authorisation, as a rule, is considered as granted except in special cases where there are overriding reasons of public interest including the legal interests of third parties. The principle of tacit authorisation has been introduced in the legal system of Cyprus through the SD.

2.9 Articles 14, 15, 16 SD

The above Articles were transposed into the respective articles of the Horizontal (Framework) Law and formed part of the screening exercise carried out by Cyprus.

2.10 Articles 14–19 SD

Relevant discussions as regards these articles took place in the context of the methodology to be followed with regard to the screening exercise.

2.11 Articles 22–27 SD

Articles 22-27 of the SD were transposed through Articles 22-26 of Section V of the Horizontal (Framework) Law. Articles 24 and 25 of the SD were part of the national Screening exercise.

2.12 Articles 28 ff. SD: Administrative Cooperation

Administrative assistance with other Member States (MSs) in areas such as taxation and customs existed prior to the SD. The domestic administrative assistance foreseen in national legislation is not extensive and sophisticated.

The SD provided substantial encouragement for administrative cooperation, both domestically and among Member States, through the Internal Market Information System (IMI).

Despite the considerable administrative burden brought about by the SD, there are no provisions for financial compensation.

The data protection provisions of the national law are in line with the respective requirements of the SD.

2.13 Problems and Discourses on Administrative Cooperation

Given that the SD has been implemented only very recently, it is too early to draw conclusions on any practical problems concerning administrative cooperation in general and the provisions of Article 29 in particular.

2.14 Convergence Programme (Chapter VII of the Services Directive)

Due to other priorities, so far no time could be made available for any internal discussions on Article 37.

3 Assessment of the Impact of the Services Directive

3.1 Extent of the Impact

A Guide has been prepared and circulated by the Planning Bureau to the Ministries/relevant authorities to assist them with the screening exercise, Working groups have been established per Ministry with representatives from the Law Office of the Republic, the Planning Bureau, other broad public sector organisations including local authorities as well as competent bodies of the private sector. A two-stage approach was followed, the first stage being the analytical examination and assessment of the national laws and the administrative procedures. The second stage being the identification of the requirements that shall remain applicable provided that they could be justified according to the provisions of the Directive (i.e. non-discrimination provisions, provisions of necessity and proportionality). In the second stage, these provisions were checked against the provisions of the Directive in a structured way and they were discussed in the respective working groups. Once the screening exercise was finalised, the competent authorities proceeded with the necessary amendments to legislation. Although there were many changes were necessary for many administrative procedures in various laws, the competent authorities reported that they did not face any obstacles to implement the directive.

3.2 Assessment of the Transposing Legislation

The SD is viewed as a substantial contribution towards the overall policies of simplification, modernisation and acceleration of proceedings; the improvement of transparency and quality of services; the protection of consumers and the encouragement of service providers within a more competitive business environment.

3.3 Most important and Profound Changes Induced by the Services Directive

The simplification of national legal and administrative practices, the establishment of the Point of Single Contact and the administrative cooperation of Member States through the IMI are considered as substantial benefits for a service economy like Cyprus.

Implementation of the Services Directive in the Czech Republic

Filip Křepelka

1 General Remarks on the Transposition Strategy and General Understanding of the Implementation

1.1 Main References Used in this Research

Zákon č. 222/2009 Sb., o volném pohybu služeb (the Act on the Free Movement of Services, also translated in other English texts addressing the implementation of the Services Directive as the Act on the Freedom to Provide Services), and *Zákon č. 223/2009 Sb., kterým se mění některé zákony v souvislosti s přijetím zákona o volném pohybu služeb* (the Act Amending Certain Acts in Connection with the Adoption of the Act on the Free Movement of Services, henceforth 'the Amending Act') implement the Services Directive.

Both acts were adopted as formally separated by the Parliament of the Czech Republic on 17 June 2009 (final approval by the Senate). Their entry into force was expected for the day required by the Services Directive, that is, 28 December 2009. There was no intention to either apply implementing legislation earlier, or to delay the implementation for some reason.

The author is Associate Professor at Masarykova Univerzita, Brno

F. Křepelka (✉)
Masarykova Univerzita, Brno, Czech Republic
e-mail: filip.krepelka@law.muni.cz

U. Stelkens et al. (eds.), *The Implementation of the EU Services Directive*,
DOI: 10.1007/978-90-6704-840-8_6,

Both acts have been published as legal documents of national importance in the *Sbírka zákonů* (the Collection of Acts).[1] They can also be found on the Internet as a website presentation of the Parliament of the Czech Republic.[2]

Relevant acts of the Parliament and other legal documents are often also published on the Internet by a competent ministry or other central authority. The *Ministerstvo průmyslu a obchodu* (the Ministry of Industry and Trade) was charged with the implementation of the Services Directive. Such documents are translated into foreign languages only scarcely. Nevertheless, the Act on the Free Movement of Services was translated into English by this Ministry for the presentation of its implementation even before its adoption.[3]

Both pieces of legislation have been proposed to the Parliament by the *Vláda* ('the Government', i.e. the council of ministers) together with the required explanatory reports. These reports are studied and cited because they form the first commentary of adopted legislation. The reports are, however, of varying quality. As regards implementation of the Services Directive, contributions and costs are calculated in detail and legislative options addressing several aspects are explained. The Directive is mentioned as a sole cause for the adoption of the legislation. According to the methodology for the preparation of legislation, the relations of particular paragraphs of draft legislation to articles of the Directive are indicated in an explanatory report. Nevertheless, the provisions of the proposed legislation are mostly explained only in a general manner.

The Ministry also prepared and commissioned several opinions on the Services Directive project as presented by the European Commission. These documents focused on the purported economic impact of the Directive and its implementation in Member States. Evaluation of the Directive project was optimistic. The Ministry commissioned a study from a Czech subsidiary of a globally operating consultant firm.[4] The study calculated potential increase of international trade in services, gross domestic product, and employment.

Repudiation of the principle of country of origin and the introduction of sector exceptions in the process of approval by the Council of Ministers and the European Parliament was regretted as an unnecessary abandoning of the original intent to totally liberalise trade in services within the European Union. Nevertheless, the legal aspects of implementation were analysed in these government documents to a limited extent.

---

1 For an online version, see http://www.sbirka.cz.

2 Website of the *Poslanecká sněmovna* (the Chamber of Deputies) which is lower house of the Parliament (http://www.psp.cz) provides information about legislative process related to every act of the Parliament. The role of the *Senát* is limited.

3 See http://www.mpo.cz/zprava68963.html.

4 See KPMG Česká republika, s.r.o. (2006).

1.2 Impact of the Services Directive

Despite early proclamations by the Ministry and its representatives, implementation of the Service Directive has contributed to the simplification of Czech laws regulating services and other economic activities to a limited extent. Such an effect is most apparent in changes of the existing legislation brought about by the Amending Act.

It should be noted that Czech legislation applicable to business and trade is generally perceived as complicated, burdensome, and inconsistent. From time to time, politicians launch campaigns promising its reduction, simplification, and clarification.

Preparation of legislation in the Czech Republic includes questioning (the so-called *připomínkové řízení*, i.e., reminder proceedings) all ministries, other central agencies, and superior courts. The specific advisory body of the Government (the Council of Ministers)—*Legislativní rada* (the Legislative Council)—is consulted on legal aspects. Furthermore, economic and social partners are asked for comments, albeit their responses are often ignored if they oppose government policy.

As regards implementation of the Services Directive, *Hospodářská komora České republiky* (the Chamber of Commerce of the Czech Republic) and *Svaz průmyslu a dopravy* (Association of Industry and Transportation) were consulted, among others. There is no evidence of consultation with national representation of trade unions, whose West European counterparts contributed to the reshaping of the Services Directive, claiming its negative impact on social stability.

1.3 (National) Scope of Application

In my opinion, the Services Directive is applicable only in a transnational context. It addresses cross-border services as defined in the case law of the Court of Justice interpreting the provisions of the Treaties.[5] Such a limitation is based on the wording of Article 1, which mentions the freedom of establishment and the free movement of services. It is hard to claim that these words have a different meaning from that in the Treaty provisions. Furthermore, the Services Directive is based on provisions related to the internal market.

5 See Articles 49–55 of the Treaty establishing the European (Economic) Community (numbered before the Treaty of Amsterdam as 59–65) and Articles 56–62 of the Treaty on the Functioning of the European Union.

Finally, the Services Directive was implemented in the Czech Republic as a regulatory measure for cross-border services only. This limitation results from the wording of section (paragraph) 1 of the Act on the Free Movement of Services.[6]

Therefore, it is difficult to claim that domestic providers—including nationals and companies of other Member States of the European Union which exercise freedom of establishment, and foreign nationals and companies enjoying openness of the Czech Republic towards immigration and foreign business—can rely on simplifications brought about by the implementation while serving clients in the Czech Republic.

Nevertheless, the Amending Act has repealed several temporal limitations of licences for both foreign and domestic service providers. Finally, the impact of implementing legislation is thus a broader than the intent expressed in it.

As regards the scope of application of the implementing legislation in relation to everybody, the answer is also not easy. The Act on the Free Movement of Services is applicable solely to cross-border services and their providers or consumers. Such an approach effectively excludes its general application to individuals and legal entities in other fields.

There is, however, an interesting exception in practice. Points of single contact, established by the Act on the Free Movement of Services for implementation of the Services Directive solely for the simplification of the cross-border movement of services, in reality also assist foreign subjects considering establishment in the Czech Republic, and even nationals and domestic companies interested in business at home.

The Act on the Free Movement of Services does not include a provision establishing unequal treatment. On the contrary, the principle of equal treatment and the exclusion of non-proportional and unnecessary requirements are underlined in a general way.[7]

The Amending Act changed dozens of acts addressing many service sectors. First, it removed remaining bans and restrictions imposed on providers settled abroad. Second, it introduced into these acts tacit consent with the temporary provision of service on territory of the Czech Republic if decision within a prescribed time is missing.

Delivery of service by a provider settled in another Member State is excluded only in exceptional cases. For example, legislation on atomic energy adjusted by the Amending Act explicitly excludes the professional education of experts from

[6] According to the ministerial translation of the Act into English: "This Act transposes the relevant legislation of the European Communities and regulates the cross-border provision of services, the rights and obligations of service providers, the rights of service recipients, the points of single contact, their activities and structure, the establishment of authorisations to provide services under the law, and the supervision of service providers on the internal market of the European Union."

[7] See sections 4 and 5 of the Act on the Free Movement of Services.

the liberalisation of services brought about by implementing legislation.[8] In other cases, implementation of the Directive led to a clarification of requirements. For example, it introduced the clear duty of land surveyors (geodesists) to notify their activities on territory of the Czech Republic to competent authorities.[9]

The legislation is based on a screening of existing Czech legislation. Dozens of Czech acts were analysed. Many provisions excluding or discriminating against foreign providers were removed or adjusted to the principle of equality.

On the other hand, explanatory reports reveal that little attention was paid to whether the existing requirements related to services and their providers were proportional. Until now, nobody has indicated in legal journals or otherwise any example of such deficiency.

Provisions on the free movement of services in the Treaties can enjoy a direct effect and precedence over purported incompatible legislation of the Czech Republic. Furthermore, the Services Directive can be applied directly in these cases because it addresses the relation between an individual and the Member State (vertical effect).

As already mentioned, implementing legislation addresses solely cross-border services. Cross-border establishment which is also addressed with the Directive despite its full name (Directive on Services in the Internal Market) remains almost unaffected with cited implementing legislation. Even explanatory reports do not mention the freedom of establishment or the Directive's requirement to simplify its exercise.

From this point of view, we can ask whether implementation of the Services Directive is sufficient. Certainly, the principle of equal treatment of nationals and companies of other Member States results also from provisions of the Treaties. Czech laws usually do not discriminate against foreign subjects if they decide to settle in the Czech Republic for business. Nevertheless, the Directive also requires the simplification of establishment.

1.4 Incorporation of Transposing Legislation

The Czech Republic has decided to implement the Directive—at least its general provisions and provisions related to the cross-border movement of services—with the specific Act on the Free Movement of Services. This act establishes rules for the simplification of cross-border trade in services, specific procedures (recognition of authorisations issued by other Member States, recognition of insurance, and cooperation of Czech and foreign authorities in the supervision of domestic service

[8] See Part 11 of the Amending Act adjusting *zákon č. 18/1997 Sb., o mírovém využívání atomové energie a ionizujícího záření* (Act on the Peacetime Exploitation of Atomic Energy and Ionizing Radiation).

[9] See Part 9 of the Amending Act changing *zákon č. 200/1994 Sb., o zeměměřičství* (the Act on Geodesy).

providers abroad and foreign service providers active on the territory of the Czech Republic), and specific institutions (points of single contact).

According to one ministerial officer involved in the implementation of the Services Directive, the relation between the Act on the Free Movement of Services and sector legislation for various economic activities shall not be simplified to the statement that the act is *lex specialis* towards other legislation.[10] The principle of the free movement of services shall be perceived as *lex generalis*. Specific sector legislation can contain its own provisions on cross-border services and their providers and consumers. Such cases are, however, not usual. Furthermore, since there is no regulation of administrative cooperation, the act shall be perceived as *lex generalis* in procedural issues. On the hand, tacit consent introduced by the Amending Act into many acts for various sectors and also mentioned in the Act on the Free Movement of Services is to be understood as *lex specialis* towards general regulatory regimes.

The Act on the Free Movement of Services is accompanied with the act amending provisions of thirty-six acts establishing the standards and requirements for various economic activities. Most of the acts introduce the rights of authorised foreign providers to deliver services after simplified authorisation and tacit consent.

Proposals to establish required procedures and instruments, that is, points of single contact, the simplified recognition of documents issued by other Member States, and tacit consent after an elapsed delay for requests for remaining authorisations in a new codification of administrative proceedings, *zákon č. 500/ 2004 Sb., správní řád* (administrative code), were allegedly turned down by the Ministry of the Interior and its legislative experts as 'compromising their newly shaped masterpiece'.[11]

1.5 The Relationship of the Services Directive to Primary EU Law

Czech politicians and journalists often described the Services Directive project, both before and during its implementation, as a new legal framework that would finally establish the freedom to provide services across the internal borders of the European Union. They largely ignored existing provisions on the free movement of services in the Treaties.

This interpretation of the Service Directive project even enjoyed some influence with the Ministry of Industry and Trade and the institutions it consulted.

---

[10] I have discussed the issue with Ms. M. Brandejská from the Ministry of Industry and Trade.

[11] According to Ms. M. Brandejská (see above). Compare this with Germany, which implemented administrative measures of the Services Directive in its *Verwaltungsverfahrengesetz*. Electronic communication, European administrative cooperation, and the assistance of points of single contact were introduced in this federal code of administrative proceedings.

This resulted in exaggerated expectations and even disappointment after removal of the principle of the country of origin and the exclusion of several services in the process of adoption of the Services Directive.

Only few experts familiar with European Union law reminded that the free movement of services was established in primary law decades ago and that sector legislation contributes to the realisation of this basic economic freedom in various sectors (transportation, banking, insurance, telecommunication, attorneys, television etc.). Furthermore, before its accession to the European Union, the Czech Republic had implemented sector regulations and directives to numerous pieces of legislation addressing various sectors of the Czech economy.

Incidentally, the existence of the free movement of services was addressed upon accession of the Czech Republic to the European Union in 2004 in a general way in *zákon č. 451/1991 Sb., živnostenský zákon* (Act on Trade Licences/*Gewerbegesetz*), applicable in businesses unregulated by specific legislation with general standards. Its specific free movement of services provision[12] largely excludes its own application, thus establishing the general recognition of foreign authorisations to provide services in the Czech Republic.[13]

It is also well known that the scope of the Services Directive is restricted because several important services are excluded (e.g. health care, social services, transportation, financial services, and telecommunications).

There is no known judgment of the Czech courts directly applying provisions of the Treaties on the free movement of services. In general Case law on basic economic freedoms is rare. Therefore, frequent judicial application of the Directive as an instrument of interpretation of unclear implementation provisions and other legislation (indirect effect of directives), and eventually as an instrument of the correction of inconsistent and deficient Czech law (vertical direct effect) cannot be expected.

1.6 Screening

The Ministry organised the screening of Czech legislation addressing various service branches in an elaborate procedure.[14] Few cases of discrimination against foreign providers were identified. In other cases, unnecessary or doubtful

[12] Section 69a was introduced a few days before accession, obviously as an emergency solution. Commentaries remain largely silent about consequences of this provision.

[13] It is interesting that nobody mentioned the provision during the implementation process of the Services Directive. I suggest interpret this section a forgotten piece of legislation from the early days of the Czech Republic in the European Union.

[14] The Ministry started the screening with legislation in its competence in 2007. Screening of legislation administered by other ministries started in 2008. Elaborate procedures for communication and negotiations among the ministries were established and a special task force was created.

requirements were identified. The screening included cooperation with other ministries. In several cases, these ministries insisted on existing requirements and restrictions. The Ministry accepted them in some cases, sometimes after difficult debate. Nevertheless, in general, the Ministry pushed for liberalisation. The screening was generally carried out on an inter-ministerial level. Chambers and associations were informed and consulted. The reaction to the results of the screening comprises the Amending Act.

2 Individual Articles of the Services Directive

2.1 Article 6 SD: Point of Single Contact (POSC)

The Act on the Free Movement of Services established points of single contact (singular *jednotné kontaktní místo*, plural *jednotná kontaktní místa*).[15] A list of points of single contact is specified in the ministerial decree expected in the act.[16]

Points of single contact are not expected to decide on application and notifications. The Czech Republic has not gone beyond the requirements of the Directive, which does not want to redistribute competences at the national level with the establishment of points of single contact. Czech points thus have two principal tasks. First, they are expected to provide information. Second, they are expected to accept applications and distribute them to competent authorities.

Thirteen points of single contact have been established in every regional capital, and two in the capital, Prague. In general, this organisation reflects the territorial division of the Czech Republic, which is composed of thirteen regions (singular *kraj,* plural *kraje*) and a separate capital. The country has ten million inhabitants. One point of single contact thus serves an area consisting of five hundred thousand to one million inhabitants. Nevertheless, authorisations of economic activities allow business in the entire territory of the country in most cases. Therefore, all fifteen points of single contact handle inquiries and applications related to services and business on the entire territory of the Czech Republic.

Points of single contact have not been established as new agencies. They consist of small units in selected offices of the general administration of economic activities (singular *živnostenský úřad*, *Gewerbeamt* in German and Austrian law). There are more than two hundred administrations of this kind in the Czech Republic.[17] Therefore, in most cases the fifteen points of single contact distribute

---

[15] The points of single contact are established according to its sections 13–17.

[16] See *Vyhláška č. 248/2009 Sb., kterou se stanoví seznam jednotných kontaktních míst* (Decree of the Ministry of Industry and Trade Establishing the List of the Points of Single Contact).

[17] See *Zákon č. 570/1991 Sb, o živnostenských úřadech* (the Act on Offices of Economic Administration).

applications and notifications to other parts of this general administration of economic activities. If specific legislation is applicable and special administration is competent, points of single contact transmit applications to competent ministries and agencies.

A significant part of the enforcement of national (statewide) law is left to the regions and selected larger municipalities, i.e. cities and towns (*přenesená působnost,* transferred competence). The general administration of economic activities is vested in these municipalities. A total of two hundred municipalities thus administer economic activities with their *živnostenský úřad*. Fourteen cities—regional capitals in most cases—are thus charged with an agenda of point of single contact, and Prague has two points of single contact due to its economic importance and the presence of all ministries.

In accordance with the explanatory report, dozens of newly engaged or reassigned officers[18] have been charged with the business of point of single contact. These individuals—usually younger lawyers with a sufficient knowledge of European Union law and English—are often indicated by name in the city administration's website.

While private partners were consulted in the preparation of legislation for the implementation of the Services Directive, they were not involved in the establishment of the points of single contact according to the Act on the Free Movement of Services. Probably, there was little interest in taking over this agenda. Points of single contact, above all, serve foreign providers of services on Czech Republic territory, and the Chamber of Commerce serves Czech business, which has little desire to face foreign competitors.

However, the *Hospodářská komora České republiky* (Chamber of Commerce of the Czech Republic), and regional and district branches of it have launched its own system under similar names (mostly *informační* or *kontaktní místa pro podnikatele,* information/contact points for entrepreneurs) for the consultation of various business administrative aspects. This system is not established with to Czech law, and not mandated by the state. There was communication between the Ministry and the Chamber on whether such label is acceptable (even whether the state was to have a 'trademark' for these words *ex lege*) because the similar naming of similar activities easily leads to confusion.

Legislation for implementation of the Services Directive does not contain specific provisions on liability in case of the misconduct or inappropriate administration of the points of single contact. Specific legislation exists on state liability for damages caused by the exercise of public power.[19] As regards the

[18] For example, two lawyers in my home city Brno (Brünn). Both are former students of my faculty; for contact see http://www.brno.cz/informace/archiv/zivnostensky-urad-mesta-brna-zumb/jednotne-kontaktni-misto/.

[19] *Zákon č. 82/1998 Sb., o odpovědnosti za škodu způsobenou při výkonu veřejné moci nesprávným rozhodnutím nebo nesprávným úředním postupem* (the Act on Liability for Damage Caused in Connection with the Exercise of Public Power for Incorrect Decision or Incorrect Administration).

exercise of the above-mentioned transferred competence, the state is liable for failures of the points of single contact. It can, however, reclaim damages from the municipality in question. The Czech Republic should thus be held liable for failures of points of single contacts that result in damages.

However, there is little experience with disputes related to the improper administration of business activities.[20] Czech courts inconsistently adjudicate claims for the compensation of lost profits. Liability cases related to the activities of points of single contact may be extremely rare or absent at all. First, tacit consent enables the delivery of services, even in cases of passivity of the authorities. Furthermore, Czech law provides various administrative and judicial steps (complaints, actions) against the inactivity of authorities. Finally, the Act on the Free Movement of Services does not expect that the points of single contact are always capable to providing perfect information about foreign laws,[21] and or even about remedies and actions, or related social security and taxation (see below). It would thus be hard to successfully complain about improper advice.

2.2 *Article 7 SD: Right to Information*

Information for foreign providers required by the Directive is described generally as the first task of the points of single contact in the Act on the Free Movement of Services.[22] Furthermore, generalised information shall be provided on remedies (complaints, appeals, actions) against decisions on applications and notifications. Points of single contacts are also expected to provide general information about the legal conditions of the delivery of services in other Member States, about consumer protection, and about consumer protection institutions and associations in those states.

I think that the legal framework describing the role of the points of single contact does not require more than the Services Directive. Nevertheless, the policy of the Ministry charged with the supervision, guidance, and assistance of the points of single contacts goes significantly beyond the legislative definition of their tasks.

The Ministry's Internet presentation, aimed at individual and corporate entrepreneurs,[23] provides an overview of the most important concepts of law and describes the administrative practices applicable to service providers. The services are broken down into approximately 180 categories. Numerous forms can be

---

[20] Apart from investments disputed and adjudicated by the International Centre for Settlement of Investment Disputes or by arbitrators in accordance with bilateral investment treaties.

[21] Section 14 letter b requires provision of "general information on the requirements in other Member States relating to the acquisition of authorisation to provide services".

[22] Section 14 mentions 'the information required to obtain authorisation to provide a service, including, in particular, the particulars of the application and the contact details of administrative bodies competent to handle the application under other legislation'.

[23] See http://www.businessinfo.cz.

downloaded, including those related to the posting of workers, social security, and taxation. This information is available to everyone, including domestic providers and individuals and companies with the intent to conduct business. The website is labelled an electronic point of single contact.[24]

It is hard to determine whether points of single contact are capable of providing perfect information about the standards and procedures related to all services and their providers. Czech legislation is perceived as complicated, inconsistent, and unpredictable.

The Act on the Free Movement of Services does not mention the scope of the information provided in other languages. English is the foremost foreign language due to its status as a language of international communication. German and Polish are also suitable because they are the languages of neighbour countries.[25] The amount of information in English is limited in reality. Information in German and Polish is completely absent. Presentation in these languages is obviously not a priority for the Ministry. Recruitment to the newly established positions of points of single contact included the requirement of certified knowledge of the English language; analysing and preparing information in English is thus expected.

An officer of a contacted point of single contact[26] underlined that in most cases the single contact point answers questions related to intent to provide temporary services and/or to establish business on a permanent basis in Austria and Germany. In most cases, individual craftsmen ask for the information. The cooperation of German points of single contact and other agencies is appreciated when compared to that of Austrian ones. Temporary restrictions on cross-border trade in selected services with Austria established in the Treaty of Accession shall not be forgotten here.[27] Limited knowledge of the German language, however, makes analyses of the laws of both neighbour countries attractive for Czech providers and entrepreneurs difficult.

The number of foreign subjects seeking information and assistance about the legal conditions of temporary and permanent business in the Czech Republic is small. Reminders related to social security (coordination) and taxation (bilateral tax treaties, value-added tax) accompany information on legislative framework, necessary applications, and notifications.

There has been little experience with corporate providers of services. Perhaps, big companies are capable to learn about foreign laws otherwise. Few also consult posting of workers in the Czech Republic and in other countries.

---

[24] Sections 13–17 of the Act on the Free Movement of Services do not mention any electronic point of single contact. Such a label is thus unofficial.

[25] The Slovak and Czech languages are mutually intelligible and, at least in the Czech Republic, nobody expects or requires translation between the two.

[26] I thank Ms. *Z. Softičová* from the point of single contact in Brno for fruitful discussion about various legal and practical aspects of implementation of the Services Directive in the Czech Republic in general and about activities of the points of single contact in particular.

[27] See Annex V: List referred to in Article 24 of the Act of Accession: Czech Republic, point 13.

2.3 Article 8 SD: Procedures by Electronic Means

The website of the Ministry of Industry and Trade has already been mentioned as a general source of information for foreign providers. Fifteen points of single contact have their own websites and can be easily reached by e-mail or phone.

According to the Act on the Free Movement of Services, points of single contact accept and transfer the requests for authorisations and notifications of foreign providers.[28] No mention is made about the form of these requests; therefore, the normal rules on forms of communication and the exchange of information are applicable.

Official communication with points of single contact can be carried out with mail and with certified communication tools according to specific legislation on electronic communication.[29] Nevertheless, official electronic communication (electronic signatures) in accordance with this legislation is less efficient, in general, in the Czech Republic than expected due to various reasons. Problems and deficiencies accompanying the introduction of compulsory notifications to companies, other legal entities, and individual entrepreneurs made e-government unpopular. Therefore, mail and direct contact continue to be standard means of communication for foreign providers of services barely familiar with the requirements of Czech law.

The introduction of electronic communication in the Czech Republic, in general, and in its administration and judiciary, in particular, has been generally realised. Implementation of the Services Directive did not play a specific role. On the other hand, unofficial communications are electronic to a great extent.

First, the exchange of information between Czech authorities charged with the supervision of service providers and the authorities of other Member States is expected to be electronic.[30]

Second, the informative role of the points of single contacts is realised by electronic means, in general. The Act on the Free Movement of Services, indeed, does not push for the use of electronic communication. Conventional mails and visits by providers or their representatives are not excluded or discouraged. Nevertheless, e-mails and phone calls are obviously the preferred methods of communication with the points of single contact, according to the experience of consulted professionals.

---

[28] See section 15 of the Act on the Free Movement of Services.

[29] *Zákon č. 227/2000 Sb., o elektronickém podpisu* (Act on the Electronic Signature) a *Zákon č. 300/2008 Sb., o elektronických úkonech* (Act on Electronic Acts), which established tools for the verified communication of individuals with the public authorities and compulsory electronic communication for the institution of public administration and for companies and individual entrepreneurs.

[30] See section 26 of the Act on the Free Movement of Services. The Internal Market Information System established with European Commission decision no. 2008/49/EC is mentioned.

Individuals and representatives of companies download, print, and fill out forms and send them by conventional mail to the point of single contact they have selected if they decide to do business in the Czech Republic and must therefore submit notifications and applications.

2.4 Article 9 SD: Authorisation Schemes

The Act on the Free Movement of Services does not explicitly address the freedom of establishment in the Czech Republic. Therefore, answers are relevant to cross-border services and their providers.

The Amending Act introduced tacit consent into numerous acts addressing various service branches, if a request for authorisation or notification of intent is not decided upon within a prescribed period, with the temporary activity of service providers from other Member States on the territory of the Czech Republic.[31]

The lawmaker relaxed the authorisation procedures in several sector acts. Nevertheless, it is hard to claim that the Directive generally switched Czech law from advance authorisations to mere subsequent (a posteriori) inspections. Similarly, there was no general shift from authorisations to mere notifications. From this point of view, the wording and intent of the Directive were not carefully respected.

Implementation of the Services Directive touches existing authorisation schemes for service providers for establishing business in the Czech Republic. Many service providers must be authorised according to above-mentioned general legislation on economic activities. Several service providers require authorisation according to specific legislation. Several services must be approved in every case. It is impossible to provide more than a simplified overview here.

There is general legislation on economic activities and specific legislative frameworks for specific economic activities. The general framework for economic activities is the *zákon č. 451/1991 Sb., živnostenský zákon* (Act on Licensing of Trade, *Gewerbegesetz* in German law). Economic activities are divided into three groups. The first group comprises of activities that can be launched by both individuals and companies after simple notification. The second group comprises of activities that can be launched after notification accompanied by an expected certificate of qualification. The third group comprises of activities requiring permission after an evaluation of personal, material, financial, or other conditions. Nevertheless, in most cases permission is granted if the conditions are met. Denial can be questioned via judicial action. Similarly, specific laws establish comparable

---

[31] Periods are set in general or sector legislation for administrative proceedings. Nevertheless, section 30 of the Act on the Free Movement of Services established several modifications to these periods.

regimes of permission. However, many standards are vaguely formulated and thus enable the discretion of the competent administrative authority.[32]

As explained, acts implementing the Services Directive do not explicitly address the freedom of establishment. Therefore, it is possible to debate whether Czech law complies with requirements of the Directive. Conditions of establishment in the Czech Republic are essentially liberal. Discrimination against foreign companies and individuals is exceptional in the legislation addressing business. The Czech Republic has not been criticised before or since accession for discrimination against foreign operators. Even companies from the non-Member States are generally allowed to do business in the Czech Republic. The most frequent case is, however, incorporation of a Czech company by foreign nationals, companies, or investors. From regulatory point of view, the enterprise is thus domestic.

Under such conditions, there is no debate by legal experts on the interpretation of vague provisions of the Services Directive that set limits for permission regimes of the Member States. Nobody has analysed whether simple notifications and registrations should also comply with the Directive's requirements. I agree with affirmative answer because these requirements can also become a burden for subjects from abroad. Nevertheless, they can more easily meet the requirement of proportionality than requirements of permission.

2.5 Article 10 SD: Conditions for the Granting of Authorisation

The Amending Act introduced the recognition of foreign authorisations in several sector acts. Nevertheless, Czech law implementing the Services Directive cannot be interpreted in the way that such recognition generally applicable for all established providers of services.

The Czech Republic is a unitary state. Regional and local governments are involved in the enforcement of national laws. Nevertheless, they cannot set, in most cases, specific rules for business in their territory (exceptions: taxi drivers, slot machines). Certainly, different regimes for economic activities result from zone planning and environmental protection. Many areas are the subject of regimes that exclude numerous businesses.

In most cases, licences based on the discretion of the authorities are excluded. Persons and companies meeting all conditions are entitled to an authorisation. Since 2003, a judicial review of administrative refusals of authorisation is

---

[32] Summarized in English in section 'The Czech Republic', published by the European Commission for Mutual Evaluation expected in the Services Directive—Stakeholders' Consultation; see http://ec.europa.eu/internal_market/consultations/2010/services_directive_en.htm.

available.[33] According to generally applicable rules on administrative proceedings, refusal to grant authorisation should be motivated and this motivation can be subject to administrative and judicial review.

2.6 Articles 11 SD (Duration of Authorisation) and 12 SD (Selection from Among Several Candidates)

As mentioned above, establishment is not addressed. Nevertheless, mistakenly, unlimited validity is mentioned in the Act on the Free Movement of Services. Similarly, the requirement of transparent selection between several applicants is mistakenly repeated here.[34]

2.7 Article 13 SD: Authorisation Procedures

The maximum duration of administrative procedures is prescribed in a general manner in legislation on administrative proceedings (*zákon č. 500/2004 Sb., správní řád*) and for many specific situations in special laws, including these addressing various economic sectors. Implementation of the Directive did not contribute to any adjustment of these time limits. Certainly, the introduction of tacit consent in numerous specific acts addressing various economic activities creates an implicit time limit for the authorities.

Tacit authorisation as a general consequence of the inactivity of administrative authority is a novel tool in Czech administrative law related to the general supervision of economic activities. Few permissions result—as in, for example, individual construction activities—from the sole notification and lack of intervention of a competent authority within a prescribed period of time.

Legislation implementing the Directive uses different wording for tacit consent, *Vznik oprávnění uplynutím lhůty*, that is, the 'establishment of authorisation upon expiration of a time limit'. This establishment is mentioned as a general measure implementing the Directive in the Act on the Free Movement of Services.[35] Confirmation of competent authority and registration *ex officio* for necessary legal

[33] Two-tier administrative judiciary consisting of departments of administrative judiciary in *krajské soudy* (regional courts) and independent *Nejvyšší správní soud* (the Supreme Administrative Court) was established in 2003 in accordance with the *zákon č. 150/2002 Sb., soudní řád správní* (Code of Administrative Justice).

[34] See sections 4 (4) and 4 (2), respectively, of the Act on the Free Movement of Services.

[35] See the wording of section 28 of the Act on the Free Movement of Services in the ministerial translation into English: '(1) Where so provided by other legislation, authorisation to provide a service shall be deemed granted upon expiration of the time limit for the delivery of a decision'.

certainty is expected in such cases.[36] Nevertheless, such an approach is applicable only if such a solution was introduced with the Amending Act into specific acts.

2.8 Articles 14, 15, 16 SD

According to screenings, few prohibited measures were identified and removed with the Amending Act. On the other hand, many requirements whose assessment was demanded were left unexamined. The screening focussed on discrimination against foreign providers. Proportionality of requirements was questioned and resulted in the reduction or removal of requirements in only a few cases. At least this is the conclusion that can be drawn from the absence of opposite claims in explanatory reports and other accompanying documents.

The screening of Czech law was presented as careful by the Ministry and its experts, even in unofficial discussions. No discussion about the reliability of this claim followed.

2.9 Articles 22–27 SD

The Act on the Free Movement of Services includes provisions modelled after requirements of the Services Directive on information to be provided by service providers to consumers in general or upon request.[37] The Act on the Free Movement of Services does not describe specific sanctions for failure to do so.[38] No mention is also made about the language of the information. General rules of Czech law seem to be applicable. Presumably the legislator expects that providers will inform their clients voluntarily to avoid distrust in their services.

Similarly, the legislator reproduced the provision related to liability insurance required by Czech legislation.[39] Although many Czech statutes require liability insurance, the conditions are not described in a detailed manner. Knowledge that the results of economic activities should be covered by insurance is limited.

The expert from a point of single contact said that nobody has discussed the validity of imported insurance or the extension of insurance abroad. If consulted, I would suggest pay attention to the territorial limitations of policies.

---

[36] See sections 28 (2) and 30 of the Act on the Free Movement of Services.

[37] See sections 10 and 11 of the Act on the Free Movement of Services.

[38] If compared with the implementation in Poland, see *Ustawa o swiadczeniu uslug na terytorium Rzeczypospolitej Polskiej (Dziennik ustaw nr. 47, poz. 278, 2010), rozdzial 4—przepisy karne.*

[39] Section 8 of the Act on the Free Movement of Services merely summarizes Article 23 of the Directive.

The voluntary standardisation and settlement of disputes remain unmentioned by implementing legislation of the Services Directive. I interpret these provisions as recommendations. Therefore, they need not necessarily be implemented by laws.

2.10 Articles 28 ff. SD: Administrative Cooperation

Provisions of the Directive on the administrative cooperation of authorities charged with the control of both foreign providers operating temporarily in the territory of the Czech Republic and domestic providers operating in other Member States are reflected in the implementation.[40] However, formulations of the Act on the Free Movement of Services are even less elaborate than the wording of the Directive.

Many problems will arise if these provisions are applied, especially in cases involving sanctions to both domestic and foreign providers. The relation of these specific rule sets to the generally applicable rules, standards, and principles of administrative proceedings is unclear. People with experience in the general administration of economic activities admit unofficially that Czech authorities face troubles with enforcing sanctions on Czech subjects if high fines are not a threat. At least the point of single contact I have consulted has no experience with cross-border administrative cooperation related to the supervision and sanctioning of both Czech providers doing business abroad and foreign providers operating on the territory of the Czech Republic.

I am convinced that administrative cooperation should be described in a more detailed manner at the level of the European Union. First, competence to restrict or to ban the temporary activity of a service provider from another Member State should be clarified. Second, the feasibility of sanctioning for noncompliance with laws abroad, including noncompliance with the laws of a host country only, will be examined. In addition, the extent of the applicability of the laws of the host country of a temporarily present service provider should be identified. The debate about the principle of country of origin has confused many. It should be noted that, according to the Treaties, the law of a Member State is applicable where the service is provided.[41] Last but not least, the relation with the criminal law of Member States and the coordinating competence of the European Union is to be clarified.

---

[40] See sections 18–26 of the Act on the Free Movement of Services.

[41] See Article 57 (3) of the Treaty on the Functioning of the European Union (former Article 50).

3 Assessment of the Impact of the Services Directive

The Services Directive was presented as an important step towards the further liberalisation of trade among Member States of the European Union. Therefore it and its implementation in Member States were also cheered by several Czech right-wing liberal politicians, who are, in other cases, sceptical about European integration.

Nevertheless, the legal implications of the Services Directive were discussed to a limited extent in the Czech Republic. Approximately ten papers and articles in journals have been written from 2006 to 2010 about the Directive. These papers and articles are short (three to seven pages) and summarise the content of the Directive or its crucial political aspects.[42] No detailed legal analyses have been published by Czech authors, and the implementing legislation is too new to be commented upon, with the exception of theses written by law students.[43] Interestingly, interest in European Union law is waning and little demand now exists for such commentaries.[44]

The Ministry of Industry and Trade has realised the expected screening of existing legislation and prepared the abovementioned implementing legislation. I am convinced that the original intentions of using the Directive's implementation for a profound reorganisation of the Czech system of control of economic activities were forgotten. As mentioned in the report, the legislator focussed solely on the free movement of services provided temporarily on the territory of the Czech Republic. Freedom of establishment is addressed accidentally or in practice only.

I share doubts about the Directive's contributions.[45] It addresses with a single set of measures extremely different services with different economic, social, political, and legal aspects. However, one size does not fit all.[46]

Furthermore, I do not believe in the expectations expressed by studies commissioned by the European Commission because natural obstacles to providing services temporarily in Europe have not been ascertained or measured.

Europe's multilingualism is the most obvious obstacle also for administration. Communication in foreign languages is limited to preliminary information. Applications and notifications require some knowledge of the host country's

---

[42] See Basedow (2006), pp. 53–60; Foltýn (2005a), pp. 13–17; Foltýn (2005b), pp. 14–18; Hradil (2006), pp. 10–16; Leszay (2006), pp.151–153.

[43] A thesis written by Smejkal-Brandejská (2009).

[44] Several Czech textbooks on European Union law are available. Nevertheless, there is limited number of experts capable to write monographs addressing uncountable topics of this supranational law. Furthermore, there is little demand for such books. Publishers are thus not interested. Commentary of the Services Directive comparable to German 489 pages book Schlachter and Ohler (2008) cannot be reasonably expected in the Czech Republic for both reasons.

[45] Křepelka (2008), p. 348 I prepare the text for publication after evaluation of the Directive's implementation. It will be (probably) the first monograph about free movement of services in the European Union in Czech language and addressing participation of the Czech Republic.

[46] Barnard (2004), pp. 370–372.

language. Ultimately, the proper provision of many services requires at least a basic knowledge of such languages.

Finally, I am convinced that the principle of the administrative control of providers abroad and from abroad is troublesome because state administrations have only limited interest in the operations of their providers abroad.

Directive project is an example of the activism of the European Union elites and bureaucrats. Expectations were exaggerated. Its results will be modest. From the point of view of service providers from abroad, administrative obstacles are not reduced to zero with the Directive's implementation because they cannot be if services are administered at national level.

Implementation of the Services Directive in the Czech Republic shows unsatisfactory law-making in this new Member State. Provisions of the Act on the Free Movement of Services are formulated vaguely, confrontation of sections reveals inconsistencies, and several important legal aspects of inter-state trade in services are not addressed at all.

This law-making can be excused with deficiencies and ambiguity of the Services Directive only partially. Both conditions of ministries (underpaid and fluctuating experts) and poor academic reflection should be blamed.

References

For legislation, jurisprudence and websites please refer to 1.1 of the report and footnotes directly.

Barnard C (2004) The Substantive Law of the EU—The Four Freedoms. Oxford University Press, Oxford

Basedow J (2006) Princip země původu a mezinárodní právo soukromé na evropském vnitřním trhu služeb. Právní forum 4:53–60

Foltýn V (2005a) Návrh směrnice o službách na vnitřním trhu—I. díl. Jurisprudence 1:13–17

Foltýn V (2005b) Návrh směrnice o službách na vnitřním trhu—II. díl. Jurisprudence 2:14–18

Hradil J (2006) Princip země původu—změny v oblasti volného poskytování služeb. Právni rozhledy 1:10–16

KPMG Česká republika, s.r.o. (2006) Analýza ekonomických dopadů návrhu směrnice o službách na vnitřním trhu pro Czech Trade (Analysis of the Economic Consequences of the Draft of the Directive on Services in the Internal Market for Czech Trade, i.e., for the Ministerial Agency for the Promotion of exports). Available at: http://www.mpo.cz/dokument2857.html

Křepelka F (2008) Evropská a světová liberalizace obchodu službami (European and Global Liberalization of Trade in Services), submitted for habilitation at Masarykova univerzita in Brno and defended there in 2009

Leszay L (2006) Směrnice o službách na vnitřním trhu. Ad notam.

Schlachter M, Ohler C (eds) (2008) Europäische Dienstleistungsrichtlinie—Handkommentar. Nomos, Baden–Baden

Smejkal-Brandejská M (2009) Směrnice o službách na vnitřním trhu a její implementace do českého právního řádu (directive on Services in the Internal Market and its Implementation in the Czech legal order), submitted in 2009 and defended in 2010 at Masarykova univerzita in Brno.

Implementation of the Services Directive in Denmark

Michael Gøtze

1 General Remarks on the Transposition Strategy and General Understanding of the Implementation

1.1 Main References Used in this Research

The Services Directive[1] was transposed into Danish law by means of the horizontal Law on Services in the Internal Market, which was adopted by the Danish Parliament on 7 May 2009. The act entered into force on 28 December 2009. Denmark was the first country in the EU to adopt a new law implementing the Services Directive. The Danish law ensures the right to freedom of establishment for companies in Denmark and ensures that companies established in the EU have the right to provide services in Denmark on a temporary basis. It obliges Danish authorities to accept documents issued in other EU countries. The law prohibits discrimination against service providers on the grounds of nationality or residence.

The Danish Law on Services in the Internal Market is available in English on the website of the responsible authority, the Internal Market Centre in Copenhagen, within the Danish Enterprise and Construction Authority (DEACA),[2]

The author is Professor of Law, PHD, Centre of Legal Studies in Welfare and EU Market Integration (WELMA), Faculty of Law, Copenhagen University.

[1] 2006/123/EC (2006), OJ, L 376, p. 36.
[2] See http://www.deaca.dk, last visited July 2010.

M. Gøtze (✉)
Centre of Legal Studies in Welfare and EU Market Integration (WELMA),
Faculty of Law, Copenhagen University, Copenhagen, Denmark
e-mail: Michael.Gotze@jur.ku.dk

U. Stelkens et al. (eds.), *The Implementation of the EU Services Directive*, 159
DOI: 10.1007/978-90-6704-840-8_7,

at http://www.deaca.dk/file/38199/Danish_law_on_services_EN_110509.pdf. The Danish Internal Market Centre coordinates the implementation of the Services Directive in Denmark. The translated document containing the Danish act is produced by the Danish authorities, but the translation is explicitly unofficial and non-binding.

The preparatory works of the Law of Services include a number of considerations as to the relation between the Services Directive and Danish law.[3] The parliamentary documents can be found on the website of the Danish Parliament (*Folketinget*) at www.folketinget.dk and on the website of the Danish legal information database at https://www.retsinformation.dk/Forms/R0710.aspx?id=123269. The preparatory works of the Law on Services in the Internal Market are available only in Danish.

An official and concise account of the situation in Denmark—so far—as to the implementation of the Services Directive can be found at the website of the European Commission, the EU Single Market, Mutual evaluation foreseen by the Services Directive—Stakeholders' consultation, at http://ec.europa.eu/internal_market/consultations/2010/services_directive_en.htm.

As part of this research the author contacted the relevant persons at the Danish Internal Market Centre, who willingly contributed with information on the Danish implementation process so far.

Danish implementation of the Services Directive has not in itself given rise to much debate in the Danish legal literature, and the following is based on the existing analyses in articles on the various aspects of the Danish implementation process. The articles were produced by civil servants in the responsible Danish ministry and by practising lawyers, respectively. Both articles are mainly descriptive and are available only in Danish.[4]

Background information and statistics on Denmark's economy can be found at the website of the Danish Ministry of Economic and Business Affairs at http://www.oem.dk. These are available in English. Denmark is the 15th largest exporter of services in the world, and the service sector plays an increasing role in the Danish economy and for Danish exports.[5]

---

[3] Bill of 4 February 2009 proposed by the Danish Ministry of Economic and Business Affairs (*Lovforslag L 122 af 4. februar 2009, fremsat af Erhvervs- og økonomiministeren*).

[4] See T. Frydenberg, M. Bresson, and J. Them Parnas (2009) (the authors of the article are civil servants from the Danish Ministry of Economic and Business Affairs), available at http://www.djoef.dk/Udgivelser/Juristen/Juristen2009/Juristen-nr-9-2009/Servicedirektivet-og-lov-om-tjenesteydelser-i-det-indre-marked.aspx, last visited July 2010, and H. Peytz and L. Spangsberg Grønfeldt (2009), p. 36 (the authors are practising lawyers). A general analysis, produced by Danish academic lawyers prior to the implementation—can be found in U. Neergaard, R. Nielsen, and L. M. Roseberry (eds) (2008).

[5] See also the economic analysis in *Economic effects of liberalising international trade,* DEACA, Copenhagen, December 2005. The report is available in English.

1.2 Impact of the Services Directive

1.2.1 Profound Cause of Changes to National Law? Impact on Danish General Administrative Laws

The Services Directive is incorporated into Danish law by the adoption of the horizontal Law on Services in the Internal Market. This law contains provisions on the following:

- Scope of application (Article 1)
- Definitions (Article 2)
- Information requirements for service providers (Articles 3 and 4)
- Rights of service recipients (Articles 5 and 6)
- Documents (Articles 7 and 8)
- Freedom of establishment (Articles 9 and 10)
- Temporary provision of services (Articles 11 and 12)
- Administrative cooperation (Article 13)
- Other precautionary measures (Article 14)
- Reporting requirements (Article 15)
- Setting up a point of single contact (hereafter POSC; Article 16)
- Penalties (Article 17)
- Entry into force (Articles 18 and 19)

The act is a specific act concerning the area of services only, and, from a Danish administrative law perspective, the act represents a sectoral regulation in its own right. Thus, the directive did not cause an alteration of Danish general administrative laws and the directive has not sparked a discussion on the European influence on Danish administrative law via the Services Directive. Generally, there is a tradition that general administrative law adheres to a predominantly national focus, and there has been no profound reconstruction or rethinking of Danish general administrative law—apart from the area of the rules on the processing of data—as a result of European Union law until now.

The general legal framework for Danish administrative law is the Danish General Administrative Procedures Act,[6] which is considered the normative cornerstone within administrative law. Seen from an international perspective, Danish administrative law has traditionally been relatively informal. There are only few general requirements concerning procedure. Until 1987 a few unwritten principles applied concerning incapacity, collection of information, notice to the citizen of administrative acts, and so on. In a few special areas of regulation, unwritten rules were supplemented by specific statutory requirements concerning administrative procedure.[7] In 1985, a distinct step was taken in the direction of more formalised

---

6 Act No. 571 on General Administrative Procedures (*Forvaltningslov*) of 19 December 1985 with amendments.

7 For a general introduction to Danish General Administrative Law, see Dahl et al. (2002), p. 145.

legal requirements as to administrative procedures when the Danish Parliament adopted the General Administrative Procedures Act. The act came into force in 1987 as to state authorities, and in 1989 as to regional and local authorities.

The General Administrative Procedures Act is not particularly comprehensive, since it only lays down a rather narrow selection of basic rules concerning administrative procedure. The basic requirements of the act are, first and foremost, the right to unbiased administration, the right to a prior hearing, the right of the parties to a case of access to documents, and the obligation of a public authority to give reasons. The Danish General Administrative Procedures Act does not contain any general provisions on, for example, the duration of administrative procedure or tacit authorisation by public authorities. The General Administrative Procedures Act applies to all cases in which administrative decisions (*Verwaltungsakten,* or *actes administratifs*) are taken by authorities. Conversely, the act does not apply to service functions such as educational activities or medical treatment and surgeries at hospitals. These do not represent decisions in the Danish administrative law approach to the concept of decision.

As comments to the Danish General Administrative Procedures Act vis-à-vis a possible alteration due to the Services Directive, the following characteristics are noted.

1. A narrow normative focus on decisions. The General Administrative Procedures Act has in itself traditionally made the legal horizon of Danish administrative law rather narrow, in the sense that the primary focus is formal administrative *decisions* rather than services and administrative activities in a functional sense. The concept of administrative decision has been broadened in a dynamic way in various areas, in particular by the Danish Parliamentary Ombudsman in a number of ombudsman opinions, but the concept of decision is still the primary gateway into Danish general administrative law. As to the Services Directive, it contains a number of specific procedural requirements—for example, the obligation to accept documents form other EU Member States—that are altogether outside the current scope of the Danish General Administrative Procedures Act. It would require a fundamental reconstruction and rethinking of the act to 'incorporate' the Services Directive.
2. A strong focus on procedure. Furthermore, the Danish General Administrative Procedures Act contains no substantive principles such as, for example, a fundamental principle of anti-discrimination or proportionality within public administration. Such principles apply according to traditional Danish administrative law primarily as unwritten and judge-made principles. The scope of the Danish Act is thus much narrower than, for example, the European Code of Good Administrative Behaviour (*Der Europäische Kodex für gute Verwaltungspraxis,* or *Le Code européen de bonne conduite administrative*) of the European Ombudsman comprising both substantive and formal requirements.[8]

[8] The European Code of Good Administrative Behaviour was approved in September 2000 by the European Parliament, and the code plays a significant role in practice in relation to the

So far the Danish General Administrative Procedures Act has been amended seven times—in 1991, twice in 2002, in 2004 and in 2005, and twice in 2009—and the purely *procedural* scope of application of the act has never been extended.[9] On the one hand, the procedural focus of the present General Administrative Procedures Act can make an alteration due to the Services Directive relatively easy, because the Services Directive states a number of procedural requirements. On the other hand, however, the act has so far been quite resistant to European impulses, and its alteration due to the Services Directive appears, given that backdrop, less likely.

3. A predominantly national focus. This leads us to the third fundamental characteristic of the current General Administrative Procedures Act. The focus of the act is—and has consistently been—national. None of the seven act amendments was spurred by European regulations or directives. Most of the amendments consist of highly technical revisions and adjustments, in particular on the right of parties to access to documents. The amendment of the act in 2002 deals with the digitalisation of public administrative information. The most recent amendment, in 2009, deals with the internal exchange of information within public administration, and its purpose is to simplify the interplay between the Danish General Administrative Procedures Act and the Danish Act on the Processing of Personal Data.[10] The latter implements Directive 95/46/EC on the protection of individuals with regard to the processing of personal data and on the free movement of such data, and one might perhaps claim that this amendment of the General Administrative Procedures Act represents a kind of Europeanisation. However, the amendment is highly technical and does not change the fundamental structure or framework of the General Administrative Procedures Act.

To sum up, the Services Directive has not caused an alternation of general Danish administrative laws, neither profound nor marginal. The General Administrative Procedures Act is untouched by the Services Directive. There are no considerations in the preparatory works to the Danish Law on Services in the Internal Market of a possible spill-over effect on general administrative law in Denmark. There has been no discussion of an alteration scenario in Danish administrative law.

As to the current relation between the Danish General Administrative Procedures Act and the Danish Law on Services in the Internal Market, the General

(Footnote 8 continued)
maladministration of the European Ombudsman. See www.ombudsman.europa.eu, last visited July 2010.

[9] See Amendments No. 347 of the General Administrative Procedures Act of 6 June 1991, No. 215 of 22 April 2002, No. 382 of 6 June 2002, No. 215 of 31 March 2004, No. 553 of 24 June 2005, No. 501 of 12 June 2009, and No. 503 of 12 June 2009.

[10] Act No. 429 on the Processing of Personal Data (*Lov om behandling af personoplysninger*) of 31 May 2000, with amendments.

Administrative Procedures Act is explicitly based on a modified principle of *lex specialis*. This means that the Danish public authorities are obliged to comply with the Law on Services in the Internal Market as *lex specialis* only if the law provides service providers with a *better* legal protection than the General Administrative Procedures Act. If the latter provides a higher level of protection, the public authorities are under an obligation to comply with the general act. Due to the fact that the Danish Law on Services in the Internal Market contains a number of requirements that are not regulated at all in the—relatively narrow—Danish General Administrative Procedures Act, there will, in practice, only very rarely be a conflict between the two acts. In practice, the Law on Services in the Internal Market is without doubt the primary regulatory framework when Danish public authorities deal with service providers.

1.2.2 Involvement in the Transposition Process

The Danish Internal Market Centre—organised under the Danish Ministry of Economics and Business Affairs and the DEACA—is responsible for the implementation and application of rules concerning EU's single market. The Internal Market Centre coordinates the implementation of the Services Directive in Denmark. Danish authorities are obliged to send notifications of technical rules in accordance with the Services Directives via the Internal Market Centre. To facilitate the implementation process, the Internal Market Centre set up a working group with the participation of the other ministries and agencies affected by the Directive. The working group met on a regular basis to discuss the Directive. The compulsory screening of Danish legislation is conducted within this working group.

The Danish implementation process requires that all competent authorities be responsible for the necessary adjustment of specific legislation and specific administrative regulations within their respective areas of competence. So far, among others, the Danish Departments of Justice, Culture, Environment, Nutrition, and Transport and Economics made alterations in existing legislation and administrative regulations to comply with the requirements of the Services Directive. In specific terms, the Danish Law on Services in the Internal Market caused amendments in sectoral laws, such as the law on the sale of real estate, the law on electricians, the law on gas installation, the law on trade, the law on maritime training, the law on professional diving activities, the law on copyright, and the law on marketing. Most amendments are carried out in the technical 'package deal' of one single act.[11]

[11] All those mentioned were amended by Law No. 364 of 13 May 2009 (*Ændring af næringsloven, markedsføringsloven, erhvervsfremmeloven and forskellige andre love på Økonomi- og Erhvervsministeriets område*), Act No. 510 on Copyright (*Ophavsretslov*) of 12 June 2009, and Act No. 498 of 12 June 2009 (*Ændring af lov om inkassovirksomhed og lov om vagtvirksomhed*).

1.3 (National) Scope of Application

1.3.1 Transnational and Domestic Service Providers

The Danish Law of 7 May 2009 on Services in the Internal Market regulates the situations of both transnational and domestic service providers. According to Article 1, the Law applies to (1) service providers who are nationals of or established in an EU/EEA Member State who wish to establish themselves or are already established in Denmark and (2) service providers established in a EU/EEA Member State who wish to deliver or who deliver services on a temporary basis in Denmark. Thus the Law on Services in the Internal Market as well as the administrative regulations implementing it applies to *all* services providers, whether transnational or domestic. The intention of the Danish Parliament was to make the Law on Services in the Internal Market a highly precise implementation of Article 2 (1) of the Services Directive. It appears to follow from the preparatory works to the Danish Law that this scope of the Law is a result of the Directive, and that the Danish legislator thus seemingly construes the Directive as applicable to both transnational and domestic actors within the service sector.

According to Article 2 of the Law on Services in the Internal Market, the Law does not apply to (1) the liberalisation of services of general economic interest, reserved to public or private entities, (2) the privatisation of public entities providing services, (3) the abolition of monopolies providing services, (4) aids granted by Member States that are covered by Community rules on competition, (5) definitions, in conformity with Community law, of what is considered to be services of general economic interest, (6) the organisation and financing, in compliance with the state aid rules, of services of general economic interest and the specific obligations they should be subject to, (7) measures taken, in conformity with Community law, to protect and promote cultural and linguistic diversity and media pluralism, (8) the rules of criminal law, (9) labour law, including rules regulating health and safety at work, (10) social security legislation, (11) the exercise of fundamental rights, (12) the field of taxation, (13) the rules of private international law, and (14) the provisions of another Community act governing specific aspects of access to or exercise of a service activity in specific sectors or for specific professions in conflict with the provisions of this law.

1.3.2 Parallel Scope of Application of Administrative Regulations

Both the horizontal Law on Services in the Internal Market and the administrative regulations implementing the Law concerns all services providers, whether transnational or domestic. It is explicitly stated in three of the four administrative regulations that their scope of application and legal definitions are the same as the ones contained in the Law on Services in the Internal Market.[12]

1.3.3 Sector Standards in the Transposing Legislation

The Law on Services in the Internal Market and the administrative regulations are based on a sector and specific scope of application and they do not create general or universal standards for the way Danish authorities deal with all citizens or with all economic stakeholders. Denmark chose not to let the Law on Services in the Internal Market apply to sectors that are excluded from the scope of application of the Services Directive.

1.4 Incorporation of Transposing Legislation

1.4.1 Implementation of Administrative Requirements

The administrative requirements of the Services Directive are implemented into Danish law by the Danish Law on Services in the Internal Market, the aforementioned amendments in various existing sector legislations, and four specific administrative regulations.

1.4.2 New Legislation

As to the administrative regulations implementing the Danish Law on Services in the Internal Market, they are as follows: Regulation 1361/2009 on the duty of notification to the EC Commission,[13] Regulation 1362/2009 on the Electronic POSC,[14] Regulation 1363/2009 on Administrative Cooperation within the EC/EEA,[15] and Regulation 1372/2009 on the Obligation of Service Providers to Give Information.[16]

---

[12] See *infra* n. 14–16.

[13] Regulation No. 1361 of 15 December 2009 (*Bekendtgørelse om pligt til indrapportering af krav til Europa-Kommisionen*), issued on the basis of the Danish Law on Services in the Internal Market.

[14] Regulation No. 1362 of 15 December 2009 (*Bekendtgørelse om elektronisk kontaktpunkt*), issued on the basis of the Law on Services in the Internal Market.

[15] Regulation No. 1363 of 15 December 2009 (*Bekendtgørelse om administrativt samarbejde med kompetente myndigheder i andre EU/EØS-lande*), issued on the basis of the Danish Law on Services in the Internal Market.

[16] Regulation No. 1372 of 16 December 2009 (*Bekendtgørelse om tjenesteyderes pligt til at give oplysninger til tjenestemodtagere*), issued on the basis of the Danish Law on Marketing.

1.5 The Relationship of the Services Directive to Primary EU Law

In conformity with Article 16 (1) of the Services Directive, Article 11 of the Danish Law on Services in the Internal Market provides that the provision of services by other Member States can only be restricted when justified by one of the four mandatory grounds mentioned in the Services Directive. Thus, the enumeration of Article 16 of the Services Directive is conclusive. Article 11 of the Danish Law on Services in the Internal Market applies only to service providers established in other Member States who deliver services in Denmark, and thus does not apply to foreign providers established in Denmark.

Various stakeholders proposed excluding additional areas from the scope of the Danish Law on Services in the Internal Market, such as education and the association of practising lawyers. Whereas education, which is wholly or mainly financed through the public purse in Denmark, is excluded from the Law on Services in the Internal Market, educational courses, which are mainly financed through private means, fall within the Danish Law on Services in the Internal Market. Excluding the latter from the scope of the Law was, according to the Danish legislator, held in breach of the Services Directive.

1.6 Screening

To comply with the Services Directive[17] and the principles of an internal market, a comprehensive screening of approximately 120 approval procedures and more than 140 administrative requirements was conducted in Denmark. The screening of Danish legislation was coordinated and conducted by the working group under the Danish Internal Market Centre. The core element in the concrete screening process was to ask the competent authority to explain in writing how a specific approval procedure and/or administrative procedure fulfilled the European requirements of necessity, non-discrimination, and proportionality. The overall and official impression—according to civil servants in the Danish Ministry of Economics and Business Affairs[18]—is that only relatively few adjustments were necessary during the screening process.

[17] Cp. Articles 9 (2) and 39 (5) of the Services Directive.

[18] See T. Frydenberg, M. Bresson, and J. Them Parnas (2009).

2 Individual Articles of the Services Directive

2.1 Article 6 SD: Point of Single Contact (POSC)

2.1.1 Establishment of the POSC

The requirement of a POSC in Article 6 of the Services Directive was achieved in Denmark by establishing a portal on the website of BusinessInDenmark at www.virk.dk. The POSC is part of the EUGO network in the EU.[19] The website presented itself in the following way:

> "Virk.dk is a business internet portal monitored by the public sector in Denmark. Center for Virk.dk manages and controls the portal and handles communication with the parties interested in the portal, such as companies and both local and national authorities. The overall objective of Virk.dk is to relieve Danish companies from administrative burdens and to provide a single entrance to the public sector. This is obtained by making it easier for companies to find business forms and applications to the public sector and information from the public sector. By delivering a number of fully digital solutions companies will be relieved from administrative burdens. You can find every business related form from any given authority in Denmark at Virk.dk. By using a digital signature companies can gain direct access to a number of specified services and online administrative systems. Furthermore, you can find other business relevant information from the Danish authorities at Virk.dk. The purpose of Virk.dk is to meet the needs of companies and ease communication with local and national authorities."

2.1.2 Subjective Understanding and Competence Structure

The Danish authorities have set up only *one* POSC. The POSC is regulated in article 16 of the Danish Law of Services in the Internal Market, empowering the Minister for Economic and Business Affairs to issue further rules to meet the requirements of the Services Directive. The Minister for Economic and Business Affairs issued a specific regulation on the Danish POSC, Regulation 1362/2009 on the Electronic Point of Single Contact.[20] The regulation entered into force on 29 December 2009. According to the regulation, the overall responsible authority for establishing the POSC is the Danish Enterprise and Constructions Authority, who ensures that authorities within their areas of competence are given access to applications and documents from companies.

Substantively, the POSC at www.virk.dk contains information for service providers on authorisation schemes and on administrative requirements in Danish law as to the services covered by the Services Directive.[21] Service providers from

---

[19] http://ec.europa.eu/internal_market/eu-go, last visited July 2010.

[20] See *supra* n. 14.

[21] http://www.virk.dk/English/businessindenmark, last visited July 2010.

EU/EEA Member States are given the opportunity to file the necessary applications and documents online to obtain an authorisation to provide services within the scope of application of the Law on Services in the Internal Market.

The competent authorities are, according to Article 5 of Regulation 1362/2009, obliged to ensure that the following information on their respective authorisations schemes is available in an updated version on the POSC: (1) application formulas, (2) application guidelines, (3) information on all requirements that must be met by service providers, (4) contact information such as name, address, phone, e-mail address, and websites of competent authorities in the application process, (5) how to access public databases on services, (6) relevant complaints bodies, and (7) contact information for relevant associations and organisations where service providers and receivers can obtain practical assistance and guidance. It is required that all the information be available in English.

The general procedure is that all applications and documents can be filed online via the website at www.virk.dk as electronic and scanned documents with scanned signatures. There is no general requirement that applications be translated by a certified linguist. When an application is filed online, the relevant authority is obliged to handle the application case. The calculation of the duration of handling an application does not start until a complete application with all the necessary supporting documents is received on the website. The competent authority is obliged to send a reply to the applicant who has submitted an application on the website by electronic mail if the applicant has given a mailing address.

2.1.3 Authorities with POSC-Function

The task of running the POSC at www.virk.dk is attributed to the Danish Commerce and Companies Agency. The website and agency existed prior to the implementation of the Directive. The establishment of the POSC did not in itself imply a reallocation of administrative competences.

2.1.4 Involvement in the Establishment of the POSC

The POSC at www.virk.dk is a joint ministerial enterprise with the participation of a vast number of relevant public authorities. The daily management of the website is attributed to the Danish Commerce and Companies Agency.[22]

---

22 The establishment of the website was already envisaged in the report Action Plan for the Global Marketing of Denmark by the Danish Ministry of Economics and Business Affairs, Copenhagen, April 2007, p. 47, on the establishment of a 'quick service desk'. The plan is available in English at www.oem.dk, last visited July 2010.

2.1.5 Liability of the POSC

It has not been clarified who will be responsible for mistakes of the POSC. That will depend on the character of the mistake. The relevant authorities feeding the POSC with factual information on, for example, application procedures are, as a starting point, responsible for erroneous information within their respective fields of competence. It can be stressed that it is the competent authorities who, in substance, are responsible for dealing with applications, and that the POSC itself is 'solely' given a coordinating role as an informative mediator between applicants and the relevant public authority.

It has not been clarified to what degree the website can be responsible for purely technical errors. The following disclaimer is stated by BusinessInDenmark at www.virk.dk:

> "The English text on BusinessInDenmark, incl. links to other websites, have been drawn up and translated in good faith and with every endeavour to ensure the accuracy of the content. However the editor shall not be liable for any kind of damages that may derive from errors or omissions from the content on BusinessInDenmark or any page that BusinessInDenmark links to."

2.2 Article 7 SD: Right to Information

Rights to information were not extended into other parts of Danish legislation, for example, Danish administrative legislation, during the transposition process.

The Services Directive was a significant incentive in the establishment of the current website at www.virk.dk, but the scope of the website goes beyond that of the Services Directive. The website represents the general access of companies—in all fields—to the relevant Danish public authorities.

2.3 Article 8 SD: Procedures by Electronic Means

As mentioned above, Article 8 is implemented in Danish law by setting up a POSC at www.virk.dk in accordance with Regulation 1362/2009.

The Directive has given impetus to a digital development that was already in progress. Thus, electronic administrative procedures existed in a number of significant areas prior to the implementation of the Directive. As an example, current real estate registration is a purely online service as a result of a reform of the Danish judiciary in 2007.

Where it is explicitly provided by law—for example, as to the provision of services—that administrative procedures are electronic, online access can replace traditional administrative procedures. When there is no such legal basis, it is normally a requirement in Danish administrative law that it shall (also) be possible for companies and citizens to make written applications if they wish.

2.4 Article 9 SD: Authorisation Schemes

Article 9 of the Directive is implemented in Article 9 of the Danish Law on Services in the Internal Market. The article is pivotal and ensures that service providers have the right to establish themselves in Denmark. In addition, it sets up four basic requirements for an authorisation scheme. The scheme and the conditions for granting an authorisation must (1) be made public in advance and (2) be justified by an overriding reason relating to the public interest and non-discriminatory; (3) the authorisation scheme and the conditions for granting the authorisation must also be appropriate for the purpose of achieving the objective pursued, and (4) the purpose may not be possible to achieve by means of less restrictive means. All relevant Danish authorisations schemes have been screened according to these principles in Article 9 of the Danish Law on Services in the Internal Market.

2.4.1 Means of Less Restrictive Measure

As an example of insufficient a posteriori inspection, the preparatory works of the Law on Services in the Internal Market state that beforehand inspection can be required as to services if it will be subsequently impossible to ascertain if the service in question suffers from defects. There are no concrete examples in the preparatory works.

2.4.2 Existing Authorisation Schemes/Procedures

As examples of authorisation schemes imposed on service providers established in Denmark, the following should be mentioned. There are authorisation schemes in the field of construction and related services, such as for building experts, plumbers, electricians, sewage contractors, energy consultants, and inspectors of heating and cooling systems. The activities of real estate agents and the letting of holiday homes are subject to authorisation. An authorisation is also required for retail and wholesale sales of food. In addition, authorisations are required for education services, such as training related to hunting, food hygiene, transportation, and maritime safety. Moreover, authorisation schemes apply to the provision of educational services in private schools and universities.[23]

The Directive and the Danish Law on Services in the Internal Market caused amendments in sector legislation such as, for example, the law on the sale of real

---

[23] A concise survey of the amendments of Danish acts resulting from the Directive can be found at http://ec.europa.eu/internal_market/consultations/docs/2010/services_directive/denmark_en.pdf, last visited July 2010.

estate, the law on electricians, the law on gas installation, the law on trade, the law on maritime training, the law on professional diving, the law on copyright, and the law on marketing. A number of these amendments deal with the question of debts to the Danish state. As to electricians, for example, until 2009 it was a requirement that an applicant for an authorisation not have considerable debts to the state. Requirements of this type have been abolished during the implementation process, because they did not comply with the necessity principle in Article 9 of the Services Directive.

2.4.3 Simple Notifications

It has not been clarified in Danish law whether simple notification requirements are contrary to Article 9 of the Services Directive.

2.5 Article 10 SD: Conditions for the Granting of Authorisation

2.5.1 Recognition of Requirements

Article 10 (2) of the Directive is implemented in Article 9 (3) of the Danish Law on Services in the Internal Market. The provision states the following: When a competent authority investigates whether a service provider meets the conditions for granting an authorisation, it must observe the requirement that the service provider is already subject to in another EU/EEA Member State or in relation to another Danish authorisation if these requirements are equivalent or essentially equivalent to the conditions for granting the Danish authorisation in question. The competent authority cannot require the same condition to be fulfilled several times. It is stated in the preparatory works of the Law on Services in the Internal Market that the Services Directive does not prevent competent authorities from setting up their own requirements in authorisation schemes. The Directive requires, however, that the competent authorities are obliged to take similar requirements from the country of origin of a service provider into consideration.

2.5.2 Granting Authorisation Throughout the Whole National Territory and Exceptions

Regarding the imposed duty to grant authorisation throughout the whole national territory and exceptions pertaining to 'overriding reasons to the public interest' there is no official information on this aspect at this time.

2.5.3 Entitlement to Grant Authorisation, Court Review of Administrative Decisions

According to Danish administrative law, some authorisations are based on very fixed criteria, whereas others have a discretionary nature. If an applicant fulfils all the fixed criteria, the applicant is entitled to the authorisation. However, if an authorisation implies a discretionary assessment of, for example, the applicant's qualifications, it is up to the authority to decide whether or not all conditions are met. Generally, Danish courts will perform a somewhat cautious review of administrative discretion, but there are no written or general principles on the intensity of review. The courts assess discretion on a case-to-case basis. If a rejection of an authorisation is of vital importance to a service provider, and if the service provider, as a plaintiff, can identify a plurality of legal mistakes, this can intensify the court's review and assessment of the case at hand. So far, there has been no published court decision on the Services Directive, and the Directive has—so far—caused no change in the current Danish court review of, for example, administrative discretion.

2.5.4 Reasoning of Administrative Decisions

According the Danish General Administrative Procedures Act, a public authority is obliged to give full reasons if it denies an application from a citizen or a company. There was no need to change Danish law because of Article 10 (6) of the Services Directive.

2.5.5 Allocation of Competences

The Danish legislator did not change the allocations of the administrative competence in the context of Article 10 of the Services Directive.

2.6 Article 11 SD: Duration of Authorisation

Article 11 of the Services Directive was not transposed in the Danish Law on Services in the Internal Market, but must be complied with by all authorisation schemes. There is no general regulation of the validity of authorisations in Danish administrative law, and the duration of the validity of an authorisation is dealt with on an individual case basis.

2.7 *Article 12 SD: Selection from Among Several Candidates*

Article 12 of the Services Directive is not transposed in the Danish Law on Services in the Internal Market, and did not cause a change in Danish law. The selection of applicants is required to comply with general administrative requirements of, for example, objectivity, reasonableness, and equal treatment. It is a legal requirement that applicants be assessed and selected on an individual case basis.

2.8 *Article 13 SD: Administrative Procedures*

2.8.1 A priori Determination of the Duration of Administrative Procedures

Only in certain—relatively few—areas has the Danish legislator determined and 'fixed' the maximum duration of an administrative procedure. Otherwise the responsible authority determines the duration of the concrete administrative procedure.

2.8.2 General Rule for the Duration

There is no general rule in Danish law on the duration of administrative procedures. The Danish General Administrative Procedures Act does not regulate the question. However, the duration of administrative procedures must comply with a basic and unwritten requirement of expediency. This requirement applies to all administrative areas. There is a considerable element of flexibility in the basic requirement of expediency, and it goes without saying that it is not contrary to the principle of expediency that the handling and assessment of a complex case last longer than for a routine case. Specific administrative laws lay down the time span for specific procedures, such as applications for access to documents that must be dealt with within 10 days. Outside the scope of these specific acts, it is up to the responsible authority to determine the duration of the administrative procedure with respect to the basic principle of expediency. The duration of administrative procedures can be reviewed and sanctioned by, for example, the Danish courts.

2.8.3 Exceptions to the General Rule for the Duration

If the legislator has determined the duration of administrative procedures, there can be no divergence from the fixed duration of procedures, except under special circumstances. In Denmark, the duration of administrative procedures was not laid down in the Law on Services in the Internal Market. In contrast, each competent authority had to assess the duration of the administrative procedure for each scheme. In this respect, the relevant ministries proposed amendments to existing legislation and/or amended existing regulations or adopted new ones. The prescribed duration starts from the moment the contact point receives the application duly completed.

2.8.4 Tacit Authorisation in the National Legal Order so Far

Tacit authorisation is not usual in Danish law, and the public authority typically needs to take explicit and formal action to grant such an authorisation. The question of tacit or formal authorisation is not dealt with in the Danish General Administrative Procedures Act.

The predominant requirement in specific legislation is an explicit authorisation. In a few areas, there is a legal basis for a tacit and informal granting of an authorisation, for example, within environmental law. There are only very few areas of tacit authorisation in current Danish law. If a public authority handles a case with illegal inexpediency and refrains from reaching a decision altogether, the authority can in certain circumstances be made responsible and given, for example, economic sanctions, but the passivity of the authority does not per se produce tacit authorisation.

2.8.5 Formal and Substantive Effects of the Tacit Authorisation

If there is a legal basis for tacit authorisation from a public authority, the authorisation has both formal and substantive effects.

2.8.6 Rules of Formally Granted Authorisations Applicable To Tacit Authorisations

Tacit authorisation is given the same legal effects as an explicit and formal authorisation, unless the specific act on tacit authorisation determines otherwise.

2.9 Articles 14, 15, 16 SD

Article 14 of the Services Directive is implemented in Article 10 of the Danish Law on Services in the Internal Market. According to Article 10 of the Law, competent authorities cannot impose any of the following requirements on a service provider: (1) discriminatory requirements based directly or indirectly on nationality or, in the case of companies, the locations of the registered office, (2) a prohibition on having an establishment in more than one Member State or on being entered in the registers or enrolled with the professional bodies or associations of more than one Member State, (3) restrictions on the freedom of a provider to choose between a principal establishment or a secondary establishment, particularly an obligation on the provider to have a principal establishment in their territory, or restrictions on the freedom to choose between establishment in the form of an agency, branch, or subsidiary, (4) conditions of reciprocity with the Member State in which the provider already has an establishment, (5) the case-by-case application of an economic test making the granting of authorisation subject to proof of the existence of an economic need or market demand, an assessment of the potential or current economic effects of the activity, or an assessment of the appropriateness of the activity in relation to the economic planning objectives set by the competence authority, (6) an obligation to provide or participate in a financial guarantee or to take out insurances from a provider or body established in their territory, and (7) an obligation to have been pre-registered for a given period in the registers held in their territories or to have previously exercised the activity for a given period in their territory.

Article 15, particularly Article 15 (7), of the Services Directives is transposed in Article 15 of the Danish Law on Services in the Internal Market empowering the Minister of Economic and Business Affairs to issue further rules. The Minister of Economic and Business has, on that basis, issued an administrative regulation, Regulation 1361/2009[24] on the obligation to report to the Commission. Notification is administered by the Danish Internal Market Centre.

2.10 Articles 14–19 SD

In Denmark it seems that Articles 14 and 15 of the Services Directive are also deemed applicable to the freedom of services. Indeed, Article 4 of Regulation 1361/2009 requires Member States to report to the Commission any new requirements imposed on the temporary provision of services. Articles 16 and 17 of the Services Directive are implemented in Articles 11 and 12 of the Danish Law on Services in the Internal Market.

2.11 Articles 22–27 SD

Articles 22 and 27 of the Services Directive are implemented by a specific regulation, Regulation No 1372/2009, on the obligation of service providers to give information to service recipients.[25]

---

[24] See *supra* n. 13.

[25] See *supra* n. 16.

The procedural requirements of these articles in the Services Directive did not have an impact on the Danish General Administrative Procedures Act and did not invoke a discussion on the interplay between the Directive and general administrative law.

2.12 Articles 28 ff. SD: Administrative Cooperation

2.12.1 Transnational Administrative Cooperation Prior to the Implementation of the Services Directive

Article 28 of the Directive is implemented in Article 13 of the Law on Services in the Internal Market, empowering the Minister of Economic and Business Affairs to issue further rules concerning the procedures for administrative cooperation with the competent authorities in other EU/EEA Member States, including the electronic exchange of information about service providers. The Minister has, on that basis, issued a specific regulation, Regulation 1363/2009, on administrative cooperation between competent authorities of the EU.[26] Administrative cooperation is supported by the Internal Market Information System (IMI) which was introduced in 2007. The IMI is a secure online application that allows national, regional, and local authorities to communicate quickly and easily with their counterparts abroad. The scope of Regulation 1363/2009 is the area of services.

2.12.2 Re-Arrangement with National Rules on Administrative Cooperation

The requirements of the Services Directive changed a number of procedures within the area of services but did not trigger a general rearrangement of administrative assistance.

2.12.3 Provisions on Financial Compensation for Transnational Administrative Cooperation

The Regulation 1363/2009 does not contain provisions on financial compensation for assistance.

---

[26] See *supra* n. 15.

2.12.4 Adaptation of the Rules on Data Protection and Professional Secrets

The Regulation 1363/2009 is applied in conformity with the Danish Act on the Processing of Personal Data[27] according to Article 12 of the Regulation. The Services Directive did not create a need to change the rules on data protection or professional secrets.

2.13 Article 29 SD: Mutual Assistance—General Obligations for the Member State of Establishment

There is no discussion in Danish law, for example, in the preparatory works of the Law on Services in the Internal Market regarding the confirmation of unlawful business.

3 Assessment of the Impact of the Services Directive

Although it is difficult at this preliminary stage to asses the full and precise impact of the Services Directive and its Danish implementation, it is common ground that the Services Directive has already caused a number of substantive and procedural changes and improvements within its ambit. In an overall description in legal terms, the Danish implementation of the Directive had been twofold. It has been carried out in the form of a horizontal act—the Law on Services in the Internal Market supplemented by four administrative regulations comprising a pillar of the most significant provisions—and a variety or 'mosaic' of sector implementations of the requirements of Directive—in the form of the analysed amendments to existing Danish acts. From the perspective of responsible Danish authorities, the new legislation and the multitude of amendments represent important legal changes within the area of services in the EU and Denmark, and the Directive is perceived as a major and ongoing challenge to legal disciplines such as European law, Danish health law, Danish labour law, and Danish social security law.

3.1 Extent of the Impact

From a Danish general administrative law perspective, conversely, the Services Directive has played a less prominent role. So far the Directive has simply been taken out of the administrative law equation. Thus, the Directive has had no impact

[27] See *supra* n. 10.

on Danish general administrative laws and has sparked no discussion of its direct or indirect impact till now. Contrary to administrative law frameworks in, for example, Germany, there is a tradition in Danish administrative law of a predominantly national focus on a distinct catalogue of administrative law questions and principles, that is, the current catalogue of procedural requirements in the Danish General Administrative Procedural Act. This tradition seemingly still exists, in spite of the challenges of e.g. the Services Directive. At this time, moreover, there is no indication in legislative, administrative, political, or academic debates in Denmark that the Services Directive aspires to implementation or conceptualisation in a future version of the Danish General Procedures Administrative Act. A completely new regulatory model in Danish law is not likely in the future if the present implementation model of the Services Directives in practice ensures an effective implementation.

3.2 Assessment of the Transposing Legislation

According to the responsible Danish authorities, the implementation of the Services Directive has, to a wide extent, been successful. There are no records of cases in, for example, the Danish courts, the relevant complaint authorities, or the European Court of Justice concerning the Danish implementation of the Services Directive, and it would be premature to conclude whether the implementation has been successful, less successful, or unsuccessful.

3.3 Most Important and Profound Changes Induced by the Services Directive

Generally, the establishment of a POSC is an interesting and significant legal development. The Services Directive requirement of a Danish POSC does not represent a novelty as such, but it has enhanced a digital evolution that was already taking place in various areas. Nonetheless, the rights of the service providers to easy access to the variety of relevant public authorities in Denmark and the right to a single online point of contact can create strong incentives to further evolution and further simplifications as to the interrelations between private actors and public authorities. Even though there is no legal obligation to provide the same level and quality of single point contacts with administrative authorities in areas other than the area of services, a spill-over effect is likely to occur over the years.

References

For legislation, jurisprudence and websites please refer to 1.1 of the report and footnotes directly.

Dahl B, Melchior T, Tamm D (eds) (2002) Danish Law in a European Perspective. Thomson Publisher, Copenhagen, p 145

Danish Enterprise and Construction Authority (DEACA) (2005) Economic Effects of Liberalising International Trade. Copenhagen

Frydenberg T, Bresson M, Them Parnas J (2009) The Services Directive and the Law on Services in the Internal Market (Servicedirektivet og lov om tjenesteydelser). Juristen 9 (Danish Law Journal). Available at http://www.djoef.dk/Udgivelser/Juristen/Juristen2009/Juristen-nr-9-2009/Servicedirektivet-og-lov-om-tjenesteydelser-i-det-indre-marked.aspx, last visited July 2010

Latrup-Petersen T (2010) The Danish Law on Services in the Internal Market with annotations ("Lov om tjenesteydelser i det indre marked"). In: Karnov Collection 2010 of Annotated Legislation

Neergaard U, Nielsen R, Roseberry LM (eds) (2008) The Services Directive, consequences for the Welfare State and the European Social Model. DJØF Publishing, Copenhagen

Peytz H, Spangsberg Grønfeldt L (2009) The Services Directive—New EU Law on Services in Denmark and the Internal Market (Den nye EU-ret om tjenesteydelser i Danmark og det indre marked). Revis og regnskabsvæsen (Danish economic and legal Journal) 11: 36

The Implementation of the Services Directive in Estonia

Carri Ginter

1 General Remarks on the Transposition Strategy and General Understanding of the Implementation

1.1 Main References Used in this Research

The SD has been mainly implemented by the law implementing the Services Directive (SD), "*Euroopa Liidu teenuste direktiivi rakendamise seadus*", [1] and the explanatory memorandum to the law implementing the SD.[2] It is to be followed up by the general part of the economic activity act "*Majandustegevuse seadustiku üldosa seadus*" (MTSÜS), which is at the time of reporting currently being drafted. The new act will replace the law implementing the SD.

Carri Ginter—Associate Professor of EU Law at the Faculty of Law at Tartu University and partner of Sorainen Law Firm. Law students Virgi Kobin, Irene Isküll, and Merili Oja provided valuable input in the drafting process of this report.

[1] Available in Estonian online at: https://www.riigiteataja.ee/ert/act.jsp?id=13245846 (06 Feb 2010).

[2] Available in Estonian online at http://www.riigikogu.ee/?page=pub_file&op=emsplain&content_type=application/rtf&file_id=798634&file_name=EL%20teenuste%20direktiivi%20rakendamise%20seletuskiri%20(606).rtf&file_size=542110&mnsensk=603+SE&fd=(06 Feb 2010).

C. Ginter (✉)
Faculty of Law, Tartu University, Tartu, Estonia
e-mail: carri.ginter@ut.ee

C. Ginter
SORAINEN Law Firm, Tallinn, Estonia

U. Stelkens et al. (eds.), *The Implementation of the EU Services Directive*,
DOI: 10.1007/978-90-6704-840-8_8,

1.2 Impact of the Services Directive

1.2.1 Profound Cause of Changes to National Law?

In Estonia the transposition of the SD has largely been limited to the wording of the directive and has not led to significant changes beyond the directive's scope. However, the MTSÜS draft will significantly affect administrative law (e.g., by introducing tacit authorisation as a rule).

1.2.2 Involvement in the Transposition Process

The draft law was largely prepared by the Ministry of Economic Affairs and Communications. Public discussion remained limited. One can say that there was no significant cooperation on several levels of administration, for example, on the municipal level. Mainly, involvement of other levels was limited to introductory meetings, which focused on providing information. For instance, during the presentation of the Internal Market Information System (IMI), a large portion of the participants had not heard of the directive and had difficulties in understanding what was being introduced. Public discussion was limited to briefing about the current status of the implementation and did not raise any discussion. There is no information about administrative practices or how the directive will, in practice, affect access to services. There is no analysis of practical effects and benefits.

1.3 (National) Scope of Application

1.3.1 Scope of the Services Directive

There has been no wide discussion about the scope of the directive. According to its wording, the new law is applicable to service providers from Estonia as well as from other contracting states in the provision of services. The true effect of the law will have to be clarified in practice. In the absence of any limiting provisions, the law could also be applied to domestic services. The MTSÜS will clearly extend the SD principles to the domestic service providers as well.

1.3.2 Application of Transposing Laws to Domestic Service Providers and Beyond

Estonia implemented the SD by adopting a new law. This should also allow domestic service providers and potentially every citizen to claim these new rights and proceedings. This argument is further supported by the constitutional right to nondiscrimination. The MTSÜS reiterates that the rules will also be applicable to domestic service providers.

1.3.3 Equal Treatment of Domestic and Transnational Service Providers

According to the law implementing the SD all service providers are treated equally.

1.4 Incorporation of Transposing Legislation

In Estonia the directive was implemented by adopting a new separate law referring clearly to the SD. Thus, even though the law may have indirect effects due to the reform of administrative processes, it does not expressly affect contexts outside the scope of the law.

1.5 The Relationship of the Services Directive to Primary EU Law

1.5.1 Relationship to Articles 49 and 56 TFEU

There has been no widespread discussion about the potential conflict between primary and secondary EU law on services. The Estonian Supreme Court (*Riigikohus*) has recognised supremacy and direct effect as general principles of EU law. A question of contradiction between the treaty provisions and the SD would most likely be referred to the Court of Justice of the European Union in the context of a preliminary rulings procedure (Article 267 TFEU). As a general principle of EU law, such a contradiction should lead to the primary law prevailing over the secondary. It can indeed be noted that the positions adopted in the SD may in fact attempt to limit the scope of Article 56 TFEU (ex Article 49 EC) and thus be contrary to the treaty provisions in light of the interpretations given to them earlier by the Court of Justice of the EU.

1.5.2 Problems in This Context

There have been no specific problems identified in this context.

1.6 Screening

According to the Eurochambers report, Estonia has more or less implemented the directive.[3] In Estonia every ministry was responsible for amendments in their area of responsibility.

---

[3] http://www.eurochambres.eu/Content/Default.asp?PageID=1&DocID=2205.

2 Individual Articles of the Services Directive

2.1 Article 6 SD: Point of Single Contact (POSC)

2.1.1 Establishment of the POSC

The new law foresees expressly the establishment of POSCs. According to the Commission homepage, the one POSC in Estonia is the website www.eesti.ee.[4] According to the law, applications or documents filed via a POSC shall be deemed as having been received by the competent authority within three working days. The website contains information and access to e-services for entrepreneurs under the menu *Entrepreneur*. Entrepreneurs can get all the necessary information regarding the establishment of a company, taxes and customs, required contacts, and so forth. The website also provides links to other websites containing more information about different procedures and actions, as well requirements. Entrepreneurs can complete procedures at a distance via the submenu *Services*. The website includes a portal called X-Road that provides other possibilities to obtain more information about the different procedures, as well as ways to complete them. It also includes official forms, official e-mail addresses, and other necessary procedural electronic documentation.

This website has existed for a longer period being very similar to the POSCs. It remains unclear what the substantial requirements are for an electronic POSC in the sense of clarity of structure and whether or not it can serve as a page referring to other web pages containing the necessary information. According to the Ministry of Economic Affairs and Communications, they do not provide assistance in POSCs concerning filling the documents, finding a lawyer, and so forth. In some cases the document templates have instructions for their completion, but this depends on the authority providing the templates.

2.1.2 Subjective Understanding, Competence Structure, Authorities with POSC-Function, Liability

In Estonia there is one POSC. There was no reallocation of administrative competences. The POSC was established via the domain www.eesti.ee and the tasks have been attributed to already existing authorities.

Standard provisions on the liability of the state apply. The functioning of the POSC is the liability of the Ministry of Economic Affairs and Communications.

[4] http://ec.europa.eu/internal_market/eu-go/index_et.htm#ee (6 Feb 2010).

2.2 *Article 7 SD: Right to Information*

Comparing the wording of the SD and that of the existing law, one does not observe a general extension of the rights to information. The POSC enables access to more information than required by the SD; however, this was also the case before implementation. Therefore the implementing law did not go beyond what was required by Article 7 Section 1 of the SD.

2.3 *Article 8 SD: Procedures by Electronic Means*

In Estonia there were no difficulties with the electronic procedures. Electronic access to most public services has been available for some years now. Electronic signatures are considered valid and binding.

It seems that the transposition did not lead to any great innovative impact beyond standard progress. Estonia has traditionally been very open to technological and IT solutions in the government sector. The validity of digital signatures and the ability to communicate with official authorities, including e.g., registries, courts, and so forth, has already been possible prior to the implementation of the SD.

2.4 *Article 9 SD: Authorisation Schemes*

2.4.1 Means of Less Restrictive Measure

Such areas are listed in the report of Estonia filed with the Commission. An example is railway construction.

In Estonia many fields of activity require registration with the Register of Economic Activities (*Majandustegevuse register).* Estonia's report to the Commission contains a long list of activities, where registration with that registry is required (e.g., dry cleaning and copy machine maintenance). The report refers to the fact that such registration is one of the simplest authorisation schemes, and essentially automatic. No prior control is exercised. This position may be disputable, since, in principle, prior notification would not be sufficient if it is not followed up with an actual registry entry. In practice, this should not be a problem, since registrations are provided liberally and quickly.

2.4.2 Existing Authorisation Schemes/Procedures

As mentioned in the previous point, many fields of activity require registration with the Register of Economic Activities. It did not have to be abolished or altered due to the reasons mentioned above. The MTSÜS introduces tacit authorisation as a rule.

2.4.3 Simple Notifications

There is no clear national understanding if the simple notification requirements are included in Articles 9 ff. SD and if simple notification can be considered as an authorisation scheme in the meaning of Article 4 (6) SD. However, some have expressed the opinion that simple notification as an obligation to the service providers included in the SD is not allowed according to Article 16 (2) (g) SD in relation to Article 19 (a) SD. According to Article 19 (a) SD, a Member State may not impose an obligation to obtain authorisation from or to make a declaration to their competent authorities. Following the opinion, the definition of "declaration" provided in Article 19 (a) SD also includes simple notification and, according to Article 16 (2) (g) SD, restrictions on the freedom to provide the services referred to in Article 19 are not allowed. In light of this, the MTSÜS foresees simple notification rules only for domestic service providers, whereas cross-border service providers are exempted from this obligation.

2.5 Article 10 SD: Conditions for the Granting of Authorisation

2.5.1 Recognition of Requirements

The law states that if a service provider has authorisations, the control of which is mainly in conformity with similar control in Estonia, duplicate rules will not be instated. Estonia does not have a federal system and was not faced with problems arising from the particularities of such a system.

2.5.2 Granting Authorisation Throughout the Whole National Territory and Exceptions

Granting authorisation throughout the whole country was not difficult in Estonia due to the fact that Estonia is not a federal state.

The law includes a list of 13 items referring to the case law of the Court of Justice of the EU as regards justification of regional authorisation only. The wording of the list is taken from Article 4 (8) SD.

2.5.3 Court Review of Administrative Decisions

In Estonia the courts review such decisions in case of an application by an affected party. Review of discretion is limited in scope to following rules exercising discretion and does not permit the court to "replace" the discretion of the authority with the discretion of the judge.

2.5.4 Reasoning of Administrative Decisions

There has been no need to change existing law at this point, because this obligation existed previously. The authorities are obliged to fully reason their decisions so all the parties can understand their grounds.

2.5.5 Allocation of Competences

There has been no new allocation of competences in this regard.

2.6 Article 11 SD: Duration of Authorisation

There was no general principle of unlimited validity of authorisations. The law now clearly states that, as a general rule, authorisations are of unlimited validity.

The law does not list specific fields, but merely the criteria by which the legislator can decide that a certain field justifies a limited term for authorisations, basically rephrasing the text of the SD. The MTSÜS will add that the limited term for authorisation is also justified, if the entrepreneur has asked for it in the application.

2.7 Article 12 SD: Selection from Among Several Candidates

The new law introduced the requirement of a competition. Similar requirements could have been deducted from earlier specific laws.

2.8 Article 13 SD: Authorisation Procedures

2.8.1 A Priori Determination of the Duration of Administrative Procedures

The duration of particular proceedings is regulated according to the particular authority involved. In some instances the law foresees specific timeframes. Such deadlines can often be prolonged. In other instances the authorities are required to act within a reasonable time. In most cases the deadlines start with the filing of the application.

The law implementing the SD states that deadlines can only be prolonged once, and then for a limited term. The same rule will also be stated in the MTSÜS, but the MTSÜS will foresee that the decision has to be made within 30 days of the application's filing, if it has not been stated differently by a law.

2.8.2 General Rule for the Duration

The law implementing the SD did not establish a general rule on the duration of the procedures. However, this will be covered by the MTSÜS (see above). This general rule also applies beyond the scope of the application of the SD.

2.8.3 Exceptions to the General rule for the Duration

Currently it is possible to deviate from the prescribed duration of procedures and the possibility is also used. However, as the MTSÜS will foresee a general rule on the duration of the procedures and does not state an exemption, it is not possible to deviate from the prescribed duration of procedures.

2.8.4 Tacit Authorisation in the National Legal Order So Far

Tacit authorisations are uncommon so far in Estonia, but the MTSÜS foresees tacit authorisation as a rule. According to the MTSÜS, there is a general obligation to notify the registrar about initiating economic activities, but this obligation does not restrict the economic activities. Cross-border service providers are exempted from this obligation (see question 2.4.3).

2.8.5 Formal and Substantive Effects of Tacit Authorisation

Currently there is no practice that allows conclusions on this topic.

2.8.6 Further Information on the National Implementation of Tacit Authorisation

The new law does not list instances where tacit authorisation is not accepted, but it does include a general reference to overriding matters of public interest. In my opinion, the provisions of the directives on tacit authorisation could be applied directly in case of lacking of wrongful implementation, since the criteria for direct effect seem to be met. As mentioned before (2.8.1), the MTSÜS will foresee that the decision has to be made in 30 days of the application's filing, if it is not been stated differently by a law. Until then the criterion of reasonable time can be applied.

2.9 Articles 14, 15, 16 SD

The legislator did not identify a need to adapt new national law as regards these provisions of the SD but, instead, included a list of such provisions from the directive into the text of the new law. Furthermore there has been no significant public discussion about the "self-screening" of the Member States.

2.10 Articles 28 ff. SD: Administrative Cooperation

Prior to the implementation of the SD there have been no provisions on transnational administrative assistance in Estonia.

And the SD did not give a cause to rearrange the provisions for administrative assistance in a general or uniform way. Transnational administrative cooperation is provided for in Paras 19–23 of the law implementing the SD. The wording is largely limited to the SD and has information added where necessary (e.g., who is responsible for the POSC).

Neither rules on financial compensation of administrative assistance have been introduced, nor a need for altering rules on data protection and professional secrets has been detected.

3 Assessment of the Impact of the SD

In Estonia the impact of the SD has not yet been realised. It is my estimate that the impact will be more significant once an understanding of the directive becomes more widespread. However, the impact may be less notable due to the general openness of the economy and the legal system, which is already very apt to allow business from another MS.

In general, there is an impression that the transposition occurred without sufficient debate and attention. This is also illustrated by the transposition method—adopting a new law. This means that formally the SD has been implemented; however it is difficult to assess whether substantive changes to the system happened as well or will happen without further reform. It is also possible that many of the solutions foreseen by the SD already existed in Estonia and therefore received less attention.

I believe that the SD is one of the few instruments where the purely EU nature of the law can be clearly seen. This greatly contributes to an understanding of the presence of EU law and its effect on day-to-day business. The introduction of POSCs, tacit licences, mutual recognition principles, and so forth will also inevitably lead to a change in the mind frame of the authorities and lead to a spillover effect to other areas where there is currently less cooperation.

The Implementation of the Services Directive in Finland

Lauri Railas

1 General Remarks on the Transposition Strategy and General Understanding of the Implementation

1.1 Main References Used in this Research

The main reference is the Act (1166/2009) on the Provision of Services (later "the Act 1166/2009"), adopted on 22 December 2009 with entry into force on 29 December 2009.[1] The government proposal or bill (HE/216/2009 vp) for the Act and on the amendment of certain other related statutes is of relevance as well as constituting the main *travaux preparatoires*. As the Act touches only upon issues of general relevance, a substantial part of the implementation consists of amending sector-specific legislation, which was not finalised by the time this report was written and therefore cannot be reported in detail. I shall, however, mention the findings made at the elementary stage on the acceptability of the authorisation schemes (see Attachment 1).

The author is Attorney-at-Law, LL.D., Krogerus Attorneys Ltd.; last updated 20 January/8 June 2010.

[1] The deadline for implementation was 28 December 2009; the deadline was exceeded by two days, which should be de minimis.

L. Railas (✉)
Krogerus Attorneys Ltd, Helsinki, Finland
e-mail: lauri.railas@krogerus.com

U. Stelkens et al. (eds.), *The Implementation of the EU Services Directive*,
DOI: 10.1007/978-90-6704-840-8_9,

1.2 Impact of the Services Directive

1.2.1 Profound Cause of Changes to National Law?

No fundamental changes have yet been made to the legislation, other than the implementing legislation. However, it was seen as necessary to appoint a committee to amend general administrative laws to provide for consequences of delay in the administrative procedures.

1.2.2 Involvement in the Transposition Process

The main responsibility was placed on the Ministry of Employment and Economy, but each ministry and body of central administration was responsible for its own sector. The Ministry of Employment and Economy coordinated the work with other ministries and constituted a channel towards the Commission. A committee consisting of relevant ministries and business organisations was established with a term of two years in March 2008 to administer the implementation.

Even before adoption of the Directive, the Ministry of Employment and Economy (in its former organisation) commissioned a report on the implementation of the Directive. The report, entitled "The Services Directive and Finland" ("*Palveludirektiivi ja Suomi*"), was written by the author of this report together with another writer.

1.3 (National) Scope of Application

1.3.1 Scope of the Services Directive

The general perception in Finland is that the Directive is intended to regulate transnational activities and that domestic relations in the field of provision of services are not touched upon by it. However, this perception has not been spelled out expressly anywhere.

However, Act 1166/2009 makes no distinction between domestic and service providers from other EEA countries in its scope.

We might add that we carried out additional study of the definition of services, since the definition of the Treaty (former Article 50) is very general and is built on *e contrario* notions as compared to free movement of goods, capital and labour. A distinction must be drawn even to agriculture, including fisheries. The principal dividing line is whether the provisions relate predominantly to the actual selling activity of either goods or financial instruments, and not to the subject-matter sold or its qualities, and in the first mentioned case, services should be concerned. However, the case law of the European Court of Justice is not consistent in this area and neither are its interpretations. The fact that, for instance, agriculture or mining is done against remuneration for others is determinant, not the activity as such. One must also mention that there is no uniform concept of service: in the Services Directive there is one, in VAT law there is another, in the legal framework for public procurement there is a third, and in sales law there is yet anothers and so on.

1.3.2 Application of Transposing Legislation to Domestic Service Providers

The matter whether the transposing laws are also applicable beyond the transnational scope of the Directive is not expressly addressed in the implementing legislation, but as no distinction is made as to scope, and as circumstances in which domestic service providers refer to the law may arise, there exist few arguments against applying the implementing legislation, even in a domestic setting.

1.3.3 Application of Transposing Legislation Beyond Service Providers

The implementation did not go that far that also citizens or other economic stakeholders can make use of the new implementing legislation. The relationships between citizens and authorities in other respects are not touched upon by the implementing legislation, although it is not excluded that someone might claim rights on the basis of analogy.

1.3.4 Equal Treatment of Domestic and Transnational Service Providers

As Act 1166/2009 does not make an express distinction between transnational and domestic service providers, no reasons for an equal treatment of domestic and transnational service providers can be found, and therefore no grounds for it are expressed. The government proposal is silent on any distinction. A Finnish MEP, Anneli Jäätteenmäki, raised this issue in a major conference on the possible extension of the regime of the Directive to medical services, but this intervention did not raise express repercussions. One can state that equality is embedded in the wording of the implementing legislation.

1.4 Incorporation of Transposing Legislation

Finland implemented expressly the authorisation procedures, such as the acknowledgement of receipt and the procedure of tacit consent. Therefore a new codification was passed, but some amendments with a limited scope are to be made to individual statutes.

The new codification is of a much smaller magnitude than the Directive, and the intellectual model for it may be found in the Finnish act (458/2002) implanting the E–Commerce Directive (2000/31/EC). Much of the contents of the Directive either already exist in Finnish statutory law, or are carried out by administrative measures.

1.5 The Relationship of the Services Directive to Primary EU Law[2]

The matter of the relation of the Services Directive to Articles 49 and 56 TFEU has received little attention, and no statement is expressed on it in the implementing legislation. However, there are now standards for activity based on establishment, and Member States can apply different criteria for the freedom to provide services.[3]

The author of this report views Article 49 and Article 56 TFEU, as applied in the jurisprudence of the ECJ, as having significance in parallel with the Directive. This is evident in areas which are excluded from the scope of the Directive. The Directive gives the provisions of the Treaty a more concrete meaning in the circumstances it addresses, and Member States are requested to take a number of measures to safeguard the fulfilment of the objectives of the Directive. This does not change the fact that independent interpretations and applications may be made on the basis of the Treaty. One may ask whether level of interpretation is not something on which the European Court of Justice should take a position.

Altogether no problems have been identified thus far.

1.6 Screening

Each sector screened its own requirements, but the Ministry of Employment and Economy led the process by coordinating the activity. In some sectors such as technical safety legislation, external consultants were used for screening, and your writer served as one such consultant.

---

2 Due to the entry into force of the Lisbon Treaty the numbering of the Articles of the Treaty contained in this report and the underlying Questionnaire has changed.

3 Finnish officials noted with interest during preparations for the implementation, the idea of British authorities responsible for the preparation of implementation, whereby national law would not make a distinction between freedom of establishment and freedom to provide services when regulating the possibilities of the Member State imposing limitations on the service activity. To comply with the Directive, a less interventionist approach (in practice, that designed for the freedom to provide services in Article 16 et seq) would have to apply. In Finland at least, this approach was not followed in the end.

2 Individual Articles of the Services Directive

2.1 Article 6 SD: Point of Single Contact (POSC)

2.1.1 Establishment of the POSC

Finland builds POSCs on existing and emerging systems for providing information to companies and electronic government. The system is based on a multi-channel service model, and the main entry or access to the system is the "Enterprise Finland" network service. The system includes the call centre of Enterprise Finland, known as the Contact Centre, as well as the services of various competent authorities. Enterprise Finland already existed prior to the implementation, but its functions have been extended to cover the tasks of POSC as prescribed in the Directive. The website of Enterprise Finland will contain sections that serve the functions of POSC. Links are also created, where necessary, to the sites of individual authorities.

The linguistic framework for the POSC and the call centre is made up of the official languages of Finland, Finnish and Swedish, and, in addition, the English language is covered.

2.1.2 Subjective Understanding, Competences Structure, Authorities with POSC-Function, Liability, and Involvement of Private Partners

The Finnish POSC is built on as a unitary system with central access, and it is a technical solution between the different authorities and the service provider. There has existed since 2003 a legal framework for e-government in Finland, and the POSC is perceived only as a technical solution with no legal implications as such. There is much information available through the POSC regarding authorisations and other administrative procedures relating to the provision of services. However, the technical facilities to apply authorisations only electronically are not yet in place. This is stated in the Government Proposal for the Act 1166/2009. My understanding is that where no special forms are used in the application procedure, electronic communications through the POSC should be valid, but obviously any reluctance of the authorities to study such communications would hamper the procedure.

There will be no special project to implement electronic procedures in a Pan–European context only. Electronic procedures will be taken into use domestically following a comprehensive government plan for the deployment of IT in public administration. This work will include the creation of a central database for electronic forms used in various procedures. In Finland, there are no stringent requirements for electronic signatures. The Act on Electronic Communications with Public Authorities (2/2003) prescribes that electronic signatures are needed only when there is doubt about the authenticity of communications.

No administrative competences are allocated to the POSC and neither are any administrative tasks reallocated between the authorities because of the establishment of the POSC.

There are no express provisions as to the impact of using the POSC on the calculation of administrative time limits, but the Government Proposal refers to section 20 of the Administration Act, which makes ultimate reception of the relevant authority determinant.

The impact of EU law on the interpretation of national law could be used to argue that reception of information by the POSC should be relevant, rather than reception by the relevant authority. However, there is no express statement to this effect, and the *travaux preparatoires* of the Act 1166/2009 are not in agreement with this interpretation, but rather with the contrary. One can of course state that outside procedural law, time limits tend to have less meaning than in procedural law and that the use of electronic communications would reduce the delay between the receipt of applications by the POSC on the one hand and by the POSC on the other irrelevant.

The tasks of POSC were given to an existing information body by expanding its activities as stated above and no private bodies were used in establishing the POSC, save for IT consultants.

The issue of liability has not been specifically addressed in public services law. The state is in principle responsible for the mistakes of the POSC following the general principles of tort law. The POSC is used by the state to perform given public functions, and the operation of the POSC in relation to service providers and different authorities is merely technical. Enterprise Finland as the POSC is a function of the state, and the differentiation between it and other authorities may have only a procedural impact, if any. Different situations might arise when it comes to the exercise of public authority proper, and other functions carried out by the state through the POSC such as informative functions. This distinction is relevant considering the variety of functions and activities of the state.

According to the Finnish Delictual Liability (Tort) Act (412/74), the state is responsible for pure economic loss in case of the exercise of public authority, whereas in other situations pure economic loss is usually not compensated. However, the state is not liable for the exercise of public authority, "where the requirements for the given activity have reasonably been complied with". This restriction is meant to reduce the liability of the public authority to exceptional situations. It is anticipated that most functions of the POSC would benefit from this restriction.

2.2 Article 7 SD: Right to Information

"The rights to information" were not mentioned at all in the implementing legislation and their scope therefore follows from the Directive, which has a direct effect in the vertical relationship (a POSC is a function of a public authority, and there exists a vertical relationship between the service provider and the public authority). The implementation of the provisions relating to the functions and duties of the POSC and the state running it are not found in the legislation, but the establishment of the POSC has been merely an administrative matter. The Government Proposal for Act 1166/2009 contains a section on the POSC but there is no "black-letter" text on POSCs in the Articles of the Act. Thereby the implementation is done through an interpretative approach, rather than reiterating the text of the Directive in all respects.

Considering the aforementioned, the "rights to information" have not been extended beyond the scope of the Directive. It should be added that general administrative law imposes on the authorities an obligation to provide information to companies and citizens, but a breach of this general obligation in connection with the POSC could not be referred to as a fault of the authorities in any specific case.

2.3 *Article 8 SD: Procedures by Electronic Means*

Electronic administration has been in place for a number of years already but its scope has been very limited in practical terms. Very few, if any, license or registration matters can be filed electronically and, correspondingly, very rarely can administrative decisions be made electronically.

The government has responded to this challenge by establishing the state IT Service Centre to develop IT services centrally. The key issue is development of a common platform solution, on which various authorities can add their own solutions, such as electronic application forms. The first results from this effort have been expected in 2010 or 2011.

It can be stated that the implementation of the Directive has certainly accelerated the development procedure for e-government, although roadmaps to more e–government already existed. But there has never been an intention to make the administration all-electronic.

2.4 *Article 9 SD: Authorisation Schemes*

The review of authorisation schemes is not yet finalised. It is anticipated that the list of authorisations prevailing prior to entry into force of the Directive will prevail. See Attachment 1.

Generally, there are few authorisation schemes that need to be abolished altogether. Probably one must look more closely into the services of real estate and rental brokering, debt collection, goldsmiths, lost property offices and chimney-sweeping especially when it comes to nondiscrimination. In these cases, an overriding reason relating to the public interest and, in most cases, the inefficacy of a *posteriori* control can be shown to exist.

According to our national understanding, notification and authorisation requirements are distinct issues; we have, however, noted the wide description of authorisation schemes in the Directive and screen our legislation accordingly.

There may, however, exist notification requirements that were introduced as substitutes for authorisations when the latter were abolished, but in practice a reply by the relevant authority was a precondition for commencement of the service activity. It is understood that this is not correct.

2.5 Article 10 SD: Conditions for the Granting of Authorisation

2.5.1 Recognition of Requirements

An express recognition of authorisations granted by other Member States is not mentioned in the implementing legislation. However, section 14 of Act 1166/2009 states that where the applicant is domiciled or established in another state belonging to the European Economic Area, Finland cannot impose requirements that are the same or pursue the same objectives as requirements imposed by the applicant's country.

Moreover, documents originating from other Member States must be recognised, and the freedom to provide services must exist. This freedom can, in individual cases, be limited by courts and authorities under sector-specific criteria as well as the general criteria of the Directive (necessary for public security, public safety, public health or the environment, non-discriminatory and proportionate).

2.5.2 Granting Authorisation Throughout the Whole National Territory and Exceptions

There are examples of authorisation schemes such as debt collection where a selected regional authority grants authorisations for the entire country. In many cases, however, a regional authority grants licenses to its administrative territory only. This aspect needs to be taken care of by screening the legislation and making necessary amendments. The best way forward is the model of debt collection above. Given that Finland is not a federal state, the change is merely a technical one and not politically difficult.

'Overriding reasons relating to the public interest' to justify regional authorisation only were not used in Finland. The need to amend legislation in the case of regional authorisations was accepted.

2.5.3 Entitlement to Grant Authorisation

The principle established in Article 10 (5) is not a universal principle in Finnish administrative law, since the authorities retain discretion in several fields, such as pharmacies and taxi licenses. These fields of service are outside the scope of the Directive. However, in the fields covered by the Directive, the evaluation of need of services should normally not be relevant. Only lost property offices, commercial shooting ranges and chimney-sweeping may be subjected to the evaluation of need before authorisation is granted. It is not known whether these exceptions will be maintained or not, but in the case of commercial shooting ranges the objective of maintaining public security may effectively be referred to in the context of several tragic mass murders committed by disturbed people.

2.5.4 Reasoning of Administrative Decisions

Article 10 (6) SD did not cause a need to change national law, as full reasoning of decisions is also required by the national administrative laws.

2.5.5 Allocation of Competences

This matter is not yet established, but it is necessary to widen the competences of regional authorities granting authorisations to cover the entire country, or to re-allocate the granting of authorisations otherwise.

2.6 Article 11 SD: Duration of Authorisation

There have been authorisations of limited validity in Finland. It is not yet certain whether these are to be maintained or not, but it is assumed that authorisations will be unlimited, unless public security and public safety reasons require otherwise.

2.7 Article 12 SD: Selection From Among Several Candidates

No transposition was made as regards Article 12 SD as it was thought that national regulations and practice were seen as adequate. However the requirement of the Directive did not have a precise counterpart in Finnish legislation.

2.8 Article 13 SD: Authorisation Procedures

2.8.1 A Priori Determination of the Duration of Administrative Procedures

The responsible authority determines a *priori* the duration of an administrative procedure.

2.8.2 General Rule for the Duration

No general rule on the duration of the procedure was established for situations envisaged in the Directive or otherwise. No sector-specific maximum durations exist. However, the law requires that administration must operate expeditiously. As stated earlier, a Committee was established to study this question on a horizontal basis. The results of its work are not yet at hand.

2.8.3 Tacit Authorisation in the National Legal Order So Far

Tacit approval was not known in Finnish administrative law before.

2.8.4 Formal and Substantive Effects of Tacit Authorisation

The difference between formal and substantive effects was probably not recognised when implementation was carried out, but it is submitted that only formal effects are created. Otherwise, the authorities could not withdraw authorisations, even in clear cases of abuse such as money laundering.

2.8.5 Rules on Formally Granted Authorisations Applicable to Tacit Authorisation

The issue whether the same rules apply to tacit authorisations as apply to formally granted authorisations is not addressed anywhere, but in my view it is obvious that the same rules apply.

The authorities are required to issue a document confirming the tacit consent.

2.9 Articles 14, 15, 16 SD

2.9.1 Need of Adaptation?

The screening is still ongoing and the results are not yet certain.

We note that Finnish law implementing the EEA Treaty and amending the Act (122/1919) on the right to carry out business in Finland gave persons domiciled and companies established in other EEA countries the right to provide services in Finland based on the freedom to provide services only when these establish a branch in Finland. This requirement was withdrawn via separate statute after intervention of the Commission immediately after the Directive had come into force. We also identified the issue ourselves, but it was originally probably a mistake of the legislator rather than an intended restriction, since no application was noticed to have taken place during the years of its validity.

In the case of car security inspections, there is a requirement that the service provider must be registered as a legal person in Finland, which presupposes the establishment of at least a subsidiary in Finland; using freedom to provide services as a ground for operations in Finland is not possible, or carrying out the operation through a branch.

2.9.2 Discourses on these Articles

We have studied with interest the UK idea that the criteria for freedom to provide services are extended to cases of establishment, thus reducing the possibilities of a Member State to interfere.

Finnish officials noted with interest during the preparations for implementation the idea of British authorities responsible for their preparation of implementation, whereby national law would make no distinction between freedom of establishment and freedom to provide services when regulating the possibilities of the Member State concerned to impose limitations on the service activity. To comply with the Directive, a less interventionist approach (in practice, that designed for the freedom to provide services in Article 16 *et seq*) would have to apply. In Finland at least this approach was not followed in the end. Dual regimes for requirements are very complex and it is sometimes difficult to say when a company is established since a company can have office facilities in a country without being established there.

There was some consideration of inclusion in the implementing legislation the concepts of establishment and freedom to provide services, but the result was less far-reaching.

2.10 Articles 14–19 SD

We have paid attention to the fact that the list of grounds for national interference in Article 16 (1), para 3, does not include consumer protection as did the allowed derogations of the Internal Market Clause (Article 3, para 4) of Directive 2000/31/EC on E-Commerce.

2.11 Excursus: Articles 20 and 21 SD

Article 20: the author of this report has examined Article 20 and its impact on relationships between companies. Private companies do not usually have an obligation to contract with another company or consumer, unless they are in a dominant position, such as many energy companies.

However, no discrimination may take place for reasons of nationality. It was conceived that the present legislative framework would be sufficient to cover all aspects of discrimination, even between companies. The author had traced some *lacunae* in this respect that companies may not only be prohibited in their contracting policy and terms from discrimination on national grounds, but may also occasionally even be obligated to serve clients across national frontiers. This approach is now expressly touched upon in Proposal No. 5 of Communication from the Commission to the European Parliament, the Council, the Economic and Social Committee and the Committee of the Regions entitled "Towards a Single Market Act, For a highly competitive social market economy, 50 proposals for improving our work, business and exchanges with one another", COM (2010) 608 final.

2.12 Articles 22–27 SD

The information requirements imposed on the service provider are implemented by Act 1166/2009 and constitute five out of the 19 substantive articles of the Act. These have been implemented almost word-by-word. As the recipient of the service may be a company, these requirements are not part of consumer protection law, or at least not solely consumer protection law. These provisions have had no impact on administrative law.

Codes of conduct may be of a private or, at least indirectly, public origin. It is very difficult for an administration to force business to adopt codes of conduct unless the threat of mandatory legislation is raised. Our implementing statute mentions only private codes of conduct. Codes of conduct should be soft law in all cases. The state can try to force or persuade private organisations into drafting codes of conduct, but this does not alter the nature of these codes.

2.13 Articles 28 ff. SD: Administrative Cooperation

2.13.1 Transnational Administrative Cooperation Prior to the Implementation of the Services Directive

Finland had no general provisions on administrative assistance. Obviously there are a number of provisions based on international conventions or EU legal acts requiring administrative cooperation in individual fields.

2.13.2 Re-Arrangement of Administrative Cooperation

The requirements of the SD gave cause to arrange the provisions for administrative assistance in a general way. The task of the coordination of assistance was given to the Consumer Agency. The relevant Finnish authorities are included in a network that is connected to the Internal Market Information System.

2.13.3 Provisions on Financial Compensation for Transnational Administrative Cooperation

The relevant administrations were allocated more funds. However, there are no provisions as to billing other Member States for extensive cooperation.

2.13.4 Adaptation of the Rules on Data Protection and Professional Secrets

In Finland, access to public documents is mentioned in the Constitution. There are of course exceptions to the main rule of transparency, and data protection and protection of business secrets are recognised parts of Finnish law. However, data protection or protecting commercial secrets are objectives that have not been considered in particular when implementing the Directive, and it is submitted that this is explained by transparency of public administration and the fact that the POSC was created without black-letter text in legislation.

Moreover, the authorities should be bound by special legislation on data protection (see Article 43 of the Directive) and the same must apply to the law on business secrets without specifically mentioning it. It should be added, moreover, that the Finnish implementation Act for Directive 2002/58/EC of the European Parliament and of the Council of 12 July 2002 concerning the processing of personal data and the protection of privacy in the electronic communications sector (Directive on privacy and electronic communications) also regulates so called "Corporate subscribers", which means that the POSC as a corporate subscriber (as distinct from a network operator) must in its electronic information network protect personal data as well as the data of companies enjoying legitimate protection, as the EC Directive mentions in particular.

The author of this report raised the issue of confidentiality in a seminar with a view to pointing out the problem to the authorities. A service provider from abroad might use the authorities to convey information on its potential competitors in Finland in fields where authorisations or notice formalities are needed. As described above, much of this is public information, but there may be limits to disclosure. When it comes to exchange of information between authorities, the problem is less acute than in the situation just described.

2.14 *Article 29 SD: Mutual Assistance—General Obligations for the Member State of Establishment*

We have experienced no problems in this regard, but practical application will follow and may lead to problems, particularly when it comes to the gravity of the unlawfulness. For comparison, see the procedures for public procurement, where contracting authorities may require the bidder to provide documentation proving innocence of certain fraud crimes. When it comes to alerting the authorities of other Member States, the threshold need not be high, since the authorities of the other Member States cannot interfere in *de minimis* cases in the provision of services by such company.

2.15 *Problems and Discourses on Administrative Cooperation*

No real problems were experienced, but organisation of cooperation needed to be done.

2.16 *Convergence Programme (Chapter VII of the Services Directive)*

No real discussions took place. One can, however, mention that, like in many other countries, some authorisation schemes in Finland are managed by private organisations such as chambers of commerce, and may or may not be prescribed by law. Therefore regulation by private organisations has different dimensions.

3 Assessment of the Impact of the Directive

3.1 *Extent of the Impact*

From the point of view of Finland, the impact of the Directive has not been as crucial as in Germany, and this is said with a view to the limited scope of the general implementing Act 1166/2009 and the administrative law in general. On the other hand, the Directive has already forced the state to consider time limits with respect to administrative decision-making in general, which is an indication of influence on law beyond the scope of the Directive.

The Directive is an expression of a legal approach that has not been in conformity with traditional national law approaches, as EU law and national law have different working methods and objectives. Some lawyers say Finland should revise its Constitution to account for the fact that the country is now a member of the EU, and many legal rights and obligations emanate therefrom.

It is thought by the author of this report that the real impact will be recognised later. One can easily ask: are we to streamline national administration only when requested by a transnational community and only to the extent requested by it? The resources available for implementation are scarce, and only minimum implementation has taken place thus far. Perhaps many questions will be studied only later, when they have become acute.

Probably the most important impact of the Directive was that the administration became more aware of the requirements of the Treaty and the case law of the ECJ. Further, the need for defined time limits is an important additional impact.

The impact of the Directive on the promotion of e-government must be crucial since an obligation to comply with advanced requirements often enhances progress.

3.2 Assessment of the Transposing Legislation

The transposition of the Directive was a minimal one. At a certain stage, it was thought that no general implementation would be necessary at all, but that screening of individual provisions would be sufficient. However, this minimalist approach did not gain much support.

Little by little, ideas emanating from the Directive must become more central, as services are regarded more and more critical to the generation of wealth and income.

3.3 The Most Important and Profound Changes Induced by the Services Directive

It remains to be seen how much effect the Directive will have in Finland. The first significant effect is the accelerated development of e-government. There exist no lobbies to demand a more profound implementation, even beyond the scope of the Directive, save the delay aspect of administration. The implementation of similar ideas in the health sector has, however, received particular attention, as it has within the EU. However, the scope of the implementing legislation has not been widened. In the fields excluded by the Directive, notably in gambling legislation, the state is fiercely defending the monopoly of authorised operators.

As stated above, it is submitted that the effects of the Directive may manifest in greater detail over time.

Attachment 1: Finnish authorisation schemes as of 2010

There are nowadays some 20–30 services or independent professions that require authorisation. Some authorisations are granted by the authorities in the relevant field, some are granted by the regional administrative authorities. Authorisation schemes are mostly motivated by arguments such as public safety or public security. The number of professions/services that need authorisation has been reduced during the 1990s. A new industry requiring authorisation is debt collection.

A list of services requiring authorisation in Finland follows.

1. ***Authorisation by a sector-specific authority is required for:***

- Car security surveys (the relevant authority: the Finnish Vehicle Administration AKE);
- Driver examinations, these can be organised by the AKE itself or by private or public bodies authorised by AKE, selection is made through open public procurement procedure, but the pricing of the examination related services is legally bound, similar regime applies to the recording equipment envisaged in Council Regulations No. 561/2006, 3821/1985 and 2135/1998;
- Real estate and rental brokering are subject to authorisation and competence requirements based on national law; these will have to be assessed through the tests of necessity and proportionality;
- Debt collection, which is however subject to an exemption through Article 17 of the Directive;
- Alcoholic drinks and products: their production, import, exports, wholesale and special sale and special (industrial) use requires authorisation; as regards compliance with the Directive, reference is made to case *C-434/04, Ahokainen and Leppik*, judgement 28.9.2006.
- The production, importation, distribution and sale of pharmaceutical products: to the extent these are covered by the Directive, which remains an issue due to the obscurity of wording, changes are apparently not needed;
- The production of poison, which can be motivated by public safety;
- Goldsmiths and precious metals: these are subject to detailed rules and authorisation schemes in many EU countries; however, one can raise the question whether retail sales should at all be subject to authorisation schemes;
- Mining and ore finding are subject to detailed authorisation schemes and a number of authorities are involved in these fields; it has been questioned, whether these fields are subject to the Services Directive at all, and if this is the case, the Directive has a major impact although the same would follow from the Treaty; mining laws have been under revision recently for other reasons
- Fertilizers, animal foods and seeds are subject to detailed EC legislation and the authorisations derive their legitimacy from these provisions;
- Professions with weapons are subject to extensive EC legislation, the requirement, according to which the establishment of a commercial shooting

range must be motivated by the applicant, needs to be examined; the number mass killings in Finland and other countries may undermine any liberalization efforts

- Electric installations and reparations: a private company issues a professional qualifications certificate which literally speaking falls within the exclusions of the Directive, but the procedure may have to be evaluated in order to avoid discrimination; one may also evaluate the need for authorisation in general
- Dangerous chemicals and explosives: public security and public safety are the motivations here as well; and
- Package travels are subject to *Council Directive 90/314/EEC of 13 June 1990 on package travel, package holidays and package tours*. However, this directive is a minimum directive, and Finland has gone beyond its requirements. The existence of a minimum directive in a field short of full harmonisation does not preclude the tests of nondiscrimination, necessity and proportionality being applied. For instance, there is a requirement that a package tours operator must have a branch in Finland. The general consumer law of the EU goes into the direction full harmonisation, which obviously reduces the possibility for manoeuvre by national authorities.

2. ***Authorisations granted by the regional authorities:***

- Sale of alcohol, this activity has been largely exempted by case law (C-434/04);
- Driving schools are subject to a number of requirements but, given the mutual recognition of driver's licenses within the EU, one could ask whether driving school training obtained abroad should be held equivalent to a Finnish one (free movement of services/or by virtue of Article 19);
- Lost property offices: the establishment of a lost property office requires authorisation which is based on evaluation of need;
- Private social and health organisations;
- Chimney-sweeping, this can be carried out by a public municipal system or by private enterprises selected through public procurement mechanisms; the problem is that chimney-sweeping fees are fixed by regulations, and the inspection system is compulsory, so that there is little to compete about;
- Animal protection: certain services related to animal protection such as the organisation of animal tests are subject to an authorisation. These requirements are in line with the Directive; and
- Gravel pits that are motivated by environmental concerns.

The Implementation of the Services Directive in France

Marie Gautier Melleray and Marion Ho-Dac

1 General Remarks on the Transposition Strategy and General Understanding of the Implementation

1.1 Main References Used in this Research

Legislation adopted in view of the transposition of the Services Directive:

- Décret n° 2010-1310 du 2 novembre 2010 relatif au registre spécial des agents commerciaux, http://www.legifrance.gouv.fr/affichTexte.do;jsessionid=BE2EDC770B899C464D674F78C4AC9861.tpdjo08v_3?cidTexte=JORFTEXT000022992790&dateTexte
- Arrêté du 24 août 2010 modifiant l'arrêté du 28 janvier 1999 modifié relatif aux conditions de ramassage des huiles usagées, http://www.legifrance.gouv.fr/affichTexte.do?cidTexte=JORFTEXT000022806796&dateTexte=
- LOI n° 2010-853 du 23 juillet 2010 relative aux réseaux consulaires, au commerce, à l'artisanat et aux services, http://www.legifrance.gouv.fr/affichTexte.do?cidTexte=JORFTEXT000022511227&dateTexte=

Prof. Dr. Marie Gautier Melleray—Currently professor of Public Law at the Faculty of Law in Bordeaux. Dr. Marion Ho-Dac—Currently working at the European Court of Justice as Administrator in the Research and Documentation Directorate.

M. Gautier Melleray (✉)
Faculty of Law, University Montesquieu-Bordeaux IV, Pessac, France
e-mail: gautiermc@hotmail.com

M. Ho-Dac
European Court of Justice, Luxembourg, Luxembourg
e-mail: marionhodac@hotmail.com

U. Stelkens et al. (eds.), *The Implementation of the EU Services Directive*,
DOI: 10.1007/978-90-6704-840-8_10,

- Décret n° 2010-780 du 8 juillet 2010 adaptant le livre II du code rural et de la pêche maritime à la directive 2006/123/CE relative aux services dans le marché intérieur, http://www.legifrance.gouv.fr/affichTexte.do?cidTexte=JORFTEXT000022454800&dateTexte=
- Décret n° 2010-699 du 25 juin 2010 relatif à l'accréditation des organismes de mesures et de vérifications mentionnés à l'article L. 4722-2 du code du travail, http://www.legifrance.gouv.fr/affichTexte.do?cidTexte=JORFTEXT000022392666&dateTexte=
- Décret n° 2010-561 du 27 mai 2010 portant diverses mesures réglementaires de transposition de la directive 2006/123/CE relative aux services dans le marché intérieur, http://www.legifrance.gouv.fr/affichTexte.do?cidTexte=JORFTEXT000022275388&dateTexte=
- Décret n° 2010-484 du 11 mai 2010 relatif à la liberté d'établissement des architectes, http://www.legifrance.gouv.fr/affichTexte.do?cidTexte=JORFTEXT000022205381
- Arrêté du 12 avril 2010 modifiant l'arrêté du 20 septembre 2006 relatif à la sélection, à la production, à la circulation et à la distribution des matériels de multiplication végétative de la vigne, http://www.legifrance.gouv.fr/affichTexte.do?cidTexte=JORFTEXT000022127415&dateTexte=
- Arrêté du 19 mars 2010 relatif au régime de déclaration préalable des manifestations commerciales, http://www.legifrance.gouv.fr/affichTexte.do?cidTexte=JORFTEXT000022013695&dateTexte=
- Décret n° 2010-210 du 1er mars 2010 relatif aux centres de formalités des entreprises, http://www.legifrance.gouv.fr/affichTexte.do?cidTexte=JORFTEXT000021898028&dateTexte=
- Arrêté du 1er mars 2010 pris en application du III de l'article R. 123-1 du code de commerce, http://www.legifrance.gouv.fr/affichTexte.do?cidTexte=JORFTEXT000021898116&dateTexte=
- Arrêté du 18 février 2010 portant approbation de diverses dispositions complétant et modifiant le règlement de sécurité contre les risques d'incendie et de panique dans les établissements recevant du public, http://www.legifrance.gouv.fr/affichTexte.do?cidTexte=JORFTEXT000021898126&dateTexte=
- Arrêté du 9 février 2010 modifiant l'arrêté du 30 avril 2002 relatif à l'habilitation des identificateurs dans les espèces chevaline et asine, http://www.legifrance.gouv.fr/affichTexte.do?cidTexte=JORFTEXT000021841620&dateTexte=
- Décret n° 2009-1668 du 28 décembre 2009 relatif à l'identification des équidés et à l'enregistrement et à la certification de la parenté des bovins, http://www.legifrance.gouv.fr/affichTexte.do?cidTexte=JORFTEXT000021540859&dateTexte=
- Décret n° 2009-1652 du 23 décembre 2009 portant application de la loi n° 2009-888 du 22 juillet 2009 de développement et de modernisation des services touristiques, http://www.legifrance.gouv.fr/affichTexte.do?cidTexte=JORFTEXT000021530009&dateTexte=
- Décret n° 2009-1650 du 23 décembre 2009 portant application de la loi n° 2009-888 du 22 juillet 2009 de développement et de modernisation des services touristiques,

http://www.legifrance.gouv.fr/affichTexte.do?cidTexte=JORFTEXT000021529652&dateTexte=

- Arrêté du 9 décembre 2009 modifiant l'arrêté du 11 décembre 2007 relatif aux conditions d'agrément pour les vérifications réglementaires prévues dans les établissements recevant du public et les immeubles de grande hauteur, http://www.legifrance.gouv.fr/affichTexte.do?cidTexte=JORFTEXT000021491298&dateTexte=
- Arrêté du 15 octobre 2009 modifiant l'arrêté du 25 octobre 2007 relatif aux conditions de conduite des coches de plaisance nolisés et à la délivrance de l'agrément pour leur nolisage, http://www.legifrance.gouv.fr/affichTexte.do?cidTexte=JORFTEXT000021190183&fastPos=1&fastReqId=1176500530&categorieLien=id&oldAction=rechTexte
- Arrêté du 15 septembre 2009 modifiant l'arrêté du 30 mars 1999 relatif à l'organisation et au fonctionnement de la Commission nationale consultative pour la faune sauvage captive, http://www.legifrance.gouv.fr/affichTexte.do?cidTexte=JORFTEXT000021113589&fastPos=2&fastReqId=806340359&categorieLien=id&oldAction=rechTexte
- Loi n° 2009-888 du 22 juillet 2009 de développement et de modernisation des services touristiques, http://www.legifrance.gouv.fr/affichTexte.do?cidTexte=JORFTEXT000020893055&fastPos=3&fastReqId=806340359&categorieLien=id&oldAction=rechTexte
- Décret n° 2009-883 du 21 juillet 2009 pris pour l'application de l'article L. 413-2 du code de l'environnement, http://www.legifrance.gouv.fr/affichTexte.do?cidTexte=JORFTEXT000020887067&fastPos=4&fastReqId=806340359&categorieLien=id&oldAction=rechTexte
- Décret n° 2009-697 du 16 juin 2009 relatif à la normalisation, http://www.legifrance.gouv.fr/affichTexte.do?cidTexte=JORFTEXT000020749979&fastPos=5&fastReqId=806340359&categorieLien=id&oldAction=rechTexte
- Décret n° 2009-696 du 15 juin 2009 modifiant le règlement et le code des devoirs professionnels de la profession de géomètre expert, http://www.legifrance.gouv.fr/affichTexte.do?cidTexte=JORFTEXT000020749868&fastPos=6&fastReqId=806340359&categorieLien=id&oldAction=rechTexte
- Décret n° 2009-681 du 12 juin 2009 relatif à l'activité de contrôle technique de la construction, pris pour l'application de l'article L. 111-25 du code de la construction et de l'habitation, http://www.legifrance.gouv.fr/affichTexte.do?cidTexte=JORFTEXT000020736488&fastPos=7&fastReqId=806340359&categorieLien=id&oldAction=rechTexte
- Arrêté du 26 janvier 2009 relatif aux modalités d'agrément des organismes de contrôle technique des manèges, machines et installations pour fêtes foraines ou pour parcs d'attractions, http://www.legifrance.gouv.fr/affichTexte.do?cidTexte=JORFTEXT000020380424&fastPos=9&fastReqId=806340359&categorieLien=id&oldAction=rechTexte
- Loi n° 2008-776 du 4 août 2008 de modernisation de l'économie, http://www.legifrance.gouv.fr/affichTexte.do?cidTexte=JORFTEXT000019283050&fastPos=10&fastReqId=806340359&categorieLien=id&oldAction=rechTexte

Draft Legislation to be adopted in view of the transposition of the Services Directive:

- Projet de loi portant fusion des professions d'avocat et d'avoué près les cours d'appel, http://www.legifrance.gouv.fr/affichLoiPreparation.do;jsessionid=36FF9689B9358E49DA2754350AA54ADF.tpdjo11v_2?idDocument=JORFDOLE000020691292&type=general

Other documents:

- Summary of the French responses to the European Commission's consultation of stakeholders on mutual evaluation foreseen by the Services Directive, http://ec.europa.eu/internal_market/consultations/docs/2010/services_directive/france_en.pdf
- Directive 2006/123 CE relative aux services dans le marché intérieur—Rapport de synthèse sur la transposition, 20 janvier 2010, Secrétariat Général des Affaires Européennes (SGAE 2010), http://www.sgae.gouv.fr/gcp/webdav/site/sgae-internet-sgae/shared/03_Autorites_FR_et_UE/Autres-positions/Directive_services/201001-Rapport_synthese_dir_services.pdf.
- Rapport d'information fait au nom de la commission des affaires européennes sur l'état de la transposition de la 'directive services', par Jean Bizet, n° 199 (2007–2008) du 7 février 2008, http://www.senat.fr/noticerap/2007/r07-199-notice.html
- Rapport d'information fait au nom de la commission des affaires européennes sur l'état de la transposition de la 'directive services', par Jean Bizet, n° 473 (2008–2009) du 17 juin 2009, http://www.senat.fr/noticerap/2008/r08-473-notice.html
- M.-J. Palasz (2009), « Le défi de la transposition de la directive services : une chance à saisir », Courrier juridique des finances et de l'industrie, n° 55, premier trimestre, pp. 45–49

1.2 Impact of the Services Directive

1.2.1 Profound Cause of Changes to National Law?

In general, the transposition of the directive in France did not greatly alter administrative laws. No concrete information was officially publicly disclosed on the content and the progress of the transposition of the Services Directive (SD).[1] The overall process lacked transparency. The French regulator transposed the

[1] Directive 2006/123/EC of 12 December 2006 on Services in the Internal Market, OJEU L 376, p. 36.

Services Directive as such (i.e., with no further changes to the French legal system other than those imposed by the Directive).

Despite the extremely large scope of the Services Directive, a sectoral transposition of the text was carried out. This means that there is no general framework for transposing the SD but, rather, a collection of regulations governing specific business areas. Hence, there has been no major reform of French administrative law.

1.2.2 Involvement in the Transposition Process

The Ministry of the Economy led the process (as per a decision of 22 June 2008). A dedicated task force in charge of the SD transposition was created to coordinate the work of the different bodies involved in the transposition process.

Business stakeholders were not consulted before mid-2008, when the establishment of Point of Single Contacts (hereafter POSCs) was discussed. All stakeholders were consulted through local chambers of commerce. No dedicated website was created. It seems that local authorities and trade unions were not involved sufficiently in the consultation process.[2]

1.3 (National) Scope of Application

This issue has not been officially discussed, but the regulator's transposition method implicitly deals with this issue.

The adjustment of French regulation to the SD provisions[3] (Articles 5–15) shows that the French regulator restricts its action to extending pre-existing rules (which initially only referred to purely national service providers) to the providers mentioned in the SD (i.e., EU transnational providers). The regulations implementing the SD are limited to business areas covered by the Directive. This means that no general/horizontal standards were promoted.

---

[2] See Senate Report n° 473, pp. 11 and 35, at http://www.senat.fr/noticerap/2008/r08-473-notice.html.

[3] See Article 8 V of Law n° 2008-776 of 4 August 2008 on economic modernisation (the so-called LME) modifying Article 2 of Law n° 94-126 of 11 February 1994 related to individual enterprise initiative applicable as of 1 December 2009. The provision can be consulted at: http://www.legifrance.gouv.fr/affichTexteArticle.do;jsessionid=6EB41D7A3818FE9ADFC25BD5A79A9C12.tpdjo14v_3?idArticle=LEGIARTI000019289117&cidTexte=JORFTEXT000000165840&dateTexte=20091201.

1.4 Incorporation of Transposing Legislation

SD requirements related to administrative proceedings were transposed using *inter alia* regulations, decrees, and sectoral orders. There has been no new codification but, rather, an adaptation of pre-existing rules.

1.5 The Relationship of the Services Directive to Primary EU Law

The relation of the Services Directive and primary EU law has not been discussed.

1.6 Screening

The task force in charge of the SD transposition was given the task of 'screening'. Following Senate report n° 473,[4] the screening took place in summer 2008. No further information is available. There was no specific communication from the regulator on the screening process or the transposition in general.

2 Individual Articles of the Services Directive

2.1 Article 6 SD: Point of Single Contact (POSC)

2.1.1 Establishment of the POSC

POSCs were added to pre-existing centres for business administrative proceedings[5] (*Centres de formalités des entreprises,* or CFE).

According to Article 8 of the French law on economic modernisation, POSC missions were transferred to pre-existing centres for business administrative proceedings. A state council decree n° 2010-210 was adopted to specify the exact missions of the POSCs.[6] However, this decree brings very few changes to the former regulation of the pre-existing centres for business administrative

[4] Consult the report at http://www.senat.fr/noticerap/2008/r08-473-notice.html.

[5] See the official website of the centres for business administrative proceedings at: http://www.entreprises.ccip.fr/web/formalites/accueil.

[6] See Articles R 123-1 through R 123-30 of the Commercial Code (decree n° 2010-210 du 1er mars 2010), available at: http://www.legifrance.gouv.fr/affichCode.do;jsessionid=1A3B2BFF6A113BEFAC2048C833664233.tpdjo11v_3?idSectionTA=LEGISCTA000006161451&cidTexte=LEGITEXT000005634379&dateTexte=20110115.

proceedings.[7] In France, POSCs will have an *electronic* and a *physical* aspect, therefore going beyond the duties laid down in the Directive. The *electronic aspect* involves the creation of a new website that plays the role of a unique virtual point of contact. The *physical aspect* relates to the traditional reception centres in the administrative offices concerned.

2.1.2 Subjective Understanding, Competence Structure

As regards physical points of contacts, France has decided to transfer the new missions of the POSCs to a pre-existing structure: the *centres for businesses administrative proceedings*. Theses centres have not been modified, but their competences have been extended to cross-border providers. There are seven networks of centres for businesses administrative proceedings, depending on the providers' activities (e.g., commercial or industrial etc.).[8] These centres have many offices in French territory. For example, as regards commercial providers, there is one centre per region hosted by the local chamber of commerce. As regards electronic points of contacts, a project for a unique electronic portal (for all types of providers) is being studied. For the time being, it seems that such a portal is only open to commercial and agricultural providers (http://www.cfenet.cci.fr/).

2.1.3 Authorities with POSC-Function

POSCs were created within pre-existing French *centres for businesses administrative proceedings*. These centres are managed by seven different types of organisations,[9] depending on the providers' activities:

- Chambers of commerce and industry
- Chambers of craftsmen
- Chambers of inland water shipping
- Commercial/civil courts and offices
- Health protection offices
- Chambers of agriculture
- Tax offices

---

7 See former Articles R 123-1–R 123-30 of the Commercial Code (decree n° 2007-431 of the 25 march 2007), available at: http://www.legifrance.gouv.fr/affichCode.do;jsessionid=4E9590BF943359A9ADF7DC40F758A58F.tpdjo11v_3?idSectionTA=LEGISCTA000006161451&cidTexte=LEGITEXT000005634379&dateTexte=20100115.

8 See Article R123-3 of the Commercial Code. Providers can consult a summary of existing centres and procedures at: http://annuaire-cfe.insee.fr/AnnuaireCFE/html/MissionCFE.htm.

9 See Article R123-3 of the Commercial Code.

2.1.4 Involvement of Private Partners, Liability of the POSC

The legal forms of POSCs depend on the network to which they are attached. By correlation, the relevant legal regime depends on its legal form.

- Chambers of commerce and industry, chambers of craftsmen, chambers of agriculture and chambers of inland water shipping are all public administrative bodies, and therefore public entities. They are responsible for the POSCs linked to their network. In this case, traditional administrative liability rules apply.
- Commercial/civil courts and offices and tax offices are devolved state administrations. The state is responsible for POSCs linked to courts and tax offices.
- Finally, health protection offices are private legal bodies in charge of administrative public services. Private liability applies here.

Following the traditional continental dichotomy under French law, public (i.e., state) liability falls under administrative rules. Administrative judges have jurisdiction over any related litigation. However, private responsibility falls under private law rules, where civil courts have jurisdiction. Both responsibility regimes share common elements, but the rules are not always identical.[10] This means that three different types of rules are potentially applicable, depending on the network to which the POSCs are linked.

2.2 Article 7 SD: Right to Information

Rights to information already existed, with pre-existing French centres for businesses administrative proceedings. These rights will be extended to transnational providers. The question whether the rights to information should be extended beyond the transnational scope of the Services Directive has not been discussed, given that no general framework was foreseen.

2.3 Article 8 SD: Procedures by Electronic Means

As it stands and as regards those pre-existing French centres for businesses administrative proceedings that are linked to chambers of commerce, proceedings have been fully dematerialised since February 2009. Proceedings to create undertakings/businesses are available online at http://www.cfenet.cci.fr. See all available online proceedings at www.cfenet.cci.fr/mode_emploi (in French only).

For those pre-existing French centres for businesses administrative proceedings that are linked to other types of bodies (other than chambers of commerce), a

[10] See Deguergue (2004), pp. 195–218.

portal is still expected to be set up. It is still unclear whether there will be one unique portal for all types of centres or several coexisting ones. It is also unclear whether or not the dematerialisation of proceedings originates from the SD transposition—this is not mentioned in the current website. The website did exist before the SD transposition but was dedicated to other administrative requirements. Other means of administrative proceedings have not been abolished. Physical points of contacts will remain.

2.4 Article 9 SD: Authorisation Schemes

Given that the screening process has not been transparent and the SD transposition not horizontal, it is very difficult to identify for which specific services the French regulator will ask for an authorisation mechanism to be maintained. We note that some regulations are currently being discussed without any reference to the SD transposition.[11] Nevertheless, the summary report on the transposition of the Directive published by the European Affairs General Secretariat provides information. For those sectors where authorisation is still required, it must be obtained from the authority in charge of the said sector.

Additional regulations adopted after the Directive and that refer to it seem to maintain the authorisation regime.[12] For example, child care centres must be authorised by the administrative commission in charge of child protection. Similarly, public and private hospitals must be authorised by the relevant administration in charge (Law 21 July 2009 on hospital reform).

In other cases, authorisation regimes are maintained but the prerequisites are more lenient.[13] For example, commercial stores must always obtain authorisation from the commission in charge of commercial development (*Commission Départementale d'Aménagement Commercial,* or CEDAC). However, authorisation is no longer compulsory for stores of less than one thousand square metres (previously three hundred square metres before the amendment of the Commercial Code).

---

[11] See, for example, the removal of the position of the Court of Appeals attorney, which will be merged with that of the Attorney General. This reform aims primarily at simplifying the existing system. The SD transposition had a very limited influence on the process. The legislative act is available for consultation at: http://www.assemblee-nationale.fr/13/dossiers/fusion_avocat_avoue_CA.asp.

[12] See, for example, ship renting or ship free lending activities (*arrêté du 15 octobre 2009 modifiant l'arrêté du 25 octobre 2007 relatif aux conditions de conduite des coches de plaisance nolisés et à la délivrance de l'agrément pour leur nolisage*).

[13] See, for example, wildlife shows for which compulsory qualifications certificates were removed (*arrêté du 15 septembre 2009 modifiant l'arrêté du 30 mars 1999 relatif à l'organisation et au fonctionnement de la Commission nationale consultative pour la faune sauvage captive*).

Further horizontal authorisation regimes remain, such as the requirement that all companies register with the commerce and companies register. However, the authorisation for the opening of hotels was removed by the 2008 legislation for economic modernisation.

Finally, we can confirm that the professional prerequisites for some activities are made easier due to the application of the mutual recognition principle and/or have less strict terms of access. For instance, in keeping with the mutual recognition principle, a number of activities, such as tour operators[14] or surveyors,[15] are more accessible.

2.5 Article 10 SD: Conditions for the Granting of Authorisation

2.5.1 Recognition of Requirements

As regards the integration of the mutual recognition principle in connection with the transposition of Article 10 (3) of the SD, no general response can be provided due to the sectoral transpositions and absence of a general framework.

Only a few examples may be given as regards the review of professional prerequisites in view of their adaptation to the freedom to provide services and the freedom of establishment, as reiterated by the SD.[16] In these examples, mutual recognition of access to and performance of activities is compulsory.[17]

For instance, the State council decree n° 2010-561 changes the professional obligations of commercial agents exercising their freedom of providing services in France. As opposed to national providers, cross-border providers—not established in France—do not need any more to declare their activities to the French competent authority.[18]

---

[14] Law n° 2009-888 of 22 July 2009 on the modernisation and development of tourism services.

[15] State council decree n° 2009-696 of 15 June 2009 modifying the surveyor's professional code.

[16] See for example State council decree n° 2010-561 of 27 may 2010 on the implementation of some provisions of the SD.

[17] See for example Law n° 2009-888 of 22 July 2009 on modernisation and the development of tourism services, Sections 5 and 6. On this topic, see Batteur (2010).

[18] See new Article R-134-7 (last paragraph) of the Commercial Code available at: http://www.legifrance.gouv.fr/affichCodeArticle.do;jsessionid=F38A1D06055534C3A469873A46F474B6.tpdjo17v_1?idArticle=LEGIARTI000023379484&cidTexte=LEGITEXT000005634379&dateTexte=20110116.

2.5.2 Granting Authorisations Throughout the Whole National Territory and Exceptions

The issue of granting authorisations throughout the whole national territory has not been discussed.

Under French administrative law, a clear distinction is made between authorisations to conduct a business in a specific field and authorisations to exercise a profession. Those granted to conduct a business in a specific field are usually delivered by local authorities and are only valid in the related local territory. For example, this is the case for child care centres, which must be authorised by the local administrative commission in charge of child protection. These authorisations are not valid throughout the whole national territory. The second type of authorisation is valid for the whole national territory, as in the case for an authorisation to exercise the profession of architect.

2.5.3 Entitlement to Grant Authorisation, Court Review of Administrative Decisions

The mentioned issues have not been discussed. In principle, the discretionary powers of the authorities and any review by the courts vary, depending on the authorisation mechanism.

In the areas where the authorisation regime was modified to transpose the Directive, two situations now coexist. In the first situation, discretionary power was removed (e.g., for travel agents and health professionals). In the second situation, discretionary power was maintained but the authorisation regimes were simplified and transparency improved (e.g., in the area of commercial town planning).

2.5.4 Reasoning of Administrative Decisions

There has been no need to change current regulations in force. A general duty to provide explanations for all negative individual administrative decisions currently exists.

2.5.5 Allocation of Competences

Following the SD transposition, authorisations will be granted by the same administrative authorities, given that transposition of the Directive in France is sectoral. A possible modernisation of authorisations regime may be foreseen.[19]

[19] See, for example, the authorisation regime for tourist guide after Law n° 2009-888 of 22 July 2008 on the modernisation and development of tourism services, Article L 141-3 of the Tourism Code (relocation of competence), and, for the registration of tourism services providers, see the new Article L 141-2 of the Tourism Code.

2.6 Article 11 SD: Duration of Authorisation

The principle of unlimited authorisations was not transposed. Under French law, time-limited authorisations are possible. For example, all authorisations related to the management of centres for children or the elderly are valid for a limited time period of 15 years. Under French law, authorisations without explicit time limitations are, in principle, unlimited when they are *non in personam* (e.g., an authorisation for the opening of commercial stores). Those *in personam* authorisations without explicit time limitations end upon the death of the beneficiary (e.g., authorisation for the exercise of a specific professional activity).

2.7 Article 12 SD: Selection from Among Several Candidates

This issue of possible changes of national law induced by Article 12 SD was not discussed within the sectors on which the transposition focused (e.g., tourism professionals). As regards public contracts and the delegation of public services, French law[20] adopted in view of the transposition of secondary EU law and also French[21] and EU case law[22] already address this point. However, the rules governing several specific areas (e.g., the occupation of state property, or *domaine public et domaine privé des personnes publiques*)[23] might contradict these requirements of candidate selection/competition. This is because the administrative authorities have total discretionary power. There are no requirements for publicity or competitive calls for offers.

[20] See the Public Contract Code (*Code des marchés publics*), http://www.legifrance.gouv.fr/affichCode.do?cidTexte=LEGITEXT000005627819&dateTexte=20091202) and Law n° 93-122 of 29 January 1993 on the fight against corruption and on the transparency of the economic life and of administrative proceedings (so-called law "Sapin") http://www.legifrance.gouv.fr/afficheTexte.do?cidTexte=JORFTEXT000000711604&fastPos=2&fastReqId=465858747&categorieLien=cid&oldAction=rechTexte).

[21] See Conseil d'Etat, 3 November 1997, Million et Marais, http://www.legifrance.gouv.fr/affichJuriAdmin.do?oldAction=rechJuriAdmin&idTexte=CETATEXT000007955138&fastReqId=24529709&fastPos=1).

[22] See ECJ, 7 December 2000, Teleaustria, case C-324/98, and the ECJ's order, 3 December 2001, Bent Mousten Vestergaard, case C-59/00.

[23] See Berthon (2009), p. 483.

2.8 Article 13 SD: Authorisation Procedures

2.8.1 A Priori Determination of the Duration of Administrative Procedures

The duration of an administrative procedure can be set by a legislative text, which is rare, or, more often, by the courts. The duration is set in line with the notion of 'reasonable delay'. For the time being, most sectoral transposition acts do not foresee specific time limits for authorisation procedures.[24] A limited number of transposition acts include specific time limits for the validity of authorisation procedures. This is the case for commercial town planning, where decisions must be made by the relevant authority within a limited period of time. There can be no tacit authorisations, unless allowed by a specific text.

2.8.2 General Rule for the Duration

There are no rules on the length of administrative procedures. There is no plan to establish any.

2.8.3 Tacit Authorisation in the National Legal Order So Far

Tacit authorisation has not been usual in French administrative law.

If there is no reply from the administration for a period of two months, this signifies, in principle, that the request has been denied, except if regulated differently by a specific text. It is worth mentioning that there are more and more exceptions to this rule. However, this does not cover the full scope of the SD. There is no general tacit authorisation regime. In principle, under French administrative law, tacit authorisation mechanisms are treated as conflicting with the rights of third parties (a key principle of administrative law). In this context, tacit authorisation mechanisms can only be allowed if provided for by a specific sectoral derogatory provision.

2.8.4 Further Information on Tacit Authorisation

There are no further aspects on tacit authorisation which are worth mentioning in the context of the SD transposition.

We are of the opinion that Article 13 (4) of the SD could not have any direct effect. No reasonable delay is foreseen by the text, which shows that much room for interpretation is left to the Member States. Additionally, if the EU and national laws do not foresee any specific delay, direct effect is therefore impossible.

---

[24] See, for example, Law n° 2009-888 of 22 July 2008 on the modernisation and development of tourism services, which does not foresee any legal delay for the administrative proceeding.

2.9 Articles 14, 15, 16 SD

Due to the lack of information on the screening process, we cannot provide an answer to the question whether the national legislator did identify the need to adapt national law according to these provisions of the Services Directive or not.

French law may be in contradiction with several requirements of the SD (Articles 14–16), for instance, as regards the establishment or residence requirements to obtain access authorisations. We can therefore anticipate further sectoral modifications on these points.[25] This is especially the case for travel agents. For some other sectors, burdensome requirements of access and professional exercise were retained despite some legal adaptations (e.g., for accounting experts[26]).

2.10 Articles 14–19, 22–27 SD

Again due to a lack of transparency of the transposition process no further discussions are perceptible.

2.11 Articles 28 *ff.* SD: Administrative Cooperation

Aspects related to administrative cooperation have been transposed by Law n° 2010-853 of 23 July 2010 on the networks of the chambers of commerce, commerce, craft industry and services. This law includes a specific chapter VII transposing provisions on transnational administrative assistance called "administrative and criminal cooperation in the field of services".[27]

The provisions transposing the chapter related to administrative cooperation follow strictly the SD.[28] The provisions notably include:

- A general principle of cooperation between competent French authorities and competent authorities of other EU and EEA Member States.

---

[25] See State council decree n° 2010-561 of 27 May 2010 on the implementation of some provisions of the SD.

[26] See changes to the pre-requisites and conditions to perform the activities of accounting expert by law n° 2010-853 of 23 July 2010 on the networks of the chambers of commerce, commerce, craft industry and services. On that topic, see "Assouplissement des modalités d'exercice de la profession d'expert-comptable", La Semaine judirique Entreprise et Affaires, n° 35, 2 Sept 2010, Act. 447.

[27] See Article 32 and consecutive articles of law n° 2010-853.

[28] See Senat report n° 507 (2009–2010) from Gérard Cornu, 27 may 2010, available at: http://www.senat.fr/rap/l09-507/l09-507.html.

- The possibility for French competent authorities to collect information on the conditions under which a services provider established in France conducts his activities.
- A duty to inform the European Commission and other EU and EEA Member States of any conduct or specific acts by a provider established in France or which provides services in France that could cause serious damage to the health or safety of persons or to the environment.
- A duty to respond to any information requests and requests to carry out any checks, inspections and investigations from other EU and EEA Member States.

Additionally, a system of electronic communication is created for French competent authorities to respond to information requests addressed by other EU and EEA Member States.

There has been no rearrangement of provisions for administrative assistance in general.

The law n° 2010-853 of 23 July 2010 on the networks of the chambers of commerce, commerce, craft industry and services amends the Criminal proceedings Code to allow the circulation of data on criminal records in cases mentioned by the Directive. Other elements are already covered by regulation n° 78-17 of 1978 on personal data protection. In accordance with that regulation, French competent authorities must respect the confidentiality of all information exchanged on services providers with the European Commission and other EU and EEA Member States.

2.12 Problems and Discourses on Administrative Cooperation

No problems or discourses were perceptible, except for the late transposition, as mentioned above.

3 Assessment of the Impact of the Services Directive

As mentioned previously, this is not the case in France, where the impact of the transposition has been reduced as much as possible. This is because of the extremely negative impact of the Bolkenstein's Directive on French public opinion and fears of social dumping, which led to a cautious and discreet transposition.

From this perspective, no gold-plating is foreseen. Where possible, French authorities have preferred to adapt existing mechanisms rather than create new processes. This also explains the absence of a general transposition framework in favour of sectoral reviews, which are included in wider reforms (such as the law on economic modernisation, the law on hospital reform, and the law on judicial and legal professions), avoiding wide media coverage. Such a method is not in breach of the Directive as such but certainly goes against its objective, since the expected simplification has not yet been achieved. Some time is needed before all transposition acts are adopted. A post-reconstruction might shed more light on the overall reform.

References

For legislation, jurisprudence and websites please refer to 1.1 of the report and footnotes directly.

Batteur A (2010) La règlementation applicable à la vente de voyages et de séjours depuis l'entrée en vigueur de la loi du 22 Juillet 2009 et de ses décrets d'application. Revue de droit des transports n° 5, Mai 2010, étude 6

Berthon G (2009) Le Régime de passation des concessions domaniales à la croisée des chemins. Revue française de droit administratif (RFDA), p 483

Bizet J (2007–2008) Rapport d'information fait au nom de la commission des affaires européennes sur l'état de la transposition de la 'directive services', n° 199 du 7 février 2008. Available at: http://www.senat.fr/noticerap/2007/r07-199-notice.html

Bizet J (2008–2009), Rapport d'information fait au nom de la commission des affaires européennes sur l'état de la transposition de la 'directive services', n° 473 du 17 juin 2009. Available at: http://www.senat.fr/noticerap/2008/r08-473-notice.html

Cornu G (2009–2010), Senat report n° 507 from 27 may 2010. Available at: http://www.senat.fr/rap/l09-507/l09-507.html

Deguergue M (2004) L'Exhorbitance du droit de la responsabilité administrative. In: Melleray F (ed) L'Exhorbitance du droit administratif en question(s). Librairie Générale de Droit et de Jurisprudence (LGDJ), Paris, pp 195–218

Palasz M-J (2009) Le défi de la transposition de la directive services: une chance à saisir. Courrier juridique des finances et de l'industrie, n° 55, premier trimestre, pp 45–49

Secrétariat Général des Affaires Européennes (SGAE) (2010) Directive 2006/123 CE relative aux services dans le marché intérieur—Rapport de synthèse sur la transposition, 20 janvier 2010. Available at: http://www.sgae.gouv.fr/gcp/webdav/site/sgae-internet-sgae/shared/03_Autorites_FR_et_UE/Autres-positions/Directive_services/201001-Rapport_synthese_dir_services.pdf

La Semaine judirique Entreprise et Affaires (2010) n° 35, 2 September 2010, Act. 447. Assouplissement des modalités d'exercice de la profession d'expert-comptable

The Implementation of the Services Directive in Germany

Michael Mirschberger

1 General Remarks on the Transposition Strategy and General Comprehension of the Implementation

1.1 Main References Used in this Research

ON FEDERATION LEVEL

Viertes Gesetz zur Änderung verwaltungsverfahrensrechtlicher Vorschriften (4. VwVfÄndG), Gesetz vom 11.12.2008—Bundesgesetzblatt Teil I 2008 Nr. 58, 17.12.2008, S. 2418 [Fourth law on changing the Administrative Procedures Law].

Gesetz zur Umsetzung der Dienstleistungsrichtlinie im Gewerberecht und in weiteren Rechtsvorschriften, Gesetz vom 17.07.2009—Bundesgesetzblatt Teil I 2009 Nr. 44, 24.07.2009, S. 2091 [Law on implementing the Services Directive in the German Trade, Commerce and Industry Regulation Act (GewO) and further legal acts].

Gesetz zur Umsetzung der Dienstleistungsrichtlinie auf dem Gebiet des Umweltrechts sowie zur Änderung umweltrechtlicher Vorschriften, Gesetz vom 11.08.2010—Bundesgesetzblatt Teil I 2010 Nr. 43, 17.08.2010, S. 1163 [act on

Michael Mirschberger, Ass. Jur., during the research project, research assistant at the Chair of Public Law, German and European Administrative Law (Prof. Dr. U. Stelkens), German University of Administrative Sciences Speyer and at the German Research Institute for Public Administration Speyer (mirschberger@foev-speyer.de). For valuable discussions on the draft of this report I thank Joachim Kliemann, Administration of the Senator for Interior and Sport of the federal state of Berlin. For valuable support I thank Mrs. Ohliger. The report is based on the implementation in June 2010, partially up-dated later on.

M. Mirschberger (✉)
German Research Institute for Public Administration Speyer, Speyer, Germany
e-mail: mirschberger@foev-speyer.de

U. Stelkens et al. (eds.), *The Implementation of the EU Services Directive*,
DOI: 10.1007/978-90-6704-840-8_11,

implementation of the Services Directive in environmental law and other changes of environmental provisions].

Verordnung über Informationspflichten für Dienstleistungserbringer—Dienstleistungs-Informationspflichten-Verordnung—DL-InfoV, Verordnung vom 12.02.2010, Bundesgesetzblatt Teil I 2010 Nr. 11, 17.03.2010, S. 267 [statutory instrument on information obligations of service providers].

Verordnung zur Umsetzung der Dienstleistungsrichtlinie auf dem Gebiet des Umweltrechts sowie zur Änderung umweltrechtlicher Vorschriften, Verordnung vom 09.11.2010—Bundesgesetzblatt Teil I 2010 Nr. 56, 15.11.2010, S. 1504 [statutory instrument on implementation of the Services Directive in environmental law and other changes of environmental provisions].

Verordnung zur Anpassung gewerberechtlicher Verordnungen an die Dienstleistungsrichtlinie, Verordnung vom 09.03.2010, Bundesgesetzblatt Teil I 2010 Nr. 11, 17.03.2010, S. 264 [statutory instrument on adoption of statutory instruments based on the German Trade, Commerce and Industry Regulation Act to the requirements of the Services Directive].

Achtundachtzigste Verordnung zur Änderung der Außenwirtschaftsverordnung, Verordnung vom 08.12.2009, Bundesanzeiger—Amtlicher Teil, Nr. 188, 11.12.2009, S. 4180 f. [statutory instrument on changing the statutory instrument on foreign trade].

ON FEDERAL STATE LEVEL
Baden Wuertemberg

Gesetz zur Änderung des Landesverwaltungsverfahrensgesetzes und anderer Gesetze vom 30.07.2009, BW GVBl 2009, S. 363

Gesetz über Einheitliche Ansprechpartner für das Land Baden-Württemberg (EAG BW) vom 01.12.2009, BW GVBl 2009, S. 679-681; Bekanntmachung des WM GBl 2010, S. 33

Free State of Bavaria

Gesetz zur Änderung des Bayerischen Verwaltungsverfahrensgesetzes und anderer Rechtsvorschriften vom 27.07.2009 Bay GVBl 2009, S. 367-379

Gesetz über die Zuständigkeit für die Aufgaben des Einheitlichen Ansprechpartners im Freistaat Bayern (Bayerisches EA-Gesetz—BayEAG) vom 22.12.2009, Bay GVBl 2009, S. 626

Ausführungsverordnung Einheitlicher Ansprechpartner (AVBayEAG) vom 28.04.2010, Bay GVBl 2010, S. 224

Gewerbedurchführungsverordnung (GewerbedurchführungsVO—GewV) vom 09.02.2010 Bay GVBl 2010, S. 103

Berlin

Gesetz zur Umsetzung der Richtlinie 2006/123/EG über Dienstleistungen im Binnenmarkt vom 18.11.2009, Bln GVBl 2009, S. 674

Gesetz über den Einheitlichen Ansprechpartner für das Land Berlin (EAG Bln) vom 18.11.2009, Bln GVBl 2009, S. 674

Dienstleistungsrichtlinie-Ausführungsverordnung (DLR-VBundR) vom 15.12.2009, Bln GVBl 2009, S. 843, corr. 2010, S. 198

Brandenburg

Gesetz zur Einführung des Einheitlichen Ansprechpartners für das Land Brandenburg und zur Änderung weiterer Vorschriften vom 07.07.2009, Bbg GVBl 2009, S. 262-271

Gesetz über den Einheitlichen Ansprechpartner für das Land Brandenburg (BbgEAPG) vom 07.07.2009, Bbg GVBl 2009, S. 262-264

Bremen

Gesetz zur Änderung des Bremischen Verwaltungsverfahrensgesetzes vom 03.11.2009, BremGbl. 2009, S. 446-448

Mitteilung des Senats zur "Umsetzung der EU-Dienstleistungsrichtlinie (EU-DLR) im Land Bremen—Verortung der Einheitlichen Ansprechpartner" vom 02.06.2009, LT-Drs. 17/813

Hamburg

Siebtes Gesetz zur Änderung des Hamburgischen Verwaltungsverfahrensgesetzes vom 07.04.2009, HmbGVBl 2009, S. 113-114 [law on changing federal state Administrative Procedures Law]

Hamburgisches Gesetz zur Umsetzung der Europäischen Dienstleistungsrichtlinie und über weitere Rechtsanpassungen vom 15.12.2009, HmbgGVBl 2009, S. 444-450

Hamburgisches Gesetz über die Durchführung der Aufgaben des Einheitlichen Ansprechpartners (HmbEAG) vom 15.12.2009, HmbgGVBl 2009, S. 444-445

Hesse

Gesetz zur Änderung verwaltungsverfahrens- und verwaltungskostenrechtlicher Vorschriften vom 09.07.2009, Hesse GVBl 2009, S. 253-255 [law on changing federal state Administrative Procedures Law]

Hessisches Gesetz zur Umsetzung der Richtlinie 2006/123/EG des Europäischen Parlaments und des Rates vom 12. Dezember 2006 über Dienstleistungen im Binnenmarkt und zur Änderung von Rechtsvorschriften vom 15.12.2009, Hesse GVBl 2009, S. 716-728

Gesetz über den Einheitlichen Ansprechpartner Hessen (EAHG-Gesetz—EAHG) vom 15.12.2009, Hesse GVBl 2009, S. 717-718

Mecklenburg–Western Pomerania

Gesetz zur verwaltungsrechtlichen Umsetzung der EG-Dienstleistungsrichtlinie in das Landsrecht von Mecklenburg-Vorpommern (EG-DLRG M-V) vom 02.12.2009, M-V GVBl. 2009, S. 666-671

Gesetz zur Umsetzung der Richtlinie 2006/123/EG über Dienstleistungen im Binnenmarkt in Mecklenburg-Vorpommern vom 17.12.2009, M-V GVBl 2009, S. 729-737

Gesetz zur Errichtung von Stellen mit der Bezeichnung "Einheitlicher Ansprechpartner" und zur Übertragung von Aufgaben auf die Wirtschaftskammern-(Einheitlicher-Ansprechpartner-Errichtungsgesetz Mecklenburg-Vorpommern) (EAPG M-V) vom 17.12.2009, M-V GVBl 2009, S. 729-731

Lower Saxony

Gesetz zur Änderung verwaltungsverfahrensrechtlicher Vorschriften vom 24.09.2009, NS GVBl 2009, S. 361

Niedersächsisches Gesetz über Einheitliche Ansprechpartner (NEAG) vom 16.12.2009, NS GVBl 2009, S. 481

North Rhine-Westphalia

Gesetz zur Änderung verwaltungsverfahrens-, zustellung- und gebührenrechtlicher Regelungen zur Umsetzung der EU-Dienstleistungsrichtlinie in das Landesrecht Nordrhein-Westfalen und weiterer Anpassungen vom 12.05.2009, NRW GVBl 2009, S. 269-298

Gesetz zur Bildung Einheitlicher Ansprechpartner in Nordrhein-Westfalen (EA-Gesetz NRW) vom 08.12.2009, NRW GVBl 2009, S. 748-750

Verordnung zur Anpassung dienstleistungsrelevanter Verfahren an die EG-Dienstleistungsrichtlinie (Dienstleistungsrichtlinien-Anpassungsverordnung – DLRL-AnpV) von 12.01.2010, NRW GVBl 2010, S. 24.

Rhineland-Palatinate

Erstes Landesgesetz zur Umsetzung der Richtlinie 2006/123/EG des Europäischen Parlaments und des Rates vom 12. Dezember 2006 über Dienstleistungen im Binnenmarkt vom 27.10.2009, RhP GVBl 2009, S. 355-357

Zweites Landesgesetz zur Umsetzung der Richtlinie 2006/123/EG des Europäischen Parlaments und des Rates vom 12. Dezember 2006 über Dienstleistungen im Binnenmarkt vom 27.10.2009, RhP GVBl 2009, S. 358-363

Landesgesetz über die einheitlichen Ansprechpartner in Verwaltungsangelegenheiten vom 27.10.2009, RhP GVBl 2009, S. 355-356

Saarland

Gesetz zur Änderung des Saarländischen Verwaltungsverfahrensgesetzes vom 11.03.2009, Amtsblatt Saarland 2009, S. 674

Verordnung über die Bestimmung der Zuständigkeit als Einheitlicher Ansprechpartner nach der Richtlinie 2006/123/EG des Europäischen Parlaments und des Rates über Dienstleistungen im Binnenmarkt vom 19.01.2010, Amtsblatt Saarland 2010, S. 8 [valid until 31.07.2010]

Saxony

Gesetz zur Umsetzung der Dienstleistungsrichtlinie im Freistaat Sachsen (Sächsisches Dienstleistungsrichtliniengesetz—SächsDRG) vom 13.08.2009, Sächs GVBl 2009, S. 438-445

Gesetz über den Einheitlichen Ansprechpartner im Freistaat Sachsen (SächsEAG) vom 13.08.2009, Sächs GVBl 2009, S. 446-447

Saxony-Anhalt

Gesetzes zur Umsetzung der EG-Dienstleistungsrichtlinie in Sachsen-Anhalt vom 16.12.2009, LSA GVBl 2009, S. 700

Gesetz über den einheitlichen Ansprechpartner, zur Regelung der europäischen Verwaltungszusammenarbeit sowie zur verwaltungskostenrechtlichen Umsetzung der europäischen Dienstleistungsrichtlinie in Sachsen-Anhalt (Einheitlicher-Ansprechpartner-Gesetz—EAG LSA) vom 16.12.2009, LSA GVBl 2009, S. 700

Schleswig–Holstein

Gesetz zur Änderung des Landesverwaltungsgesetzes, des Landesmeldegesetzes und des Landesstatistikgesetzes vom 17.09.2009, SH GVBl 2009, S. 573-576

Gesetz über die Errichtung einer Anstalt öffentlichen Rechts "Einheitlicher Ansprechpartner Schleswig–Holstein" (Errichtungsgesetz Einheitlicher Ansprechpartner) vom 17.09.2009, SH GVBl 2009 S.577-582

Thuringia

Thüringer Gesetz zur Umsetzung der Richtlinie 2006/123/EG des Europäischen Parlaments und des Rates vom 12. Dezember 2006 über Dienstleistungen im Binnenmarkt vom 08.07.2009, Th GVBl 2009, S. 592-603

Gesetz über die Errichtung einer einheitlichen Stelle nach dem Thüringer Verwaltungsverfahrensgesetz und zur Umsetzung des Artikels 6 der Richtlinie 2006/123/EG (Thüringer ES-Errichtungsgesetz) vom 08.07.2009, Th GVBl 2009, S. 596-598

For further explanatory documents, e.g., parliamentary documents throughout the legislation process and journal articles, please see the List of References.

1.2 Impact of the Services Directive

1.2.1 Profound Cause of Changes to National Law?

In Germany, one can say prima facie, that the implementation of the Services Directive (SD) potentially could trigger simplification, modernisation and acceleration of administration, or better administrative proceedings, on the legislative level.

On the level of the Federation, implementation of the SD has been used to promote changes in administrative law which have long been sought but could not be carried out.[1] This might explain why, as regards the implementation of procedural requirements of the SD, there has not been a one-to-one implementation; this represents a decisive deviation from the former principle of one-to-one transposition of directives in Germany. This principle has been adhered to strictly in the past. The SD yields an important improvement in this context. Hence, the SD has been transposed into German law beyond its minimum requirements. The scope of application of the new rules and regulations implementing the SD has been extended to domestic service providers or potentially even to citizens, at least with respect to procedural requirements. Generally, novel and generally applicable rights and procedures have been introduced into German law in accordance with the rules and requirements of the SD. Accordingly, innovations in general administrative law become an occasion and a cause for modernising parts of the statutes on administrative proceedings.[2] Several rules in the Administrative Procedures Law (Verwaltungsverfahrensgesetz—VwVfG) have been altered and adapted. These legislative adaptations were always implemented as general rules, not limited to the scope of the SD, but are basically applicable to all fields of administrative law/proceedings.

It must be mentioned that, due to the federal system of governance in Germany, implementation must occur on several different levels: the community level, the federal state level, and the Federation level and beyond, also on the level of different chambers. The "legislators" on these levels, competent with respect to implementation in their fields, tried to implement the requirements of the SD using a common approach, but this approach has in some ways failed, as will be described later in this document.[3]

1.2.2 Involvement in the Transposition Process

The transposition process in Germany has been quite complex, due to Germany's federal system and the fact that most administrative proceedings are subject to the legislation of the sixteen "Bundesländer" (federal states). Steady coordination has therefore been necessary. Despite the federal state system, the Federal Ministry of

---

1 U. Stelkens, in: Stelkens et al. (2011/2012), Europarecht para 239; Compare also BR-Drs. 284/1/09, 7.

2 Schliesky (2008), 30 ff.

3 See also Schliesky (2010b), 1 ff., 3 ff., 15 ff.

Economics and Technology took, together with the so-called Conference of Ministers of Economics,[4] the decisive supervising position in the implementation process.[5]

This constellation of supervision indicates the huge necessity for coordination between the federal states and the federal government/legislator. In several steps,[6] the Conference of Ministers of Economics decided on decisive points of the implementation process and decided in its session of December 7th/8th, 2006 in Dessau[7] to mandate the so-called "Bund-Länder-Ausschuss Dienstleistungswirtschaft" (Committee of the Federation and the Federal States on Service Economy) to supervise the implementation process for the Conference and to report on the proceedings.

Aside from the federal states and the "Bund" (Federation), municipalities and various chambers and their corresponding organisations had to be involved in the implementation process. In addition, NGOs and other affected institutions have been involved in the normal way of consultation on new laws.[8]

Thus, one can say that the federal system in Germany, which provides different legislative competences for the implementation process, led to close and regular cooperation on all levels of administration. This cooperation consisted of several level-groups and was in some ways hierarchically structured. This included the cooperation of the Federation and the federal states (Conference of Ministers of Economics and Conference of the Minister-Presidents of the Federal States), and cooperation within the federal states organised by the federal state governments coequal with the municipalities and chambers. At all levels of the process, all other

---

[4] An assembly of all Federal State Ministers of Economics deciding on common economic policies.

[5] Decision of the Federal Government (Chancellor Dr. Angela Merkel) and the Minister-Presidents Conference of December 19th 2007 at a common conference in Berlin. Inter alia see: BT-Drs. 17/728, 2.

[6] Decisions and reports on the implementation of the SD at the sessions at Eisenach (June 4th/5th 2007), Darmstadt (November 19th/20th 2007), Regensburg (June 9th/10th 2008), Weimar (December 15th/16th 2008), Potsdam (June 18th/19th 2009), Lübeck (December 14th/15th 2009); all available at http://www.bundesrat.de/cln_171/nn_8796/DE/gremien-konf/fachministerkonf/wmk/wmk-termine.html. (All Websites in this report have been checked in July 2011 again).

[7] Protocol of the decisions of this session available at: http://www.bundesrat.de/cln_171/DE/gremien-konf/fachministerkonf/wmk/Sitzungen/06-12-07-08-WMK/06-12-07-08-beschluesse,templateId=raw,property=publicationFile.pdf/06-12-07-08-beschluesse.pdf.

[8] See e.g., BT-Drs. 17/728, 7 ff.

affected ministries of the Federation and the federal states and their corresponding national conferences[9] have been informed and involved, as far as is appropriate.[10]

1.3 (National) Scope of Application

1.3.1 Scope of the Services Directive

In Germany, most legal scholars assume that the SD is directly applicable only to transnational, not domestic, services and establishments. This is based on the general argument that the competences of the European Union are limited to transnational services in this particular case.[11]

Furthermore, Recital 5 underlines this perception, as it states that the SD aims for the removal of barriers in the internal market, i.e., the transnational context is stressed.

Moreover, the principle of conferred powers in EU Law demands a legal basis for the SD, which is derived from Articles 49, 56, 53 (2), 62 TFEU (former: Articles 43, 49, 47 (2), 55 ECT).[12] Whether Article 53 (2) TFEU can also be seen as a basis for legal actions in purely domestic cases[13] has not been widely discussed during the implementation process. Apparently, only Luch and Schulz discuss this problem intensively.[14] The German legislator seems to be aware of

---

[9] In Germany's political system there is regularly an assembly of the ministries of corresponding policy sectors of the states together with the federal minister in this sector (Sector-Specific Conferences of Ministers). These conferences are not government bodies but are essential links between the federal government and the responsibilities of the different state governments. Thus unity on important topics can be achieved. One sector-specific conference is the Conference of Ministers of Economics (the single ministries might have different notations, decisive is their competence for economy policy, justice…). The conferences are usually prepared by the Head Civil Servant of each ministry. They meet shortly before the conference and prepare the conference of the ministers. This group is in turn supported by special mixed committees of experts of the states and the federation.

[10] Statement of the Conference of Ministries of Economics: Protocol of the session in Darmstadt 2007, on topic 2.1, p. 3 (http://www.bundesrat.de/cln_171/DE/gremien-konf/fachministerkonf/wmk/Sitzungen/07-11-19-20-WMK/07-11-19-20-beschluesse,templateId=raw,property=publicationFile.pdf/07-11-19-20-beschluesse.pdf); Protocol of the session in Weimar 2008, on topic 2.1, p. 1 (http://www.bundesrat.de/DE/gremien-konf/fachministerkonf/wmk/Sitzungen/08-12-15-16-WMK/08-12-15-16-beschluesse,templateId=raw,property=publicationFile.pdf/08-12-15-16-beschluesse.pdf).

[11] Compare representative: Schmitz and Prell (2009a), 2; Windoffer (2007), 496, fn. 4; against a purely transnational perception: obviously Commision Handbook under 5. and 6.; Luch and Schulz (2008a), 33 ff., 38 ff.

[12] Streinz (2008), 97; Streinz and Leible, in: Schlachter and Ohler (2008), Introduction para 24.

[13] This is controversially discussed: Streinz (2003), Article 47 EGV para 12, fn.23.

[14] Luch and Schulz (2008a), 33 ff.

this discussion but does not go into any further detail about it.[15] In accordance with the great emphasis the German legislator places upon the fact that the procedural requirements of the SD (especially in regard to Article 6 SD) are transposed into German law in a general way, which means that these regulations are applicable for domestic service providers as well, one can suppose that the legislator shares, in the end, the perception of most scholars in this field. Otherwise, emphasising this instance would be obsolete, as it is binding.

1.3.2 Application of Transposing Legislation to Domestic Service Providers and Beyond

The German legislator transposed the requirements of the SD regarding administrative procedures (Articles 5 to 8 SD), as mentioned above, in a very general way. The changes were implemented by the Fourth Law on changing the Administrative Procedures Law,[16] passed at the end of 2008.

The directive's requirements were mainly implemented by creating new rights and procedures in the codified general provisions of administrative law, in particular, the Administrative Procedures Law. Based on this general approach of procedural requirements transposition, the German legislation allows not only transnational service providers, but also domestic service providers[17] and, even beyond that, potentially every citizen (in case a specific administrative law statute refers to the new provisions) to claim these new rights and procedures. This effect is accomplished by implementing, especially as regards Article 6 SD, new and general means of administrative procedure by introducing the new §§ 71a-71e VwVfG into the Administrative Procedures Law. This approach of transposition has the advantage of providing basic rules which are applicable to everyone—even outside the assumed scope of the SD—whenever a specific administrative law (e.g., the German Trade, Commerce and Industry Regulation Act) refers to these general procedural provisions. Hence, constant repetition through repeated introduction of the same regulations in every specific administrative law could be prevented.[18] This guideline of implementation strategy has also been used with respect to implementation of tacit (fictitious) authorisation, the duration of administrative procedures, and certain rights to information.[19]

---

[15] BT-Drs. 16/10493, 12: "... zumindest für grenzüberschreitende Sachverhalte ..." ("at least for transnational cases").

[16] Viertes Gesetz zur Änderung verwaltungsverfahrensrechtlicher Vorschriften (4. VwVfÄndG), Gesetz vom 11.12.2008—Bundesgesetzblatt Teil I 2008 Nr. 58, 17.12.2008, 2418.

[17] Only one federal state did not provide equal treatment to domestic service providers and deviated from this principle in general for the POSC procedure: Bavaria; compare: BayLT-Drs. 16/2627, 1, 5; this is often also reported for the Free State of Saxony, but to my view § 1 s. 3 SächsEAG opposes that point of view. Compare also SächsLT-Drs. 4/14874, B. § 1 zu Satz 3.

[18] On this complex see inter alia BT-Drs. 16/10493, 1, 12 ff.; Schmitz and Prell (2009a), 3.

[19] Besides §§ 71a-71e VwVfG, also § 42a VwVfG and § 25 VwVfG. More on this topic later on.

Furthermore, it should be stated here that the above-mentioned extensions of the scope of the SD and the general approach of implementation are only applied where possible and useful. Accordingly, there is still a difference, as regards the implementation of non-procedural requirements, between domestic and transnational service providers (e.g. in regard to Article 16 SD).[20] As is evident below, there are several provisions of the German Trade, Commerce and Industry Regulation Act (Gewerbeordnung—GewO) that are no longer applied to transnational service providers, but that are still valid for domestic service providers. Thus, in this regard there has been no change to domestic service providers, this is reasoned by the fact that service providers of other Member States are already subject to the establishment regulations of their own Member State, whereas for German service providers, these regulations are in fact the business requirements of their Member State and hence their own establishment requirements.[21] In some ways the originally abolished "principle of the home country" is, in this way, still perceptible.[22]

1.4 Incorporation of Transposing Legislation

Implementation in accordance with administrative proceeding requirements has been introduced, as mentioned above, by establishing a new section in the pre-existing Administrative Procedures Law. This section (§§ 71a-71e VwVfG) provides a new type of procedure with its own procedural rights.

The specific administrative laws within the scope of the SD (e.g., the German Trade, Commerce and Industry Regulation Act) must declare the new section applicable by reference; other administrative laws (e.g., planning laws) may also refer to it. In the latter case, it depends on the discretion of the legislator whether the new provisions apply or not. Thus, the new administrative procedure prompted by the implementation of the SD may be applied in relation to citizens and even in contexts outside the SD's scope of application.

Accordingly, the new administrative procedure fits well into existing administrative legislation in Germany, which consists of general codification on procedures (Administrative Procedures Law) and specific administrative laws regulating special fields of administration via provision for material standards and/or peculiar procedural rules in addition to general rules. Hence, for transposition of the SD and its procedural requirements, there has been no implementation via separate codification; rather, there is incorporation into existing administrative law via amendment of such laws.

[20] This seems quite clear, but as it differs from the general approach it should be mentioned. The Commission Handbook agrees in 7.1.2.

[21] BT-Drs. 16/12784, 12; Schönleiter (2009), 386.

[22] See Streinz and Leible, in: Schlachter and Ohler (2008), Introduction para 30 ff.

As regards non-procedural requirements, a homogeneous implementation such as this is missing. The German GewO is based on a broad approach for business conduct in Germany.[23] Indeed it is a sectoral act, but in fact it covers most parts of business conduct regulated by administrative law. Given this, the legislator apparently tried to implement the requirements using a horizontal approach within one field of specific administrative law, especially the German GewO.[24]

1.5 The Relationship of the Services Directive to Primary EU Law

The relation of the SD and primary EU Law has been discussed in Germany, but not extensively. Only a few publications deal explicitly with this topic and it seems that this question is not regarded as problematic—despite one exception.

Due to the small number of publications on this matter[25] the opinion on the mentioned relation is as follows:[26]

The SD is a specification of primary EU Law, in concreto of Articles 49 and 56 TFEU. Therefore, the SD must be assessed and interpreted in light of primary EU Law and corresponding jurisdiction of the Court of Justice of the European Union (ECJ). Despite this basic assessment, the SD, as a special distinction of primary law, is seen as paramount. This rests on the basic principle of "lex specialis derogat legi generali" which, as applied in this particular case, means that as long as the provisions of the SD are in harmony with primary EU Law, the SD is the terminal source of law for its scope. This again is based on the assessment that the SD is, within its scope, a terminal codification for the field of services. In doubtful cases, the provisions of the SD must be interpreted strictly in concert with primary EU Law.[27]

Regarding these basic principles, roughly speaking, there is only one particular article of the SD under discussion: Article 16 SD. This discussion arises (and by the way the European legislator should have known this and given more help in this regard), as Article 16 (1) sp. 3, (3) SD restricts the current jurisdiction of the ECJ in respect of "overriding reasons to the public interest".[28] Although the SD itself does in several cases allow the whole scale of overriding reasons to the public interest (e.g., Article 9 (1) lit.b) SD), regarding the freedom to provide services (Article 16 SD) the justifications for national requirements for services

---

[23] Inter alia Tettinger et al. (2011), Introduction para 1–3.

[24] Compare BT-Drs. 16/12784, 9; Mann (2009), 94.

[25] Especially one commentary on the SD: Streinz and Leible, in: Schlachter and Ohler (2008), Introduction para 67 ff.; see also Streinz (2008), 97 ff.

[26] For all following assessment see: Streinz and Leible, in: Schlachter and Ohler (2008), Introduction para 67 ff.

[27] Streinz and Leible, in: Schlachter and Ohler (2008), Introduction para 85 ff.

[28] See Recital 40 and Article 4 no. 8 SD.

provision are restricted to four: reasons of public policy, reasons of public security, reasons of public health, and protection of the environment.

However, this restriction is not seen as problematic with respect to the relation of the SD to primary EU Law, because for the service provider this restriction is in fact not a restriction, but an enlargement of its freedom to provide services.[29] From the point of view of the service provider, the SD minimises the possibility of national requirements obstructing its freedom to provide services. Hence, the service provider's freedom is enlarged, not neutralised[30] Article 16 (1) sp. 3, (3) SD therefore is in harmony with Article 56 TFEU. Given the considerations described above, recourse to primary EU Law regarding further requirements justifying overriding reasons in the public interest is not possible. This is only assessed different in the case of Article 17 SD, as this exception of Article 16 SD should not annul the application of Article 56 TFEU.[31]

Instead of discussing the relation of the SD to primary EU Law, there have been more discussions about the relationship of the SD and the Directive on the recognition of professional qualifications[32] and labour law in general.[33]

1.6 Screening

The SD commits the Member States in several articles to review national legislation in regard to its compatibility with the requirements of the SD. The fundamental statement in this context is found in Article 5 SD, especially Article 5 (1) SD. As the title states, Article 5 SD aims for "simplification of procedures" in the Member States' national laws. This very broad and vague formulation must be substantiated by other provisions of the SD.[34] These specifications are general in nature: Article 9 (2) SD, Article 10 SD, Article 11 SD, Article 12 SD, Article 13 SD, of course Article 14 SD, and with confirming screen order Article 15, (1) SD, Article 16 SD, Article 19 SD, and Article 24 (1) SD.

Because of its federal system, Germany had to bear a huge burden in this regard.[35] Besides federal administrative law, all laws affected by the scope of the

---

29 Streinz and Leible, in: Schlachter and Ohler (2008), Introduction para 85 ff.

30 Streinz and Leible, in: Schlachter and Ohler (2008), Introduction para 85 ff.

31 Streinz and Leible, in: Schlachter and Ohler (2008), Introduction para 85 ff.; different emphasis, but according to this question consenting: Korte (2007), 252 ff.

32 Directive 2005/36/EC of the European Parliament and of the Council of 7 September 2005 on the recognition of professional qualifications, OJ L no. 255 of 30.09.2005, 22-142.

33 See Schlachter, in: Schlachter and Ohler (2008), Before Article 19 SD; Körner (2007), 233 ff.

34 Ziekow and Windoffer, in: Schlachter and Ohler (2008), Article 5 SD para 2, 3.

35 Falke (2009), 199 ff., 211 ff.; very illustrative also the presentation of the Committee of the Federation and the States on Service Economy, 28.02.2008, available at: http://www.dienstleisten-leicht-gemacht.de/DLR/Redaktion/PDF/normenpruefung-verstehen-und-durchfuehren,property=pdf,bereich=dlr,sprache=de,rwb=true.pdf.

SD in all 16 federal states, the local laws (e.g., municipal ordinances) of more than 10,000 municipalities[36] and of the partially mandatory chambers (234; e.g., chambers of commerce) had to be screened according to their compatibility with the SD's requirements.[37] The screening has been done in a level- and sector-specific way, i.e., every level of government and legislation screened their own provisions. On each of these levels the corresponding competent authorities (e.g., ministries) screened their own sector-specific provisions. According to the scope of the SD, the screening had to take place in at least two steps. First, the laws within the scope of the SD had to be identified; second, the procedures and material regulations had to be screened in the light of the provisions of the SD. To conduct the screening properly and in a homogeneous way (keeping in mind the various levels), a proof raster has been elaborated by the work group "Normenscreening".[38] Chambers and municipalities have been incorporated in the discussion process of the screening as well.[39] The proof raster consists of about 50 DIN A4-paper pages of questions. Going through these questions and answering them will show whether the proofed norm fulfils the requirements of the SD, and thus whether it must be altered. To make this process more comfortable and easier, the Free State of Bavaria worked out a database version of the raster, coincidentally providing a basis for the later report to the Commission.[40]

The raster is aligned along four basic principles, which are specified in detail throughout the raster:[41]

- Is the scope of the SD at issue?
- No discrimination
- Is justification according to the provisions of the SD possible?

---

36 One topic in regard of municipal ordinance that often occurs in the discussion has been the changes of cemetery statutes. Intensively discussed by Schulz (2009), 441 ff.

37 Figures are taken from the presentation mentioned in *supra* note 35, p. 11.

38 http://www.dienstleisten-leicht-gemacht.de/DLR/Navigation/umsetzung,did=264134.html; a draft sample of this raster is available at: http://www.verwaltungsmodernisierung.brandenburg.de/sixcms/media.php/4055/Raster_fuer_die_Normenpruefung.pdf.

39 Referred to in a speach on this topic by Dr. Eckhard Franz (Head of Division, Small and Medium-Sized Businesses, Federal Ministry of Economics and Technology), available at: http://www.dienstleisten-leicht-gemacht.de/DLR/Redaktion/PDF/grusswort-franz,property=pdf,bereich=dlr,sprache=de,rwb=true.pdf .

40 Referred to in a speach on this topic by Dr. Eckhard Franz (Head of Division, Small and Medium-Sized Businesses, Federal Ministry of Economics and Technology), available at: http://www.dienstleisten-leicht-gemacht.de/DLR/Redaktion/PDF/grusswort-franz,property=pdf,bereich=dlr,sprache=de,rwb=true.pdf; the electronic raster is not available public, the online portal is: http://www.norman-dlr.de/; the Handbook for NormAN-Online is e.g., available at: http://www.schleswig-holstein.de/cae/servlet/contentblob/674952/publicationFile/norman.pdf.

41 Committee of the Federation and the States on Service Economy, Frequently Asked Questions—Screening, 10.04.2008, p. 27, no. 60; available at: http://www.dienstleisten-leicht-gemacht.de/DLR/Redaktion/PDF/faqs-normenpruefung,property=pdf,bereich=dlr,sprache=de,rwb=true.pdf.

- Is the norm proportional?

This method of screening started in 2008.

Up to now, the outcome of the screening has not been published on a nationwide basis in detail. For the laws of the Federation, there has been an enumeration of altered laws in a written report from the federal government in response to an official request from a Member of Parliament.[42] According to Schönleiter, the German Trade, Commerce and Industry Regulation Act has been identified as a major piece of legislation for adaption in federal law as regards material, not procedural, changes.[43] Germany reported 211 legal acts that have been changed or set up to implement the SD in Germany to the European Commission.[44]

The European Commission announced that Europe-wide, about 16,000 requirements pertaining to the freedom of establishment, and over 19,000 requirements pertaining to freedom of service provision in the SD have yet to be communicated to Brussels by Member States, whereas 600 legislative acts have been modified thus far.[45]

2 Individual Articles of the Services Directive

2.1 Article 6 SD: Point of Single Contact (POSC)

The basic provision for the establishment of POSCs has been introduced by the changes in the Administrative Procedure Law (§§ 71a-71e VwVfG). However, as mentioned above, the Federation is rarely competent in these changes of administrative procedure.[46] Competences for changing administrative procedures and the organisation of administration are nearly entirely held by the 16 federal states. Hence, all sixteen federal states[47] had to introduce the SD requirements into their own Federal State Administrative Procedures Acts (which are basically identical to the federal one, which acts as a prototype). Taking into consideration that the federal states are not bound to federal changes in Administrative Procedures

42 BT-Drs. 17/728, 13 ff.

43 Without reference: Schönleiter (2009), 385.

44 These laws are listed at http://eur-lex.europa.eu/LexUriServ/LexUriServ.do?uri=CELEX:72006L0123:EN:NOT#FIELD_DE.

45 http://ec.europa.eu/internal_market/services/docs/services-dir/implementation/20100301_council_en.pdf; SEC (2011) 102_final, 9, speaks of "more than 34 000 requirements" altogether.

46 Except for purely federal administration.

47 Five of the sixteen federal states did not impose own Administrative Procedure Acts but installed a dynamic reference to the respective current version of the Administrative Procedures Act of the Federation. So these five federal states basically did not have to change anything in this regard.

Law,[48] while implementing the requirements of the SD regarding POSCs, one might expect several different provisions at the end of the implementation process. And indeed there are small deviations, but overall, the federal states and the federal government agreed on a harmonised implementation to assure common standards in the whole country.[49] For implementing the POSC, the federal states and the Federation did also elaborate a common framework for the duties of the POSC ("Anforderungsprofil für 'Einheitliche Ansprechpartner'"),[50] but there was no common approach for the establishment of the POSC.

Besides this basic division of competences, the establishment of the POSCs had to be conducted by law in every single federal state. And in this regard huge differences pertaining to the establishment and form of the POSC are evident.[51] The different approaches are explained as follows:

Basically as a national common platform, a website has been introduced by the Federal Ministry of Economics and Technology. This platform, called "German Business Portal" with its subpages "EU Service Market" and "Point of Single Contact",[52] guides the visitor of another Member State to the corresponding POSC for providing services and also provides a form for direct contact. Direct contact is also possible via the federal state platforms, which guide users within the state to the competent POSC.

As shown below, POSC implementation in Germany is very heterogeneous. This instance already indicates that the German legislator agrees on a subjective understanding of the need to establish POSCs.[53] Otherwise one should expect only one POSC for the whole country. This question and all associated questions have been scientifically examined by experts of the German Research Institute for Public Administration Speyer,[54] as mandated by the Federal Ministry of Economics and Technology. This examination of 2006 gives profound insight into all possibilities and legal frameworks for the introduction of POSCs in the federal system of Germany.

---

48 Sachs, in: Stelkens et al. (2008), Introduction para 47–49, 60, 65.

49 E.g., Protocol of the Conference of Ministers of Economics at its session in Eisenach (June 4th/5th 2007) on topic 2.2, available at: http://www.bundesrat.de/cln_171/DE/gremien-konf/fachministerkonf/wmk/Sitzungen/07-06-04-05-WMK/07-06-04-05-beschluesse-berichte,templateId=raw,property=publicationFile.pdf/07-06-04-05-beschluesse-berichte.pdf.

50 Available in German at: http://www.dienstleisten-leicht-gemacht.de/DLR/Redaktion/PDF/anforderungsprofil-fuer-einheitliche-ansprechpartner,property=pdf,bereich=dlr,sprache=de,rwb=true.pdf.

51 On the implementation in concreto see inter alia: Schliesky et al. (2010), 249 ff.

52 Available under: http://www.german-business-portal.info/GBP/Navigation/en/eu-service-market.html; German website: http://www.dienstleisten-leicht-gemacht.de/.

53 Explicitly inter alia: Anforderungsprofil "Einheitlicher Ansprechpartner", 6; available at: http://www.dienstleisten-leicht-gemacht.de/DLR/Redaktion/PDF/anforderungsprofil-fuer-einheitliche-ansprechpartner,property=pdf,bereich=dlr,sprache=de,rwb=true.pdf.

54 Ziekow et al. (2006) available in German at: http://www.dienstleisten-leicht-gemacht.de/DLR/Redaktion/PDF/gestaltungsoptionen-und-anforderungen-an-einheitliche,property=pdf,bereich=dlr,sprache=de,rwb=true.pdf.

On the basis of a solely subjective understanding of the POSCs,[55] the German federal states—who as mentioned above are responsible for the administrative procedures—used this freedom intensively:[56]

The federal state of Baden Wuertemberg introduced the POSC by attributing this task to the existing chambers of Baden Wuertemberg (e.g., chambers of commerce and industry, bar association) and additionally (after notification at the Ministry of Economics Baden Wuertemberg and publication in the law gazette) the local authorities (Landkreise ~ counties, districts; Stadtkreise ~ municipalities not subject to any district government). A quite similar introduction has been chosen by the Free State of Bavaria. The only remarkable differences are that there is a probational period of two years for the establishment of POSCs at local authorities and that Bavaria established the POSCs only for transnational service providers within the scope of the SD, not for purely domestic service providers, as the Bavarian legislator assumes that for national service providers without a transnational component, existing instruments for providing services are sufficient.[57] As well as attributing the tasks of the POSCs to chambers, but only to them: the federal state of Hamburg,[58] the federal state of Mecklenburg—Western Pommerania[59] and the Free State of Thuringia.[60] Although of course there are always certain special features in every corresponding federal state law, these five states—roughly speaking—chose a chamber-model for establishing their POSCs. But one particular feature of this variety of establishment is notable: In Thuringia the establishment of POSCs by private legal entities is explicitly permitted, if the competent federal state ministry agrees.

In addition to the various chamber models, two federal states assigned the tasks of the POSCs to local authorities only. This way was chosen by the federal states of Lower Saxony[61] and North Rhine-Westphalia.[62] In Lower Saxony, besides the various state-typical local authorities (except one type of municipality), the ministry competent for economics can be a POSC.[63]

A third category is constituted by those federal states that attributed the POSCs to existing regional authorities/entities or authorities/entities with special duties.

The federal state of Bremen attributed the tasks of the POSC to existing private legal entities responsible for economic development and comparable tasks

---

[55] Also for a subjective understanding: Commission Handbook 5.2.1.

[56] See Schliesky et al. (2010), 249 ff., 292 ff.

[57] LT-Drs. 16/2627, 1, 5.

[58] § 2 HmbEAG.

[59] § 1 EAPG M-V.

[60] § 1 Thüringer ES-Errichtungsgesetz.

[61] § 1 NEAG.

[62] § 1 EA-Gesetz NRW.

[63] § 1 (1) s. 1, 3 NEAG.

("Wirtschaftsförderung Bremen GmbH, WFB, and BIS Bremerhaven").[64] The federal state of Hesse attributed the POSC to its three "Regierungspräsidien" (~ state authorities for administrative districts), which are authorities between the local and federal state authorities competent for supervision of local authorities and further, over-regional matters.[65]

The federal state of Rhineland-Palatinate, however, attributed the POSCs' tasks to its two "Struktur- und Genehmigungsdirektionen Nord/Süd" (~ public authorities competent for structural planning; one for the northern and one for the southern part of the state).[66]

The federal state of Saxony attributed the duties of the POSC to its "Landesdirektion Leipzig", which is a state authority for administrative districts.[67] Comparably the federal state of Saxony-Anhalt attributed the POSC tasks to the "Landesverwaltungsamt", which is as well a state administration office.[68]

A fourth branch is the implementation strategy in the federal states of Berlin, Brandenburg and Saarland. Overall, these federal states implemented the POSC by building up an internal division in the federal state ministry competent for economics.[69] In the federal state of Saarland, there is one POSC which is maintained by the chambers of the Saarland, but the Federal State Ministry of Economics and Science is the authority in charge of this POSC.

Finally, the federal state of Schleswig–Holstein has chosen a unique method of implementation. In Schleswig–Holstein, an independent statutory body ("rechtsfähige Anstalt des öffentlichen Rechts") has been introduced to fulfil the tasks of the POSC.[70] This statutory body is maintained by the federal state of Schleswig–Holstein, the local governments and all chambers of handicrafts and chambers of commerce and industry in Schleswig–Holstein.

These very different ways of introduction seem to be problematic with respect to the aim of the SD, which primarily is to lower hurdles for foreign service providers in other Member States.[71] In a nutshell, the current legislation would allow the establishment of at least 301 POSCs, there will probably be about 150 up to 200.[72]

---

64 Bürgerschafts-Drucksache 17/813; Beschlussprotokoll 17/48; Schliesky et al. (2010), 295 f. specify the establishment in Bremen as a local authority model.

65 § 1 EAHG.

66 § 2 (1) RPL EAP.

67 § 1 SächsEAG.

68 § 2 (1) EAG LSA.

69 § 1 (1) EAG Bln; § 2 BbgEAPG and ministerial order of October 6th 2009 in conjunction, Bbg.GVBl. vom 16.07.2009, 262 ff.; § 1 EA-Gesetz Saarland.

70 § 1 (1) EhAsprPErG SH.

71 See e.g., Recital 4 to 7, 12.

72 An estimated amount of 160 POSCs is listed in a 2009 published survey of Eurochambers, 21, available at: http://www.eurochambres.eu/Content/Default.asp?PageID=1&DocID=1917; another recent survey of the RKW speaks of up to 200 POSCs in Germany, p. 34, available at: http://www.rkw-kompetenzzentrum.de/fileadmin/media/Dokumente/Publikationen/2010_Doku_Einheitlicher-Ansprechpartner.pdf.

While introducing the POSCs in this way, the legislature(s) did not re-allocate administrative competences, but left these competences untouched, which has been criticised sporadically. Quite in contrast, the legislator mainly attributes the tasks of the POSCs to existing authorities or institutions. The only exception is the establishment of the new statutory body in Schleswig–Holstein. Private partners or legal entities under private law have been involved so far only in Bremen, but might become involved in other federal states as well in the future, as the legal provisions of some federal states include the possibility of involving private partners (e.g., Saarland and Thuringia).

As regards the liability of the POSCs, the usual principles of state liability[73] are applied. There are no special rules for POSCs.[74] This means that each POSC is reliable for its own actions according to § 839 BGB (Civil Code) and Article 34 GG (Basic Constitutional Law). There are only a few provisions which regulate the duties and liability in the relation-competent authority and POSC.[75]

Regarding supervision of the POSCs there are basically two options for the legislator: specialist supervision or judicial supervision. Taking the differences according to the introduction of the POSCs in the different federal states into consideration, it is not surprising that the answer to the question whether specialist or judicial supervision is administered is heterogeneous as well.

One additional point (not asked for) on this matter: As regards charges for POSC use, the picture is again heterogeneous. Most acts of the federal states establishing the POSC-system do have provisions for charges for using the POSC procedure, but they are not homogeneously formulated.

Aside from these organisational differences, there are also differences in the range of authorisations that can be performed by a POSC. In the wide field of the German GewO for instance, one basic rule (§ 6b GewO) states that all administrative procedures of the GewO can be driven over the POSC, but the federal states can deviate from this basic principle in accordance with the services provided in Article 2 (2) SD. Furthermore § 6b GewO does not distinguish between transnational and purely domestic service provision. To avoid discrimination against domestic service providers, the POSC-system in general should be open for them as well in the eyes of the federal legislator.[76] Deviations according to § 6b s. 2 GewO in regard of Article 2 (2) SD have been made by several states.[77] In some federal states, the POSCs have been imposed for additional administrative procedures in certain cases (e.g., "Eichordnung" [statutory instrument on calibration

[73] For a comprehensive presentation of state liability in Germany see e.g.: Grzeszick (2010) § 43–48, 931 ff.

[74] See Huck, in: Bader and Ronellenfitsch (2010), § 71a VwVfG para 19.

[75] See e.g., Article 3 (2) BayEAG.

[76] BT-Drs. 16/12784, 15; also Schönleiter (2009), 387; exception see footnote 17.

[77] E.g., § 3 BayGewV; § 2 DLRL-AnpV NRW; §9 SächsGewODVO.

regulations]).[78] There are also federal states which opened the POSC procedure for annex procedures combined with an originally SD-scoped authorisation.[79]

2.2 Article 7 SD: Right to Information

In Germany the requirements of Article 7 SD have been implemented as provisions in the newly created administrative procedure (§§ 71a-71e VwVfG) which is explained above. This new section contains one provision for the "rights to information", § 71 c VwVfG. In § 71c (1) VwVfG the requirements of Article 7 (1) SD and Article 7 (4) SD have been transposed; § 71c VwVfG does not extent the "rights to information" laid down in Article 7 (1), (4) SD. It moreover contains the duty of providing the necessary information for service providers without application to special cases, but only general information.[80] One specialty in this concern might be that the German legislator assumes that Article 7 (4) SD is not precise enough, as the requests of applicants cannot be "faulty or unfounded" themselves.[81] The German legislator therefore assumes that this provision must be interpreted the way that Article 7 (4) SD means cases where the applications are not precise enough. Therefore, § 71c (1) s. 2 VwVfG sets forth the duty to inform the applicant immediately about the fact that its application is not precise enough. § 71c (2) VwVfG states that the competent authorities must give detailed information about all details regarding the request/application of the service provider inclusive of the prevailing opinion on the interpretation of uncertain provisions. In this respect, § 71c (2) SD refers also to the general (altered with respect to SD requirements[82]) information provision for authorities, § 25 VwVfG.[83]

As shown above, the new procedure in the Administrative Procedures Law implementing the procedure of the POSCs can be used in domestic cases as well (as long as specific administrative laws refer to it).

This means that for all procedures run by POSCs, the "rights to information" are binding. Beyond that, the new provision of § 25 (2) VwVfG is applicable to all administrative procedures. This provision commits the authority to give information about necessary documents for a successful application and it must provide information on how the procedure can be completed. The authority also must provide information about the projected duration of the application procedure and the completeness of the application documents. Furthermore, the "rights to

[78] E.g., § 1 Bln DLR-VBundR; § 1 DLRL-AnpV NRW.

[79] § 2 (3) s. 2 EAG Bln and § 3 (1) EAG LSA; see also on the whole procedure: Luch and Schulz (2010), 225 ff., 228.

[80] BT-Drs. 16/10493, 20.

[81] BT-Drs. 16/10493, 20.

[82] BT-Drs. 16/10493, 7, 15.

[83] BT-Drs. 16/10493, 20.

information" must be obeyed, if the applicant is applying directly to the competent authority and not to the POSC. This is ordered by § 71a (2) VwVfG.[84]

2.3 Article 8 SD: Procedures by Electronic Means

2.3.1 Introduction of Electronic Procedures

In Germany, regulations on electronic administrative procedures existed prior to implementation of the SD. But these previous regulations did not give the applicant an enforceable right of access to an electronic procedure. Giving access to electronic procedures was rather a decision at the discretion of the authority (§ 3a (1) VwVfG).[85] Now the authority is obliged to use electronic procedures, if the applicant so requires. This obligation is laid down, again, in one article of the newly established POSC procedure, § 71e VwVfG.[86] Nevertheless the applicant must achieve a signature card, if the specific administrative law serving as the source of the application requires "legal requirement of writing" (§ 3a (2) s.2 VwVfG is referred to in § 71e s.2 VwVfG).[87] The "legal requirement of writing" is of course a hurdle for European service providers as currently there are no common standards for this requirement in the European Union.[88] Nevertheless, this requirement is consistent with EU law[89] as the "Commission Decision of 16 October 2009 setting out measures facilitating the use of procedures by electronic means through the 'points of single contact' under Directive 2006/123/EC of the European Parliament and of the Council on services in the internal market"[90] states in Article 1 (1). This Commission Decision shows that the problem of different systems of certified advanced signatures

[84] BT-Drs. 16/10493, 18.

[85] Kopp and Ramsauer (2008), § 3a VwVfG para 5; Schmitz, in: Stelkens et al. (2008), § 3a VwVfG para 6 ff.

[86] If the POSC procedure is ordered to be applicable by a specific administrative law. Then again the electronic procedures apply also in the direct relation applicant—competent authority because of § 71a (2) VwVfG.

[87] Schulz (2010a), 205 ff., 216 f.; but recognition of qualified signatures issued by other Member States is ruled in directive 99/93 EC and in § 23 (1) s.1 SigG; compare also BT-Drs. 16/10493, 20.; a new development in 2011 has also established a "DE-Mail-System", which means that one can obtain a special protected email postbox of an official certificated provider to receive official documents of authorities; see: BT-Drs. 17/3630, also Gesetz zur Änderung von De-Mail-Diensten und anderer Vorschriften vom 28.04.2011—Bundesgesetzblatt Teil I Nr. 19 vom 02.05.2011, 666-675.

[88] Schulz (2010a), 205 ff., 216 f.

[89] Compare e.g., Schmitz and Prell (2009b), 1121 ff., 1127; Schulz (2010a), 205 ff., 216 f.

[90] Commission Decision of 16 October 2009 setting out measures facilitating the use of procedures by electronic means through the 'points of single contact' under Directive 2006/123/ EC of the European Parliament and of the Council on services in the internal market, OJ L no. 274 of 20 October 2009, 36 f.

has been recognised on the European level. The decision tries to find a solution by acceptance of foreign certificates and listing "trusted certificates" of each Member State (Article 1 (2-4) and Article 2 Decision).

The German legislator assumes that it is not necessary that the service provider explicitly declare its wish to use electronic means for its application procedure. Implied actions, such as contacting the POSC by email, would be sufficient for a stated choice.[91] As the administrative procedure can, but need not be, set up at the POSC and thus the competent authorities behind the POSC can be contacted for application purposes further on, these competent authorities must provide electronic procedures as well, including for their own internal communications.[92]

2.3.2 Impact of the Services Directive on Electronic Procedures in Germany

As in many other countries, so-called "eGovernment" has been a vital and broadly discussed issue for more than ten years.[93] Local governments and authorities, in particular, have increased their options for electronic procedures[94]; nevertheless, probably because of the discretion of the authorities as to whether to open up access to electronic procedures in combination with costs for the corresponding electronic infrastructure, the use of eGovernment so far has been in need of further development.[95]

The SD gives an impulse to establish special electronic means in the whole administrative sector, not just in selected sectors as before. Therefore the implementation of this electronic infrastructure and various system options has been discussed intensively.[96] The most ambitious duty in this respect seems to be to tackle the problem of the coherency of all systems.[97] By adding one module to the existing initiative "Deutschland-Online", a common frame and a role model for the implementation of eGovernment structures throughout all different levels of authorisation has been elaborated under the auspices of the federal states of Baden Wuertemberg and Schleswig–Holstein. But according to the division of competences, this basic alignment is not binding on the federal states.[98] Another important legal change should be mentioned here, although it is not directly connected to the implementation of the SD. In 2009 the "German Grundgesetz"

---

[91] BT-Drs. 16/10493, 20.

[92] BT-Drs. 16/10493, 21; Ziekow and Windoffer, in: Schlachter and Ohler (2008), Article 8 SD para 4.

[93] Compare e.g.: Kopp and Ramsauer (2008), § 3a VwVfG para 3 fn. 8.

[94] Luch and Schulz (2009), 219 ff., p. 235.

[95] Luch and Schulz (2009), 219 ff., 234 ff, 248 f.

[96] Compare e.g.: Eckert (2009), 115 ff.

[97] See also: Ziekow and Windoffer, in: Schlachter and Ohler (2008), Article 8 SD para 8.

[98] Information on the project as well as the final report is available at: http://www.it-planungsrat.de/DE/Projekte/AbgeschlosseneProjekte/DLR/Dienstleistungsrichtlinie.html?nn=1335606.

(German Constitutional Act) was amended[99] and changed.[100] One change has been the establishment of Article 91c GG, which allows working out common standards and cooperation in IT-systems of the Federation and the federal states. Although the reasoning behind the act does not particularly refer to the SD,[101] this article surely plays a decisive role in future cooperation in the field of eGovernment and IT-systems related to the implementation of the SD, especially Article 8 SD.[102]

Nevertheless, the obligation to open administrative procedures to electronic means in such an extensive way (as not only the application, but also the communication between POSC and the competent authority must be done in an electronic way) and the broad discussion about it shows the great impact of the SD in this area.

Thus eGovernment discussion and further establishment gets a fruitful impulse from the requirements of the SD.[103] But several topics remain to be discussed and cleared up.

2.3.3 Removal of Other Means

The possibility of running an administrative procedure electronically is meant as an additional option in Germany.[104] So further on the service provider can submit its application and necessary documents as papers, but electronically as well.

No conventional means of running administrative procedures is abolished; rather, an additional means has been made available.

2.4 Article 9 SD: Authorisation Schemes

2.4.1 Means of Less Restrictive Measure

The question of whether there are less restrictive means throughout German law of providing authorisation schemes has been discussed among German scholars intensively.

[99] Mainly due to the results of a commission bearing the duty to modernise the fiscal relations of the Federation and the federal states, but also as regards the cooperation of the Federation and the federal states.

[100] Draft act with reasoning: BT-Drs. 16/12410; Gesetz vom 29.07.2009—Bundesgesetzblatt Teil I 2009 Nr. 48 vom 31.07.2009, 2248-2250.

[101] Only to an increasing number of EU norms in this area and the objective to tackle the link between the German and the EU networks; BT-Drs. 16/12410, 9 f.; on the whole topic and procedure of introducing Article 91c GG: "Die gemeinsame Kommission von Bundestag und Bundesrat zur Modernisierung der Bund-Länder-Beziehungen, Hrsg. Deutscher Bundestag and Bundesrat (2010), Berlin, 175–204; profound on the whole topic of Article 91c GG: Siegel (2010), 299-322.

[102] On this topic in general: Siegel (2009), 1128 ff.

[103] Schliesky (2009a), 99 ff., 107 ff., 122 ff.

[104] So as well: BT-Drs. 16/10493, 21.

Quite early Ziekow[105] discussed these matters and concluded that there could be changes in the field of special authorisation schemes of §§ 35 ff. GewO (German Trade, Commerce and Industry Regulation Act) and in statutes governing restaurants serving alcoholic drinks (more simply, "statutes governing restaurants").[106]

Altogether Ziekow identifies a parallelism between Article 9 SD and the German law according to § 35 or § 38 GewO, which regulate 'a posteriori instruments' of authorities regarding unreliable businessmen. Nevertheless, Ziekow expected strict handling on the part of the European Commission in these cases and therefore some regulations might need adaptation.[107]

Kluth also mentioned the German Handicrafts Regulation Act and obligatory registration of the Role of Craftsmen for certain businesses as fields of law which must be changed to sustain the requirements of the SD.[108] Kluth also identified areas of §§ 30 ff. GewO which can stay "untouched" by the SD's requirements and therefore he does not see a general, but a specific need of adoption in §§ 35 ff. GewO. Nevertheless, he also stresses that especially the statutes governing restaurants (since 2006 a federal state, not federal competence) would probably have to be adapted to Article 9 (1) SD.[109]

Similar conclusions are drawn by Cornils[110] and Krajewski.[111]

The Handbook of the European Commission seems to underline Ziekow's attitude towards a strict handling of the European Commission regarding the requirements of Article 9 SD. It clearly expresses this under 6.1.1:

> Article 9 not only requires Member States to evaluate their authorisation schemes and to abolish or modify those schemes which are not justified, but also to report to the Commission the reasons why they consider that the remaining ones are compatible with the criterion of non-discrimination, are justified by an overriding reason relating to the public interest and are proportionate.

Although the requirements of Article 9 SD are already legally binding under the jurisdiction of the ECJ, which developed the three criteria of the quote,[112] the mentioned law fields have been identified as those that must be adapted.

Nevertheless, apparently there have been only minor or few changes by the legislator so far. Even the strictly criticised provisions of the "Gaststättengesetze"

---

105 Ziekow (2007a), 217; see also Schulz (2008), 175 ff., 193 ff.

106 Ziekow (2007a), 217.

107 Ziekow (2007a), 217; see also Schulz (2008), 175 ff., 193 ff.; against this general expectation: Stober (2008), p. 148 f.

108 Kluth (2008), 131 ff., 149.

109 Kluth (2008), 131 ff., 149.

110 Cornils, in: Schlachter and Ohler (2008), Article 9 SD para 46; comprehensive on the whole subject and consequences of the SD's requirements for the German rules of authorisation schemes: doctoral thesis of Hissnauer (2009), 143 ff., especially 260 ff.

111 Krajewski (2009), 929 ff., 930 f.

112 Krajewski (2009), 930.

(statutes governing restaurants) have remained almost untouched thus far. In the federal state of Bremen for instance, it is still necessary to get an authorisation before opening a restaurant[113]; the federal states of Brandenburg and Thuringia both abolished this requirement, replacing it with by notification before opening a restaurant.[114] But these changes were passed before the SD and were due to "Föderalismusreform", a reform reallocating competences of the Federation and the sixteen federal states,[115] by which the federal states gained the competences for passing their own statutes for governing restaurants. So this change had nothing to do with Article 9 SD.[116] In the state of Saarland an own statute governing restaurants has been recently passed which provides also a notification requirement only,[117] but the reasoning does not ground on the SD again, but more on earlier agreements on deregulation.[118] Nevertheless the POSC procedure has been installed in § 4 (8) SGastG. Furthermore the Free State of Saxony passed an own statute governing restaurants in a comparable manner.[119] The state of Baden-Wuerttemberg passed an own statute governing restaurants; but this statute more or less only refers to the provisions of the "old" law of the Federation and therefore no profound change took place. None of the other 10 federal states have passed their own laws and therefore the federal statute governing restaurants still applies in them, which still requires an authorisation before starting a restaurant business.

There may be further changes in the future. However, currently no changes are prominent and apparent in regard of Article 9 SD. This is different in regard to the freedom of providing services and Article 16 SD, as shown below.

2.4.2 Existing Authorisation Schemes/Procedures

There are three types of authorisation or notification regarding the establishment of service businesses: two different types of authorisation and the notification.[120] But business conduct usually nevertheless falls within the German Trade, Commerce and Industry Regulation Act and is possible without authorisation and is derived from the freedom of business conduct granted by the Basic Constitutional Law. Nevertheless, there are (quite a lot of) exceptions.[121]

---

113 § 2 (1) BremGastG.

114 § 2 (1) BbgGastG; § 2 (1) ThürGastG.

115 Bundesgesetzblatt Teil I vom 28.08.2006, 2034.

116 Compare reasoning of the changes e.g., in Thuringia: http://www.thueringen.de/imperia/md/content/homepage/politisch/rpk/thueringer_gaststaettengesetz.pdf.

117 § 3 (1) SGastG.

118 Compare S-LT-Drs. 14/317, 1 f.

119 § 2 (1) SächsGastG.

120 Ziekow (2007b), § 5 para 12 ff.; Ruffert (2010), § 21 para 51 ff.

121 Ruthig and Storr (2008), § 3 para 218.

1. "Präventives Verbot mit Erlaubnisvorbehalt"

(= preventive prohibition with reservation in regard to granting permission)

This principle means that before establishing a service business one has to apply for authorisation from the competent authority. Starting without this authorisation would be illegal, even if all necessary preconditions were theoretically fulfilled and all documents were present.

This type originally applies, if the legislator assumes that it is better to have preventive proof of all necessary instances before granting an authorisation because of possible harmful outcomes in case of ineligible potential service providers. Such authorisations are basically regulated in the German Trade, Commerce and Industry Regulation Act[122] and the Handicraft Regulation Act or the statute governing restaurants.[123]

2. "Ausnahmebewilligung/Verbot mit Befreiungsvorbehalt"

(= exceptional leave/prohibition with conditional discharge)

This type is the most rigid form of authorisation procedure, but usually does not apply anymore in Germany. The basic concept is that a particular activity is not allowed at all due to its hazards. Only in specific, very restricted cases can the service activity be allowed. However, contrary to the first type, there is no claim to get authorisation granted. The decision on whether authorisation is granted is at the discretion of the authority.[124] The authority determines whether there is a need for the applied-for business. As already noted, this type is nearly nonexistent in Germany today, so (1) has to be seen as the most prevalent authorisation scheme in Germany.

3. "Anzeigepflichten"

(= notifications)

Finally, there are different provisions which stipulate notification requirements. A central provision in this case is § 14 GewO. This provision of simple notification of § 14 GewO says that the starting of a particular business must be noticed to the competent authority, but no material examination goes along with it.

One can distinguish the simple notification from the special/qualified notification, which requires further material proceedings or the submission of particular documents together with the notification form. The difference with respect to (1) in case of special notification is therefore that until a possible prohibition of the authority—hence the time between notification and interdiction—the performance is not illegal,

---

[122] The German Trade, Commerce and Industry Regulation Act basically allows every business without any authorisation (§ 1 (1) GewO). But there is quite a wide range of exceptions ordered by law to this basic statement.

[123] Compare e.g.: Ruthig and Storr (2008), § 4 para 398; Schliesky (2003), 229.

[124] Ziekow (2007b), § 5 para 11 ff.

but legally done. The notification itself makes it legal. In cases of simple notification, the notification is only an accessory obligation, but does not—if the business must be authorised anyway—give legal cause for business operation.[125]

2.4.3 Simple Notifications

The question of the relation of simple notifications and the requirements of the SD has been discussed in Germany—and somehow surprisingly—has been controversial.[126]

Even if one must admit that this question was first discussed in regard to Article 16 SD, the question arose also in the discussion about authorisation schemes,[127] as the scope of the term "authorisation" had to be cleared up. Hissnauer deals with this question in a very clear and distinct way.[128] He compares the directive's definition of Article 4 no. 6 SD and Recital 39 with the German perception of the term "authorisation schemes" and concludes logically that only provisions requiring legal action by the competent authority can be subject to the term "authorisation". Therefore he sees simple notifications such as § 14 GewO as outside the scope of Article 9 SD.[129]

Cornils clarifies this question further by stating more precisely that one must distinguish between simple notifications and qualified notifications, as the latter are a precondition for legal business performance, whereas the former are, as mentioned above, only accessory obligations.[130]

2.5 Article 10 SD: Conditions for the Granting of Authorisation

2.5.1 Recognition of Requirements

In Germany, the requirements of recognition of authorisations granted by other Member States have been transposed by the new provision of § 13b GewO.[131]

§ 13b GewO says in its first clause that documents issued by authorities of other Member States according to reliability and financial circumstances of a service provider must be acknowledged by German authorities. Nevertheless, the German authorities can demand a certificated German transcription of these documents. If

[125] Cornils, in: Schlachter and Ohler (2008), Article 9 SD para 20.

[126] Hissnauer (2009), 144 ff.; Luch and Schulz (2008b), 82 f.; Schliesky et al. (2008), 157; against: Stober (2008), 149.

[127] Schliesky et al. (2008), 157.

[128] Hissnauer (2009), 144 ff.

[129] Hissnauer (2009), 146.

[130] Cornils, in: Schlachter and Ohler (2008), Article 9 SD para 20.

[131] BT-Drs. 16/12784, 16.

other Member States do not normally issue such documents, the missing documents can be substituted by comparable documents of the other Member State or by affirmation in lieu of oath (§ 13b (1) s.2 GewO). Furthermore, § 13b (2) GewO provides comparable regulations for professional indemnity insurance.

Except for § 36 GewO, all SD requirements according to industrial business authorisation schemes have been implemented by § 13b GewO.[132]

§ 36a (1) GewO stipulates—also as a new provision—according to the requirements of training and capability, proof of technical expertise comparable to what is provided by § 13b GewO. In case no comparison in regard to other Member States is possible, an additional aptitude test or a training course can be demanded by the authority, (§ 36a (2) GewO). § 36a (3) GewO states that comparable (even if different from German) requirements and achievements must be acknowledged analogously to § 13b GewO.

As the above-described requirements/authorisation schemes (reliability, financial circumstances, professional indemnity insurances, public appointment of technical experts) are seen as the only ones in regard to the provisions of the SD which are affected by Article 10 (3) SD, the transposition by parliamentary law is seen as sufficient and complete by the legislator.[133]

A further change was made by statutory instrument of the federal government and the "Bundesrat" (second chamber of parliament, representing the federal state governments).[134] By this statutory instrument, several other statutory instruments have been amended in this regard. So e.g., § 2 Makler- und Bauträgerverordnung (statutory instrument for brokers and builders) has been amended by adding a sixth clause which determines the acknowledgement of bonds and insurances in this field.

Furthermore, the new statutory instrument implementing the requirements of the SD in environmental law[135] contains certain changes in specific administrative laws according to the acknowledgement of documents and capabilities.[136] Even if the reasoning of the new provisions refers to other provisions of the SD, these changes can, from my point of view, also be seen as implementation of Article 10 (3) SD.

---

[132] BT-Drs. 16/12784, 16.

[133] Coincidentally implementing requirements of directive 2005/36 EC; BT-Drs. 16/12784, 17 f.

[134] BR-Drs. 25/10 of January 20th 2010.

[135] See Sect. 1.1.

[136] Examples would be also: clause 8 of § 6 "Altholzverordnung" (statutory instrument on used wood); clause 8b of § 3 "Bioabfallverordnung" (statutory instrument on biological waste); clause 2, 3 of § 9a "Chemikalien-Klimaschutzverordnung" (statutory instrument on chemicals in regard of climate protection); clause 5 of § 5 "Chemikalien-OzonschichtVO" (statutory instrument on chemicals in regard of the ozone layer); clause 5 of § 21 and clause 3 of § 24 "Deponieverordnung" (statutory instrument on dumpsites); clause 8 of § 9 "Gewerbeabfallverodnung" (statutory instrument on business waste).

2.5.2 Granting Authorisation Throughout the Whole National Territory and Exceptions

Germany is a federation with three main levels of government and legislation: the Federation, the sixteen federal states and the local municipalities.

Taking this very basic and rough order into consideration, it seems obvious that granting authorisations throughout the whole country would provoke problems.[137]

Hence one must distinguish between three levels to answer this question. For regulations of federal law, nation-wide validity—even if federal state authorities carry out the federal regulations—seems not to be problematic.[138] The only problematic cases seem to be authorisations attached to plant- and facility-based authorisations which only grant authorisation for a specific area. But according to the prevailing opinion, such authorisations can be justified by Article 10 (4) SD, as there would be overriding reasons in the public interest in these cases.[139] In this respect, Recital 59 is considered especially important. Authorisation based on personal criteria has been assessed as hardly justifiable.[140]

But more problematic are regulations of the federal states. Their validity is limited to the respective federal state borders. Therefore a solution transposing Article 10 (4) SD had to be found. As a solution, usually the mutual acknowledgement of granted authorisations by the federal states—in their general Administrative Procedures Law or in each specific administrative law within the scope of the SD—is seen as the proper means to solve this problem.[141]

According to local rules/statutes (e.g., cemetery statutes) this solution would, roughly[142] said, be possible as well. Contrarily, Schulz states that the huge number of municipalities (12,554)[143] probably makes this solution impossible. Therefore, his solution is to withdraw the concerned regulations, even if they are in conformance with Article 9 SD, as they are not compatible with Article 10 (4) SD.[144] Against this point of view, one can argue that usually the municipalities lean on prototypes of local statutes elaborated by a municipal organisation or ministry. The problem should therefore only arise, if the prototype is elaborated correctly, if the municipality decides to deviate from the prototype. A third way would be a

---

[137] Articles on this topic: Schulz (2008), 175 ff.; Ziekow (2007a), 179–189, 217–225, 218.; Krajewski (2009), 929 ff., 931 f.; Cornils, in: Schlachter and Ohler (2008), Article 10 SD para 29 ff.; Hissnauer (2009), 153 f.

[138] Krajewski (2009), 931 f.

[139] Cornils, in: Schlachter and Ohler (2008), Article 10 SD para 37 f.; Krajewski (2009), 931, also referring to the Commission Handbook 6.1.5.; critical on this topic: Ziekow (2007a), 218 f.

[140] Krajewski (2009), 931.

[141] Schulz (2008), 190 f; Krajewski (2009), 932; Cornils, in: Schlachter and Ohler (2008), Article 10 SD para 35.

[142] You would further on have to divide two different areas of competences in municipalities, which should not be mentioned, as not handled here.

[143] Schulz (2008), 199.

[144] Schulz (2008), 199.

directive by the federal state legislator,[145] but this solution might be problematic in light of the principle of self-government of municipalities stated in Article 28 (2) GG (Basic Constitutional Law).[146]

In particular, the obligation to be member of a special chamber competent for only a certain regional area has been discussed in this regard, but has mainly been seen as compatible with Article 10 (4) SD.[147]

Apparently, adaption on this issue is still ongoing. It is not possible to show all different fields. But it should be mentioned, as an example, the recognition of engineers who are members of the chamber of engineers in another federal state: they are now allowed to submit building plans in other federal states as well without being listed for this purpose in the listing of the other federal state chamber of engineers. The recognition of such provisions has been implemented in several fields and in nearly all federal states.[148]

The principles stated above seem to be the only possible ones compatible with the SD and the German state order, which in accordance with Article 10 (7) SD should not be altered by Article 10 (4) SD. A similar problem arose with respect to Article 6 SD and Article 6 (2) SD.

As already mentioned, the prevailing opinion[149] seems to assume that with respect to plant- and facility-based authorisations, the existing local limitation can be maintained. This is, first, based on Recital 59, which says that

> [f]or example, environmental protection may justify the requirement to obtain an individual authorisation for each installation on the national territory.

Plant- and facility-based authorisation would always concern the local environment and has certain demands concerning infrastructure.[150] Cornils stresses these local infrastructure requirements and refers, as well as Krajewski, in this regard, to the Commission Handbook, which states that

> [i]ndividual authorisations for each establishment will normally be justified in cases where the authorisation is linked to a physical infrastructure (...) because an individual assessment of each installation in question may be necessary.[151]

Cornils also identifies other overriding reasons in the public interest, such as protection of health and life to justify regional limited authorisation in German law.[152]

---

145 Schliesky (2008b), 62.

146 Schliesky (2008b), 61.

147 Kluth (2008), 131 ff., 151 f.

148 Compare e.g., survey on the changes in building codes of the states as regards engineers, available at: http://ikth.de/files/info/Synopse_VB_BIngK_2010.pdf.

149 Cornils, in: Schlachter and Ohler (2008), Article 10 SD para 38; Krajewski (2009), 931, who also refers to the Commission Handbook 6.1.5.; Kluth (2008), 152; critical: Ziekow (2007a), 218 f.

150 Cornils, in: Schlachter and Ohler (2008), Article 10 SD para 38.

151 Commission Handbook 6.1.5.

152 Cornils, in: Schlachter and Ohler (2008), Article 10 SD para 38.

Bigger problems arise with respect to authorisations which are not plant or facility based, but related to personal criteria for granting authorisation.[153] In these cases authorisations are granted only if the applicant is, for example, enrolled in the Role of Craftsmen, and even then only for the area of the chamber of handicrafts he/she is enrolled in.[154] So, in these cases it is assumed that justification of such regional authorisation will be difficult to maintain.[155]

Furthermore, in Germany there are mixed types of authorisation, combining plant- and facility-based and personal authorisations. In these cases, it is argued that only in respect of the infrastructural conditions can personal criteria be assessed. Therefore the regional limitation can be maintained, as it is comparable with plant- and facility-based authorisations.[156]

2.5.3 Entitlement to Grant Authorisation, Court Review of Administrative Decisions

As far as the implementation of Article 10 (5) SD is concerned, no further need of adaption or transposition has been identified.[157] The existing regulations already cover this requirement of the SD. This is, as already mentioned, based primarily on the principle of freedom of business conduct set forth in Article 12 GG (Basic Constitutional Law) in Germany. If someone fulfils the requirements of a business provision, he/she is entitled to authorisation.[158] Discretion might in such cases only play a role as regards additional conditions to the granted authorisation.[159]

As regards the judicial review of decisions on the granting of authorisations, the German provisions and jurisdiction takes the following approach: Administrative courts review administrative acts only according to their compliance with legal provisions. The discretion itself, if there is any (compare above), is not subject to further review, but the courts control whether the legal provisions defining such discretion are met and whether this discretional use is in compliance with the teleological meaning of the parent act.[160] It should be mentioned that the court is not allowed to replace the discretion decision of the authority if it only dissents with the authority's opinion deriving from certain possible and legal conclusions. Only if there is abuse of discretion, i.e., in specific cases (e.g., exceeding discretionary powers), can the authority's decision be withdrawn and the authority must

---

[153] Krajewski (2009), 931.

[154] Krajewski (2009), 931.

[155] Contrary Cornils, in: Schlachter and Ohler (2008), Article 10 SD para 40.

[156] Schulz (2008), 194 f., 200.

[157] Cornils, in: Schlachter and Ohler (2008), Article 10 SD para 41 f.; Ziekow (2007a), 219; Oertel (2006), 159; Hissnauer (2009), 154 f.

[158] Inter alia: Ruthig and Storr (2008), § 3 para 224.

[159] Inter alia: U. Stelkens, in: Stelkens et al. (2008), § 36 VwVfG para 117.

[160] Decker, in: Posser and Wolf (2008), § 114 VwGO.

then decide again in a new discretionary procedure while taking the opinion of the court into consideration.[161]

2.5.4 Reasoning of Administrative Decisions

Also in regard to Article 10 (6) SD, no adaption obligation has been identified.[162] In Germany § 39 VwVfG already provides the obligation for all authorities to reason their formal decisions in an extensive way. For those clauses of § 39 VwVfG that might be insufficient with respect to Article 10 (6) SD, an interpretation of § 39 VwVfG in the light of European law must take place and hence no further transposition is needed.[163] Luch and Schulz even state that German administrative law does "over-satisfy" ("(über)erfüllt") this requirement already.[164]

2.5.5 Allocation of Competences

Although implementation of the SD might have been a good chance to alter competences in this regard (possibly also in regard of Article 6 (2) SD), the German legislator(s) obviously did not want to change the historical, built-up structure of competences in the Federation. This is understandable, as there would have been much ado about such reallocation, but by sticking to the given order the implementation has been more complex.

2.6 Article 11 SD: Duration of Authorisation

First, it should be mentioned that scholars in Germany see this provision in relation to Article 10 (3), (4) SD. These regulations would provide a principle of "once-only-authorisation" ("Grundsatz der Einmalgenehmigung"), whereupon Article 10 (3), (4) SD determine this principle in a territorial way and Article 11 SD in a temporal way.[165]

Article 11 SD is also seen as plain sailing according to transposition needs.[166] And it can be expected that the European Commission will be strict in this respect,

---

[161] Kopp and Schenke (2011), § 114 VwGO para 1, 4 ff.

[162] Very profound examination on this topic: Hissnauer (2009), 155 ff., p. 173 f.; also: Luch and Schulz (2008b), 59 ff., 85; Cornils, in: Schlachter/Ohler 2008, Article 10 SD para 43.

[163] Hissnauer (2009), 173 ff.

[164] Luch and Schulz (2008b), 85.

[165] Cornils, in: Schlachter and Ohler (2008), Article 11 SD para 1; Krajewski (2009), 932.

[166] Ziekow (2007a), 219; Krajewski (2009), 932.

especially in accordance with Article 11 (4) SD, as a possibly less severe intervention compared to temporarily limited authorisations.[167] Ziekow refers to the fact that for most of the potential cases in this regard the SD is not applicable.[168]

In Germany the principle of unlimited validity usually applies to the regular case of authorisation. This is connected with the aforementioned entitlement to receive authorisation if all requirements are fulfilled. These requirements are proved only at the time of application and cannot be imposed by additional conditions placed on the applicant.[169] But some exemptions are made in specific fields of law. Most probably, as Ziekow states, there have been no changes yet, as most cases where Article 11 SD and its implementation could become relevant are outside the scope of the SD (e.g., public licenses for taxis).[170]

2.7 Article 12 SD: Selection from Among Several Candidates

With respect to Article 12 SD, German scholars primarily refer to Recital 62 as further explanation.

Kluth demands an introduction of a new section into the Administrative Procedures Law, not only for the cases covered by Article 12 SD, but also for other proceedings combined with a selection by the authority.[171] But this very broad demand has not been fulfilled by the legislator.

Actually there is already a provision in the German Trade, Commerce and Industry Regulation Act in this regard (§ 70 GewO). This provision stipulates in clauses 2 and 3 that applicants can be excluded from fairs, exhibitions and markets.[172]

Kluth identifies a need for specialisation of this provision as the particular criteria are not listed in the provision text, which speaks only of exclusion because of "factual justifying reasons".[173] Thus far, § 70 GewO has not been altered or amended. But one must see that there is settled jurisdiction and administrative practice on this provision, which specifies the requirement in a quite detailed manner.[174]

Ziekow and Krajewski stress that Article 12 (1) SD is based on the existing jurisdiction of the ECJ concerning selection decisions, especially in public procurement law.[175] But Ziekow also demands a particular procedural provision for

---

167 Commission Handbook 6.1.4.

168 Ziekow (2007a), 219.

169 Compare U. Stelkens, in: Stelkens et al. (2008), § 36 VwVfG para 122 ff.

170 Ziekow (2007a), 219.

171 Kluth (2008), 131 ff., 154.

172 Schliesky (2003), 220 f.

173 Kluth (2008), 131 ff., 153 f.; critical also: Schliesky (2008a), 26.

174 Ruthig and Storr (2008), § 3 para 351.

175 Ziekow (2007a), 219; Krajewski (2009), 932.

the allocation of scarce authorisations ("eines Verfahrensrechts der Verteilung knapper Genehmigungen").[176]

As mentioned above, as far as perceptible, this has not happened yet and it is not foreseeable if the legislator will do as recommended. Probably this will not be the case.

2.8 Article 13 SD: Authorisation Procedures

2.8.1 A Priori Determination of the Duration of Administrative Procedures, General Rule for the Duration and Exceptions of the General Rule for the Duration

The requirements of Article 13 SD have been transposed in § 42a VwVfG. Thus, again a general clause has been established which builds a consistent regulation on its own, but does not mandate which specific authorisation procedure (in or outside the scope of the SD) applies to it.[177]

Altogether, the federal legislator assumes that the below-treated topic of tacit authorisation will become increasingly common.[178]

§ 42a (2) s.1 VwVfG says that the usual period of time for working on an application is three months, wherein the time does not run out before all necessary information/documents have been submitted to the authority (§ 42a (2) s.2 VwVfG). With respect to the beginning of the decision period—within the scope of the SD—it must be acknowledged that for procedures driven using the POSC, the documents are seen as passed on to the competent authority three days after their receipt at the POSC (§ 71b (2) VwVfG). For the decision period, the competent authority must also take into consideration that according to § 71b (6) VwVfG for authorisations which shall be announced abroad via post, a period of one month for tacit announcement is already included in the three months, so effectively only two months for the authority decision remain.[179]

According to § 42a (2) s.3 VwVfG the decision period can be prolonged once, if this is justified by the difficulties of deciding the case. Such a prolongation must be reasoned and announced to the applicant in due time, § 42a (2) s.4 VwVfG.

In Germany there has been a discussion among scholars on the question "quis iudicabit" concerning the completeness of application documents, as this will mark the starting point of the decision period.[180] The prevailing opinion, as far as it is possible to speak of one in this concern, is correct when it states that the only

[176] Ziekow (2007a), 219 f.

[177] BT-Drs. 16/10493, 15.

[178] BT-Drs. 16/10493, 15.

[179] On the whole complex: BT-Drs. 16/10493, 16; Schmitz and Prell (2009a), 8.

[180] Schmitz and Prell (2009a), 8; Krajewski (2009), 933; Bernhardt (2009), 101 f.

possible, SD-conforming solution can be the point of time when objectively all necessary documents for the decision of the application are submitted. Other starting points would give the competent authorities discretion with respect to the starting point of the decision period. This would not fulfil the strict requirements of Article 13 (3) SD.[181]

Considering the aforementioned issues, it is clear that currently the duration is basically and in general fixed by law. But it might happen that there are changes in the future. As already mentioned, specific adaption of the decision time can be stipulated by specific administrative laws. In these cases, e.g., Schmitz and Prell state that these alternative decision times—shorter or longer depending on the specific needs and the complexity of the different fields of administrative law and authorisation—may also be enacted through publishing decision-time-plans by the competent authorities, which have been previously mandated by a provision of a specific administrative law.[182] Ramsauer[183] argues against this point of view and is probably correct when he says that wording and system of the SD probably argues more for fixation by law.

But obviously even the legislator allows explicitly[184] such sub-law-level organisation of decision times, which makes it more difficult to find the appropriate period of time for certain authorisations. Apparently, the legislator in fact has used the ordinance by law so far.[185]

As implementation has been carried out, again via a general rule in the Administrative Procedures Law, the regulation of tacit authorisation after three months without a decision by the competent authority can also be potentially applied beyond the scope of the SD. The legislator seems to welcome this opportunity and states that he will probably apply this provision in cases beyond the scope of the SD.[186]

There have been recommendations to deviate from the three-month-period in specific administrative laws on the level of the Federation,[187] but up to now there seem to be—as far as apparent by the huge amount of altered acts—only deviations in specific administrative laws of some federal states.[188] On the Federation level for

---

[181] Krajewski (2009), 933; Schmitz and Prell (2009a), 8; also tending for this solution: Commission Handbook 6.1.8. on the intention of Article 13 SD; also the wording of Article 13 (6) and (3) s. 2 SD; Cornils, in: Schlachter and Ohler (2008), Article 13 SD para 1, also on the intention of Article 13 SD.

[182] Schmitz and Prell (2009a), 8.

[183] Ramsauer (2008), 417 ff., 423.

[184] BT-Drs. 16/10493, 16.

[185] E.g., § 6a (1) GewO, which sticks to the three months for authority decision, although the German Bundestag first wanted to reduce this period to two months only (BT-Drs. 16/12784, 6, 15).

[186] BT-Drs. 16/10493, 15.

[187] For the German Trade, Commerce and Industry Regulation Act in BT-Drs. 16/12784, 6, 15; for the Handicrafts Code in BT-Drs. 16/12784, 7.

[188] E.g., in the federal state of Berlin as regards some provisions of the firearms act the duration is six months; § 2 (2) Nr. 1 DLR-VBundR, Bln. GVBl. 2009, 843 and Bln. GVBl. 2010, 198.

instance, no aberration took place in several statutory instruments based on changes demanded by the SD so far.[189] But the act on implementation of the SD in environmental law and other changes of environmental provisions foresees a period of four months in some provisions of the Federal Immissions Control Act.[190] However, generally there has so far been a coherent system of three months, which makes it easier for the applicant, but provokes the question of why the possibility of aberration had arisen at all when nearly all laws stick to the basic period of three months. In this case, a terminated provision might have been clearer, if the legislator wishes not to deviate from the three-month standard. But on the other hand, a strict period might not be sufficient for all administrative procedures.

2.8.2 Tacit Authorisation in the National Legal Order So Far

That the tacit authorisation was "usual" in the German system before the SD would be too strong a word. But there have been already single provisions that stipulated tacit authorisation after a certain decision period for the competent authority.[191] Such provisions are, for example, common in certain building laws of the federal states.[192]

A general provision—such as § 42a VwVfG implementing Article 13 SD in the Administrative Procedures Law—did not exist prior to the implementation of the SD. In this regard, it must be stressed again that § 42a VwVfG only provides a general and consistent procedure, but does not stipulate the application of tacit authorisation to all administrative procedures per se, but by reference in specific administrative laws. This provision would allow application to the whole scale of administrative laws.

Furthermore, it should be mentioned—although not explicitly asked for, but discussed by Krajewski—that the German implementation in this connection builds a reverse scheme to the intended standard-exception-relation of the SD.[193] The SD says in Article 13 (4) s.1 that

"[f]ailing a response within the time period set or extended in accordance with paragraph 3, authorisation shall be deemed to have been granted."

So the standard is that automatically, without any further step, the (tacit) authorisation is granted and only in exceptional cases would this not be the case. In

---

189 No deviation of the standard period of three months took place for example in the new § 9a (1) s.1 statutory instrument in chemicals and climate protection or new § 21 (4) statutory instrument on dumpsites, both in BT-Drs. 17/862, 7 f.

190 BT-Drs. 17/2148, 2 f., 9, 11.

191 Schmitz and Prell (2009a), 7; Krajewski (2009), 934; Hissnauer (2009), 219; profound on the whole topic of tacit authorisation: Caspar (2000), 131 ff.; see also: Kopp and Ramsauer (2011), § 42a VwVfG para 1; Guckelberger (2010), 109 ff.

192 Hissnauer (2009), 219: e.g., in Rhineland-Palatinate for certain buildings underlying only a simple planning authorisation procedure a decision by the authority has to be made within one month (!) after all documents have been submitted (§ 66 (4) s.2 RhPlz-BauO).

193 Krajewski (2009), 933.

Germany this principle is somehow implemented upside-down.[194] The standard is that tacit authorisation usually does not apply. Only in cases of established references in specific administrative laws does tacit authorisation occur. For Krajewski—who refers to this instance and he is probably correct—this instance is not problematic in accordance with the requirements of the SD, so long as in all fields of the scope of the SD a corresponding reference to § 42a VwVfG is installed.[195]

2.8.3 Formal and Substantive Effects of Tacit Authorisation

In this regard, the legislator and nearly all scholars are in consent and are clear[196]: The (tacit) authorisation has only formal, but no substantive effect. This means that the legal fiction only indicates that an authorisation was granted, but not that this authorisation would be legal.

This reception depends on the German system of authorisation by administrative act (§ 35 VwVfG). At the end of an authorisation procedure, the decision of the authority is given to the applicant by positive (granting) or negative (refusal) administrative act. The administrative act constitutes such an important cornerstone in German administrative law that the Administrative Procedures Law provides several specific sections on the character and handling of administrative acts. And there are strict rules according to nullity, revocability and other matters of administrative acts (§§ 35–53 VwVfG). Among these are also provisions to revoke or withdraw an administrative act (§§ 48, 49 VwVfG). A question in accordance with § 48 VwVfG is, whether a fictitious authorisation—which as mentioned above already existed in German administrative law before the implementation of the SD—can be withdrawn because of illegality.[197]

The likely prevailing opinion argues that a fictitious authorisation cannot have more authority than an authorisation granted under the usual procedure.[198] Against this and other arguments on this concern, which cannot be discussed here any further, argues Ziekow who assumes a material/substantive effect of a fictitious authorisation as at least possible.[199] Taking this controversial discussion, already underway before the implementation of the SD, into consideration, it is nearly unavoidable that this discussion becomes even more controversial during the implementation process of Article 13 SD.[200] Although Ziekow doubts that a purely

[194] Bernhardt (2009), 102.

[195] Krajewski (2009), 933 f.

[196] Very broad and distinguished: Hissnauer (2009), 226 ff.; see also U. Stelkens, in: Stelkens et al. (2008), § 35 VwVfG para 68.

[197] See e.g., Caspar (2000), 131 ff., 138.

[198] E.g., Jäde (2009), 169 ff., 170.

[199] Ziekow (2007a), 222.

[200] Cornils, in: Schlachter and Ohler (2008), Article 13 SD para 21.

formal effect is in concert with Article 13 (4) SD,[201] apparently other scholars stick to this purely formal understanding.

That the legislator followed the prevailing opinion can be seen in the new provision of § 42a (1) s. 2 VwVfG, which stipulates that all regulations of authority of administrative acts and the remedy procedure must be applied analogously to fictitious authorisations as well.[202] This means that § 48 VwVfG too will have to be applied and by that it is clear that the legislator follows the prevailing opinion. The grounding of the new provision also states as much. Only the authorisation is fictitious, not its legality.[203]

2.8.4 Rules of Formally Granted Authorisations Applicable to Tacit Authorisations

As already mentioned in the context above, § 42a (1) s.2 VwVfG declares all provisions valid for formally granted administrative procedures for analogous applicable to tacit (fictitious) authorisations as well. So basically all provisions of §§ 36-53 VwVfG can be applied to tacit (fictitious) authorisation.

The legislator states in its reasoning in the draft law that the absence of a decision of the authority is (of course) not a reason for withdrawal of a tacit (fictitious) authorisation, because the intention of Article 13 SD and § 42a VwVfG would thus be thwarted.[204]

The analogous application also means that it is possible to impose collateral additional conditions later on for fictitious authorisation without touching the authorisation itself.[205] This reasoning also stresses that the interest worthy of protection of the beneficiary to maintain the tacit (fictitious) authorisation must be especially protected.[206] In this regard, scholars discuss whether the discretion of the authority given in § 48 VwVfG for withdrawing the tacit (fictitious) authorisation has to be limited to be in consent with the SD's requirements.[207] Such scholars say that the discretion must obey failures of the authority and/or the interest worthy of protection of the applicant/beneficiary for which the tacit (fictitious) authorisation is maintained.[208] In this way, the danger of simple and fast

---

201 Ziekow (2007a), 222; he argues that the "effet utile" requires a material effect as well—anyway between the authority and the applicant—and therefore the European regulation cannot be "weakened" by the opportunity of withdrawel in § 48 VwVfG.

202 See also U. Stelkens, in: Stelkens et al. (2008), § 35 VwVfG para 67.

203 BT-Drs. 16/10493, 15 f.

204 BT-Drs. 16/10493, 16.

205 BT-Drs. 16/10493, 16.

206 BT-Drs. 16/10493, 16.

207 Cornils, in: Schlachter and Ohler (2008), Article 13 SD para 26 ff.; Krajewski (2009), 934.

208 Cornils, in: Schlachter and Ohler (2008), Article 13 SD para 26 ff.; Krajewski (2009), 934.

withdrawal of tacit (fictitious) authorisations in cases of failures by the authority through the authority can be banned.[209]

The analogous application also applies as regards appeal procedures and legal actions.[210]

2.8.5 Further Information on the National Implementation of Tacit Authorisation

In regard to the implementation of Article 13 SD, the other clauses seem to be non-problematic as regards existing German law.[211]

Article 13 (1) SD is seen as a common principle of the rule of law.[212] Although there are different forms of administrative procedure in Germany, it is assumed that in all of them the requirements of Article 13 (1) SD are fulfilled and no implementation is needed.[213]

This is seen differently as regards Article 13 (2) SD.[214] In Germany, the costs of administrative procedures are legally implemented on the Federation level by the "Verwaltungskostengesetz (VwKostG)"[215] [act on costs of administrative procedures].[216] Of course, no amounts are stipulated there in particular, but the principles for calculating the costs of non-court administrative procedures are spelled out. In § 3 S. 1 VwKostG a system of equivalence of administrative costs is laid down, which builds on the very basic principle of the German system of administrative charges, and means that besides the factual costs, aspects such as the benefit of the administrative decision for the applicant or the economic value, are considered to get a proportionate charge rate. So in this case, the charges can exceed the costs of the procedures. § 3 s. 2 VwVfG builds on the opposite principle, where charges must not be higher than the factual costs for administration. But the latter principle applies only when an act explicitly declares this principle valid, otherwise the first principle must be applied. For this reason, the

---

[209] This seems to be the incitement for Ziekow's different and distinguishing opinion; Ziekow (2007a), 222 f.

[210] BT-Drs. 16/10493, 16.

[211] Ziekow (2007a), 223.

[212] Cornils, in: Schlachter and Ohler (2008), Article 13 SD para 2 ff.

[213] Cornils, in: Schlachter and Ohler (2008), Article 13 SD, para 5; Oertel (2006), 165 ff.

[214] See as a short survey by the Federal Ministry for Economics and Technology in German at: http://www.dienstleisten-leicht-gemacht.de/DLR/Redaktion/PDF/gebuehrenrechtliche-vorgaben,property=pdf,bereich=dlr,sprache=de,rwb=true.pdf.

[215] Verwaltungskostengesetz vom 23.06.1970, Bundesgesetzblatt Teil I 1970 Nr. 59 vom 26.06.1970, 821-825 in the current version of 2011. For the corresponding acts of the federal states see: http://www.saarheim.de/Gesetze%20Laender/verwkosten_laender.htm.

[216] It is not possible to show all options of charging systems and laws of the federal states in this report. Therefore only the act of the Federation shall be elucidated. But the regulations in the federal states usually do not deviate largely from these principles.

legislator(s)[217] had to implement at least within the scope of the SD either legal references declaring the second principle applicable[218] or had to implement a general clause in their act on charges for administrative procedures which states that in case of corresponding EU law, the first principle does not apply insofar as EU law requires this.[219] As regards the Federation level, the way of legal reference has been chosen.[220]

The requirement of Article 13 (5) SD has been implemented by § 42a (3) VwVfG. No particulars need to be mentioned. Article 13 (6) SD has been implemented in the new section about the POSC (§ 71b (4) VwVfG). This provision must also be acknowledged, if the applicant does not use the POSC for his procedure, but "only" applies directly at the competent authority (§ 71a (2) VwVfG). Article 13 (7) SD can be seen as being implemented by changing § 25 VwVfG and the introduction of § 71c VwVfG as a general information duty.[221]

2.9 Articles 14, 15, 16 SD

2.9.1 Need of Adaptation?

First, it must be stated that especially Articles 14 and 15 SD and partly Article 16 SD are built from existing requirements stated by the ECJ[222]or Article 56 TFEU. Therefore, one might think that there should be no loose ends which have to be implemented. But on the other hand, Article 16 SD partially goes far beyond Article 56 TFEU or ECJ jurisprudence.[223]

However, the German legislator indeed identified needs of adaption of national law in this regard. The central aim of the law on implementing the SD in the German Trade, Commerce and Industry Regulation Act and further legal acts[224] is

---

[217] Again all federal states had to do so due to their competences.

[218] Compare e.g., Article 1 Nr. 19 b) bb) of Viertes Gesetzes zur Änderung des Sprengstoffgesetzes vom 17.07.2009, Bundesgesetzblatt Teil I 2009 Nr. 44 vom 24.07.2009, 20.

[219] Article IV of Gesetz zur Umsetzung der Richtlinie 2006/123/EG über Dienstleistungen im Binnenmarkt vom 18.11.2009, Bln GVBl 2009, 674, amending § 8 (1) s. 3 and (6) GebBeitrG [act on charges for administrative charges in the federal state of Berlin] with a general clause. See e.g., also Article 2 of Gesetz zur verwaltungsrechtlichen Umsetzung der EG-Dienstleistungsrichtlinie und zur Umsetzung von Bundesgesetzen in das Landesrecht von Mecklenburg-Vorpommern vom 02.12.2009, GVOBl. M-V 2009, 666.

[220] See footnote 215; the act of the Federation on charges for administration procedure has not been amended with a general clause in case of corresponding EU law so far.

[221] Ramsauer (2008), p. 419, sees § 71c VwVfG alone not as sufficient. But by the amendment of § 25 VwVfG to my view his demands should be fulfilled.

[222] Cornils, in: Schlachter and Ohler (2008), Article 14 SD para 1; Article 15 SD para 1; Article 16 SD para 3.

[223] E.g., Krajewski (2009), 934 f.

[224] See Sect. 1.1.

to transpose the requirements of Article 16 SD into German provisions for business activities, especially the German Trade, Commerce and Industry Regulation Act.[225] This law introduces a new § 4 in the German Trade, Commerce and Industry Regulation Act which stipulates that certain enumerated authorisations or provisions are generally not applied to service providers settled in another Member State of the EU or a state of the EEA.[226] This provision is strict, as the German legislator does not see that any of the possible justifying reasons (Article 16 (3) SD) are applicable for most authorisation provisions of the German Trade, Commerce and Industry Regulation Act.[227]

Among the provisions which do not apply for foreign service providers is, for instance, § 34 (1) s.1 no. 1 GewO, which stipulates an authorisation for running a broker business. Further exceptions are laid down in § 4 (1) s.2 GewO for the case that the service provision is not subject to Articles 2 (2) or 17 SD. These exceptions altogether constitute notification obligations,[228] such as the duty of simple notification laid down in § 14 GewO. This is mentioned here, as there has been much discussion about the need to abolish § 14 GewO for transnational service providers settled in another Member State.[229]

It should also be mentioned that the German legislator at first did not precisely distinguish between temporary and permanent service provision in this regard. This assessment is based on the difficulties of distinguishing between the freedom of establishment and the freedom of providing services in accordance with ECJ jurisprudence. The legislator stated that temporary service provision is mentioned in Recital 77, but does not elaborate the definition of "establishment" in Article 4 no.5 SD.[230] But during the legislative process—demanded by the Bundesrat—the feature "temporarily" has been introduced for more clarity in this regard.[231] The federal government was strictly against the introduction of this feature, as it states that the feature "temporarily" is not a definite criterion for distinguishing between the freedom of establishment and the freedom of providing services anymore, and therefore cannot help any further in the application of § 4 GewO based only on transnational service provision without establishment in Germany. Furthermore it argues that Article 4 no. 5 SD speaks of a "stable infrastructure" as a precondition for an establishment. By narrowing the scope of Article 16 SD only to temporary transnational service providers, those service providers who constantly provide services in Germany but have no stable infrastructure would be outside the application of Article 16 SD, respectively, § 4 GewO and thus be assumed as being

[225] BT-Drs. 16/12784, 1.

[226] The old § 4 GewO has been abolished, so this paragraph was not reserved and could be used for this basic and new provision; compare: Schönleiter (2009), 384 ff., 386.

[227] BT-Drs. 16/12784, 11.

[228] Schönleiter (2009), 386.

[229] BT-Drs. 16/12784, 12 f.; BR-Drs. 284/09, 3; BT-Drs. 13190, 6.

[230] BT-Drs. 16/12784, 12.

[231] BR-Drs. 284/09, 1 f.

established in Germany, which is not in concert with the definition of Article 4 no. 5 SD.[232] The argument of the federal government seems compelling, nevertheless the legislative chambers decided differently.

A particular feature of § 4 GewO might be clause 2, which stipulates that clause 1, which provides the exceptions for foreign EU-service providers as mentioned above, is not applicable in case of misuse. If a service provider does provide its services only from another Member State to escape the duties enumerated in clause 1, these exceptions shall not be applied to such providers. In its reasoning, the legislator justifies this clause with existing jurisdiction of the ECJ (e.g., 15/12/2005, Nadin, Nadin-Lux and Durré Rs. C-151/04 and C-152/04) and Recital 79.[233] The impetus for this clause seems to be the fear that German legal standards could be undermined by service providers who might easier establish themselves in another country, or service providers of other Member States with more than one establishment, among them one in Germany, but acting from another establishment.[234] Whether this fear is realistic and whether the clause is really in consent with European law[235] cannot be discussed here, but seems nevertheless doubtful. This fear does—anyway partly—only arise because Germany chose a one-to-one transposition for implementing the requirements of Article 16 SD. For service providers of other Member States outside the scope of the SD and for German service providers, the requirements remain the same as before implementation of the SD.

Further, service providers within the scope of the SD, but established in Germany, will have to fulfil the existing requirements, if they provide the services from their domestic establishment.[236]

That the exceptions of § 4 (1) GewO do not apply to domestic service providers is reasoned by the legislator as associated with the actually abolished country-of-origin principle.[237] As foreign service providers are subject to the provisions and supervision of their home country, further examination by German authorities is not necessary. For German service providers of course, Germany with its legal provisions and supervision is their home country and therefore unequal treatment on this point would be justified.[238]

Based on the changes through § 4 GewO, there will be some follow-up changes in statutory instruments. The current statutory instrument for implementing these changes passed on March 9, 2010.[239]

---

232 BT-Drs. 16/13190, 6.

233 BT-Drs. 16/12784, 14.

234 BT-Drs. 16/12784, 14.

235 Assessing this regulation as in line with EU law: Schönleiter (2009), 386.

236 BT-Drs. 16/12784, 11 f.; Schönleiter (2009), 386.

237 BT-Drs. 16/12784, 12.

238 BT-Drs. 16/12784, 12; Schönleiter (2009), 386; Krajewski (2009), 935.

239 BR-Drs. 25/10; Verordnung vom 09.03.2010, Bundesgesetzblatt Teil I 2010 Nr. 11 vom 17.03.2010, 264.

Furthermore, it should be mentioned that in Germany, Article 16 (2) SD is mainly seen as a so-called black-list, which means that these requirements must be fulfilled strictly and cannot be justified by the choice of overriding reasons to the public interest in Article 16 (3) SD.[240] The reduction of overriding reasons to the public interest is discussed below.

Changes due to the requirements of Articles 14, 15 SD are possible and in some fields probably necessary.[241] But there are no changes to the general approach and regulation. As these requirements are just provisions built up by ECJ jurisprudence, the implementation dimension is assessed as small.[242]

2.9.2 Discussion on the Self-Screening of the Member States

As is evident from the answer above concerning screening in general,[243] this process was a huge challenge for the German authorities.

But apparently there is no statement concerning the exchange of screening subjects. Prior to the SD, the European Commission had to identify offences against European law or ECJ jurisdiction; now the Member States themselves must actively comb through their public (possibly even civil) law. Probably this exchange and the assessment towards this exchange have always been assessed in the implementation process and in the discussion about this process, as it has always been stated as being complicated and a lot of work. But there has not been substantive discussion on this particular point of the SD's requirements.[244]

2.10 Articles 14–19 SD

During the implementation process, many topics pertaining to several provisions of the SD have been discussed.

To answer this question, one must first discuss the relations among the given articles. The first particular in this regard might be that Cornils is of the opinion that the provisions of Articles 14 and 15 SD are applicable not only as regards authorisation in the field of freedom of establishment, but also in regard to the freedom of providing services as far as the provision suits this.[245] The reasoning

---

240 Inter alia: Cornils, in: Schlachter and Ohler (2008), Article 16 SD para 52; Roth (2008), 205 ff., 215; different: Krajewski (2009), 935; Heidfeld (2009), 1471 ff.; not clear: Commission Handbook 7.1.3.4.

241 Hissnauer (2009), 259 f.

242 Kluth (2008), 155.

243 See Sect. 1.6.

244 Callies and Korte (2009), 65, 91 f.; Lemor and Haake (2009), 70.

245 Cornils, in: Schlachter and Ohler (2008), Article 14 SD para 2; Article 9 SD para 11 f.

behind this opinion lies in "argumentum a maiore ad minus". If the (prohibited) requirements of Articles 14, 15 SD are prohibited for establishing a service business, they must also be prohibited if there is only temporary service provision, because the hurdles for the freedom of service provision must be even lower. Although this opinion "weakens" the strict distinction between the freedom of establishment and the freedom of providing services that the Commission Handbook stresses,[246] this argument is striking.

Herresthal argues that for a coherent system of the freedom to provide services, the same exemptions as for temporary service providers must be applied to recipients of services. Hence, the exemptions of Article 17 SD must be applied to Article 19 SD.[247] Herresthal later argues with Recitals 84, 85, 87–90, which also do not distinguish between service providers and recipients of services, but refer solely to the freedom of providing services which encompasses both sides—the provider side and the recipient side.[248] The close connection and reciprocity would also be expressed by Article 16 (2) lit.g) SD, which refers to Article 19 SD. The Commission Handbook states on this matter that by restricting the freedom of recipients of services, the freedom of service providers is restricted as well.[249] This also supports the opinion of Herresthal, which has to be assessed as consequential and correct.

Also discussed is the relation between Article 16 SD and Article 18 SD. One opinion sees Article 18 SD as not self-justifying, but only a special executive competency.[250] Another opinion sees Article 18 SD as a special reason to justify deviations from Article 16 SD.[251] This opinion is entirely consistent with the wording of Article 18 SD, which states, in clause 1: "By way of derogation from Article 16 ...". Although there is no question about the fact that one can of course see only an executive competency in Article 18 (1) SD, it seems that the wording and the connection to Art. 16 SD speak more for the assumption that Article 18 (1) SD is a reason to justify an exemption to Article 16 SD.[252]

Finally it should be stated here that Article 16 (1) lit.b), (3) SD are seen as terminal in Germany.[253] As a result, no other possible overriding reasons to the public interest[254] can be used to justify restrictions in this respect. Even recourse to primary EU Law is seen as not possible.[255]

---

246 Commission Handbook 6.; 6.2.; 6.3.; 7.1.1.

247 Herresthal, in: Schlachter and Ohler (2008), Article 19 SD para 8.

248 Herresthal, in: Schlachter and Ohler (2008), Article 19 SD para 8; stressing the two sides of one medal also: Commission Handbook 7.2.; basically to the freedom of providing services: Craig and de Búrca (2008), 813 ff., 818.

249 Commission Handbook 7.1.3.

250 Schmidt-Kessel, in: Schlachter and Ohler (2008), Article 16 SD para 42.

251 Ohler, in: Schlachter and Ohler (2008), Article 18 SD para 1.

252 See also: Commission Handbook 7.1.5., where an executive role is only seen for clause 2.

253 Schmidt-Kessel, in: Schlachter and Ohler (2008), Article 16 SD para 42, with further references; Krajewski (2009), 934 f.

254 Recital 40; Article 4 no. 8 SD.

255 For reasoning see above Sect. 1.5.

2.11 Articles 22–27 SD

Art. 22 and 27 SD, as well as the requirements of Article 20 (2) SD, were implemented by the statutory instrument on duties to inform recipients of services (short: DL-InfoV).[256] There have already been obligations to inform customers with respect to specific laws (e.g., § 35 a GmbHG) in Germany. Despite these, the legislator chose a general implementation strategy, as the given duties to inform customers were only specific to particular cases, but not given in general before. If existing specific provisions go beyond the requirements of the statutory instrument, they must be applied (§ 2 (1) DL-InfoV). The legislator implemented eleven duties to inform recipients of services and four additional information duties, if requested by the recipient (§ 2 (1), § 3 DL-InfoV). The provided service must be within the scope of Article 2 SD (§ 1 (1) DL-InfoV). The legal basis of the statutory instrument is § 6c GewO, which was introduced by the Law on implementing the SD in the German Trade, Commerce and Industry Regulation Act and further legal acts.[257] This law also provides a horizontal approach by adding a clause 1a to § 6 GewO, which stipulates that § 6c GewO is also applicable to all business providers and other providers with respect to Article 4 no.2 SD. So there is one central provision which declares the DL-InfoV applicable and thus this application need not be implemented repeatedly in each specific law.[258]

Via this implementation, an impact is perceptible insofar as there is now one basic regulation with respect to information duties regarding services. Nevertheless, the existing special provisions remain and are still in force. There might be a coherent system now, but the system is difficult to comprehend.[259]

The information duties were apparently not extended beyond the requirements of the SD.[260]

§ 5 DL-InfoV stipulates that there must not be discrimination, in accordance with the requirements of Article 20 (2) SD, with respect to general conditions of access to a service. To ensure the conduct and observance of the information provisions, fines can be imposed (§ 6 DL-InfoV).

The "Nationaler Normenkontrollrat (NKR)" (National Regulatory Control Council) refers to the huge costs of these information duties and therefore demands an evaluation with the aim of further concentration of various information duties of specific laws and the general DL-InfoV.[261] These costs are still subject to discussion after publication of the draft of the DL-InfoV.[262]

---

[256] BR-Drs. 888/09; Bundesgesetzblatt Teil I Nr. 11 vom 17.03.2010, 264 f.

[257] See Sect. 1.1; see also: Schönleiter (2009), 387.

[258] BT-Drs. 16/12784, 5 f., 14 f.

[259] Lindhorst (2010), 145.

[260] BR-Drs. 888/09, 12-17.

[261] Annex to BR-Drs. 888/09; also the Economic Council of the Bundesrat, in: BR-Drs. 888/1/09, 2.

[262] E.g., Lindhorst (2010), 145.

As regards Article 23 SD, an implementation took place partially by § 13b (2) GewO[263]; whereas the other clauses of Article 23 SD have been seen as not necessary to be transposed.[264]

Generally, one can assume that the requirements of the SD in this regard must be seen as compensation for the abolition of certain authorisation schemes or of prohibited or restricted requirements.[265]

As regards Article 26 SD, the leading position in the process of establishing common standards for quality of services has been taken over by the "Deutsches Institut für Normung e.V. (DIN)",[266] in particular its "Koordinierungsstelle Dienstleistungen (KDL)".[267] DIN, together with KDL, along with various expert groups, are working on common standards for the quality of services and are examining whether European standards can be useful in certain fields of service. Furthermore, the KDL coordinates the communication to all affected bodies and organisations.[268] DIN is an entity under private law, but is mandated by the federal government by contract[269] as the national institute for the elaboration of standards.

Excursus:

At this stage, it might be advisable to provide a brief review on the implementation of the requirements of Article 21 SD. Article 21 SD has been implemented on the Federation level. To ensure constant and qualified information for service recipients, a web-portal[270] has been established by "Germany Trade & Invest",[271] an agency of the Federation for Business Development and investment in Germany, and the "Bundesamt für Verbraucherschutz und Lebensmittelsicherheit" (= The Federal Office of Consumer Protection and Food Safety).[272] The portal gives detailed information on the themes listed in Article 21 (1) SD for the other Member States. It is also possible to directly contact the operators of the portal.

---

263 Also introduced by the German Trade, Commerce and Industry Regulation Act, see Sect. 1.1.

264 Schmidt-Kessel, in: Schlachter and Ohler (2008), Article 23 SD para 10.

265 Schulz (2010b), 27 ff., 32 ff. with further references; Schmidt-Kessel, in: Schlachter and Ohler (2008), Vorbemerkung zu Articles 22 ff. SD para 2.

266 http://www.din.de/cmd?level=tpl-home&contextid=din.

267 http://www.kdl.din.de/cmd?level=tpl-home&contextid=kdl

268 http://www.kdl.din.de/cmd?level=tpl-rubrik&menuid=78794&cmsareaid=78794&menurubricid=78822&cmsrubid=78822&languageid=de

269 http://www.din.de/sixcms_upload/media/2896/Vertrag_BRD_DIN.pdf

270 www.portal21.de.

271 http://www.gtai.com/web_en/homepage.

272 http://www.bvl.bund.de/EN/Home/homepage_node.html.

2.12 Articles 28 ff. SD: Administrative Cooperation[273]

2.12.1 Transnational Administrative Cooperation Prior to the Implementation of the Services Directive

Prior to implementation of the SD, provisions on administrative assistance were part of the German Administrative Procedures Law (§§ 4 ff. VwVfG).[274] But these provisions were applicable only to domestic assistance of authorities[275] and thus were not seen as sufficient in accordance with the requirements of Articles 28 ff. SD. Furthermore, it is well known that § 4 VwVfG is limited to additional help in singular exceptional cases beyond the competence of the assistance-seeking authority. Long-term assistance is usually introduced by legal provision, as consequences for the system of competences have been feared. As it is likely that assistance will increasingly be demanded along with an increasing amount of transnational service provision, new provisions only for assistance in European contexts had to be introduced.[276] Furthermore, this solution gives the advantage of a clear and comprehensible regulation of such assistance cases without discussion on the—possibly analogous—application of such cases to §§ 4 ff. VwVfG.

Remarkable in accordance to the newly introduced section named "European Administrative Cooperation" (§§ 8a-8e VwVfG) is that it has not been introduced by the Fourth Law on changing the Administrative Procedures Law, implementing the procedural and formal requirements of the SD, but by the law on implementing the SD in the German Trade, Commerce and Industry Regulation Act and further legal acts.[277] The Council of Economics and Technology of the German parliament demanded and drafted the mentioned new section,[278] which was later passed by the whole parliament.[279] The reason for this might be[280] that there has been a discussion on whether the requirements of Articles 28 ff. SD should really be incorporated into the Administrative Procedures Act(s),[281] or whether there should be an own codification for the implementation of transnational administrative assistance.

In some federal states, the changes in their acts on administrative procedures, corresponding to changes on the Federation level (§§ 8a-8e VwVfG), additional provisions for the use of the Internal Market Information System (IMI)[282] have

---

[273] On the whole topic see inter alia: Schmitz and Prell (2009b), 1121 ff.

[274] For basic information see: Kopp and Ramsauer (2008), § 4 VwVfG; Stelkens et al. (2008), § 4 VwVfG.

[275] Kopp and Ramsauer (2008), § 4 VwVfG para 8, 9-9b.

[276] Schönleiter (2009), 390; BR-Drs. 16/13399, 12.

[277] For both laws see Sect. 1.1.

[278] BT-Drs. 16/13399, 5 f.

[279] BT-PlPr. 16/227, 25264 A.

[280] Anyway according to Schliesky and Schulz (2010), 309 ff., 314.

[281] As supported e.g., by Windoffer (2008), 797 ff., 801.

[282] http://ec.europa.eu/internal_market/imi-net/index_en.html.

been established by law. These additional provisions, which mainly regulate organizational competences of authorities in regard to the IMI, go along with provisions on data protection.

2.12.2 Re-arrangement with National Rules on Administrative Cooperation

The new introduced section on "European Administrative Cooperation" is consistent and terminal.[283] The new section did not cause an alteration or amendment of the existing assistance provisions of §§ 4 ff. VwVfG. The new provisions were additionally introduced. Thus there is one section for domestic and one section for European assistance; a uniform regulation does not exist, but § 8a (3) VwVfG refers to provisions of §§ 4 ff. VwVfG, which should be analogously applied, if European law is not in opposition.

2.12.3 Provisions on Financial Compensation for Transnational Administrative Cooperation

Indeed, there are new provisions on financial compensation which have been introduced by adding the new section on European assistance to the Administrative Procedures Law.

In the past, there usually has been no charge for administrative assistance due to comity in public international law and to acts of EC Law.[284] Germany has now introduced a new paragraph 8c VwVfG, which stipulates the reimbursement of administrative expenses. But the reimbursement only takes place if demanded by legal acts of the EU. While reasoning this provision, the legislator stresses that basically the own administrative assistance relates to the administrative assistance of the Member States and therefore no charges are required. Only if EU Law by itself declares that expenses of administrative assistance must be reimbursed should the German authorities do so. Besides that, the legislator also stresses the provision of Article 28 (7) SD, and therefore identifies the need of chargeable administrative assistance in case of consultancy of registers, if German authorities are charged for consultancy of registers as well.[285]

2.12.4 Adaptation of the Rules on Data Protection and Professional Secrets

Apparently there has been—so far—no profound change in regard to rules on data protection and professional secrets. But recently the attitude towards necessary

[283] See also Schliesky (2010b), 1 ff., 12-15.

[284] Ohler, in: Schlachter and Ohler (2008), Article 28 SD para 28.

[285] On the whole complex: BT-Drs. 16/13399, 6, 14.

changes in the field of data protection, especially due to the IMI, became under increased discussion.

The attitude that basically there is no need for additional changes in the field of data protection is probably based on the assumption that Ohler gives in commenting on Article 28 SD.[286] As the SD provides no requirements with respect to data protection and professional secrets for the authority in a material manner, other provisions of EU Law must be applied.[287] This would be stressed first by the SD itself, as Article 43 SD orders the application of directive 95/46/EC[288] and directive 02/58/EC.[289] Further on, in the case of unregulated situations, European fundamental rights should apply.[290]

Particularly for personal data, there is one main codification of data protection on the Federation level in Germany[291] which has yet not to be amended throughout the implementation process. As Ohler states, fundamentally, one must acknowledge that there are two sides to consider in cases of administrative assistance and data protection.[292] The Member State providing the information must obey European legislation and its own national requirements for transferring information to foreign authorities. As regards the usage of such information by foreign authorities, this is a question of the laws of the information-receiving Member State.[293]

As regards the data protection laws of the federal states, some changes are evident. For example, one act on the application of the IMI in the federal State of Berlin has been under discussion in the Berlin Parliament,[294] which foresees, on the one hand, rules for the application of the IMI in an organisational way and, on the other hand, in § 3 of the law, special rules on data protection. But altogether this amendment on data protection, which on the one hand refers to the Commission Decision of 12 December 2007 concerning the implementation of the IMI as regards the protection of personal data[295] in its first sentence and, on the other hand, gives an additional requirement for categorised use of personal data in case

[286] Ohler, in: Schlachter and Ohler (2008), Article 28 SD para 29 ff.

[287] Ohler, in: Schlachter and Ohler (2008), Article 28 SD para 33.

[288] Directive 1995/46/EC of 24 October 1995 on protection of individuals with regard to the processing of personal data and on the free movement of such data (OJ L 281, 23.11.1995, 31-50).

[289] Directive 2002/58/EC of 12 July 2002 concerning the processing of personal data and the protection of privacy in the electronic communications sector (OJ L 201, 31.07.2002, 37-47).

[290] Ohler, in: Schlachter and Ohler (2008), Article 43 SD para 1 ff.

[291] Bundesdatenschutzgesetz, Bundesgesetzblatt Teil I Gesetz vom 20.12.1990, 2954; until today several changes.

[292] Ohler, in: Schlachter and Ohler (2008), Article 28 SD para 30.

[293] Weiß (2006), 263 ff., 267.

[294] Bln-Drs. 16/3266, now passed: Gesetz vom 08.07.2010, Bln GVBl 2010, 361; comparable regulation in Rhineland-Palatinate, Article 2 Erstes Landesgesetz zur Umsetzung der Richtlinie 2006/123/EG des Europäischen Parlaments und des Rates vom 12. Dezember 2006 über Dienstleistungen im Binnenmarkt, vom 27.10.2009, RhP GVBl 2009, 355-357.

[295] *OJ L no. 13, 16.1.2008, 18–23.*

of the alert mechanism (Article 32 SD), does not provide real or new regulation with respect to the data protection act of the Berlin Parliament. In fact, the amendment clearly refers to the regulations of the Berlin act on data protection. This amendment clause on data protection in the Berlin law seems to be more or less simply an affirmation of the usual data protection act slightly amended by the reference to the Commission Decision and a concretion as regards the alert mechanism of Article 32 SD.[296] A real (profound) change in data protection law would look much different. But § 3 of the law nevertheless gives a special legal source for using and working with personal data in accordance with the rules of the Berlin data protection act, and hence provides more legal certainty for the affected authority. One final remark on the law in Berlin: According to § 2 of the draft law, the IMI system is also applied in certain fields of national administration, not just in the transnational transmission of data.

As a result, there are slight amendments and more detailed regulations on data protection in the federal states or for the Federation—sometimes also in the acts establishing the POSC[297]—but according to the current state of practice and discussion, this will probably not lead to a profound change in the system of data protection in Germany.

Aside from the general law on data protection, three additional provisions must be acknowledged. One is newly introduced into the above-mentioned new section of the Administrative Procedures Law as § 8d VwVfG. In its first clause, this paragraph stipulates the duty of competent authorities to provide information about facts and persons as far as required by legal acts of the EU. This information should be provided "ex officio".[298] This clause therefore especially pertains to the implementation of Article 29 (3) and Article 32 (1) SD.[299]

Clause two of § 8d VwVfG stipulates the duty for the competent authority to inform the person whose information was requested by the other Member State as to the transmission of information, but again only if legal acts of the EU so require. The character of the information, its purpose and the legal means of transmission must be communicated to the relevant person. This clause is meant as a transposition of information duties, such as outlined in Article 33 (1) s.2 SD.[300]

Reasoning on § 8d (2) VwVfG, the legislator stresses that, generally, the source for data protection in cases of information transmission due to clause 1 is the specific EU Law provision amended by directive 95/46/EC or the national transposition laws of the Member States and specific national law provisions amended by the subsidiary law on data protection.[301]

---

[296] Compare also the reasoning of the law: Bln-Drs. 16/3266, 9.

[297] Compare e.g., § 8 Thüringer ES-Errichtungsgesetz, § 19 Errichtungsgesetz Einheitlicher Ansprechpartner.

[298] BT-Drs. 16/13399, 14.

[299] BT-Drs. 16/13399, 14.

[300] BT-Drs. 16/13399, 14.

[301] BT-Drs. 16/13399, 14.

The other provision of interest in this regard is § 11b GewO, which provides special and hence paramount regulations for regulated professions in accordance with transmission of personal data in the EU/EEA. Although applicable to regulated professions,[302] it should be mentioned that § 11b GewO has not been implemented because of the SD, but because of the directive[303] on the recognition of professional qualifications,[304] and therefore is valid only for regulated professions under directive 200/36/EC.

Schönleiter stresses another important difference between § 8d VwVfG and § 11b GewO, specifically: the latter usually does not apply ex officio, but only on demand of a foreign authority.[305] From this principle, § 11b (1) s.2 GewO makes only one exception: if there are actually leads that the information is needed by the foreign competent authority to carry out its given task. But this should always be the case in the scope of the SD, so this difference should not really matter.[306]

Because of the European directives on data protection, there is no violation of data protection through administrative assistance; in fact they constitute the justifying reasons for the assistance.[307]

2.13 Article 29 SD: Mutual Assistance—General Obligations for the Member State of Establishment

As mentioned above, implementation of Article 29 (3) SD has been achieved through the introduction of § 8d (1) VwVfG. Altogether there has been no further discussion about the implementation of Article 29 SD. § 8a VwVfG, which states the principle of European assistance in German administrative law, can be seen as further implementation as well.

Apparently there was—astonishing if one considers the discussions before the passage of the SD[308]—no discussion of Article 29 (1) SD as far as "not unlawful business conduct" is concerned.

[302] Schönleiter (2009), 390 f.

[303] Directive 200/36/EC of 7 September 2005, OJ L no. 255, 30.09.2005, 22-142; meanwhile several corrigenda.

[304] BT-Drs. 16/12784, 15.

[305] Schönleiter (2009), 390 f.

[306] Schönleiter (2009), 391.

[307] Ohler, in: Schlachter and Ohler (2008), Article 43 SD para 4; comparabel: Kopp and Ramsauer (2008), § 8d VwVfG para 3.

[308] Streinz and Leible, in: Schlachter and Ohler (2008), Introduction para 30 ff.

2.14 Problems and Discourses on Administrative Cooperation

Perhaps it should be mentioned that the alert mechanism of Article 32 (1) SD has been implemented by the new paragraph 1 of § 8d VwVfG in the section "European Administrative Cooperation".

For implementation of the new section, it should be mentioned again that a general provision has been introduced into the German Administrative Procedures Law, avoiding fragmentation through specific law implementation.[309]

§ 8a (3) VwVfG declares provisions of the originally domestic administrative assistance system for applicable[310] as far as EU Law does not oppose. By this reference other requirements of Chapter VI can be implemented. So by analogous application of § 7 VwVfG (conduct of assistance), the requirements of Article 29 (2) s.2 SD and Article 31 (3) s.2 SD can be seen as implemented.[311] The requirements of Article 35 SD are (as a further example) introduced by the application of § 8a (2) s.2, (3) VwVfG in accordance with § 5 (1) VwVfG.[312] This system of references has the additional positive aspect that the German authorities can deal with already known provisions and principles.[313]

2.15 Convergence Programme (Chapter VII of the Services Directive)

Apparently no discussions about Chapter VII on Convergence took place. Only Article 43 SD has been discussed with respect to data protection in the Member States. This has already been treated above.

3 Assessment of the Impact of the Services Directive

3.1 Extent of the Impact

Indeed the impact of the SD in Germany has been severe, not only for service providers within the scope of the SD, but even beyond, as shown above. The instance of consequent screening of all provisions of administrative law in regard to their accordance with the freedom of establishment and the freedom to provide

309 Schmitz and Prell (2009b), 1123.

310 The analogous applicable rules are §§ 5, 7, 8 (2) VwVfG.

311 BT-Drs. 16/13399, 13.

312 Schmitz and Prell (2009b), 1124.

313 BT-Drs. 16/13399, 13.

services seems to have built a new awareness of burdens for service providers and, moreover, the netting of provisions became once more the focus of discussion. This on its own would be a great achievement, but beyond the general implementation strategy, it seems to be an ambitious basis for further modernising reforms in the administrative sector. Therefore, the SD gives great impulse—just think for example of the IT-infrastructure that has to be built up and of course, when such a standard is achieved, it will also be applied in additional areas of administrative law—and hopefully it will be a further, decisive step in modernising administrative (procedure) law. Nevertheless, one has to say that implementation in a general way, as chosen in Germany, only provides the chance of further improvement. The legislator must not remain on the currently achieved status, but must make use of the general provisions (especially as regards the POSC and the tacit authorisation) by reference to administrative law outside the scope of the SD and should even take on the evaluation duties as incentive for steady renewal and proof of its administrative law canon.[314]

3.2 Assessment of the Transposing Legislation

The discussion whether the transposition of the SD in Germany can be assessed as great improvement has continued to be quite lively in Germany. Some scholars think that the implementation has not been sufficiently ambitious, because there has been no deviation from the given order of the SD and the single requirements have been implemented as far as needed, but not beyond.[315] This might be correct, if only the specific requirements are examined, along with the respectively implemented provisions, but this cannot constitute the overall assessment. Of course, one could have wished that by implementing the POSCs, competence structures would have been changed or the rights to information would have been extended compared to the requirements of the SD during the implementation process. And of course one could have maintained the hope that the material provisions, especially the changes in the Law on implementing the SD in the German Trade, Commerce and Industry Regulation Act and further legal acts, would be applied to domestic business persons as well, and not only the procedural provisions. But again, one must observe the overall implementation, and consider the approach; especially in the field of administrative procedure one must say that the SD released great impulse for German administrative law. This assessment is based primarily on the following conditions:

All provisions of German law had to be screened as to their compatibility with the SD's requirements. Those provisions not in concert with the SD had to be

---

314 So also Schliesky (2010a), 273 f.

315 E.g., Ernst (2009), 953, 960; to some extent also Schliesky (2010a), 272 ff.; Schliesky (2010b), 1 ff., 19 ff.

altered, amended or abolished. The Administrative Procedures Law remains a basic resource for all administrative procedures and has taken on new sections, potentially applicable to every relation. Hence, these new rights are basically open for actions in every field of action of an authority. The legislator wanted this broad and open implementation and therefore did not want a one-to-one implementation as regards the procedural requirements of the SD.[316] This means that the POSC section and the section on rights to information and tacit information can be applied potentially in every possible relation. This is a substantial achievement. Possibly with respect to material requirements—especially regarding statutes governing restaurants (see above)—a more ambitious implementation would have been desirable. Nevertheless the improvement in administrative procedures is incontrovertible, and the basis for an even more ambitious reform is quite well established.

One must also take into consideration that there has been a deviation from the "doctrine" of one-to-one transposition of directives in Germany as regards administrative procedures. Again it should be stressed that it seems that the SD is seen as a good cause—at least for the federal legislator or government—to induce changes that might were desired before, but that have not been politically enforceable.[317] However, at the same time, one must say that, especially with respect to the POSCs but also beyond them, a homogeneous way of implementation has not been achieved in a sufficient way.[318] This situation should be based basically on the federal system of Germany and accordingly some chances have been missed aside from the commonly implemented procedural rights of the SD. This twofold situation led obviously to different views on implementation in Germany.

3.3 *Most Important and Profound Changes Induced by the Services Directive*

The most important change is the implementation of procedural rights as general rules in the Administrative Procedures Law. With this broad implementation the first step towards new administrative procedures beyond the service sector has been made. Aside from the POSCs, tacit authorisation especially can build an instrument for further improvement in administrative procedural law. The POSCs and the corresponding new procedures in the Administrative Procedures Law give the possibility of establishing such front-office-models throughout the whole administration and thus great improvement for the applicant can be achieved. These changes—if they are cultivated by the legislator(s)—sustainably affect subsequent developments in administrative law. Besides this very important aspect

[316] BT-Drs. 16/10493, 12.

[317] U. Stelkens, in: Stelkens et al. (2011/2012), Europarecht para 239.

[318] Critical also inter alia Schliesky (2010a), 269 ff.

of German implementation, another one is the progress in eGovernment structures in Germany. As this analysis is based on laws, the whole branch of eGovernment support induced by the implementation of the SD cannot be shown in this report. But on the whole, there has been a lot of factual work on this issue and a lot of discussion among administration groups on this topic. The SD opened the gate to a new decisive step towards a real "eGovernment" structure, although today for a full functioning "eGovernment", there are still many things to be done.

References

For legislation, jurisprudence and websites please refer to 1.1 of the report and footnotes directly.

Journal Articles

Bernhardt D (2009) Fingierte Genehmigung nach der Dienstleistungsrichtlinie—Möglichkeiten der Regelung und Einschränkung. In: Gewerbearchiv (GewArch), pp 100–106

Callies C, Korte S (2009) Die Dienstleistungsfreiheit und ihre Umsetzung in Deutschland. In: Europarecht (EuR), pp 65–92

Caspar J (2000) Der fiktive Verwaltungsakt—Zur Systematisierung eines aktuellen verwaltungsrechtlichen Instituts. In: Archiv des öffentlichen Rechts (AöR), pp 131–153

Ernst C (2009) Die Einführung eines einheitlichen Ansprechpartners i.S. der EU-Dienstleistungsrichtlinie durch das 4. Gesetz zur Änderung verwaltungsverfahrensrechtlicher Vorschriften. In: Deutsches Verwaltungsblatt (DVBl.), pp 953–961

Guckelberger A (2010) Die Rechtsfigur der Genehmigungsfiktion. In: Die Öffentliche Verwaltung (DÖV), pp 109–118

Heidfeld C (2009) Abschaffung der gewerberechtlichen Aufnahmeüberwachung für grenzüberschreitend tätige Dienstleistungserbringer. In: Neue Zeitschrift für Verwaltungsrecht (NVwZ), pp 1471–1473

Jäde H (2009) Die verwaltungsverfahrensrechtliche Genehmigungsfiktion. In: Umwelt- und Planungsrecht (UPR), pp 169–173

Körner M (2007) EU-Dienstleistungsrichtlinie und Arbeitsrecht. In: Neue Zeitschrift für Arbeitsrecht (NZA), pp 233–238

Korte, S (2007) Was bleibt vom herkömmlichen Verständnis der Dienstleistungsfreiheit?—Zur Überlagerung der Art. 49 f. EG durch die Art.16 ff. der Dienstleistungsrichtlinie. In: Europäisches Wirtschafts- und Steuerrecht (EWS), pp 246–255

Krajewski, M (2009) Anforderungen der Dienstleistungsrichtlinie an Genehmigungsregelungen und ihre Umsetzung im deutschen Recht. In: Neue Zweitschrift für Verwaltungsrecht (NVwZ), pp 929–935

Lemor F, Haake K (2009) Ausgesuchte Rechtsfragen der Umsetzung der Dienstleistungsrichtlinie. In: Europäische Zeitschrift für Wirtschaftsrecht (EuZW), pp 65–70

Lindhorst H (2010) Vorhang auf zum nächsten Akt: Die Dienstleistungsinformationspflichten-Verordnung. In: Multimedia und Recht (MMR), pp 145–146

Luch AD, Schulz SE (2010) Die Gesetzgebung der Bundesländer zur Einrichtung Einheitlicher Ansprechpartner nach Art. 6 DLR. In: Gewerbearchiv (GewArch), pp 225–230

Mann T (2009) Randnotizen zur Umsetzung der Dienstleistungsrichtlinie im Gewerberecht. In: Gewerbearchiv (GewArch), pp 93–97

Ramsauer U (2008) Änderungsbedarf im Verwaltungsverfahrensrecht aufgrund der Dienstleistungsrichtlinie. In: Zeitschrift für Öffentliches Recht in Norddeutschland (NordÖR), pp 417–425

Schliesky U (2010a) Die Richtlinie über Dienstleistungen im Binnenmarkt—Gemeinschaftsrechtlicher Anstoß zu einer gescheiterten Verwaltungsreform? In: Deutsche Verwaltungspraxis (DVP), pp 266–274

Schliesky U, Luch AD, Schulz SE (2008) Überlegungen zum Anwendungsbereich der Dienstleistungsrichtlinie. In: Wirtschaft und Verwaltung (WiVerw), pp 151–175

Schmitz H, Prell L (2009a) Verfahren über eine einheitliche Stelle – Das Vierte Gesetz zur Änderung verwaltungsverfahrensrechtlicher Vorschriften, in: Neue Zeitschrift für Verwaltungsrecht (NVwZ), pp 1–12

Schmitz H, Prell L (2009b) Europäische Verwaltungszusammenarbeit – Neue Regelungen im Verwaltungsverfahrensgesetz. In: Neue Zeitschrift für Verwaltungsrecht (NVwZ), pp 1121–1128

Schönleiter U (2009) Das neue Gesetz zur Umsetzung der Dienstleistungsrichtlinie in der GewO. In: Gewerbearchiv (GewArch), pp 384–391

Schulz SE (2009) Kommunale Friedhofssatzung und EU-Dienstleistungsrichtlinie—eine unendliche Geschichte. In: Kommunaljurist (KommJur), pp 441–448

Siegel T (2009) IT im Grundgesetz. In: Neue Zeitschrift für Verwaltungsrecht (NVwZ), pp 1128–1131

Siegel T (2010) Neue Querschnittsaufgaben und Gewaltenteilung – Zur Vereinbarkeit der neuen IT-Strukturen und damit verbundener Beschaffungen mit der vertikalen und horizontalen Gewaltenteilung. In: Der Staat Bd. 49, pp 299–322

Stober R (2008) Die Bedeutung der Dienstleistungsrichtlinie (DLR) für das Wirtschaftsverwaltungsrecht. In: Wirtschaft und Verwaltung (WiVerw), pp 139–150

Weiß W (2006) Grundrechtsschutz im EG-Kartellverfahren nach der Verfahrensnovelle, in: Europäische Zeitschrift für Wirtschaftsrecht (EuZW), pp 263–268

Windoffer A (2007) Die Implementierung einheitlicher Ansprechpartner nach der EU-Dienstleistungsrichtlinie—Problemfelder und Anpassungsbedarf im nationalen Recht. In: Neue Zeitschrift für Verwaltungsrecht (NVwZ), pp 495–501

Windoffer A (2008) Die Gesetzgebungsvorhaben des Bundes und der Länder zur verwaltungsverfahrensrechtlichen Umsetzung der EG-Dienstleistungsrichtlinie. In: Die Öffentliche Verwaltung (DÖV), pp 797–801

Ziekow J (2007a) Die Auswirkungen der Dienstleistungsrichtlinie auf das deutsche Genehmigungsverfahrensrecht. In: Gewerbearchiv (GewArch), pp 179–183, 217–255

Books

Bader J, Ronellenfitsch M (2010) Beck'scher Online-Kommentar VwVfG, 6th edn.

Böhret C, Grunow D, Ziekow J (eds) (2006) Der Vorschlag zu einer Richtlinie des Europäischen Parlaments und des Rates über Dienstleistungen im Binnenmarkt—Regelungsgehalt-Problemfelder-Akteurpositionen, Speyerer Forschungsbericht Nr. 241

Craig P, De Búrca G (2008) EU Law: Text, Cases and Materials, 4th edn. Oxford University Press, Oxford

Deutscher Bundestag, Bundesrat (eds) (2010) Die Gemeinsame Kommission von Bundestag und Bundesrat zur Modernisierung der Bund-Länder-Finanzbeziehungen—Die Beratung und ihre Ergebnisse. Berlin

Erichsen H-U, Ehlers D (eds) (2010) Allgemeines Verwaltungsrecht, 14th edn. Walter de Gruyter Verlag, Berlin

Graf C, Paschke M, Stober R (eds) (2009) Die europäische Dienstleistungsrichtlinie—Turbo für die Wirtschaft oder Sturm im Wasserglas?, Verlag Dr. Kovac

Hissnauer D (2009) Auswirkungen der Dienstleistungsrichtlinie auf das deutsche Genehmigungsverfahrensrecht, Nomos-Verl.-Ges

Kopp FO, Ramsauer U (2008) Verwaltungsverfahrensgesetz—Gesetzeskommentar, 10th edn. C.H. Beck Verlag

Kopp FO, Ramsauer U (2011) Verwaltungsverfahrensgesetz—Gesetzeskommentar, 12th edn. C.H. Beck Verlag

Kopp FO, Schenke R (2011) Verwaltungsgerichtsordnung—Gesetzeskommentar, 17th edn. C.H. Beck Verlag

Leible S (ed) (2008) Die Umsetzung der Dienstleistungsrichtlinie—Chancen und Risiken für Deutschland, JWV Jenaer Wiss. Verl.-Ges

Posser H, Wolf HA (2008) Verwaltungsgerichtsordnung—Gesetzeskommentar. C.H. Beck Verlag

Ruthig J, Storr S (2008) Öffentliches Wirtschaftsrecht, 2nd. edn. C.F. Müller Verlag

Schilling P (2009) Neuland EU-Dienstleistungsrichtlinie. Beuth Verlag

Schlachter M, Ohler C (eds) (2008) Europäische Dienstleistungsrichtlinie—Gesetzeskommentar. Nomos-Verl.-Ges

Schliesky U (2003) Öffentliches Wirtschaftsrecht, UTB Taschenbuch, 2nd edn. C. F. Müller Verlag

Schliesky U (ed) (2008) Die Umsetzung der EU-Dienstleistungsrichtlinie in der deutschen Verwaltung—Teil I: Grundlagen, Lorenz-von-Stein-Institut für Verwaltungswiss. an der Christian-Albrechts-Universität

Schliesky U (ed) (2009) Die Umsetzung der EU-Dienstleistungsrichtlinie in der deutschen Verwaltung—Teil II: Verfahren, Prozesse, IT-Umsetzung, Lorenz-von-Stein-Institut für Verwaltungswiss. an der Christian-Albrechts-Universität

Schliesky U (ed) (2010) Die Umsetzung der EU-Dienstleistungsrichtlinie in der deutschen Verwaltung—Teil III: Information, Wissen und Verantwortung, 2010, Lorenz-von-Stein-Institut für Verwaltungswiss. an der Christian-Albrechts-Universität

Stelkens P, Bonk HJ, Sachs M (eds) (2008) Verwaltungsverfahrensgesetz—Gesetzeskommentar, 7th edn. C.H. Beck Verlag

Stelkens P, Bonk HJ, Sachs M (eds) (2011/2012) Verwaltungsverfahrensgesetz—Gesetzeskommentar, 8th edn. forthcoming, C.H. Beck Verlag

Streinz R (2003) EUV/EGV—Gesetzeskommentar. C.H. Beck Verlag

Tettinger PJ, Wank R, Ennuschat J (2011) Gewerbeordnung—Kommentar, 8th edn. C.H. Beck Verlag

Ziekow J (2007b) Öffentliches Wirtschaftsrecht. C.H. Beck Verlag

Book Chapters

Eckert K-P (2009) IT-Architektur als Rahmen für die Realisierung der DLRL. In: Schilling, Neuland EU-Dienstleistungsrichtlinie, Beuth Verlag, pp 115–141

Falke J (2009) Umsetzung der Dienstleistungsrichtlinie—statt befürchteten Sozialdumpings erhoffte Verwaltungsreform? In: Fischer-Lescano et al. (eds) Europäische Gesellschaftsverfassung—Zur Konstitutionalisierung sozialer Demokratie in Europa, Nomos-Verl.-Ges, pp 199–225

Grzeszick B (2010) Staatshaftungsrecht. In: Erichsen and Ehlers (eds) Allgemeines Verwaltungsrecht, 14th edn. Walter de Gruyter Verlag, pp 931–1040

Kluth W (2008) Auswirkungen der Dienstleistungsrichtlinie auf die Handwerks- und Gewerbeordnung. In: Leible S (ed) Die Umsetzung der Dienstleistungsrichtlinie—Chancen und Risiken für Deutschland, JWV Jenaer Wiss. Verl.-Ges, pp 131–156

Luch AD, Schulz SE (2008a) Der personelle Anwendungsbereich der EU-Dienstleistungsrichtlinie—Verpflichtung zur einheitlichen Umsetzung der Vorgaben für inländische und grenzüberschreitende Sachverhalte. In: Schliesky U (ed) Die Umsetzung der EU-Dienstleistungsrichtlinie in der deutschen Verwaltung—Teil I: Grundlagen, Lorenz-von-Stein-Institut für Verwaltungswiss. an der Christian-Albrechts-Universität, pp 33–58

Luch AD, Schulz SE (2008b) Der sachliche Anwendungsbereich der EU-Dienstleistungsrichtlinie—Zur Abgrenzung von dienstleistungsspezifischen Genehmigungen und solchen allgemeiner Natur. In: Schliesky U. (ed) Die Umsetzung der EU-Dienstleistungsrichtlinie in der deutschen Verwaltung—Teil I: Grundlagen, Lorenz-von-Stein-Institut für Verwaltungswiss. an der Christian-Albrechts-Universität, pp 59–116

Luch AD, Schulz SE (2009) Vorgaben der EU-Dienstleistungsrichtlinie zur elektronischen Verfahrensabwicklung—Gemeinschaftsrechtlicher Zwang zur Verrechtlichung des eGovernment und Chance für einen kohärenten und effektiven IuK-Einsatz in der öffentlichen Verwaltung? In: Teil II: Verfahren, Prozesse, IT-Umsetzung, Lorenz-von-Stein-Institut für Verwaltungswiss. an der Christian-Albrechts-Universität, pp 219–324

Oertel M-P (2006) Teil 4: Problemfeldanalyse, B. Beschreibung ausgewählter Problemfelder. In: Böhret C, Grunow D, Ziekow J (eds) Der Vorschlag zu einer Richtlinie des Europäischen Parlaments und des Rates über Dienstleistungen im Binnenmarkt—Regelungsgehalt-Problemfelder-Akteurpositionen, Speyerer Forschungsbericht Nr. 241, pp 138–211

Roth W-H (2008) Die Dienstleistungsrichtlinie und der Verbraucherschutz, in: Leible (ed), Die Umsetzung der Dienstleistungsrichtlinie—Chancen und Risiken für Deutschland, JWV Jenaer Wiss. Verl.-Ges., pp 205–235

Ruffert M (2010) Verwaltungsakt. In: Erichsen, Ehlers (eds) Allgemeines Verwaltungsrecht, 14th edn. Walter de Gruyter Verlag, pp 669–755

Schliesky U (2008a) Das Ende der deutschen Verwaltung?—Die europäische Dienstleistungsrichtlinie - Anstoß zur Verwaltungsmodernisierung und Zwang zur Verwaltungsreform. In: Schliesky (ed) Die Umsetzung der EU-Dienstleistungsrichtlinie in der deutschen Verwaltung—Teil I: Grundlagen, Lorenz-von-Stein-Institut für Verwaltungswiss. an der Christian-Albrechts-Universität, pp 1–32

Schliesky U (2008b) Der einheitliche Ansprechpartner und die Grenzen der Verbandskompetenz. In: Leible (ed) Die Umsetzung der Dienstleistungsrichtlinie—Chancen und Risiken für Deutschland, JWV Jenaer Wiss. Verl.-Ges., pp 43–72

Schliesky U (2009a) E-Government: Neuer Schub durch die Richtlinie? In: Graf et al. Die europäische Dienstleistungsrichtlinie—Turbo für die Wirtschaft oder Sturm im Wasserglas? Verlag Dr. Kovac, pp 99–160

Schliesky U (2010b) Die Umsetzung der EU-Dienstleistungsrichtlinie als (gescheiterter) Innovationsprozess?—Wissen, Information und deren Management als Zukunftsaufgabe und wesentlicher Faktor der Verwaltungsmodernisierung. In: Schliesky (ed) Die Umsetzung der EU-Dienstleistungsrichtlinie in der deutschen Verwaltung—Teil III: Information, Wissen und Verantwortung, Lorenz-von-Stein-Institut für Verwaltungswiss. an der Christian-Albrechts-Universität, pp 1–25

Schliesky U, Schulz SE, Neidert A (2010) Bewertung der Richtlinienumsetzung in Deutschland—Der Einheitliche Ansprechpartner im Verfahrens- und Organisationsrecht. In: Schliesky (ed) Die Umsetzung der EU-Dienstleistungsrichtlinie in der deutschen Verwaltung—Teil III: Information, Wissen und Verantwortung, Lorenz-von-Stein-Institut für Verwaltungswiss. an der Christian-Albrechts-Universität, pp 249–307

Schliesky U, Schulz SE (2010) Bewertung der Richtlinienumsetzung in Deutschland—Die europäische Amtshilfe der §§ 8a ff. VwVfG und das Internal Market Information System. In: Schliesky (ed), Die Umsetzung der EU-Dienstleistungsrichtlinie in der deutschen Verwaltung—Teil III: Information, Wissen und Verantwortung, Lorenz-von-Stein-Institut für Verwaltungswiss. an der Christian-Albrechts-Universität, pp 309–339

Schulz SE (2008) Die bundesweite Geltung von Genehmigungen nach der EU-Dienstleistungsrichtlinie— Art. 10 Abs. 4 DLR als Herausforderung für die Verbandskompetenz. In: Schliesky (ed) Die Umsetzung der EU-Dienstleistungsrichtlinie in der deutschen Verwaltung—Teil I: Grundlagen, 2008, Lorenz-von-Stein-Institut für Verwaltungswiss. an der Christian-Albrechts-Universität, pp 175–201

Schulz SE (2010a) Bewertung der Richtlinienumsetzung in Deutschland: Elektronische Verfahrensabwicklung und IT-Umsetzung. In: Schliesky (ed) Die Umsetzung der EU-Dienstleistungsrichtlinie in der deutschen Verwaltung—Teil III: Information, Wissen und Verantwortung, Lorenz-von-Stein-Institut für Verwaltungswiss. an der Christian-Albrechts-Universität, pp 205–248

Schulz SE (2010b) Reichweite der Informationsverpflichtungen staatlicher Stellen aus der EU-Dienstleistungsrichtlinie. In: Schliesky (ed) Die Umsetzung der EU-Dienstleistungsrichtlinie in der deutschen Verwaltung—Teil III: Information, Wissen und Verantwortung, Lorenz-von-Stein-Institut für Verwaltungswiss. an der Christian-Albrechts-Universität, pp 27–82

Streinz R (2008) Die Ausgestaltung der Dienstleistungs- und Niederlassungsfreiheit durch die Dienstleistungsrichtlinie - Anforderungen an das nationale Recht. In: Leible S (ed) Die Umsetzung der Dienstleistungsrichtlinie—Chancen und Risiken für Deutschland, JWV Jenaer Wiss. Verl.-Ges., pp 95–129

Online Document

European Commission Handbook. English version available at: http://ec.europa.eu/internal_market/services/docs/services-dir/guides/handbook_en.pdf

Ziekow J, Beck D, Bohne E, Hill H, Jansen D (2006) Gestaltungsanforderungen an "Einheitliche Ansprechpartner" des Vorschlages einer EU-Dienstleistungsrichtlinie im föderalen System der Bundesrepublik Deutschland. Available in German at: http://www.dienstleisten-leicht-gemacht.de/DLR/Redaktion/PDF/gestaltungsoptionen-und-anforderungen-an-einheitliche,property=pdf,bereich=dlr,sprache=de,rwb=true.pdf

Documents of the *parliament* are available at: http://dipbt.bundestag.de/dip21.web/bt or for documents of the *second chamber* (Bundesrat; BR-Drs.): http://www.bundesrat.de/cln_152/nn_8336/DE/parlamentsmaterial/berat-vorg/suche-beratungsvorgaenge-node.html?__nnn=true

The Implementation of the Services Directive in Hungary

Anita Boros

1 General Remarks on the Transposition Strategy and General Understanding of the Implementation

1.1 Main References Used in This Research

Parliamentary documents: http://www.parlament.hu/internet/plsql/internet_irom

- Electronic list of laws: on DVD (called "Jogtár" = database of laws) and at www.magyarorszag.hu (free official website with the actual laws). These databases contain the Hungarian legal acts in force. Since many legal acts were affected by the implementation, and several new ones were adopted, it would be difficult to highlight only one or two.
- Reports of the central and local public administration.
- Coordination materials of the regional public administration office (e.g., http://www.darkh.hu/belso-piaci-szolgaltatasi-iranyelv).
- Study of the project 'Preparation of the project on the implementation of the 2006/123/EU directive on inner market services' (http://www.ekk.gov.hu/hu/ekk/sajtokozlemenyek/20090330_sajtokozlemeny).

Assistant Professor Anita Boros, Ph.D., L.L.M., Faculty of Public Administration, Corvinus University Budapest (anita.boros@uni-corvinus.hu). This document was audited by the experts of the Hungarian Foreign Ministry. I wish to thank them for their excellent work.

A. Boros (✉)
Faculty of Public Administration, Corvinus University Budapest, Budapest, Hungary
e-mail: anita.boros@uni-corvinus.hu

U. Stelkens et al. (eds.), *The Implementation of the EU Services Directive*,
DOI: 10.1007/978-90-6704-840-8_12,

1.2 *Impact of the Services Directive*

1.2.1 Profound Cause of Changes to National Law?

The transposition itself was a huge challenge with an enormous workload in every Member State (MS). In Hungary most of the laws on Public Administration was affected by the Services Directive (SD) so these had to be screened one by one, in depth. It was a great opportunity for the experts responsible for the screening to concentrate not only on the three most significant sets of articles of the SD (screening, deregulation/single points of contact, and electronic procedures/ administrative cooperation) but also on Article 5 (simplification of procedures), and thus be able to eliminate unnecessary and complicated administrative burdens on service providers. This exercise resulted in several cases in faster, simpler, and one-step administrative procedures.

The period of the implementation of the SD furthermore coincided with the general political intention to modify the legal basis of the public administration to create a more modern, client-friendly, electronic-based public administration. The Ministry of Justice and Law Enforcement therefore drafted the law on the law amendments relative to Act CXI of 2008 (hereinafter referred to as the Ket-novel) amending Act CXL of 2004 (hereinafter referred to as Ket) on the general rules of administrative procedures and services and its sectoral modification.

In light of the number of acts concerned, it was appropriate to arrange for the adoption of such amendments in a package. The so-called Act Omnibus[1] was adopted in parallel with the Framework Act, and other legal acts have also been amended (e.g., acts on justice matters and construction matters). This act (Act LVI of 2009) was adopted by the Hungarian Parliament on 20 June 2009 and entered into force on 1 August 2009 and 1 October 2009.

Nevertheless, due to the horizontal and framework nature of the Directive, it was clear in the very first phase of the implementation that its provisions cannot be implemented by merely amending sectoral legislation, but require the adoption of a framework act, which would contain the fundamental principles, procedural rules, as well as requirements laid down in the Directive, in a way that adapts to the provisions of the Directive. The Framework Act (Act LXXVI of 2009) was adopted by the Hungarian Parliament on 22 June 2009, the third among MS.

Although the deadline for transposing the Directive was 28 December 2009, the entry into force of the Framework Act was set for 1 October 2009, in accordance with the date of entry into force of the law aimed at the wide-ranging restructuring of domestic (national) public administration procedures. Bearing in mind that in several cases a number of provisions regulated by the Directive arise within public administration procedures, these two laws are closely interconnected, and their

[1] Act LVI of 2009 on the amendments relating to the entry into force of the Ket-novel on the amendment of Act CXL of 2004 on the general rules of administrative proceedings and services, and to the transposition of Directive 2006/123/EC on services in the internal market.

rule schemes are complementary. Accordingly, many requirements (e.g., deadlines, procedural requirements and formalities, liaising via electronic means) for the granting of authorisations, for example, do not appear in the Framework Act but in the act on the general rules of administrative proceedings and services.[2]

As a result of the SD implementation, Hungarian central and local law was reviewed.

i. In the course of and parallel to the preparation of the Framework Law, the Ministry of Justice and Law Enforcement Affairs drafted the law on the law amendments relative to the Ket-novel amending the Act CXL of 2004 on the general rules of administrative procedures and services coming into effect, and to the transposition of the Directive 2006/123/EC on internal market services, which was also passed on 22nd June 2009 by Parliament, and entered into force on 1 July 2009 (Act LVI. 2009, Statute Law Revision). This act includes all statutory changes necessary to ensure conformity with the Directive (about 100 laws are involved). Furthermore, to ensure compliance between the directive and the laws, a separate package of amendments has been proposed to the government and the National Assembly (e.g., Act LXXV of 2009 on the amendment of particular laws on judicial services relative to legal professions and Act LVII of 2009 on the amendment of particular laws on facilitating construction investments).
ii. Act LXXVI of 2009 on general rules of service start-up and continuation (framework) is a framework act that—in order to uniformly meet the requirements of the Directive—contains the basic rules that shall be applied in every respect of service activities under the effect of the Directive, and shall be uniformly applied in the sectoral laws on regulating these activities, as well as in official procedures in specific cases. This is the most important act of the Hungarian implementation of the Directive. However, we must not forget that the implementation of the Directive resulted in the modification of several other regulations as well. In this aspect, the law is closely related to the regulation implemented in the Ket-novel on amending Act CXL of 2004 on the general rules of administrative procedures and services, and relies fully on its regulation applied from 1 October 2009 onward; it only contains the basic divergences and supplementary regulations. The Ket-novel is enshrined in the objectives and is fully compatible with the reduction of administrative burdens, ensuring opportunities for electronic administration and the elimination of double authorisation requirements, and the relevant provisions of the Directive—also on a horizontal basis—are, actually, transposed by the Ket. This fact justifies particular provisions of the law entering into effect on 1 October 2009 instead of 28 December 2009, the deadline defined by the Directive.

[2] Act CXL of 2004 on the general rules of administrative proceedings and services, and the Ket-novel on its amendment.

iii. Modifications of government decrees necessary for the implementation of the SD was also submitted to the government in a single proposal by the Ministry of Justice and Law Enforcement (about 100 government acts were involved).
iv. The modifications of the ministerial decrees were prepared by the ministries within their spheres of competence.
v. Pursuant to the Constitution of the Republic of Hungary on Act XX of 1949, specifically § 44/A (2) thereof, local governments may issue decrees, which may not infringe higher level legislation.

In line with Act XI of 1987 on legislation § 10, the local government may issue ordinances

(1) To set detailed regulations in accordance with local and regional features vested by law, on the one hand, and
(2) On the other hand, to settle social relations not regulated in higher level laws.

Taking into account the Hungarian horizontal framework law on services, only laws or government decrees issued in the scope of the primary legislator can regulate authorisations or notification schemes, in both cases of services activities provided in an establishment and cross-border cases. In this respect, local government decrees shall not contain such regulations.

1.2.2 Involvement in the Transposition Process

Background

As soon as Directive 2006/123/EC on services in the internal market entered into force in December 2006, Hungary began developing an internal coordination scheme for transposition and, in line with the relevant national legislation, executing the tasks involved in transposing the Directive into Hungarian law.

The wide range of services covered by the Directive and the fact that the national legislation—and thus the regulation of services—is essentially sectoral in nature meant that these were the tasks of the individual ministries. To ensure that national legislation was in line with the Directive by 28 December 2009, all ministries were involved in the process through regular expert meetings coordinated by the Ministry of Foreign Affairs.

The expert group working on transposition of the Directive had widely conciliated views—not only within the framework of Hungarian public administration, but also with the interested professional bodies and interest groups—informing them of the course of legal deregulation and of the screening of the legal system involved in transposing the Directive.

The Screening Process

In the case of EU legislation requiring internal legislation, and thus in case of the SD, what needs to be assessed first and foremost is which internal legislation might be affected during implementation of the Directive. According to the Hungarian rules on legislation, rights and obligations with general effect can only be provided for by legislation, the two main groups thereof being legislation drawn up at the national level (i.e., laws, government decrees, and ministerial decrees) and that at the local level (i.e., municipal decrees). During the transposition of the SD, these legal acts need to be screened.

With regard to both main legislation groups, the screening process was started at the very beginning of the transposition, according to a single methodology. As far as legislation adopted at the national level is concerned, the screening process was coordinated by the Ministry of Foreign Affairs, in close cooperation with the Ministry of Justice and Law Enforcement and other concerned ministries, while the coordination of screening municipal decrees drawn up at the local level was carried out by the Ministry of Local Government, having competence in the matter, informing at the same time the Ministry of Foreign Affairs.

In May 2008, in the middle of the transposition period, the Hungarian government adopted a government decision on tasks arising from the implementation of Directive 2006/123/EC on services in the internal market. The government in the above-mentioned decision identified four main tasks concerning the implementation of the SD.

As a starting point, a proposal for legal harmonisation, which, according to Hungarian legislation, is a prerequisite for each adopted EU legal act, was drawn up to provide compliance with the provisions of the Directive. Within the framework of this procedure, every ministry checked the legislative acts within their spheres of competence that might be affected by the provisions of the Directive, and thus a preliminary list of affected national legislation was framed.

This preliminary list of national legislative acts affected by the provisions of the Directive served as a basis for the screening process carried out in 2007 and 2008. Within this process, relevant legislative acts were checked systematically according to a methodology adopted beforehand, as a result of which the following information was identified: the exact number and title of the legal act concerned, the legal basis of the legislation, the government body (ministry) responsible for the legislation, the relevant provision of the SD, the provision of the national legislation affected by the deregulation, whether or not there is a reporting obligation under Article 39(1) and/or (5) of the Directive for the given provision within the Interactive Policy Making (IPM) system serving this purpose, the competent authority, and other information relevant to the legal act in question.

Based on the above, approximately 350 legal acts adopted at the national level were identified and screened up through the summer of 2008, and then Hungary had an exact inventory at its disposal on what provisions of what pieces of legislation could be maintained, required amendments, or needed to be repealed and, with regard to all this, which legal acts were affected by the reporting obligation.

In light of the huge number of legal acts requiring amendments, a decision was made to have most of the necessary amendments of laws and government decrees adopted by the government, and, in the case of laws, by the Hungarian Parliament in one package, instead of one by one. As far as ministry decrees are concerned, as a result of the screening, from August 2008, each ministry had a perfect knowledge of which legal acts, covered by its responsibilities and competence, needed to be amended, and in which directions, so they could schedule their tasks accordingly.

Not only legal acts (laws, government decrees, ministry decrees) but, logically, also legislation at the local level, that is, municipal decrees were affected by the screening obligation arising from the Directive. Municipal decrees needed to be screened accordingly, to verify whether or not they were contrary to the provisions of the Directive. This task was performed by the local municipalities, and according to the legislation in force, the screening process carried out to make municipal decrees compatible with the Directive was coordinated by the Ministry of Local Government, which regularly informed the members of the SD implementation expert group on the state of play of the process.

Sectoral Amendments

Adoption of the Framework Act and amendments of laws (see point "Profound Cause of Changes to National Law?" above) unavoidably implied the necessary amendment of legislation ranking at a lower level. Within the legislative hierarchy, right after laws, this concerned government decrees. Here too, in light of the number of legal acts concerned, it seemed appropriate to adopt amendments to government decrees and repeal certain provisions in a single package.[3]

As regards legislation ranking at a lower level, ministry decrees were amended by the ministries concerned, subject to legislative hierarchy, of course, and always in accordance with the Framework Act and the amendments of laws.

Adoption of the Framework Act and amendments of laws necessarily implied the appropriate amendment of municipal decrees.

1.3 (National) Scope of Application

1.3.1 Scope of the Services Directive

We understand that the scope of the SD and the scope of its application are very clearly laid down in the SD itself. Therefore our national implementation followed the same structure indicated in the SD. It is clear that in the case of establishment (Article 9) the overriding reason relating to the public interest is a wider category than the four (public policy, public security, public health, protection of the environment) in the case of cross-border services (Article 16). The scope and provisions of the Framework Act cover both service providers established in Hungary and those established in another EEA country, be it within the framework of an establishment or provided as a cross-border service. This issue, however, was

[3] Government Decree 182/2009 (IX.10) amending and repealing certain government decrees in the context of the entry into force of the Ket-novel amending Act CXL 2004 on the general rules of administrative proceedings and services, and the transposition of Directive 2006/123/EC on services in the internal market.

brought together with the need to distinguish between establishment and cross-border service provision in Hungarian legislation.

1.3.2 Application of Transposing Legislation to Domestic Service Providers

As already mentioned in section "Scope of the Services Directive" above, Hungarian legislation implementing the SD, in particular the Framework Act, is applicable to not only service providers established in another EEA country but also service providers established in Hungary to the extent that they provide their services in Hungary (regardless of the nationality of the service provider).

Articles 3 and 4 of the Framework Act contain the rules relevant to the transposition of the rules on authorisation schemes provided for in Article 9 of the Directive. According to these articles, it is stipulated by law that within the framework of establishment, as a general rule, no authorisations are needed to take up and pursue a service activity as a service provider, and no notification is needed regarding taking up a service activity. This last requirement, that is, notifying the authorities of the taking up of a service activity, appears as a new category in the Hungarian legislation, and the detailed rules thereof are laid down in Articles 21–25, 27 and 28 of the Framework Act (see below for further details).

It was stipulated as a safeguard clause that, similar to the provisions of the Directive, service provision in establishment cases can be restricted only on the basis of overriding reasons relating to the public interest, and that such a restriction can only be provided for in laws ranking highest in the hierarchy of legal acts or, for activities not regulated by laws, in government decrees issued through an original competence. This means that in all such cases where the legislator deems it justified to require an authorisation for taking up or pursuing a service provision by becoming established, or a notification as regards taking up a service provision, covered by the Directive (Framework Act), the legal basis thereof can exclusively be regulated through laws and original government decrees.

The provision under Article 14 of the Framework Act constitutes another simplification for the service provider. According to it, within the framework of procedures necessary to take up or pursue a service activity, always maintaining safeguard rules, no other competent authorities or authorities responsible for the proceedings can be designated in case of misconduct on the part of a competent authority or the responsible authority, the consent of the competent authority shall be deemed granted, and the service provider shall have the right to take up and pursue the activity applied for.

Another important new element of the Framework Act is the regulation of notification as a legal institution. Through its introduction, the authorisation of certain services was replaced by a simple declaration, that is, a notification. The fundamental objective of the legislator was to reach aims relating to public interests through the least restrictive means. To abolish the previous authorisation procedure, in the cases of certain service activities a notification scheme was introduced as a new legal institution.

Notification is not considered an authorisation scheme within the meaning of the Directive, since the main point of the notification is so that a service provider can start providing services, regardless of the notification, if satisfying the relevant legal requirements. In itself, the absence of notification does not result in the loss of rights to pursuit an activity. The authority responsible for the supervision of the service in question shall, immediately upon receipt of the notification, verify whether the notification satisfies the legal requirements or not (verifying of formalities). If the notification complies with the above-mentioned requirements, the notifying party shall be informed thereof by being sent the verification. If the notification does not satisfy the legal requirements, the service provider's attention is drawn to deficiencies. Within the framework of the notification procedure, the authority responsible for the supervision of the service in question registers the service provider *ex officio*, whether or not it has verified that the service provider effectively fulfils the provisions on entitlement laid down in the relevant legislation. Irrespective of the notification, as soon as the entitlement requirements are fulfiled, the service provider can start activities. Should the authority responsible for the supervision of the service in question establish during the verification that the service provider is effectively providing an activity subject to notification, it imposes a penalty, and, where the service provider otherwise satisfies all relevant legal provisions concerning the taking up and pursuit of the service activity in question, the authority shall register him *ex officio*. Neither the receipt of the verification on the notification nor the registration can serve as conditions to take up and pursuit an activity.

Thus, subject to recital (39) and Article 4 (6) of the Directive, the notification scheme cannot be considered an authorisation scheme but only a 'simple declaration'.

Transposition of the relevant regulation concerning requirements under Article 15 of the Directive can be found in Article 52 of the Framework Act containing the requirements, that is, the requirements to be evaluated, under Article 15 (2) of the Directive. Here the Framework Act practically takes over the text of the Directive. As regards the regulation of these requirements, it follows from the Hungarian Constitution that these can only be regulated in legislation or on the basis of an authorisation granted in legislation.

1.3.3 Application of Transposing Legislation Beyond Service Providers

The scope of the Hungarian Framework Act covers the taking up and carrying out of a service provision provided by a service provider established in Hungary or in another EEA country; therefore, it stipulates general standards in relation to these issues.

1.3.4 Equal Treatment of Domestic and Transnational Service Providers

The SD itself distinguishes between establishment and cross-border service provisions, and the Framework Act follows the same logic. 'Equal treatment' could have happened only if we had applied the stricter (i.e., cross-border) requirements also for establishment cases, an approach we find to be a bit premature. It is not by chance that the European legislation has not taken this step either.

1.4 Incorporation of Transposing Legislation

The Framework Act implements the articles of the SD relating to administrative procedures. For example, the provision under Article 14 of the Framework Act constitutes simplification for the service provider, according to which within the framework of procedures necessary to take up or pursue a service activity, always maintaining safeguard rules, no other competent authorities or authorities responsible for the proceedings can be designated in case of misconduct on the part of a competent authority or the responsible authority, the consent of the competent authority shall be deemed granted, and the service provider shall have the right to take up and pursue the activity applied for. Article 15 implements the ban on double inspection, and Article 16 lays down the provisions of Article 5 of the SD. The act also implements professional liability insurance and guarantees in Article 17.

Provisions of a horizontal nature of the SD were implemented in the Framework Act, and several new acts were also adopted (e.g., on the notification scheme provided for in Article 15 (7) SD, on administrative cooperation, and the Internal Market Information System (IMI), on the point of single contact (POSC)). Otherwise, existing legislation was amended and brought in line with the regulations of the SD.

1.5 The Relationship of the Services Directive to Primary EU Law

1.5.1 Relationship to Article 49 and 56 TFEU

The need for adopting SD back in 2006 derived from the fact that many obstacles to the principle of free provision of services existed in practice despite EC Treaty regulation. In many cases European Court of Justice (ECJ) case law was integrated into the SD regulations, thus providing for the proper application of the principle.

1.5.2 Problems in This Context

There have been no problems identified in this context.

Main objective of the Directive is to provide one of the four economic freedoms defined by the Treaty establishing the European Community (hereinafter referred to as TEC, now TEU and TFEU), the freedom of services through secondary law enforcement. The fundamental objective of the TFEU is to create a single internal market that removes obstacles from the free movement of goods, persons, services, and capital. The provision of services under the TFEU is administered in two ways: through establishment and through cross-border provision. For the former case Articles 43–48 of Chapter 2 TEC (the right of establishment, now: 49–55 TFEU) are relevant, and for the latter Articles 49–55 of Title III, Chapter 3 TEC (Services, now: 56–62 TFEU) are relevant.

In this regard, the problem of interpretation did not come up under the implementation process.

1.6 Screening

See section "Involvement in the Transposition Process" ("The screening process") for details on the Hungarian screening procedure.

2 Individual Articles of the Services Directive

2.1 Article 6 SD: Point of Single Contact (POSC)

2.1.1 Establishment of the POSC

The central electronic service system within the framework of electronic government operates an integrated administrative and information point, the Hungarian POSC. The central service system within the framework of electronic government operates with an integrated contact information centre, in an electronically accessible, transparent, and in some service activities, according to uniform criteria, systematic way.

(a) The POSC provides free and unlimited information.

- (i) It establishes each standard of the service providers for launching and continuing business, service initiation, and conduct activities on the procedures and the authorities responsible for such procedures, as well as the service providers in matters relating to the taking or continuing the provision of practical assistance organisations and their availability,
- (ii) It provides information about the requirements on the start and continuation of specific service activity for service users, as well as about the

organisations offering practical help in service activity cases for consumers and their availability,
- (iii) It provides information about the legal remedy on the start or continuation of the service activity available to service providers and service users, as well as other generally available methods of settling disputes regarding legal disputes on service activities; and

(b) The POSC ensures that the service provider is in connection with the start or continuation of the specific service activity.

- (i) The POSC ensures that all the necessary procedural activities for the procedures of registration and data change are in line with the act on company publicity, the liquidation procedure of companies, as well as the procedure of establishing private businesses;
- (ii) The POSC provides directly applicable legislation or the general rules of the EU, which provide mandatory reporting on a single interface, and to finish the necessary procedures as soon as possible—in the simplest and fastest way;
- (iii) The POSC ensures public access to official records and the data of public service registers and to provide information on data requirement conditions from such registers.

In addition, the integrated administrative and information point provides general information for the service recipients:

(a) It provides the applicable requirements in each EEA country about the launch and continuation of service activities, in particular the provisions relating to consumer protection.
(b) In case there is a dispute between the provider and the recipient of some of the other EEA countries in accordance with the law, it provides information about available methods for settling disputes and remedies.
(c) It provides information about other EEA States regarding services related to the provision of practical assistance in matters dealing with major organisations and their contact details, such as the European Consumer Centres Network operation.[4]

2.1.2 Subjective Understanding, Competence Structure, Authorities with POSC-Function, Involvement of Private Partners

The option and requirement of 'POSC' is possibly implementable in multiple dimensions. According to national regulation, taking into account such pre-existing single point of contacts, we may find the administration of the building authorisation system

[4] The quote comes from the Framework act (Article 31), implementing the provisions of the SD on the POSC. Furthermore, Gov. Decree 160/2010 (V. 06.), on the detailed rules of the operation of the integrated administrative and information point entered into force 7 May 2010, contains the detailed implementing rules of the Framework Act on services.

(which was subject to significant revisions and a high degree of simplification in 2008) and the Ket-novel too established a body of law through authorities that provides a concentration of all the service procedures for one official authority. In this case, after the application of certain specific sectoral rules within the scope of procedures and a specific examination of their relations, another authority can be involved. The single point does not involve any new authority or the establishment of new administrative powers. The integrated information and communication system as an intelligent portal (www.magyarorszag.hu) ensures that each of the necessary procedures can be accessed in one place. It does not pose a procedural deviation from the general rules.

The framework law—in consideration of all these options and the available resources and ongoing developments—lays down the rules of the latter solution. The framework of the central electronic service system establishes an administrative and information point, which is electronically available and transparent. Each of the service activities systematically provide, according to uniform criteria transparency and accessibility to providers and recipients—on the basis of unrestricted and freely available information. It also ensures a context of procedures, including company publicity, court procedures for companies, registration procedures, and data changes.

This solution builds on the existing electronic administration law provisions of the Ket effective from 1 October 2009 onwards, which means that the operation of the portal and the underlying knowledge base do not need further maintenance of resources.

The integrated contact and administration point—beyond the complex information function—will basically mean the facility and support of a complex system of electronic communication, but the procedural rules of the electronic administration are included in the Ket. However, the life-event-based approach and the required comprehensive and well-structured information system may facilitate administrative services.

In this context, it is necessary to draw attention to the Directive and the subsequent rules, since sometimes they overlap each other in certain horizontal or sectoral legislation, such that, in order to achieve coherence in the legal system, these legal regulations should be harmonised and adjusted to the necessary extent.

The Operation of the Consumer Centres Network from Ket § 33/A

The integrated administrative and information point—in cooperation with the supervising authorities—provides general information to the services to start and continues applicable requirements related to the normal enforcement practices.

Where requests for the exercise of a right can be submitted collectively if so provided in an act or government decree, at an authority designated by such act or government decree ('participating authority'), this authority shall transmit such requests within eight working days to the authorities vested with powers and jurisdiction for adopting the relevant decisions.

The administrative time limit shall commence on the day when the requests are delivered to the authorities vested with powers and jurisdiction.

Unless otherwise prescribed by an act or government decree,

(a) The client shall be liable to pay the applicable duties and fees to the participating authority;
(b) The participating authority shall check the request and shall advise the client to remedy any deficiencies; this, however, shall have no bearing on the right of the authority vested with powers and jurisdiction to request missing information;
(c) The participating authority shall be entitled to reject the request without substantive examination;
(d) The participating authority shall have powers to terminate the proceedings.

An act or government decree may confer other procedural functions upon the participating authority.

If the participating authority has advised the client to remedy certain deficiencies pursuant and the deadline prescribed has not yet expired, the competent authority may extend the deadline and request additional information.

If the participating authority has released a notice requesting the missing information and the client complied in due time, the competent authority may not issue another notice pertaining to the contents and enclosures of the request.

Where so prescribed in an act or government decree, or upon the consent of the client who has submitted a request for the opening of proceedings, a certification body specified by law may participate in the process of ascertaining the relevant facts of the case. The authority must accept the certificate issued by the certification body in accordance with the relevant legislation in ascertaining the relevant facts of the case, and shall conduct no further procedural steps in respect of the facts certified.

The introduction of POSC has basically been—just like the implementation of the SD—a governmental task; however, its implementation and establishment were carried out with the involvement of contractors awarded in procurement procedures.

2.2 Article 7 SD: Right to Information

Article 7 of the SD was implemented in Article 31 of the Framework Act. It declares that the central electronic service system under regulation of the central government body operates an integrated administrative and information point. For details, please see section "Establishment of the POSC".

In the context of information, the integrated management and general information section points provide the following information to the recipients:

(a) Applicable requirements of the launching and continuation of service activities in each EEA country, in particular the provisions relating to consumer protection,
(b) A dispute between the provider and the recipient in some of the EEA countries in accordance with the law is available for settling disputes and remedies, as well as
(c) Certain other EEA States in services related to the provision of practical assistance in matters dealing with major organisations and their contact details, such as the European Consumer Centres Network operation.

In line with the Ket, the authority and the participating authority mentioned shall publish the public sector information specified in the Freedom of Electronic Information Act by electronic means.

In addition to the data specified in the Freedom of Electronic Information Act, the electronic information provided by the authority and the participating authority referred to in Section 38/A shall contain the following:

(a) The names of the officers handling the various types of official proceedings and their contact information, or contact information for the customer service representative from whom this information can be obtained;
(b) The time limit prescribed in the relevant legislation for administrative services;
(c) Information relating to the rights of clients relating to procedural steps and the obligations of clients;
(d) The duties and charges—including the duties and charges payable for the proceedings of special authorities—and information relating to payment procedures;
(e) Information relating to communication by electronic means, such as the conditions for using the central system, the availability of the request and petition forms, other standard forms, and similar means of information technology required for the opening of proceedings, and instructions for filling out and sending these forms;
(f) Information relating to setting up a customer port of entry for the purpose of electronic communication; and
(g) Information relating to the technical requirements for electronic communication and on system malfunctions.

The authority and the participating authority referred to in Article 38/A shall ascertain that the information published is authentic, accurate, updated, and continuously available online, over the Internet.

The minister in charge of supervising the national security services shall have authority to derogate from this act—upon consultation with the data protection commissioner—relating to information to be made public by the national security services.

2.3 Article 8 SD: Procedures by Electronic Means

Within the central electronic service system, the body (KEKKH = Office of Public Administration and Electronic Services)—appointed by the Government—operates an integrated administration and information point that is accessible online. It is transparent and systematised based upon consistent viewpoints of the service activities. It

(a) provides unrestricted and freely available information;

(b) ensures that the service provider can carry out all the procedural acts necessary to start and provide the given service activities, all on a unified website, in the shortest time, and in the easiest way; and
(c) ensures access to the public data of authorities regarding the service activity, and provides information on the conditions for applying for data from such databases

Given that the POSCs should operate electronically, after extensive negotiation between the governmental organisations and professional business associations, it was decided to use the existing government website (www.magyarorszag.hu). A study of the POSC's possible options was completed in 2008. The government passed a special project financed with EU resources to ensure the financial resources necessary for the realisation of the system in March 2009.

The electronic procedures can be seen as a great innovation, but the period of the implementation of the SD coincided favourably with the general political intention to modify the legal (and technical) basis of public administration to create a more modern, client-friendly, electronic-based public administration.

We did not remove other means of administrative proceedings. It is still possible to arrange administrative procedures personally, as a choice.

Thanks to the principles of Ket on e-processes, unless otherwise prescribed by law, clients and other parties to the proceeding shall not be required to establish contact with the authority by electronic means.

Unless otherwise prescribed by law, in proceedings opened upon their request, clients and other parties to the proceeding shall have the right to change the means of communication they originally selected on one occasion without any explanation, and with reasonable justification thereafter.

Administrative authorities are required to conduct interdepartmental communications by electronic means or electronic mail, no other means of communication may be engaged.

2.4 Article 9 SD: Authorisation Schemes

2.4.1 Means of Less Restrictive Measures

We understand that it is not areas of administrative law but there are different types of service activities where authorisation schemes were maintained. In accordance with the provisions of the Framework Act and those of the Directive, Hungary is maintaining and has reported, within the framework of the IPM system, an authorisation scheme for several service activities. There is no case in Hungarian legislation where authorisation is regulated only in cases of the cross-border provision of services. In all such cases Hungary is convinced that the underpinning justifying requirements are met.

2.4.2 Existing Authorisations Schemes/Procedures

In a great number of cases Hungarian legislation has moved towards notification and has replaced previous authorisation schemes by a simple declaration. This happened in more than 50 cases altogether, in cases of establishment. See also the instantly following remarks.

2.4.3 Simple Notifications

A notification scheme cannot be seen as an authorisation scheme according to the SD, thus it cannot fall under Article 9. An important new element of the Framework Act is the regulation of notification as a legal institution. Through its introduction, authorisation of certain services was replaced by a simple declaration, that is, a notification. The fundamental objective of the legislator was to reach aims relating to public interests through the least restrictive means. To abolish the previous authorisation procedure, in the case of certain service activities a notification scheme was introduced as a new legal institution.

Notification is not considered an authorisation scheme within the meaning of the Directive, since the main point of the notification is for a service provider to start providing services, regardless of the notification, if satisfying the relevant legal requirements. In itself, the absence of notification does not result in the loss of rights to pursue an activity.

Hungarian law distinguishes between licencing and notification procedures. Before the SD entered into force, hundreds of different licencing procedures were possible. After the SD 'arrived', amendments were reviewed, as was each of the Procedure Acts in the public sector related to the SD. As a result,

(a) Activities that need notification or require a licence were determined,
(b) To ensure a single (easy and fast) procedure the amendment or repeal should not include any procedural rule that causes duplication or confusion or is contrary to the objectives of the SD.

According to the framework, the service supervisor monitors the reporting obligation.

If the control authority finds out that a provider is actually carrying out an activity requiring a licence without notification, it will impose a fine and

(a) If the service is in conformity with the entitlement to statutory requirements of launching and continuing of service, take to its own record/report or note data changes to a register, or
(b) If the provider does not comply with the statutory requirements of launching and continuing a service, until proof or justification of the right to provide said service activity is prohibited.

To start or continue the service activity, an authorisation process is required by the service supervisor and at the same time the authority by office is registering the service provider.

2.5 Article 10 SD: Conditions for the Granting of Authorisation

2.5.1 Recognition of Requirements

Article 15 of the Framework Act stipulates that whenever a service provider in the country of establishment has met the requirements or equivalent requirements set out for the taking up or pursuit of service activities, its activity shall be presumed legal. So Article 15 explicitly implements Article 10 (3) SD on the prohibition of double authorisation.

Since this provision presupposes that the competent authorities have sufficient knowledge about the other EEA state requirements and their actual control mechanisms, provisions had to be made on liaison points (Article 28 SD), which can be found in Article 32 of the Framework Act.

On the other hand, so that the competent authorities of each different MS can easily communicate with each other (administrative cooperation, Article 28 of the Directive and Articles 39–48 of the Framework Act), Internet-based software was developed by the Commission. The IMI is a secure online application that allows national, regional, and local authorities to communicate quickly and easily with their counterparts abroad. Hungary participates actively in this project. A government decree setting out rules on the use of the IMI is already available in Hungary and we have also identified all IMI coordinators and competent authorities at the national, regional, and territorial levels. We have registered and trained all of the coordinators and competent, national-level authorities to use the IMI as well.

2.5.2 Granting Authorisation Throughout the Whole National Territory and Exceptions

The transposition of the duty to grant authorisations throughout the whole country was not difficult. In Hungary in most of the cases the scope of the authorisation covers the whole territory of the country. We reported in the IPM a territorial restriction in 11 cases, since this requirement falls under Article 15 (2) SD. Most are justified by public security being an overriding reason of public interest.

2.5.3 Entitlement to Grant Authorisation, Court Review of Administrative Decisions

The principle of *lex specialis derogat lex generalis* applies also in the relation between the Framework Act on services and the Act on General Administrative Procedures. In the case of granting an authorisation, no specific rules as to the implementation of Article 10 (5) are set out, and thus the relevant regulations of the act on general administrative procedures apply. The act on services regulates that the client initiating the procedure must be informed on the inducement of the authorisation procedure, and this must contain information on the possibilities for remedy and the conditions of tacit authorisation.

In the case of notification (see the detailed explanation on this institution above), which is not considered an authorisation scheme according to Article 4 number 6 SD, this institution was introduced by the act on services, and thus all specific rules on that (including deadlines) are set out therein.

Administrative courts review concern whether the decision was brought about lawfully and whether there has been procedural failure.

2.5.4 Reasoning of Administrative Decisions

There have also been no problems as regards the duty to reason administrative decisions. According to the general administrative procedure, every decision should be justified in Hungary.

2.5.5 Allocation of Competences

The SD did not modify the allocation of competences.

2.6 Article 11 SD: Duration of Authorisation

In the screening process, in some cases we came across the limited validity of authorisations, but such authorisations were abolished and replaced with either an automatically renewable authorisation scheme or an authorisation granted for an unlimited period. Simple notification is valid for an unlimited period of time (except for cross-border cases, where notification is valid for five years). The authorisation is in principle valid for an unlimited period of time, except for special cases where, according to the sectoral legislation and on the basis of overriding reasons relating to the public interest, it is possible for an authorisation to be for a limited period of time.

2.7 *Article 12 SD: Selection from Among Several Candidates*

Taking into account the general rules regulating the decision-making process of the authorities, there was no need to transpose this requirement.

2.8 *Article 13 SD: Authorisation Procedures*

2.8.1 A priori Determination of the Duration of Administrative Procedures

It is not the authority but the legislation that lays down the general rules on the duration of an administrative procedure. The general time limit is 30 days[5] in the case of authorisation schemes. (As mentioned previously, the provisions on the notification regime—a notification not being an authorisation—are to be found in the act on services, according to which the service provider may start service activities when notifying the authority.) Neither the receipt of the verification of the notification nor the registration can serve as conditions to take up and pursue an activity. The general regulation can be found in Act CXL of 2004 on the general rules of administrative proceedings and services.

Resolutions, rulings for the termination of the proceedings, and the rulings of appellate authorities for the annulment of decisions of the first instance and for reopening the case shall be adopted within 30 days[6] from the date specified at the beginning of the process and measures shall be taken to have the decision published within the same time limit. A shorter time limit may be established by any form of legislation, whereas a longer one may be established only by an act or government decree. Where this act fails to prescribe the time limit for the execution of any procedural step, the authority shall take measures without delay, but within five working days, for having the procedural step in question carried out.

The administrative time limit shall be reckoned from the date of delivery of the petition to the competent authority or on the date of the opening of the proceedings if launched *ex officio*. This provision shall also apply where a petition for proceedings to be conducted by a Hungarian authority has to be submitted to an authority other than Hungarian.

2.8.2 General Rule for the Duration

As clarified just before, we have a horizontal act on the general rules of administrative proceedings and services, which is the *lex generalis* in this respect. Furthermore we have the Framework Act on services, which is the *lex specialis*

---

[5] According to the new modification of Ket effective from 01 01 2011.

[6] According to the new modification of Ket effective from 01 01 2011.

and serves as a basis for services only. As mentioned above, the general rule on the duration is found in the horizontal act on administrative procedures, whereas the rules on notification specifically introduced for procedures falling under the Framework Act on services can be found in the latter.

2.8.3 Exceptions of the General Rule for the Duration

Since the general rules on the duration of procedures are to be found in the horizontal act on the general rules of administrative proceedings (see above), it is this legislation that regulates the possibility to differ from the general time limit of procedures. Accordingly, a shorter time limit may be established by any form of legislation, whereas a longer one may be established only by an act or government decree.

The institution of tacit authorisation, on the one hand, was an already regulated institution in the horizontal act governing general rules on administrative procedures; on the other hand, as a result of implementing the SD, it can be found explicitly in the act on services as well. The provision under Article 14 thereof constitutes simplification for the service provider, according to which, within the framework of procedures necessary, to take up or pursue a service activity, always maintaining safeguard rules, no other competent authorities or authorities responsible for the proceedings can be designated in case of misconduct on the part of a competent authority or the responsible authority, the consent of the competent authority shall be deemed granted, and the service provider shall have the right to take up and pursue the activity applied for.

2.8.4 Tacit Authorisation in the National Legal Order So Far

Tacit authorisation existed previously in our general administrative procedure law, that is, Act CXL of 2004 on the general rules of administrative proceedings and services. The Framework Act on service provision only followed the pre-existing regulation in Hungary.

2.8.5 Formal and Substantive Effects of Tacit Authorisation

Tacit authorisation has substantive effects. The service provider has the right to take up and carry out its service provision.

2.8.6 Rules of Formally Granted Authorisations Applicable to Tacit Authorisations

The same rules as for formally granted authorisations apply to tacit (fictitious) authorisations.

2.9 Articles 14, 15, 16 SD

Apparently the legislator identified a need to adapt national law to implement these articles, since these articles are the heart of the SD, besides the general rules on authorisation systems in Article 9. All three articles were implemented in our Framework Act. Article 4 (2) implements Article 14 on prohibited requirements, Article 52 of the Framework Act contains requirements, that is, the requirements to be evaluated, under Article 15 (2) of the Directive. Here, the Framework Act, practically, takes over the text of the Directive. As regards the regulation of these requirements, it follows from the Hungarian Constitution that these can only be regulated in legislation or on the basis of an authorisation granted in legislation. Articles 7–9 of the Framework Act contain the transposing rules for Article 16 of the SD. According to these, it was laid down in law that, as a general rule, in case of the cross-border provision of service, neither authorisations are needed to take up and pursue a service activity, nor are notifications required to take up the service activity.

2.10 Articles 14–19 SD

There have been no discussions with regard to prohibited requirements/restrictions and further exceptions. These questions were implemented in the Hungarian law. The reconciliation of the issue was not a problem.

2.11 Articles 22–27 SD

Act III determines the requirements for dealing with complaints and sets out the rules on basic information provided to the recipients by the service providers in general, relative to every service covered by the act. In this part, the law will take over the provisions of the Directive, but the violation of these provisions and the penalisation of the violation are vested in the competence of authorities, with legal rulings to be found in the following places: The Community rules on consumer protection law in context, and in particular the internal market for business customers from unfair trading practices, as well as Council Directives 84/450/EEC 97/7/EC, 98/27/EC, 2002/65/EC, and 2006/2004 of the European Parliament and the Council amending Regulation 2005/29/EC of the European Parliament and Council, consumers as users of the proceedings of the consumer against unfair trade practices on the Prohibition of Act XLVII of 2008, and the Law on Consumer Protection Act CLV of 1997 (hereinafter referred to as the Consumer Act).

No problems occurred concerning Article 22–27 SD. These articles were implemented in the Framework Act, that is, in Articles 34–38, 6, and 17.

The question of legislative changes during the preparation process did not cause any particular problem.

Since the State has the opportunity to determine or establish more detailed and stringent requirements for service providers in its territory, where appropriate, in some cases the domestic legislation contained more stringent requirements for cases of complaint handling and service fees, such as the Consumer Protection Act.

2.12 Articles 28 ff. SD: Administrative Cooperation

2.12.1 Transnational Administrative Cooperation Prior to the Implementation of the Services Directive

There was and still is international legal assistance as a legal instrument used for cross-border administrative cooperation in Hungary. The idea is the same in cases of national and international legal assistance; however, international cooperation used to be a complicated and time-consuming process.

The Framework Act on services stipulates that in connection with the administrative procedure of service provisions within its scope, the general rules on international legal assistance in the Ket (equivalent to horizontal law on administrative procedures) should be applied with derogations laid down in Chapter IV of the Framework Act on services.

International legal aid/assistance rules, of course, are not unknown to Hungarian law. According to the Ket, legal aid/assistance means the following.

National legal assistance	International legal assistance
Legal assistance may be requested: (a) If any procedural step is necessary outside the area of jurisdiction of the requesting authority, (b) If it is justified by the client's lawful interests or for reasons of cost efficiency, (c) Where any data or document is required for the requesting authority to discharge its duties is in the possession of another authority, government, or local body, or—in connection with certain specific types of cases as specified in an act—another agency or person.	Where the Republic of Hungary has an agreement for mutual administrative assistance with any state, or if there is reciprocity existing between the states, or it is permitted under multilateral international agreement, the authority may contact a foreign authority to request legal assistance accordingly, and shall fulfil any request for legal assistance received from abroad. In the assessment of reciprocity, the position of the minister in charge of foreign policies shall be authoritative, and it will be formulated in agreement with the minister having competence in connection with the case on hand.
The request referred to in (a) and (b) shall be made, depending on the nature of the case, to a body vested with similar powers and	Unless otherwise provided for in an act or government decree, the Hungarian and foreign (international) authorities involved in a request

(continued)

(continued)

National legal assistance	International legal assistance
competences as the requesting authority, or, failing this, to the notary of the competent local government. In proceedings opened upon request, the client's consent for the processing of personal data for the purpose of providing legal assistance shall be presumed, including personal data transmitted to the extent required. In connection with proceedings opened and conducted *ex officio*, the authority shall be entitled to transmit personal data, from among the data that may be processed on the strength of law, to the requested body to the extent required for the purposes of legal assistance.	for international legal assistance shall be in direct contact. If the Hungarian authority is unaware of the authority of the foreign state that is competent for satisfying its request for legal assistance in accordance, the request shall be sent via the competent supervisory organ to the minister in charge of foreign policies. The minister in charge of foreign policies shall forward the request for legal assistance in accordance through the ministry of the foreign state responsible for handling foreign affairs to the competent authority. The requested authority, if lacking competence to provide the legal assistance requested, shall forward the request to the competent authority and shall notify the requesting authority accordingly.
The requested body or person may refuse to comply with the request only if it constitutes any violation of the law. If another authority is vested with powers to provide the legal assistance requested, the requested body or person shall forward the request to this body without delay, not to exceed five days from the date of receipt of the request, and shall inform the requesting authority accordingly. The request shall be satisfied within 15 days in the cases specified under (a) and (b), or within eight days in the case specified under (c). The requested body shall communicate its ruling on the extension of the administrative time limit to the requesting authority. The requesting authority shall inform the client concerning the ruling for the extension of the time limit for legal assistance.	The authority shall refuse to fulfil the request of a foreign authority if it is likely (a) To jeopardise the national security of the Republic of Hungary or public safety, (b) To jeopardise any fundamental right of any person affected, or (c) To infringe upon any law. When a foreign request is refused, the requesting authority shall be informed, with the reasons communicated

But, as mentioned above, in the case of mutual administrative assistance falling under the SD (based on the use of the IMI), the provisions of the act on services act as *lex specialis*.

2.12.2 Rearrangement with National Rules on Administrative Cooperation

The requirements of the SD did not give a cause to (re)arrange the provisions for administrative assistance in a general way. The provisions on administrative cooperation of the SD were implemented in the Framework Act and not in the Ket. This means that the special rules on administrative cooperation of the SD (especially the use of the IMI) apply only regarding service activities, service providers, and procedures in the scope of the Framework Act.

The framework assesses that in the launching and continuation of service-related cases related to the administrative authorities, the general rules of procedure of the law on international legal aid/assistance shall be applied.

In international legal aid cases, the authority of the other EEA state shall find the competent authorities and make contact via the electronic network in the IMI.

According to the framework, the requests from any EEA states are not subject to reciprocity. The authorities shall increase cooperation with the competent authority of another EEA state in processing requests, as well as the relevant domestic authorities.

The requested authority shall fulfil the requirements of the request within the time limit specified therein, and to the extent necessary to find a solution for a problem if the request is substantiated and the reasons for the request and the request for information or action requested is properly justified.

If it is not possible to comply with a request, the requested authority shall notify this fact to the requesting authority and inform it of the time within which the anticipated request can be met.

In cases of border service providers in other EEA states or providers established/settled in the Republic of Hungary, the competent authority certifies that the service is actually established in the Republic of Hungary and the providers continue to service their business legally.

In a request—where a detailed inquiry must be justified and its purpose clearly defined—addressed to another EEA state's competent authority, the request for action, the measure deemed necessary, and the request must also indicate the underlying legal articles.

2.12.3 Provisions on Financial Compensation for Transnational Administrative Cooperation

Administrative cooperation under the Framework Act (i.e., changing information between competent authorities in different MSs) is free of charge.

2.12.4 Adaptation of the Rules on Data Protection and Professional Secrets

The privacy provisions of the Data Protection Act have not been modified, since the Hungarian data protection rules are among the most stringent in Central and

Eastern Europe. However, special rules on data handling regarding administrative cooperation were set out in the Framework Act on services.

2.13 Article 29 SD: Mutual Assistance—General Obligations for the Member State of Establishment

Article 29 SD is not seen problematic at all especially, since the IMI is in full operation and the necessary IMI structures have been set up in every MS.

2.14 Problems and Discourses on Administrative Cooperation

There have been no problems and discourses on Chapter VI of the SD which would be worth mentioning.

2.15 Convergence Programme (Chapter VII of the Services Directive)

As regards Chapter VII of the SD there have also been no discussions or discourses which would be worth mentioning. Codes of conduct in Article 37 are assessed as regulation under the scope of the SD.

According to Chapter VII, the establishment of a behaviour, also called the ethical codex, is under process (e.g., the existing codes have been adjusted in areas such as consumer protection and laws connected to advertisements).

3 Assessment of the Impact of the SD

3.1 Extent of the Impact

We fully agree with the opinion that the impact of the SD can be assessed as severe. The screening of the national legislation, the setting up of the POSCs, and the use of the IMI in administrative cooperation are such achievements that will definitely help exploit the full potential of the services sector and will have, according to our expectations, far-reaching effects throughout the EU. The implementation of the SD was the result of a long-term conciliation process: The implementation of the general rules of procedure has changed significantly and created the sectoral procedural requirements for electronic and procedural rules and opportunities for further simplification of the procedure.

3.2 Assessment of the Transposing Legislation

The transposition of the SD is assessed as a success story in Hungary that was brought together with measures (e.g., the setting up of the POSCs or the significant simplification in the field of authorisations and notifications) that are crucial and indispensable for a well-functioning service sector.

Under the implementation of the SD all the rules have been transposed into domestic legislation: The implementation is considered detailed mainly in light of the framework and the adoption of a number of procedural amendments.

The implementation was considered to be successful because all the ministries that were involved not only supervised the general rules of procedures but also reviewed each sectoral procedure system under the scope of the SD.

3.3 Most Important and Profound Changes Induced by the Services Directive

The approach of both the legislation (legislator level) and the competent authorities in public administration (application level) has changed. In most cases, we managed to switch from an ex ante check to an ex post control, which may ease service providers' lives significantly.

Thanks to the SD, the totality of Hungarian administrative procedural rules has been revised. Such a comprehensive, unified, and detailed review has probably never appeared at the same time in almost every sector before 2006 in Hungary.

The Implementation of the Services Directive in Ireland

John Biggins and Catherine Donnelly

1 General Remarks on the Transposition Strategy and General Understanding of the Implementation

1.1 Main References Used in this Research

The Services Directive (SD) was transposed into Irish national law on 10 November 2010 primarily through a statutory instrument, the *European Union (Provision of Services) Regulations 2010*[1] (the Statutory Instrument). The discussion in this chapter regarding this transposition will derive from: the Statutory

John Biggins, BA, LL.M (Dub)—Research Associate, Centre for Regulation and Governance, University College Dublin. Catherine Donnelly, LL.B. (Dub)—B.C.L. (Oxon); LL.M. (Harv); D.Phil. (Oxon); Barrister, Blackstone Chambers, London, Law Library, Dublin; Attorney at Law, New York; Lecturer in Law, Trinity College, Dublin., latest update July 2011.The authors wish to thank the Department of Jobs, Enterprise and Innovation for helpful guidance regarding the transposition of the SD in Ireland. The views expressed herein are the authors' alone and do not necessarily represent the views of any other individual or organisation. Errors and omissions also remain the authors' alone.

[1] S.I. No. 533/2010 (the Statutory Instrument)—http://www.djei.ie/trade/marketaccess/singlemarket/european_union%20%28provision_%20of_%20services%29_regulations.pdf (last accessed 23 July 2011). See also Sect. 1.4.2 herein.

J. Biggins (✉)
Research Associate, Centre for Regulation and Governance,
University College, Dublin, Ireland
e-mail: john.biggins@ucd.ie

C. Donnelly
Trinity College, Dublin, Ireland
e-mail: catherine.donnelly@tcd.ie

U. Stelkens et al. (eds.), *The Implementation of the EU Services Directive*,
DOI: 10.1007/978-90-6704-840-8_13,

Instrument itself; materials published on the website of the Department of Jobs, Enterprise and Innovation (named the Department of Enterprise, Trade and Innovation during the period of the transposition process)[2]; the Draft Services in the Internal Market Regulations 2010[3] (the Draft Regulations); and a Regulatory Impact Analysis (the RIA). These last two documents were prepared in the lead up to the official transposition,[4] and will serve as important reference points in the following responses. Reference will also be made to parliamentary debates, parliamentary questions and inputs from stakeholders. These will be referenced individually as they arise but are all available to browse online on a website specifically dedicated to the transposition of the SD in Ireland at http://www.djei.ie/trade/marketaccess/singlemarket/servicesdirective.htm.[5] Aside from the Statutory Instrument, other specific pieces of Irish legislation will also be referenced throughout this report. These can be viewed in more detail on the official online database of Irish legislation at http://www.irishstatutebook.ie/.[6]

1.2 Impact of the Services Directive

1.2.1 Profound Cause of Changes to National Law?

From the outset, it is important to emphasise the fact that Ireland is, by and large, immersed in a different legal tradition from that of the vast majority of its European Union (EU) partners. As a common law jurisdiction, the Irish legal system shares much in common with the legal systems of the United Kingdom, United States, Canada, Australia and New Zealand. An important aspect of the Irish system in terms of the nature of administrative law is that most economic sectors are governed by individual pieces of legislation rather than by an overarching legislative scheme establishing administrative rules generally applicable to most or all sectors, which may be the case in many Continental Civil Law jurisdictions. In Ireland, where sector-specific legislation does not elaborate on certain matters, for example, on issues regarding the manner in which a competent authority

---

[2] Please note that, by the time of the final draft of this chapter, the Department of Enterprise, Trade and Innovation had been renamed the Department of Jobs, Enterprise and Innovation. This Department has also previously been named the Department of Enterprise, Trade and Employment. These names will appear interchangeably herein, though all reference the same department.

[3] See, *Consultation Document*—http://www.djei.ie/trade/marketaccess/singlemarket/09serv030FINAL.pdf (last accessed 23 July 2011).

[4] See, *Regulatory Impact Analysis* (the RIA)—http://www.djei.ie/trade/marketaccess/singlemarket/09RIA007a.pdf (last accessed 23 July 2011).

[5] Last accessed 23 July 2011.

[6] Last accessed 23 July 2011.

exercises its functions and discretionary powers, the Irish courts have either applied established common law principles, or they have developed or applied principles found in other common law jurisdictions, most usually the United Kingdom. In this sense, "judge-made law" has constituted the dominant source of administrative law in Ireland. This judge-made law has usually arisen out of judicial review proceedings in the courts.[7]

Judicial review under the common law in the Irish context is a procedure whereby an applicant can petition the High Court of Ireland for review of a decision of a public authority. Judicial review tests public authority action for compliance with a variety of standards, such as "openness, fairness, participation, impartiality, accountability, honesty and rationality".[8] It is concerned with establishing whether a public authority, when exercising its functions, including its discretion, has both adhered to the explicit requirements of sector-specific legislation and also to generally established common law principles,[9] ultimately aiming to ascertain whether a public body has acted *intra vires*. Irish administrative law is therefore essentially a combination of sector-specific legislation and legal principles established by the courts. The transposition of the SD has not provided a spur to the legislator to alter administrative laws and principles generally. A literal approach to transposition has been adopted, involving the introduction of a horizontal law transposing the vast majority of the SD itself.

1.2.2 Involvement in the Transposition Process

The formal consultation process[10] and auxiliary matters were handled by the Department of Enterprise, Trade and Innovation. There was input from the Department of Transport, Department of Communications, Energy and Natural Resources and the Department of Arts, Sport and Tourism, and the Department of Enterprise, Trade and Innovation, but this participation was mandated in any event by the requirements of the screening process. An individual opposition T.D., the Irish Congress of Trade Unions and the competent authority with responsibility for the registration of chartered surveyors, the Society of Chartered Surveyors, also made written representations to the Department of Enterprise, Trade and

[7] See, generally, Delany (2008), Hogan and Gwynn Morgan (2010), de Blacam (2009).

[8] Taggart (1997), pp. 1, 3.

[9] These principles include reasonableness, proportionality and appropriate exercise of discretion.

[10] However, it has been pointed out by the Department for Jobs, Enterprise and Innovation that the Department had extensive contact both within the Department, with other government departments and external stakeholders during the approximately seven years in which the SD was negotiated. Email correspondence with the Department of Jobs, Enterprise and Innovation (on file with authors).

Innovation regarding the transposition of the SD.[11] The transposition process was concentrated in the Department of Enterprise, Trade and Innovation. There was a good degree of vertical engagement between government departments regarding specific aspects of the SD, though there does not appear to have been an extensive formal engagement from other stakeholders.[12] The Minister for Enterprise, Trade and Innovation indicated in 2005 that his department had contacted at least 50 stakeholder organisations seeking comments on initial drafts of the SD, an invitation which was subsequently repeated.[13] These invitations, by and large, do not appear to have translated into formal written submissions, at least not according to publicly available information. The Irish Congress of Trade Unions, the competent authority responsible for chartered surveyors and an opposition political party appear to have constituted the only formal responses from stakeholders to the Government consultation document.[14]

1.3 (National) Scope of Application

1.3.1 Scope of the Services Directive

Subject to the exemptions set out in the SD, Articles 5–15, now transposed through the Statutory Instrument, have equal application and binding effect regardless of whether the service provider is of domestic or transnational character. This is set out in Regulation 3 (1) of the Statutory Instrument which stipulates: "Subject to para (2) and (3), these Regulations apply to services supplied by providers established in the State or established in any other Member State".

1.3.2 Application of Transposing Legislation to Domestic Service Providers

The attitude of the Irish authorities on this question was initially indicated in the Draft RIA published during the transposition process which provided that,

---

[11] See, *Response from Irish Congress of Trade Unions*, 21 October 2009—http://www.djei.ie/trade/marketaccess/singlemarket/09serv284.pdf (last accessed 23 July 2011); *Response from the Society of Chartered Surveyors*, 21 October 2009—http://www.djei.ie/trade/marketaccess/singlemarket/scs_response.pdf (last accessed 23 July 2011); *Response from Arthur Morgan T.D. on behalf of Sinn Féin*, 21 October 2009—http://www.djei.ie/trade/marketaccess/singlemarket/09serv256a.pdf (last accessed 23 July 2011) (Responses).

[12] Though, according to the Department, there was reportedly a good degree of informal engagement. Email correspondence with Department of Jobs, Enterprise and Innovation (on file with authors).

[13] *The Minister for Enterprise, Trade and Employment answered a Parliamentary question on the draft Directive*, 18 April 2005—http://www.djei.ie/trade/marketaccess/singlemarket/servicesdirective.htm (last accessed 23 July 2011).

[14] See, Responses above n. 11.

> [t]hese articles do not... draw any distinction between domestic and non-domestic providers. Therefore, they apply in the same way to service providers established in another Member State and to services established (or willing to establish) in Ireland.[15]

The legislator therefore seems to have followed the opinion and guidance of the European Commission on this matter.[16] Accordingly, the legislator has implicitly accepted the jurisdiction of the EU to legislate in relation to domestic, as well as transnational, service providers as indicated by the provisions of Regulation 3 (1) of the Statutory Instrument, outlined in the previous answer.[17]

1.3.3 Application of Transposing Legislation Beyond Service Providers

The Statutory Instrument does not provide explicitly for general and universal standards. Nonetheless, it could be inferred that, as there has been no distinction drawn by the legislator between the rights of domestic and transnational service provides, this suggests that some or all of these standards might be extended, in practice, to other economic stakeholders and citizens more generally who happen to deal with the relevant competent authorities. However, whether or not citizens and economic stakeholders could sustain a legal *right* to enjoy these standards from the outset is not elaborated in the Statutory Instrument. That could conceivably be a matter for future judicial clarification.

1.3.4 Equal Treatment of Domestic and Transnational Service Providers

As indicated in the preceding answers, the Statutory Instrument has rendered the SD applicable to both domestic and transnational service providers.

1.4 Incorporation of Transposing Legislation

1.4.1 Implementation of Requirements Relating to Administrative Proceedings

The Irish Government was late in transposing the SD into national law. Transposition occurred on 10 November 2010, considerably overshooting the transposition due date of 28 December 2009. Moreover, it has been indicated by the Department of

---

[15] The RIA above n. 4, p. 30.

[16] See, *Handbook on the Implementation of the Services Directive*—http://ec.europa.eu/internal_market/services/docs/services-dir/guides/handbook_en.pdf (last accessed 23 July 2011).

[17] Though the Department has interpreted this simply as compliance with the text and spirit of the SD itself. Email correspondence with the Department of Jobs, Enterprise and Innovation (on file with authors).

Enterprise, Trade and Innovation that further work will be required throughout 2011 in terms making a final decision on exactly which legislation is to be amended in light of the transposition of the SD and in terms of formally activating certain provisions of the Statutory Instrument itself.[18] However, the Department of Enterprise, Trade and Innovation did conclude the consultation period by 16 October 2009. The Minister for Enterprise, Trade and Innovation subsequently indicated some time prior to the formal transposition that the administrative work in transposing the SD had "reached a point where it can be applied administratively, to a considerable extent, ahead of the coming into force of the legislation".[19] The administrative application of the SD in advance of formal transposition principally referred to the fact that the point of single contact was in operation by February 2010, well in advance of the formal transposition of the SD. However, the establishment of the point of single contact itself still overshot the SD transposition due date. In April 2010, the perspective of officials within the Department of Enterprise, Trade and Innovation on this matter was expressed in the following terms:

> Work on the non-legislative aspects of the transposition process is sufficiently well advanced to allow the Department to apply the Directive administratively (the Commission, other Member States and stakeholders know this) ... In summary, Ireland is open for business as far as the Services Directive is concerned but the necessary legal and administrative work involved in the transposition process has not yet completed. Every effort is being made to complete the work as soon as possible.[20]

In light of the formal transposition of the SD, it is clear that the stipulations of the SD as regards administrative proceedings were fully transposed by virtue of the provisions set out under Part 3 through Part 5 of the Statutory Instrument. Given the absence of a generally applicable administrative law statute governing the services sector in Ireland, the legislator indicated during the transposition process that it was reviewing already existing sector-specific legislation in light of the provisions of the SD. Examples of legislation which were indicated as requiring examination in the context of compliance with the SD included[21]:

- Beach Bye Laws for the Administrative Area of Clare County Council, made pursuant to the Local Government Act 2001[22]

---

[18] For example, according to the Department of Enterprise, Trade and Innovation, Regulation 11(2) of the Statutory Instrument has not yet been formally activated by the Minister. Email correspondence with the Department of Enterprise, Trade and Innovation (on file with authors).

[19] See, *The Tánaiste and Minister for Enterprise, Trade and Employment answered a question from Deputy Michael D. Higgins on the Services Directive*, 2 February 2010—http://www.djei.ie/trade/marketaccess/singlemarket/servicesdirective.htm (last accessed 23 July 2011).

[20] See, *The Minister for Enterprise, Trade and Employment answered a question from Deputy Joe Costello on the Services Directive*, 1 April 2010—http://www.djei.ie/trade/marketaccess/singlemarket/servicesdirective.htm (last accessed 23 July 2011).

[21] For further information on this point see http://ec.europa.eu/internal_market/consultations/docs/2010/services_directive/ireland_en.pdf (last accessed 23 July 2011).

[22] No. 37/2001.

- Bray Promenade Esplanade and Seashore Bye Laws, made pursuant to the provisions of the Public Health (Amendment) Act 1907
- Donegal County Council Regulation and Control of Certain Beaches Bye Laws, made pursuant to the Local Government Act 2001
- Employment Agency Act 1971[23]
- Employment Agency Regulations 1972–1993
- Irish Horse Racing Industry Act 1994[24]
- Kerry County Council Amended (Beach) Bye Laws, made pursuant to the Local Government Act 2001
- Limitation of Emissions of Volatile Organic Compounds Due to the Use of Organic Solvents in Certain Paints, Varnishes and Vehicle Refinishing Products Regulations 2007[25]
- Mayo County Council Newport Harbour Bye Laws, pursuant to the Local Government Act 2001
- Occasional Trading Act 1979[26]
- Petroleum Vapour Emissions Regulations 1997[27]
- Property Services (Regulation) Bill 2009
- Road Traffic (Driver Instructor Licensing) (No. 2) Regulations 2009[28]
- Tourist Traffic Acts 1939–1940
- Transport (Tour Operator and Travel Agents) Act 1982[29]
- Video Recordings Act 1989[30]

It does not appear that the legislator has yet executed specific amendments to the listed legislation in parallel to the transposition of the SD. The Department of Enterprise, Trade and Innovation has, at time of writing, indicated that it shortly intends to settle on a final list of individual pieces of legislation requiring amendment and would likely publish such a list accordingly.[31] In any event, blanket provisions have been inserted into the Statutory Instrument which purport that any inconsistencies between sector-specific legislation and the Statutory Instrument will be overridden by the provisions of the Statutory Instrument itself. This is set out under Regulation 4 (2) and (3) of the Statutory Instrument:

> 4 (2) Every enactment relating to the provision or availing of a service shall, subject to any other rules of law relating to the construction of that enactment, be construed in a manner which is consistent with these Regulations.

---

23 No. 27/1971.

24 No. 18/1994.

25 S.I. No. 199/2007.

26 No. 35/1979.

27 S.I. No. 375/1997.

28 S.I. No. 203/2009.

29 No. 3/1982.

30 No. 22/1989.

31 Email correspondence with the Department of Enterprise, Trade and Innovation (on file with authors).

> 4 (3) If it is not possible to construe an enactment referred to in paragraph (2) in a manner consistent with these Regulations, then, in so far as the enactment is inconsistent with a provision of these Regulations, the enactment does not apply to the extent of the inconsistency.

Furthermore, the legislator indicated in the RIA that there are aspects of the SD which may not require transposition at all,[32] although it has not explained what exactly is being referenced here. The Department of Jobs, Enterprise and Innovation has since clarified with the authors that it is referring to provisions which are already in force in Ireland as well as other administrative issues yet to be resolved between the European Commission and Ireland.[33]

1.4.2 Incorporation or New Codification

Ireland implemented the vast majority of the SD through the Statutory Instrument with horizontal effect. However, the legislator also opted to transpose Article 42 of the SD, in combination with the Injunctions Directive,[34] through a separate statutory instrument, the *European Communities (Court Orders for the Protection of Consumer Interests) Regulations 2010*,[35] promulgated on 23 November 2010. According to the Departmental website, the reasons for transposing Article 42 of the SD separately in this way were taken on the grounds of "transparency" as the SD is listed among the Directives covered by the Injunctions Directive in terms of the protection of consumer rights.[36] This statutory instrument in turn repealed the *European Communities (Protection of Consumer Collective Interests) Regulations 2001*.[37]

Also of some relevance in this context is the *Electronic Commerce (Certification Service Providers Supervision Scheme) Regulations 2010*,[38] promulgated on 31 May 2010. This statutory instrument was principally introduced to give effect to a requirement on the Minister for Communications, Energy and Natural

---

[32] The RIA above n. 4, p. 60.

[33] Email correspondence with the Department of Jobs, Enterprise and Innovation (on file with authors).

[34] Directive 98/27/EC of the European Parliament and of the Council of 19 May 1998 on injunctions for the protection of consumers' interests [1998] OJ L 166/51. This directive and subsequent amendments have been codified in Directive 2009/22/EC of the European Parliament and Council of 23 April 2009 on injunctions for the protection of consumers' interests (Directive on injunctions for the protection of consumers' interests) [2009] OJ L110/30.

[35] S.I. No. 555/2010—http://www.djei.ie/publications/sis/2010/si555.pdf (last accessed 23 July 2011).

[36] http://www.djei.ie/trade/marketaccess/singlemarket/servicesdirective.htm (last accessed 23 July 2011).

[37] S.I. No. 449/2001.

[38] S.I. No. 233/2010—http://www.djei.ie/trade/marketaccess/singlemarket/10serv082.pdf (last accessed 23 July 2011).

Resources to prescribe a scheme of supervision of Certification Service Providers (CSP's), in accordance with Annexes I and II of the *Electronic Commerce Act 2000.*[39] *The Electronic Commerce Act 2000* in turn transposed the *Electronic Signatures Directive.*[40] In accordance with this legislation, the relevant Minister is obliged to maintain lists of CSP's established in Ireland who are issuing qualified certificates, based on notification and evidence of certification forwarded. The Department of Enterprise, Trade and Innovation and the Department of Communications, Energy and Natural Resources have therefore indicated that further administrative work will be necessary in the wake of the transposition of the SD which will permit Ireland to make certain information available to the Commission on this matter as recently requested.[41] The transposition of the SD in Ireland appears to have been literalist in nature. This is somewhat unsurprising, given that the legislator had previously indicated it was not in favour of a "gold plated" transposition.[42]

By way of explanation as to the means of transposition of the SD, a statutory instrument is a form of delegated legislation and can be passed into law by the legislator subject, in principle, to parliamentary accountability, but without requiring anywhere near the usual levels of scrutiny from the Irish national parliament (Oireachtas) than would be the case if, for example, an Act of Parliament were utilised as the transposing mechanism.[43] The reasons previously given by the Minister for Enterprise, Trade and Innovation for the decision to transpose the SD through statutory instrument was to facilitate transposition by the due date, though this did not materialise in reality. It was further suggested by the Minister that implementation by way of statutory instrument is entirely in line with the traditional manner in which EU Directives have generally been transposed in Ireland, pursuant to the provisions of the *European Communities Act 1972.*[44] The Irish

---

[39] No. 27/2007.

[40] Directive 99/93/EC of the European Parliament and of the Council of 13 December 1999 on a Community framework for electronic signatures (Directive on a Community framework for electronic signatures) [2000] OJ L13/12.

[41] See, *Transposition of Article 8 of the Directive on Services in the Internal Market*—http://www.djei.ie/trade/marketaccess/singlemarket/servicesdirective.htm (last accessed 23 July 2011).

[42] See the RIA above n. 4, p. 61. Although a senior official at the Department of Jobs, Enterprise and Innovation has also pointed out to the authors that this Statutory Instrument transposing the SD was still one of the most difficult and complex pieces of legislation that they had to draft in their many years of experience, exacerbated by the relatively few persons allocated to work on the transposition at the Department, coupled with administrative responsibilities in establishing the NPSC and so forth. Email correspondence with the Department of Jobs, Enterprise and Innovation (on file with authors).

[43] See, in particular, the requirements of section 4 of the *European Communities Act 1972* (No. 27/1972). For a more general discussion of delegated legislation in Ireland see, e.g., Coakley and Gallagher (2005), pp. 218–219.

[44] No. 27/1972; See, *The Tánaiste and Minister for Enterprise, Trade and Employment answered three questions from Arthur Morgan T.D. on the Services Directive*, 6 October, 2009—http://www.djei.ie/trade/marketaccess/singlemarket/servicesdirective.htm (last accessed 23 July 2011).

Supreme Court has upheld the validity of transposing EU Directives by way of statutory instrument, regardless of the fact that these frequently effect changes to Acts of the Oireachtas.[45]

Nonetheless, in the context of a controversial EU directive such as the SD, it may be worth highlighting that concerns were expressed by the Constitution Review Group of Ireland (CRG) in 1996 regarding possible implications in terms of the increasing use of statutory instruments in the transposition of EU law. In recommending a review of the oversight role played by the Oireachtas in the context of statutory instruments, the CRG observed, *inter alia*:

> The extensive use of statutory instruments to implement directives has meant that hundreds of statutory provisions, some important, have been expressly or impliedly repealed by statutory instruments often with a minimum of publicity. The use of statutory instruments ensures speedy and effective implementation of EC law but often at the expense of the publicity and debate which attends the processing of legislation through the Oireachtas. In this respect the operation of the 1972 Act might be said to contribute to an 'information deficit' and possibly a 'democratic deficit'.[46]

The method of transposition of the SD through statutory instrument has been criticised in some quarters, particularly by an opposition political party and the Irish Congress of Trade Unions.[47] The appropriateness of this transposition method has also been raised directly with the Minister for Enterprise, Trade and Innovation in Dáil Éireann (Lower House of the Oireachtas).[48]

1.5 The Relationship of the Services Directive to Primary EU Law

1.5.1 Relationship to Articles 49 and 56 TFEU

There appears to have been no substantial assessment of this particular issue in the Irish context. The effect of the SD has been conceptualised primarily in terms of its potential role in complementing the provisions set out under the EU Treaties, thus providing legal certainty in the exercise of the fundamental freedoms thereunder. This is elaborated by the legislator in the Draft RIA in the following terms:

> The objective of the Services Directive is to create a single market for services, similar to the single market for goods that has operated for the past 15 years or so. It aims to

---

[45] See, *Meagher* v *Minister for Agriculture* [1994] 1 IR 329.

[46] See, *Report of the Constitution Review Group* 1996—http://www.constitution.ie/reports/crg.pdf (last accessed 23 July 2011).

[47] See, Responses above n. 11.

[48] See, *The Tánaiste and Minister for Enterprise, Trade and Employment answered a question on the Services Directive*, 22 September 2009—http://www.djei.ie/trade/marketaccess/singlemarket/servicesdirective.htm (last accessed 23 July 2011).

> eliminate obstacles to the freedom of establishment for service providers and to the free movement of services between Member States (whether remotely or where the service provider travels temporarily to another Member State). It also aims at giving both services providers and recipients of those services the legal certainty they need in order to exercise the fundamental freedoms that are enshrined in the [TFEU].[49]

1.5.2 Problems in this Context

It does not appear that problems have been identified in this context.

1.6 Screening

The "screening process in concreto" adopted in Ireland was overseen by the Inter-Departmental Committee on the Services Directive (IDC) but it was further agreed that each government department would oversee the screening process in its own area of competence. The Internal Market Unit (IMU) in the Department of Enterprise, Trade and Innovation undertook to provide support and training where necessary. Ultimately, it was up to each government department to screen relevant legislation relating to sectors under its remit and subsequently report to the IDC on the matter which, it appears, in turn reported through the European Commission Interactive Policy Mechanism (IPM).[50] Four departments reported back after screening legislation. The results of these will be examined in more detail.

Department of Communications, Energy and Natural Resources[51]
This Department raised the issue of the Irish Postal Service (An Post). It was noted in particular that under Regulation 18 (a) (1) of the Draft Regulations—which formed the basis for transposition of the SD—derogations from the stipulations of the SD have been applied to the Irish postal sector in relation to any relevant activities falling under the *Postal and Telecommunications Services Act 1983*.[52] The Department further suggested that this derogation be applied in relation to services provided by An Post pursuant to the *European Communities (Postal Services) Regulations 2002*,[53] implementing Directive 97/67/EC,[54] as amended by

[49] The RIA above n. 4, p. 56.

[50] The RIA above n. 4, pp. 64–69.

[51] See, *Response from Department of Communications, Energy and Natural Resources*—http://www.djei.ie/trade/marketaccess/singlemarket/servicesdirective.htm (last accessed 23 July 2011).

[52] *Postal and Communications Services Act 1983* (No. 24/1983).

[53] S.I. No. 616/2002.

[54] Directive 97/67/EC of the European Parliament and of the Council of 15 December 1997 on common rules for the development of the internal market of Community postal services and the improvement of quality of service (Directive on Community postal services) [1998] OJ L15/14.

Directive 2002/39/EC.[55] This legislation primarily relates to the role of An Post in the handling of cross-border mail between Ireland and other EU Member States.[56] It appears that this omission was simply an oversight on the part of the legislator when drafting the original Draft Regulations and this Department was merely highlighting it, given that the exemption is now found in Regulation 7 (a) (i) of the Statutory Instrument.

Department of Arts, Sport and Tourism[57]

This Department referred to the proposal to exclude service providers engaged in the gambling industry from the scope of the SD. It was noted under Regulation 3 (2) (h) of the Draft Regulations that the relevant national legislation excluded from the ambit of the SD, would be the *Gaming and Lotteries Acts 1953–2002* and the *National Lottery Act 1986*.[58] This Department further suggested that the *Betting Act 1931*[59] (the 1931 Act) also be excluded from the scope of the SD. Provisions of the 1931 Act remain operational and are relevant to the Irish horseracing and greyhound racing industry. However, it was pointed out by this Department that, strictly speaking, the latter piece of legislation fell within the remit of the Department of Finance. The Department of Finance does not appear to have raised issues in relation to this piece of legislation, at least not publicly. In any event, a seemingly wide derogation for the gambling industry has been introduced in the Statutory Instrument in Regulation 3 (2) (h), reflecting the provisions of the SD.

The Department of Arts, Sport and Tourism also raised an issue regarding the compatibility of Regulation 14(5) of the Draft Regulations (transposing Article 13 SD) and the *Tourist Traffic Acts 1939–2003*. There is particular concern over how the SD, when transposed, could potentially override the checks currently in place under this legislation, which, *inter alia*, prohibits the entry of a provider of tourist accommodation on to the register of accommodation in the absence of explicit approval from the Irish National Tourism Development Authority (Fáilte Ireland). This Department suggested that the prospect of "tacit approval" occurring in the tourist accommodation market would be intolerable with regard to potential damage to the public interest. These concerns have not been reflected in the Statutory Instrument.

This Department also lobbied that "reasonable time periods" for the purposes of Regulation 14 of the Draft Regulations (transposing Article 13 SD) regarding authorisation procedures should be extended to one month in most cases, although

---

[55] Directive 2002/39/EC of the European Parliament and of the Council of 10 June 2002 amending Directive 97/67/EC with regard to the further opening to competition of Community postal services (Directive on competition in Community postal services) [2002] OJ L176/21.

[56] An Post is the designated Universal Service Provider under the 2002 Regulations. See, in particular, Regulation 4 (2) (a).

[57] See, *Response from Department of Arts, Sport and Tourism*—http://www.djei.ie/trade/marketaccess/singlemarket/servicesdirective.htm (last accessed 23 July 2011).

[58] No. 28/1986.

[59] No. 27/1931.

recognising that best practice will usually dictate a turnaround of seven days. The legislator ultimately went beyond these recommendations, as evidenced by the provision of Regulation 18 (2) of the Statutory Instrument. This indicates that "… a period that exceeds 60 days is not reasonable".

Department of Transport[60]

The Department of Transport considered the implications of the SD within its particular areas of authority also. This Department gave an undertaking that the requirements of the SD had been noted in the context of Maritime Divisions within this Department, and that they would thus be "factored in" to any future procedures with regard to maritime matters. The Department also raised questions over the status of the Dublin Airport Authority[61] for the purposes of the SD, and noted the stipulations of Regulation 3 (2) (d) of the Draft Regulations (transposing Article 2 SD), that "transport services, including port services, falling within the scope of Title V of the Treaty establishing the European Communities" (now Title VI of Treaty on the Functioning of the European Union (TFEU)) were excluded from the scope of the SD. Consequently, this Department was of the opinion that the SD, although not directly referencing airports in this part, implicitly referenced airports, such that the activities with regard to the administration and management of Irish airports were deemed to be excluded from the scope of the SD, unless the legislator at some future point wished to make the SD applicable in this area. This has not been specifically elaborated in the Statutory Instrument one way or the other.

At the same time, this Department was of the view that the exclusion should not be applicable to other services which, although embodying a transport element, were not definable as "transport services" (i.e., did not fall strictly within the definition of transport services such as port, air transport, rail) for the purposes of the exclusion. Such services are suggested to include car rental services, funeral services and aerial photography services which are viewed as coming within the ambit of the SD. Again, this issue has not been specifically addressed in the Statutory Instrument.

In relation to the Irish taxi industry, this Department was of the view, having consulted Recital 21 of the SD and with the Irish Commission for Taxi Regulation, that the SD would not be applicable within this realm of economic activity. The Commission for Taxi Regulation has apparently received clarification that it will not be considered a "competent authority" for the purposes of the Directive. This Department also discussed the applicability of the SD to the National Transport Authority (NTA)[62] which is responsible for the research, co-ordination and

[60] See, *Response from Department of Transport*, 21 October 2009—http://www.djei.ie/trade/marketaccess/singlemarket/servicesdirective.htm (last accessed 23 July 2011).

[61] The Dublin Airport Authority is responsible for the administration and management of Dublin International Airport. The Dublin Airport Authority is also responsible for the administration of Shannon and Cork International Airports. Accordingly, Dublin Airport Authority retains considerable powers to influence the running of the three major airports within the Republic of Ireland. See, generally, the *State Airports Act 2004* (No. 32/2004).

[62] See http://www.nationaltransport.ie/ (last accessed 23 July 2011).

development of transportation strategies in Ireland. This Department notes that it considers the NTA exempt from the scope of the SD by virtue of the exclusions under aforementioned Regulation 3 (2) (d) of the Draft Regulations (transposing Article 2 SD) and Regulations 2 (2) and 2 (3) of the Draft Regulations (transposing Article 3 SD) which exclude the applicability of the SD to public utilities and already existing monopolies. Nevertheless, this Department contended that the procedures adopted by the NTA are effectively in compliance with the SD in many respects anyway.

Department of Enterprise, Trade and Innovation[63]
This Department recommended that a definition of "consumer" be explicitly included within the definition of a "recipient" in the transposing Statutory Instrument. The Department pointed out that EU measures routinely make the distinction between "consumers and others", which serves to facilitate enforcement at national level. This recommendation was accepted by the legislator and the definition of consumer forwarded by the Department now appears in Regulation 2 (1) of the Statutory Instrument as follows: "In these Regulations—'consumer' means a natural person who is acting for a purpose that is outside the scope of the person's business, trade or profession". This Department also made recommendations that the word "consumer" be incorporated into the provisions of Article 7 of the SD, in relation to information provided by a point of single contact, when this came to be transposed into the Statutory Instrument. However, this appears not to have been accepted by the legislator. The word "consumer" does not appear after the term "recipient" pursuant to Regulation 29 (3) of the Statutory Instrument relating to the information obligations of the point of single contact. Similarly, this Department had recommended that the term "consumer" be inserted into the wording of Article 22 SD regarding information assistance obligations on service providers. This was not accepted by the legislator either. The provisions of Regulation 22 of the transposing Statutory Instrument make reference to the information rights of service recipients without distinguishing between recipients and consumers in that regard. This Department also recommended that the term "consumer" be included in Articles 26 (1), (2) and (3) as well as Article 27 (1), 27 (2) and Article 28 SD, relating to information obligations on service providers, when these came to be transposed in the Statutory Instrument.[64] The legislator similarly did not accept those recommendations.

This Department is also responsible, *inter alia*, for the management of policies in relation to trading in public places and requested local authorities to conduct a review of all bye laws relating to casual trading in order to ensure that those bye

[63] See, *The Services Directive and Casual Trading*, 18 December 2009—http://www.nationaltransport.ie/ (last accessed 23 July 2011).

[64] See, *The Consumer Policy Section of the Department of Enterprise, Trade and Employment has produced a paper looking for a definition of consumer to be included in the draft Directive*—http://www.djei.ie/trade/marketaccess/singlemarket/servicesdirective_dev.htm (last accessed 23 July 2011).

laws were in compliance with the requirements of the SD. The Department has instructed local authorities that it considers each of them to be "competent authorities" for the purposes of the SD and that it is thus up to each local authority to ensure compliance with the SD in regard to the management of casual trading policy. Accordingly, this Department has set out the various requirements of the SD for the local authorities and the applicability of its provisions to casual trading. This includes discussion of the criteria for licensing, authorisations, fees, information requirements and so on.

All of the above comments were subsequently forwarded to the Office of the Attorney General for consideration in the drafting of the Statutory Instrument, which was reportedly subject to numerous drafting revisions thereafter.[65]

2 Individual Articles of the Services Directive

2.1 Article 6 SD: Point of Single Contact (POSC)

2.1.1 Establishment of the POSC

The POSC has been introduced in Ireland, at least initially, in the form of a new National Point of Single Contact (NPSC). The NPSC is currently administered by the IMU in the Department of Enterprise, Trade and Innovation. The website address of the NPSC is http://www.pointofsinglecontact.ie.[66] The website also maintains an email address, telephone and fax numbers as well as providing a postal address.[67]

2.1.2 Subjective Understanding, Competence Structure

It appears that the legislator has preferred the option of a single point of contact with national competence but this is likely best understood in the context of the fact that Ireland is not a federal state, rather than as an inherent aversion to a subjective understanding of Article 6. Under Regulation 31 (1) of the Statutory Instrument, the Minister is empowered to designate further points of single contact:

> 31 (1) The Minister may designate by notice in writing a person to carry out the functions of a point of single contact under these Regulations with respect to a particular service activity, on such conditions as the Minister deems appropriate and in accordance with these Regulations.

---

[65] Email correspondence with the Department of Jobs, Enterprise and Innovation (on file with authors).

[66] Last accessed 23 July 2011.

[67] See, http://www.pointofsinglecontact.ie/contact.htm (last accessed 23 July 2011).

While it is possible that further points of single contact may be established for certain sectors, it has been indicated that this would be unlikely.[68] Administrative inefficiencies might arise if there were a proliferation of points of single contact given the relatively smaller sectoral size of the Irish economy in comparison to larger Member States, such as Germany, France and the UK. The exact nature of the relationship between a prospective point of single contact established for a certain sector and the NPSC is not specifically addressed in the Statutory Instrument. The nature of such relationships, if or when they occur in future, will be defined by Ministerial prerogative in accordance with Regulation 31 (1) of the Statutory Instrument.

There is no mention of points of single contact being established to deal with domestic and foreign providers separately, though this could conceivably be a future possibility by virtue of Regulation 31 (1) of the Statutory Instrument. It also does not appear that the NPSC is expected to assume responsibilities which are enjoyed by competent authorities. Instead, the NPSC operates as a "general information service", according to its website.[69] There has not been a reorientation of administrative responsibilities to the NPSC. However, where the Minister proposes to establish additional points of single contacts for specific sectors, Regulation 31 (2) of the Statutory Instrument mandates the Minister to consult with the competent authority (if any) in that sector before doing so:

> 31 (2) Where there is a relevant competent authority in the State in respect of a particular service activity, the Minister shall consult with the authority before designating a person under paragraph (1).

This could be interpreted as an indication that where new points of single contact are to be established in the future, there is the theoretical prospect that certain responsibilities might be transferred to the new point of single contact away from an existing competent authority.[70]

2.1.3 Authorities with POSC-Function

On 5 February 2010, it was announced that, notwithstanding the ongoing work at transposing the SD, the website of the NPSC had been established in order to bring the SD into effect administratively. The NPSC does not appear, at present, to provide for the completion of online processes on its website, but does provide links to the websites of competent authorities involved in "selected service activities", thus ruling out the reallocation of administrative competences to the NPSC itself.[71]

---

[68] Email correspondence with the Department of Jobs, Enterprise and Innovation (on file with authors).

[69] See http://www.pointofsinglecontact.ie/ (last accessed 23 July 2011).

[70] Though it has been indicated that this is unlikely to happen. Email correspondence with Department of Jobs, Enterprise and Innovation (on file with authors).

[71] http://www.pointofsinglecontact.ie/aboutus.htm (last accessed 23 July 2011).

In addition to the foregoing, it should be highlighted that a virtual national single point of contact for businesses (whether domestic or transnational), the Business Access to State Information and Services (BASIS),[72] already exists in Ireland. This provides an electronic interface and generic information to businesses, including service providers, primarily pertaining to relevant government and public services resources and regulations. BASIS was established pursuant to an e-government Action Plan launched by the Irish government in 2000. The mandate of BASIS is described as deliverance of,

> Government information and services to business 24 h a day, seven days a week, from a single access point and with a consistent look and feel ... Information on the website is structured around the "life events" of a business, e.g., business start-up and development, paying taxes and employing staff.[73]

This demonstrates that the notion of a single point of contact for information provision is not alien to Ireland. BASIS may therefore have established best practice which the new NPSC in the IMU may perhaps emulate in terms of its operation. It is not entirely clear as to why BASIS itself was not simply designated as the NPSC in Ireland.[74]

2.1.4 Involvement of Private Partners

Private partners did not play a role in the establishment or initial operation of the NPSC. It also does not appear likely at this stage that private partners will play a role in the operation of the NPSC, certainly not in the short or medium term. The licensing and accreditation of points of single contact are not addressed in the Statutory Instrument.

2.1.5 Liability

Liability of the POSC is not addressed in the Statutory Instrument. Insofar as the NPSC is based in the IMU, it is presumed that the Minister for Enterprise, Trade and Innovation could be vicariously liable[75] for errors on the part of the NPSC. It is also likely that the NPSC will be susceptible to judicial review in the usual way.[76]

---

[72] See, *BASIS* http://www.basis.ie/home/home.jsp?pcategory=10055&ecategory=10055&language=EN (last accessed 23 July 2011).

[73] See, http://www.basis.ie/home/home.jsp?pcategory=10079&ecategory=10082&language=EN (last accessed 23 July 2011).

[74] The authors are aware of anecdotal evidence suggesting that BASIS may have been effectively mothballed, though the authors were not in a position to definitively confirm this at time of writing.

[75] The notion that a Government Minister could be held liable in analogous fashion to a corporation sole was illustrated, for example, in *Maccauley* v *Minister for Posts and Telegraphs* [1966] I.R. 345.

[76] See discussion of the principles of judicial review in Ireland herein at text nn. 7–9.

2.2 Article 7 SD: Right to Information

2.2.1 Right to Information in the National Legislation

Regulations 29 and 30 of the Statutory Instrument transpose Article 7 SD. Regulation 11 of the Statutory Instrument transposes Article 21 of the SD. The European Consumer Centre Ireland[77] and the Galway Chamber of Commerce[78] will fulfil the relevant functions for the purposes of Regulation 11 (1) (c)[79] of the Statutory Instrument, transposing Article 21 (1) (c) SD. Regulation 11 (1) (c) of the Statutory Instrument provides:

> 11 (1) Every recipient in the State is entitled to obtain the following information from an information officer…(c) information as to the contact details of organisations including the European Consumer Centres Network, from which providers or recipients (or both) may obtain practical assistance.

Regulation 11 (2) of the Statutory Instrument establishes the position of "information officer". The Department of Enterprise, Trade and Innovation has indicated that information officers will not be attached to the NPSC.[80] The Department of Enterprise, Trade and Innovation has also indicated that Regulation 11 (2) has, at time of writing, not yet been "formally activated" by the Minister. The Department of Enterprise, Trade and Innovation has indicated that the European Consumer Centre Ireland and Galway Chamber of Commerce will instead carry out the requirements of Regulation 11 (1) of the Statutory Instrument in lieu of the activation of Regulation 11 (2). The Department has indicated that it has had an agreement in place with the European Consumer Centre Ireland and Galway Chamber of Commerce in this regard dating to before the transposition of the SD.[81] The delegation of these functions to such bodies is line with the stipulations of Article 21 (2) SD which provides:

> Member States may confer responsibility for the task referred to in paragraph 1 on points of single contact or on any other body, such as the centres of the European Consumer Centres Network, consumer associations or Euro Info Centres.

Most of the functions allocated to the information officer under the Statutory Instrument relate to the handling of requests by service recipients based in Ireland who are seeking services sector information pertaining **to other Member States**,

---

[77] http://www.eccireland.ie/ (last accessed 23 July 2011).

[78] http://www.galwaychamber.com/ (last accessed 23 July 2011).

[79] See, *The European Commission has published a list of Article 21 bodies under the Services Directive*, 28 January 2010—http://ec.europa.eu/internal_market/services/docs/services-dir/guides/bodies_designated_en.pdf (last accessed 23 July 2011).

[80] Email correspondence with Department of Enterprise, Trade and Innovation (on file with authors).

[81] Email correspondence with Department of Enterprise, Trade and Innovation (on file with authors).

as mandated by Article 21 SD. However, under Regulation 11 (10) and (11) of the Statutory Instrument the role of the information officer has seemingly been marginally extended beyond the requirements of Article 21 SD to include intermediation of requests, by service recipients, for advice and step-by-step guides from a relevant supervisory or regulatory competent authority in Ireland regarding a service provided **in Ireland**.

But it also appears that Article 21 has not been correctly transposed by Regulation 11. Pursuant to Article 21(1) SD, there is an obligation to ensure that advice from competent authorities regarding services provided in other Member States shall, where appropriate, include a simple step-by-step guide; while information and assistance shall be provided in a clear and unambiguous manner, shall be easily accessible at a distance, including by electronic means and shall be kept up to date. By contrast, Regulation 11 (11) specifically applies only this obligation to information furnished in respect of services provided in Ireland and it is not applied to information furnished in respect of services in other Member States.[82]

The notion of a "right to information" under Article 7 SD may be a new concept, although only in certain respects, in the Irish context. Up until this point, competent authorities have been under an existing statutory obligation to release records on request, subject to certain exceptions, pursuant to the *Freedom of Information Acts 1997 and 2003* (Freedom of Information Acts)[83] and/or the *Data Protection Acts 1988 and 2003* (Data Protection Acts).[84] The Freedom of Information Acts confer a right of access to records held by public bodies,[85] subject to various exceptions.[86] Data protection legislation confers rights of information to individuals as against most organisations which may hold records specifically about them, including public authorities and other such bodies. This differs from freedom of information legislation in that only information pertaining to an individual may be requested.[87]

Regulation 30 of the Statutory Instrument, transposing Article 7 (2) SD largely reflects the pre-existing scheme in relation to rights to records in Ireland; the subtle difference is that the right of access is now to **information** rather than to **records.**

---

[82] The Department of Jobs, Enterprise and Innovation has since suggested that this may be because it deems that Ireland cannot force competent authorities in other Member States to provide this information. Email correspondence with the Department of Jobs, Enterprise and Innovation (on file with authors).

[83] *Freedom of Information Acts 1997 and 2003* (No. 13/1997 and No. 9/2003)—http://www.irishstatutebook.ie/2003/en/act/pub/0009/index.html (last accessed 23 July 2011).

[84] *Data Protection Acts 1988 and 2003* (No. 25/1988 and No. 6/2003)—http://www.dataprotection.ie/documents/legal/compendiumAct.pdf (last accessed 23 July 2011).

[85] See, section 6 of the *Freedom of Information Act 1997*, as amended by section 4 of the *Freedom of Information (Amendment) Act 2003*.

[86] See, sections 19–32 of the *Freedom of Information Act 1997*, as amended by sections 14–23 of the *Freedom of Information (Amendment) Act 2003*.

[87] See, section 4 of the *Data Protection Act 1988*, as amended by section 5 of the *Data Protection (Amendment) Act 2003*.

In addition, the requirements of Regulation 30, transposing Article 7 (2) SD as well as Regulation 11, transposing Article 21 SD, appear to replicate already existing structures. Firstly, this can be detected in terms of the establishment of the post of information officer, which mirrors personnel who typically administer requests pursuant to the Freedom of Information Acts.[88] Secondly, in terms of the substance of Regulation 11 and Regulation 30, these could be considered to reinforce the "information on request" spirit prevalent under existing legislation.

2.2.2 Implementation Within the Scope of the Services Directive

Rights to information were extended in national legislation by virtue of the transposition of the SD, though the legislator did not go beyond the substantive requirements of the SD itself. One minor subtlety of note is the requirement under Regulation 29 of the Statutory Instrument which mandates that the competent authorities not only make the relevant information available through the NPSC but also to the Minister.

2.3 Article 8 SD: Procedures by Electronic Means

2.3.1 Transposing Legislation

Regulation 32 of the Statutory Instrument transposes Article 8 SD in literal fashion.

2.3.2 Electronic Means in the Irish Legal System

It is not unusual for electronic procedures to be utilised in the Irish context in terms of registrations or applications to relevant competent regulatory authorities within particular sectors. However there has traditionally been no blanket statutory obligation upon competent authorities to adhere to electronic procedures in terms of registrations and applications. Some competent authorities may require adherence to electronic procedures to some extent or other regarding registrations and applications and others may not at all. As an illustration of the varying extent to which electronic procedures are currently utilised, the following procedures in some sectors can be highlighted:

1. **Chartered Building Surveyors:** Pursuant to the *Building Control Act 2007*[89] (the 2007 Act), the Society of Chartered Surveyors (SCS) is now the competent

---

[88] See, the provisions of section 4 of the *Freedom of Information Act 1997*, as amended by section 3 of the *Freedom of Information (Amendment) Act 2003*.

[89] No. 21/2007.

authority in Ireland for governing the registration of persons as quantity surveyors and building surveyors. According to its website the SCS hosts electronic registration procedures.[90] Nevertheless, there may be variations in the electronic application depending on the type of registration sought and it is unclear whether new procedures would entirely preclude hard copy applications. The 2007 Act itself does not appear to mandate electronic procedures for the purposes of registration; nonetheless, as mentioned, the competent authority has indicated that it intends to embrace such procedures.

2. **Tourist Accommodation:** Under the *Tourist Traffic Acts 1939–2003*,[91] Fáilte Ireland is the competent authority for governing a situation where an accommodation service provider wishes to enter the register of accommodation in Ireland and obtain quality assurances and classifications. Under Section 26 (2) (a) of the *Tourist Traffic Act 1939*[92] it is stipulated that: "Every application under this section for the registration of any premises shall—(a) be made in writing in the prescribed form and manner". It appears that, to date, Fáilte Ireland has subcontracted aspects of this role to third parties. While the legislation governing this sector does not presently mandate the use of electronic procedures, nevertheless it is clear that at least one of the subcontractors utilises electronic procedures in fulfilling its functions regarding the registration of tourist accommodation service providers.[93] This obviously does not preclude the necessity for hard copy elements to be retained and it is highly likely that this is indeed the case, given the nature of the sector.
3. **Auctioneers and House Agents:** Currently, Auctioneers and House Agents are required, as per the *Auctioneer and House Agents Acts 1947–1973* to go through quite an onerous legalistic process, involving court clearance, before they may be licenced to practice in Ireland. The whole system is set for overhaul shortly with the Property Services Regulatory Authority (PSRA) assuming primary responsibility for licensing as a competent authority.[94] At the time of writing, the relevant legislation establishing entirely new procedures in this sector are transiting through the Houses of Parliament (Oireachtas) in the form of the *Property Services (Regulation) Bill 2009* (the 2009 Bill).[95] This particular piece of legislation, as currently structured, does not appear to

---

[90] *Society of Chartered Surveyors* https://registrationbody.scs.ie/registration/ (last accessed 23 July 2011).

[91] *Tourist Traffic Acts 1939–2003* http://www.attorneygeneral.ie/slru/Restatement_Tourist_Traffic_Acts_1939_to_2003.PDF (last accessed 23 July 2011).

[92] No. 24/1939.

[93] *Tourist Accommodation Management Services Limited*—http://www.tams.ie/mis/login.asp?messageStr = (last accessed 23 July 2011).

[94] *Property Services Regulatory Authority*—http://www.npsra.ie/website/npsra/npsraweb.nsf/page/whatwedo-licensing-en (last accessed 23 July 2011).

[95] See, *Property Services (Regulation) Bill 2009* (the 2009 Bill) (Second Stage, Dail Eireann) http://www.oireachtas.ie/viewdoc.asp?fn=/documents/bills28/bills/2009/2809/document1.htm (last accessed 23 July 2011).

explicitly mandate that electronic procedures shall be made available, ultimately allowing the competent authority (i.e., the PSRA in this case) discretion to determine what form applications should take. This is evidenced, in particular, under Section 31(1) of the 2009 Bill which specifies, *inter alia*, that, "[a] person may make an application in the specified form to the Authority for a licence...". Therefore, according to the legislation as currently proposed, the competent authority will ultimately be responsible for determining the form which applications will take and methods available. At present, the website of the PSRA provides no outward indication that electronic procedures are currently available or are to be established.[96] This will need to be reviewed in light of the requirements of the SD. Notwithstanding this, there are clear indications that aspects of a hard copy process will be retained, particularly in relation to a requirement to obtain police clearance etc. before a licence may be granted by the PSRA.[97]

4. **Aquaculture:** Aquaculture and foreshore licencing in Ireland are governed by the *Foreshore Act 1933*[98] and the *Fisheries (Amendment) Act, 1997*.[99] Neither of these pieces of legislation specifies the particular form which applications for licences must take. The relevant competent authority here is the Department of Agriculture, Fisheries and Food and according to its website, such applications for licences must be completed on a downloadable application form. The directions on the application form specify that these should then be returned in hard copy format to the address of the competent authority in question.

These examples are intended to demonstrate that in Ireland electronic procedures have historically not been required by legislation governing individual service sectors, but may be utilised at the discretion of the relevant sector. Consequently, while the idea of applications being conducted electronically is not a new concept in the Irish context, unless at least some semblance of electronic procedure is introduced into those sectors which do not currently embrace this, questions of compliance of Ireland with Article 8 SD may arise. In sum therefore, the notion of electronic procedures may be a novel concept for some sectors and less so for others.

2.3.3 Removal of Other Means

The Statutory Instrument does not mandate the complete removal of other means of administrative proceedings. It remains very likely that other means of administrative proceedings (especially hard copy means) will not be entirely abolished. It may be—as a result of the varying practices among the sectors illustrated by the

[96] http://www.npsra.ie/website/npsra/npsraweb.nsf/page/whatwedo-licensing-en (last accessed 23 July 2011).

[97] See, in particular, section 31 (3) (b) of the 2009 Bill above n. 95.

[98] No. 12/1933.

[99] No. 23/1997.

examples set out above—that during the transposition process the legislator branded Article 8 as "the most difficult article of the Directive to transpose because it imposes obligations on the Member States that are very challenging".[100]

2.4 *Article 9 SD: Authorisation Schemes*

2.4.1 Means of Less Restrictive Measure

It does not appear usual for *a posteriori* inspections to take precedence over formal authorisations in the Irish context. More usually, *a posteriori* inspections of an undertaking might arise in conjunction with a formal authorisation requirement rather than instead of it. Regulation 13 of the Statutory Instrument transposes Article 9 SD in literal fashion. The Statutory Instrument does not therefore specify in exactly which service sectors a formal authorisation scheme will be retained in favour of *a posterioi* inspection. This may become clearer if or when individual pieces of legislation are amended in light of the SD.

2.4.2 Existing Authorisation Schemes/Procedures

In the Irish context, it appears that primarily two types of authorisation tend to prevail. The first, and predominant, type is where it is necessary to get prior approval for certain activities, without which commencing operations is prohibited.[101] The second type can be a simple notification system where, in the absence of good cause, no material examination of the operation will be conducted.[102] In some instances, no authorisation is required at all.[103]

---

[100] The RIA above n. 4, p. 62.

[101] See, e.g., section 19 *Video Recordings Act 1989* (No. 22/1989); section 5 *Transport (Tour Operators and Travel Agents) Act 1982* (No. 3/1982).

[102] See, e.g., registration of company names under section 21 (as amended) of the *Companies Act 1963*, the *Companies Acts 1963–2010*—http://www.cro.ie (last accessed 23 July 2011). See also Competition Authority decisions regarding non-threatening mergers under the *Competition Act 2002* (No. 14/2002). It is recognised that these examples do not necessarily constitute authorisations for the provision of services within the understanding of the SD, they have been utilised solely for purposes of illustrating that the general principle of notifications can apply in some areas of Irish law.

[103] Certain waste activities under the *Waste Management Acts 1996—2008*. See, http://www.epa.ie/whatwedo/licensing/waste/who%20needs%20a%20waste%20licence/wastemanagementactexemptions/ (last accessed 23 July2011).

2.4.3 Simple Notifications

The question whether simple notifications have to be seen as included by Articles 9 ff. SD is not elaborated in the Statutory Instrument transposing the SD.

2.5 Article 10 SD: Conditions for the Granting of Authorisation

2.5.1 Recognition of Requirements

It appears that the requirements of Article 10 (3) SD have been transposed in literal fashion by Regulation 15 (3) of the Statutory Instrument. It does not appear that further problems occurred in this context.

2.5.2 Granting Authorisations Throughout the Whole National Territory and Exceptions

The Statutory Instrument does not indicate any particular difficulty in this regard. It is unlikely that this provision will cause difficulty, given that Ireland is not a federal state and most competent authorities in each Irish service sector tend to retain a national competence regarding authorisations within their particular sector. In any event, the circumstances of an authorisation will make clear the exact conditions under which the activity can be conducted.

Regulation 15 (7) of the Statutory Instrument transposes Article 10 (4) SD. Regulation 15 (7) does not explain exactly when a set of circumstances might warrant a regional authorisation only. It might be speculated that concerns regarding dislocation in the Irish economy could constitute a potential public interest ground justifying regional authorisations only, especially in the context of the recent economic crisis, but this is a speculative observation.

2.5.3 Entitlement to Grant Authorisation, Court Review of Administrative Decisions

It does not appear that an entitlement to acquire authorisation to conduct a service activity once all of the conditions are met is a fundamental divergence from most provisions in Irish administrative laws. It should be highlighted, however, that some authorisations in the Irish context are awarded pursuant to quite open-ended and vague criteria. The schemes for the granting of such authorisations display a lack of concrete conditions; rather they can be dependent upon a large range of ill-defined criteria with the possibility for a considerable amount of decision-making discretion.[104]

It will continue to be possible for applicants seeking an authorisation to petition the Irish High Court on judicial review should they be dissatisfied with the manner in which a refusal or withdrawal of authorisation is reached by a competent public authority.[105] It is also well-established that the Irish courts are willing to permit a challenge to a decision of a competent authority itself on the basis, for example, that the decision is alleged to be unreasonable.[106] Alternatively, for example, a decision of a competent authority can be substantively challenged on the basis that it violates some fundamental right. The proportionality of the decision itself may thus be scrutinised by the Courts on this basis.[107] Accordingly, insofar as an authorisation is refused or withdrawn, Regulation 15 (10) of the Statutory Instrument simply emphasises the status quo in that this will be amenable to judicial review in the usual way. Regulation 15 (8) (a) and (b) and Regulation 15 (9) of the Statutory Instrument transpose the provisions of Article 10 (5) and (6) SD.

2.5.4 Reasoning of Administrative Decisions

It does appear that an "entitlement" under Article 10 (6) SD to the reasoning of a competent authority when applications are refused or withdrawn will be a new departure in Irish law, in some respects. At present, the onus is usually placed upon the individual who wishes to secure the information to actively request it.[108] The common law rule in Ireland has traditionally held that individuals are not automatically entitled to the reasoning of competent public authorities,[109] though increasingly exceptions are made due to concerns about the right to natural or constitutional justice.[110] Moreover, the courts have often held that reasons are

---

[104] For example, see section 10 of the *Public Transport Regulation Act 2009* (No.37/2009). The authors are aware of the exemption for transport services under the SD; this example is merely intended to illustrate the general point.

[105] For an example of an authorisation having being refused and this decision subsequently challenged see, e.g., *Genmark Pharma Limited* v *Minister for Health* [1997] IEHC 121; [1998] 3 IR 111. For an example of an authorisation having been withdrawn and this decision subsequently challenged see, e.g., *Agrichem BV* v *Minister for Agriculture and Food* [2005] 1 IEHC 99.

[106] See, *The State (Keegan)* v *Stardust Victims Compensation Tribunal* [1986] IR 642; *O'Keeffe* v *An Bord Pleanala & Ors* [1993] 1 IR 39.

[107] See, e.g., *Meadows* v *Minister for Justice, Equality and Law Reform* [2010] IESC 3.

[108] See also the discussion regarding information rights and freedom of information legislation in response to Question 2.2 above.

[109] See, e.g., *McCormack* v *Garda Complaints Board* [1997] 2 IR 489; [1997] 2 ILRM 321.

[110] See, e.g., *Anheuser Busch* v *Controller of Patents, Designs and Trademarks* [1987] IR 329; *Rajah* v *Royal College of Surgeons of Ireland* [1994] IR 384; *F.P and A.L* v *Minister for Justice, Equality and Law Reform* [2002] 1 IR 164; *Prenderville* v *The Medical Council* [2007] IEHC 427; see discussion in Delany (2008), pp. 306–309.

required if necessary to render judicial review proceedings effective,[111] which is not hugely dissimilar from the situation created by the Statutory Instrument, in which the duty to give reasons has been transposed with a reference to judicial review as the mechanism to challenge refusal or withdrawal of an authorisation. Additionally, a statutory-based entitlement to reasoning is not entirely unusual and may be explicitly provided for in some individual pieces of legislation or within voluntary codes.[112]

2.5.5 Allocation of Competences

The Statutory Instrument transposing the SD does not reallocate administrative competencies with regard to which authorities are responsible for granting authorisations.

2.6 Article 11 SD: Duration of Authorisation

Regulation 16 of the Statutory Instrument transposed Article 11 SD in literal fashion through a generally applicable regulation. The Statutory Instrument does not delineate specific examples of exceptions to unlimited authorisations. At present in Ireland, time-limited authorisations do arise and appear to be more usual than authorisations of unlimited validity[113]; as such, this provision might be expected to have a significant impact as authorisations for a limited period will have to be justified by an overriding reason related to the public interest.

2.7 Article 12 SD: Selection from Among Several Candidates

The notion of applying selection criteria and opening up certain sectors to tender and selection from among several applicants is not unusual in the Irish context. For example, this would appear to already operate within certain sectors such as in the

---

[111] Hogan and Morgan (2010), para 14–121.

[112] See, e.g., *Kings Inns Regulation of Applications from EU Member States* http://www.kingsinns.ie/website/prospective_students/special/eu.htm (last accessed 23 July 2011); *Conditions for registration as a Foreign Lawyer with the Law Society of Ireland* http://www.lawsociety.ie/Pages/Public-Becoming-a-Solicitor-CMS/Overseas-Applicants/EU-Registered-Lawyers/ (last accessed 23 July 2011). See also Regulation 40 of the *Social Welfare (Consolidated Supplementary Welfare Allowance) Regulations 2007* (S.I. No. 412/2007).

[113] However authorisations of unlimited validity have arisen in specific contexts: see, e.g., Regulation 4(1) *Wireless Telegraphy (Ship Station Radio Licence) Regulations 2006* (S.I. No. 414/2006).

granting of prospecting licences (PLs) by the State for particular mining activities. The grant of licences in this sector, usually contingent upon a competition (as it would not be feasible to have a proliferation of prospectors working in the same geographical area regarding the same mineral), is principally governed by Section 9 of the *Minerals Development Act 1940*[114] and legislation enacted subsequent to this, particularly the *Minerals Development (Amendment) Regulations 1994*[115] and the *Minerals Development Act 1995.*[116] The already established principles and procedures established in sectors such as mining could likely be quite easily projected into a situation where the number of authorisations in a particular service sector must be limited. Nonetheless, the legislator opted to transpose the requirements of Article 12 SD by Regulation 17 of the Statutory Instrument. The Draft RIA indicated that it was expected that Article 12 would "have very limited applicability in Ireland".[117] However, it was not further explained why this may be the case.

2.8 Article 13 SD: Authorisation Procedures

2.8.1 A Priori Determination of the Duration of Administrative Procedures

In Ireland, the determination of the duration of an administrative procedure may be referenced in legislation in general terms such as, "as soon as possible" etc. but the exact duration of each individual procedure is usually left to the discretion afforded to individual public competent authorities.[118]

2.8.2 General Rule for the Duration

During the transposition process the legislator had suggested that the, "period of time … does not have to be the same for every service …".[119] Consequently, the Department of Enterprise, Trade and Innovation invited submissions from stakeholders, especially competent authorities, in relation to what should constitute "reasonable periods" and "as quickly as possible".[120] The Department of Arts,

---

[114] No. 31/1940.

[115] S.I. No. 319/1994.

[116] No. 15/1995.

[117] The RIA above n. 4, p. 35.

[118] For example, note the absence of duration in the procedure when applying for a licence under Regulation 4 of the *Wireless Telegraphy (Digital Terrestrial Television Licence) Regulations 2008* (S.I. No. 198/2008).

[119] The RIA above n. 4, p. 26.

[120] The RIA above n. 4, p. 26.

Sport and Tourism had suggested that in relation to the registration of tourist accommodation providers, for example, three (3) months should be the appropriate time period for the purposes of Regulation 14 (3) of the Draft Regulations proposing to transpose Article 13 (3), while one month should be the appropriate time limit under Regulation 14 (6), (7) and (8) of the Draft Regulations proposing to transpose Article 13 (5), (6) and (7).[121]

Ultimately, the legislator inserted sixty (60) days as a reasonable time period for the purposes of Article 13 (3) SD as reflected in Regulation 18 (2) of the Statutory Instrument. However, this is further qualified by the provisions of Regulation 18 (4) of the Statutory Instrument which permits a twenty eight (28) day time extension, reflecting allowances for such time a time extension also pursuant to Article 13 (3) SD. In sum, therefore, the legislator has established general maximum durations on administrative procedures but only within the scope of such procedures specifically falling under the Statutory Instrument transposing the SD i.e., applications by service providers for authorisations. It would thus appear to be a matter for individual competent authorities as to whether they wish to apply these time limits in terms of other activities falling outside the scope of the SD.

2.8.3 Exceptions to the General Rule for the Duration

It is possible to differ from the prescribed duration of procedures. By virtue of Regulation 18 (7) of the Statutory Instrument transposing Article 13 (4) SD, different arrangements may be put in place by competent authorities for "overriding reasons relating to the public interest (including the legitimate interest of third parties)". The Statutory Instrument does not elaborate on what exactly should be interpreted as "overriding reasons relating to the public interest".

2.8.4 Tacit Authorisation in the National Legal Order So Far

Tacit or fictitious authorisations are not usual within Irish law but may occur in some instances.[122] Generally speaking, there is concern regarding such authorisations due to possible public interest issues. Such concerns may include, for example, that certain tourist accommodation service providers might be able to enter the register of accommodation without having complied with necessary quality controls associated with securing a licence to do so. Similarly, other concerns might be, for example, that persons might be able to secure tacit or

[121] See, *Response from Department of Arts, Sport and Tourism*—http://www.djei.ie/trade/marketaccess/singlemarket/servicesdirective_trans.htm (last accessed 23 July 2011).

[122] As an example, under Irish competition law, if the Competition Authority fails to respond to a merger notification within the relevant time period set down in legislation, this effectively results in a tacit authorisation for the merger to proceed.

default authorisation to sell certain video recordings without having satisfied the usual criteria for grant of a licence. Such video recordings might include material deemed detrimental to the public interest. It has been clarified that Ireland interprets this provision as at least partly placing an onus on competent authorities to ensure efficient and speedy authorisation processes are put in place.[123]

2.8.5 Formal and Substantive Effects of Tacit Authorisation

Tacit authorisations—insofar as they exist in Ireland—appear to embody both formal and substantive effects.

2.8.6 Rules of Formally Granted Authorisations Applicable to Tacit Authorisations

The same rules would appear to apply to tacit authorisations. In the absence of misconduct/offences, it seems that an authorisation cannot be revoked arbitrarily.

2.8.7 Further Remarks

There is nothing further to mention on this point. It must be emphasised that this does not appear to be a common phenomenon in Irish law.

2.9 Article 14, 15, 16 SD

Articles 14 and 15 of the SD relate to the lists of measures in which Member States are prohibited or restricted from engaging in order to facilitate the free movement of services. Prohibitions on measures contained in the black and grey lists have been transposed through Regulations 20 and 21 of the Statutory Instrument which are generally applicable. The stipulations of Articles 14 and 15 are recounted in literal fashion. Article 16 SD has principally been transposed through Regulation 6 of the Statutory Instrument, again in literal fashion.

Regulation 21 (5) and (6) of the Statutory Instrument transposing Article 15 (7) SD accepts the self screening requirement therein.

2.10 Articles 14–19 SD

There are no further issues to report on these articles.

---

[123] Email correspondence with Department of Jobs, Enterprise and Innovation (on file with authors).

2.11 Articles 22–27 SD

Regulation 22 of the Statutory Instrument transposes Article 22 SD in a literal manner. An additional provision appears in Regulation 22 (4) which does not seem to appear in Article 22 SD (though such additional requirements are permitted by Article 22 (5)):

> In giving a description of a service by means of an information document, the provider shall ensure that the information referred to in paragraph (3) [transposing Article 22 (3) SD] is also included in that information document.

Regulation 24 of the Statutory Instrument transposes Article 23 SD. This provides that the Minister for Enterprise, Trade and Innovation may, after consultation with the Minister for Finance and any other relevant Minister of the Government, give a direction in writing to a particular service provider to obtain and maintain professional liability insurance in light of a particular risk identified by the Minister. Although essentially a discretionary provision, this may add a new imperative to Irish law in some service sectors more than others. While professional indemnity insurance is an existing feature of most professional services sectors, obligations in this regard currently appear to arise out of a combination of already existing statutory provisions and/or voluntary codes adopted by individual competent authorities.[124]

Regulation 25 of the Statutory Instrument transposes Article 24 SD literally. Article 24 (1) of the SD requires that total bans on advertising (termed "commercial communications" in the text of the SD) by regulated professions must be removed. While it does not appear that any such bans exist in Ireland, in legislation at least, this matter was flagged for investigation by government departments during the screening process.[125] Previously, there was a complete ban on advertising services as a solicitor in Ireland, though this blanket ban was subsequently removed in the mid-1990s.[126] While certain restrictions on advertising still remain in the context of the solicitor's profession, arguably they could not be construed as constituting a total ban and, as such, they would not be expected to fall within the meaning of Article 24 SD. However, it may be possible that restrictions on advertising imposed upon barristers in Ireland pursuant to Article 6.1 of the Bar

---

[124] For example, solicitors are required to avail of professional indemnity insurance as per *The Solicitors Acts 1954 to 2002 (Professional Indemnity Insurance) Regulations 2007* (S.I. No. 617/2007); Similarly, chartered accountants must also avail of professional indemnity insurance as clearly set out in Bye Laws promulgated by the Chartered Accountants of Ireland. http://www.charteredaccountants.ie/General/About-Us/Charter-Bye-laws-Rules-of-Professional-Conduct-and-Code-of-Ethics/ (last accessed 23 July 2011).

[125] The RIA above n. 4, p. 47; *Consultation Document* above n. 3, p. 49.

[126] See section 71 of the *Solicitors Act 1954* (No. 36/1954), as amended by section 69 of the *Solicitors (Amendment) Act 1994* (No. 27/1994).

Code of Conduct[127] may fall foul of the SD. Barristers in Ireland are entitled to post biographical information upon a website maintained by the Bar Council—regarded by the Bar Council as form of advertising—but barristers cannot engage in advertising within the media in the usual sense. Accordingly, the key test will likely be as to what constitutes a "total prohibition" on advertising under EU law and as to whether the Bar Council Code of Conduct is in compliance with Article 24 (2), in particular, which stipulates:

> Member States shall ensure that commercial communications by the regulated professions comply with professional rules, in conformity with Community law, which relate, in particular, to the independence, dignity and integrity of the profession, as well as to professional secrecy, in a manner consistent with the specific nature of each profession. Professional rules on commercial communications shall be non-discriminatory, justified by an overriding reason relating to the public interest and proportionate.

It is possible that the rules adopted by competent authorities for the regulated professions, especially in terms of the legal profession example invoked above, may now require revision in light of the transposition of the SD.

Regulation 26 of the Statutory Instrument transposes Article 25 SD with no further additions arising. With regard to Article 26 of the SD, it had been suggested by the legislator during the transposition process that it was "largely aspirational but not completely so…". Consequently, the legislator made it clear from the outset that Article 26 SD was viewed as essentially optional in the Irish context, apart from Article 26 (2) SD. Therefore, only Article 26 (2) SD was transposed through Regulation 27 of the Statutory Instrument. Nevertheless, the Department of Enterprise, Trade and Innovation has invited submissions from stakeholders as to how the general service quality aspirations in Article 26 might be achieved.

Regulation 23 of the Statutory Instrument transposes Article 27 SD. The legislator generally followed the wording of Article 27 SD. However, under Regulation 23 (3) (a) and (b)—transposing Article 27 (1) SD—fourteen (14) days is specified as the time period within which service providers must acknowledge receipt of a complaint from a recipient in writing. It is also mandated that such complaints be resolved satisfactorily and without delay. Nevertheless, the Regulation states that "vexatious" complaints are not expected to be resolved satisfactorily and without delay. This particular provision does not appear in Article 27.

In relation to the obligation under Article 27 (3) SD for Ireland to respect financial guarantees to respect judicial decisions lodged in credit institutions in other Member States, it had been suggested by the legislator during the transposition process that this, "technical provision will need careful examination by the Department of Enterprise, Trade and Innovation, the Department of Finance and the Financial Regulator, at the transposition stage".[128] However, in the final

[127] *Code of Conduct for Barristers*, promulgated by the Bar Council of Ireland—http://www.barcouncil.ie/documents/memberdocs/CodeOfConductAdopted050710.pdf (last accessed 23 July 2011).

[128] The RIA above n. 4, p. 49.

transposition, Regulation 23 (5) of the Statutory Instrument ultimately recounted the wording of Article 27 (3) SD.

2.12 *Articles 28 ff. SD: Administrative Cooperation*

2.12.1 Transnational Administrative Cooperation Prior to the Implementation of the Services Directive

Transnational administrative assistance already exists to some degree within the Irish context and this may be partly attributable to the peculiar political situation which has prevailed in Ireland. For example, pursuant to the Belfast (Good Friday) Agreement 1998, InterTrade Ireland was established.[129] This organisation engages in both policy and research activities but also practical initiatives to foster cross-border service activities between the Republic of Ireland and the area of Northern Ireland constituting part of the United Kingdom.[130] Examples of this include the establishment of the "All Ireland Software Network" aiming to promote the development of integrated Information Communication Technology on a cross-border basis with the view to encouraging business activity and growth. InterTrade Ireland has also established the "All Ireland Polymer and Plastics Network", to encourage the growth of this particular sector North and South, and the "North West Science and Technology Partnership", to develop research and development and business activity in the areas of science and technology in the north-west of Ireland. InterTrade Ireland also provides general assistance to service providers North and South with regard to, *inter alia*, financial and sales programmes coupled with an advisory service. There also exists another organisation established on a cross-border basis, the Centre for Cross Border Studies.[131] This organisation aims to encourage greater practical co-operation between policy-makers North and South, tending be more pre-occupied with macro policy initiatives, whether social, economic or commercial, than Inter-Trade Ireland which is more heavily oriented towards developing micro-level benefits for service providers North and South. The Centre for Cross Border Studies is managed by the Special EU Programmes Body.

2.12.2 Re-Arrangement Together With National Rules on Administrative Cooperation

It does not appear that the requirements of the SD provide cause to (re)arrange the provisions for administrative assistance in general or uniform terms. Pursuant to

---

[129] See http://www.intertradeireland.com/aboutus/ (last accessed 23 July 2011).

[130] This includes the geographical area of Ireland comprising the six north-eastern counties of Antrim, Armagh, Derry, Down, Fermanagh and Tyrone.

[131] See http://www.crossborder.ie/ (last accessed 23 July 2011).

Regulations 33-43, the Statutory Instrument purports to address transnational administrative assistance only to the extent of the requirements of the SD.

2.12.3 Provisions on Financial Compensation for Transnational Administrative Cooperation

No provision for compensation arises in the Statutory Instrument.

2.12.4 Adaptation of the Rules on Data Protection and Professional Secrets

There already exists fairly robust data protection legislation in Ireland. Regulation 50 of the Statutory Instrument transposing Article 43 SD recounts the reference to respect for the Privacy[132] and Data Protection Directives[133] therein.

2.13 Article 29 SD: Mutual Assistance—General Obligations for the Member State of Establishment

Regulation 37 and Regulation 42 of the Statutory Instrument transpose Article 29 SD. No further discussions have arisen on the matters set out therein.

2.14 Problems and Discourses on Administrative Cooperation

No problems or discourse surrounding Chapter VI of the SD have been highlighted in the Irish context.

2.15 Convergence Programme (Chapter VII of the Services Directive)

Seemingly, codes of conduct under the Statutory Instrument are conceptualised as a matter for the competent authorities and providers, rather than the State as such, particularly in terms of rendering these available to providers and recipients where applicable.

---

[132] Directive 2002/58/EC of the European Parliament and of the Council of 12 July 2002 concerning the processing of personal data and the protection of privacy in the electronic communications sector (Directive on privacy and electronic communications) [2002] OJ L201/37.

[133] Directive 95/46/EC of the European Parliament and of the Council of 24 October 1995 on the protection of individuals with regard to the processing of personal data and on the free movement of such data (Directive on personal data) [1995] OJ L281/31.

3 Assessment of the Impact of the SD

In similar spirit to other Member States, concerns had been raised Ireland in relation to earlier drafts of the SD, particularly regarding the operation of the Country of Origin Principle (COP) and the potential challenges this was considered to pose to domestic employment standards and wage rates. These concerns were especially pertinent during parliamentary debates discussing the SD in 2006. Left wing political parties and Independent parliamentary representatives were especially vocal in challenging the Government on these matters. The Government did not necessarily disagree with opposition political representatives on this issue, recognising that substantial amendments to the SD were warranted and likely to occur at EU level.[134] Nevertheless, Government representatives deemed it necessary to publicly address the fears of the trade union movement in Ireland on the COP issue. These concerns took place against the backdrop of considerable public controversy surrounding the plight of workers employed by Irish Ferries who faced degradation of their employment terms and conditions following the decision of that company to "reflag" in Cyprus.[135] This controversy had coincidentally erupted around the time of the initial SD debates. In reality, this action by Irish Ferries was actually permitted by the subtleties of international commercial maritime law but was utilised by opponents as a backdrop to the debate on the SD at the time and the COP in particular.

By late 2006, the Government had indicated that it was somewhat disappointed with the proposal being presented at that stage and that it would have preferred a more ambitious measure. The Minister for Enterprise, Trade and Innovation expressed particular disappointment at the fact that temporary employment agencies were set to be exempt from the SD, which was seen as an important growth sector for Ireland at that time. The Minister provided his perspective on the likely effects of the SD generally in blunt terms:

> 'On the European Internal Market, we are not holding our breath in terms of the impact of the new services directive. We think it is a fairly neutered measure at best and its impact will not be fundamental … our assessment is that it may not represent the Holy Grail that might have been originally suggested … the advice to me is that the services directive is not a huge step forward and that is also my assessment of it'.[136]

---

[134] See, *Address by Mr Tom Kitt T.D. at SIPTU Seminar*, 13 January 2006—http://www.djei.ie/trade/marketaccess/singlemarket/servicesdirective_dev.htm (last accessed 23 July 2011); *Services Directive Debate in the Dail*, 25 and 26 January 2006—http://www.djei.ie/trade/marketaccess/singlemarket/servicesdirective_dev.htm (last accessed 23 July 2011); *Employment Issues Debate in the Seanad*, 25 January 2006—http://www.djei.ie/trade/marketaccess/singlemarket/servicesdirective_dev.htm (last accessed 23 July 2011).

[135] See, R. Riegel, S. Molony and A-M. Walsh, "Ferry Row Could be Economic Disaster—Harney", *Irish Independent* (29 November 2005)—http://www.independent.ie/national-news/ferry-row-could-be-economic-disaster–harney-233334.html (last accessed 23 July 2011).

[136] *The Minister for Enterprise, Trade and Employment answered a Paliamentary Question on the Draft Services Directive*, 11 October 2006—http://www.djei.ie/trade/marketaccess/singlemarket/servicesdirective_dev.htm (last accessed 23 July 2011).

The national policy advisory body for enterprise and science (Forfas) operating under the auspices of the Department of Enterprise, Trade and Innovation has recently provided its perspective on the likely impacts of the SD in terms of growth in the Irish services sector. It is guardedly optimistic that the transposition of the SD in Ireland has the potential to spur increases in exports and net employment theoretically, potentially increasing net welfare in Ireland by around 816 million euro per annum. However, there are also deemed to be obstacles in achieving these goals. Forfas particularly highlights, inter alia, the need for Ireland to maintain international competitiveness in terms of wage and production costs in line in with EU counterparts in order to render these goals achievable.[137] Ironically, the recent economic crisis in Ireland triggering decreases in average wages may actually increase the likelihood that the SD will exert positive effects in the long term. The maintenance and development of skills which are relevant to the services sector are also considered crucial, though this may now prove challenging in a tightened fiscal environment in the Irish context, necessitating curbs on government spending, including in education. Ultimately though, it will be necessary for Ireland to embrace the SD as part of a multifaceted approach towards recovery from the unprecedented economic crisis now facing it. This was affirmed by the Minister for Enterprise, Trade and Innovation in a press release accompanying the transposition of the SD. Therein, the Minister indicated his view that, "the transposition of the directive will have a significant impact on our economic recovery prospects".[138]

In terms of the legal implications surrounding the transposition of the SD, it is worth highlighting that the preference of Irish Governments over the years has been oriented towards a "light touch regulation" agenda. Service providers from other Member States have thus traditionally established themselves in Ireland in roughly the same manner as domestic providers. The SD may serve to remove any residual hardships which transnational service providers might have experienced in Ireland when attempting to conform to rules which may have suited domestic service providers marginally better than transnational providers.

In terms of the transposition of the SD, the "gold plated" approach which might prevail in other Member States has been explicitly ruled out by the Irish Government. The reasoning for this offered by the Irish Government is that this, "can have the effect of putting businesses in the 'gold plating' Member State at a competitive disadvantage in relation to other EU states where directives are implemented more literally".[139] It has been considered that going beyond the requirements of the SD in Ireland would be a contradiction of the aims of the SD in

---

[137] *Forfas Input into the Services Directive Regulatory Impact Analysis*, September 2010—http://www.forfas.ie/media/forfas100930-input_to_services_directive_impact.pdf (last accessed 23 July 2011).

[138] See, *Press Release on the European Union (Provision of Services) Regulations 2010 S.I. 533 of 2010*, 11 November 2010—http://www.djei.ie/press/2010/20101111a.htm (last accessed 23 July 2011).

[139] The RIA above n. 4, p. 61.

breaking down barriers to transnational business and that this would be detrimental to the "better regulation" agenda in Ireland.[140]

References

For legislation, jurisprudence and websites please refer to 1.1 of the report and footnotes directly.

Books

Coakley J, Gallagher M (2005) Politics in the Republic of Ireland. Routledge, London
de Blacam M (2009) Judicial Review, 2nd edn. Dublin, Tottel
Delany H (2008) Judicial Review of Administrative Action, 2nd edn. Dublin, Round Hall
Hogan G, Gwynn Morgan D (2010) Administrative Law, 4th edn. Dublin, Sweet and Maxwell

Book Chapter

Taggart M (1997) The Province of Administrative Law Determined? In: Taggart M (ed) The Province of Administrative Law. Oxford, Hart

Special Online Sources

Commission Handbook on the Implementation of the Services Directive (2007) Available at http://ec.europa.eu/internal_market/services/docs/services-dir/guides/ handbook_en.pdf
Department of Enterprise, Trade and Employment Ireland Regulatory Impact Analysis (the RIA) (2009) Available at: http://www.djei.ie/trade/marketaccess/singlemarket/09RIA007a.pdf (from March 2009)
Department of Enterprise, Trade and Employment Ireland Consultation Document on the EU Services Directive (2009) Available at: http://www.djei.ie/trade/marketaccess/singlemarket/09serv030FINAL.pdf (from August 2009)
Forfas (National Policy Advisory Body for Enterprise and Science) Input into the Services Directive Regulatory Impact Analysis (2009) Available at: http://www.forfas.ie/media/forfas100930-input_to_services_directive_impact.pdf (from September 2010)
Report of the Constitution Review Group (1996) Available at: http://www.constitution.ie/reports/crg.pdf

[140] The RIA above n. 4, p. 61.

The Implementation of the Services Directive in Italy

Simone Torricelli

1 General Remarks on the Transposition Strategy and General Understanding of the Implementation

1.1 Main References used in this Research

The research focussed on the legislation that passed.

As we describe later, the transposition process was conducted in two steps. First, specific interventions modified regulations on single issues (see, in particular, Article 9 of Law no. 69/2009,[1] Article 38 of Law Decree no. 112/2008,[2] and Article 9 of Law Decree no. 7/2007[3]). Second, and with a certain delay, the government[4] adopted a legislative decree designed to provide for a complete

Professor Simone Torricelli, Università degli Studi di Firenze, Dipartimento Diritto Publico (simone.torricelli@unifi.it).

[1] Published in the Official journal n. 140, 19 June 2009—Suppl. Ord. n. 95; available at http://www.parlamento.it/parlam/leggi/09069l.htm.
[2] Published in the Official journal n. 147, 25 June 2008—Suppl. Ord. n.152/L; available at http://www.camera.it/parlam/leggi/decreti/08112d.htm.
[3] Published in the Official journal n. 26, 1 February 2007; available at http://www.parlamento.it/parlam/leggi/decreti/07007d.htm.
[4] On the base of the law of delegation 7 July 2009, n. 88, published in the Official Journal n. 161, 14 July 2009; available at http://www.parlamento.it/parlam/leggi/09088l.htm.

S. Torricelli (✉)
Dipartimento Diritto Publico, Università degli Studi di Firenze, Florence, Italy
e-mail: simone.torricelli@unifi.it

U. Stelkens et al. (eds.), *The Implementation of the EU Services Directive*,
DOI: 10.1007/978-90-6704-840-8_14,

transposition in all the sectors covered by the directive (Legislative Decree of 26 March 2010, no. 59, '*Attuazione della direttiva 2006/123/CE relative ai servizi nel mercato interno*'[5]). These laws are the main source of our analysis, and any regional laws, where existing, were also considered.[6]

Specific information on the implementation process was obtained from the website of the Department for EU Policies,[7] and, namely, from the guide "*Guida per il monitoraggio relative alla direttiva servizi*"[8] as well as from a website specifically created as a national point of single contact (POSC).[9]

As for implementation at the regional level, important elements are provided in a publication by the Interregional Legislative Observatory on "*L'attuazione della Direttiva servizi 2006/123/CE (Bolkenstein). Lo stato dell'arte delle Regioni*"[10] Concerning relations between national and regional legislations, some clarifications are contained in the resolution of the Department for Enterprise and Internationalisation of 6 May 2010.[11]

1.2 Impact of the Services Directive

1.2.1 Profound Cause of Changes to National Law?

The transposition process has not yet concluded, and it systematic effects are just starting to become apparent, so an evaluation of the impact is necessarily incomplete. At the moment, it seems to exclude the fact that the Services Directive (SD) has altered Italian administrative law in a significant way for at least three reasons.

The first (and main) reason is that Italian legislation already provided, before the transposition process, many of the simplification mechanisms imposed by the

---

[5] http://www.governo.it/GovernoInforma/Dossier/direttiva_servizi/decreto_legislativo.pdf

[6] See, as examples, Regional Law Piemonte, 30 December 2009, n. 38, "Disposizioni di attuazione della direttiva 2006/123/CE del Parlamento europeo e del Consiglio relativa ai servizi del mercato interno", published in the Official Bulletin n. 1, 7 January 2010 (available at http://www.regione.piemonte.it/artig/dwd/lr38_09.pdf); Regional Law Emilia Romagna, 12 February 2010, n. 4, "Norme per l'attuazione della direttiva 2006/123/CE relativa ai servizi nel mercato interno e altre norme per l'adeguamento all'ordinamento comunitario", published in Official Bulletin n. 20, 12 February 2010 (available at http://demetra.regione.emilia-romagna.it/al/monitor.php?urn=er:assemblealegislativa:legge:2010;4); Regional Law Umbria, del 16 February 2010, n. 15, published in the Official Bulletin, Suppl. Ord. n. 3, serie generale n. 9, 24 February 2010 (available at http://www.consiglio.regione.umbria.it/ sicor/mostra_atto_stampabile.php?file=lr2010-15.xml).

[7] http://www.politichecomunitarie.it/attivita/?c=direttiva-servizi

[8] http://www.politichecomunitarie.it/attivita/15696/storia

[9] http://www.impresainungiorno.gov.it/index_it.html

[10] http://www.consiglio.regione.toscana.it/leggi-e-banche-dati/Oli/Relazioni-monografiche/ANNO-2009/settembre%202009/ALL2a-sett-09.pdf

[11] Prot. 3635/C, N. 0045166, available at http://www.fipe.it/fipe/Area-legis/Area-pubbl/Somministr/direttiva-servizi.pdf.

directive. The second reason clearly depends on the fact that Legislative Decree no. 59/2010 is extremely generic: It often reproduces the content of the dispositions of the directive. Furthermore, in many cases the decree delegates to a future governmental intervention the concrete fulfilment of the directive's requirements. As a third reason, we observe that the passed laws concern exclusively economic activities, without any extension to other areas of administrative law.

The real impact of the directive appears modest, but is not totally negligible. We anticipate that it can be estimated in connection with the directive's transposition, acceptance, and generalisation of the principle according to which an activity can be commenced on the basis of a simple notification (a principle already existing in the system), but without any delay (whereas before the applicant usually had to wait 30 days for public administration control).[12]

1.2.2 Involvement in the Transposition Process

The complexity of the Italian system, regarding the distribution of legislative powers between the State and the Regions and of administrative functions between the State, Regions, and other local authorities, explains the number of different public subjects involved in the process.

The first phase, the screening of existing regulations, was organised by the Department for EU Policies, but the Department for Regional Affairs, the Regions, and the local authorities also participated in defining both subsequent proceedings and the evaluation criteria. In the same phase, the Ministry for EU Policies formed a technical panel composed of representatives of the different departments and several professional associations[13] to discuss the issue.

As for the legislative process at the national level, Parliament delegated the task of implementation to the government. Even in this case the Regions were consulted: In fact, the legislative decree the government adopted previously obtained the advice of the Permanent Conference State-Regions. Nevertheless, due to the fact that the directive concerns issues that belong to either the regional or state legislative competence, the legislative decree is applicable to the Regions only until they adopt autonomous regulations.[14] The Regions therefore participated in the process with their own laws.[15] According to the general principles, regional laws can even deviate from state legislation, but within limits: In particular, they cannot reduce the level of competition established by the national legislator.[16]

We observe, in conclusion, that close cooperation has definitely taken place.

---

[12] See *infra* point 1.4, and particularly fn. 20.

[13] Decree 23 September 2009 (http://www.politichecomunitarie.it/attivita/16875/tavolo-tecnico-di-confronto).

[14] Article 84 of the legislative decree n. 59/2010.

[15] See *supra* fn. 6.

[16] See the resolution of the Department for the enterprises and for the internationalisation, 6 May 2010.

1.3 (National) Scope of Application

On these subjects, as well as many others concerning the SD, the doctrinal debate is nonexistent[17]; the legislator was left alone to decide matters. Concerning the scope of the application of the new legislation, the choice was both vast and strict at the same time. It was vast because Legislative Decree no. 59/2010 extends the new rules to all economic activities consisting of the exchange of goods or provision of services, even of an intellectual nature, whether domestic or transnational.[18] It is strict because, as mentioned, it has not created new standards to be applied to all administrative activities, even beyond those concerning economic activities (but with the non-negligible exception indicated in the following point).

1.4 Incorporation of Transposing Legislation

Since the main procedural mechanisms provided by the directive were already in existence in the Italian general law on administrative procedure,[19] the legislator, while transposing the directive, simply stated applied the provisions indicated by the general law on administrative procedure. Nevertheless, under the pressure of the directive, a residual clause was also introduced in the general law on administrative procedure, stating the principle that, provided no different provisions exist, services covered by the directive can be provided on the basis of a simple notification and that the activity can be commenced at the same time as the notification, without any delay. A subsequent modification of the same general law extended this principle to all regulated activities, such that the specific reference to the directive in that law has disappeared.[20]

As we will see later, POSCs also already exist within the Italian system: Legislative Decree no. 59/2010 delegated the government to modify their existing regulation and to adapt it to the new EU requirements.[21]

---

[17] Among the few contributions, Si Nitto and Cataldi (2010), Panetta (2010), Colavitti (2009), Preto (2007), Miranda (2007), Pappadà (2007), Cafari Panico (2006), Santagata (2006).

[18] See, in particular, Article 1 of the decree. Anyhow, a different treatment of national and transnational providers would cause a constitutional problem: see *infra* Sect. 2.5.

[19] Law 7 August 1990, n. 241, published in the Official Journal 18 August 1990, n. 192, as several time modified, available, in the text in force, at http://www.bosettiegatti.com/info/norme/statali/1990_0241.htm.

[20] See Article 49, para 4 bis, decree law 31 May 2010, n. 78, as converted into the law n. 30 July 2010 (published in the Official Journal GU n. 176 of 30 July 2010—Suppl. Ordinario n.174), both available at http://www.normattiva.it/dispatcher?service=213&datagu=2010-07-30&annoatto=2010&numeroatto=122&task=ricercaatti&elementiperpagina=50&redaz=010G0146&aggatto=si&&afterrif=yes&newsearch=1&fromurn=yes&paginadamostrare=1&tmstp=1283071604515).

[21] See Sect. 2.1.

Italy incorporated the new rules/regulations into existing statutes and passed new codifications. As mentioned in Sect. 1.1, at least at the state level, the implementation was ensured by (a) a specific decree of transposition, (b) other new laws implementing the directive in specific fields, and (c) some modifications of existing laws.

1.5 The Relationship of the Services Directive to Primary EU Law

There has not been any debate on this issue in Italy.

1.6 Screening

As stated above (in Section "Involvement in the Transposition Process"), the screening was organised by the Department of EU Policies and arranged in cooperation with other institutional and professional subjects. *In concreto*, the department devised a questionnaire requiring first a screening of the procedures by each administration (local, regional, or national) and then a verification of their compatibility with the provisions of the directive.

In a public audition, the Ministry of EU Policies declared that more than 300 administrative procedures were screened, but the results have not been published.[22] Some results are codified in Legislative Decree no. 59/2010, where a specific section is dedicated to provide new and simpler regulations to specific service providers (beauticians, shipping agents, hairdressers, etc.). However, in the report of the Interregional Legislative Observatory, it appears that most Regions decided to keep existing regulations, considering that they do not contrast with the directive. It is hard to say if this depends on a "defensive" approach of Italian administrations or on the fact that the Italian legislation, which eliminated many prior authorisation requirements, was already in line with the aims of the SD. Both factors probably contributed.

2 Individual Articles of the Services Directive

2.1 Article 6 SD: Point of Single Contact (POSC)

2.1.1 Establishment of the POSC, Subjective Understanding, Competence Structure, Authorities with POSC-Function

Entities similar to the POSCs requested by the directive have existed in the Italian system since 1998, when the legislator created the so-called "*Sportello unico delle*

[22] http://www.politichecomunitarie.it/ministro/17248/audizione-del-ministro.ronchi

attività produttive".[23] Even if the competences concerning the construction, extension, closure, localisation, and re-localisation of certain productive activities are often shared by different bodies, Law no. 112/1998 prescribes that the entire proceeding must be in charge of one only administrative entity. Inside the competent structure, a POSC must be established,[24] while, under the general provision of the law on administrative procedure,[25] a specific civil servant must be personally liable for conducting the procedure and the official's name must be formally communicated to the applicant.

However, this regulation does not refer to all the formalities demanded of the provider to commence activities, namely, it does not include either inscription in the register of undertakings or other fiscal and social security formalities. As for the latter aspects, Article 9 of Law Decree no. 7/2007 allows the applicant to submit (usually electronically) only one communication, which is valuable both for inscription in the register of undertakings and for obtaining the fiscal and VAT codes, as well as for other fiscal, insurance, and social security aspects. When the administration receives this communication, it issues a receipt that allows the applicant to immediately commence activities.

It appears, therefore, that even if this legislation were already close to fulfilling the EU requirement, its main criticism concerns the necessity of (at least) two applications, each requiring several authorisations or acts but addressing two different bodies. Implementation of the directive demands intervention on this issue. With this aim, the legislator delegated the government to simplify the system, following the directive provisions, and to rationalise the current regulation of POSCs to ensure the right of providers to complete, through the POSC and electronically, all procedures and formalities needed.[26] However, up until today, this duty to adapt the existing rules has not been accomplished.

In concreto, POSCs were introduced by the creation of specific offices internal to the local public authorities, namely, the municipalities, which are in charge of receiving applications and declarations, however named, and submitting them to the competent authorities. The POSCs, therefore, do not affect the rules on competence. Nevertheless, Law Decree no. 59/2010[27] states that if the local administrations have not created POSCs, the authorisation for administrative functions must be considered as automatically delegated to the Chamber of Commerce. In this case, the transposition seems indeed to determine a reallocation of competences. For another example of reallocation, see the following point.

At the central level, the government created a national POSC, operating through a website that is supposed to be in charge of supporting the network of local

---

[23] In the Italian text of the directive, the expression POSC is literally translated as "Sportello unico".

[24] D'Orsogna (2003), Piperata (2002), Gardini and Piperata (2002); Torchia (1999).

[25] Articles 4, 5 and 6 of the law n. 241/1990.

[26] Article 25 (1) of the legislative decree n. 59/2010.

[27] Article 25 (4) of the legislative decree n. 59/2010.

POSCs.[28] Many of the functions of the website that should be fulfilled, however, have not yet been activated, such that providers needing information must contact a call centre or send e-mails. On the other hand, a linked website[29] arranged and managed by the government allows the submission of certain applications concerning specific administrative requirements, but it does not cover all those needed to commence all activities.

2.1.2 Liability

In case of mistakes of the POSCs, the general rules of public liability apply. This means that the applicant can sue for damages against the public body (or also against civil servants, in case they acted with malice or with particularly evident negligence). Nevertheless, it must be underlined that, despite the fact that public liability should be governed by the same principles as private liability (Article 2043 of the Civil Code, which demands, as requirement for private liability, a whatever kind of negligence), case law limits it to cases where the mistake is evident, or inexcusable.

The civil servant responsible for the mistake can also suffer disciplinary consequences.

2.1.3 Involvement of Private Partners

Article 38 of Legislative Decree no. 112/2008 provides that the charge to verify the existence of the legal conditions to start, modify, transfer, or close an undertaking may be delegated to private entities. In the case this verification does not imply the exercise of discretionary power, their declaration that the activity fulfils the legal conditions is equivalent to an authorisation. In the other case, these private entities' function is to support the POSCs. The conditions and modalities for these private entities to obtain accreditation will be regulated by a government act that has not yet been adopted.

2.2 Article 7 SD: Right to Information

Before the transposition, the right of information was not expressly affirmed in the Italian legislation. Nevertheless, the general law on administrative procedure provides that public bodies must indicate, by acts that must be published, which office is in charge of each type of procedure. Even if a duty to inform has not

28 www.impresainungiorno.gov.it

29 www.impresa.gov.it

expressly been established, it is implicit that this office will provide information to satisfy the needs of any citizen, for whatever reason.

Furthermore, Article 10 of Legislative Decree no. 165/2001 (and, before, Article 10 of Legislative Decree no. 29/1993) adds that every public body must create a specific office in charge of relations with the public whose competence includes the duty to inform about the acts and the goings-on of procedures, as well as to promote initiatives to assure the knowledge of legislations, services, and structures. With specific reference to economic activity, Article 11 of Legislative Decree no. 82/2005 imposes the duty on all public offices to communicate to the Department for Productive Activities the list of administrative requirements established as necessary for the commencement and exercise of each economic activity. These requirements should have been published in a register to be consulted on the website of the Department for Productive Activities, but this provision does not seem to have been implemented.

As we can see, the Italian system has faced the problem of information even before the SD. Legislative Decree no. 59/2010 (Article 26) introduces for the first time in an express way the right to address the competent authorities to obtain all information on the procedural steps to follow and the conditions to fulfil, and the right to be assisted in carrying out the administrative requirements. The content of this right corresponds perfectly to what Article 7 of the SD requires, without any extension. The scope of this right corresponds to the scope of the decree, so it is not limited to the provision of services, but extends to all economic activities.[30]

As for the online publication of the information concerning the requirements for providing a service, the issue is connected with the aforementioned reform of the POSCs. It is foreseeable that once the national POSC website is completely operational, it will be the main online source of information.

2.3 *Article 8 SD: Procedures by Electronic Means*

The legislator has not clarified how to establish electronic procedures *in concreto*, but delegated regulation on this topic to a subsequent act to be adopted by the government. The only indications given (following Article 8 (2) SD) are that, for overriding reasons relating to the public interest, the public authorities can require an interview of the applicant or an inspection, thus introducing an exception to the rule that the procedure must be carried out entirely electronically. Nevertheless, it must be considered that even in this case, Italian legislation (and especially Legislative Decree no. 82/2005, the Code of the Electronic Administration[31]) has in many aspects anticipated the directive. The code affirms the right of citizens to

---

[30] See Sect. 1.3.

[31] Published in the Official journal n. 112, 16 May 2005—Suppl. Ord. n. 93, available at http://www.camera.it/parlam/leggi/deleghe/testi/05082dl.htm).

require public bodies to use electronic instruments and, in particular, to establish an electronic' "dialogue" with public entities, as well as to exercise in the same way the right to view administrative documents. The code also imposes that the POSCs offer their services, even electronically, and accept electronically submitted applications. The implementation of this regulation is nevertheless modest and heterogeneous; hopefully, the directive and European supervision will be a propulsive factor. In this context, it is clear that traditional proceedings have not been removed.

2.4 Article 9 SD: Authorisation Schemes

2.4.1 Means of Less Restrictive Measure

Since 1990, the law on administrative procedure has replaced all existing authorisations with a simple notification of the start of the activity, provided that (a) the delivery of the authorisation does not imply the exercise of discretionary powers, (b) there are no limits on the number of authorisations public authorities can deliver, and (c) the activity is not subject to public plans or programs.[32]

However, some areas are excluded from this mechanism and the authorisation scheme is still maintained. This is the case for authorisations that must be delivered by public administrations operating in the field of national defence, public security, immigration, asylum, citizenship, finance, health, cultural and environmental assets, and the environment. A further exception concerns cases when the authorisation is required by EU law. Others exceptions are then provided by special legislation.

This last point is crucial. Services are often governed by specific regulations deviating from the general principles, and these can also be different in different regions. We nevertheless observe that the Italian system exhibits an autonomous trend to overcome the authorisation scheme that does not originate from EU input, but which the EU has alimented.

2.4.2 Existing Authorisation Schemes/Procedures

According to the regulation described, public control of the existence of legal requirements for private activities can assume three different forms. First, we have the classic authorisation scheme. The procedure to be respected is always the ordinary procedure regulated by Law no. 241/1990, so that it is not possible to distinguish different authorisation schemes. The only variation on the model can appear when a public authority does not adopt an act (positive or negative) within

[32] Article 19 of the law n. 241/1990.

the time limit for the conclusion of the procedure, because sometimes this "silence" is equivalent to a tacit authorisation, but important exceptions are provided.[33] As for requirements imposed by Article 10 of the SD, they correspond to general principles of Italian administrative law, such that no new conditions are introduced for the legality of the procedure. As seen, this scheme is rarely utilised, particularly in the field of economic activities.

The second model is that of the notification of the beginning of an activity, which can assume two different forms. Prior to implementation of the SD, the general law on administrative procedure provided that the applicant had to wait 30 days so that the public authorities can verify the existence of the legal requirements. Once the delay expired, the activity could commence, but the public authorities did not lose their power: They could make the control on requirements even later on, but only within a reasonable term; furthermore, since the activity has already started and the public authorities' behaviour has created on the applicant a legitimate expectation about its legality, the decision to interdict it depends on the presence of a specific public interest, prevailing on the private interest of the applicant.

This model survived only in some special regulations, but it is not the more general one.

Implementation of the directive brought about a modification of the general law of administrative procedure: A simple notification attributes the right to immediately commence an economic activity. Public authorities must control its legality by a delay of 60 days and can interdict the activity; after that time limit, the interdiction is admitted only when the activity can be a danger to the artistic or cultural patrimony, the environment, the public health, public security, or national defence.

As mentioned above,[34] it is interesting that these modification first concerned services included in the scope of the directive and was then extended to all other cases, in both economic and non-economic fields. This model, which was introduced in the implementation of the SD, is now the general model to be applied to economic activities. This seems to be an indirect impact of the SD.

2.4.3 Simple Notifications

Italian legal scholars tend not to consider the simple notification requirement included in an "authorisation scheme", because in that case the applicant does not "ask" anything: The applicant only declares that all the requirements to which the activity is subordinated are completed and that therefore he or she will begin exercising it. This perspective led the Italian authorities to ask the Commission if the screening should also cover those regulations not requiring prior authorisation,

---

[33] Article 20 of the law n. 241/1990. See *infra* Section 2.8.

[34] See Sect. 1.3.

but the answer involved the duty to screen all concerns, even those.[35] Indeed, the question should be treated as EU matter and not as a national one.

2.5 Article 10 SD: Conditions for the Granting of Authorisation

2.5.1 Recognition of Requirements

No specific rules consider the hypothesis of authorisations granted by other Member States (MSs), which are left to the application of the general principle of mutual recognition. The only provision concerning this issue is specifically referred to in the regulated professions, for which Legislative Decree no. 59/2010 confirms the previous legislation requiring a national decree of recognition of the professional title.[36]

A particular problem arising from the application of the mutual recognition principle concerns the case where an MS grants an authorisation according to less restrictive requirements than those demanded by Italian legislation. This question was brought up to the Constitutional Court, which declared (in a non-recent case) that since Italian legislation was more demanding than that of other countries regulating other providers operating in Italy, in application of the mutual recognition principle, Italian law should be considered in breach of the Constitution and therefore annulled because it causes an "inverse" discrimination.[37]

2.5.2 Granting Authorisation Throughout the Whole National Territory and Exceptions

Legislative Decree no. 59/2010 states, in (apparent) general terms, that authorisation allows providers to carry out their activity all over the national territory, with the exception of cases where overriding reasons of public interest limit its efficacy. When this can happen is not clear (and specific areas of exceptions are not identified), so that the disposition can be understood in the sense that authorisations have a general territorial efficacy (general principle) if other laws do not expressly limit them (with exceptions to be expressly provided). Such applications can result, however, in great complications, because of the need to verify in every single case, by analysing the legislation of the specific fields (limitations are, e.g., provided for the activity of private vigilance, for tourist guides), whether the specific authorisation submits to the general rule or if an exception is provided.

---

[35] As mentioned in the interregional legislative Observatory Report on "L'attuazione della Direttiva servizi 2006/123/CE (Bolkenstein). Lo stato dell'arte delle Regioni", fn. 10.

[36] Article 46 of the legislative decree n. 59/2010.

[37] Constitutional Court, n. 443/1997, available at www.giurcost.org.

2.5.3 Entitlement to Grant Authorisation, Court Review of Administrative Decisions

In Italian law, every administrative procedure must be concluded within a time limit established by a law or established in advance by each administration.[38] On the other hand, there is no rule imposing the conclusion of a procedure and the granting of an authorisation once all the investigations have been completed, even if a similar rule can be derived from the general principle of "good administration" stated by Article 97 of the Constitution (which is interpreted as containing the obligation for public bodies to act as quickly as possible). Besides, general law on administrative procedure also provides that a specific civil servant should be in charge of the procedure, and that one of the duties is to ensure that the procedure be carried out quickly.

As for the extent of judicial control on the granting or denial of an authorisation, it is limited. Basically, the judge verifies the regard of the laws and of other principles guiding administrative discretion—first of all, the principle of reasonableness—and also that the power was correctly exercised in view of the public interest indicated by the law. A review beyond these limits is not usually permitted (the extent of Italian administrative court control is therefore not different from that assured by the Court of justice on EU administrative acts). Article 10 of the SD does not seem to have incurred any change.

2.5.4 Reasoning of Administrative Decisions

The requirement to fully reason administrative decisions in Article 10 (6) SD did not cause a need to change national law. Article 3 of Law no. 241/1990 provides that all individual administrative acts must indicate the reasons justifying their adoption.

2.5.5 Allocation of Competences

There has been no change in the allocation of competences in this regard.

2.6 *Article 11 SD: Duration of Authorisation*

Legislative Decree no. 59/2010[39] simply reproduced the contents of Article 11 of the SD, concerning both the principle of unlimited validity and its exceptions. It is

---

[38] See *infra* Section 2.8.

[39] Article 11 of the legislative decree n. 59/2010.

disputable, however, whether the limitation of this authorisation's validity must be provided in general terms by specific laws or whether the administration in charge of delivering it could itself introduce a limitation by invoking the existence of an overriding reason relating to the public interest or by preferring to replace the unlimited validity clause with one providing for the authorisation's automatic renewal.

No general prohibitions on time limit authorisations existed previously.

2.7 Article 12 SD: Selection from Among Several Candidates

The obligation to carry out a selection corresponds nowadays to a general principle (inspired by EU Treaties[40]) to be applied every time public authorities provide a whatever benefit to a specific citizen (the principle is also applicable to licences and authorisations when their numbers are limited, e.g., taxi licences). Article 12 of Legislative Decree no. 59/2010 reproduces this principle, but the directive and its implementation did not introduce anything new.

2.8 Article 13 SD: Authorisation Procedures

2.8.1 A Priori Determination of the Duration of Administrative Procedures and General Rule for the Duration

Law no. 241/1990 states that all public bodies must establish, by general acts, a time limit within which each type of proceeding must be concluded, and that if the authority does not fulfil this obligation, the time limit for the conclusion of the procedure is 30 days. Different delays are sometimes provided by specific regulations.

As for the time limit to control in the case of a simple notification, see "Simple Notifications" above.

2.8.2 Exceptions of the General Rule for the Duration

Law no. 241/1990 allows a public entity to differ from the prescribed duration of a procedure, but only once, for not more than 30 days, to obtain information or certifications about facts, conditions, or qualities that do not issue from acts it owns or that are owned by other public authorities.

---

[40] See Consiglio Stato sez. VI, 21 May 2009, n. 3145.

2.8.3 Formal and Substantive Effects, Applicable Rules, Exceptions

The following concerns only the case of a priori authorisation requirements (in the case of a simple notification, the lack of subsequent control does not interfere with the exercise of the activity). The general rule, applicable in case the authority does not respond to a filed application in time, is that silence is equivalent to a tacit authorisation.

This tacit authorisation has not only formal but also substantial effects, because once it is formed, public authorities that oppose it must quash it. However, following Article 21 nonies l no. 241/1990, the power to annul a fictitious act can be exercised only by a reasonable delay and after a comparative evaluation of all the affected interests (i.e., there must be public interest requiring its annulment prevailing on the private interest in keeping it). In this sense, tacit authorisation is submitted to the same regime of authorisations that are formally granted.

However, the mechanism of tacit authorisation does not apply in all cases. In general terms, it is excluded from the areas of national defence, immigration, citizenship, public security, health, and the environment; there are then specific dispositions introducing other exceptions. In all these cases, in the face of silence from the public authorities, the applicant can sue the administration before the administrative court. The judge, first, orders the adoption of the act, then, in cases of further inactivity, can nominate a commissioner who takes the act in substitution of the public authority.

2.9 Articles 14, 15, 16 SD

As for Article 14 of the SD, one effect of the implementation of the directive (and more so, in general, in the application of EU principles) concerned the authorisation for the activity of private vigilance. The law[41] submitted its delivery to an evaluation of market demand: the law was reformed and this condition abolished in 2008.[42]

Concerning Article 15 of the SD, Legislative Decree no. 59/2010 reproduces a list of forbidden requirements and specifies, as does the directive, that these requirements are admitted only for overriding reasons relating to general interests; it provides, furthermore, that all public bodies must communicate to the government any new dispositions introducing similar requirements.[43] It is interesting that the provision of the decree specifically concerning discriminatory requirements

---

[41] Article 136 decree n. 773/1931: see, as an example of its application, Consiglio di stato, sez. IV, 28 March 1992, n. 349.

[42] Law 6 June 2008, n. 101, published in the Official Journal 7 June 2008, n. 132.

[43] Articles 12 and 13 of the legislative decree n. 59/2010.

states not only that similar requirements are forbidden, but also that all provisions of law containing them are automatically abolished.[44]

2.10 Articles 14–19 SD

There have been no discussions with regard to prohibited requirements/restrictions (Articles 14, 15, 16, 19 SD) and further exemptions (Articles 16 (3), 17, 18 SD) in Italy.

2.11 Articles 22–27 SD

There have been also neither discussions nor discourses on Articles 22–27 SD.

No initiatives were taken regarding the issue of the Member States as initiator of private regulation during the transposition.

2.12 Articles 28 ff. SD: Administrative Cooperation

Prior to the transposition of the SD, there was no specific legislation in Italy concerning transnational administrative cooperation (with the exception of certain networks of authorities in specific sectors, such as telecommunications, which is indeed something new). The lack of previous regulation can perhaps explain the fact that the legislator considered it necessary, for a correct transposition, to provide very analytical regulation on the issue, to which Legislative Decree no. 59/2010 dedicates several articles (Articles 36–43).

The requirements of the SD caused no general (re)arrangement of provisions for administrative assistance. There have been no new rules on financial compensation introduced. Furthermore rules on data protection and professional secrets remained unaltered.

2.13 Article 29 SD: Mutual Assistance—General Obligations for the Member State of Establishment

This article does not seem problematic.

---

[44] Article 29 of the legislative decree n. 59/2010.

2.14 Problems and Discourses on Administrative Cooperation

There have been no problems or discourses as regards Chapter VI (administrative cooperation) which are worth mentioning.

2.15 Convergence Programme (Chapter VII of the Services Directive)

The transposition did not impose a general obligation for providers to adopt codes of conduct and, besides, public authorities do have not a role in the creation of similar codes.

3 Assessment of the Impact of the Services Directive

From the Italian perspective the impact of the SD on administrative procedure law, administrative law for business activities, and even beyond cannot be assessed as severe as in Germany (See Sect. 1).

Due to the lack of doctrinal debate, it is difficult to describe the perception of how the transposition was carried out; besides, the fact that the transposition process has not yet ended prevents definitive conclusions. However, see "Profound Cause of Changes to National Law?".

The most interesting effect produced by the transposition process can perhaps be identified by the generalisation of an instrument that previously had but a limited place in the legal system: the notification to the public authorities of the existence of legal conditions as the only formal requirement to complete before commencing an economic activity. This is a conceptual model, introduced by EU law, able to change in general terms the paradigm of the relation between economic freedoms and public powers. In this scheme, the provider does not have to wait for a formal authorisation, or even experience, after notification, any delay, such that the provider has the right to exercise his or her freedom before the public authorities and, in general, the community have the opportunity for any kind of verification. In this sense, the provider is wholly liable with respect to the law, while the administration tends to lose its paternal role in saying what is allowed or not. Whatever the evaluation of this phenomenon, it appears to be a remarkable step towards a veritable liberalisation of the market.

References

For legislation, jurisprudence and websites please refer to 1.1 of the report and footnotes directly.

Cafari Panico R (2006) La liberalizzazione dei servizi tra il regime vigente e la direttiva bolkestein, Diritto pubblico comparato ed europeo, pp 1880–1893
Colavitti G (2009) La direttiva bolkestein e la liberalizzazione dei servizi professionali, Rassegna forense, pp 481–520
D'Orsogna M (2003) Unificazione funzionale e sportello unico, Giornale di diritto amministrativo, p 471
Gardini G, Piperata G (2002) Le riforme amministrative alla prova, lo sportello unico per le attività produttive. Giappichelli, Torino
Miranda M (2007) Dal principio del paese di origine alla clausola "libera prestazione di servizi", l'art. 16 della direttiva 2006/123/CE. Quali novità per la libera circolazione dei servizi nel mercato interno?, Contratto e impresa. Europa, fasc. 2, pp 918–933
Panetta S (2010) L'impatto della direttiva servizi sulle attività commerciali, Disciplina del commercio e dei servizi, pp 45–57
Pappadà D (2007) Il diritto di stabilimento delle società nella nuova direttiva sui servizi nel mercato interno, Contratto e impresa. Europa, pp 972–980
Piperata G (2002) Lo sportello unico, Rivista Trimestrale di Diritto Pubblico, p 41
Preto A (2007) la direttiva 2006/123/ce: dal principio del paese d'origine alla libera prestazione dei servizi, Contratto e impresa. Europa, pp 886–917
Santagata R (2006) La nuova direttiva sui servizi: le ripercussioni nel diritto del lavoro, Diritti lavori mercati, pp 591–620
Si Nitto T, Cataldi C (2010) Note sugli sportelli unici dopo la direttiva «servizi»: le riforme in atto in Italia, Francia, Gran Bretagna e Spagna, at <www.astrid-online.it>
Torchia L (1999) Lo sportello unico per le attività produttive, Giornale di diritto amministrativo, p 109

Special Online Sources

Dipartimento Politiche Comunitarie (2007) Guida per il monitoraggio relative alla direttiva servizi, Octobre (2007). Available at: http://www.politichecomunitarie.it/attivita/15696/storia
Regione Piemonte—Direzione Affari Istituzionali e Avvocatura (2009) L'attuazione della Direttiva servizi 2006/123/CE (Bolkenstein). Lo stato dell'arte delle Regioni, Settembre 2009. Available at: http://www.consiglio.regione.toscana.it/leggi-e-banche-dati/Oli/Relazioni-monografiche/ANNO-2009/settembre%202009/ALL2a-sett-09.pdf

The Implementation of the Services Directive in Latvia

Agris Repšs and Valts Nerets

1 General Remarks on the Transposition Strategy and General Understanding of the Implementation

1.1 Main References Used in this Research

The study on the implementation of the Directive 2006/123/EC of the European Parliament and of the Council of 12 December 2006 on services in the internal market[1] (hereinafter—the Services Directive) was based on the following sources:

Agris Repšs—Advocate and Partner of law firm SORAINEN and Board Member at Riga Graduate School of Law; he also lectured at the Stockholm School of Economics in Riga.Valts Nerets—Legal Counsel and Associate at law firm SORAINEN and Lecturer at Riga Graduate School of Law.

[1] Directive 2006/123/EC of the European Parliament and of the Council of 12 December 2006 on services in the internal market. OJ L 376, 27.12.2006, pp. 36–68.

A. Repšs (✉) · V. Nerets
SORAINEN, Riga, Latvia
e-mail: agris.repss@sorainen.com

V. Nerets
e-mail: valts.nerets@sorainen.com

U. Stelkens et al. (eds.), *The Implementation of the EU Services Directive*,
DOI: 10.1007/978-90-6704-840-8_15,

1. Parliamentary documents:

   Annotation of the Law on the Free Provision of Services[2];

2. Laws, Cabinet orders:

   (a) Law on the Free Provision of Services,[3]
   (b) Cabinet Order No. 90 (2009) 'On Plan of Actions for Simplification of Administrative Procedures in Service Sectors in relation with the Directive 2006/123/EC of 12 December 2006 of the European Parliament and of the Council of 12 December 2006 on services in the internal market',[4]
   (c) Cabinet Order No. 342 (2009) 'On the Implementation of Concept of "points of single contact" pursuant to provisions of the Directive 2006/123/EC of 12 December 2006 of the European Parliament and of the Council of 12 December 2006 on services in the internal market'[5];

3. Reports by the Ministry of Economics:

   (a) Informative report of 11 January 2010 'On implementation process of form models 1 and 3 of "points of single contact" pursuant to provisions of the Directive 2006/123/EC of 12 December 2006 of the European Parliament and of the Council of 12 December 2006 on services in the internal market',[6]

---

[2] Annotation of the Law on the Free Provision of Services. Available on the Internet at http://titania.saeima.lv/LIVS/SaeimaLIVS.nsf/0/B77396F3F860A4E8C225768D0041EC56?OpenDocument (last accessed at 8 April 2011), hereinafter—the Annotation.

[3] Law on the Free Provision of Services (in Latvian: Brīvas pakalpojumu sniegšanas likums). Official publication: "Latvijas Vēstnesis", No. 62 (4254), 20.04.2010., in force from 04.05.2010. Available on the Internet (in Latvian only) at: http://www.likumi.lv/doc.php?id=208269 (last accessed at 8 April 2011), hereinafter—the Law.

[4] Cabinet Order No. 90 'On Plan of Actions for Simplification of Administrative Procedures in Service Sectors in relation with the Directive 2006/123/EC of 12 December 2006 of the European Parliament and of the Council of 12 December 2006 on services in the internal market' (in Latvian: Par Pasākumu plānu administratīvo procedūru vienkāršošanai pakalpojumu sniegšanas jomā saistībā ar Eiropas Parlamenta un Padomes 2006.gada 12.decembra Direktīvas 2006/123/EK par pakalpojumiem iekšējā tirgū ieviešanu). Official publication: "Latvijas Vēstnesis", No. 23 (4009), 11.02.2009. Available on the Internet (in Latvian only) at http://www.likumi.lv/doc.php?id=187626 (last accessed at 8 April 2011), hereinafter—the Cabinet Order No. 90.

[5] Cabinet Order No. 342 (2009) 'On the Implementation of Concept of "points of single contact" pursuant to provisions of the Directive 2006/123/EC of 12 December 2006 of the European Parliament and of the Council of 12 December 2006 on services in the internal market' (in Latvian: Ministru kabineta rīkojums Nr. 342 Par koncepciju "Vienas pieturas aģentūras principa ieviešana atbilstoši Eiropas Parlamenta un Padomes 2006.gada 12.decembra Direktīvā 2006/123/EK par pakalpojumiem iekšējā tirgū noteiktajām prasībām"), with amendments. Official publication: "Latvijas Vēstnesis", No. 85 (4071), 02.06.2009. Available on the Internet (in Latvian only) at http://www.likumi.lv/doc.php?id=192695 (last accessed at 8 April 2011), hereinafter—the Cabinet Order No. 342.

[6] Informative report of 11 January 2010 'On implementation process of form models 1 and 3 of "points of single contact" pursuant to provisions of the Directive 2006/123/EC of 12 December

(b) Informative report of 29 July 2010 'On implementation process of form models 1 and 3 of "points of single contact" pursuant to provisions of the Directive 2006/123/EC of 12 December 2006 of the European Parliament and of the Council of 12 December 2006 on services in the internal market'[7];

4. Other sources:

Website of the Ministry of Economics at www.em.gov.lv, website of Point of Single Contact for Services and Products at www.latvija.lv, and website of the Cabinet of Ministers of the Republic of Latvia at www.mk.gov.lv.

1.2 Impact of the Services Directive

1.2.1 Profound Cause of Changes to National Law?

Neither the government nor the Latvian Parliament set up a specific goal of altering the legislation beyond the one-to-one transposition of the SD. During the transposition process of the SD the legislature discovered that several legal provisions already existed in Latvian laws, thus these provisions were not transposed.[8] The Latvian Parliament chose to define some terms more widely than stipulated in the SD, also taking into account the case law of the European Court of Justice.[9]

(Footnote 6 continued)
2006 of the European Parliament and of the Council of 12 December 2006 on services in the internal market' (in Latvian: 11.01.2010. Informatīvais ziņojums par vienas pieturas aģentūras 1. un 3.formas modeļa ieviešanas gaitu atbilstoši Eiropas Parlamenta un Padomes 2006.gada 12.decembra Direktīvā 2006/123/EK par pakalpojumiem iekšējā tirgū noteiktajām prasībām). Available on the Internet (in Latvian only) at http://polsis.mk.gov.lv/view.do?id=3018 (last accessed at 8 April 2011), hereinafter—the Informative report of 11 January 2010.

[7] Informative report of 29 July 2010 'On implementation process of form models 1 and 3 of "points of single contact" pursuant to provisions of the Directive 2006/123/EC of 12 December 2006 of the European Parliament and of the Council of 12 December 2006 on services in the internal market' (in Latvian: 29.07.2010. Informatīvais ziņojums par vienas pieturas aģentūras 1. un 3.formas modeļa ieviešanas gaitu atbilstoši Eiropas Parlamenta un Padomes 2006.gada 12.decembra Direktīvā 2006/123/EK par pakalpojumiem iekšējā tirgū noteiktajām prasībām). Available on the Internet (in Latvian only) at http://polsis.mk.gov.lv/view.do?id=3018 (last accessed at 8 April 2011).

[8] E.g., the right provided in Article 10 (6) of the SD to challenge decisions of competent authorities before the courts or other instances of appeal is stipulated in Section 76 (2) of the Administrative Procedure Law (in Latvian: Administratīvā procesa likums). Official publication: "Latvijas Vēstnesis", No.164 (2551), 14.11.2001; "Ziņotājs", No. 23, 13.12.2001., with amendments. Available on the Internet at http://www.likumi.lv/doc.php?id=55567 (last accessed at 12 April 2011), hereinafter—the APL.

[9] E.g., under Section 1, subparagraph 9 of the Law, "services" means also economic activities provided without remuneration. See also: the Annotation, *supra* note 2, p. 19, with reference to, e.g., C-385/99 *V.G. Müller-Fauré v Onderlinge Waarborgmaatschappij OZ Zorgverzekeringen UA and E.E.M. van Riet v Onderlinge Waarborgmaatschappij ZAO Zorgverzekeringen*, European Court reports 2003 p. I-04509.

1.2.2 Involvement in the Transposition Process

The process of implementation of the SD, which is still ongoing, is a result of the cooperation of various state institutions, primarily controlled by the Cabinet of Ministers, the Ministry of Economics as the main ministry responsible for the transposition, and other ministries which are responsible for the analysis of their respective fields.

For coordination purposes, the draft Law was sent to the Small- and Medium-Sized Enterprises and Crafts Consultative Committee of the Ministry of Economics of the Republic of Latvia, the National Economy Committee, the Latvian Chamber of Commerce and Industry, and the Employers' Confederation of Latvia.[10] No objections or suggestions to the draft Law, however, were received from these organisations. No special informative campaigns or consultations with experts were carried out.[11] Thus, a close cooperation and coordination took place in the transposition process, with governmental and non-governmental organisations involved.

1.3 (National) Scope of Application

The requirements of the SD are binding not only for providing transnational services or for transnational establishment, but also compulsory with regard to purely domestic services or establishment.

The implementing laws and regulations are applicable also to domestic service providers to their full extent. The Law does not contain any specific restrictions regarding domestic or non-domestic service providers. Section 3 (2) of the Law states that the Law regulates economic activity in the provision of services to the extent that it does not contradict norms of *lex specialis* stipulated in other laws.

The Law engenders general and universal standards for the way authorities deal with all citizens and all economic stakeholders, thus they may be claimed by everybody. Article 20 of the Directive is implemented in Section 6 (2) of the Law and stipulates that the recipients may not be made subject to discriminatory requirements based on their nationality or place of residence.[12]

1.4 Incorporation of Transposing Legislation

Most of the requirements relating to the administrative proceedings were implemented in the Law one-to-one. Some of the required norms were already included

---

[10] The Annotation, *supra* note 2, p. 37.

[11] Ibid.

[12] See also the Annotation, *supra* note 2, p. 21.

in the APL.[13] However, the provision of Article 13 (4) of the SD stating that failing a response within the set time period authorisation shall be deemed to have been granted was not implemented in the Law pursuant to second sentence of Article 13 (4) and due to the fact that this proposition would be contrary to already existing provisions of the APL.[14]

For transposition of the main issues of the SD the Law was adopted. However, a number of changes in other laws were made[15] and new Cabinet Regulations and Cabinet Orders were issued.[16]

1.5 The Relationship of the Services Directive to Primary EU Law

Pursuant to the established practice of the ECJ[17] the Latvian Parliament has included the concept of a "short-term service provider" in Sections 15 and 16 of the Law. Currently no problems have been identified in this context.

1.6 Screening

The screening process was performed by the respective ministries under the guidance of the Ministry of Economics. As a result of the screening process 69 legal acts to be amended were identified.[18]

---

[13] The APL, *supra* note 8. See, e.g., Section 63 of the APL corresponds to Article 10 (5) of the SD; Sections 67 and 75–77 of the APL correspond to Article 10 (6) of the SD; Section 64 of the APL corresponds to Article 13 (3) of the SD.

[14] See Section 64 (2) of the APL. See also the Annotation, *supra* note 2, p. 24.

[15] E.g., Cabinet Regulations No. 184 (2003) "Requirements for Activities with Biocidal Products" (in Latvian: "Prasības darbībām ar biocīdiem"). Official publication: „Latvijas Vēstnesis", No. 83 (2848), 04.06.2003. Available on the Internet at http://www.likumi.lv/doc.php?id=75744 (last accessed at 13 April 2011), in Latvian, with amendments. Also available at http://www.vvc.gov.lv/export/sites/default/docs/LRTA/MK_Noteikumi/Cab._Reg._No._184_-_Requirements_for_Activities_with_Biocidal_Products.doc (last accessed at 13 April 2011), in English, without amendments.

[16] E.g., the Cabinet Order No. 342, *supra* note 5.

[17] See the Annotation, *supra* note 2, pp. 18–20, with references to e.g., C-55/94 *Reinhard Gebhard v Consiglio dell'Ordine degli Avvocati e Procuratori di Milano*, European Court reports 1995, p. I-04165, para 39; C-215/01 *Bruno Schnitzer. Reference for a preliminary ruling: Amtsgericht Augsburg—Germany*. European Court reports 2003, p. I-14847, para 28.

[18] The Informative report of 11 January 2010, *supra* note 6, p. 3.

2 Individual Articles of the Services Directive

2.1 *Article 6 SD: Point of Single Contact (POSC)*

2.1.1 Establishment of the POSC

The provisions of the SD regarding the POSC were implemented in the fifth chapter of the Law—"The unified state and municipal service web portal and its operator". The chapter also includes provisions for principles of operation of the portal and states the responsibilities of the curator of the portal, e.g., to organise the operation of the unified state and municipal service web portal in cooperation with the responsible institutions and in accordance with the principle of good governance.[19]

Section 17 of the Law sets forth that the portal provide all information about the authorities responsible for procedures regarding the provision of services and their competences, as well as the necessary actions to receive authorisation from responsible authorities. The website address of the portal is https://www.latvija.lv.

The portal was developed in 2006[20] as a joint state and municipal e-services site. Therefore, there was no need to create a completely new web portal to introduce the POSC and instead the information regarding the POSC was added in a special section. The portal allows service providers to obtain information through a single entry point and electronically complete required administrative procedures in order to commence provision of services in a chosen business sector in Latvia.

The website of the POSC states that through the POSC its user can

(a) obtain all the information about the procedures which must be completed for the specific services activity, and
(b) obtain all the information regarding formalities needed for carrying out specific activities.[21]

The website contains descriptions of the services, electronic submission forms, and links to legislative acts and public registers, while also stating the means of redress available in the event of a dispute and detailed contact information and providing step-by-step instructions for the use of the POSC.[22] Much of the information on the website, however, is available only in Latvian. The information on www.latvija.lv is free of charge.[23]

---

[19] See Section 18 (2) of the Law.

[20] Latvia State Portal. https://www.latvija.lv/EN/WebLinks/portal/about_portal (last accessed at 13 April 2011).

[21] https://www.latvija.lv/EN/WebLinks/Portal/services_directive.htm (last accessed at 13 April 2011).

[22] https://www.latvija.lv/NR/rdonlyres/E84E1846-191E-4056-87CB-9D9F292D710B/773/step_by_step.pdf (last accessed at 13 April 2011).

[23] Section 19 (1) of the Law.

Cabinet Regulations No. 480 (2010) prescribes the order in which the exchange of information between the operator of the portal and the responsible institutions is carried out and the order in which the information included in the unified service web portal in the sphere of application of the Law is updated.[24] According to Section 4 of Cabinet Regulations No. 480, the operator of the unified service portal is the State Regional Development Agency (SRDA).

2.1.2 Subjective Understanding, Competence Structure

Only one POSC was introduced in Latvia. The administrative competences were not re-allocated, leaving them with the respective ministries.

2.1.3 Authority with POSC-Function

The functions of the POSC were attributed to an existing institution—the SRDA.

2.1.4 Involvement of Private Partners

The private partners were not involved in the introduction of the POSC.

2.1.5 Liability

Section 18 (1) of the Law stipulates that the operator is responsible for the maintenance and development of the portal. However, Section 12 of Cabinet Regulations No. 480 provides that the responsible institution shall ensure that accurate and credible information is provided in the services catalogue. The section explicitly states that the director of the respective institution is responsible for the correctness and timely provision of the information in the portal. Thus, the liability for mistakes at the POSC depends on whether there is a mistake in the portal as such or whether there is a mistake in the services catalogue provided in that portal.

[24] Cabinet Regulations No. 480 (2010) "Information exchange order of the unified service portal" (in Latvian: Vienotā pakalpojumu portāla informācijas apmaiņas kārtība). Official publication: "Latvijas Vēstnesis", No. 88 (4280), 03.06.2010. Available on the Internet (in Latvian only) at: http://www.likumi.lv/doc.php?id=211207 (last accessed at 13 April 2011), hereinafter—the Cabinet Regulations No. 480.

2.2 Article 7 SD: Right to Information

The rights to information were not extended as a result of the implementation. Article 7 of the SD is currently being implemented only within the scope of application of the SD.

2.3 Article 8 SD: Procedures by Electronic Means

A new, innovative electronic communications system was introduced during the implementation of the SD. It is possible to log on to system in a number of ways, depending on the seriousness of the task—for instance, using an authorisation system of a bank, using a special “e-signature” (requiring special devices—electronic card and card reader), or “mobile id”, which is a possibility to connect through a mobile phone connected to a certain operator. It is also possible to establish a simple account on the website www.latvija.lv. However, through this account the user will have only limited access to the contents of the portal.

To some extent, there were established electronic procedures in Latvia. Thus, in this context the transposition of the SD did not have a great innovative impact.

The implementation of electronic procedures did not replace other means of administrative proceedings. Therefore, the service provider or recipient still has discretion to decide the manner in which information will be provided to him or her.

2.4 Article 9 SD: Authorisation Schemes

2.4.1 Means of Less Restrictive Measure

According to Annex 3 of Cabinet Order No. 90 a posteriori inspection is not seen as sufficient for provision of services for which the concept of ‘overriding reasons relating to the public interest’ applies, e.g., for blasting works or pyrotechnic services (for national armed forces), gathering and storage of unexploded ordnance, geodesic work, or cartographic work. For reasons of fiscal monitoring and to prevent the provision of services for fraudulent purposes, or for financing terrorism, a posteriori inspection is not seen as sufficient for services concerning precious metals and stones, installation of cash registers, professional activities of certified auditors, etc. Many other services are listed in Annex 3 of Cabinet Order No. 90 for which an authorisation scheme applies, e.g., construction services (business operators); retail and wholesale trade in tobacco products, alcoholic beverages, beer and oil products; various services involving animals; trade in tractor machinery, trailers, and units thereof bearing identification number; placing on the market of plant protection products; water resources management; end-of-life vehicle management; waste management; special aerial works (landscape caption and aerial photography); trade in vehicles and units thereof bearing identification numbers; publishing services; organisation of public events; recruitment services; education services such as higher education, vocational education, and general education; trade in natural gas; trade in electricity; trade at markets, fairs, driving shops, and street shops; certain tourism services (tour operators, tourism agencies, package tourism services, and tourism accommodation), sale and use of explosives; trade of arms.

2.4.2 Existing Authorisation Schemes/Procedures

In Latvia there are several coexisting authorisation schemes or procedures: licensing, certification, registration, coordination, accreditation (for educational institutions), and notification. Licensing or registration is usually the applicable procedure. Due to the requirements of the SD, authorisation procedures were altered or abolished, e.g.,[25] an unlimited duration license instead of temporary license for blasting works or pyrotechnic services (for national armed forces), simplification of procedures for obtaining a license for the establishment of shooting-galleries, abolishing licensing for customs broker services. For various services (e.g., purchase of ferrous and nonferrous metals and scrap) the service provider will be entitled not to hand in such information or documents which are already available to the respective authorities. Application of simpler procedures for other services is being discussed among the responsible authorities.

2.4.3 Simple Notifications

For provision of several services a simple notification is still required, e.g., for animal competitions, markets, auctions, exhibitions, and other events with the participation of animals. Notification procedure is applied to ensure animal health and welfare as well as the safety of persons.

2.5 *Article 10 SD: Conditions for the Granting of Authorisation*

The recognition of authorisations granted by other MS has been implemented in Section 14 (5) and Section 22 of the Law.[26] There is no information about any problems concerning the implementation of this requirement.

---

[25] Cabinet Order No.90, *supra* note 4, Section 5.

[26] See also the Annotation, *supra* note 2, p. 23.

There is no information regarding any difficulties in granting authorisations which give access to the service activity, or to exercise that activity, throughout the whole national territory of Latvia.

Latvia has not identified any areas of "overriding reasons relating to the public interest" to justify only regional authorisation.

There is no difference between the provision of Article 10 (5) of the SD and Section 63 of the APL.[27] Decisions of an institution may be disputed at a higher institution and, afterwards, before the court. Both the higher institution and the court of first and second instance will re-adjudicate the matter on the merits in general or in the part to which the objections of the submitter are applicable.[28] Pursuant to Section 103 (1) of the APL, the courts also review the use of discretion by authorities.[29] Thus, the transposition of Article 10 (5) of the SD did not change the existing provisions of Latvian administrative law.

There was no need to change provisions of the APL due to the obligation to fully reason the decision of the authority pursuant to Article 10 (6) of the SD. The existing provisions of the APL regarding form and component parts of administrative acts and right to dispute administrative acts already prescribed the obligation to fully reason decisions of the authorities.[30]

The Latvian legislator did not change the allocation of competences in the context of Article 10 of the SD.[31]

2.6 Article 11 SD: Duration of Authorisation

The principle of unlimited validity was transposed in Section 13 of the Law. Pursuant to this section, an authorisation may be issued for a limited period of time only if its renewal is subject to continued fulfilment of requirements, the number of available authorisations is limited due to the insufficient availability of natural resources or technical capacities, or when a limited period of time is justified by

---

27 Section 63. Decision regarding Issue of an Administrative Act or Termination of a Matter

(1) After determination of all necessary facts and hearing of the participants in the administrative proceeding, an institution shall without delay assess the facts of the matter and [...] make a decision regarding issuance of an administrative act or termination of a matter.

(2) An institution shall notify a submitter, as well as other participants in the administrative procedure, if they have been called to express their opinion, of the decision to terminate the matter and of the reasons thereof.

28 Pursuant to Section 81 (1), Section 103 (1) of the APL, *supra* note 8.

29 Section 103. Substance of Administrative Procedure in Court.

(1) The substance of administrative procedure in court shall be court control of the legality and validity of administrative acts issued by institutions or actual actions of institutions within the scope of freedom of action, as well as the determination of public legal duties or rights of private persons and the adjudication of disputes arising from public legal contracts.

30 See, in particular, Section 67 and Sections 75–77 of the APL, *supra* note 8.

31 See also the Annotation, *supra* note 2, p. 22.

overriding reasons relating to the public interest. In particular, the term 'automatic renewal' was not included in the Law.[32] Previously there was no exact prohibition on time-limited authorisations in the Latvian legal system.

2.7 *Article 12 SD: Selection from Among Several Candidates*

Article 12 of the SD was transposed in Sections 13 (4) and 14 (1) of the Law. The existing law did not confer any advantages on the providers whose authorisations have just expired or on any persons having any particular links with those providers. The transposition of Article 12 of the SD into the Law, however, has now created an exact prohibition on conferring advantages on the providers whose authorisations have just expired. Again, however, the providers whose authorisations have just expired were not in a more advantageous situation than other providers prior to the transposition of Article 12 of the SD. Thus also after the transposition of the SD, and in accordance with the existing provisions of the law, authorisations are granted based on clear, comprehensive, objective, fair, equal, and public requirements.

2.8 *Article 13 SD: Authorisation Procedures*

2.8.1 A Priori Determination of the Duration of Administrative Procedures

The duration of an administrative procedure is prescribed by law. According to Section 64 of the APL, an institution shall take a decision regarding the issuance of an administrative act within a month from the day the submission is submitted.[33]

2.8.2 General Rule for the Duration and Exceptions

According to Section 64 of the APL, duration of administrative procedures must not exceed a month from the day the submission is made to the institution. According to Section 5 (3) of the Law on Submissions, the institution must provide a substantive reply within a reasonable time, having regard for the urgency of the matter of the

---

[32] See also the Annotation, *supra* note 2, pp. 23–24.

[33] Section 64. Time Periods regarding Issuing of Administrative Acts.

(1) If an administrative matter is initiated on the basis of a submission, an institution shall take a decision regarding the issue of an administrative act within a month from the day the submission is submitted, provided that a shorter term is not prescribed in a regulatory enactment. [...].

submission, but not later than within one month from the day when the submission was made, if not otherwise prescribed by law.[34] Thus, duration of one month for the procedures may be considered as a general rule. Different durations are prescribed in specific laws and Regulations of the Cabinet.[35]

There is a possibility to differ from the prescribed duration of procedures. According to Section 64 (2) of the APL,[36] due to objective reasons an institution may extend the one-month time limit for a period not exceeding four months or, if a lengthy determination of facts is necessary, the time period for taking a decision may be extended for up to one year. In urgent cases, however, the submitter may apply to the institution with a substantiated submission and request that time period for the issue of the administrative act be abbreviated.[37]

2.8.3 Tacit Authorisation in the National Legal Order So Far

Tacit (fictitious) authorisation is not typical in the Latvian legal system. It can, however, be the situation that the provider has not received an answer from the responsible institution within the time limit prescribed by law. In this case the participant in the administrative proceeding may submit a complaint to a higher institution or to a court.[38] If an institution fails to comply, within the set time period, with the decision of a higher institution or the court, the relevant procedural action shall be deemed to have been performed, if it is practically and legally feasible. If it is not practically and legally possible, participants in the administrative proceedings for whose benefit the relevant time period has been stipulated have the right to claim compensation; moreover, failure to comply with the time period shall in itself be considered as moral harm within the meaning of the APL.[39] If, however, the APL or other regulatory enactment specifies a time period within which, in the course of an administrative proceeding, an institution is required to carry out a procedural action unfavourable to the submitter or the potential addressee of an administrative act, then such procedural action may no longer be carried out after expiration of the time period.[40]

[34] Law on Submissions (in Latvian: Iesniegumu likums). Official publication: "Latvijas Vēstnesis", No. 164 (3740), 11.10.2007.; Ziņotājs, 22, 22.11.2007.), with amendments. Available on the Internet at http://www.likumi.lv/doc.php?id=164501 (last accessed at 26 April 2011).

[35] E.g., 10 working days for registering an animal cemetery (pursuant to Cabinet Regulations No. 1114 (2009)); up to 90 days for obtaining a category A or B permit for polluting activities (pursuant to Cabinet Regulations No. 1082 (2010), issued on the basis of provisions of the Law on Pollution).

[36] The APL, *supra* note 8.

[37] Ibid, Section 64 (3).

[38] The APL, *supra* note 8, Section 49 (2).

[39] Ibid, Section 49 (3).

[40] Ibid, Section 49 (4).

2.8.4 Formal and Substantive Effects of Tacit Authorisation

Tacit (fictitious) authorisation has more formal than substantive effects because an institution which has received a submission usually answers such submissions within the time limit prescribed by law. These provisions have practical importance and have been applied by courts and parties to the dispute[41]; however, the situations stipulated in Sections 49 (3) and 49 (4) are not likely to occur very often.

2.8.5 Rules of Formally Granted Authorisations Applicable to Tacit Authorisation

As prescribed in Section 49 (3) of the APL, "if an institution fails to comply, within the set time period, with the decision of a higher institution or the court [..], the relevant procedural action shall be deemed to have been performed, if that is practically and legally feasible. If that is not practically and legally possible, participants in the administrative proceedings for whose benefit the relevant time period has been stipulated have the right to claim compensation [..]." Thus, the rules applicable to tacit (fictitious) authorisation will depend on whether the performance of the relevant procedural action is "practically and legally feasible". If not, then in accordance with provisions of Section 49 of the APL, no tacit authorisation in the respective situation is possible.

2.8.6 Further Information on Tacit Authorisation

Latvia has not included a definition of "tacit (fictitious) authorisation" in the Law. As stated in the Annotation,[42] this term has not been implemented in the Law on the basis of Article 13 (3) of the Directive so as "not to create controversies with the APL, and interpretation and application problems".[43]

2.9 *Articles 14, 15, 16 SD*

The Latvian Parliament did not identify a need to adapt national law to implement these articles and there is no discussion about the self-screening of Latvia.

---

[41] See, e.g., Judgment of Administrative Appeal Court of 20 December 2010 in case No. A42581807. Available on the Internet at www.tiesas.lv/files/AL/2010/.../AL_2012_apg_AA43-1391-10_18.pdf (last accessed at 27 April 2011).

[42] The Annotation, *supra* note 2, p. 24.

[43] Ibid.

Furthermore there are no further problems or discourses regarding these articles in Latvia.

2.10 Articles 14–19 SD

There were no special discussions organised with regard to prohibited requirements and restrictions of the SD in Latvia, but the draft Law was sent to various non-governmental institutions for review. However, no objections or suggestions to the draft Law were received from these organisations.[44]

2.11 Articles 22–27 SD

There were no special discussions with regard to these articles of the SD. With implementation of the SD the use of electronic means for submitting applications to the institutions has developed through the simplification of the submission process. Otherwise the SD has not influenced the modernisation of administrative law generally or the APL in particular. There is no information regarding the incentives of the Latvian government to encourage professional bodies, as well as chambers of commerce and craft associations and consumer associations, to cooperate at the Community level in order to promote the quality of service provision.

2.12 Articles 28 ff. SD: Administrative Cooperation

There were no provisions on transnational administrative assistance in Latvia prior to the transposition of the SD. The requirements of the SD did not give a cause for rearranging the provisions for administrative assistance. There are no provisions on financial compensation for the quite wide range of assistance. And furthermore there was no need to change rules on data protection and professional secrets.

2.13 Article 29 SD: Mutual Assistance—General Obligations for the Member State of Establishment

Article 29 of the SD has not been seen as problematic. There have been no discussions regarding the respective article.

[44] See Sect. 3.2, *infra*.

2.14 Problems and Discourses on Administrative Cooperation

There have been no further problems or discourses as regards Chapter VI.

2.15 Convergence Programme (Chapter VII of the Services Directive)

There are no worth-mentioning discussions that have taken place in Latvia regarding Chapter VII of the SD. There is no information on the role of the Latvian government as an initiator of private regulation in Article 37.

3 Assessment of the Impact of the Services Directive

3.1 Extent of the Impact

As the SD was mostly implemented one-to-one by introducing the Law, the impact has been rather moderate to minor, depending on the field. This may be due to the fact that the APL is very well-drafted and thus Latvian administrative law did not need to be changed much for the transposition of the SD.

3.2 Assessment of the Transposing Legislation

Given the reaction of the society in general, minimal press coverage, and the lack of discussions during the implementation, one could conclude that the implementation of SD was perceived neutrally, as "another EU directive".

3.3 Most Important and Profound Changes Induced by the Services Directive

First of all, it is necessary to note the changes in the licensing system, which made it easier to obtain authorisations in many fields. Secondly, the introduction of the POSC has made cooperation with state authorities substantially easier. These could be named as the most important and notable changes brought up with the introduction of the SD.

The Implementation of the Services Directive in Lithuania

Danguolė Bublienė and Skirgailė Žalimienė

1 General Remarks on the Transposition Strategy and General Understanding of the Implementation

1.1 Main References Used in this Research

The research about implementation of the Services Directive (SD) in Lithuania was based on information found in the following sources:

1. The Ministry of Economy's website, www.ukmin.lt;
2. The website of the Parliament of the Republic of Lithuania, www.lrs.lt;
3. The website Business Gateway (a website of a Point of Single Contact for Services and Products), www.verslovartai.lt;
4. http://www.paramaverslui.eu/go.php/lit/Paslaugu_direktyva_reglamentas_del_apibu/233;
5. The website of the Government of the Republic of Lithuania, www.lrvk.lt; and
6. The website of the Ministry of Interior Affairs, www.vrm.lt.

Dr. Danguolė Bublienė, Vilnius University and Advocate at Baltic Legal Solutions (Danguole.Bubliene@lt.blslawfirm.com); Prof. Skirgailė Žalimienė, Vilnius University and Judge at the Supreme Administrative Court of Lithuania (szalimiene@lvat.lt).

D. Bublienė (✉)
Baltic Legal Solutions, Vilnius, Lithuania
e-mail: Danguole.Bubliene@lt.blslawfirm.com

D. Bublienė · S. Žalimienė
Vilnius University, Vilnius, Lithuania
e-mail: szalimiene@lvat.lt

S. Žalimienė
Supreme Administrative Court of Lithuania, Vilnius, Lithuania

U. Stelkens et al. (eds.), *The Implementation of the EU Services Directive*,
DOI: 10.1007/978-90-6704-840-8_16,

The authors of this report also used the method of interview, where the authors contacted the relevant persons, namely, Ms. Jolita van Otterlo, head of the Division of Services Policy of the Ministry of Economy, and Ms. Lina Sabaitienė (public organisation Enterprise Lithuania), head of the Point of Single Contact for Services and Products.

1.2 Impact of the Services Directive

1.2.1 Profound Cause of Changes to National Law?

The question of whether the transposition of the SD gives a profound cause to the Lithuanian legislator to alter—beyond the minimum requirements and a one-to-one transposition of the SD—administrative laws in general can be answered both positively and negatively.

Positively, because the legal norms of the Law on Services do not draw any distinction between national and transnational activities. Besides, the Conception on the Services Law adopted by the Regulation of the Government, clearly indicated that the new services law will provide the provisions according to which Lithuanian providers would be in a equal position as providers of other Member States (MSs). This means that the same requirements and principals will apply to all service providers. It has been stressed that the aim of these provisions is to avoid discrimination against Lithuanian providers when stricter conditions apply to Lithuanian providers aiming to exercise services in Lithuania.

Moreover, implementation of the SD will finally lead ('will' because not all legal acts are harmonised with the SD at this moment) to some modernisation and simplification of the administrative proceedings. This huge work was done by identifying the requirements of the legal acts that fell within the scope of the SD and revising them. Now, the huge work consists of changing these legal acts. However, it should be noted that some requirements established in the SD already existed in the legislation of Lithuania, for example, the requirement regarding unlimited terms of licence and the requirement concerning maximum time limits for the issuing of the licence (Article 2.79 of the Civil Code of the Republic of Lithuania, hereinafter the **Civil Code**[1]).[2]

---

[1] The English version of the Civil Code is published at the website http://www3.lrs.lt/pls/inter3/dokpaieska.showdoc_l?p_id=377611&p_query=&p_tr2.=

[2] Article 2.79 of the Civil Code provides the following:

1. Where the requirements specified in the regulations of licensing are fulfilled an open-ended licence shall be issued.
2. Except as otherwise provided by law, licence for the engagement in a certain activity or a written motivated refusal to issue a licence shall be submitted to an applicant within thirty days as of the day on which the documents for the issuance of a licence were produced.

Negatively, because of the following reasons. *First*, neither the Lithuanian legislator, nor the Government of the Republic of Lithuania (hereinafter the **Government**) brought this ambitious aim—to go beyond the minimum requirements of the SD—in their agenda. Moreover, a separate commission consisting of the representatives of state institutions, non-governmental organisations, businesses, and other interested persons was established (the so-called Sunrise Commission), and various subgroups of this commission were formed. The main task of this commission is to present recommendations related to the development of the administration and administrative proceedings. The activity of this commission is not related to the implementation of the SD. Therefore, the SD was not a profound cause for implementing the modernisation, simplification, and effectiveness of the whole administration and administrative proceedings.

Second, the SD was implemented by adopting a new law—the Law on Services (hereinafter the **Services Law**), but not by changing the Law on Public Administration[3] (hereinafter the **Public Administration Law**). Therefore, a unified system of requirements in the administration and administrative proceedings was not created.

Third, the SD was understood as the legal act regulating economic activity but not administration and administrative proceedings. This was why responsibility for the implementation of the SD was assigned to the Ministry of Economy, notwithstanding the fact that the Ministry of Interior Affairs is the main institution in Lithuania responsible for public administration. The mission of the Ministry of Interior Affairs is to serve society, guarantee its safety, efficient and professional public administration (emphasis made by the authors of this report) based on information technologies, and also create conditions for sustainable regional development, not to mention that the strategic goals of the Ministry of Interior Affairs are related to public administration (one of the strategic goals is optimising the public administration system based on professional civil service and the development of an information and knowledge society).[4] Meanwhile, the mission of the Ministry of Economy is to develop a positive legal and economic

(Footnote 2 continued)

3. Refusal to issue a licence may not be based on the inexpediency of activities and has to be motivated.
4. Information on the issuance of a licence, its revocation and withdrawal shall be stored in the register of legal persons. The licensing authority must notify the register of legal persons about the issuance, revocation and withdrawal of licences in accordance with the procedure established by the regulations of the register of legal persons.
5. Upon the issuance of a licence a legal person must supply information specified in the licensing requirements and related to the licensed activities or conditions predetermining the issuance thereof and allow the institution for the supervision of licensed activities to verify it.
6. Stamp tax for the issuance of a licence shall not exceed the costs of the issuance of a licence and supervision thereof.

[3] With the exception of small amendment that establish the rule that special rules regarding institutional cooperation can be established in the Services Law.

[4] Information was taken from the website www.vrm.lt.

environment for economic development and to ensure public welfare and employment. By implementing its mission, it places the major focus on the promotion of innovations, the improved administration of European Union (EU) structural funds, and small and medium-sized business development.[5]

Finally, the scope of services regulated in the Services Law was not expanded compared with the SD. This means that economic activity that goes beyond the definition of services provided in the SD does not fall within the scope of the Services Law. In this case, general law—the Public Administration Law—should be applied.

Therefore, it can be concluded that the SD on the political level was not understood as a measure giving profound cause to simplify or modernise administrative procedures, or at least all initiatives have not been coordinated and have not led to the one and same purpose to modernise, simplify, and accelerate administrative proceedings.

1.2.2 Involvement in the Transposition Process

The process of transposition of the SD into Lithuanian legislation started in 2008 and is still ongoing. The Ministry of Economy has been responsible for implementation of the SD. It has also been coordinating the whole process of implementation. It organized the training for the representatives of the state institutions and municipalities and explained the purpose and requirements of the SD, as well as drafted the questionnaires and guidelines for the screening of legal acts. The process of reviewing national legislation was implemented using the special information system TAPIS, which was created for the purposes of the screening. The representatives of the institutions that participated in the screening process were instructed on how to use this system.

The implementation of the SD was organized in four stages: (i) At the first stage requirements and legal acts that fell within the scope of the SD were identified. A total of 72 laws and about 800 other legal acts that fell within the scope of the SD were found. (ii) At the second stage all identified legal acts were revised and evaluated to identify necessary amendments. This work was accomplished by filling out the questionnaire prepared by the Ministry of Economy. According to this questionnaire, the revision of legal acts should be done while seeking to identify whether the requirements of the particular legal acts conform to the requirements of the SD provided in Articles 9, 14–16, 24, and 25 of the SD. However, in a self-assessment report, the Ministry of Economy provided that at this stage the legal acts were also evaluated to ascertain whether they were in conformity with Articles 5, 8, 10–13, 20, 23, and 27 of the SD. (iii) At the third stage the relevant amendments were drafted and coordinated with interested institutions. (iv) At the fourth stage (which was performed simultaneously with the

[5] Information was taken from the website www.ukmin.lt.

third stage) the representatives of state institutions were instructed to use the specific Internet system (IPM) prepared by the European Commission that helps provide the screening results to the European Commission.

In the process of the implementation of the SD, a law firm was hired to provide assistance regarding the identification of legal acts that needed amendment according to requirements of the SD. In addition, an analysis was prepared regarding how the activity of the points of single contact (POSCs) should be implemented (analysis regarding of the system should be used and cost evaluation).

The identification and revision of legal acts were accomplished by more than 100 state institutions following the plan approved in the meeting of the state secretaries of the ministries. Not only state institutions (ministries, state institutions subordinate to ministries, and other state institutions) but also municipalities were involved in this process.

The Services Law was drafted by a working group established in 2008 by order of the prime minister.[6] This working group consisted of the representatives of various institutions: the Ministry of Economy, the Ministry of Justice, the Department of European Law under the Ministry of Justice, the Office of the Government, and the Association of Local Authorities in Lithuania. It should be noted that the representatives of the Ministry of Interior Affairs was not included in this working group.

In the screening process the Ministry of Economy tried to involve various associations of business; however, they were not very active in this process. Only the Association of the Chambers of Commerce, Industry and Crafts demonstrated discernible interest in this process, and this institution was involved in the screening process.

It can be concluded that during the process of the transposition of the SD into Lithuanian legislation, close cooperation and coordination took place between the several levels of administration. However, the leading position in the process of the SD was attributed not to the Ministry of Interior Affairs, which, as was mentioned, is responsible for the public administration area, but to the Ministry of Economy. At least both ministries should be a leader of the process of the implementation of the SD.

1.3 (National) Scope of Application

There are no discussions (at least not in public) or articles in Lithuania about the scope of the SD.

As was commented in Sect. 1.2.1, the Services Law does not make any distinction between national and transnational services or establishment. On the contrary, the aim of the legislator was to expand the implementation of the SD to

---

[6] Order No. 83 of the Prime Minister was adopted on 3 March 2008.

national service providers as well and to treat transnational and domestic service providers equally. Therefore, not only transnational service providers can refer to the laws/regulations implementing the SD, but also domestic service providers can benefit from all implementing laws/regulations of the SD. The reason for this expansion was not the understanding that the SD provides such a requirement, but the legislator's understanding that the opposite decision would infringe on the principle of equality, and as a result could be evaluated as breaching the Constitution of Lithuania. Certainly, from the political perspectives, it was also an attractive decision.

1.4 Incorporation of Transposing Legislation

Two methods for the transposition of the SD into the Lithuanian legal environment have been considered in Lithuania.[7] The Conception on the Services Law provided that the first method for implementation of the SD is an amendment of the existing legislation which falls within the scope of the SD. The second method is an adoption of general law—the Services Law and the amendment of sectoral laws. After assessment of the advantages and disadvantages of these two approaches, the second way was chosen. It should be noted that a third method—an amendment of two general laws, the Public Administration Law and the Civil Code[8]—that could cover the requirements of the SD was not considered (at least this method was not provided as possible in the Conception on the Services Law).

Lithuania implemented the SD into Lithuanian legislation using a horizontal method and a vertical method.[9] The horizontal method means that a general law ('umbrella' law) is adopted that comprises the general principles and requirements of the SD (*horizontal approach*). The vertical method means that laws (indicated in the screening process as contradicting the provisions of the SD) regulating particular economic activities have been amended (*vertical approach*).

Horizontal approach

As was mentioned above, the Lithuanian legislator implemented the SD mainly by adopting a new special law, the Services Law.[10] Therefore, Lithuania chose to implement the SD not by codifying existing laws but by incorporating new rules into the legal system of Lithuania. However, this method of implementation can create

---

[7] The Conception on the Services Law adopted by the Regulation of the Government of 15 April 2009, No. 330.

[8] The Civil Code provides the requirements for the proceedings of the licensing of economic activities of legal persons.

[9] The self-assessment report, prepared by the Ministry of Economy.

[10] The Law on Services adopted by the Law of 15 December 2009, No. XI-570 (http://www3.lrs.lt/pls/inter3/dokpaieska.showdoc_l?p_id=361342&p_query=&p_tr2=).

some legal uncertainty, because there is no clear distinction between the Services Law and the Public Administration Law.[11] There is no article or discussion (at least not in public) on that issue in Lithuania. Court practice shows how this method of implementation will be realised in practice. However, some issues should be pointed out: First, there is no clear understanding as to which law may be considered as general legal norm and which as special. Second, the definition of the services will always be under consideration. There are no reasonable grounds to exclude other economic activities from the regime of legal norms provided in the Services Law (accordingly from the scope of Services Law). The implementation of the SD through the Public Administration Law would allow one to apply the same legal regime to all economic activities (with the exception of very specific activities).

It should be taken into consideration that the Public Administration Law also regulates administrative services and provides some requirements for these services (according to Article 1 of the Public Administration Law, this law shall create the necessary preconditions for the implementation of the provision of the Constitution of the Republic of Lithuania stipulating that all state institutions shall serve the people; shall establish the principles of public administration, the spheres of public administration, the system of entities of public administration, and the basics of organising administrative procedures; and shall guarantee the right of persons to appeal against the acts or omissions or administrative decisions of entities of public administration, as well as the right to statutory and impartial consideration of applications, complaints, and statements submitted by persons). Besides, it should be noted that the general requirements of the procedure for issuing licences (authorisation requirements) are also regulated by the Civil Code. Therefore, now two laws regulate the general requirements of authorisations. From the viewpoint of legal technique, it is highly doubtful that this is a very good method for the transposition of the SD.

The Services Law consists of seven chapters: General Provisions, Exercise of the Freedom of Establishment, Exercise of the Freedom to Provide Services, Assurance of Service Quality, Administrative Simplification, Administrative Cooperation, and Final Provision. The detailed analyses of the provisions of the Services Law are provided by answering the questions indicated in the second part of this questionnaire.

The SD, in principal, was implemented in the Lithuanian Services Law mostly by copying the relevant provisions of the SD. Only a few additional (or more specific) provisions were established, for example, the specific term for the issuance of authorisations was provided. Besides, it should be noted that most legal norms of the Services Law do not directly establish legal requirements but, rather, indicate that these requirements (principles) should be established while preparing and adopting other legal acts that specifically regulate some economic activity. Therefore, this method of implementation makes it necessary to transpose the SD

---

[11] The Public Administration Law was adopted by the Law of 17 June 1999, m. No. VIII-1234 (http://www3.lrs.lt/pls/inter3/dokpaieska.showdoc_l?p_id=363063).

using not only the horizontal approach but also the vertical approach. This also means that examination and evaluation of whether the SD is implemented correctly in Lithuanian laws can only be made after a revision of all the legal acts that fall within the scope of the SD.

Vertical approach

It should be noted that during the process of the revision of the legal acts in light of the SD, the Ministry of Economy revealed that for full implementation of the directive, 302 legal acts (42 laws, 137 other legal acts, and 123 legal acts approved by municipalities) would have to be amended, taking into account the requirements of the SD (and the requirements of the Services Law, which implements the provisions of the SD). However, as yet[12] only several of them were adopted. Moreover, it should be noted that the Services Law was adopted only on 15 December 2009 and came into force on 28 December 2009. The Government and its authorised institutions were obliged to adopt all legal acts necessary for the implementation of the Services Law. However, this work is not yet finished.

1.5 The Relationship of the Services Directive to Primary EU Law

It appears that Chapter III of the SD codifies the case law of the European Court of Justice (ECJ) as it concerns the freedom of establishment in two sections: prior administrative authorisation for establishment and other requirements that restrict or may restrict establishment. The most important rule applicable to prior authorisation schemes seems to be an obligation to mutually recognise requirements complied with in another MS. This is an obligation already imposed by the Treaty, and the SD introduces a set of operative principles to guarantee that the conditions for an authorisation scheme are fulfilled, which adds value by reference to existing case law. The main added value may come from the 'screening process', whereby each MS must examine existing and future authorisation schemes to check if they comply with the conditions laid down in the SD.

As regards the freedom to provide services, the prohibition of restrictions on that freedom within the Community is already enshrined in the Treaty, and the key question lies in the differences between the Treaty and the SD. Article 16 (1) of the SD, in addition to laying down the obligation to ensure the free access and free exercise of service activities, allows MSs to restrain such freedoms by imposing requirements that respect the principles of non-discrimination, necessity, and proportionality. In that sense, Article 16 is clearly inspired by existing case law and, although the SD does not explicitly mention the obligation of mutual recognition—contrary to its provisions on freedom of establishment—it could be considered that

[12] The end of July 2010.

such an obligation is implicitly incorporated into the obligation of proportionality. However, the SD provides for a limited list of available justifications for exceptions to the freedom to provide services: public policy, the public, security, public health, and protection of the environment. This contrasts with the non-exhaustive list of justifications recognised in the case law of the Court of Justice. For some more considerations on Article 16 of the SD and its relation with case law on Treaty provisions regarding the freedom to provide services, please see Sect. 2.10.

1.6 Screening

The process of screening was described in Sect. 1.2.2. Additionally, it should be noted that Article 5 of the SD was implemented without any additional explanations. The Ministry of Economy does not comment in detail on Article 5 of the SD. Therefore, the assessment about "not sufficiently simple" regulation was done on the ground of own understanding of the institution which reviewed the legal act, and accordingly prepared the amendment to the relevant legal act.

However, it should be noted that the Conception on the Services Law shows that simplification of the administrative proceedings was understood as the establishment of points of single contact (hereinafter the POSCs) and the inclusion of electronic services in the administrative proceedings. The provision of Article 5 of the SD regarding the simplicity of regulations was not directly implemented in the general law, the Services Law. The chapter Administrative Simplification was introduced in the Services Law, however, since (as will be shown below) it deals with matters of the POSC and electronic procedures of administrative services.

2 Individual Articles of the Services Directive

2.1 Article 6 SD: Point of Single Contact (POSC)

2.1.1 Establishment of the POSC

The provisions of the SD regarding the **POSC** were implemented in the fifth chapter of the Services Law (called Administrative Simplification). Part 2 of Article 18 sets forth that providers and recipients shall have a right to use the services of the POSC or to contact the competent authorities of the Republic of Lithuania directly. The law provides that the institution performing the functions of the POSC shall be designated by the Government. The Government's decision has not been adopted yet. However, practically, it is understandable that the functions of POSC will be attributed to the public organisation Enterprise Lithuania (*Viešoji įstaiga 'Eksportuojančioji Lietuva'*). Lithuania has absorbed the model of the Dutch POSC.

A public organisation (or public institution/public establishment[13]) is a specific type of legal person. A public organisation can be established by a private or state[14] legal person or/and natural person. This type of legal person differs from a budgetary institution, which may exceptionally be established only by state or municipality and, as a general principle, its activity may be financed only by the state or municipality budget (accordingly, the rules of the establishment of public organisations differ from those regulating the establishment of budgetary institutions). Pursuant to the Law on Public Establishments,[15] a public establishment shall be a non-profit public legal person of limited civil liability whose aim is to satisfy public interests by carrying out educational, training and scientific, cultural, health care, environmental protection, sports development, social, or legal aid provisions, as well as other activities useful to the public. A public organisation as a type of legal person belongs to the group of public legal persons (in Lithuania there are two groups of legal persons: private and public). The founders of a public organisation should establish its capital and they are the owners of the relevant part of this capital (after registration of the public establishment in the register of legal persons, the founders become stakeholders of the established public organisation). A public organisation has the right to pursue economic and commercial activities that are not prohibited by law and which are inseparably connected with the objectives of activities thereof. In practice, there are many public organisations in Lithuania that pursue very different types of economic and commercial activity.

The fifth chapter of the Services Law lays down the functions of the POSC, the scope of information that should be provided by the POSC and other competent institutions, and the order in which the information should be provided.

The functions of the POSC were attributed to the public organisation Enterprise Lithuania. A new division was established in this organisation—the POSC for Services and Products—and a new website—Business Gateway[16]— was created. Business Gateway is a website of the POSC for Services and Products. The website of the POSC announces that the POSC provides (i) information on permits and licences enabling the provision of services in Lithuania, (ii) information on the technical requirements applicable to products sold on the Lithuanian market,[17] (iii) general information for business, (iv) contact information of competent

[13] The translation of the law provided on the Seimas website uses the word establishment. Other sources use either the word organisation or institution.

[14] A state legal person is understood to be an institution, organisation established by the state or other state institution, as well as municipality or institution, or organisation established by a municipality whose main aim is public administration or public services.

[15] The English version of the law is published at http://www3.lrs.lt/pls/inter3/dokpaieska.showdoc_l?p_id=372028&p_query=&p_tr2=.

[16] http://www.verslovartai.lt/

[17] This function of the POSC implemented the Regulation (EC) No 764/2008 of the European Parliament and of the Council of 9 July 2008 laying down procedures relating to the application of certain national technical rules to products lawfully marketed in another Member State and repealing Decision No 3052/95/EC.

institutions; and (v) information on the POSCs of the EU MSs. Therefore, it can be concluded that a virtual POSC has been established in Lithuania (an Internet portal on electronic basis).

The Services Law does not explicitly provide the financing source for the performance of POSC functions. However, considering that POSC functions are state functions, they should be financed by the state budget. To date, the functions of the POSC are financed by the structural funds of the EU.

The Services Law does not provide any fee system for using POSCs.

2.1.2 Subjective Understanding, Competence Structure, Authorities with POSC-Function

As was described, in Lithuania only one POSC was introduced and its functions were attributed to the public organisation. The national legislator did not reallocate the administrative competences or responsibilities of state institutions. The POSC has the function of intermediary among providers, recipients, and competent public institutions. The POSC does not fulfil the functions of the competent authority or institution. The competent authority or institution is the subject of public administration, which has a supervisory or regulatory role in relation to service activities, including, in particular, administrative authorities, courts, and professional bodies that, in the exercise of their legal autonomy, regulate access to service activities or the exercise thereof.

In accordance with the procedure prescribed by the Government, the POSC grants providers and recipients an opportunity to perform all the procedures and legal formalities related to access to service activities and exercise thereof

1. To submit all the necessary applications and documents to receive the authorisations, as well as declarations, notifications, and applications, addressed to the competent authorities of the Republic of Lithuania for entry into a register, list, or database or for registration with a professional body or association, as well as applications and documents necessary to terminate economic activities;
2. To obtain the authorisations and other documents issued by the competent authorities;
3. To receive and provide the information specified in the Services Law.

Pursuant to the Services Law, these procedure and formalities can be fulfilled over a distance or/and by electronic means (however, this does not apply when the legislation provides for the right or obligation of the competent authorities of the Republic of Lithuania to inspect the premises where the service is provided, the equipment used by the provider, the physical capability of the provider, or the personal honesty of the provider or its employees). However, in practice, the POSC provides its services only by electronic means. The employees of the POSC maintain the website Business Gateway and provide consultations over the phone. However, they do not provide information in paper form.

The Services Law provides the order and procedure that the POSC and competent institutions should follow in an attempt to provide relevant services to providers or recipients. The POSC and the competent authorities of the Republic of Lithuania must ensure that a response to a request for information or assistance is given within five working days, calculated from the day the request was received. If the request is erroneous, the applicant shall be informed about this within five working days of the receipt of the request. If the request is submitted in disregard of the competence, the POSC or competent institution shall refer this request to the relevant institution and the applicant shall be informed of this within five working days of the receipt of the request. The POSC or competent institution shall explain to the applicant the reasons of the request's referral. The POSC or the competent institution shall provide the information indicated in the law orally, in writing, or by electronic means. The information supplied must be relevant.

The Services Law establishes the principle of cooperation between the POSC and the competent institution. The law provides that upon receipt of a request from a provider or supplier to perform specific procedures and formalities, the POSC shall, within two working days, transfer this request and accompanying documents to the competent authority of the Republic of Lithuania, which shall take the action prescribed in the legislation of the Republic of Lithuania. Having performed the actions prescribed in the legislation of the Republic of Lithuania (e.g., having decided to issue an authorisation or supply information), the competent authority, within the time period specified in the legislation, shall directly or via the POSC respond to the provider or recipient who submitted the request and/or other documents. If a request was submitted to the POSC in electronic form, the competent authority shall also respond in electronic form or, if the recipient or provider so requests, in paper form.

As was provided above, the functions of the POSC are attributed to the existing institution. In the process of drafting the Services Law and coordinating this law with other interested institutions and persons, there were considerations to attribute the functions of the POSC to the Association of the Chambers of Commerce, Industry and Crafts or to the Register of Legal Persons.

2.1.3 Involvement of Private Partners

Private partners were not involved in the introduction of the POSC.

2.1.4 Liability

The Services Law does not regulate the issue of liability of the institution for which functions of the POSC were attributed. As was mentioned, the functions of the POSC were attributed to the public organisation. The common practice in the Lithuanian legal system is that a public organisation is not a public administration institution. However, according to the Public Administration Law, a public organisation can be authorised by laws to fulfil administrative functions. Considering that the public organisation Enterprise Lithuania is authorised to fulfil the functions of the POSC by Government decision, it would be treated as a public administration institution, that is, an institution that realises state management functions. The liability of institutions engaged in public administration is regulated by the Civil Code. Therefore, the public organisation Enterprise Lithuania would be liable for mistakes related to the activities of the POSC according to civil liability rules provided in the Civil Code. Claims regarding the illegal activity or omission of the POSC shall be presented to the administrative courts of Lithuania. The same courts are authorised to solve claims where damages arise as a result of illegal actions or omissions of the POSC. However, it should be noted that the POSC is not liable for the accuracy of the information or data or documents provided by the competent institutions. Therefore, the scope of POSC liability is quite narrow.

It should be noted that political liability for POSC activity belongs to the Minister of Economy, since the Minister of Economy is responsible for the implementation of the SD, as well as for the internal market and free movement of services, and the Ministry of Economy is the founder of the public organisation Enterprise Lithuania.

2.2 Article 7 SD: Right to Information

According to the Services Law, the POSC shall supply the providers or recipients with the following information:

1. Information on the requirements applicable to the providers of services in the Republic of Lithuania, including procedures and legal formalities that must be performed to obtain access to service activities or to exercise such activities;
2. The contact details of the competent authorities of the Republic of Lithuania;
3. The means of and conditions for accessing public registers and databases;
4. Information on the means of redress generally available in the event of dispute between the competent authorities of the Republic of Lithuania and the provider or the recipient, between a provider and a recipient, or between providers;
5. The contact details of the associations or organisations of the Republic of Lithuania, other than the competent authorities of the Republic of Lithuania, from which providers or recipients may obtain practical assistance; and
6. General information about the criteria for the evaluation of the quality of services.

It also provides a tool for the online completion of business-related procedures and formalities.

It should be noted that the scope of the information provided by the POSC indicated in points 1–5 is the same as is regulated in Article 7 of the SD. In addition, Part 2 of Article 19 reflects the requirement of Article 7 (2) of the SD, which indicates the requirement to provide information on the way in which the requirements applicable to providers are generally interpreted and applied. Additionally, the Services Law provides that this right does not cover the right to legal consultation in specific cases.

As was mentioned above, the scope of the Services Law goes beyond the SD because the Services Law does not distinguish between national and international services or establishment. However, it does not go beyond the scope of the definition of services.

2.3 Article 8 SD: Procedures by Electronic Means

As was mentioned, the procedure and formalities in relation to accessing service activities or the exercise thereof can be fulfilled over a distance or/and by electronic means. The Services Law provides that the Government or a Government-authorised institution shall prescribe the procedure of exercising the rights mentioned. To date, this procedure has not been adopted. However, the draft of the government decision has been prepared. From a technological point of view, the public organisation Enterprise Lithuania is ready to implement the electronic administrative procedure. In practice the service provider may provide the documents and receive information by electronic means.

On the website www.verslovartai.lt are instructions on how services providers or recipients can log into a message box. By using this message box, service providers and recipients are able to provide the required documents. Service providers will be able to sign the documents by using qualified electronic signatures, and state institutions will have the possibility to check their identity. Service providers aiming to use the message box should be identified by using the banking system or a digital certificate.[18] Lithuania has introduced the Dutch message box solution, which is a secure electronic communication system that enables applicants to apply for permits or licences (or other authorisations) and complete administrative procedures with the competent authorities online.

The implementation of electronic procedures does not replace traditional methods of administrative procedure. The service provider or recipient has the discretion to decide which way of providing information is acceptable. However, as

[18] On the website www.verslovartai.lt, if a service provider wants to use the services provided by the e-government portal, he or she must be one of the users of the Internet banking system of the listed commercial banks or have a class 2 or class 3 personal digital certificate, issued by a qualified e-mail service provider. If the service provider is using a bank that is not included in the list, he or she must connect through a previous portal version. It is also provided that the service provider's personal data (name, surname, personal ID) existing in the bank or certification Centre will be used for registration in the portal. Any other information existing in the bank or certification centre (e.g., accounts and money operations) is not provided from the bank or certification centre.

was mentioned above, in practice, the POSC provides services only by electronic means. The competent institutions provide information in the traditional way.

2.4 Article 9 SD: Authorisation Schemes

It can be said that the implementation of the provisions of Article 9 (1) of the SD (authorisation schemes) to the Services Law was not literal. Article 5 of the Services Law, which is relevant in this regard, provides that substantial requirements applicable to the granting of authorisations, the suspension thereof, cancellation of the suspension, and withdrawal of the authorisations, as well as the requirements applicable to the providers that were granted an authorisation, are to be established by laws in accordance with the principles laid down in Article 4 of this law. Article 4 (1) of the Services Law provides that to ensure the freedom of establishment, the requirements applicable to the access to a service activity or the exercise thereof provided for in the legislation must comply with the following principles: (1) nondiscrimination, that is, the requirements may not directly or indirectly discriminate against the provider on the grounds of nationality, place of residence, or the MS in which the provider is established; (2) necessity, that is, the requirements must be justified by an overriding reason relating to the public interest; and (3) proportionality, that is, the requirements must be proportional and suitable to achieve their purpose and must not restrict the right to provide services or the service activity more than is necessary to achieve the respective purpose. Therefore neither the obligation to consider 'a less restrictive measure' nor the imperative to establish the insufficiency of 'an a posteriori inspection' are expressly mentioned in the Services Law.

As regards the general process and results of the screening, please see Sect 1.2.2 of this report. The licensing of certain types of activities not justified by the necessity and proportionality principles—for example, the manufacture and technical maintenance of firefighting equipment, trading in antiques—was eliminated as inconsistent with the SD. The outcome of the screening, specifically relating to Article 9 of the SD, may be laid down as follows.

The most important authorisation schemes that have been maintained by the legislator of Lithuania following the implementation of the SD are related to the arms, explosives, and civilian pyrotechnics circulation sector, the commercial services sector, the education and training sector, and the alcohol and tobacco trading sector.[19]

Taking into account the particularities of each sector of activity, its social importance, and the necessary level of security and control, the Lithuanian

[19] The preliminary list of authorisations granted in Lithuania may be found at http://www.ukmin.lt/lt/veikla/veiklos_kryptys/paslaugu-direktyva/. However, in the meantime, this list has not been updated and includes authorisations that were to be abolished due to implementation of the SD. This list is available only in Lithuanian.

authorities examined the validity and necessity of existing authorisations falling within the scope of the SD and suggested priority alternatives and less restrictive control measures than the issuing authorisations. The Government agreed to the abolition of the following licences/certificates:

1. Licence to carry out burial services (Law on the Burial of Human Remains),
2. Licence for the manufacturing and technical maintenance of firefighting equipment (Law on Fire Safety),
3. Authorisation to carry out aerial photography (Law on Geodesy and Cartography);
4. Licence to carry out geodetic surveys of cadastral objects (real property; Law on the Land Register),
5. Requirement for the manager of a legal entity to hold a receiver's certificate (Law on Corporate Receivership),
6. Declaration on the temporary provision of tour operator services (Law on Tourism),
7. Rural tourism, bed and breakfast, and tourist camping ground certificates (Law on Tourism),
8. Authorisation for external assessors of livestock (Law on Animal Breeding),
9. Licence to act as an intermediary for Lithuanian citizens and persons residing in Lithuania seeking employment abroad (Law on the Approval, Entry into Force and Implementation of the Lithuanian Labour Code; Labour Code),
10. Licence to trade in antiques (Law on the Protection of Cultural Goods),
11. Authorisation to provide postal services (Law on Post).

No type of authorisation scheme or procedure as such was generally abolished. However, to reduce the administrative burden for service providers, the Government agreed to the following:

1. The permission for topographic and cartographic activities and the permission for geodetic activities are replaced by the requirement to hold a qualification certificate (Law on Geodesy and Cartography).
2. The authorisation to provide receivership services is replaced by the requirement to register on the list of persons providing corporate receivership services (Law on Corporate Receivership),
3. The authorisation to provide restructuring services is replaced by the requirement to register on the list of persons providing corporate restructuring administration services (Law on Corporate Restructuring), and
4. Tour operator, travel agent, and agency certificates are to be replaced by registration on the list of tour operators, travel agents, and travel agencies (Law on Tourism).

Following the implementation of the SD, there are several types of authorisations (in the broad sense of the definition) in Lithuania:

1. A licence or a permission to carry out a certain activity (e.g., to provide cremation services or to trade in explosives),

2. A requirement to obtain a qualification or other certificate (e.g., the qualification certificate of an assessor of real property or of a business, the travel agency certificate, and the audit enterprise certificate),
3. A requirement to be included in a certain list (e.g., entry to the list of court experts and entry to the list of persons providing potable water), and
4. A notification (e.g., notification of the provision of courier services).

According to the Lithuanian understanding, simple notification requirements are not in prejudice with the provisions of the SD and were maintained.

2.5 *Article 10 SD: Conditions for the Granting of Authorisation*

The provisions of Article 10 (3) of the SD that imply the recognition of authorisations granted by another MS were transposed into Article 6 (3) of the Law on Services:

> In those cases when an authorisation is required before taking up service provision in the Republic of Lithuania, repeated satisfaction of the same or essentially similar requirements and/or controls which the provider has already satisfied in another Member State or in the Republic of Lithuania while seeking another authorisation may not be required. When presenting an application for authorisation, the provider shall, directly or via the point of single contact, present all the necessary information on the said requirements/controls satisfied by the provider in another Member State or in the Republic of Lithuania.

The requirement of the validity of authorisations throughout the whole national territory is implemented through the provisions of Article 8 (3) of the Services Law:

> Authorisation granted entitles the provider to provide services throughout the territory of the Republic of Lithuania. The right to provide services is also granted to the branches and subsidiaries established in the Republic of Lithuania by the provider which received the authorisation if they pursue the activities for which the provider is granted authorisation. The laws may require providers to obtain separate authorisations or the validity of authorisations may be restricted to a certain part of the territory of the Republic of Lithuania, if such exceptions are justified by overriding public interests.

While Lithuania is a unitary state, the requirement related to the validity of an authorisation throughout the whole state territory did not cause particular problems.

As is clear from the wording of Article 8 (3) of the Services Law, there is a possibility to justify regional authorisation only, on the basis of overriding reasons relating to the public interest. At the moment, however, it seems that there are no laws enacted that would make use of this possibility. Additionally, it could be mentioned that in the Services Law, ‘overriding public interests’ are perceived as reasons provided for by the EU law that justify the imposition of certain requirements, including public policy; public security; public safety; public health; preserving the financial equilibrium of the social security system; the protection of consumers, recipients of services, and workers; fairness of trade transactions; combating fraud; protection of the environment and the urban environment; animal health; intellectual property; conservation of the national historic and artistic heritage; and social policy objectives and cultural policy objectives (Article 2 (13) of the Services Law). This definition of overriding public interests corresponds to the respective definition contained in Article 4 (8) of the SD.

The provision of Article 10 (5) of the SD is implemented by Article 7 (1) of the Services Law, which provides that a competent authority of the Republic of Lithuania must deliver an authorisation or a written reasoned refusal of an authorisation to the applicant within 30 days, except when the laws reasonably prescribe a longer period. This period shall start to run from the day the POSC or the competent authority of the Republic of Lithuania (if the applicant applies to the competent authority of the Republic of Lithuania directly) receives all the documents duly executed and the information necessary to obtain an authorisation.

Until enactment of the Services Law, a general time limit for the procedure of granting the authorisations was set in the Civil Code of the Republic of Lithuania. Except as otherwise provided by law, a licence for engagement in a certain activity or a written motivated refusal to issue a licence is to be submitted to an applicant within 30 days, as of the day on which the documents for the issuance of the licence were produced (Article 2.79 (2) of the Civil Code). Such a time limit was normally transposed into the legislation concerning particular sectors of service provision (e.g., trading in tobacco or alcohol products).

What concerns the revision of the decisions to grant an authorisation, a provision of Article 10 (6) of the SD is implemented in Article 6 (5) of the Services Law which provides that decisions of competent authorities of the Republic of Lithuania related to the granting, the suspension or the cancellation of suspension and the withdrawal of authorisations may be appealed against in accordance with the procedure prescribed by the laws of the Republic of Lithuania.

Article 15 (1) of the Law on Administrative Proceedings, which defines the competence of administrative courts, provides that administrative courts shall decide cases, *inter alia*, relating to the lawfulness of legal acts passed and actions performed by entities of public administration and municipal administration, as well as the legality and validity of refusal by said entities to perform the actions within the remit of their competence or delays in performing the said actions. The issue of the lawfulness of legal acts covers the issue of the discretion of the authorities that passed those acts; therefore the courts do review the discretion of the authorities. Upon hearing a case, the administrative court may satisfy the complaint and revoke the contested act (or a part thereof) or obligate the appropriate public authority itself to remedy its committed violation or to carry out other orders of the court (Article 88 of the Law on Administrative Proceedings).

The condition established in Article 10 (6) of the SD, that decisions from the competent authorities concerning the refusal or withdrawal of an authorisation must be fully reasoned, was transposed to Article 6 (4) of the Services Law.

However, the general requirement that an individual administrative act must be based on objective facts and provisions of legislation and that measures applied must be reasoned already existed in Article 8 of the Law on Public Administration.

It also seems that the implementation of the provisions of the SD did not in any way influence the allocation of administrative competences with regard to the granting of authorisations.

2.6 Article 11 SD: Duration of Authorisation

The requirement related to the unlimited validity of authorisations and the exceptions of this rule, provided for in Article 11 (1) of the SD, were transposed to Article 8 (1) of the Services Law. It provides that a competent authority of the Republic of Lithuania shall grant authorisation to the provider for an unlimited period of time, except where

1. Authorisation is extended automatically or is related to regular satisfaction of the requirements specified in the authorisation scheme,
2. The limited number of available authorisations is justified by overriding public interests,
3. The number of available authorisations is limited because of the scarcity of natural resources or technical capacity, or
4. The limited authorisation period is justified by overriding public interests.

It should be noted that the list of exceptions laid down in Article 11 (1) was supplemented with that related to the scarcity of natural resources and technical capacity; however, in any case, this exception is expressly provided for in the following provision of the SD (Article 12 (1)).

Before implementation of the SD, the Civil Code of the Republic of Lithuania provided that where the requirements specified in the regulations of licensing are fulfilled, an open-ended licence shall be issued (Article 2.79 (1)).

2.7 Article 12 SD: Selection from Among Several Candidates

The provisions of Article 12 of the SD relating to the selection from among several candidates were implemented by Article 8 (1), (3) of the Services Law, cited above in Sect. 2.6, and Article 8 (2) of the Services Law. Article 8 (2) provides that where the number of authorisations available for a given activity is limited because of the scarcity of available natural resources or technical capacity, the competent authorities of the Republic of Lithuania must apply *an impartial and transparent selection procedure* to the applicants. In those cases, the authorisation shall not be open to automatic renewal nor confer any other advantage on the provider whose authorisation has expired no later than 10 days ago[20] or on the provider which is closely linked to that provider either in the form of control or participation or when those providers are spouses, close relatives, or related by marriage. In establishing the rules for the selection procedure, the provisions of Articles 5 and 6 of this law must be complied with and overriding public interests may be taken into account.

The granting of licences in various sectors of economic activities related to the scarcity of available natural resources or technical capacities has been regulated by the laws and other acts enacted in those particular sectors. Existing regulations provide for various schemes for the granting of authorisations where the number of licences must be limited due to the need to preserve natural resources or due to the insufficiency of technical capacities. For instance, the Law on Fisheries provides for an auction of licences for commercial fishing in inland waters; thus in certain cases such licences must be granted, if other relevant conditions are satisfied, to applicants that offer the highest bid. It may be noted that, according to the legislation in force, the right to exploit a fishing plot may be also granted without an auction to the last user of the fishing plot if it complied with the obligations set for commercial fishing in that water body. The impartiality and transparency of existing procedures and the compatibility of similar provisions, as cited above, with the new Services Law should be examined when deciding the upcoming amendments of the laws and other acts in relevant sectors.

2.8 Article 13 SD: Authorisation Procedures

2.8.1 A Priori Determination of the Duration of Administrative Procedures and General Rule for the Duration

The provisions of Article 13 (3) of the SD concerning the duration of an administrative procedure were implemented by Article 7 of the Services Law. Article 7 (1) of this law provides that a competent authority of the Republic of Lithuania must deliver an authorisation or a written reasoned refusal of an authorisation to the applicant within 30 days, except when the laws reasonably prescribe a longer period. This period shall start to run on the day the POSC or the competent authority of the Republic of Lithuania—if the applicant applies to the competent authority directly—receives all the documents duly executed that are necessary to grant an authorisation.

[20] The relevant provision of the SD (Article 12 (2)) has the wording 'the provider whose authorisation has just expired'. It can be argued whether or not the strict period of 10 days is in line with the sense of Article 12 (2) of the SD. In any case, it appears that the Lithuanian provision is not linguistically clear enough, because it is not obvious which period covering the moment of expiration of an authorisation is meant, a maximum of 10 days before the given moment or a minimum.

The term provided for in Article 7 (1) of the Services Law is applicable to the authorisation procedures within the limits of the scope of the Services Law as defined in Article 1 of this law, which appears to coincide completely with the scope of the SD as defined in Article 2 of this directive.

It should be noted that, according to Article 7 (2) of the Services Law, in exceptional cases specified by law, the period of 30 days set in para 1 of this article may, due to important reasons, be extended once for up to 30 days. In such a case, the competent authority that decided to extend the period referred to in para 1 must, prior to the expiry of the period specified in para 1 of this article, notify the applicant of the extension of the term and the reasons why it was extended.

2.8.2 Tacit Authorisation

Article 7 (3) of the Services Law provides that if there is no response during the prescribed period to the application for authorisation which is duly executed and followed by all documents and information necessary for the grant of authorisation, *an authorisation shall be deemed to be granted,* except for cases specified by law when failure to respond to an application for authorisation shall not be equated with granting of an authorisation, and such an exception is justified by overriding public interest, including the legitimate interests of third parties. Here it should be noted that sectoral laws shall be free to provide exceptions of the general rule of tacit authorisations if such exceptions are based on overriding public interests. This is, however, in line with Article 13 (4) of the SD.

On the whole, a tacit (fictitious) authorisation was not provided for by the existing laws regulating the grant of authorisations. The Services Law does not envisage any special effects with regard to tacit authorisation, and that fact most probably implies that tacit authorisations would not differ from formally granted administrative authorisations. The law does not explicitly provide for any form of confirmation issued by the competent authorities to confirm fictitious authorisation; however, this does not mean that applicants would be prevented from applying for such confirmations.

What concerns the meaning of 'response' in Article 13 (4) of the SD (and Article 7 (3) of the Services Law), attention could be drawn to Article 7 (4) and (3), which provides that the competent authority of the Republic of Lithuania that receives an application for authorisation shall, within five working days of the receipt of the application, send the applicant a confirmation that the application has been received. The confirmation of receipt must include, *inter alia,* the statement that in the absence of a response within the period specified, the authorisation shall be deemed to have been granted. This implies that the response should be understood as a reply consisting of a decision to grant an authorisation or a decision to extend a period for the examination of the application and not merely as a letter from the authorities that the application is being dealt with, etc.

2.9 Articles 14, 15, 16 SD

Requirements related to the freedom of establishment for providers which are prohibited or subject to evaluation are dealt with in Articles 14 and 15 of the SD, and the provisions of those articles have been implemented by relevant provisions of the Services Law. The content of Article 14 of the SD (prohibited requirements) was, in principle, literally transposed to Article 3 of the Services Law.

Article 15 (3) of the SD, which lays down the conditions that the requirements subject to evaluation need to satisfy (nondiscrimination, necessity, and proportionality), is implemented by Article 4 (1) of the Services Law. The latter provides that the requirements of the legislation in the Republic of Lithuania that are applicable to access to service activities and the exercise thereof must correspond to the following principles: (1) nondiscrimination, i.e. the requirements may not directly or indirectly discriminate against the provider on grounds of nationality, place of residence, or the MS in which the provider is established; (2) necessity, that is, the requirements must be justified by overriding public interest; and (3) proportionality, that is, the requirements must be proportionate and suitable to achieve the desired result, and must not restrict the right to provide services or the exercise thereof more than is necessary to achieve the respective purpose. A captious comparison of the provisions of the SD and the Services Law may reveal a slightly different implementation of Article 15 (3) (c) of the SD without expressly mentioning the obligation to check if a less restrictive measure could obtain the same result.

Article 15 (2) of the SD, which lists the requirements to be evaluated, was transposed to Article 4 (2) of the Services Law. During the screening some inconsistencies of Lithuanian law with Article 15 of the SD were identified and eliminated: for instance, a provision permitting a licensed activity to be pursued only by legal persons, which prevents natural persons from pursuing the same activity, or a provision permitting a certain activity to be pursued only by legal persons of a certain legal form, for example, public institutions. Such requirements were either abolished or justified in accordance with the principles of nondiscrimination, necessity, and proportionality.

What concerns the freedom to provide services and the principles with which requirements applicable to the access to or exercise of a service activity must comply, and which are laid down in Article 16 (1) of the SD, those principles were, in principle, literally transposed to Article 9 (3) of the Services Law. However, provisions of Article 16 (2) of the SD, which lays down the requirements that a MS may not impose on a provider established in another MS, were *not* transposed to the Services Law. These prohibited requirements concerning the freedom of establishment were only laid down in the Recommendations on the draft of amendments to the laws and legislation implementing the laws not complying with the provisions of the European Parliament and Council Directive 2006/123/EC of

12 December 2006 on services in the internal market[21] (para 28). Moreover, para 28 of those Recommendations provides that the competent authorities of the Republic of Lithuania must ensure that (while amending or making proposals for the amendments of legislation) the requirements applicable to providers having established in another MS and temporarily providing services in Lithuania would be nondiscriminative, necessary (i.e., justified by reasons of public policy, public security, public health, or the protection of the environment) and proportionate to the purpose sought. Para 28 further provides the list of such requirements that coincide with those listed in Article 16 (2) of the SD. Following the logic of the Recommendations, such requirements may be subject to the evaluation of the competent authorities in light of the principles of nondiscrimination, necessity, and proportionality as provided for in Article 9 (3) of the Services Law (and Article 16 (1) of the SD). Therefore it appears highly doubtful that such a scheme of regulation chosen by the legislator of Lithuania is in line with the purport of the SD.

As regards the substantive effect of Article 16 of the SD in Lithuania, it could be mentioned that, according to the screening results, Lithuanian legislation does not contain provisions that are applicable solely to services providers established in other MSs. However, the situation in which requirements in relation to Article 16 of the SD are applicable to service providers established in other MSs as well as to Lithuanian service providers was identified during the legislative screening of some Lithuanian legal acts. For instance, such a requirement is contained in the Law on the Control of Alcohol: A licence to engage in the wholesale and retail trade in alcoholic beverages must be issued to both service providers established in Lithuania and service providers established in another MS. Analogous requirements that both service providers established in Lithuania and those established in other MSs be granted licences for wholesale and retail trading in tobacco products, according to the representatives of the competent authorities, are to be incorporated into the Law on the Control of Tobacco. In this case it may be also disputed whether such requirements would not be in prejudice to Article 16 (2) (b) of the SD, which prohibits an obligation on the provider to obtain an authorisation from the competent authorities of the MS in which services are to be provided, and if such requirements may be justified by any other provisions of the SD or other instruments of Community law, as provided for by Article 16 (2) (b) of the SD.

2.10 Articles 14–19 SD

First, it appears that the discussions could concern the regulation of the freedom to provide services, that is, the rather complex and therefore confusing scheme of

[21] Valstybės žinios, 16 May 2009, Nr. 57-2245, Order of the Minister of Economy of the Republic of Lithuania of 8 May 2009, No. 4-216; repealed as of 1 January 2010; see http://www3.lrs.lt/pls/inter3/dokpaieska.showdoc_l?p_id=343970.

Article 16 of the SD. While it may be interpreted that Article 16 (2) of the SD blacklists the requirements that would always restrict the freedom to provide services in case the provider is established in another MS, and which could in no way be justified by reasons related to overriding public interests, it may be noted (as was described, in Sect. 2.9) that in Lithuania the legislator and the authorities responsible for the screening and drafting of proposals to amend the legislation so that it would meet the conditions of the SD have the opposite opinion. As was mentioned above (in the fourth para of Sect. 2.9), the provisions of Article 16 (2) of the SD that lay down the requirements which MSs may not impose on a provider established in another MS were *not* transposed to the Services Law; nor were any possible justifications for deviating from Article 16 (2) of the SD transposed either.

Second, the wording and system of Article 16 of the SD do not appear to clarify the relation between Articles 16 (1) and Article 16 (3) of the SD. It is not clear what the purpose was of the latter provision to rewrite the principles of necessity (availability to justify the requirements for reasons of public policy, public security, public health, and protection of the environment) into the first sentence of Article 16 (3) of the SD. Does the fact that the second sentence of Article 16 (3) of the SD allows the MS, in accordance with Community law, to apply its rules on employment conditions, including those laid down in collective agreements, and that this provision is situated after the possible justifications on the basis of necessity imply that the MS may invoke the provisions of collective agreements in order to justify possible requirements applicable to the freedom to provide services without having to justify such requirements by the principles of necessity?

Third, it is not obvious why the meaning of the necessity principle in Article 16 (1) (b) of the SD is made different from that provided for in Article 9 (1) (b), which requires the authorisation scheme to be justified by an overriding reason relating to public interest. The overriding reasons relating to public interest, as defined in Article 4 (8) of the SD, mean reasons recognised as such in the case law of the Court of Justice, including but not limited to public policy, public security, and public health. However, only these three types of relevant public interest, which are provided for in the Treaty, with the supplement of the sole interest of the protection of the environment, as regards the interests recognised later by the case law of the Court of Justice, are mentioned in Article 16 (1) (b), apparently leaving overboard all the other interests developed by the Court of Justice. It is even more surprising in the light of Recital 40 in the preamble of the SD, which lays down in detail the 'at least' possible reasons that are covered by the concept of overriding reasons relating to the 'public interest' according to the case law of the ECJ.

2.11 Articles 22–27 SD

Articles 22–27 of the SD, relating to the quality of services, were transposed to the Articles 13, 14, 15, 16, 19, 13, and 17 of the Services Law.

As regards Article 26 of the SD and the measures to encourage providers to take action on a voluntary basis in order to ensure the quality of service provision, it could be mentioned that some of such measures are already provided in the existing legislation. For instance, Article 11 (1) of the Law on Electronic Signature provides that certification service providers may voluntarily accredit themselves with an institution of signature supervision. Accreditation is the assessment of a certification service provider's ability to perform his functions. Accreditation is not a required condition of certification service providers.

2.12 Articles 28 ff. SD: Administrative Cooperation

What concerns the provisions of transnational administrative assistance in Lithuania prior to the transposition of the SD and, in particular, Article 28 (7) of the SD, which provides that MSs shall ensure that registers in which providers have been entered, and which may be consulted by the competent authorities in their territory, may also be consulted, in accordance with the same conditions, by the equivalent competent authorities of the other MSs, it may be mentioned that Article 18 (1) of the Law on State Registers provides that register data shall be provided to legal and natural persons of EU MSs in accordance with the same procedure established for the provision of such data to legal and natural persons of the Republic of Lithuania.

On the whole, it appears that the requirements of Article 28 of the SD were fully transposed into Articles 22 and 8 of the Services Law. It seems that, apart from international agreements and European regulations on transnational administrative cooperation, there were no other comprehensive provisions for transnational administrative assistance in Lithuanian law prior to the transposition of the SD.

It also seems that no particular changes as regards the rules on data protection and professional secrets are envisaged at the moment, and no intention to require financial compensation from the authorities of other MSs for the meantime was presented.

2.13 Article 29 SD: Mutual Assistance—General Obligations for the Member State of Establishment

Article 29 of the SD is implemented in the SD using "copy to" technique of the implementation of the directives into the national law. As can be seen from the Conception on the Services Law, *travaux préparatoires,* and other documents issued in the process of the adoption of the Services Law in the Parliament of the Republic of Lithuania, there were no particular discussions regarding the confirmation of not unlawful business conduct.

2.14 Problems and Discourses on Administrative Cooperation

As can be seen from the Conception on the Services Law, *travaux préparatoires,* and other documents issued in the process of the adoption of the Services Law in the Parliament of the Republic of Lithuania, there were no particular problems or discourses regarding Chapter VI (administrative cooperation).

2.15 Convergence Programme (Chapter VII of the Services Directive)

There were no particular discussions (at least not in public) in Lithuania regarding Chapter VII of the SD. As regards the codes of conduct, it should be noted that there is no tradition of the codes of conduct in Lithuania. The legislation does not provide any mechanism encouraging the creation and adoption of such codes. The Services Law also does not provide any particular provisions for initiating codes of conduct. By implementing the provisions of the Directive 2005/29/EC of the European Parliament and of the Council of 11 May 2005 concerning unfair business-to-consumer commercial practices in the internal market and amending Council Directive 84/450/EEC, Directives 97/7/EC, 98/27/EC, and 2002/65/EC of the European Parliament and of the Council and Regulation (EC) No. 2006/2004 of the European Parliament and of the Council (Unfair Commercial Practices Directive; OJ, 2005 L 149, p. 22) with the Law on Prohibition of Unfair Business-To-Consumer Commercial Practices the latter law provides that the authority shall promote the development of the codes of conduct and shall cooperate with the code owners and other commercial operators who have assumed or are planning to assume the obligations stipulated in the codes of conduct. However, no such mechanism was implemented in practice.

3 Assessment of the Impact of the Services Directive

3.1 Extent of the Impact

There were no broad discussions (at least not in public) about the SD or the draft of the SD. The discussions were only between the ministries that participated in formulating the Lithuanian position. Different positions regarding the SD were observed in the Ministry of Economy and the Ministry of Justice.

It remains to be seen what the real practical effects of the SD and its implementation will be. It may be said, however, that much unclear and inconsistent drafting of the SD left a number of issues open and at the same time may have led to some uncertainties in the Law on Services, which is used to implement the SD in Lithuania. Article 16 of the SD and corresponding provisions of the Law on Services could serve as an example to illustrate the legal uncertainties that unfortunately arose in this context.

However, the impact of the SD on administrative procedure law should already be assessed as severe, primarily due to the huge amount of screening work done, the elimination of certain authorisations, and the establishment of POSCs, which *in concreto* are already at the disposal of foreign and national businesses.

3.2 Assessment of the Transposing Legislation

In Lithuania the SD was considered as another additional legal act of *acquis communautaire* that had to be implemented. It was definitely a quite complicated act that led to an enormous amount of administrative work. However, as was mentioned above, there was no political aim to tie the implementation of the SD to the reform of administrative proceedings.

3.3 Most Important and Profound Changes Induces by the Services Directive

The most important and most profound change induced by the transposition of the SD was the establishment of the POSC and providing the ability to receive administrative services by electronic means. However, the effect of the latter instrument will depend on the practical implementation of the provisions of the Services Law. It was an effective impulse to realise the principle of 'one point' (one desk) in practice and to finally create the capability of receiving administrative services over a distance. In addition, it should be mentioned that the system of tacit authorisation was quite a big challenge and an important step in the Lithuanian public administration system.

The Implementation of the Services Directive in Luxembourg

Aurélie Melchior

1 General Remarks on the Transposition Strategy and General Understanding of the Implementation

1.1 Main References Used in this Research

The research regarding the implementation of the services directive (SD) in Luxembourg was based on information found in public sources (i.e., the website of the Parliament of Luxembourg and the website of the "Service central de legislation", the website of the Ministry of the Middle Classes (*Ministère des classes moyennes*), and that of the Ministry of Economy and Foreign Trade (*Ministère de l'économie et du commerce extérieur*). The information found at the time this report was written consists of the following:

- The bill of the (framework) law regarding the services within the internal market (hereinafter the 'Bill'), dated May 24, 2011 (Mémorial A No. 108 May 26, 2011).[1] The Bill was enacted to implement the general principles of the SD.

Please note that the answers to this questionnaire were given at the state of the law in Luxembourg as of 21 July 2011. Please note that the Services Directive (SD) has not yet been fully implemented as of the date of this report in Luxembourg and that some answers below were given on the basis of a draft bill that is still under discussion in Parliament. I cannot exclude the possibility that some amendments would be fulfilled.

[1] http://www.chd.lu/wps/PA_1_084AIVIMRA06I432DO10000000/FTSShowAttachment?mime=application%2fpdf&id=1092429&fn=1092429.pdf.

A. Melchior (✉)
Faculty of Law, Economics and Finance, University of Luxembourg, Luxembourg, Luxembourg
e-mail: aurelie.melchior@uni.lu

U. Stelkens et al. (eds.), *The Implementation of the EU Services Directive*,
DOI: 10.1007/978-90-6704-840-8_17,

(The original timing foresaw that the draft Bill should have been passed by Parliament before the deadline of 28 December 2009, but an amendment to the draft Bill has been introduced by the Ministry of Economy and Foreign Trade [*Ministère de l'économie et du commerce extérieur*]).

- The law of 29 May 2009 abolished the obligation to provide a certified copy of an original document.[2] This law entered into force on 8 June 2009. Indeed, a certified copy of an original document delivered by a Luxembourg administrative authority or an administrative authority from another Member State (MS) of the European Union (EU) to be submitted in an administrative procedure of the state, a municipality, or any other public person of public law can no longer be requested. In case of doubt of the validity of the produced copy, the authorities may request the presentation of the original, provided that such a request indicates the reasons thereof.
- The draft bill no. 6158[3] introduced by the Ministry of the Middle Classes (*Ministère des classes moyennes*) regarding modification of the current law of 28 December 1988, called the law on the right of establishment, which basically governs access to and the practice of activities, subject to the authorisation by the Minister of the Middle Classes to comply with the provision of the SD.

1.2 Impact of the Services Directive

1.2.1 Regarding the POSC

Even before the Bill has been adopted, the Luxembourg government has already put in place some comprehensive points of contact that can be qualified as points of single contact (POSCs) under the meaning and requirements of the SD.

---

[2] See http://www.chd.lu/wps/portal/public/!ut/p/c1/jczJDoIwFIXhZ_EJ7u1lapdMVkAxpakBNqQxhJAwuDAa315Wxp3mLP98B1rYttjHONj7uC52ghpav0souVSZSygD5SLlaR4YXTqc-1tv_I4415UMT6kQJsIMY6ZTFRFm9I_-dB6LzUh1LGLmodTOD10e1rmHBtrg60Pke6SSacPV2SmYB83UD_b6gtts6uca7t6WzK08/dl2/d1/L0lJSklna21BL0lKakFBRXlBQkVSQ0pBISEvWUZOQTFOSTUwLTVGd0EhIS83X0QyRFZSSTQyMDg5SkYwMk4xU1U4UU8zSzE1Lzc6blJtNjc4MzAwMDc!/?PC_7_D2DVRI42089JF02N1SU8QO3K15_action=list#7_D2DVRI42089JF02N1SU8QO3K15.

[3] See http://www.chd.lu/wps/portal/public/!ut/p/c1/jczJDoIwFIXhZ_EJ7u1lapdMVkAxpakBNqQxhJAwuDAa315Wxp3mLP98B1rYttjHONj7uC52ghpav0souVSZSygD5SLlaR4YXTqc-1tv_I4415UMT6kQJsIMY6ZTFRFm9I_-dB6LzUh1LGLmodTOD10e1rmHBtrg60Pke6SSacPV2SmYB83UD_b6gtts6uca7t6WzK08/dl2/d1/L0lJSklna21BL0lKakFBRXlBQkVSQ0pBISEvWUZOQTFOSTUwLTVGd0EhIS83X0QyRFZSSTQyMDg5SkYwMk4xU1U4UU8zSzE1L1FIZnhEOTQ3MDA1NQ!!/?PC_7_D2DVRI42089JF02N1SU8QO3K15_action=list#7_D2DVRI42089JF02N1SU8QO3K15.

1.2.2 Regarding the Notice for Administrative Authorisation

Article 11 (7) of the Bill stipulated that in case no answer is given within a three-month period, it is deemed that the required authorisation was granted. This principle of tacit authorisation is a restriction to the general principle fixed by the law dated November 7, 1996.

The Bill provision is therefore the opposite of the existing administrative rules currently into force.

This provision has been somewhat criticised, since this new provision applies only to activities and service providers that fall under the scope of the Bill. In that respect, some commentators suggested extending (as initially foreseen in the initial draft Bill) this new rule to apply not only to service providers and activities falling within the scope of application of the Bill and, respectively, the SD, but also to everybody for each activity. However, an amendment has been proposed to the original draft Bill by the Ministry of Economy and Foreign Trade (*Ministère de l'économie et du commerce extérieur*) to restrain the scope of the principle of tacit authorisation to and within the framework of the SD and it is that amended version that has been adopted.

In my opinion, this amendment, which is a general provision with no specialisation, represents a severe setback to the requirements of the SD regarding administrative proceedings, since it now provides for the contrary, that is, that silence means refusal in all cases related to the protection of the 'human and natural environment'.

In my opinion, it seems that most of the so-called operating licences would thus likely (depending of the interpretation of that restriction that will be done by the competent authorities) fall under such a restriction and that therefore such a general restriction is contrary to the fundamental aim of the SD regarding administrative proceedings. This means that, in practice, the current rule will likely remain the main rule and that the rule proposed by the Bill will become the exception, even in the scope of application of the Bill and thus of the aims and provisions of the SD.

Moreover, it is my opinion that such an amendment could be considered as irrelevant and unjustified, since it could be considered from the European Court of Justice (ECJ) as already under the scope of the public interest.

1.2.3 Regarding the Freedom of Establishment for Providers and the Freedom of Provision of Services in the EU

The text proposed by the government for the implementation of the SD regarding the freedom of establishment for providers and the freedom of provision of services in the EU was the subject of many criticisms from commentators on the draft Bill. Indeed, the main criticisms were that (i) the wording of the proposed text is unclear and causes more problems than it solves questions raised by the implementation of the provision of the SD, and (ii) Article 7 (1) of the draft Bill could be considered in contradiction with Article 7 (2). Even Articles 8 and 9 of the draft Bill with the proposed wording were stricter and more restrictive than the directive, and therefore do not provide any breathing room for the national authorities to impose limitations on the freedom of provision of services as allowed by the SD.

Indeed, Article 7 (1) provided that 'the freedom to provide services within the Community shall not be restricted' (this formulation is more restrictive than the drafting used in Article 16 (1) of the SD).

Article 7 (2) provided in substance that the free access and the free exercise of a service activity can be restrained only by imposing requirements that respect the principles of nondiscrimination, necessity, and proportionality.

Article 7 (3) provided that paras 1 and 2 do not concern national rules regarding the employment conditions, including those announced in the collective agreement applied to all services provided on national territory in conformity with EU law.

Finally, after discussions, Luxembourg decided to implement *mutatis mutandis* Articles 16 and 17 of the SD.

1.2.4 Regarding the Establishment of an Effective Administrative Cooperation Among Member States

The Bill does not allow the identification of the competent authorities who participate in administrative cooperation, train these authorities, and register them in the internal market information system (IMI) system and therefore there is a lack. However, according to information made available on the website of the Ministry for Public Service and Administrative Reform (*Ministère de la fonction publique et de la réforme administrative*),[4] it seems that this ministry is the competent authority.

In conclusion, and at this stage of implementation of the SD into Luxembourg legislation, I am therefore of the opinion that the transposition of the SD did not profoundly motivate, for the time being, the national legislator to alter—beyond the minimum requirements and a one-to-one transposition of the SD—administrative laws in general.

On 16 March 2007, the Luxembourg government decided to involve the following ministries in the process of the implementation of the SD:

- The Ministry of State (*Ministère d'état*) and
- The Ministry of Economy and Foreign Trade (*Ministère de l'économie et du commerce extérieur*),

both of which was assisted by an interdepartmental committee (*Comité interministeriel*) composed of representatives of the Ministry of the Middle Classes (*Ministère des classes moyennes*), the Ministry of Tourism and Housing (*Ministère du tourisme et du logement*), the Ministry for Public Service and Administrative Reform (*Ministère de la fonction publique et de la réforme administrative*), as well as departments and administrations involved in the process regarding the access to and exercise of services activities. There is, however, a lack of information regarding the cooperation and coordination between the administrations involved.

[4] See http://www.fonction-publique.public.lu/fr/annuaire/mfpra/mfpra-imi/index.html.

1.3 (National) Scope of Application

1.3.1 Scope of the Services Directive

According to parliamentary discussions, the prevailing opinion is that the requirements of the SD are also seen as compulsory with regard to purely domestic services/establishments falling within the scope of application of the SD.

1.3.2 Application of Transposing Legislation to Domestic Service Providers

According to Article 1 (1) of the Bill, the implementing laws should be applicable also to domestic service providers, given that they fall under the scope of the directive.

1.3.3 Application of Transposing Legislation Beyond Service Providers

According to parliamentary discussions and the Bill, it seems clear that it is not the intention of the Luxembourgish government to extend the new rules regarding administrative procedure (i.e., that silence means authorisation) to everybody, but only to activities and services providers falling within the scope of application of the SD, even though this approach was envisaged in earlier stages of the legislative procedure.[5] However, according to parliamentary works, it seems that it is the intention of the Luxembourg government to extend the new rules regarding POSCs to everybody (even domestic providers and non-service providers), it being understood that a recognised electronic signature delivered by LuxTrust S.A.[6] is required.

There was a discussion into whether the field of the new administrative procedure law (i.e., silence means authorisation) had to be extended to everybody to ensure equal treatment of all operators, that is to say, between those falling into the scope of application of the SD and for service providers including services not covered by the SD.

1.4 Incorporation of Transposing Legislation

For the time being and due to the lack of hindsight on the administrative practise regarding the restriction provision of the Bill (i.e., that silence means refusal in all cases related to the protection of the 'human and natural environment'), no clear

---

[5] For more details regarding that point, please refer to the initial draft bill no. 6022.

[6] For more details regarding this electronic signature, please refer to its development in the answer to question 2.1.1.

answer can be given to the question how and to which extent the requirements of the SD relating to administrative proceedings will be implemented.

Indeed, in the Bill, most of the requirements of the SD relating to administrative proceedings are supposed to be fulfilled. However, because of the restriction provision (i.e., that silence means refusal in all cases related to the protection of the 'human and natural environment') in the Bill, it seems to me that the requirements of the SD regarding administrative proceedings will likely not be fulfiled. Indeed, the proposed amendment provides now for very contrary SD requirements regarding administrative proceedings, that is, that silence means refusal in all cases *inter alia* related to the protection of the human and natural environment. This means, in my opinion, that most of the so-called operating licences would thus potentially fall under such a restriction and that this amendment is therefore a severe setback to the requirements of the SD regarding administrative proceedings.

1.5 The Relationship of the Services Directive to Primary EU Law

According to parliamentary works and the prevailing opinion in the various chambers in charge of giving their opinion of the Bill, the fields that are not covered by the SD and therefore by the Bill and all areas that constitute a derogation of the scope of application of the SD shall be governed by Articles 43 and 49 of the EC Treaty (now Articles 49 and 56 TFEU).

According to parliamentary works, the SD is seen as concluding secondary legislation for establishment and services, and thus derogates the application of primary law within the scope of the SD.

In that context, the main problem that has been identified regards activities having an impact on the human and natural environment. Indeed, as mentioned hereof, it seems that the requirements of the SD regarding administrative proceedings will not be fulfiled, since they now provide for a contrary result, that is, that silence means refusal in all cases related to the protection of the human and natural environment, which is to say, in my opinion (depending of the application of this provision by the competent administrative authority), potentially most activities.

1.6 Screening

Luxembourg informed the European Commission that the screening process was complete. However, it must be noted that the national authorities lack information on the details of this screening, and it seems that the screening concerning vertical transposition has not been totally completed. For the time being, no significant vertical legislation is available.

2 Individual Articles of the Services Directive

2.1 Article 6 SD: Point of Single Contact (POSC)

2.1.1 Establishment of the POSC

e-POSCs

Luxembourg has already implemented several highly comprehensive contact points, including most notably the *portails entreprises* available at www.entreprises.public.lu (hereinafter referred to as the 'Business portals') launched by the Luxembourg government in November 2004. This website plays the role of a POSC, within the meaning of the SD, since it was integrated into the broader portal website guichet.lu (www.guichet.lu), which was launched by the Luxembourg government on 17 November 2008.

The purpose of the website guichet.lu is to offer a virtual POSC to complete all online proceedings and formalities in relation to Luxembourg administration. It must be noted that it is not the intention of the Luxembourg government that this website replace, in practice, traditional physical counters and offices and that the scope of action is broader than that of the POSC in the meaning of the SD, since it is not to access a service or to exercise it. The POSC is therefore both an e-front desk that forwards applications by service providers to the relevant administration and a space where service providers can find assistance, even if administrative competences have not been reallocated.

In concreto, the website is divided into two main sections: the first one for individuals and the other for businesses. These two sections were developed as an online interactive platform for administrative formalities that enabled one to download documents and file them online, as well as send them to the administration via secured electronic means.

Besides this website, the Luxembourg government has launched an e-TVA application and an e-tax return application that enable the declaration of taxes online.

An online service enabling service providers to declare new employees to health security for health benefits is also available.

All documentation and online forms have to be electronically signed before being sent to the relevant authorities and therefore require a public key infrastructure (PKI)[7] certificate delivered by a company named LuxTrust. LuxTrust is a

---

[7] A public key infrastructure is based on a technology linking a private key, held only by the user, and a public key, known by everyone. These two keys form a single pair and a third person can check, using the public key, if a message or signature indeed originates from a specific private key. LuxTrust, as a certification authority, adds to this technology very involved procedures of user identification before giving out a private key. It then creates a digital certificate containing the user's public key as well as data relating to the user's identity. LuxTrust electronically signs this certificate so that it can no longer be amended and to ensure that the third identification procedures of the user have been met. The high standards that LuxTrust selected for the technology used and its procedures guarantee that a third person, for example, the application provider, can trust the contents of the certificate and may at any time check its validity with LuxTrust.

certification authority established on 18 November 2005 between the Luxembourg government and major private sector actors in Luxembourg, particularly the financial sector. LuxTrust helps meet a need for increased security in electronic commerce for both the government and the financial sector and other actors in the Luxembourg economy, thus retaining an international vocation through the adoption of standards recognised worldwide.

Since June 2006 LuxTrust has the status of *professionnel du secteur financier* (PSF), or professional of the financial sector, which allows the company to work closely with the financial sector. Supervision by the *Commission de Surveillance du Secteur Financier* (CSSF, www.cssf.lu) benefits all LuxTrust customers.

The security solutions offered not only allow the sharing of costs, but also take into account the rapidly changing technological and legal environments.

It should be noticed that the Luxembourgish government also launched mobile POSC via an application for mobile phones.

Physical POSC

The Bill foresees a conventional delegation to the Luxembourg Chamber of Professional Trades and the Luxembourg Chamber of Commerce. The latter will have privileged access to the government's electronic/virtual POSC and the EU will be notified thereof.

For consumers, the CEC Luxembourg[8] is the physical POSC.

2.1.2 Subjective Understanding, Competence Structure, Authorities with POSC-Function

As already mentioned, from a practical point of view, Luxembourg has undertaken several actions to meet the requirements of the SD regarding this matter even before the adoption of the Bill. Several POSCs have already been created to provide entrepreneurs with the necessary information enabling them to conduct their business in Luxembourg, including the following:

- The Centre des Formalités PME, created by the Luxembourg Chamber of Professional Trades (*Chambre des métiers*), particularly its website,
- The *Espace Entreprises* of the Luxembourg Chamber of Commerce (*Chambre de commerce*), also through its website,
- The *Guichet Unique PME* created on the initiative of 21 communes of the North of Luxembourg, together with the Luxembourg Chamber of Professional Trades and the Luxembourg Chamber of Commerce, and
- The guichet.lu, available at www.guichet.lu, launched by the Luxembourg government.

---

[8] *Centre Européen des Consommateurs GIE de Luxembourg.*

Therefore, and in my opinion, it seems that Luxembourg agrees on a subjective understanding of POSCs. The tasks of the POSCs are attributed to already existing authorities. The Luxembourg Chamber of Commerce (*Chambre de commerce*) and the Luxembourg Chamber of Professional Trades (*Chambre des métiers*) are in charge of the physical POSCs for the companies. For the customers, CEC Luxembourg is in charge of the physical POSC. Regarding the e-POSC, the Luxembourg government remains in charge.

2.1.3 Involvement of Private Partners

The Bill provides for an accreditation of the private partners involved in the introduction of POSCs.

Some critics have mentioned that the wording used in the Bill is not clear enough to fulfil the requirement of EC and Luxembourg laws that provide that a law shall be taken to have a convention delegation of a competence from the state to another public entity.

For the time being, no by-law or amendment to the Bill has been proposed nor a draft of a law. Therefore, for the time being, I cannot anticipate how this problem will be resolved.

2.1.4 Liability

In Luxembourg, a legislative and judicial system of state liability already exists and it seems that there is no need to adapt this system further to the implementation of POSCs. This is a system based on the liability of the state for the faulty operation of the state's services.[9]

2.2 Article 7 SD: Right to Information

According to information available in the Bill, the 'rights of information' will be implemented *mutatis mutandis* and, therefore, this right should not be extended (as far as I know and on the basis on the draft bill and current legislation) in the Luxembourg national legislation during the transposition process.

It must be noted that a limited right to information already exists in Luxembourg. Indeed, Article 26 of the current law on the right of establishment dated 28

9 Law of 1 September 1988—Loi du 1 septembre 1988 relative à la responsabilité civile de l' état et des collectivités publiques (Mémorial A no. 51 du 26 septembre 1988), modifiée par la Loi du 13 juin 1994 relative au régime des peines (Mémorial A no. 59 du 7 juillet 1994).

December 1988 and that organises the information in favour of third parties provides that the mention of the profession and the issue number of the governmental authorisation must be indicated on all letters, estimates, invoices, building site panels, and shop windows.

It seems, therefore, that the pre-existing right to information will be extended to all service providers, but it also seems that it is not the intention of the Luxembourg government to go further.

Since Luxembourg decided to implement the provision regarding the rights to information *mutatis mutandis*, these rights should only concern the scope of application of the SD, without prejudice to any further draft bill that could be proposed in the process of the implementation of the SD in Luxembourg.

2.3 Article 8 SD: Procedures by Electronic Means

Luxembourg has not yet enacted a legal framework that specifically determines the requirements that documents issued or presented to the administration need to meet. Luxembourg has implemented Directive 1999/93/EC on a Community framework for electronic signatures and has planned out the technical requirements for certain online administrative procedures and formalities, such as those accessible to individuals but not relating to the access to a service and those accessible to entrepreneurs relating to VAT declarations. A PKI framework has been established recently, relying largely on the accredited certification service provider (CSP) LuxTrust to enable the use of e-documents towards public administrations.

As Luxembourg has not yet enacted a legal framework that specifically determines the requirements that documents issued or presented to the administration need to meet, in this perspective, the implementation of the SD will be considered as an improvement, especially as a by-law should be taken in that respect.

However, on the one hand, Luxembourg has implemented Directive 1999/93/EC on a Community framework for electronic signatures. On the other hand, from a practical view point, Luxembourg has planned out the technical requirements for certain online administrative procedures and formalities, such as those accessible to individuals but not relating to the access to a service and those accessible to entrepreneurs.

Implementing Directive 1999/93/EC on electronic signatures, the Luxembourg law of 14 August 2000 relating to ecommerce, as amended, defines an electronic signature as a set of data, inseparable from the document, that guarantees its integrity and identifies its signatory and shows his or her agreement to the contents of the document (Article 1322-1 § 3 of the Luxembourg Civil Code).

To be valid, an electronic signature must be created by a secured system based on a qualified certificate that the signatory can maintain under his or her sole control (Article 13 of the Law of 14 August 2000 relating to e-commerce, as amended). According to Article 2 § 1 of the Luxembourg Regulation of 1 June 2001 on electronic signatures, qualified certificates must contain the following:

- An indication that the certificate is issued as a qualified certificate,
- The identification of the CSP and the state in which it is established,
- The name of the signatory, or a pseudonym, which shall be identified as such,
- Signature verification data that correspond to signature creation data under the control of the signatory,
- An indication of the beginning and end of the period of validity of the certificate,
- The identity code of the certificate, and
- The advanced electronic signature of the CSP issuing it.

Pursuant to Article 3 § 1 of the Luxembourg Regulation of 1 June 2001 on electronic signatures, CSPs must do the following:

- Demonstrate the necessary reliability for providing certification services;
- Ensure the operation of a prompt and secure directory and a secure and immediate revocation service;
- Ensure that the date and time when a certificate is issued or revoked can be determined precisely;
- Verify, on production of an official document of identity, the identity and, if applicable, any specific attributes of the person to whom a qualified certificate is issued;
- Employ personnel who possess the expert knowledge, experience, and qualifications necessary for the services provided, in particular competence at the managerial level, expertise in electronic signature technology, and familiarity with proper security procedures (they must also apply administrative and management procedures that are adequate and correspond to recognised standards);
- Use trustworthy systems and products that are protected against modification and ensure the technical and cryptographic security of the processes they support;
- Take measures against the forgery of certificates and, in cases where the CSP generates signature creation data, guarantee confidentiality during the process of generating such data;
- Maintain sufficient financial resources to operate in conformity with the requirements laid down in the applicable laws and regulations, in particular to bear the risk of liability for damages, for example, by obtaining appropriate insurance;
- Record all relevant information concerning a qualified certificate for an appropriate period of time, in particular for the purpose of providing evidence of certification for the purposes of legal proceedings (such a recording may be done electronically);
- Not store or copy the signature creation data of the person to whom the CSP provided key management services; and
- Use trustworthy systems to store certificates in a verifiable form.

In our point of view, the transposition should not release great innovative impact because it falls under the willingness of the simplification of the administrative proceedings developed by the government in 2004.

It seems that it is not the intention of Luxembourg government to remove the other means of administrative proceedings but, rather, to have both systems coexist.

2.4 Article 9 SD: Authorisation Schemes

Articles 9 (1) and (3) of the SD are implemented by Articles 7 (1) and (3) of the Bill. Luxembourg, as already mentioned, needs to adapt its law concerning the establishment authorisation in order to comply with the requirements of the directive.

The Luxembourgish government intends to make the authorisation scheme comply with the provision of Article 9 of the SD and the wording of Article 28 of the initial draft law concerning the establishment authorisation seems to align with that. However, this draft bill of law is still under discussion and currently we cannot anticipate the final result of the discussions.

2.5 Article 10 SD: Conditions for the Granting of Authorisation

Article 10 of the SD is implemented by Articles 8 of the Bill. Luxembourg, as already mentioned, needs to adapt its law concerning the establishment authorisation in order to comply with the requirements of the directive.

It is the willingness of the Luxembourg government to make the authorisation scheme comply with the provision of Article 10 of the SD and the initial draft law concerning the establishment authorisation seems to go in that way. However, this draft bill of law is still under discussion and we cannot anticipate how the final result of discussion at the time this report is written will be. Due to the lack of hindsight and of the vertical transposition, I am not in a position to give further information as of today.

2.6 Article 11 SD: Duration of Authorisation

Article 11 of the SD is implemented by Articles 9 of the Bill. Luxembourg, as already mentioned, needs to adapt its law concerning establishment authorisation in order to comply with the requirements of the directive.

Due to the lack of hindsight and of the vertical transposition, I am not in position to give further information as of today.

2.7 Article 12 SD: Selection from Among Several Candidates

Article 12 of the SD is implemented by Articles 10 of the Bill. Luxembourg, as already mentioned, needs to adapt its law concerning establishment authorisation in order to comply with the requirements of the directive.

Due to the lack of hindsight and of the vertical transposition, I am not in position to give further information as of today.

2.8 Article 13 SD: Authorisation Procedures

2.8.1 A Priori Determination of the Duration of Administrative Procedures

According to Article 11 (4) of the Bill, the duration of an administrative procedure is determined by decision of the responsible authority. However, it must be noted that Article 11 (7) of the Bill states that, by derogation to the principle fixed in the modified law dated November 7, 1996 regarding the proceeding in front of the administrative jurisdiction, in case the authority does not answer to the filed application within the prescribed time, the authorisation is deemed to have been granted to the provider.

2.8.2 General Rule for the Duration and Exceptions

The Bill does not foresee for a fixed duration of the procedure but provides for a 'reasonable duration' (Article 11 (4)) of the Bill. This duration shall be fixed in advance and shall be made public. A ceiling duration is, however, given by Article 11 (4) and confirmed by Article 11 (7) the Bill, which stipulates that in case no answer is given within a three-month period, it is deemed that the required authorisation was granted.

Article 11 (6) of the Bill foresees that the competent administration can postpone the deadline for a limited period of time and just once, in case the complexity of a file requires such an extension. This decision shall be duly reasoned and notified.

2.8.3 Tacit Authorisation in the National Legal Order So Far

In the Luxembourgish legal system, tacit authorisation did not exist before the adoption of the Bill. Such tacit authorisation is considered by most of the commentators as a major innovation in administrative procedure law that will allow one to reduce the duration of the procedure granting administrative authorisation in the field of services.

2.8.4 Formal and Substantive Effects of Tacit Authorisation

Pursuant to the system implemented by Article 11 (7) of the Bill, it seems that such tacit authorisation will have substantive effects.

2.8.5 Rules of Formally Granted Authorisations Applicable to Tacit Authorisation

The drafting of the Bill does not provide for an express answer to the question whether the same rules will apply for formally granted as for tacit authorisations. However, it seems that the same rules apply.

2.9 Articles 14, 15, 16 SD

2.9.1 Need of Adaptation?

Certain changes in specific sectors are intended. Luxembourg identifies a need to adapt the law regarding the authorisation of establishment dated December 28, 1988 to implement these articles. The law regarding the authorisation of establishment is by nature horizontal and therefore covers most of the activities covered by the SD. The Ministry of the Middle Classes (*Ministère des classes moyennes*) has submitted a draft law to parliament to adapt this law to the requirement of the SD and to make the law of establishment consistent notably with the dispositions of the SD.

2.9.2 Discussion on the Self-Screening of the Member States

Due to the lack of information regarding screening, I am not in a position to give information whether there are discussions or not.

These articles are implemented under Chapter 3 of the Bill.

2.10 Articles 14–19 SD

Initially, there was a lack of implementation of these articles in the draft Bill.

Finally, after several discussions regarding more the fact to have these articles implemented in this Bill or in another law, it has been decided to implement these articles in Article 12 ff.

2.11 Articles 22–27 SD

No problems regarding the transposition of these articles have been identified pursuant to our study of parliamentary works. It appears that there were no particular discussions on that point.

Article 20 of the Bill (quality policy) provides that the Luxembourgish Institute of Standardisation, accreditation, security and quality of products, and services encourages the services providers to warranty the quality of the services. It has to be noted that this certification is not compulsory.

2.12 Articles 28 ff. SD: Administrative Cooperation

2.12.1 Transnational Administrative Cooperation Prior to the Implementation of the Services Directive

Stricto sensu, there were no provisions on transnational administrative assistance in Luxembourg prior to the provision of the Bill.

2.12.2 Re-Arrangement Together with National Rules on Administrative Cooperation

The requirements of the SD did not give a cause to (re)arrange the provisions for administrative assistance in a general or uniform way. It only gives a general legal framework on transnational administrative assistance.

2.12.3 Provisions on Financial Compensation for Transnational Administrative Cooperation

There are no provisions on financial compensation for transnational assistance.

2.12.4 Adaptation of the Rules on Data Protection and Professional Secrets

According to the information made available to us, it does not seem that a change in the rules on data protection and professional secrets due to the wide range of information obligations is foreseen at this stage. It has been suggested that the transfer of information should be done within the context of the rules regarding data protection and professional secrets in each MS.

2.13 *Article 29 SD: Mutual Assistance—General Obligations for the Member State of Establishment*

Article 29 of the DS is implemented by Article 26 of the Bill.

There was some discussion as it was considered by the State Council (*Conseil d'Etat*) in its complementary advice that the wording and drafting of para 2 is problematic as it does not fall within the competence of a foreign authority to impose to national authorities to proceed to verification or inspections that are perhaps not foresee in the Luxembourgish legislation.

2.14 *Problems and Discourses on Administrative Cooperation*

No problem or discourses regarding Chapter VI have been identified pursuant to our study of parliamentary works. It appears that there were no particular discussions on that point.

2.15 *Convergence Programme (Chapter VII of the Services Directive)*

According to the information made available to us, it seems that no discussion on that chapter has taken place.

3 Assessment of the Impact of the Services Directive

Because of the restriction to the principle of tacit authorisation and according to the fact that for the time being we have no hindsight of the final interpretation of the text by the competent authority, it is not possible to give a final answer to the question, if the impact of the SD on administrative procedure law, administrative law for business activities, and even beyond can be assessed as severe in the Luxembourg view. If the interpretation of the restriction contained in the Bill is strict (as it should be, according to me and considering the case law of the CJEU), the impact of the SD on administrative procedure law could be considered significant.

For the time being and due to the delay in the legislative process to implement the SD, it is difficult to say whether the Luxembourgish transposition is to be considered a success, since this judgement should be made once a significant hindsight on the application of the Bill and more precisely regarding the application of the restriction to the principle of tacit authorisation in all cases related to the protection of the 'human and natural environment' could have been done. Indeed, depending on the respective application (restrictive or not) of the restriction, the transposition could be considered a real improvement or, on the contrary, a minimum transposition of the SD.

In our view, the most important and significant change induced by the implementation of the SD in Luxembourg involves administrative procedure law and the rule of Article 11 (7) of the Bill providing that silence means authorisation, since this will allow a significant reduction in the duration of the instruction of files by the competent administration. However, this significant change will not have the expected effect in the case where the rule according which that silence means refusal in all cases related to the protection of the human and natural environment is interpreted in an extensive manner by the competent administrative authority.

The Implementation of the Services Directive in Malta

Peter G. Xuereb

1 General Remarks on the Transposition Strategy and General Understanding of the Implementation

1.1 Main References Used in this Research

The sources used for the purposes of compiling this report include the relevant draft legislation and reports of parliamentary debates, press reports, interviews, information disseminated and documentation issued in public seminars, and the laws themselves. The Services Directive (SD) was transposed into Maltese law via an 'omnibus' act of Parliament with the short title of Services (Internal Market) Act 2009 (hereinafter 'SIMA'). It was promulgated on 29 December 2009. The bill presented to the house was bill number 32 of 2009, published on 2 October 2009 and available online at http://www.doi.gov.mt/EN/Bills/2009. The act is Act No. XXIII of 2009 and is available at http://www.lawsofmalta.gov.mt.

It is a horizontal law that transposes the general framework and obligations of the Directive. As such, it takes precedence over specific laws in matters covered by the Directive, and therefore provides a safeguard in the event that any law or legal provision may have been overlooked in the screening process. Its scope extends to

Prof. Dr. Peter G. Xuereb. Professor of European and Comparative Law, Jean Monnet Professor, and Head of the Department of European and Comparative Law in the Faculty of Law, and also Chairman of the European Documentation and Research Centre (Jean Monnet European Centre of Excellence) at the University of Malta. Latest update of the report July 2010.

P. G. Xuereb (✉)
Department of European and Comparative Law,
European Documentation and Research Centre, University of Malta, Msida, Malta
e-mail: peter.g.xuereb@um.edu.mt

U. Stelkens et al. (eds.), *The Implementation of the EU Services Directive*,
DOI: 10.1007/978-90-6704-840-8_18,

all services covered by the Directive, even if no particular Maltese legislation exists regulating a particular service. Of course, every attempt has been made by the government to identify all laws that require amendment and to remove any incompatible provisions from extant Maltese legislation. The act thus makes these amendments. Much has been left, however, to be regulated in delegated legislation to be issued at the same time as or soon after the promulgation of the SIMA. As of 15 January 2010, much of such delegated legislation was still in the pre-legislative phase, but this was remedied by the adoption of several pieces of subsidiary legislation in the first half of 2010.

1.2 Impact of the Services Directive

The transposition exercise cannot be said to have had a radical impact on the essence of Maltese administrative law. However, it has involved a major review, covering a large number of Maltese laws. Furthermore, it has had two most salutary effects: First, in most cases there was no deadline for the granting of authorisations; second, every decision must now be fully reasoned. The opportunity has been taken to clarify and strengthen the roles of competent authorities and their obligations of impartiality and timely and efficient service (Article 4 of the Act). The process of screening existing law for compatibility, or otherwise, with the Directive started in June of 2007, with the work being coordinated first by the Ministry of Finance, Economy, and Investment (hereafter 'MFEI'), through an interministerial group of seven government ministries and the involvement of some 20 competent authorities affected by the Directive. Moreover, the opportunity was seized to generally streamline processes for the supervision of providers and for consumer access to appropriate remedies. The implementation of 'procedural' obligations provided an important opportunity, in the setting up of the electronic point of single contact (POSC), to modernise the delivery of administrative procedures and remedies. It is reported that the MFEI worked closely with other government entities and all relevant competent authorities to ensure full delivery of a modern, responsive, and efficient service in this regard.

1.3 (National) Scope of Application

The scope of the Directive is wide and not limited to the provision of transnational services. The SIMA is expressed to be passed to establish general provisions facilitating the exercise of freedom of establishment for service providers and the free movement of services in the internal market and to implement the SD. On its terms, and in light of the definition provisions in the Act (Part II of the Act), it is clear that the Act has followed the Directive very closely and applies to the establishment and provision of services within the meaning of the SD. Article 4 of the Act provides that competent authorities are to be under certain specific obligations of the simplification of procedures, impartial action, the provision of information, and so on,

> "further to the fulfilment of the powers, functions and responsibilities attributed to the competent authority, in the founding and enabling legislation concerning the area of competence, and without prejudice to the allocation of functions and powers vested among authorities within the national administrative system".

Important additional clarification and possibly development of the law is taking place in a manner that applies to both the core matters and cases covered by the Directive in implementation of the Treaty rules, as well as in purely domestic situations. It is thus possible to say that the implementation and the manner of implementation engender general and universal standards.

1.4 Incorporation of Transposing Legislation

The general approach was that of adopting a horizontal Act, the Services (Internal Market) Act 2009, which is an enabling law and therefore substantially transposes the Directive. The Act amends various pieces of existing 'primary' legislation (acts of Parliament) as they relate to the various areas of activity or sectors covered by the Directive (and the Act). The transposition exercise was completed by the enactment of a number of sets of new or amending regulations (subsidiary legislation enacted under the main acts of Parliament and published as Legal Notices) enacted within three to six months of the enactment of the main law. Generally, the amendments made to the other acts of Parliament or legal codes affected, and made by the SIMA itself, refer to the powers and obligations of the respective authorising (competent) authorities as set out in those pieces of legislation. Often, cross-references are now made in those other Acts to the provisions of the Services (Internal Market) Act, for example, as to definitions. In effect, two codes (the Commercial Code and the Code of Organisation and Civil Procedure) and some 12 acts of Parliament dealing with various services and trades have been amended, as well as six others dealing with various professions and the conferring of professional qualifications.

1.5 The Relationship of the Services Directive to Primary EU Law

This issue is not thought to be problematic. The SD has been transposed through the exercise of powers within the scope of the Maltese Act of Parliament, which made (and makes) the Treaties applicable law in Malta (the European Union Act of 2003, Act No. V of 2003, Chapter 460 of the Laws of Malta, as amended).

In virtue of that law, the Services (Internal Market) Act will be construed in accordance with the SD. The new provisions inserted into other laws by SIMA often refer directly to the SD, or even to the relevant Treaty articles.

1.6 Screening

The process of screening existing laws for compatibility, or otherwise, with the Directive started in June 2007, with the work being coordinated first by the MFEI through an interministerial group of seven government ministries and the involvement of some 20 competent authorities affected by the Directive. It would appear that some competent authorities responded more quickly than others and that some were not as proactive as they might have been in the early stages. It is also true that the drafting of many of the legal notices (delegated legislation) that would supplement SIMA itself, as well as the affected acts of Parliament, and be made in legal terms under the provisions of the main act and those other acts, is yet to be completed, and their promulgation was delayed to 2010.

2 Individual Articles of the Services Directive

2.1 Article 6 SD: Point of Single Contact (POSC)

There is to be one electronic point of contact, but work on it has not yet been completed, although it is reportedly at an advanced stage and is now almost in place, according to my information. It will provide a full service via a government domain and currently works via link-up to the various competition authorities, thus ultimately providing what is envisaged to be a 'one-stop shop' delivery service. Article 12 (2) of the SIMA enabled the minister to provide for this in regulations to be adopted under Article 12 (1). There has not been any reallocation of administrative competences thus far into the process, and indeed the Act provides that all is without prejudice to the allocation of administrative competences vested among authorities within the national administrative system (Article 4 of the Act). Any liability for mistakes made by or through the POSC will follow the usual administrative law rules. It is also envisaged that a physical facility service will be provided.

2.2 Article 7 SD: Right to Information

Access to information relating to the matters at hand was available electronically as far as concerns matters within the public sphere, but less easily so regarding the regulated professions. The Act now extends the system of information and establishes clear rights to information over all activities falling within the scope of the Directive. The full scope is clearer now that the delegated legislation is published. The main mechanism that will apply to ensure that the POSC and the competent authorities respond as quickly as possible to a request for information or assistance, as required by Article 7 (4) of the Directive, is through the clear obligations of the competent authorities to furnish information and to respond without delay (Article 4 of the Act). At the time of this writing, the POSC is an electronic front desk.

2.3 Article 8 SD: Procedures by Electronic Means

Work on the completion of the POSC was still ongoing at the time of this writing. Over the last years, e-government has been one of the success stories of the Maltese public administration and government. The POSC is set to fully build upon updated electronic (e-government) means and procedures, which are being used and themselves updated at the moment. Article 12 (2) of the Act provides that the Minister may make regulations providing, *inter alia,* for the definition of the functions of a POSC and its administrative and operational set up and function, including its coordination with the relevant competent authorities and other bodies established under other laws in fulfilment of the functions assigned to it. These regulations have not, as of yet, been passed. Otherwise, this exercise can be seen as an extension of existing electronic services, but on a noteworthy scale. Existing non-electronic means and procedures have not been removed.

2.4 Article 9 SD: Authorisation Schemes

Access to all economic activities in Malta required a licence. This is attributed to the residual nature of the Trading Licences Act (Chapter 441 of the Laws of Malta), which licences all those activities that are not regulated by specific acts (mainly those establishing sector-specific authorities and regulators). Therefore, generally speaking, the areas of administrative law in which an 'a posteriori' inspection was not considered sufficient were those regulated by sector-specific regulators: tourism, resources (energy and water), regulated professionals, postal services, employment agencies, ancillary services to transport (such as VRT stations and car rentals), childcare, education services, and construction services.

Before the SD all authorisation schemes were an ex ante formality that had to be undertaken by an application through a procedure established by the competent authority, which could include inspections, interviews, and so forth. Most application forms and information concerning these schemes already existed on the respective competent authority's website. Procedure per se is pretty standard in Malta. Requirements and documents to be submitted may vary according to the type of service activity. The main changes made to the requirements included those instances where a particular document was considered 'not necessary', for example, a birth certificate when the applicant is producing an identification number or passport. The exercise was therefore one of simplification and the assessment of the necessity of the objectives pursued by the actual application/authorisation scheme. An authorisation scheme is abolished, or, rather, replaced by an 'ex post' notification in most retail and wholesale activities falling under the Trading Licences Act (Cap 441) and governed by the provisions of LN 1 of 2006 in particular, whose changes are quite significant.

As far as a national understanding is concerned, and as per the Directive, an authorisation scheme is a procedure that must be completed by the applicant before accessing the market, and all licences in Malta that are being retained fall under this definition. Authorisations continue to be required, for example, for accommodations, catering, travel services, tourist guides, and some others areas. The notification procedures that are being adopted by the legislative changes refer to ex post procedures and therefore do not fall under the definition of 'authorisation' in the SD and therefore Article 9.

2.5 Article 10 SD: Conditions for the Granting of Authorisation

In effect, the recognition of requirements and authorisations is implemented via Article 5 of the SIMA. No particular problems appear to have occurred or are envisaged on this score. Article 5 of the Act in effect transposes Article 10 of the Directive, as well as some other articles of the same. For example, it also makes provision for what is contained in Article 13 of the Directive concerning time periods for deciding on an application for authorisation. While such time periods are likely to continue to be set in the relevant service-sector–specific subsidiary legislation, these principles will nevertheless apply should the matter be left by Parliament to a competent authority.

Granting authorisation throughout the whole country was not a problem in Malta, which is not a large state; the scope of the Act covers the entire national territory, in principle (Articles 5 (4) and (11) (a) refer). The question of regional exceptions has not come up yet.

The Act establishes the entitlement to grant authorisation (Article 5 (12) (f)). This reflects Maltese law. Judicial review is available in the ordinary courts or by way of appeal to the Appeals Tribunal established by the Administrative Justice Act or another relevant tribunal, in accordance with the legislation applicable to the particular activity and its regulation. The adjudicating body will examine the decisions on the grounds of *ultra vires* and compliance with the law, the proper exercise of executive discretion, and the rules of natural justice. The Act itself provides for the designation by ministerial regulations of an 'Appeals Board' to take cognisance of complaints lodged by a provider against a competent authority in default of a procedure identified under its founding and enabling legislation (Article 12 (2) (f) of the Act).

Pertaining to the duty to fully reason administrative decisions indeed a general change in the law was carried out. The principle now applies across all activities, as per Article 5 (12) (h) of the Act, which expressly provides for full reasons and renders the decisions of the competent authorities open to challenge before the Appeals Board (see 'judicial review' above).

No alteration has so far ensued in the allocation of administrative competences in regard to the granting of authorisations.

2.6 Article 11 SD: Duration of Authorisation

Article 5 (10) (a) of the Act provides that an authorisation shall be for an indefinite period. This provision also reproduces the exceptions permitted by Article 11 of the Directive but elaborates in Article 5 (9) on the second exception by providing that a time restriction may be applied 'where the number of authorisations available for a given service activity is limited because of the scarcity of available natural resources, technical capacity or if justified by an overriding reason related to public interest'. This is the language of Article 12 (1) of the SD, the transposition of which is linked to that of Article 11 of the SD in this way. Therefore, Article 5 (10) (b) provides that in such cases an authorisation shall be granted for an appropriate limited period, and that the authorisation shall not be open to automatic renewal or confer any other advantage. There was no previous prohibition on time-limited authorisations.

2.7 Article 12 SD: Selection from Among Several Candidates

Such principles are known to Maltese law. Such procedures and principles are applied in other laws.

2.8 Article 13 SD: Authorisation Procedure and Tacit Authorisation

This is normally done by law. The SIMA now provides for decision making to be carried out as quickly as possible and in a way that does not 'unduly complicate or delay the commencement of the service activity by the provider' (Article 5 (12) (a) of the Act), and also 'within a time period which shall be fixed and made public in advance, failing which it shall be deemed that the authorisation has been granted'

(Article 5 (12) (d) of the Act). It is expected that these time periods will continue to be set in the relevant subsidiary legislation. The general rule in Maltese law was that decisions needed to be made within a reasonable time, although some legislation provided for decisions to be made within a stipulated time. Fictitious authorisations are not part of the law in general. When it comes to the provision of services, the position can differ. For example, the Veterinary Services Act (Chapter 437 of the Laws of Malta) now provides for a maximum period of two months, after which, in the absence of a decision, the service may be provided. However, appeal or other judicial procedures may be necessary if no time limit is specified by legislation or the competent authority, or where, for overriding reasons of public interest, it is provided that the absence of a reply shall not be construed to imply the automatic granting of the licence (e.g., as per the Postal Services Act, Chapter 254 of the Laws of Malta, as amended by the SIMA).

2.9 Articles 14, 15, 16 SD

Articles 14, 15, and 16 were transposed by Articles 5 and 6 of the Act. The screening process led to the removal of restrictions deemed to clash with Union law. There has been no public discussion, except in passing, about self-screening or the mutual evaluation report.

2.10 Articles 14–19 SD

No general public discussions are ongoing.

2.11 Articles 22–27 SD

There has been little or no public debate regarding these articles, or the provisions of the SIMA that implement them, on the lines that they may involve a transfer or transition of obligations away from the authorities to the private sector. Provision is made for information to be made available via the competent authorities and through the entity fulfiling the role of the European Consumer Centre in Malta, or any other entity as may be designated by the minister (Article 10 (3) of the Act, in combination with Articles 7 and 8 of the Act).

2.12 Articles 28 ff. SD: Administrative Cooperation

While the Act makes provisions for administrative cooperation, there was no pre-existing system and it is expected that further legislation may be put in place for this purpose. However, Articles 7 and 8 of the Act transpose the essential principles in the Directive, while being supplemented in procedural terms by the second, third, fourth, and fifth schedules to the Act. The Act does make a saving for 'the limitations imposed by any other law', which could be interpreted as referring to restrictions relating to data protection or professional secrets (Article 8 (6) of the Act).

2.13 Article 29 SD: Mutual Assistance—General Obligations for the Member State of Establishment

This is transposed by Article 8 and the second schedule of the SIMA. There would appear to have been no particularly difficult discussions on this matter.

2.14 Problems and Discourses on Administrative Cooperation

There seem to have been no problems with Chapter VI of the Services Directive.

2.15 Convergence Programme (Chapter VII of the Services Directive).

There seem to have been no problems with Chapter VII of the Services Directive.

3 Assessment of the Impact of the Services Directive

In terms of legal impact, I would like to highlight two main developments that affect administrative law across the board in relation to establishment and services: First, in the past authorisation schemes did not, as a rule, operate by reference to a deadline for making of administrative decisions; second, the SIMA introduced the principle that all administrative decisions must be fully reasoned. These two developments in themselves are a significant improvement in the law.

Economic experts declare that it is very difficult to say what the medium- to long-term general economic impact in Malta of the SD will be or, indeed, to say what it will be in particular sectors. Operators in some sectors remain concerned as to the inflow of the provision of services, and at least one large trade union has warned that there could be a loss of trade and jobs, but expert opinion appears to generally discount this overall.

While the impact in terms of administration is a radical one, in the sense that the SD necessitated a whole new infrastructure for the provision of information and supervision, the underlying principles have not caused any major revision of administrative law, apart from the points alluded to above.

Therefore, it is very early to say how the SD's concrete effects will play out at the level of the services sector. However, the POSC and the various provisions and mechanisms for information, once fully operational, should make a significantly positive impact on operators and on the position of recipients generally. It is against a general backdrop of positive expectations that the SIMA has been enacted in Malta.

The Implementation of the Services Directive in the Netherlands

Sacha Prechal, Sybe de Vries and Frederik van Doorn

1 General Remarks on the Transposition Strategy and General Understanding of the Implementation

1.1 Main References Used in this Research

For our main references, see the List of References. Throughout the questionnaire, the footnotes often refer to the concept of *Kamerstukken*, which entails parliamentary documents, that is, mostly explanatory (or responsive) memoranda.

Dr. Alexandra (Sacha) Prechal—Professor of European Law at the Europe Institute of the School of Law at Utrecht University, since 10 June 2010 she is Judge at the Court of Justice of the European Union. Dr. S.A. (Sybe) de Vries—Associate Professor in European Law at the Europe Institute of the School of Law at Utrecht University. Frederik van Doorn, MSc, LL.M.—Policy adviser at the Ministry of Economic Affairs, Agriculture and Innovation. Every opinion expressed in this research is strictly personal. The authors would like to thank Sophie Hiensch and Maartje Möhring for their valuable research assistance. Latest update April 2010.

S. Prechal · S. de Vries (✉)
Europe Institute of the School of Law, Utrecht University, Utrecht, The Netherlands
e-mail: S.A.deVries@uu.nl

S. Prechal
e-mail: A.Prechal@uu.nl

F. van Doorn
Ministry of Economic Affairs, Agriculture and Innovation, The Hague, The Netherlands
e-mail: F.Doorn@minez.nl

U. Stelkens et al. (eds.), *The Implementation of the EU Services Directive*,
DOI: 10.1007/978-90-6704-840-8_19,

1.2 Impact of the Services Directive

1.2.1 Profound Cause of Changes to National Law?

The main legal document implementing the Services Directive (SD) in the Netherlands is the Services Act, which will be elaborated upon below. The transposition of the SD in the Netherlands is based on the following six principles that are important for both the contents of the implementation, as well as for its scope.[1] The first principle used is that the transposition is, in principle, limited to the obligations stemming from the SD itself. That is, the implementation of the SD has been limited to the minimum requirements. Exceptions to this principle have only been made when the text of the SD itself was unclear and when discussions with the European Commission indicated a more far-reaching scope of the SD, or when extending the obligations of the SD to purely domestic services would unambiguously result in an improvement.[2] The second principle is related to the first and states that the implementation process is limited to the minimum requirements and minimum transposition measures, even when the SD explicitly hints at the possibility of extending the requirements in national law. This principle was, for example, relevant for the implementation of Article 6 SD concerning the (optional) use of the point of single contact (POSC) by service providers, as well as when deciding not to implement the optional provision of Article 23 SD. The reason for this choice of a minimum transposition is given by the Dutch legislator in its explanatory memorandum of the Services Act: This prevents the implementation process from becoming more complex than necessary and minimises the administrative costs associated with the transposition of the SD for provinces, municipalities, and undertakings.[3]

As a result of these two principles, the implementation of the SD in the Netherlands has had a limited effect on general administrative law. It has been decided to only extend the requirements of the SD into national law with regard to three subject areas. First, the tacit fictitious authorisation of Article 13(4) SD (i.e., *lex silencio positivo*) has also been introduced as a possibility in purely domestic situations. Second, the POSC is also available for Dutch service providers. Finally, the Internal Market Information system (IMI) is also used in purely domestic situations.[4] All of these issues will be further elaborated upon below, when dealing with the individual articles of the SD.

Although mentioning the first two principles of the Dutch implementation of the SD suffices for answering the question, it is useful to also mention the other

---

[1] *Kamerstukken II* 2007/08, 31 579, nr. 3, pp. 16–17. See also Hessel et al. 2009, pp. 42–45.

[2] In this context, the Dutch legislator mentions that this means that the transposition process will result in a minimum of so-called 'nationale koppen', i.e., situations where the legislator goes beyond the minimum requirements of the SD (Kamerstukken II 2007/08, 31 579, nr. 3, p. 16).

[3] *Kamerstukken II* 2007/08, 31 579, nr. 3, p. 16.

[4] BZK 2009, p. 19.

principles that have been used during the transposition process. The third principle addresses the interpretation of the SD itself and the role of the Commission's 'Handbook on the implementation of the Services Directive'.[5] The legislator emphasises that the implementation of the SD in the Netherlands is based on a Dutch interpretation, which uses the Commission's handbook as only one of various interpretative sources.[6] In this regard the legislator points out that it is generally recognised (by the Commission as well) that the handbook is not binding for the Member States (MSs).

A fourth principle that has been used during the transposition of the SD concerns the allocation of administrative competences. Corresponding with various provisions in the SD,[7] the Dutch legislator has indicated that a key issue in the implementation process is that no amendments to the allocation of competences, at the local or regional level, of authorities will be made. Next, pursuant to the fifth principle, the implementation of the SD will have a technologically neutral character.[8] That is, the legal changes needed for the implementation leave considerable room for technological developments, so that future legislative amendments are less likely to be necessary. Finally, a sixth key principle the Dutch legislator has used entails that, prior to implementation, an extensive scrutiny of domestic legislation has taken place in order to establish to what extent Dutch national law is already in conformity with EU law and therefore needs no further transposition.[9]

1.2.2 Involvement in the Transposition Process

The transposition process has been supervised by the Ministry of Economic Affairs, which is politically responsible for the implementation of the SD. Within the Ministry of Economic Affairs, a project group has been established, named the *Projectgroep Implementatie Dienstenrichtlijn* (Project Group Implementation Services Directive, PID), which has co-ordinated the entire implementation process. The PID has started a website specifically dedicated to the implementation of the SD and it has also organised informational meetings throughout the country.[10] In the implementation process, the PID has exchanged information and cooperated with the Ministry of Economic Affairs, the Ministry of the Interior and Kingdom Relations, and the Ministry of Justice. Moreover, extensive cooperation and information exchange has taken place between these parties involved and the Europe-oriented think tank *Europa Decentraal* (which might be translated as 'Europe at the decentral level').

---

[5] See http://ec.europa.eu/internal_market/services/docs/services-dir/guides/handbook_en.pdf.

[6] *Kamerstukken II* 2007/08, 31 579, nr. 3, p. 16.

[7] See e.g., Recital 48 SD, as well as Articles 6 (2) and 10 (7) SD.

[8] *Kamerstukken II* 2007/08, 31 579, nr. 3, pp. 16–17.

[9] *Kamerstukken II* 2007/08, 31 579, nr. 3, p. 17.

[10] See http://www.dienstenrichtlijn.ez.nl.

At a decentralised level, the PID worked closely with the *Vereniging van Nederlandse Gemeenten* (Association of Dutch Municipalities, VNG), the *Interprovinciaal Overleg* (Association of the Provinces of the Netherlands, IPO), and the *Unie van Waterschappen* (Dutch Association of Regional Water Authorities, UvW).[11] Furthermore, all decentralised authorities received a brochure from the PID explaining the SD itself and which tasks these decentralised authorities had to fulfil. In this context, a checklist was published so that it was relatively easy to check whether rules were in conformity with the SD.[12] Finally, the PID also cooperated with several independent associations such as the *Sociaal-Economische Raad* (Social and Economic Council, SER), *Federatie Nederlandse Vakbeweging* (Dutch Trade Union Federation, FNV), *Christelijk Nationaal Vakverbond* (National Federation of Christian Trade Unions, CNV), VNO/NCW (Confederation of Netherlands Industry and Employers), and MKB Nederland (a lobby organisation for SMEs).[13]

1.3 (National) Scope of Application

During the implementation of the SD, there have been extensive discussions as to its scope.[14] Key issues in this debate have been, on the one hand, what should be considered a 'service' and, on the other hand, to what extent the SD should apply to purely domestic situations.[15]

In the context of the first issue, Hessel mentions that the SD functions as a 'container', because the formulation of its scope includes both the freedom of services and the freedom of establishment, whereas the term *services* has been defined very broadly, that is, 'any self-employed economic activity, normally provided for remuneration, as referred to in Article 50 of the Treaty' (now Article 57 of the Treaty on the Functioning of the European Union, hereafter TFEU).[16] Moreover, there have been extensive discussions on whether the distribution of goods should be regarded as a 'service'.

The Dutch legislator has acknowledged these uncertainties as to the scope of the SD on several occasions and emphasises that, when dealing with such ambiguities, it has chosen to use its own interpretation of the SD (which, *inter alia,* includes the view that the distribution of goods is not a 'service').[17] As mentioned

[11] *Kamerstukken II* 2008/09, 31 859, nr. 3, p. 5.

[12] See http://www.dienstenrichtlijn.ez.nl/images/stories/Checklist_Aanvullende_doorlichting.pdf.

[13] See http://www.dienstenrichtlijn.ez.nl/veelgestelde-vragen-nieuw/11-algemeen/254-welke-instanties-zijn-bij-de-dienstenrichtlijn-betrokken.

[14] See e.g., Duijkersloot and Widdershoven 2007, *Kamerstukken II* 2007/08, 31 579, nr. 3, p. 10 ff.; BZK 2009, p. 24.

[15] See e.g., Duijkersloot and Widdershoven 2007, p. 192.

[16] Article 4 (1) SD. See Hessel 2007a, Hessel et al. 2009.

[17] *Kamerstukken II* 2007/08, 31 579, nr. 3, p. 13.

above, this interpretation is based on various principles, including one stating that the transposition is, in principle, limited to the obligations stemming from the SD itself and will therefore not lead to extension in national law. This interpretation can be seen in Article 2 of the Services Act, which uses a twofold method to transpose the scope of the SD. First, Article 2 (1) of the Services Act states that the Services Act only applies to those services that are included within the scope of the SD.[18] This dynamic link, so to speak, with the SD itself has been specifically introduced in order to easily—that is, without legislative changes—take into account judgements of the European Court of Justice (ECJ) on the interpretation of the scope of the SD.[19] Second, Article 2 (2) of the Services Act stipulates that the Minister of Economic Affairs can decide to declare that specific authorisation regimes and services are to be included within the scope of the SD.

As a result, according to the Dutch view, the starting point when determining the actual scope of the SD is the SD itself.[20] In this respect, the legislator points to Articles 2 (1) and 4 of the SD as important determinants of the scope of the SD, since they state that the SD 'shall apply to services supplied by providers established in a Member State',[21] whereas 'services' are to be defined as 'any self-employed economic activity, normally provided for remuneration, as referred to in Article 50 of the Treaty' (now Article 57 TFEU).[22] Hessel's view that the SD functions as a 'container' is substantiated by the fact that the SD not so much defines what is to be included in the concept of 'service', but, rather, stipulates what is not to be included. An exception is Recital 33 SD, which provides a rather extensive—though not exhaustive—list on the services covered by the SD.[23] According to Recital 33,

> "[t]he services covered by [the SD] concern a wide variety of ever-changing activities, including business services such as management consultancy, certification and testing; facilities management, including office maintenance; advertising; recruitment services; and the services of commercial agents. The services covered are also services provided both to businesses and to consumers, such as legal or fiscal advice; real estate services such as estate agencies; construction, including the services of architects; distributive trades; the organisation of trade fairs; car rental; and travel agencies. Consumer services are also covered, such as those in the field of tourism, including tour guides; leisure services, sports centres and amusement parks; and, to the extent that they are not excluded from the scope of application of the Directive, household support services, such as help for the elderly. Those activities may involve services requiring the proximity of provider and recipient, services requiring travel by the recipient or the provider and services which may be provided at a distance, including via the Internet".[24]

---

18 *Kamerstukken II* 2007/08, 31 579, nr. 3, p. 15.

19 *Kamerstukken II 2008/09, 31 579, nr. C, p. 11.*

20 *Kamerstukken II* 2007/08, 31 579, nr. 3, p. 15.

21 Article 2 (1) SD.

22 Article 4 (1) SD.

23 See also BZK 2009, p. 25.

24 Recital 33 SD.

Corresponding with the SD itself, the Dutch legislator gives considerable attention to what is to be excluded from the scope of the Directive.[25] First, the legislator emphasises that Article 1 SD excludes rules of criminal law, labour law, or social security legislation, measures concerning linguistic diversity, and the organisation of services of general economic interest. Second, the legislator embraces the view that the SD does not apply to non-economic services of general interest, financial services, electronic communications services and networks, services in the field of transport, services of temporary work agencies, healthcare services, audiovisual services (including cinematographic services), gambling activities, activities connected with the exercise of official authority, social services, private security services, and services provided by notaries and bailiffs.[26] Third, the SD specifically excludes the field of taxation.[27] Next, pursuant to Article 3 (2) SD, the Directive does not concern rules of private international law. Fifth, the legislator sees in Article 3 (1) SD another limitation of the scope of the Directive. This provision states that the SD has a complementary function, that is, in case of a conflict provisions of other Community acts will prevail. In this context the Dutch legislator points out that it is possible for a certain directive to be excluded from the scope of the SD with regard to some subject matters, but where the (legislation implementing the) SD does apply to other issues in this directive. Similarly, when going beyond a minimum implementation of a directive that deals with matters excluded from the SD's scope, the SD can nevertheless apply to those provisions that go beyond the minimum transposition of that directive.[28]

A more specific indication of what should be considered to be included in the scope of the SD is Recital 9, according to which the SD

> "applies only to requirements which affect the access to, or the exercise of, a service activity. Therefore, it does not apply to requirements, such as road traffic rules, rules concerning the development or use of land, town and country planning, building standards as well as administrative penalties imposed for non-compliance with such rules which do not specifically regulate or specifically affect the service activity but have to be respected by providers in the course of carrying out their economic activity in the same way as by individuals acting in their private capacity".[29]

Recital 9 therefore indicates that certain rules are to be excluded from the scope of the SD. The Dutch legislator illustrates (its interpretation of) the meaning of Recital 9 with case law of the Court of Justice.[30] According to the legislator, this case law shows that a rule will be outside the scope of the SD, if it applies both to

---

[25] *Kamerstukken II* 2007/08, 31 579, nr. 3, p. 11 ff.

[26] Article 2 (2) SD.

[27] Article 2 (3) SD.

[28] *Kamerstukken II* 2007/08, 31 579, nr. 3, pp. 12–13.

[29] Recital 9 SD.

[30] Case C-544/03 and C-545/03, *Mobistar SA v. Commune de Fléron*, and *Belgacom Mobile SA v. Commune de Schaerbeek* [2005] ECR I-07723, para 26–35; Case 465/05, *Commission v. Italy* [2007] ECR I-11091, para 46–48.

natural and legal persons acting as provider or recipient of a service and to natural persons acting in their private capacity. Finally, an important indicator of the SD's scope is Recital 57, which explicitly states that rules on public procurement are excluded from the scope of the SD.[31]

As to what extent the SD should apply to purely domestic situations, the Dutch legislator has chosen minimum implementation of the requirements. As a result, the requirements of the SD are perceived as merely binding for the provision of transnational services or establishment, and not for purely domestic situations. The provisions in the laws implementing the SD, most notably the Services Act and the Amendment Act SD (see below), are therefore, in principle, not applicable to purely domestic situations. As will be explained below, there are only three exceptions to this minimum transposition of the SD: the *lex silencio positivo*, the POSC, and the Internal Market Information system (IMI) have been extended to apply in purely domestic situations.

The legislator has chosen for this minimum transposition of the Directive to minimise the complexity and administrative costs associated with the implementation.[32] Only when the SD itself was unclear and when discussions with the European Commission indicated a more far-reaching scope of the SD or when extending the obligations of the SD to purely domestic situations would unambiguously result in an improvement the Dutch implementation has gone beyond the minimum requirements. This view implicitly deals with the concept of reverse discrimination, that is, when more flexible rules only apply to service providers from other MSs and not to domestic service providers. For example, as will be explained below, the problem of reverse discrimination has been recognised when dealing with the POSC (Article 6 SD). When transposing this provision into national law, the Dutch legislator has considered that mere implementation of the minimum requirements would result in an undesirable situation where domestic service providers are treated differently than service providers in another MS.[33] The problem of reverse discrimination has also been addressed by provinces and municipalities when screening their own rules.[34]

1.4 Incorporation of Transposing Legislation

Initially, the Dutch legislator had planned to implement the SD into national law in four stages, which will be described below.[35] However, as the extensive screening of national rules applying to the provision of services showed that the number (and

[31] *Kamerstukken II* 2007/08, 31 579, nr. 3, p. 15; BZK 2009, p. 28.

[32] *Kamerstukken II* 2007/08, 31 579, nr. 3, p. 16.

[33] *Kamerstukken II* 2007/08, 31 579, nr. 3, p. 29.

[34] Hessel et al. 2009, pp. 54–55.

[35] *Kamerstukken II* 2007/08, 31 579, nr. 3, p. 17 ff.

severity) of inconsistencies with the SD was limited, it was decided that three stages would suffice.[36]

The primary instrument of the implementation process is the introduction of a separate act, that is, the Services Act (*Dienstenwet*). The main objective of the Services Act is to transpose the key obligations from the SD into national law. According to the Dutch view, there are four such key obligations[37]:

1. The obligation of administrative simplification as well as the establishment of a POSC,
2. The transposition of general rules concerning authorisation schemes, insofar as these are not yet incorporated in Dutch law,
3. The protection of service recipients by imposing information obligations on service providers and ensuring that this information is available at the POSC, and
4. The promotion of cross-border administrative cooperation and information exchange between competent authorities.

These requirements are met through either individual provisions in the Services Act or—when it was decided to extend the provisions of the SD to purely domestic situations—in general laws such as the General Administrative Law Act (*Algemene wet bestuursrecht*, Awb) and the Dutch Civil Code (*Burgerlijk Wetboek*).

The second component of implementing the SD has been initiated pursuant to the screening obligation of the SD. The screening process has made visible several inconsistencies of sector-specific rules with the SD. As will be elaborated upon below, however, the number of inconsistencies of national rules with the SD found is limited, since the Netherlands have been very active in recent years in reducing ‘unnecessary’ and ‘burdensome’ economic legislation. The inconsistencies that did emerge were generally resolved by the ministry responsible for the matter. However, for some changes it was found that making various small amendments national law all at once was more effective. For this purpose the Amendment Act SD (*Aanpassingswet Dienstenrichtlijn*) was introduced.[38] This act incorporates various sector-specific changes but also gives effect to some amendments to more general legislation (e.g., the incorporation of the *lex silencio positivo* into general administrative law).

Initially, the Dutch legislator had planned to introduce a third act that would finalise the implementation process (at the central level). This so-called *Veegwet* (often translated as ‘package law’) would solve possible inconsistencies that emerged during the implementation process of the SD. However, the introduction of the Services Act and the Amendment Act SD proved sufficiently capable of bringing national law in line with the requirements of the SD. The introduction of an additional act, the *Veegwet*, was therefore not considered necessary.

---

[36] *Kamerstukken II* 2008/09, 31 859, nr. 3, pp. 3–6.

[37] *Kamerstukken II* 2007/08, 31 579, nr. 3, p. 18; BZK 2009, p. 20.

[38] *Kamerstukken II* 2008/09, 31 859, nr. 2.

The fourth and final stage of the implementation process concerns regulatory amendments at a lower government level. This stage entails amendments through an order in council, ministerial regulations, or a policy rule, taken by (decentralised) administrative authorities, with a coordinating role for the (abovementioned) IPO, the VNG, and the UvW.

1.5 The Relationship of the Services Directive to Primary EU Law

In the Netherlands, the legislator is of the opinion that the SD is largely based on the principles of the freedom of services and the freedom of establishment and, correspondingly, the case law of the Court of Justice.[39] That is, the SD entails in large part a codification of the case law of the ECJ regarding the freedom of establishment and the freedom of services,[40] which concerns Articles 49 and 56 TFEU (ex Articles 43 and 49 EC), respectively. For example, the SD explicitly refers to Article 50 EC (now Article 57 TFEU) when defining the concept of 'services'. Similarly, the distinction between the freedom of services and the freedom of establishment, which is generally not made in Dutch national law,[41] also stems from jurisprudence concerning these Treaty provisions.[42]

A final example is the concept of 'overriding reasons relating to the public interest', to which reference is made in several provisions of the SD and which has been developed by the Court of Justice in its case law on Articles 49 and 56 TFEU (ex Articles 43 and 49 EC).[43] Correspondingly, Article 1 of the Services Act does not give its own interpretation of the concept of 'overriding reasons relating to the public interest', but defines the concept as those reasons which the ECJ has recognised as such. In conclusion, the Dutch legislator emphasises that the interpretation, as well as the implementation, of the SD needs to be assessed in light of the doctrines established in primary EU law.[44]

Since the Dutch legislator is of the opinion that the SD codifies case law of the ECJ, it has argued that the provisions regarding the freedom of services and of establishment (i.e., Articles 9 and 16 SD) need no further implementation in Dutch (statutory) law. The underlying reason for this view, that there is no need for transposition into national law, is that the doctrines established by the Court apply to Treaty provisions that are directly applicable in the national legal order.[45] Since

---

[39] *Kamerstukken II* 2007/08, 31 579, nr. 3, pp. 3–6.

[40] See more extensively Hessel et al. 2009, pp. 15–37. See also Gijón 2008, pp. 369–370.

[41] Van Meerten 2008, pp. 253–254.

[42] See e.g., Case C-55/94, *Gebhard* [1995] ECR I-4165; Case C-215/01, *Bruno Schnitzer* [2003] I-14847.

[43] See especially Recital 40 of the SD.

[44] *Kamerstukken II* 2007/08, 31 579, nr. 3, p. 6.

[45] *Kamerstukken II* 2007/08, 31 579, nr. 3, p. 20.

these rules concerning the freedom of services and of establishment already needed to be complied with, no further amendments in national law were considered necessary. As will be elaborated upon below, however, some provisions have been incorporated in instructions for the legislature.

In this context, however, one important difference between the Treaty provisions and the SD should be emphasised. The Dutch legislator recognises that although Article 16 SD corresponds to a large extent with the doctrine established on the freedom of services as laid down in Article 56 TFEU (ex Article 49 EC), there is an important difference.[46] Article 16 SD stipulates that MSs shall not provide access to or allow a service activity to be exercised in their territory subject to compliance with any requirements that do not respect the principles of non-discrimination, necessity, and proportionality. With regard to the necessity requirement, however, the SD does not allow justifications other than reasons of public policy, public security, public health, or the protection of the environment, whereas the case law on Article 56 TFEU (ex Article 49 EC) did allow other justifications.[47]

This issue was addressed by both the Dutch Council of State (*Raad van State*, which, *inter alia,* advises the government and Parliament on legislation and governance) and the (abovementioned) Social and Economic Council (SER) in their advice on the implementation of the SD.[48] Both organisations acknowledged the tension between the limited number of justifications in the SD, on the one hand, and the rule of reason as formulated in the case law on Article 56 TFEU (ex Article 49 EC) on the other hand. It remains to be seen how the ECJ will deal with this tension. Notwithstanding this important difference between the SD and primary EU law, the Dutch legislator has considered that Article 16 SD needs no implementation in national statutory law, since it merely forms a prohibition for the legislator when determining authorisation schemes and can therefore be safeguarded through de facto behaviour. As a result, and as will be elaborated upon below, Article 16 SD has been (or will be) included in instructions for the legislature.

One final remark regarding the relation between primary EU law and the SD concerns the concept of services of general (economic) interest. The Directive only covers services performed for an economic consideration. Services of general interest are therefore not covered by the Directive. As to services of general economic interest, however, the legislator in the Netherlands, as well as the SER, considers that these are generally included in the scope of the SD. The SER argues that it would not make sense to place services of general economic interest outside the scope of the SD, since this is an important opportunity to ensure a good future balance between market integration and policy integration.[49] It should be noted,

[46] This is also acknowledged in the literature; see e.g., Drijber 2004, Belhadj et al. 2007, Douma 2007, Hessel 2007a, Hessel 2007b, Hessel 2007c, Gijón 2008.

[47] *Kamerstukken II* 2007/08, 31 579, nr. 3, p. 21.

[48] *Kamerstukken II* 2007/08, 31 579, nr. 4; SER 2005.

[49] SER 2004.

however, that some services of general economic interest, such as those that may exist in the field of transport and in the area of postal services, are excluded from the scope of the Directive.[50] Moreover, as will be further elaborated upon below, Article 17 (1) (a) SD excludes services of general economic interest from the scope of Article 16 SD, which stipulates the freedom to provide services.

1.6 Screening

The screening process targeted several provisions of the SD.[51] Pursuant to Article 39 (1) of the SD, MSs must present a report to the Commission by 28 December 2009 at the latest, which contains the information specified in the following provisions: (a) Article 9 (2) SD on authorisation schemes, (b) Article 15 (5) SD on requirements to be evaluated, and (c) Article 25 (3) SD on multidisciplinary activities. Moreover, pursuant to Article 39 (5) SD, this report shall also include reflections on the national requirements within the context of Articles 16 (1) and 16 (3) SD. Finally, Article 14 SD lists prohibited requirements that were also subject to the screening process.

The screening of national rules has as its objective to determine which national legislation and rules fall under the scope of the SD and to what extent adjustments need to be made to comply with the requirements stated in the SD. More specifically, the requirements in national law have been tested to ascertain whether they satisfy the criteria of non-discrimination, necessity, and proportionality. In effect, the screening process entails a conformity test of Dutch legislation and rules with the European concepts of freedom of services and of establishment as stipulated in the SD.[52] When inconsistencies are found, regulatory changes have been made.

The screening process has been undertaken at both the central and the decentralised levels of the government. Because of its importance to other screening activities, screening at the central level was already started in 2006, and concluded before other screening activities. The screening process at the decentralised level of government involved the provinces, municipalities, and water boards.[53] In the process, the decentralised government authorities have been supported in several ways.[54] The PID has distributed a brochure with an action plan for the screening process, organised several informational meetings throughout the country, and was available for questions concerning the screening. Moreover, the (abovementioned) associations VNG, IPO, and UvW have actively contributed to the screening by

[50] See also Recital 17–18 SD.

[51] *Kamerstukken II* 2007/08, 31 579, nr. 3, p. 52.

[52] *Kamerstukken II* 2007/08, 31 579, nr. 3, p. 52.

[53] *Kamerstukken II* 2007/08, 31 579, nr. 3, p. 53.

[54] *Kamerstukken II* 2008/09, 31 579, nr. 6, pp. 24–25.

coordinating the entire procedure and providing provinces, municipalities, and water boards with model rules.

As to the results of the screening process, the Dutch legislator points out that the number of inconsistencies with the SD that have been found was very limited.[55] Both at the central level and at the level of provinces, municipalities, and water boards, relatively few requirements needed adjustment.[56] As will be elaborated upon below, the reason for this limited amount of inconsistencies with the requirements of the SD is that the Netherlands had already been very active in recent years in reducing unnecessary and 'burdensome' economic legislation. Operations that promoted deregulation and competition, on the one hand, and realised a simplification of authorisation schemes, on the other hand, meant that much of the legislation and rules applying to services were already in conformity with the requirements of the SD. The inconsistencies that were found were resolved by the authority responsible. For some issues, however, it was found that making various small amendments in national law all at once was more effective. As mentioned above, these adjustments have been made by the introduction of the Amendment Act SD.

2 Individual Articles of the Services Directive

2.1 Article 6 SD: Point of Single Contact (POSC)

2.1.1 Establishment of the POSC

As mentioned above, the Dutch government has chosen to implement the SD through enactment of a separate act, that is, the Services Act (*Dienstenwet*). This act contains the general provisions, whereas amendments to sectoral legislation have been incorporated, *inter alia,* in the Amendment Act SD (*Aanpassingswet Dienstenrichtlijn*). Chapter 2 (Articles 5 and 6) and Chapter 3 (Articles 7–16) of the Services Act arrange the establishment of the Dutch (virtual) POSC, the *Dienstenloket*. The *Dienstenloket* allows service providers, *inter alia,* to electronically follow the procedures and formalities needed to legitimately provide a service. No new authority has been established to implement Article 6 SD; the service has been accommodated with the existing website 'Answers for businesses' (*Antwoord voor bedrijven*).[57]

In short, the *Dienstenloket* has three functions: the information function, the support function, and the transaction function.[58] The information function refers to

---

[55] *Kamerstukken II* 2008/09, 31 859, nr. 3, p. 4.

[56] See more extensively *Kamerstukken II* 2008/09, 31 579, nr. 6, pp. 26–27; Schiebroek 2009b, pp. 143–172.

[57] See http://www.antwoordvoorbedrijven.nl.

[58] *Kamerstukken II* 2007/08, 31 579, nr. 3, pp. 24–27; BZK 2009, pp. 21–22.

the right to information of Article 7 SD. Pursuant to the information function, the *Dienstenloket* should provide the information required for all the procedures and formalities regarding the service concerned to service providers and recipients. For consumers, additional information is available through the Dutch Consumer Authority. The support function entails an obligation to provide assistance concerning the interpretation and application of the licence regime. Finally, the transaction function refers to the obligation stipulated in Article 8 SD and therefore ensures that all procedures and formalities can be handled through the *Dienstenloket*.

As mentioned above, the establishment of a POSC is one of the three subject areas from the SD where the Dutch legislator has chosen to go beyond transposition of the minimum requirements in the SD. In its explanatory memorandum of the Services Act, the legislator states that mere implementation of the minimum requirements would result in the undesirable situation where domestic service providers are treated differently than service providers in another MS.[59] That is, the legislator in the Netherlands recognised the problem of reverse discrimination within the context of the POSC. As a result, it has been decided to extend the obligations concerning the POSC (i.e., the *Dienstenloket*) to purely domestic situations.

2.1.2 Subjective Understanding and Competence Structure

The Dutch legislator is of the opinion that the obligation to establish a POSC can be interpreted as meaning that multiple POSCs are allowed.[60] In this context, the legislator refers to Recital 48 of the SD, which states that "[t]he number of points of single contact per Member State may vary according to regional or local competencies or according to the activities concerned."[61] The Dutch government stresses, however, that considerable dispersion of the POSCs might interfere with the objective and effectiveness of the SD.

The Netherlands have chosen to establish the *Dienstenloket* as one central office, that is, a virtual one-stop shop, for service providers. All competent authorities that are relevant for the procedures and formalities of services are, pursuant to Article 14 of the Services Act, obliged to be connected to the POSC. Moreover, corresponding with the functions of the *Dienstenloket*, the competent authorities should also carry out the information, support, and transaction functions themselves. As will also be discussed below, no substantial changes regarding the allocation of administrative competences have been made.

59 *Kamerstukken II* 2007/08, 31 579, nr. 3, p. 29.

60 *Kamerstukken II* 2007/08, 31 579, nr. 3, p. 25.

61 Recital 48 SD.

2.1.3 Authorities and POSC-Function

As mentioned above, the task of the POSC has been attributed to the website 'Answers for businesses', which also existed prior to the implementation process of the SD. The *Dienstenloket* is meant to function as an intersection in the network between different administrative authorities.[62] Besides the fact that the *Dienstenloket* and several competent authorities have now specifically been given the obligation to connect to the POSC and carry out the information, support, and transaction functions, no changes in the division of powers and substantive decision making of these authorities have been made.

2.1.4 Involvement of Private Partners

Private partners such as social partners and unions were consulted during the transposition process of Article 6 SD. In this process, companies were able to sign up for an electronic message box (see below) during a trial period until June 2009 and give feedback to the government through questionnaires.

2.1.5 Liability

The responsibility for the introduction and continuous operation of the Dutch POSC lies with the Minister of Economic Affairs. The legislator in the Netherlands has recognised that questions of liability may become relevant, especially with regard to procedures by electronic means.[63] The virtual POSC (*Dienstenloket*) may, for example, be under maintenance, but it is also possible that the information, support, and transaction functions do not perform adequately. However, the Dutch legislator has been of the opinion that the nature of the obligations stipulated in the SD does not require a specific arrangement concerning liability of the POSC, since the current regime of state liability is expected to suffice.[64] In this context, it should be noted that the system of state liability in the Netherlands is, in effect, strict liability. The current regime of state liability in the Netherlands requires that the government operate according to the principles of good governance, that is, acting accurately and not unlawfully. An important aspect of the implementation of the SD in the Netherlands has therefore been to provide proper definitions of the information function, support function, and transaction function in the Services Act, on the basis of which liability will be assessed.

---

[62] BZK 2009, p. 57.

[63] *Kamerstukken II* 2007/08, 31 579, nr. 3, pp. 39–41.

[64] *Kamerstukken II* 2007/08, 31 579, nr. 3, p. 39.

2.2 Article 7 SD: Right to Information

As mentioned above, the POSC has been accommodated with an existing website (i.e., 'Answers for businesses'). As a result, prior to the implementation of the SD, information on various relevant issues for service providers and recipients was already provided online. Pursuant to the SD, however, there is now a legal obligation for competent authorities to ensure that relevant information is easily accessible to providers and recipients and that it can be accessed by the public without obstacle. Moreover, the information available should now also entail information on rules and authorisation schemes in other MSs. Any information given should be provided in a clear and unambiguous manner. In this respect, the Dutch legislator notes that the extent to which this obligation can be adequately satisfied depends on the information provision of other MSs and on the efforts of the Commission regarding the facilitation of information exchange.[65] Although neither the SD nor the Services Act stipulates that the information available should be available in foreign languages,[66] it is expected that translations of at least basic information will be given in English.[67]

The right to information as laid down in Article 7 SD has been included in the Services Act. Article 7 (a) of the Services Act stipulates that information regarding the requirements and licence regimes for the provision of services, as well as the contact details of the competent authorities, should be easily accessible through the *Dienstenloket*, and thereby codifies both Article 7 (1) (a) and Article 7 (1) (b) SD. Similarly, Article 7 (b) of the Services Act transposes Article 7 (1) (d) SD, since it stipulates that information concerning the means of redress in case of a dispute between competent authorities and a services provider or recipient, between a provider and a recipient, or between providers should be easily accessible. Next, Article 7 (c) of the Services Act gives effect to the obligation to provide easily accessible information on the means of, and conditions for, accessing public registers and databases on providers and services, and therefore transposes Article 7 (1) (c) SD. Finally, Article 7 (d) of the Services Act addresses Article 7 (1) (e) SD by stipulating that information regarding the contact details of the associations or organisations, other than the competent authorities, from which providers or recipients may obtain practical assistance must be easily accessible.

As mentioned above, implementation of the obligations concerning the establishment of a POSC has gone beyond the minimum requirements of the SD. As a result, the right to information referred to in Article 7 SD does not only apply to transnational services and the transnational establishment, but is also seen as compulsory for purely domestic situations.

---

[65] *Kamerstukken II* 2007/08, 31 579, nr. 3, p. 34.

[66] Article 7 (5) SD does, however, encourage points of single contact to make the information provided available in other Community languages.

[67] *Kamerstukken II* 2007/08, 31 579, nr. 3, p. 33.

2.3 *Article 8 SD: Procedures by Electronic Means*

2.3.1 Establishment

Prior to the SD, Dutch administrative authorities did not have the obligation to establish electronic procedures under the General Administrative Law Act, but could nevertheless use them to communicate with citizens unless procedural requirements made this impossible.[68]

As mentioned above, the obligation in Article 8 SD to establish procedures by electronic means is referred to by the Dutch legislator in the explanatory memorandum of the Services Act as the transaction function.[69] Pursuant to Article 8 SD, MSs shall ensure that all procedures and formalities relating to access to a service activity and to the exercise thereof may be easily completed, at a distance and by electronic means, through the relevant POSC and with the relevant competent authorities. As mentioned above, the Netherlands have established the virtual POSC *Dienstenloket*.

As discussed above, the Services Act stipulates the obligation for the Dutch Minister of Economic Affairs to establish a virtual POSC, whereas competent authorities are obliged to connect to and use the virtual POSC when engaged in procedures and formalities relating to access to a service activity. The *Dienstenloket* therefore functions as an electronic intersection for exchanging information between service providers and competent authorities. The *Dienstenloket* functions through the website 'Answers for businesses', where it is possible for service providers and competent authorities to exchange messages through an electronic message box (*Berichtenbox*). This message box operates in a secured electronic environment and allows service providers to complete and submit forms electronically or by printing them, filling them out manually, and then scanning and emailing them to the *Dienstenloket*.

An important issue when dealing with procedures and formalities relating to access to a service activity is the electronic signature. The *Dienstenloket* allows electronic signatures to be sent, but—depending on the procedure concerned—a scanned signature may also be required. Pursuant to the recent Commission decisions regarding the facilitation and improvement of the cross-border use of electronic signatures for completing procedures and formalities to a service activity,[70] the

---

[68] See Articles 2:13–2:17 of the General Administrative Law Act.

[69] *Kamerstukken II* 2007/08, 31 579, nr. 3, p. 27.

[70] Commission decision of 2 October 2009 setting out the practical arrangements for the exchange of information by electronic means between Member States under Chapter VI of Directive 2006/123/EC of the European Parliament and of the Council on services in the internal market, *OJ* L 263/32, and Commission decision of 16 October 2009 setting out measures facilitating the use of procedures by electronic means through the 'points of single contact' under Directive 2006/123/EC of the European Parliament and of the Council on services in the internal market, *OJ* L 274/36.

Dutch government has amended the Services Act accordingly.[71] The body responsible for the establishment, maintenance, and publication of the so-called 'trusted list' will be the Dutch telecommunications and postal regulatory authority, *Onafhankelijke Post en Telecommunicatie Autoriteit* (OPTA).

2.3.2 Innovative Impact

The Netherlands were already increasingly making use of electronic procedures, though the fact that service providers from other MSs may now also make use of this instrument appears to be a substantial innovation. That is, prior to the SD, there was a move towards e-government in the Netherlands in 1994. The Netherlands was one of the first countries in Europe to start this. The SD, however, formed an impetus to expand and professionalise these services. The EU also has initiatives in this area to improve e-government services in the MSs, such as the i2010 e-Government Action Plan.[72] Another innovation is the electronic message box, which already appears to be developing into a generic message box, meaning that it will be expanded into a communication channel not only for businesses but also for citizens. Similarly, Commission decisions concerning the facilitation of the cross-border use of electronic signatures appear to have induced the legislator to develop a legal regime covering this issue.

2.3.3 Removal of Other Means

For the time being, the electronic procedures are complementary to the existing system. The possibility exists to switch between the electronic procedures and the regular procedure at any time, regardless of the form in which the proceedings were initiated.

2.4 Article 9 SD: Authorisation Schemes

2.4.1 Means of Less Restrictive Measure

Pursuant to Article 9 SD, MSs have an obligation not to make access to a service activity or the exercise thereof subject to an authorisation scheme unless (i) the authorisation scheme does not discriminate against the provider in question, (ii) the need for an authorisation scheme is justified by an overriding reason relating to the public interest, and (iii) the objective pursued cannot be attained by

---

71 *Kamerstukken II* 2009/10, 31 859, nr. 4.

72 See e.g., COM (2006) 173 final.

means of a less restrictive measure, in particular because an a posteriori inspection would take place too late to be genuinely effective. The SD defines the concept of 'authorisation scheme' as

> "any procedure under which a provider or recipient is in effect required to take steps in order to obtain from a competent authority a formal decision, or an implied decision, concerning access to a service activity or the exercise thereof".[73]

The Dutch government is of the opinion that this includes an obligation to register in order to be allowed to provide a service.[74] As a result, because the concept of 'authorisation scheme' is defined rather broadly, it can be said that most services are regulated and require some form of authorisation.

In this context, it has been noted by Van Meerten that it is very difficult to point out which services typically require prior authorisation in the Netherlands.[75] It is therefore not very helpful to provide an overview of all services that require authorisation in the Netherlands, since this would not provide much insight in the discussions and problems of the implementation of the SD in the Netherlands. The uncertainty in determining which services require prior authorisation is partly caused by the fact that the Dutch requirements do not distinguish between 'temporary' and 'permanent' activities, that is, services and establishment. Instead, the legislation focuses on the regulation of a certain activity. In this respect, it should be noted that the Dutch legislator is of the opinion that Article 16 (2) SD, which includes a prohibition of subjecting the provision of services (not establishment) to an authorisation, contains no black list and that Article 16 (3) SD can therefore derogate from Article 16 (2) SD.[76] This issue will be further discussed below.

The implementation of the SD appears not to have made changes to the Dutch approach in regulating services. In this context Hessel points out that, similar to the situation in Germany, it is possible to require a notification that would merely serve as an information system instead.[77] Especially in light of this proportionality test of Article 9 (1) (c) SD, this obligatory notification may be a good alternative to the current authorisation schemes.[78] As of yet, it appears that the Dutch legislator has not chosen to change its approach and substitute its authorisation schemes for obligatory notifications.[79]

---

[73] Article 4 (6) SD.

[74] *Kamerstukken II* 2007/08, 31 579, nr. 3, p. 43; BZK 2009, p. 37.

[75] Van Meerten 2008, p. 252.

[76] See also Van Meerten 2008, pp. 254–255.

[77] Hessel 2007a.

[78] Hessel refers to Case C-302/97, *Klaus Konle* v. *Republik Österreich* [1999] ECR I-3099; Joined cases C-515/99, C-519/99 to C-524/99 and C-526/99 to C-540/99, *Hans Reisch and Others* v. *Bürgermeister der Landeshauptstadt Salzburg and Grundverkehrsbeauftragter des Landes Salzburg and Anton Lassacher and Others* v. *Grundverkehrsbeauftragter des Landes Salzburg and Grundverkehrslandeskommission des Landes Salzburg* [2002] ECR I-02157; Case C-425/01, *Margarethe Ospelt and Schlössle Weissenberg Familienstiftung* [2003] ECR I-09743.

[79] Hessel et al. 2009, pp. 61–62.

2.4.2 Existing Authorisation Schemes/Procedures

In general, it is possible to distinguish three types of authorisation procedures in the Netherlands. First, there is the authorisation within the concept of Dutch administrative law (*vergunning*). This concerns the authorisation procedure that is most commonly used in the Netherlands. In this context, it should be stressed that the Netherlands have been very active in recent years in reducing 'unnecessary' and 'burdensome' economic legislation.[80] An example of these legislative initiatives is the operation '*Marktwerking, Deregulering en Wetgevingskwaliteit*' (which might be translated as Competition, Deregulation, and Quality of Legislation).[81] This large-scale operation has drastically amended the regulation of economic activity with respect to many services and economic activities in general. More recently, the Dutch government initiated programmes specifically targeted at simplifying authorisation schemes, both on a central and a decentralised level.[82] In the project 'IPAL', the Dutch ministries were responsible for the reduction of the administrative burden for businesses, and it is expected that this will lead to a reduction of that administrative burden in 2011 of 25%.[83] Similarly, the operation '*Project Vereenvoudiging Vergunningen*' aimed to simplify authorisation procedures and specifically concerns the necessity and costs of authorisations as an instrument.[84] As a result, these efforts towards deregulation of economic activity have led the Dutch legislator to consider that unnecessary authorisations have already been abolished; the authorisations that remain are expected to meet the requirements of necessity and proportionality.[85] The changes that have been made to authorisation procedures therefore generally do not concern Article 9 SD, but one or more of the subsequent Articles (see especially the concept of *lex silencio positivo* of Article 13 SD, question 8 of the questionnaire, here Sect. 2.8).

An example of such an authorisation that has been mentioned within the context of the implementation of the SD (though due to an amendment following Article 13 SD) is the regulation of the mining sector. The *Mijnbouwwet* (i.e., the 'Mining Act') stipulates that an authorisation is required for depositing potential hazardous materials. The Dutch legislator considers that this authorisation satisfies the criteria stipulated in Article 9 SD, since it does not discriminate, is justified by an overriding reason relating to the public interest (i.e., the protection of the environment, public health, and public security), and is proportionate.[86] With regard to the requirement of proportionality, the legislator considers that this activity requires (ex ante) authorisation because the public interest would not be adequately safeguarded with merely an *a posteriori* (ex post) inspection.

---

[80] See also Van Meerten 2008, pp. 251–252.

[81] *Kamerstukken II* 2007/08, 31 579, nr. 3, p. 24.

[82] *Kamerstukken II* 2007/08, 31 579, nr. 3, p. 24.

[83] Van Meerten 2008, p. 251.

[84] Van Meerten 2008, p. 252.

[85] *Kamerstukken II* 2008/09, 31 859, nr. 3, p. 7.

[86] *Kamerstukken II* 2008/09, 31 859, nr. 3, p. 16.

A second type of authorisation procedure in the Netherlands concerns the obligation to register prior to legitimately providing a service. This authorisation procedure therefore also functions on an ex ante basis. Although this instrument does not fall within the concept of *vergunning* in Dutch administrative law, it is included within the concept of 'authorisation' as meant in the SD.[87] This understanding is based on the fact that sometimes authorisations are not provided upon request. A notification may, for instance, change into an authorisation if the service provider can only enter the market after a certain period of time after notification and the competent authority meanwhile issues an authorisation including certain conditions that the service provider must fulfil. It was therefore an issue needing considerable attention during the implementation procedure that the obligation to register should also be justified by an overriding reason relating to the public interest and satisfy the proportionality requirement in that it cannot be attained by a less restrictive measure.[88]

Finally, there is the instrument of a simple notification that merely serves to inform the government that the provision of a service has commenced. That is, pursuant to this simple notification, an applicant can start his activity once notified, but the authority still may materially examine the project (and may prohibit the activity on an *ex post* basis). The Dutch deregulation of economic activity has, however, primarily focussed on whether or not an authorisation procedure is justified and cost effective, and not so much—as in the European concept of proportionality—on whether the instrument that has been chosen in the procedure could have been substituted by a less restrictive alternative. Correspondingly, the implementation process has, as of yet, not led to a considerable change towards a reduction in authorisation schemes in favour of notification requirements.[89]

2.4.3 Simple Notifications

Simple notification requirements, which, by definition, merely aim to notify the competent authorities (and cannot lead to an authorisation), are, according to the Dutch view, not included in Article 9 SD.[90] According to Hessel, this view is substantiated by case law of the ECJ.[91]

---

[87] *Kamerstukken II* 2007/08, 31 579, nr. 3, p. 43; BZK 2009, p. 43; Hessel et al. 2009, p. 61.

[88] See BZK 2009, p. 37 ff.

[89] Hessel et al. 2009, p. 63.

[90] Schiebroek 2009a, p. 98.

[91] Hessel 2007a, Hessel et al. 2009, pp. 63–64. See Case C-302/97, *Klaus Konle* v. *Republik Österreich* [1999] ECR I-3099; Joined cases C-515/99, C-519/99 to C-524/99 and C-526/99 to C-540/99, *Hans Reisch and Others* v. *Bürgermeister der Landeshauptstadt Salzburg and Grundverkehrsbeauftragter des Landes Salzburg and Anton Lassacher and Others* v. *Grundverkehrsbeauftragter des Landes Salzburg and Grundverkehrslandeskommission des Landes Salzburg* [2002] ECR I-02157; Case C-425/01, *Margarethe Ospelt and Schlössle Weissenberg Familienstiftung* [2003] ECR I-09743.

2.5 Article 10 SD: Conditions for the Granting of Authorisation

2.5.1 Recognition of Requirements

The recognition of authorisations granted by other MSs has been implemented by Articles 30, 35, and 55 of the Services Act. Pursuant to Article 30 of the Services Act, a service provider automatically satisfies the requirements of an authorisation scheme if he or she has already satisfied similar criteria in another MS. Moreover, a competent authority is obliged to check whether a service provider has already satisfied similar criteria in another MS.

2.5.2 Granting Authorisation Throughout the Whole National Territory and Exceptions, Entitlement to Grant Authorisation, Court Review of Administrative Decisions, Reasoning of Administrative Decisions

Below, we will subsequently deal with implementation issues of Articles 10 (4), 10 (5) and 10 (6) SD. Article 10 (4) SD stipulates that an authorisation shall enable the provider to have access to the service activity or to exercise that activity throughout the national territory, including by means of setting up agencies, subsidiaries, branches, or offices, except where an authorisation for each individual establishment or a limitation of the authorisation to a certain part of the territory is justified by an overriding reason relating to the public interest. Pursuant to Article 10 (5) SD, an authorisation shall be granted as soon as it is established in light of an appropriate examination that the conditions for authorisation have been met. Finally, according to Article 10 (6) SD, any decision from the competent authorities, including refusal or withdrawal of an authorisation, except in the case of the granting of an authorisation, shall be fully reasoned and shall be open to challenge before the courts or other instances of appeal.

None of these provisions required specific implementation in the Netherlands, since their effects were, according to the legislator, already adequately safeguarded within Dutch law.[92] Following Article 10 (4) SD, a competent authority may not limit the service activity to a certain part of the territory. Dutch authorisation schemes are, however, granted following an application. Consequently, this application, and therefore the applicant, determines the jurisdictional scope of the authorisation. If no specific jurisdiction is mentioned in the application, the authorisation is in principle limited to the jurisdiction of the competent authority, which is in accordance with Article 10 (7) SD.[93] There are, however, two exceptions to this regime.[94] First, the legal basis for the authorisation scheme may explicitly stipulate that the scope is jurisdictionally limited, in which case the

[92] *Kamerstukken II* 2007/08, 31 579, nr. 3, pp. 22–24.

[93] See also Recital 59 SD.

[94] *Kamerstukken II* 2007/08, 31 579, nr. 3, p. 23.

conformity of the limitation with the SD has already been confirmed in previous screening operations. Second, additional requirements may be attached to the authorisation, in which case Article 3:46 General Administrative Law Act (Awb) requires proper reasoning. This will also cover the overriding reason relating to the public interest.

Next, Article 10 (5) SD stipulates that an authorisation shall be granted as soon as it is established, in light of an appropriate examination that the conditions for authorisation have been met. This is in accordance with the legal regime that existed prior to the introduction of the SD. No legislative changes were therefore necessary.[95] Correspondingly, decisions concerning the granting of authorisations are reviewed with a limited (or marginal) standard of review, that is, whether the authority has reached its conclusion in the legally correct manner. Similarly, Article 10 (6) SD, according to which authorities have an obligation to fully reason their decisions, was considered to be already sufficiently safeguarded in Division 3.7 of the General Administrative Law Act, which deals with reasons for orders. Article 3:46 of the General Administrative Law Act, for example, states that "[a]n order shall be based on proper reasons." As a result, the legislator did not see a need to implement Article 10 (6) SD.[96]

2.5.3 Allocation of Competences

Corresponding with Article 10 (7) SD, the legislator in the Netherlands has not made amendments to the allocation of the competences, at the local or regional level, of authorities granting authorisations. As mentioned before, this has been one of the main principles used during the implementation of the SD in the Netherlands.

2.6 Article 11 SD: Duration of Authorisation

Article 11 (1) of the SD has been implemented through Articles 33 (1) and 33 (2) of the Services Act. Article 33 (1) of the Services Act is a translation of Article 11 (1) SD and therefore stipulates that an authorisation granted to a provider shall not be for a limited period, except where (a) the authorisation is being automatically renewed or is subject only to the continued fulfilment of requirements, (b) the number of available authorisations is limited by an overriding reason relating to the public interest, or (c) a limited authorisation period can be justified by an overriding reason relating to the public interest. Article 33 (1) of the Services Act therefore applies to instances when the competent authority determines the

95 *Kamerstukken II 2007/08*, 31 579, nr. 3, pp. 22–23.

96 *Kamerstukken II 2007/08, 31 579*, nr. 3, pp. 22–23.

limitation of the period to which the authorisation applies. In contrast, Article 33 (2) of the Services Act applies to authorisations for which the period to which it applies is only subject to the continued fulfilment of requirements. These authorisations shall, in correspondence with Article 11 (1) (a) SD, also not be for a limited period, except in those cases stipulated in Article 33 (1) of the Services Act.[97]

Prior to implementation of the SD, Dutch law did not have a prohibition on time-limited authorisations. The implementation of the SD into national law therefore caused a need for regulatory changes regarding this matter.[98]

2.7 Article 12 SD: Selection from Among Several Candidates

Notwithstanding the general rule of Article 33 (1) of the Services Act that an authorisation granted to a provider shall not be for a limited period, Articles 33 (4) (b) and 33 (5) of the Services Act stipulate that this does not apply to situations where the number of authorisations available for a given activity is limited because of the scarcity of available natural resources or technical capacity. These provisions therefore implement the requirements of Article 12 SD.

The Dutch legislator points out that most—but not necessarily all—services for which authorisations are required but where the number of authorisations is limited for reasons mentioned above will fall outside the scope of the SD.[99] The reason is because this often involves services that are specifically excluded from the scope of the Directive, such as certain services of general economic interest, for example, those that may exist in the field of transport. Moreover, during the screening of the authorisation procedures, it was found that at the central level situations where the number of authorisations available for a given activity is limited because of the scarcity of available natural resources or technical capacity only occur sporadically, whereas at a lower level this was not a relevant issue at all.[100] As a result, the Dutch legislator concluded that there was no need for further structural implementation of the criteria regarding the selection procedure of Article 12 (1) SD, but noted that additional, sector-specific legislation (and instructions for the legislature) would be introduced if the screening process proved this to be necessary.[101]

The criteria regarding the selection procedure for authorisations that are limited because of the scarcity of available natural resources or technical capacity varies, depending on the type of allocation procedure chosen. In this context, it should be mentioned that the Dutch government makes use of various allocation procedures,

---

[97] See also *Kamerstukken II* 2007/08, 31 579, nr. 3, pp. 111–112.

[98] BZK 2009, pp. 38–39.

[99] *Kamerstukken II* 2007/08, 31 579, nr. 3, p. 112.

[100] *Kamerstukken II* 2007/08, 31 579, nr. 3, pp. 19–20.

[101] *Kamerstukken II* 2007/08, 31 579, nr. 3, pp. 19–20; Schiebroek 2009a, pp. 106–107.

including auctions, beauty contests, first-come-first-served allocation, grandfather rights, and lotteries.[102] In all of these procedures the General Administrative Law Act stipulates that the government shall act in correspondence with an adequate duty of care and shall weigh the interests of those directly involved.[103]

Although the Dutch legislator has considered that structural implementation of the criteria regarding the selection procedure of Article 12 (1) SD was unnecessary, it saw a need to implement Article 12 (2) SD.[104] Article 33 (5) of the Services Act therefore stipulates that when the number of authorisations is limited because of the scarcity of available natural resources or technical capacity, authorisation shall be granted for an appropriate limited period.

2.8 Article 13 SD: Authorisation Procedures

2.8.1 A Priori Determination of the Duration of Administrative Procedures, General Rule for the Duration and Exceptions

The duration of an administrative procedure in the Netherlands is determined by the General Administrative Law Act (*Algemene wet bestuursrecht*). Article 4:13 of the General Administrative Law Act stipulates that an administrative decision shall be made within the time limit prescribed by statutory regulation or, in the absence of such a time limit, within a reasonable period after receiving the application. This does not correspond with the requirements of Article 13 (3) SD, however, which states that the application will be processed as quickly as possible and, in any event, within a reasonable period that is *fixed* and made public in advance. As a result, for services falling within the scope of the SD, the Dutch legislator has chosen to resolve this inconsistency by introducing Article 31 of the Services Act.[105] Pursuant to this provision, an administrative decision regarding an administrative procedure within the context of the SD shall be made within a maximum time limit of eight weeks. Article 31 (2) of the Services Act incorporates the possibility stated in Article 13 (3) SD that, when justified by the complexity of the issue, the time period may be extended once, by the competent authority, for a limited time. Since changes have only been made in the Services Act and not in the General Administrative Law Act, this rule on the duration of procedures only applies within the scope of the SD. That is, the prescribed duration of the time period within the General Administrative Law Act is a *lex generalis*; different durations may be prescribed in different, specific administrative laws such as the Services Act.

---

[102] See e.g., Van Ommeren 2004.

[103] See Division 3.2 of the General Administrative Law Act concerning 'The duty of care and the weighing of interests', as well as Drahmann 2009.

[104] *Kamerstukken II* 2007/08, 31 579, nr. 3, p. 19.

[105] *Kamerstukken II* 2007/08, 31 579, nr. 3, pp. 108–109.

2.8.2 Tacit Authorisation

The issue that has probably been discussed the most during the implementation process of the SD in the Netherlands is the transposition of the provisions concerning the tacit fictitious authorisation, that is, the *lex silencio positivo* (LSP).[106] The Dutch legislator has seen a substantial improvement in the instrument of the tacit fictitious authorisation and has therefore decided to extend this into national law so that it will also apply to purely domestic situations.[107] The tacit fictitious authorisation has therefore been transposed in the General Administrative Law Act. Below, we will subsequently deal with the interpretation of the legislator concerning the LSP, the situation before implementation, and the situation after implementation before finally reflecting on some peculiarities regarding the discussion.

Pursuant to Article 13 (4) SD, the MSs have an obligation to introduce the *Lex Silencio Positivo*. That is, MSs should incorporate in their legal regime a system according to which an authorisation shall be deemed to have been granted when there has been a failure of response within the time period set or extended in accordance with Article 13 (3) SD. However, different arrangements may be put in place where justified by overriding reasons relating to the public interest, including a legitimate interest of third parties.[108] In this context, the legislator stipulates that such different arrangements could include national rules according to which, in the absence of a response of the competent authority, the application is deemed to have been rejected.[109]

Prior to the implementation of the SD, unlike in many MSs, the instrument of the *Lex Silencio Positivo* was not commonly used in the Netherlands,[110] whereas it was generally recognised that authorities exceeding the time limit formed a considerable problem.[111] The old regime did allow interested parties (or applicants) redress to an order that had not been made in due time.[112] It was one of the agreements the current Dutch government reached, however, to combat this problem of exceeding time limits. The introduction of the LSP in national law

---

106 See e.g., *Kamerstukken II* 2007/08, 31 579, nr. 3, pp. 47–52; *Kamerstukken II* 2008/09, 31 859, nr. 3, pp. 7–8; *Kamerstukken I* 2008/09, 31 579, nr. C, pp. 21–26; *Kamerstukken II* 2008/09, 31 579, nr. 14; *Kamerstukken II* 2008/09, 31 579, nr. 6, pp. 19–24; *Kamerstukken II* 2008/09, 31 579, nr. 15; *Kamerstukken II* 2008/09, 31 579, nr. F, pp. 1–5; BZK 2009, pp. 42–49; Schiebroek 2009a, pp. 99–105.

107 See e.g., BZK 2009, p. 19.

108 Article 13 (4) SD.

109 See *Kamerstukken II* 2007/08, 31 579, nr. 3, p. 49, as well as Recital 63 SD.

110 It had been used, for example, in the Dutch Competition Act.

111 Schiebroek 2009a, p. 99.

112 That is, pursuant to Article 6:2 General Administrative Law Act (Awb), the failure to make an order in due time has been equated with an order for the purposes of statutory regulations governing objections and appeals.

therefore gives effect not only to the implementation of the SD but also to the agreement of the current government coalition.[113]

As mentioned above, the concept of the tacit fictitious authorisation has been implemented in general administrative law. A new section specifically designed for the LSP (Sect. 1.4) has been included in the General Administrative Law Act. It should be mentioned, however, that the original proposal for implementation of the LSP has been amended and broadened to apply automatically to all authorisation schemes within the scope of the SD.[114] Although the *Lex Silencio Positivo* has also been introduced for purely domestic situations, the new regime does make a distinction between the application for authorisations falling under the scope of the SD and those falling outside the SD's scope.[115] On the one hand, for authorisations falling outside the scope of the SD, the instrument of the LSP does not automatically apply. The (decentralised) government can therefore decide whether or not it wants the instrument to apply. On the other hand, for authorisations that do fall under the scope of the SD, the LSP will automatically apply as of 2012. (Unfortunately, the Dutch government does not provide any explanation as to why this transition period is necessary.) That is, the Dutch legislator has introduced a transition period (in Article 65 of the Services Act) after which the *Lex Silencio Positivo* will automatically apply to authorisations within the scope of the SD, unless the legislator has explicitly specified otherwise in the law. The legislator will make such exceptions when there are overriding reasons relating to the public interest.

By contrast, the LSP will not automatically apply before 2012. The regime of Article 65 of the Services Act stipulates that, until 2012, the LSP is not to apply to authorisations granted by the decentralised government. When it appears, however, that there are no overriding reasons relating to the public interest justifying this disapplication, the competent authority will have to ensure that it does apply. For other authorisations falling under the scope of the SD but outside the group of authorisations categorically exempted by Article 65 of the Services Act, the competent authority will, prior to 2012, have to confirm that the tacit fictitious authorisation applies or does not apply, depending on whether there are overriding reasons relating to the public interest justifying disapplication.

When the *Lex Silencio Positivo* applies, the same rules apply as to formally granted authorisations. As a result, the authorisation can be revoked or nullified. The LSP will take legal effect within three days after the time limit has been exceeded. Moreover, the tacit fictitious authorisation should be confirmed by the competent authority within two weeks. If confirmation is not given in due time, the applicant is allowed to take legal action.

The implementation of the tacit fictitious authorisation has caused quite some discussion in the Netherlands. One of the issues that caused discussion in

---

[113] Schiebroek 2009a, pp. 101–102.

[114] *Kamerstukken II* 2008/09, 31 579, nr. 14.

[115] Schiebroek 2009a, p. 100.

Parliament is the effect the LSP has on third parties. The legislator has emphasised, however, that it has extensively weighed the interests of parties before determining the new regime in the General Administrative Law Act. Other issues were the fact that the instrument of the LSP is not in conformity with all requirements stipulated in general administrative law (e.g., the requirements that administrative decisions include proper reasoning and that the administrative authority shall gather the necessary information concerning the relevant facts and the interests to be weighed).[116] A third issue that has caused debate is the transposition period that has been introduced by Article 65 of the Services Act. In particular, decentralised government authorities were sometimes confused as to when the LSP should apply to a specific authorisation.[117] Despite these difficulties, it is generally expected that the introduction (and broadening) of the SD's obligation concerning the tacit fictitious authorisation will result in an improvement in administrative law.[118]

2.9 Articles 14, 15, 16 SD

2.9.1 Need of Adaptation?

The Dutch legislator is of the opinion that none of these articles need implementation in statutory law. Articles 14, 15, and 16 SD need no further implementation in national law because they form prohibitions that are to be incorporated in the framework within which the Dutch government determines requirements and authorisations. As a result, the prohibitions are to be safeguarded by de facto government behaviour, and not by statutory law.[119] With regard to Article 14 SD, the legislator points out that these prohibited requirements have already been sufficiently safeguarded within Dutch law and therefore need no transposition at all.[120] As to Articles 15 and 16 SD, the Dutch government considers that these prohibitions should be implemented in various instructions for the legislature, including a handbook for the implementation of European legislation and Instructions for Regulations (*Aanwijzingen voor de regelgeving*).[121] Furthermore, the legislator stresses that Articles 15 and 16 SD are part of an extensive screening process and will be included in the report that is, in accordance with Article 39 (5) SD, to be presented to the European Commission. According to the legislator, this will serve as an additional safeguard that these provisions will not be infringed upon.

---

[116] *Kamerstukken II* 2007/08, 31 579, nr. 3, p. 50.

[117] Schiebroek 2009a, p. 101.

[118] Schiebroek 2009a, pp. 104–105.

[119] *Kamerstukken II* 2007/08, 31 579, nr. 3, p. 21.

[120] *Kamerstukken II* 2007/08, 31 579, nr. 3, p. 138.

[121] *Kamerstukken II* 2007/08, 31 579, nr. 3, p. 21.

A remark on Article 16 SD, which has also been made when discussing Article 9 SD, is that the regulation of economic activity in the Netherlands does not distinguish between 'temporary' and 'permanent' activities, that is, services and establishment. In this respect, it was already noted that the Dutch legislator is of the opinion that Article 16 (2) SD, which includes a prohibition on subjecting the provision of services to an authorisation, contains no black list and that Article 16 (3) SD can therefore derogate from Article 16 (2) SD.[122] Moreover, it has also been mentioned that the implementation of the SD does not appear to have changed this Dutch approach in regulating services. Similar to the implementation of Article 9 SD, the legislator is of the opinion that there is no need for transposition into national law, because the doctrines established by the Court apply to Treaty provisions that are directly applicable in the national legal order.[123] As a result, no further amendments in national law were considered necessary.

The Dutch legislator does recognise, however, that although Article 16 SD corresponds to a large extent with the doctrine established on the freedom of services as laid down in Article 56 TFEU (ex Article 49 EC), there is an important difference. Article 16 SD stipulates that an MS shall not provide access to or exercise a service activity in its territory subject to compliance with any requirements that do not respect the principles of nondiscrimination, necessity, and proportionality. With regard to the necessity requirement, however, the SD does not allow justifications other than reasons of public policy, public security, public health, or the protection of the environment, whereas the case law on Article 56 TFEU (ex Article 49 EC) did allow other justifications.[124] Notwithstanding this important difference, the Dutch legislator has considered that Article 16 SD needs no implementation in statutory law, since it merely forms a prohibition for the legislature and can therefore be safeguarded through de facto behaviour.

2.9.2 Discussion on the Self-Screening of the Member States and Other Discourses

During the implementation process of the SD, the Netherlands have initiated a screening of their legislation to ascertain whether any inconsistency with the SD exists in their legal system. The screening process was divided into three parts.[125] The first part dealt with the question of whether a certain legislation was excluded from the scope of the SD. The second part asked whether the legislation that was not excluded from the SD regulated a service. The final stage concerned the screening of the legislation of Dutch municipalities and provinces. The screening operation particularly concerned the issues of necessity, proportionality, and nondiscrimination.

[122] See also Van Meerten 2008, pp. 254–255.

[123] *Kamerstukken II* 2007/08, 31 579, nr. 3, p. 20.

[124] *Kamerstukken II* 2007/08, 31 579, nr. 3, p. 21.

[125] See Van Meerten 2008, p. 253.

Especially because the Netherlands has been very active in recent years in reducing 'unnecessary' and 'burdensome' economic legislation, the amount of legislation that needed amendment was very limited.[126] When it appeared that rules needed adjustment, this would be carried out by the ministry responsible for the matter. For some changes, however, making various small amendments in national law all at once was found to be more effective. For this, the Amendment Act SD (*Aanpassingswet Dienstenrichtlijn*) was introduced.[127] With regard to the screening of the legislation of Dutch municipalities and provinces, a number of issues proved problematic and/or unclear.[128]

First, it proved to be very difficult for both municipalities and provinces to determine the exact scope of the SD and its terms and definitions, which were completely new to some civil servants. Second, as mentioned before, whereas the SD distinguishes between the freedom of services, on the one hand, and the freedom of establishment, on the other, this distinction is not made within Dutch national law. This led to some difficulties. Especially when a national measure affected both the freedom of services and the free movement of goods, problems emerged.[129] Finally, it has proven a challenging task for municipalities and provinces to justify their exceptions on Article 16 SD for the limited number of reasons provided for in Article 16 (3) SD (i.e., public policy, public security, public health, or the protection of the environment). Especially for decentralised administrative authorities, this task was rather problematic and initiated much discussion.

2.10 Articles 14–19 SD

Many of the discussions with regard to Articles 14–19 of the SD have already been outlined above, or will be explained below. Interestingly, none of these provisions have been transposed into national (statutory) law, either because the legislator considered that it was already sufficiently safeguarded within the national legal order or because it concerned instructions for de facto behaviour by the government.

One of these discussions involves the just mentioned issue that the legislator is of the opinion that there is no need to transpose Articles 14–16 SD into national statutory law. The main underlying argument for this perspective is that these provisions merely provide a framework for the legislator and can therefore be adequately safeguarded through de facto government behaviour. Articles 15 and 16 SD are, however, (to be) included in instructions for the legislature. The same argument is

[126] *Kamerstukken II* 2008/09, 31 859, nr. 3, p. 4.

[127] *Kamerstukken II* 2008/09, 31 859, nr. 2.

[128] See Hessel et al. 2009.

[129] Van Meerten 2008, pp. 253–254.

applied by the Dutch legislator when assessing Article 19 SD, which stipulates prohibited restrictions on a recipient of services supplied by a provider established in another MS. Article 19 SD is therefore merely implemented by including it in the Instructions for Regulations (*Aanwijzingen voor de regelgeving*).

As mentioned above, another key discussion in the Dutch implementation process has been on Article 16 SD. Since legislation in the Netherlands generally does not distinguish between the 'temporary' and 'permanent' activities, the difference in strictness between Articles 9 and 16 SD has raised some discussion when screening the various authorisation schemes. In this context, it has already been noted that the Dutch legislator is of the opinion that Article 16 (2) SD, which is includes a prohibition on subjecting the provision of services to an authorisation, contains no black list and that Article 16 (3) SD can therefore derogate from Article 16 (2) SD.

Van Meerten has emphasised that if Article 16 (2) SD would indeed contain a black list, the use of Article 16 (3) SD would be doubtful.[130] He also points out that the fact that the Netherlands do not distinguish between 'temporary' and 'permanent' activities might lead to incompatibility between Article 16 (2) SD and Article 9 SD if the former provision would indeed entail a black list. That is, the situation might arise in which the same authorisation scheme is permitted under Article 9 SD but prohibited under Article 16 (2) SD.[131] Concerning this matter and the tension between the limited number of justifications in Article 16 SD, on the one hand, and the rule of reason as formulated in the case law on the freedom of services, on the other, it will be interesting to see how the ECJ deals with these issues.[132]

Article 17 SD stipulates (additional) derogations from the freedom to provide services as laid down in Article 16 SD. As (the rather lengthy) Article 17 SD merely provides derogations of Article 16 SD and does not entail obligations for the MSs, the Dutch legislator points out that this provision needs, by its nature, no implementation into national law.[133] One peculiarity that has been pointed out in the literature concerns Article 17 (1) (a) SD. This provision states that Article 16 SD shall not apply to services of general economic interest (*inter alia* in the postal, electricity, and gas sectors, as well as in water distribution and supply services, wastewater services, and waste treatment).[134] It is interesting to note that where Recital 17 SD states that services of general economic interest fall within the scope of the Directive, Article 17 (1) (a) SD excludes them for one of the Directive's most important provisions, Article 16 SD. As a result, services of general economic interest, when related to the freedom of services, are to be assessed according to general Treaty rules. Moreover, the specification of a certain activity as services of general economic interest would (partially) exclude them from the scope of the SD. In this context it has already been

130 Van Meerten 2008, p. 254.

131 Van Meerten 2008, p. 255.

132 See also SER 2005, Belhadj et al. 2007.

133 *Kamerstukken II* 2007/08, 31 579, nr. 3, p. 138.

134 Belhadj et al. 2007.

mentioned that the Dutch legislator, in correspondence with the advice of the SER, did not designate certain activities of services of general economic interest to exclude them from the scope of the SD.

2.11 Articles 22–27 SD

Chapter V of the SD concerns the quality of services. Articles 22–27 SD form positively formulated obligations, that is, positive integration, and stipulate that the each MS shall make sure that service providers meet certain requirements related to their quality of service.[135] Since the Dutch legislator is of the opinion that Articles 22–27 SD concern similar obligations regarding the provision of information, it was decided to transpose them simultaneously in Articles 62 and 63 of the Services Act.

More specifically, because the Dutch legislator was of the opinion that Articles 22 (3) (e) and 27 (4) SD entailed the same obligations, although the latter provision is formulated more strictly, it has contacted the European Commission, which explained that the mere transposition of Article 27 (4) SD would indeed be sufficient to comply with both obligations.[136] Articles 22 and 27 SD concern obligations for MSs to ensure that providers make available information regarding their name, legal status, and contact details. Article 62 of the Services Act arranges the insertion of a specific section in the Dutch Civil Code (*Burgerlijk Wetboek*) that stipulates these obligations for service providers but limits them for services falling within the scope of the SD. These obligations concerning the provision of information will be enforced through both private and public law. In this context, Article 62 of the Services Act ensures that the Dutch Consumer Authority (*Consumentenautoriteit*) has the competences to enforce these information obligations from a public law perspective.[137]

The Dutch legislator has chosen not to transpose Article 23 SD, since this is not an obligation but merely a possibility for the MSs. For various reasons Articles 24 and 25 SD have also not been implemented into national law. First, similar to Articles 14–16 SD, Articles 24 and 25 SD need not be safeguarded by implementation in statutory law, since they form instructions for de facto behaviour by the government.[138] Second, Articles 24 (1) and 25 (1) SD were considered to be already sufficiently safeguarded within Dutch national law. Finally, at the time of the drafting of the Services Act, it was considered that Articles 24 (2) and 25 (2) SD might need further implementation in sector-specific legislation. However, after the screening process, it was concluded that additional implementation by the Amendment Act SD was not necessary.

---

135 Belhadj et al. 2007.

136 *Kamerstukken II* 2007/08, 31 579, nr. 3, pp. 136–137.

137 *Kamerstukken II* 2007/08, 31 579, nr. 3, pp. 136–137. See also BZK 2009, p. 23.

138 *Kamerstukken II* 2007/08, 31 579, nr. 3, pp. 20–21; BZK 2009, p. 33.

Finally, the legislator in the Netherlands argues that Article 26 SD (with the exception of the second paragraph) needs, by its very nature, no transposition into national law, since this merely concerns obligations that can be met through accompanying measures.[139] Article 26 (2) SD stipulates that MSs shall ensure that information on the significance of certain labels and the criteria for applying labels and other quality marks relating to services can be easily accessed by providers and recipients. In the Netherlands this has been implemented into national law by Articles 11 and 22 of the Services Act, which stipulate an obligation for the Minister of Economic Affairs to make this information readily accessible for service providers and service recipients, respectively. The Dutch government is of the opinion that information on labels and other quality marks related to services are primarily the responsibility of the market parties themselves, but nevertheless offers some information on these issues through *ConsuWijzer*, an initiative of the Consumer Authority, the Dutch competition authority (NMa), and the Dutch telecommunications and postal regulatory authority (OPTA).[140]

2.12 Articles 28 ff. SD: Administrative Cooperation

2.12.1 Transnational Administrative Cooperation Prior to the Implementation of the Services Directive

A large part of the Services Act has been dedicated to the implementation of Chapter VI of the SD concerning administrative cooperation. An important reason for this effort may be that, pursuant to Article 28 (8) SD, the Commission may start the infringement procedure of Article 258 TFEU (ex Article 226 EC) when MSs fail to comply with their obligation of mutual assistance.[141] Another important reason for the emphasis on administrative cooperation is that prior to the SD, Dutch national law had, in general, no provisions on transnational administrative assistance.[142] Although there were some specific provisions on this matter, *inter alia*, Articles 89g and 91 of the Dutch Competition Act (*Mededingingswet*), there was no general legal basis in Dutch law. Article 37 of the Services Act fills this gap by implementing the provisions on mutual assistance of Articles 28–31 SD. Article 37 of the Services Act states that upon request of the competent authority of another MS, the authority in charge of authorisations and notifications will provide information on the service provider. It will also carry out verifications, inspections, and investigations into the activities of a service provider if the competent

[139] *Kamerstukken II* 2007/08, 31 579, nr. 3, p. 20.

[140] *Kamerstukken II* 2007/08, 31 579, nr. 3, p. 94. See http://www.consuwijzer.nl.

[141] Schiebroek 2009a, p. 108.

[142] *Kamerstukken II* 2007/08, 31 579, nr. 3, p. 114.

authority of another MS requests so. Furthermore, all information will be provided electronically and, if possible, via the Internal Market Information System (IMI).

2.12.2 Re-Arrangement of Administrative Cooperation

Since there were no rules for transnational administrative assistance in the Netherlands prior to the SD, the implementation process created a need for a system of administrative assistance. Chapter VI of the Services Act transposes chapter VI of the SD. As a result, corresponding with the SD, the Services Act establishes a regime on administrative assistance with four different procedures.[143] First, pursuant to Articles 28 Sections 3–6, 29 and 31 SD, the Services Act establishes a basis for a general information request (Articles 37–39, 54, and 56 of the Services Act). Such a request needs to be duly motivated and the information acquired can only be used in respect of the matter for which it was requested. Second, corresponding with Article 33 SD, Articles 40–44 of the Services Act allow a competent authority to request a foreign competent authority for information on the good repute of providers. The requested information may concern information on disciplinary or administrative actions or criminal sanctions and decisions concerning insolvency or bankruptcy involving fraud. The third procedure regarding mutual assistance that has been established pursuant to the implementation of the SD does not concern a request for information, but entails the possibility of taking measures relating to the safety of services. This procedure, laid down in Articles 18–35 SD, is transposed by Articles 40–45 of the Services Act and requires a competent authority to give considerable attention to the reasoning of its request. Finally, Article 51 of the Services Act transposes the alert mechanism of Articles 29 (3) and 32 SD. This procedure stipulates that a competent authority must inform the MS of establishment, other MSs concerned, and the European Commission when it becomes aware of serious specific acts or circumstances relating to a service activity that could cause serious damage to the health or safety of persons or to the environment.

As of yet, the first three procedures should take place through the Internal Market Information System (IMI) established by the Commission. It is likely, however, that the IMI system will also be used for the fourth procedure, concerning the alert mechanism.[144] As mentioned above, the use of the IMI is one of the three subject areas of the SD that have been extended in national law to also apply to purely domestic situations. The system entails a secured electronic environment through which competent authorities of different MSs can exchange information on service providers. Moreover, the information system is also used to support the mutual assistance provisions of the revised Professional Qualifications Directive (2005/36/EC).

---

143 See also *Kamerstukken II* 2007/08, 31 579, nr. 3, pp. 58–59; BZK 2009, pp. 64–65, Schiebroek 2009a, pp.109–110.

144 *Kamerstukken II* 2007/08, 31 579, nr. 3, p. 61.

2.12.3 Provisions on Financial Compensation for Transnational Administrative Cooperation

No provisions on financial compensation for the regime of administrative assistance of Chapter VI of the SD have been included in the Services Act.

2.12.4 Adaptation of the Rules on Data Protection and Professional Secrets

In the Netherlands, rules concerning privacy and data protection have been implemented in the Personal Data Protection Act (*Wet bescherming persoonsgegevens*, Wbp). This act distinguishes between 'personal data' and 'special personal data', the latter type of data being subject to a stricter regime than the processing of ordinary personal data.[145] It is expected that the four procedures provided for by the SD and incorporated into the Services Act can be executed within the existing framework of the Personal Data Protection Act. The general information request as well as the possibility of taking measures relating to the safety of services, that is, the first and third procedures, will merely deal with personal data, and not special personal data.

By contrast, the second procedure, concerning the request of a foreign competent authority for information on the good repute of a provider, might include special personal data. The Dutch legislator argues that it is, as of yet, unclear whether the alert mechanism will deal with special personal data. This is because there is still a lot of uncertainty concerning this mechanism, since the Commission is still working on the specifics of the mechanism.[146] Regardless of this uncertainty, the alert mechanism will be executed within the existing framework of the Personal Data Protection Act.

2.13 Article 29 SD: Mutual Assistance—General Obligations for the Member State of Establishment

As mentioned above, Article 29 SD has largely been transposed into Article 37 of the Services Act. Article 29 (3) SD, however, deals with a different procedure, that is, the alert mechanism, and is therefore implemented in national law through Article 51 of the Services Act. There have been no discussions on the confirmation of unlawful business conduct.

[145] This type of information includes information on a person's religious or philosophical beliefs, race, political opinions, health, sex life, and membership of a trade union (Sauerwein and Linnemann 2001, p. 47 ff.).

[146] *Kamerstukken II* 2007/08, 31 579, nr. 3, p. 67 and pp. 123–125.

2.14 Problems and Discourses on Administrative Cooperation

One issue that has been under some discussion concerns the rather wide range of information obligations under the SD. Under the four different procedures established by Chapter VI of the SD, the information that can be exchanged may include information on criminal sanctions (see Article 33 SD). Pursuant to Article 1 (5) SD, however, the rules of criminal law are outside the subject matter of the SD.[147] The explanatory memorandum of the Services Act explains that criminal law is considered to be completely excluded from the scope of the SD and that information on Dutch juridical data and criminal records, within the scope of the Judicial Data and Criminal Records Act (*Wet justitiële en strafvorderlijke gegevens*), shall not be exchanged through the regime of administrative cooperation within the framework of the SD.[148]

The Dutch legislator is of the opinion that these types of information requests need additional safeguards, which have not been provided for in the SD. In this respect, the legislator refers to Commission initiatives regarding the exchange of criminal records as examples of how such information requests might take place while adequately safeguarding the public interests involved.[149] To act in conformity with the SD, however, the Dutch legislator has chosen to make use of the Certificate of Good Behaviour (*Verklaring omtrent het gedrag*, VoG) instead. As a result, a request for obtaining criminal records will be interpreted as a request for such a Certificate of Good Behaviour, which will be provided in accordance with the Personal Data Protection Act.[150]

Another remark concerns the implementation of Articles 30 (2) and 18 in conjunction with Article 35 SD and their relation with the country of origin principle. In this respect, it should first be noted that the Dutch government was a supporter of the original proposal of the SD, which is included this principle. Serious doubts were, however, expressed by the advisory bodies of the Council of State and the Social and Economic Council as to the limited list of public interests the MSs can rely on to restrict the free movement of services and the possible effect on longstanding regimes and rules of international private law and criminal law.[151] The final version of the SD rejects the country of origin principle.

With regard to Articles 30 (2) and 18 in conjunction with 35 SD, however, the Dutch legislator mentions that the transposition of these provisions has proven to be technically complex, since these were not formulated very clearly with regard to the rejection of the country of origin principle. Article 30 (2) SD stipulates that the MS of establishment shall not refrain from taking supervisory or enforcement measures in its territory on the grounds that the service has been provided or

[147] See also Schiebroek 2009a, pp. 110–111.

[148] *Kamerstukken II* 2007/08, 31 579, nr. 3, pp. 57–59.

[149] COM(2005) 690 final and COM(2008) 332 final.

[150] *Kamerstukken II* 2007/08, 31 579, nr. 3, pp. 116–120.

[151] See also Van Meerten 2008, pp. 264 ff.

caused damage in another MS. Similarly, Article 18 SD, in conjunction with Article 35 SD, refers to the fact that, by way of derogation from Article 16 SD and in exceptional circumstances only, an MS may, in respect of a provider established in another MS, take measures relating to the safety of services.

Although the country of origin principle has not been included in the SD, the legislator argues that the formulation of these provisions might unintentionally suggest the opposite, that is, that the Directive does embrace the country of origin principle. The legislator has therefore chosen to implement these provisions so that such an interpretation is no longer possible without harming the obligations and objectives of the SD.[152] In Articles 40–45 of the Services Act, for instance, detailed rules are laid down for measures relating to the safety of services. The competent authorities have supervisory and enforcement powers also in respect of services provided in the Netherlands by providers established in another MS.

2.15 Convergence Programme (Chapter VII of the Services Directive)

Besides the discussion mentioned above on the matter of personal data, which is related to Article 43 SD, no discussions have taken place on Chapter VII of the SD. An important reason for this absence of discussion is probably the fact that the Dutch legislator is of the opinion that, except for Articles 37 (2) and 43 SD, Chapter VII needs no implementation into national law.

By contrast, Article 37 (2) SD, pursuant to which MSs shall ensure that the codes of conduct referred to in Article 37 (1) SD are accessible by electronic means, is implemented into national law through Article 11 of the Services Act. Similar to Article 26 (2) SD regarding information on labels and other quality marks relating to services, the Dutch legislator considers that the establishment of these codes of conduct are primarily the responsibility of the market parties themselves. In this context, the legislator points out that there already has been substantial self-regulation at a European level. The codes of conduct that resulted from this self-regulation have also been made available electronically.[153] However, to ensure that Article 37 (2) SD will, in effect, be complied with, Article 11 (d) of the Services Act nevertheless stipulates the final responsibility for the Minister of Economic Affairs to ensure that the codes of conduct are accessible by electronic means.

---

[152] *Kamerstukken II* 2007/08, 31 579, nr. 3, p. 58.

[153] *Kamerstukken II* 2007/08, 31 579, nr. 3, p. 94.

3 Assessment of the Impact of the Services Directive

3.1 Extent of the Impact

As was already observed throughout this report, first, the legislator has opted for a 'minimum transposition', that is, in general it was limited to the minimum requirements laid down in the directive. Moreover, in many respects the principles and provisions of the SD directive squared well with the national policy to reduce regulatory and administrative costs and burdens. In this sense, it speeded up the already ongoing process at the national level. For these reasons the impact should not be perceived as severe.

This, however, does not mean that the implementation did not result in some important changes or may not induce changes in the long run.[154] A striking feature is the extension of various obligations to domestic services where this was believed to result in an improvement or to combat potential instances of reverse discrimination.

One of the most important innovations is, no doubt, the introduction of the tacit fictitious authorisation (the *Lex Silencio Positivo*), which has also been extended to domestic situations. It gave an important impetus to changing the rules. This was—in any case and according to many—necessary to address adequately the problem of public authorities exceeding time limits.

The same holds true for POSCs and the use of electronic procedures more in general. Both issues are not an entirely new phenomenon in Dutch law and administration. For instance, the use of electronic procedures as prescribed in the directive fit into an already ongoing process of introducing e-government. The POSC has been accommodated within an existing website.[155] However, the transposition of the SD provided an important impetus to continue on this road. It speeded up the process and also influenced the direction of this development.

The use of POSCs and, further also, the rights for information provided for in Article 7 SD and the use of the IMI have been extended beyond the scope of the SD.

It must also be stressed that a whole range of de facto steps had to be taken, such as actually connecting all the public bodies concerned with the electronic network that had to be set up under the directive and the communication facilities that had to be put in place.[156]

A final point that should be mentioned is transnational administrative assistance. In the Netherlands this was a relatively poor developed area of administrative law. No general rules were dealing with this, so, in a way, it is a novelty. While quite some transposition measures had to be enacted in this respect, the next challenge is the

---

[154] Cf. Backes 2009, who catches the assessment of the implementation in the terms 'much ado about nothing or the beginning of a new administrative culture?' On the last point he is somewhat hesitant, however.

[155] Cf. www.antwoordvoorbedrijven.nl.

[156] With one major concern remaining: the use of foreign languages. How to make the system accessible for foreign service providers?

implementation of transnational administrative assistance into the working processes of the administration.

3.2 Assessment of the Transposing Legislation

A successful minimum transposition can already be an improvement! For instance, the extensive screening of all the statutes, delegated, and other lower government legislation, and even policy rules is a valuable result of the implementation exercise. Moreover, as was indicated above, some elements of the SD were extended beyond the scope and obligations of the SD, since it was believed to be beneficial for the purely national services industry as well.

In our view, the process of transposition in the Netherlands was, as probably anywhere else, complex, time-consuming, and labourious. However, it was conducted very carefully and, insofar as it may be observed now, it was also successful. Nevertheless, as always in relation to implementation, the next challenge is to apply the new rules and to do so in a way that corresponds to the objectives pursued by the SD. This may require further training and, last but not least, a change of mentality of the administration. These are issues sometimes more difficult to achieve than the drafting and screening of legal rules.

3.3 Most Important and Profound Changes Induced by the Services Directive

See the answer to Sect. 3.1.

References

For jurisprudence please refer to the footnotes directly.

Literature

Backes CW (2009) Much ado about nothing of het begin van een nieuwe bestuurcultuur? De omzetting van de Dienstenrichtlijn. NTB 2009 10:307–317

Belhadj E, Evans SJH, van de Gronden JW (2007) De Dienstenrichtlijn: Ee gebreken van de deugden? Een eerste verkenning van de Dienstenrichtlijn. SEW 2007 4:141–152

Ministerie van Binnenlandse Zaken en Koninkrijksrelaties (2009) De Dienstenrichtlijn, Handreiking voor decentrale overheden, The Hague: BZK 2009. Available in Dutch at http://www.europadecentraal.nl/documents/dossiers/Dienstenrichtlijn/Handreiking%20 Dienstenrichtlijn.pdf

Douma WT (2007) Implementatie van de Dienstenrichtlijn: Een administratieve krachttoer ten behoeve van minder bureaucratie. RegelMaat 2007 5:181–189

Drahmann A (2009) Tijd voor een Nederlands transparantiebeginsel? Preadvies Jonge VAR 2009

Drijber BJ (2004) De bezems van Bolkestein. Nederlands Tijdschrift voor Europees Recht 2004 5:112–120

Duijkersloot APW, Widdershoven RJGM (2007) De Dienstenrichtlijn en het algemeen bestuursrecht. Regelmaat 2007 5:190–204

Gijón FF (2008) Institutional Report. In: Koeck HF, Karollus MM (eds) The New Services Directive of the European Union, FIDE XXIII Congress, Linz, vol 3. Congress Publications, Nomos, Vienna, 367–377

Hessel B (2007a) Gemeenten en de Dienstenrichtlijn (1). De Gemeentestem 2007 7269:113–125

Hessel B (2007b) Gemeenten en de Dienstenrichtlijn (2). De Gemeentestem 2007 7271:197–203

Hessel B (2007c) De Dienstenrichtlijn leidt tot hoofdbrekens voor de wetgever. RegelMaat 2007 5:205–217

Hessel B, Perton E, Schiebroek M (2009) De Dienstenrichtlijn decentraal. De gevolgen van de Dienstenrichtlijn voor decentrale overheden. Sdu, The Hague

Sauerwein LB, Linnemann JJ (2001) Personal Data Protection Act, Guidelines for personal data processors. Ministry of Justice, The Hague

Schiebroek M (2009a) De Dienstenwet en de decentrale overheden. In: Hessel B, Perton E, Schiebroek M (eds) De Dienstenrichtlijn decentraal. De gevolgen van de Dienstenrichtlijn voor decentrale overheden, Sdu, The Hague, 85–123

Schiebroek M (2009b) De toetsing van regelgeving aan de Dienstenrichtlijn: een inventarisatie van de screeningsresultaten. In: Hessel B, Perton E, Schiebroek M (eds) De Dienstenrichtlijn decentraal. De gevolgen van de Dienstenrichtlijn voor decentrale overheden. Sdu, The Hague, 143–172

Social and Economic Council (2005) The Directive on services in the internal market, SER Advisory Report 2005. Available in English at http://www.ser.nl/~/media/Files/Internet/Talen/Engels/2005/2005_07_volledig%20pdf.ashx

van Meerten H (2008) The Netherlands. In: Koeck HF, Karollus MM (eds) The New Services Directive of the European Union, FIDE XXIII Congress Linz 2008, vol 3. Congress Publications, Nomos, Vienna, 241–278

van Ommeren FJ (2004) Schaarse vergunningen. De verdeling van schaarse vergunningen als onderdeel van het algemene bestuursrecht. Kluwer, Deventer

Acts

Implementation of European law concerning the free movement of services in the internal market (Services Act). Amended proposal, Place of publication: Kamerstukken I 2008/09, 31 579, A. Available at: https://zoek.officielebekendmakingen.nl/kst-20082009-31579-A.pdf

Amendment of various laws for the implementation of Directive 2006/123/EC of the European Parliament and the European Council of 12 December 2006 on services in the internal market (PbEU L 376/6) (Amending Act Services Directive) Proposal. Place of publication: Kamerstukken II 2008/09, 31 859, number 2. Available at: https://zoek.officielebekendmakingen.nl/kst-31859-2.html

General Administrative Law Act. Available at: http://www.justitie.nl/onderwerpen/wetgeving/awb/Wettekst_awb/. This is, however, an outdated version of this act. For a complete Dutch version, see http://wetten.overheid.nl/BWBR0005537/geldigheidsdatum_07-12-2009

Parliamentary documents

Implementation of European laws concerning the free movement of services in the internal market (Services Act). Explanatory Memorandum. Place of publication: Kamerstukken II 2007/08, 31 579, number 3. Available at: https://zoek.officielebekendmakingen.nl/kst-31579-3.html

Implementation of European laws concerning the free movement of services in the internal market (Services Act). Responsive Memorandum. Place of publication: Kamerstukken II 2008/09, 31 579, C. Available at: http://www.dienstenrichtlijn.ez.nl/images/stories/090824_ServicesAct_EK_memorie_van_antwoord_150609.pdf

Implementation of European laws concerning the free movement of services in the internal market (Services Act). Further Responsive Memorandum. Place of publication: Kamerstukken II 2008/09, 31 579, F. Available at: http://www.dienstenrichtlijn.ez.nl/images/stories/090828_ServicesAct_EK_nadere_memorie_van_antwoord_230709.pdf

Implementation of European laws concerning the free movement of services in the internal market (Services Act). Letter from the Minister of Economic Affairs. Place of publication: Kamerstukken II 2009/10, 31 579, number 22. Available at: https://zoek.officielebekendmakingen.nl/kst-31579-22.html

Amendment of various laws for the implementation of Directive 2006/123/EC of the European Parliament and the European Council of 12 December 2006 on services in the internal market (PbEU L 376/6) (Amending Act Services Directive). Explanatory Memorandum. Place of publication: Kamerstukken II 2008/09, 31 859, number 3. Available at: https://zoek.officielebekendmakingen.nl/kst-31859-3.html

Other sources

Complete results of the screening of all relevant laws, Place of publication: Appendix to Kamerstukken II 2008/09, 31 579, number 6. Available at: https://zoek.officielebekendmakingen.nl/kst-31579-6.html

Advice from the Council of State concerning the Services Act (W10.08.0238/III) Place of publication: Kamerstukken II 2008/09, 31 579, number 4. Available at: https://zoek.officielebekendmakingen.nl/kst-31579-4.html

Note of amendment added to the proposal of law of amending various laws for the implementation of Directive 2006/123/EC, with explanation. Place of publication: Kamerstukken 2009/2010, 31 859, number 5. Available at: https://zoek.officielebekendmakingen.nl/kst-31859-5.html

Website of the Ministry of Economic Affairs with information on the Services Directive and its implementation in the Netherlands: http://www.dienstenrichtlijn.ez.nl/

The Implementation of the Services Directive in Poland

Piotr Stec and Przemysław Malinowski

1 General Remarks on the Transposition Straegy and General Understanding of the Implementation

1.1 Main References Used in this Research

The implementation of the Services Directive (SD) was accomplished by adoption of the Act on the Provision of Services on the Territory of the Republic of Poland (*Ustawa o świadczeniu usług na terytorium Rzeczypospolitej Polskiej*) of 2010 (hereafter the Services Act),[1] which came into force in April 2010.[2]

The author Piotr Stec is Professor of Civil and Comparative Law, University of Opole (pstec@uni.opole.pl). The author Przemysław Malinowski is Assistant Professor at the Faculty of Law and Administration, University of Opole (wpia@uni.opole.pl).

[1] Official Gazette [*Dziennik Ustaw RP*] 2010, No. 47, item 278. All relevant laws are available online at http://isip.sejm.gov.pl (Polish versions only). The draft with explanation of motives is available at http://orka.sejm.gov.pl/proc6.nsf/opisy/2590.htm and at http://bip.mg.gov.pl/Projektowane+akty+normatywne/Dzialalnosc+gospodarcza, visited 20 July 2010.
[2] For a general overview of the Act see Adamska (2010), p. 85 et seq.

P. Stec (✉)
University of Opole, Opole, Poland
e-mail: pstec@uni.opole.pl

P. Malinowski
University of Opole, Opole, Poland
e-mail: wpia@uni.opole.pl

U. Stelkens et al. (eds.), *The Implementation of the EU Services Directive*,
DOI: 10.1007/978-90-6704-840-8_20,

Other principal sources of law regulating business activities are the Constitution of the Republic of Poland (*Konstytucja Rzeczypospolitej Polskiej*) of 1997[3] and the Freedom of Economic Activity Act (*Ustawa o swobodzie działalności gospodarczej*) of 2004.[4] The new Services Act forms the 'third pillar' of Polish public economic law. These acts set out a general framework for business operations and are supplemented by numerous laws relating to certain trades and professions.

Furthermore, legislative material such as the Ministry of Economy's Assessment of the Results of the Implementation of the Directive to the Polish legal order[5] and consultation papers provided by the Polish Federation of Real Property Market (*Polska Federacja Rynku Nieruchomości*), the Polish Federation of Property Valuator Associations (*Polska Federacja Stowarzyszeń Rzeczoznawców Majątkowych*), the Polish Federation of Property Managers' Associations (*Polska Federacja Stowarzyszeń Zarządców Nieruchomości*), the Polish Federation of Property Managers (*Federacja Zarządców Nieruchomości*),[6] the Confederation of Polish Private Employers 'Lewiatan' (*Konfederacja Pracodawców Prywatnych 'Lewiatan'*),[7] and the Polish Artisans Union (*Związek Rzemiosła Polskiego*)[8] have been taken into account.

1.2 Impact of the Service Directive

The Services Act is seen as an important element of the reform of economic administrative law. Earlier stages of this reform included, among other things, a 'one-stop-shop' system of registration for entrepreneurs and civil societies and limitation of the number of administrative agencies that may control the activities of an entrepreneur at the same time. The government's main concern is to facilitate business operations and reduce regulation to an acceptable level.[9]

The Services Act constitutes a major modification of the existing system of administrative economic law, particularly by partially excluding certain services from the scope of application of the Freedom of Economic Activity Act, the liberalisation of the services sector, and other forms of economic activity. The transposition process took place in accordance with the standard procedure of draft preparation, which

---

[3] Unofficial English translation available at http://www.sejm.gov.pl/prawo/konst/angielski/kon1.htm, visited 30 April 2010.

[4] Official Gazette 2007, No. 155, item 1095 (consolidated text) as amended.

[5] Available at http://bip.mg.gov.pl/Projektowane+akty+normatywne/Dzialalnosc+gospodarcza, visited 20 July 2010.

[6] All reports available at http://bip.mg.gov.pl/Projektowane+akty+normatywne/Dzialalnosc+gospodarcza, visited 20 July 2010.

[7] http://www.pkpplewiatan.pl/opinie/prawo/3/opinia_do_projektu_ustawy_o_347wiadczeniu_us322ug_na_Terytorium_rp , visited 10 July 2010.

[8] Available at http://www.gazetaautorow.pl/index.php?option=com_content&task=view&id=5226&Itemid=35, visited 1 July 2010.

[9] The government website summarising the program can be found at http://www.mg.gov.pl/Reforma+Regulacji, visited 8 July 2010.

includes the cooperation of competent ministries and stakeholders. All legislative drafts must be consulted with stakeholders, usually non-governmental organisations (NGOs), trade unions, and associations of entrepreneurs (e.g., Commercial Chambers), which can give their opinions on the proposed legislation. Several dozens of such opinions were presented in the course of the proceedings.[10]

After consultations with employee organisations, entrepreneurs, and other stakeholders, the Ministry of Economy published the report 'Assessment of the Results of Implementation of the Directive to the Polish legal order'.[11] The report contained a complex estimate of the Directive's implementation, including compliance of the economic aspects connected with introducing changes to the internal legal system, and the influence of such changes on the following:

- The activity of public administration organs,
- Entrepreneurs,
- The competitiveness of the economy,
- Development of the labour market,
- Regional development,
- The status of public finance, and
- Consumers and households.

1.3 (National) Scope of Application

The SD deals mainly, although not exclusively, with transnational services and establishments. However, it has been obvious from the very beginning that the implementation process cannot lead to the discrimination of domestic entrepreneurs by subjecting them to more severe controls than their foreign competitors. The relevant legislation must therefore apply to both transnational and local services and establishments.

The Services Act also deals with the liberalisation of the national services industry to create a uniform playing field for all economic stakeholders. This approach is strongly backed by the constitutional principle of equality and corresponds with the simplification of Polish public economic law. The principle of equality stems from Article 32 of the Constitution of the Republic of Poland, which safeguards, among other matters, the right to equal treatment by public authorities and prohibits discrimination in political, social, and economic life. The equality of entrepreneurs has been additionally safeguarded by Article 6 (1) of the

---

[10] See *supra,* footnote 7. NGOs published an account on possible impact of the Services Directive on Polish NGO sector prepared by Blicharz (2010).

[11] Available at http://www.mg.gov.pl/Prawo/Projekty+aktow+prawnych/Dzialalnosc+gospodarcza/ visited 30 April 2010.

Freedom of Economic Activity Act by granting everyone the possibility of undertaking, conducting, and terminating economic activities under equal rights.[12]

Some provisions of the Services Act deal exclusively with transnational services providers (e.g., rules on temporary rendering services on Polish territory or intergovernmental cooperation), while others (e.g., amendments of the Freedom of Economic Activity Act and other acts) are of general use. Laws implementing the SD are applicable in relation to all economic stakeholders. The relevant provisions of the Services Act and the Freedom of Economic Activity Act apply to both national and transnational service providers. Some changes introduced by the Services Act are of a more general nature, for example, with respect to the 'tacit consent' that applies to all authorisations required by entrepreneurs.

1.4 Incorporation of Transposing Legislation

The requirements of the SD relating to administrative proceedings have been fully introduced. This is true both with respect to electronic procedures and the simplification of procedures, particularly by limiting formalities connected with business operations. Relevant changes are described below, while dealing with particular matters.

As to the implementation process, two methods, that is, the incorporation of new rules into existing statutes and the adoption of a new codification, were used. The relevant provisions were partly added to the existing Law on the Freedom of Economic Activity, and partly contained in the new Services Act. Moreover, many statutes regulating particular branches of the services industry were amended for compatibility with the provisions of the SD.[13]

The legislator decided to codify the rules for the provision of services into a separate statute, since the provisions of the SD are relevant not only to commercial service providers but also to nonprofits, which are not classified as entrepreneurs in Polish law. It should, however, be noted that the Services Act and the Freedom of Economic Activity Act are interconnected and some provisions of the latter still apply to the services sector. This method of implementation is rather unusual and has been criticised due to its awkwardness. It has been suggested that it might be better to implement the directive by including relevant provisions into the Freedom of Economic Activity Act.[14]

---

[12] The principles of equality and of freedom of economic activity are somehow limited in respect of certain foreign entrepreneurs coming from outside of European Economic Area. Such entrepreneurs may only undertake and provide economic activity in form of a limited partnership *(spółka komandytowa)*, limited joint stock partnership *(spółka komandytowo—akcyjna)*, limited liability company *(spółka z ograniczoną odpowiedzialnością)* or joint—stock company *(spółka akcyjna)*. Cf. Pazdan (2009), p. 102.

[13] The Services Act 2010 amends ca. 25 statutes.

[14] Cf. Adamska (2010), p. 90.

1.5 The Relationship of the Services Directive to Primary EU Law

Generally, the SD is considered compatible with Articles 43 and 49 of the EC Treaty (now: Articles 49 and 56 TFEU) and perceived as a way to clarify the rights of services providers. No problems in this respect have been identified so far.

1.6 Screening

Screening was carried out by the relevant ministries,[15] and an external contractor was also employed (the Law Offices of Domański, Zakrzewski, and Palinka) who prepared an opinion on the conformity of Polish economic law with the SD.[16] The opinion included a list of acts to be amended. As a result, a list of provisions incompatible with the SD was drawn up and a method of implementation (new codification plus amendments where necessary) developed.

2 Individual Articles of the Services Directive

2.1 Article 6 SD: Point of Single Contact (POSC)

2.1.1 Establishment of the POSC

By the power of the Amendment of 7 February 2004 of the Freedom of Economic Activity Act, enforced on 4 January 2009, the rule of the one-stop-shop, or 'single counter', was introduced. This rule allows entrepreneurs to submit a motion to register a business, to receive a social security number or national business registry number, or to register at the Social Insurance Agency (*Zakład Ubezpieczeń Społecznych,* ZUS). The entry must be made in the Economic Activity Records run by the communes (*Gmina* in Polish) or, in the case of commercial partnerships or companies, in the National Register of Entrepreneurs (*Krajowy Rejestr Sądowy,* KRS), which is a court register. This was intended as a first step towards the creation of an electronic information system granting access to both registers. This system will be active as of 7 January 2011. It will speed up data transfer and shorten the time for the certification of registrations. The central registry and

---

[15] Ministry of Economy as leading ministry and Ministry of Finance, Ministry of Science and Higher Education, Ministry of Agriculture and Rural Development, Ministry of Justice, Ministry of Health, Ministry of Infrastructure, Ministry of Labour and Social Policy, Ministry of Sport and Tourism, Ministry of Culture and National Heritage, Ministry of Internal Affairs and Administration, Ministry of Education, Ministry of Environment, Office for Competition and Consumer Protection.

[16] The report is available at http://polskawue.gov.pl/files/Dokumenty/Norweski%20Mechanizm%20Finansowy/ekspertyza_2008_07_UKiE_ekspertyza_20080626.pdf, visited 30 April 2010.

information on economic activity will be run by the Minister of Economy using an information technology system.

The Services Act amended the Freedom of Economic Activity Act[17] with the addition of Chapter 2a on the point of contact. The introduction of a point of single contact (POSC) is another step towards liberalisation of the rules, requirements, and procedures for registering and running a business, including a service.

Under Article 22a (5) of the Law on the Freedom of Economic Activity, a point of contact is to be maintained as a website.[18] It will present electronic procedures and information required by the Directive on services. This idea of a virtually operating public body is a novelty in Polish administrative law.

The principal language of communication with the POSC will be Polish. Information on the POSC website may, according to Article 22d (2), in addition, be prepared and published in foreign languages.

Through the POSC, it will be possible to submit to the relevant authorities applications or declarations required to undertake, conduct, or terminate business activities. Moreover, the POSC will enable notifications required in recognition of professional qualifications.

The transfer of data between the POSC and the competent authorities shall take place electronically, that is, via an electronic platform for government services or the electronic mailboxes of competent authorities. The reporting of these data is to be carried out with the use of electronic forms, as defined by Article 58 (2) of the Law on Electronic Signatures of 18 September 2001.[19] In addition, under Article 22d of that law, the Polish POSC will contain information on POSC websites located in other EU countries.

Furthermore, introduction of the POSC requires competent public authorities to allow through it the formalities and all matters related to the establishment, implementation, and termination of a business.

Additionally, the Law on the Freedom of Economic Activity requires that designated bodies accept electronic documents submitted to the POSC.

The idea of a virtual POSC is compatible with the electronic access system public authorities and entrepreneurs will have from 1 July 2011 on to information contained in the Central Records and Information on Economic Activities (CEIDG). The Register CEIDG will provide data from the Registry of Economic Activity and the National Court Register (Article 23 of the Freedom of Economic Activity Act), which will enable the provision of information on the data from the records and issuing certificates for faster entries. The CEIDG will be further integrated into a central database of records maintained by other organs. The CEIDG is to be carried out in the ICT system by the Minister of Economy.

---

[17] Official Gazette 2007, No. 155, item 1095 as amended.

[18] http://www.eu-go.gov.pl/, visited 20 July 2010.

[19] Official Gazette 2001, No. 130, item 1450 as amended.

It should be noted here that available data may refer to both businesses and entities directly or, indirectly, to their activity (e.g., agents, partners, or spouse of the entrepreneur[20]).

To sum up, it can be assumed that the POSC operation (in full) should coincide with the start of the Central Registration and Information on Economic Activity (CEIDIG). The central authority responsible for the operation of a point of contact is the Minister responsible for economic affairs, so this task has been attributed to an existing authority. One-stop-shops/single counters to help entrepreneurs, regardless of their scope of activity, register a business and facilitate contact with public authorities are operated by existing authorities responsible for the registration of businesses, that is, communes and municipalities.

2.1.2 Involvement of Private Partners

No private partners are involved in the creation and operation of the POSC. The POSC system is integrated with the registration of businesses, which traditionally has been carried out by the government. Although the privatisation of public tasks is a well-developed concept in Poland,[21] no serious attempt to privatise the registration of businesses and the provision of public data on economic activity has ever been made.

2.1.3 Liability

As far as liability for any mistakes of the POSC is concerned, the general rules of liability for public bodies will apply (Articles 417 *et seq.* of the Civil Code—*Kodeks cywilny*—of 1964). Generally, as the POSC operator, the state will be liable for delicts committed by its unlawful actions. This is a strict (causal) liability and the only subject-specific regulation that was added to the Freedom of Economic Activity Act. According to Article 22c (6) of this act, the Minister of Economy, as a competent authority for POSC operations, does not 'guarantee the honesty of a business person or his/hers employees'. This provision aims to exclude state liability for the actions of third parties. It applies, for example, if a POSC provides information on NGOs promoting business and consumer affairs, since it is supposed to maintain a database of such entities (Article 22c (1), (7) of the Services Act). Registration of an NGO is made upon request, and thus such an entity cannot be interpreted as having the status of a government-certified 'trusted third party'.

---

[20] Cf. Powałowski et al (2009), p. 168.

[21] Cf. Biernat (1994), *passim*; Zacharko (2000), *passim*.

2.2 Article 7 SD: Right to Information

Article 22b of the Freedom of Economic Activity Act implies that the POSC is to ensure, *inter alia*, access to information on the following:

- Procedures required for the establishment, implementation, and completion of economic activity on Polish territory,
- General principles for the provision of services in European Union (EU) countries (as well as in European Free Trade Association (EFTA) and European Economic Area countries),
- Contact details of public administration bodies (with an indication of their competence),
- Conditions of access to public registers and databases on businesses and entrepreneurs,
- Legal remedies available for solving disputes between an administrative body and an entrepreneur or consumer,
- Legal remedies available in a dispute between an entrepreneur and a consumer, and
- Official statements and interpretations connected with conducting and terminating business activities.

Generally, the range of information provided by the POSC does not extend the 'right of information' but makes it easier to obtain it.

As one can see, the Services Act does not extend the right to information beyond the scope of application of the SD, but it uses, however, somewhat different wording. It should be noted that entrepreneurs can also exercise the right to obtain public information on the basis of other acts, in particular, the Freedom of Information Act.

General information on running a business in Poland is also provided online by the Polish Foreign Investment Agency, a government entity. Regional and local administration usually maintains general information and contact points for both the general public and foreign entrepreneurs.

2.3 Article 8 SD: Procedures by Electronic Means

2.3.1 Electronic Procedures *in Concreto*

While mentioning procedural issues associated with setting up a business, it should be noted that until now, electronic procedures have not been fully implemented. The planned completion of the work is January 2011 (a date that coincides with the introduction of the CEIDG).

Recently enacted amendments to the Freedom of Economic Activity Act provide for the introduction of a specific system and principles governing electronic registration. Moreover, Article 22c of the Freedom of Economic Activity Act provides for the opportunity to settle all matters related to the undertaking, conducting, and termination of activities through the POSC.

The POSC will provide the competent public administration authorities with any electronically submitted documents (no later than the next business day); however, the period for the competent authority handling the case starts the working day after the reception of the application by the POSC.

Additionally, Article 22e of the Freedom of Economic Activity Act introduces a general obligation to allow the formal requirements relating to registration activities to be implemented through electronic procedures. In practice, an electronic procedure must be carried out under the following conditions and principles:

- A registration application form is specified by the Council of Ministers by way of regulation,
- A potential entrepreneur fills the form out on the website of the registered body (eventually also on the CEIDG) as well as on the POSC website),
- A request form will also comprise the registration form for inclusion in the statistic registry, tax payer identification number (NIP), and will include the payer's notification to Social Security,
- When the application is completed on the POSC website, according to the act, it will de facto be forwarded automatically to the registry of the competent local authority, which must deal with it factually, and
- On the POSC website the prospective entrepreneur will be able to use—for example, in the course of filling out the form—any information (laws, court decisions, explanations, and links to other bodies or institutions).

In this context, the proposed method of transposition will not have a great innovative impact, since it corresponds with the current implementation of other electronic procedures.

2.3.2 Removal of Other Means

The Services Act grants the right to use an electronic procedure but does not treat this as an exclusive right. Article 22c of the Economic Activity Act (as amended by the Services Act) obliges the relevant authorities to provide means for electronic procedures, but interested parties can use old-fashioned, paper-based procedures instead. Entrepreneurs may, at their discretion, apply directly to the relevant authorities without seeking help from the POSC.

2.4 Article 9 SD: Authorisation Schemes

As a general rule, undertaking and running business activities, including a service, is possible without the need to obtain certain permits, concessions, or licences (Article 6 of the Freedom of Economic Activity Act). This rule has its roots in the constitutional principle of 'economic freedom' set forth in Articles 20, 22, and 32 of the Constitution of the Republic of Poland[22] and Articles 6 and 7 of the

[22] Official Gazette 1997, No. 78, item 483.

Freedom of Economic Activity Act of 2004. According to Article 22 of the Constitution of the Republic of Poland, limitations may be imposed upon the freedom of economic activity only for important public reasons.

Restrictions on the freedom of establishment concern concessions, permits, and licences (as well as consents) that must be obtained prior to engaging in certain economic activities. In most cases, simple registration of the business is required.

Simple notification requirements are not covered by Articles 9 *et seq.* of the SD.

2.5 *Article 10 SD: Conditions for the Granting of Authorisation*

2.5.1 Recognition of Requirements

Article 9a of the Freedom of Economic Activity Act as amended by the Services Act obliges public authorities to recognise authorisations granted by other Member States, as well as certificates or other documents issued by competent authorities in other Member States. However, professional liability insurance and guarantees are accepted only if they are equivalent in scope and content to those required by Polish law (Article 9b of the Freedom of Economic Activity Act).

2.5.2 Conditions for Obtaining an Authorisation and Control of the Use of Discretion

Generally, the provision of Article 10 (5) SD is fully compatible with Polish administrative law. Public administration bodies must issue a positive decision once all conditions stipulated by law have been met. As a general rule, administrative authorities must give in writing the reasons behind their decisions to enable their control by superior authorities and/or courts.

In some, rather rare, cases, the authorities can exercise discretion or base their decision on policy grounds, referring to the notion of important public interest, public security, or public safety. For instance, according to Article 17a (2) of the Protection of Persons and Patrimony Act (*Ustawa o ochronie osób i mienia*) of 1997,[23] the minister responsible for internal affairs may refuse a concession for bodyguard services to an applicant if granting it could 'pose a threat to state security and defense abilities or security and personality rights of citizens'.

The administrative court, however, is entitled to review the use of discretion, particularly to assess whether the discretionary power has been abused. It is therefore the duty of an administrative authority to explain reasons of refusal so that such decisions are never arbitrary.

---

[23] Official Gazette 2005, No 145, item 1221 (consolidated text) as amended.

No changes in the allocation of competences in the context of Article 10 SD were made.

2.5.3 Overriding Reasons Relating to Public Policy and Regional Authorisation

Until recently, policy grounds were not defined by a statute. The Services Act, however, uses an extensive definition of *overriding reasons relating to public policy,* defined by Article 2 (1), (7) as an interest connected with public safety and order; public health; keeping a balanced social insurance system; consumer, employee, and customer protection; combating abuses; environmental protection; intellectual property; social and cultural policy; and the protection of national, historic, and artistic heritage. This definition of fields of public policy is quite vague and still leaves it for the courts to decide if particular reasons were 'overriding'.

The only example of territorial restrictions with respect to providing services relates to the sale of alcohol beverages. The number and location of premises where alcohol can be sold are restricted. Communal councils (*rady gmin*) establish the number of points of sale in such a way as to restrict excessive access to alcohol Article 12 of the Promoting Sobriety and the Prevention of Alcoholism Act (*Ustawa o wychowaniu w trzeźwości i przeciwdziałaniu alkoholizmowi*) of 1982.[24]

2.5.4 Authority's Duty to Explain a Decision

There was no need to amend the rules of appeal against the refusal of authorisation. Provisions of the Code of Administrative Procedure (*Kodeks postępowania administracyjnego*) of 1960 and the Administrative Court Procedure Act (Ustawa o postępowaniu przed sądami administracyjnymi) of 2002 that grant the right to review a decision by superior authorities and the courts are applicable in such cases.

2.6 Article 11 SD: Duration of Authorisation

The principle of unlimited authorisation was introduced as a general rule in Polish law by the Services Act. According to Article 75a of the Freedom of Economic Activity Act (as amended by the Services Act), concessions, licences, permits, and entries into records of regulated economic activity authorise the economic activity in question for an unlimited period of time. Exceptions to this rule are possible only if justified by overriding reasons relating to the public interest. Such

[24] Official Gazette 2007, No 70, item 115 (consolidated text) as amended.

exceptions exist, for instance, in cases of mining concessions, which are issued for periods of three to 50 years, as stated in Article 15 (5) of the Mining and Geology Act (*Ustawa prawo geologiczne i górnicze*) of 1994.[25]

Previously there was no prohibition on time-limited authorisations in Polish law. As a general rule, whenever an authorisation to render services was needed, the relevant licence, concession, or permit was valid for a limited period of time. The validity period was determined by a statute or administrative authority. In the latter case, relevant statutes specified the maximum and minimum validity periods. Some legal acts do not specify the duration of the authorisation, such as the Commodity Exchange Act (*Ustawa o giełdach towarowych*) of 2000.[26] In such cases, the authorisation is considered to be issued for an indefinite period of time.

2.7 Article 12 SD: Selection from Among Several Candidates

The rule of Article 12 of the SD does not constitute a major change in Polish law. It is a well-established practice to apply a selection procedure if the number of authorisations for a given activity is limited due to the scarcity of resources or technical capacities. Such procedures are always regulated by a statute and provide full guarantees of impartiality and transparency. A good example of this approach comprises Articles 51 *et seq.* of the Freedom of Economic Activity Act relating to sealed bid competitions/tenders used if only a limited number of concessions can be granted by a concession authority. The law describes the course of the proceedings and criteria to be applied in assessing the bids of competing entrepreneurs. A similar procedure is used in the case of business activities not falling within the scope of the SD, for example, concessions for the operation of casinos (Article 32 of the Gaming Act, *Ustawa o grach hazardowych*).[27]

2.8 Article 13 SD: Authorisation Procedures

2.8.1 Duration of Administrative Procedures

The duration of administrative procedures connected with granting authorisations and the conditions of granting such authorisations are defined by a statute. Statutory rules also regulate matters connected with the renewal of (or refusal to renew) an authorisation by administrative authorities.

Laws currently in force either set a specific time limit or require the authorities to issue an authorisation, licence, or permit as soon as possible (e.g., Article 11 (1)

[25] Official Gazette 2005, No 228, item 1947 as amended.

[26] Official Gazette 2010, No 48, item 284 (consolidated text) as amended.

[27] Official Gazette 2009, No 21, item 1540.

of the Freedom of Economic Activity Act). Generally, it is possible to differ from the prescribed duration of procedures, for example, if the subject matter of the motion is extremely complex and requires further analysis or an expert opinion.

2.8.2 Tacit Authorisation

Traditionally, tacit authorisations apply only in specific administrative laws. For instance, certain construction works require notification of the building authorities. If the relevant authority does not object to the planned works, authorisation is considered granted.

The Freedom of Economic Activity Act 2004 as amended by the Services Act provides for so-called 'silent consent' (tacit authorisation) as a general rule of public economic law. If competent authorities do not respond to a filed application within the prescribed time, the authorisation is considered to have been granted to the applicant (Article 11 (9) of the Freedom of Economic Activity Act). There are some statutory exceptions to this rule, as in the case of proceedings regarding animal and food health and safety, and these statutory exceptions must be justified by overriding public interest.

For example, the institution of implied consent was exempted from the following acts, in accordance with the Services Act:

- Article 3a of the Protection of Animals Act (*Ustawa o ochronie zwierząt*) of 1997[28] excludes the use of tacit consent to obtain a permit to breed or keep a dog of a breed that is deemed aggressive.
- Article 18b of the Collective Water Supply Act (*Ustawa o zbiorowym zaopatrzeniu w wodę*) of 2001[29] excludes the tacit consent of the contracting procedure in obtaining an authorisation to conduct the business of public water supply and sewage services.
- Article of the Fodder Act (*Ustawa o paszach*) of 2006[30] excludes the institution of implied consent in relation to business entities that are subject to supervision by the Veterinary Inspection.

The tacit authorisation has both formal and substantive effects, just like an administrative decision. The law does not distinguish between formally granted and tacit authorisations. Both are considered equal in this respect. It should be noted that the tacit consent system can cause problems, mostly connected with proving consent was granted. This is true in the case of an implied consent system of entrepreneur registration introduced some time ago. According to provisions of the Freedom of Economic Activity Act, if the public authority has not entered the

28 Official Gazette 2003, No 106, item 1002 as amended.

29 Official Gazette 2006, No 123, item 858 as amended.

30 Official Gazette 2006, No 144, item 1045 as amended.

entrepreneur into the register of the business-regulated activity, it is implied, then, that it made no objections to the registration of the new business.

However, the mere fact of setting up the legal basis of the so-called implicit consent does not solve the formal and legal problems of entrepreneurs. Such problems concern the impossibility of obtaining a certificate of registration from the register for use with third parties or the impossibility of obtaining information or data contained in the register that concerns the entrepreneur, all due to the fact that the data in the registry do not exist.[31] This question was not, however, raised during the implementation process. It is hoped that relevant amendments aimed at facilitating the operation of tacit consent will be proposed soon.

2.9 Articles 14, 15, 16 SD

Generally, there was no need to adapt the law to comply with Article 14 of the SD. Laws regulating services that fall within the scope of the SD do not contain prohibited restrictions. According to Article 5 of the Services Act, competent authorities cannot impose on providers of services requirements limiting access to such services, particularly relating to the authorisation of activities or restrictions in access to financial aid. Nor may competent authorities discriminate against providers of services on the basis of origin or domicile.

Numerous laws relating to services contain restrictions that fall within the scope of Article 15 of the SD. For instance, there are restrictions on the number of businesses authorised to sell alcohol, as well as restrictions on tour operators. These restrictions can mostly be justified by overriding reasons relating to the public interest.

2.10 Articles 14–19 SD

Prohibited requirements and further exemptions did not give rise to much discussion. Generally, the provisions of Articles 14–16 and 19 of the SD are compatible with a general tendency towards creating a business environment that does not discriminate against entrepreneurs. The same is true in the case of further exemptions.

[31] See further Kosikowski (2007), p. 250.

2.11 Articles 22–27 SD

There was almost no discussion with respect to the rights and duties defined in Articles 22–27 of the SD. Polish consumer law already obliges entrepreneurs to provide consumers with a wide range of information at a level not different from the standards set out by Article 22 of the SD. The same is true with respect to compulsory insurance (Article 23 SD). As far as commercial information provided by members of regulated professions is concerned, this problem has not been raised as a serious concern. Members of professions may provide information on their activities, although in some cases there are restrictions on certain forms of advertising.

Generally, it has always been possible to provide multidisciplinary services in Poland, so Article 6 (1) of the Services Act only confirms a well-established rule. It should be noted that the Services Act provides exceptions to this rule by allowing restrictions with respect to multidisciplinary services justified by the need to ensure the impartiality and independence of regulated professions. Such restrictions apply, for example, to advocates.

There are no specific rules encouraging services providers to use independent voluntary certifications, quality charters, or trademarks. Such activities are now a common practice in Poland and need almost no incentive from public bodies. Many businesses seek voluntary certification from independent and/or professional bodies, and the use of guarantee trademarks is a common practice.

2.12 Articles 28 ff. SD: Administrative Cooperation

The issue of transnational cooperation was not regulated in a specific method prior to implementation of the SD. The issues covered by Articles 28 *et seq.* of the SD are now included in Articles 11 *et seq.* of the Services Act of 2010.

The Services Act arranges for administrative assistance in cases connected with the subject matter of the Directive. The minister responsible for the economy acts as the coordinator (on Polish territory) of international cooperation in the implementation and application of the Directive.

In accordance with Article 12 of the Act, this cooperation must rely in particular on the exchange of information on providers and their services and carrying out the controls of providers. Moreover, the following applies:

- If the business of providing services will constitute a serious threat to the safety of life, health, property, or the environment, the competent authority will be able to apply to the competent authority of the state in which the service provider is established, or—in the case of natural legal persons—the place of residence, to take action to eliminate the hazard. The applicant authority will immediately inform the minister responsible for the economy.

- In case an application is received to take action to remove threats to security of life, health, property, or the environment, for service providers established or—in case of natural persons—residing on Polish territory that temporarily provide services in the territory of the requesting state, the competent authority will notify the minister responsible for economy of the above and take action to remove the threat.
- In case activities of the provider are reported that may cause injury to health or the environment or that endanger the safety of people living on Polish territory, or another Member State, the competent authority will notify the competent minister.

In accordance with Article 19, the minister responsible for the economy shall determine, by regulation, the detailed scope of international cooperation in the provision of services, with particular reference to the bodies involved in that cooperation and the determination of information and communication systems used for its implementation, with a view to ensuring proper implementation of the freedom to provide services (that regulation has not yet been issued as of this writing).

The Services Act did not introduce any fees whatsoever for assistance.

2.13 Article 29 SD: Mutual Assistance—General Obligations for the Member State of Establishment

Certain doubts may arise with respect to Article 29 (1) of the Directive, in particular, its subjective scope. During consultations, it was raised that in practice one will have to cope with interference of the public sphere into the functioning of private subjects (with any doubts being the result of the transboundary information context).

3 Assessment of the Impact of the Services Directive

The scope and contents of the SD create new duties for organs of the state and give entrepreneurs rights not covered by earlier legislation. The administrative procedure relating to international cooperation and virtual public bodies are a novelty in Polish law. The new Services Act of 2010 constitutes a major modification of the existing system of administrative economic law, particularly by the partial exclusion of services from the scope of application of the Freedom of Economic Activity Act and the liberalisation of the services sector in comparison to other forms of economic activity. This change will be achieved mostly by lifting restrictions on certain kinds of activity, mostly relating to the duration of permits and the terms and conditions of rendering services. In this respect, the implementation of the SD fits well into the general framework of economic law reform aimed at making it more business friendly.

It is hard to assess if and to what extent the transposition of the SD was successful. There are certain doubts about having the services industry regulated partly by the Services Act and partly by the Freedom of Economic Activity Act. There is no doubt that the minimum requirements of the transposition have been met. Rights granted to services providers, for example, tacit authorisation, have been extended to entrepreneurs exercising other trades and professions.

The most profound changes introduced by the Services Act are the removal of provisions related to time-limited permits to operate a business, making the lives of entrepreneurs easier, since they will not be obliged to reapply for renewal every year or two. The introduction of tacit authorisations and limitation of the duty to present original or notarised documents while applying for a permit will also be advantageous. These are perceived as introducing the 'principle of trust', that is, the statutory presumption that, *prima facie,* all information provided by an applicant is true and there is no need to supply additional original or notarised copies of the documents.

References

For legislation, jurisprudence and websites please refer to 1.1 of the report and footnotes directly.

Adamska A (2010) Świadczenie usług w Polsce a dyrektywa usługowa [Providing Services in Poland and Services Directive], 3 Prawo Europejskie w Praktyce, p 85 et seq

Biernat S (1994) Prywatyzacja zadań publicznych, [Privatisation of Public tasks], Warsaw, Państwowe Wydawnictwo Naukowe

Blicharz R/Institute of Public Affairs (2010) Account on possible impact of the Services Directive on polish NGO sector. Available at: http://www.isp.org.pl/kompas/files/9021849570051847001231406077.pdf. Accessed 30 May 2010

Kosikowski C (2007) Ustawa o swobodzie działalności gospodarczej. Komentarz [The Act of freedom of economic activity. A commentary]. LexisNexis, Warsaw, p 250

Pazdan M (2009) Prawo prywatne międzynarodowe [Private International Law]. Lexis-Nexis, Warsaw, p 102

Powałowski A et al (2009) Ustawa o swobodzie działalności gospodarczej. Komentarz [The Law on freedom of economic activity. A commentary]. Wolters Kluwer Polska—Abc 2009, Warsaw, p 168

Zacharko L (2000) Prywatyzacja zadań publicznych gminy. Studium administracyjnoprawne [Privatisation of Public Tasks of a Commune. A Study in Administrative Law], Wydawnictwo Uniwersytetu śląskiego, Katowice

The Implementation of the Services Directive in Portugal

Miguel Gorjão-Henriques

1 General Remarks on the Transposition Strategy and General Comprehension of the Implementation

1.1 Main References Used in this Research

By the time the first draft report was delivered,[1] Portugal had not yet implemented the Services Directive (SD). According to the Constitution of the Portuguese

The author is Assistant professor at the Faculty of Law at Coimbra University. He is also Partner of Sérvulo & Associados Law Firm.

[1] I expressly wish to thank Mestre Bernardo Azevedo of the Faculty of Law of the Coimbra University for his most valuable comments on the draft report. I would also like to thank my Colleagues of Sérvulo & Associados and, particularly, Professor Sérvulo Correia, for the confidence and support. I would also like to thank Mr. Ângelo Seiça Neves, coordinator of the implementation in Portugal of the SD in the Directorate-General of Economic Activities, Mr. António Maia, also of the same Directorate-General and task force, and Mrs. Sónia Santos, of AMA, I.P., for their kind availability. Any error is of course of mine responsibility.

The present report was done prior to the 2011 general elections that caused a major change in the Portuguese Government, now ruled by a Social Democrats/Christian Democrats coalition—the current structure of the XIX Constitutional Government may be found in DL 86-A/2011 of July 17.

Some major changes ocurred after the completion of the present report and are worth mentioning, although not analysed in the present report, e.g. (a) Law 17/2010, of August 4 ("*exercício da actividade de agente da propriedade industrial*"), (b) DL 32/2011, of

M. Gorjão-Henriques (✉)
Sérvulo and Associados Law Firm, Lisbon, Portugal
e-mail: mgh@servulo.com

M. Gorjão-Henriques
Coimbra University, Coimbra, Portugal

U. Stelkens et al. (eds.), *The Implementation of the EU Services Directive*,
DOI: 10.1007/978-90-6704-840-8_21,

Republic (the Portuguese Constitution) and since Constitutional Law 1/1997,[2] directives must be implemented through a decree-law (of the Government) or a law (of the parliament, the "Assembleia da República"), under Article 112 (8) of the Portuguese Constitution. Whenever the subject matter involves the reserved legislative competence of Parliament, only Parliament may act, directly or conceding a legislative authorisation to the Government. However, through Decree-Law no. 92/2010 of July 26 (hereinafter "DL 92/2010"), Portugal adopted a horizontal diploma implementing the SD.[3]

Previously, and through DL 49/2010 of May 19, implementing Directive 2007/36/EC, the Government took the opportunity to modify Article 4 of the Commercial Societies Code, stating that the obligation for foreign companies to have a permanent representation in Portugal according to Portuguese law and the regimen applicable to those not complying with those obligations were not applicable to «companies exercising its activities in Portugal under the freedom to provide services according to Directive 2006/123/EC...».[4]

1.2 Impact of the Services Directive

1.2.1 Profound Cause to Change National Law?

The SD did not cause a profound change of national administrative law beyond the requirements of the SD. However, it must be stressed that implementation of the SD will eventually have a profound impact on our administrative law, mainly due to the implementation of the tacit authorisation principle in the administrative procedure in the case of no reply in procedures intended to

Footnote 1 (continued)
March 7 ("*acesso e de exercício da actividade de organização de campos de férias*"), (c) DL 37/2011, of March 10 ("*contratos de utilização periódica de bens, de aquisição de produtos de férias de longa duração, de revenda e de troca (time sharing)*"), (d) DL 48/2011, of April 1st (the *omnibus* law, so to speak); (e) DL 61/2011, of May 6 ("*agências de viagens e turismo*"); (f) DL 69/2001, of June 15 ("*actividades de construção, mediação e angariação imobiliária*") and (g) DL 84/2011 ("*simplificação dos regimes jurídicos da deposição de resíduos em aterro, da produção cartográfica e do licenciamento do exercício das actividades de pesquisa e captação de águas subterrâneas*").

[2] Constitutional Law 1/2004 of July 24 allowed for Directives to be implemented in the autonomous regions of Azores or Madeira through a "decreto legislativo regional" in some cases.

[3] Prior to DL 92/2010, there were available references in the Directorate-General of Economic Activities website, at http://www.dgae.min-economia.pt/, including the draft Decree-Law implementing the Directive (hereinafter, the Draft Decree-Law Implementing the SD, e.g., 'Draft SDIL') and an 'Explanatory Note' (Nota Explicativa). DL 92/2010 is available at DL 92/2010, July 26.

[4] The diploma is still available at DL 49/2010—May 19.

allow access to services activities. This is in clear contraposition with the actual principle of tacit refusal under Articles 108 and 109 of the Code of Administrative Procedure. Also, the SD will have a profound impact due to the principle of the mutual recognition of habilitations (for the access and exercise of the free provision of services).

1.2.2 Involvement in the Transposition Process

The implementation procedure was coordinated by the Directorate-General of Economic Activities of the Ministry of Economy and Innovation and included all departments of the administration, whether direct (under the power of direction and strict hierarchy), indirect (to which the Government may not impose specific conducts, although some acts must be authorised or communicated to the Government), or autonomous (mainly the municipalities). A former view on the authorities involved in earlier stages of the discussion of the then draft of the SD and its initial implementation period can be found in the Portuguese report to the 2008 FIDE Congress in Austria, by Ferreira Malaquias (2008), pp. 299–307.

More recently, coordination undertaken by the Directorate-General of Economic Activities involved direct dialogue with all the governmental departments, including the "Central" Administration (including the ministries, the direct administration, hierarchically organised), other public services (indirect administration), and autonomous administration (the municipalities).

In addition, the professional orders, including lawyers, solicitors, economists, engineers, architects, biologists, veterinarians, and accountants, were also included in the procedure, at least as far as the "screening" was concerned.

1.3 (National) Scope of Application

1.3.1 Scope of the Services Directive

There is no clear answer to the question about a prevailing opinion towards the directive's scope of application. However, one may argue that the Directive's scope of application and the way Portugal intends to implement it are two different things. In fact, according to the principle of conferral laid down in Article 5 of the EU Treaty, EU law is only applicable where the situation interferes with the internal market, for instance, when a transnational element is involved. However, it is settled European Court of Justice (ECJ) case law that one cannot exclude that a situation involving only nationals may implicate the application of EU law.

1.3.2 Application of Transposing Legislation to Domestic Service Providers

DL 92/2010 also applies to service activities in Portugal carried out by service providers established in Portugal. The Portuguese Constitution establishes a principal of assimilation of nationals and foreigners, except in certain circumstances (Article 15), alongside with the principle of equality and non-discrimination (Article 13). In addition, the preamble of DL 92/2010 is based on the principle and policies of procedural simplification and *debureaucratisation*, which is considered to make the «services markets more competitive, contributing to economic growth and to job creation».

1.3.3 Application of Transposing Legislation Beyond Service Providers

Generally speaking, the laws/regulations implementing the SD are applicable also in relation to everybody, so that they could be claimed by everybody. We are not sure in how to interpret the scope of the law, in certain features, for regarding its interference over actual authorisation regimens, it seems a "framework law", establishing the principles laid down by the Directive and applicable whenever a regimen of "administrative permissions" will be created in the future. The wording of Article 4, establishing the principles of freedom of establishment and the provision of services, and the provisions of Chapter III defining cases when "permissões administrativas" ('administrative permissions') may be created allow, however, for a benign interpretation.

In other respects, it is worth noticing that several provisions of the new DL 92/2010 apply even to service providers from outside of the European Economic Area—see Article 2/2 of DL 92/2010, in relation to Articles 5 (debureaucratisation and simplification of administrative procedures), 6 (electronic points of single contact, or POSCs, and procedural dematerialisation), 7/4 (documents issued by other identified MSs), 8 (the "permissões administrativas", new administrative permissions for the exercise of the provision of services), 16 (principle of unlimited duration of "permissões administrativas", etc.), 20 (information to be provided by the service provider), and 22 (information requests and complaints).

1.4 Incorporation of Transposing Legislation

The requirements seem to have been adopted by DL 92/2010. The principle is that of the freedom of establishment or of provision of services, limited in the cases where "permissões administrativas" may be created (under Chapter III). The rules regarding debureaucratisation and procedural simplification will be applicable as of January 2011. However, a clearer picture can only be drawn when the DL 92/2010 begins to be applied and interpreted by the courts of law and relevant doctrine.

DL 92/2010 is a law of its own and does not explicitly modify any of the provisions of the Code of Administrative Procedure. However, it will eventually affect in a significant way provisions of the administrative legislation, due to its nature as a national measure implementing an EU directive. Significantly, it should be highlighted that the provision contained in the Draft SDIL (see footnote 3) establishing that the provisions of the Code of Administrative Procedure contradicting the diploma implementing the SD are revoked (Article 9 (9) of the Draft SDIL, which basically establishes that the Code of Administrative Procedure is only applicable as long as it does not contradict the SD implementing national legislation) does not appear in the new DL 92/2010.

In addition, an *omnibus* type of law was then foreseen, to adapt specific legislation that does not seem in line with the principles and rules laid down in the Draft SDIL. This law was meant to eventually modify more than 100 other laws, but it has not yet been adopted[5]. However, Chapter VIII of DL 92/2010 deals with changes in several sectoral regimens, such as

- Thermal activities (modifying DL 142/2004, of June 11),
- Dolphin and whale (et al.) observation in continental Portuguese territory (not including the Azores and Madeira—see Article 11 of Law 34/2006),
- Water for human consumption (DL 306/2007, of August 27),
- Municipal or multimunicipal public water supply and urban waste water treatment (DL 194/2009 and DL 379/93, under its current wording, given by DL 195/2009), or
- The incineration and co-incineration of waste (DL 85/2005, in its actual wording).

1.5 The Relationship of the Services Directive to Primary EU Law

In all areas not covered by the SD, Articles 49 and 56 of the Treaty on the Functioning of the EU (TFEU) remain applicable. However, in those areas covered by the SD, our reading of the ECJ case law suggests that the SD's application to any given type of service provision precludes the *direct effect* of the Treaty provisions.

Problems have not been identified in this context yet.

1.6 Screening

In each governmental department, one authority was designated to perform the screening of all the activities and administrative proceedings in force affected by the SD and the Draft SDIL.

[5] Cf. fn. 1.

As far as we know, a comprehensive report on the screening under Article 39 (1) and (5) of the SD was presented by the Portuguese government involving authorisation regimens (Article 9 (2) SD), evaluation under Article 15 (5) of the SD, and pluridisciplinary activities (Article 25 (2) SD). The results were very significant for a huge number of areas. The Annex of the DL 92/2010 provides a non-exhaustive list of activities covered by DL 92/2010 and to which the principles and rules laid down in DL 92/2010 are applicable.

2 Individual Articles of the Services Directive

2.1 Article 6 SD: Point of Single Contact (POSC)

2.1.1 Establishment of the POSC

Regarding this question, the Agência para a Modernização Administrativa, IP (Agency for Administrative Modernisation, Public Institute, hereinafter AMA, available at www.ama.pt, a public service created by Articles 5 (b) and 19 of Decree-Law 202/2006 of October 27 and implemented in 2007) expressed informally that "one of the key transformations on enterprise public services provisioning, to enhance Portugal's business climate position, is the implementation of a multi-channel approach. The POSC will be integrated into the Business Portal.

«The **Business Portal** (www.portaldaempresa.pt) is an integrated access point to the public services provided to companies. It was launched at the end of June 2006, easing access to public services provided to businesses through the Internet and all the information available in the Business Formalities Centres organized by the Business Life Cycle. It intends to be the privileged point of contact between businesses and public administration.

«In fact, the Business Portal is split into four main areas that report to the traditional cycle of business life: Creation, Management, Expansion, and Extinguishing. In each one of them, the managers will be able to find a set of information and, progressively, an extensive sample of interactive and transactional electronic services, with special attention for the following ones:

- Online process for the creation of a business, with fully digital supporting mechanisms, including upload documents and the recently launched Citizen's card;
- Online registration of business and commercial acts, such as the enterprise's social members and quotas;
- Enterprise electronic dossier, where the different processes of each enterprise with the public administration are assembled and made available to the enterprise representatives.

«The **POSC** will be available in the transaction of the Business Portal and will be available from day December 21, 2009.

«In three steps: Search, Select and View, you can find the answer to questions like: "What licenses do I need?", "What documents I need to upload?";

"Who can I contact?", "Can I submit the service online?"

«The licences are organized by activities (economic and non-economic) that the citizen/company pursues or intends to pursue. The activities are categorized into general themes for the intuitively find what you need. This research presents the name of "Search Activity".

«For each service activity there the following information:

- Possibility of access to information, guidance and contacts required for each type of licence or administrative authorisation, what procedures to perform, the necessary documents for the completion of the service and average time of execution, etc.;
- Access, with electronic authentication, to the online services that will allow companies to obtain the licences or administrative authorisations, previously identified as necessary to initiate the activity.
- Fill "smart forms" whose fields are constructed based on the search and results for indications, made by the service provider, or redirecting (via link) to the form or online service of the organism responsible for licence or administrative authorisation;
- Follow-up (monitoring) of the requested online service (time spent, where the process is, estimate time for completion, etc.). In this area information and services are clusters operated dynamically according to the user profile and the coordination process is simplified. Each user can access their personal data, the services required, the status and the documents that support them. The confidentiality of information available in this area is guaranteed for communications made between the bodies involved in the provision of services. Thus it is possible to provide public services in a way simple, transparent and safe for the entrepreneur.»

«In parallel to the electronic PSC, a physical network of single contact points providing access to procedures and formalities on activity services under the scope of the directive that will be created in the **company's Shop** (*Loja da Empresa*)."

2.1.2 Subjective Understanding, Competence Structure

In the Draft SDIL there was only supposed to be one SD POSC, the national coordinator for administrative cooperation in the area of services (*Coordenador Nacional para a cooperação administrativa na área dos serviços*—see Articles 29 and 30 of the Draft SDIL), and that POSC would not have any competences on licencing. In some cases, administrative competences may be reallocated as a result of the law simplification process, although the attributions of the POSC are very specific and mainly involve strict *coordination* attributions, with the EU and with national authorities competent in the field of authorisations, licencing, and so on. On the contrary, DL 92/2010 does not create such an entity and says, in Article

26/5, that the «ministry responsible for the area of economy indicates to the European Commission and Member States the name and address of a point of contact, in order to assure the mutual assistance coordination and the cooperation between competent administrative authorities». This looks to be an even more decentralised regimen than was in the draft SDIL.

2.1.3 Authorities with POSC-Function

The authority responsible for the management of the POSC is the AMA, identified above and established in 2007 (see also Portaria n.° 498/2007 de 30 de Abril—Define os estatutos da AMA and DL 116/2007 de 27 de Abril—Aprova a orgânica da AMA). However, the competent authorities for each licence/authorisation remain responsible for its own procedure and related information.

2.1.4 Involvement of Private Partners

Private partners have not been involved in the introduction of the POSC. Of course, private parties with specific attributions in areas covered by the SD will have to cooperate in the coordination and inter-administrative cooperation schemes to ensure the adequate functioning of the "single balcony". We have no information about if and how this kind of cooperation occurred.

2.1.5 Liability

Each competent authority is responsible for the accuracy and completeness of the contents and any other information regarding the licencing procedures it grants. The civil liability of the State and, generally, of any other public entities is regulated by Law 67/2007 of December 31. According to Law 67/2007, there is public liability (except in cases of risk responsibility or when special sacrifices may be imposed to ensure the public interest) when there are illegal actions or omissions, that is, when the violation of rules (*normas*) and legal principles are at stake. In principle, the liability is imposed on the administration service legally responsible for providing the information, independently of the internal relations between the public services involved.

2.2 *Article 7 SD: Right to Information*

Only Article 7 of the Draft SDIL recognises the rights granted by Article 7 of the SD. Of course, information rights herein established will in fact enlarge the catalogue of rights now established in our legislation. Article 6 of DL 92/2010 deals with information provided through the points of contact or service providers.

The rights apply also to national service providers, but not to business outside the scope of the SD. See our reply to "Application of Transposing Legislation to Domestic Service Providers".

2.3 Article 8 SD: Procedures by Electronic Means

2.3.1 Establishment

In Portugal the former government (XVII Constitutional Government) adopted a significant number of measures designed to dematerialise and simplify legislative (see, e.g., the *Simplex* programme) and administrative procedures. The electronic procedures established depend largely on the specific characteristics of each licence/authorisation. For example, some procedures demanded the use of digital signatures, given the risks involved in the licenced activity (e.g., lawyers), and others did not. However, guidelines have been delivered to lead the authorities in this complex process.

Electronic procedures were also thoroughly developed through the adoption of the Code of Public Contracts (*Código dos Contratos Públicos,* or CCP) implementing the public procurement directives (Directive 2004/18/EC, among others). Decree-Law 18/2008 (CCP) consecrates not only totally electronic procedures (e.g., electronic auctions) but also the systematic use of electronic platforms in the context of public contract adjudication procedures in the fields of public works contracts, public supply contracts, and public service contracts.

Article 6 DL 92/2010 formally creates a "single balcony", or single electronic point of contact, through the Internet in the already existing "Portal da Empresa" (see http://www.portaldaempresa.pt/cve/pt).

2.3.2 Innovative Impact of the Services Directive in this Regard

The implementation of the SD has an innovative impact in Portugal regarding the establishment of electronic procedures. However, Portugal already has a high level of online service sophistication. Some good examples are the ability to start a business totally online with the *On-line Firm* (*Empresa na Hora*), the dematerialisation of the Commercial Registry, industrial licences, and public contracts, etc.

2.3.3 Removal of Other Means

There has been a removal of other means of administrative proceedings. Apparently, according to Article 6 DL 92/2010, «the single electronic point of contact allows for any service provider or services recipients to accede electronically to the competent administrative authorities», giving them «the possibility to fulfil directly and immediately all acts and formalities necessary to accede to and exercise a services activity, including electronic means of payments, and the right to accede to procedures still running» (free translation, *Balcão Único Electrónico*).

2.4 Article 9 SD: Authorisation Schemes

2.4.1 Means of Less Restrictive Measure

This is one of the areas where we find it difficult to ascertain the scope of DL 92/2010. In a sense, on the one hand, looking at the question, we are inclined to say that in all areas described in the non-exhaustive annex, *a posteriori* control applies. On the other hand, the *a posteriori* regimen is not sufficient whenever the legislator feels that an "administrative permission" may be created (Article 9). This, however, must be done by the legislator according to the criteria defined in DL 92/2010.

Regarding existing regimes, the possibility of interpreting the law under the principle of *lex posterior derogate lex anterior* and uniform and coherent with the idea of the reasonable legislator (mainly with the EU law principle of indirect effect or conform interpretation) and the unity of the legal order seem to imply that the principle of freedom may be invoked by individuals or companies from the entry into force of DL 92/2010 (if not under EU law principles, even prior to this entry's into force).

2.4.2 Existing Authorisation Schemes/Procedures

When addressing this issue, we consider that the term "authorisation" is taken by the SD in a broader sense, as Recital 39 SD states:

«(39) The concept of "authorisation scheme" should cover, inter alia, the administrative procedures for granting authorisations, licences, approvals or concessions, and also the obligation, in order to be eligible to exercise the activity, to be registered as a member of a profession or entered in a register, roll or database, to be officially appointed to a body or to obtain a card attesting to membership of a particular profession».

Similarly, taking into consideration national administrative act classifications, such as that proposed by Professor Freitas do Amaral with Torgal (2001), pp. 256 et seq., we can say that among the "permissive acts" known to the doctrine one may find "authorisations" (by which the Administration allows someone to exercise a right or a pre-existent competence), "licences" (whenever the Administration allows someone to exercise a private activity relatively prohibited), "concessions" (involving the exercise of a public activity by a private party) or "admissions" (through which the Administrations empowers a private party with a certain "quality" attributing to it some rights and duties). The impact of the SD, for instance, in the duration of concessions is probably yet to be determined, although concessions, if included under EU law's principle of conferral, should generally be included in the scope of Article 12 of SD.

One main implication will be that regarding the tacit authorisation principle, which will subvert, in a sense, the administrative practices (and law) valid thus far. Many authorisation schemes are probably eliminated, but some may be created, for there are imperative reasons of public interest. Since the implementation limit period has already expired, the principle of tacit authorisation is already in force in the fields of services covered by the SD, given the principle of vertical direct effect of non-implemented EU directives. Under the Code of Administrative Procedure, administrative procedures have a general duration of 90 days and, after this period elapses, the individual may presume its claim to be denied (*indeferimento tácito*) or deferred (*deferimento tácito*). Now, although the DL 92/2010 does not in fact establish a maximum deadline for administrative procedures, it results from it, implicitly though, that even when a "permissão administrativa" is deemed necessary and created (in cases where Article 9 (1) is complied with), a tacit authorisation should be recognised. Of course, this *a maiori ad minus* argument is not exempt of criticism (and so the lack of clarity of DL 92/2010 is evident). Exceptions are overriding reasons of public interest (see Articles 8 (2) (b) and 30).

2.4.3 Simple Notifications

In my perspective, simple notification requirements, especially if they can be complied with after establishment in Portugal, are not to be considered "authorisation schemes" under the SD. Of course, the broader interpretation of the notion of "requisite" laid down in Article 4 (7) of the SD (as to include any "obligation" whatsoever) and the readings of the Handbook (p. 14, p. 2.3.1: "[the obligation to] present a declaration to the competent authorities") may lead to a different conclusion. However, we submit that a posteriori declaration obligations may be easily justified (at least) and are treated from a very different perspective by ECJ case law.

2.5 Article 10 SD: Conditions for the Granting of Authorisation

2.5.1 Recognition of Requirements

A variety of EU legislation and ECJ case law already acknowledges or imposes the principle of mutual recognition of legislations and authorisations in a variety of forms (even though more evident when we consider goods and not services—but see, e.g., a case of mutual recognition in the field of the wholesale distribution of medicines). Since the SD is barely implemented, so far there are no specific problems from the SD and this particular proviso. Article 11 (1) (a) of DL 92/2010 implements Article 10 (3) of the SD. Some problems were already identified—even before the SD—in the fields of public contractors, service providers, and vendors and in the leasing of goods in the field of public contracts.

2.5.2 Granting Authorisation Throughout the Whole National Territory and Exceptions

Article 17 of DL 92/2010 establishes the principle according to which an authorisation gives the service provider the right to accede and exercise its activity in the entirety of the national territory. For the authorisation to be limited in its geographical area, imperative reasons of mandatory public interest (overriding reasons relating to the public interest) must exist. Given our administrative organisational model and taking into consideration that the autonomous regions (Madeira and Azores[6]) and municipalities (*autarquias locais*) have scarce attributions in this areas (safe for some particular activities, due to their natural, e.g., territorial scope, such as ambulant vendors or commercial licencing), being the regulation of these activities dealt under State administration (even if indirect, as explained above) or by associations or entities integrated within the corporative autonomous administration with jurisdiction over the national territory, this issue is not likely to lead to many problems.

In DL 92/2010 no areas of 'overriding reasons relating to the public interest' (Article 10 (4) SD) to justify regional authorisation are specifically identified as such.

2.5.3 Entitlement to Grant Authorisation, Court Review of Administrative Decisions

Generally speaking, Portuguese law guarantees that, whenever the conditions for the granting of an authorisation are met, the authorisation must be granted. However, in some cases the law may recognise in some specific cases a certain level of "administrative freedom", "discretion" or "public autonomy" (Prof. Sérvulo Correia) in determining whether the requirements are met or not. In those cases, the courts may determine the legal principles that the administration must apply, but not the specific contents of the decision (Article 71 (2) of the Code of Procedure before Administrative Courts, CPTA):

«When the emission of the intended act involves the formulation of judgments typical of the administrative function and the case does not allow the identification of just one solution as legally possible, the Court may not determine the contents of the act that must be adopted, but should determine the obligations pending over

[6] Under article 228 of the Constitution, the Regions have legislative powers in the matters provided for in the "estatutos politico-administrativos" that are not reserved to the sovereign powers of the Republic.

the Administration when deciding and adopting the contested act» (free translation and adaptation).

In sum, it is fair to say that all decisions can be appealed to the administrative courts, who can review the legality but not the merits of any decision.

However, we ought to say that whenever discretionary powers are conferred to the administration (recognising its direct possibilities of action—through the expression "may" (*pode*) or the use of subjective or imprecise type concepts ("*conceitos subjectivos ou imprecisos tipo*"—through formulas such as «exceptional reasons of public interest», «strategy defined for the sector», etc.), judicial review will in fact be quite limited (error in facts, misuse of power, manifest error of appreciation, compatibility of the discretionary powers used with the general principles of administrative activity, like equality, proportionality, good faith, impartiality, justice, etc.).

2.5.4 Reasoning Administrative Decisions

Article 268 (3) of the Portuguese Constitution establishes that every act of the administration must be motivated (*fundamentação*) both expressly and in a clear way (accessible to the recipient) every time it affects rights or legally protected interests. Accordingly, the Code of Administrative Procedure, approved by the Decree-Law (DL) 442/91, of November 15, in wording resulting from DL 6/96 of January 31, also consecrates such an obligation in Articles 124 (1) (a) or (c) (cases where the motivation is mandatory) and 125 (duty to give an express reasoning and its content). The case law of the administrative courts of law is consistent with the idea that the administrative acts must be clearly and expressly reasoned, guaranteeing that the applicant can understand the foundations of the administration act. This duty of formal reasoning (indication of motives) and material reasoning (provision of sufficient and adequate reasons to substantially justify the adopted decision) must also be contextual (go alongside the adopted act). Non-compliance with these reasoning obligations turns the decision into an invalid one, except if the administration was not *obliged* (*vinculada*) or if the decision could not be different in its contents, transforming the essential formality into a non-essential formality.

2.5.5 Allocation of Competences

There has been no (re)allocation of competences in this context.

2.6 Article 11 SD: Duration of Authorisation

According to Article 16 (1) of DL 92/2010 authorisations will be granted for an unlimited duration and, whenever limited, they will be automatically renewed, assuming that all the conditions relevant to the granting of the authorisation remain fulfilled. Decree-Law DL 92/2010 excludes from these principles authorisations limited in number or duration by an overriding reason relating to the public interest, in accordance with Article 11 (1) (c) of the SD. There is no specification about the cases under which these exceptions would apply.

On the one hand, before the SD (so, for the Administration, until 28 December 2009), Portugal did not have the unlimited validity of the authorisations granted as a legal or general principle. On the other hand, no provision or principle forebodes the concession of limited duration authorisations. It could most probably be said, however, that, in principle, authorisations (in the stricter sense, i.e., pre-existing rights in the legal sphere of the recipient whose exercise is "deconditioned" by a permissive administrative act adopted by the competent administrative authority) have no pre-designed limitation in duration, and, even when that validity is limited, renovation is only dependent on the requisites that founded the original concession.

2.7 Article 12 SD: Selection from Among Several Candidates

There is no general provision corresponding to Article 12 of the SD in the national legislation. Only Article 17 (3) of DL 92/2010 implements it, imposing the application of the Code of Public Contracts (DL 18/2008, which implemented, e.g., Directive 2004/18/EC and Directive 2004/17/EC). Of course, as is pointed out in the questionnaire, ECJ case law and EU law is well known and applicable in Portugal, to the extent provided for under the EU law, namely, under Article 8 (4) of the Portuguese Constitution.

In our view, comparable regulations already exist, for instance, in certain areas outside the scope of the SD, such as telecommunications.

2.8 Article 13 SD: Authorisation Procedures

2.8.1 A Priori Determination of the Duration of Administrative Procedures

Usually the legislator determines a priori the duration of an administrative procedure. Often, the competent public authorities have the power to extend the duration of the administrative procedure, though in limited terms in duration and reason. In other cases, the duration is pre-established and it is up to the legislator to define the deadlines that, if not complied with by the competent authority for the granting of the authorisation, allows for the applicant to presume (tacit) denial in order to appeal against the tacit decision, requiring the administration to adopt the act (*acção de condenação para a prática de acto devido*).

2.8.2 General Rule for the Duration

Generally speaking, Articles 108 (2) and 109 (2) of the Code of Administrative Procedure establish a general deadline of 90 days in the case of tacit authorisation (*autorização tácita*) or tacit non-authorisation (*presunção de indeferimento*). This 90-day deadline may be, in some cases, prorogued and, whenever the beginning is dependent on the compliance of specific formalities, only when these are fulfilled do the 90 days start to count. So, in fact, the effective duration of administrative procedures is generally quite a bit longer than the 90 days specified. Of course, special laws may establish different specific deadlines for the Administration's decision, which often happens.

2.8.3 Exceptions of the General Rule for the Duration

It is not possible to differ from the prescribed duration of procedures, except if the law applicable to the procedure confers the administration the power to suspend or interrupt the, in principle, applicable deadlines. If this is not the case and if the authority does not respond to the filed application within the prescribed time, the authorisation is "deemed to have been granted to the provider" (Handbook 6.1.8).

2.8.4 Tacit Authorisation in the National Legal Order So Far

The question of tacit authorisation is very delicate in Portugal. Limiting the answer to the actual legislation in force, it must be recognised that the Code of Administrative Procedure states, in Article 108 (1) that «[w]henever the adoption of an administrative act or the exercise of a right by an individual [including e.g. companies, of course] depend on the approval or authorisation granted by an administrative organ, [these] are considered granted, except if the law provides differently, if the decision is not granted in the deadline established by law.» In Article 108 (3), the legislator nominates the cases where such tacit authorisation may happen. Some doctrine strived to increase the scope of these tacit authorisation scheme (see for instance Esteves de Oliveira et al. (1998), pp. 476–484). Alongside with the "tacit act", however, Article 109 of the same Code states that "without prejudice to the former article", the lack of decision in the deadline established by law enables the individual to presume its pretension as overruled and denied, e.g. for effect of appealing to the Courts against the Administration decision. The consistent case law of the Administrative Courts (including the Supreme, the STA) has been limiting the scope of the tacit authorisation regime under the actual legislation.

Of course, it must now be considered that, although under Article 9 (2) of the Draft SDIL it was said that to «procedures and formalities (…) applies the principle of tacit authorisation», DL 92/2010 has no specific provision in the same direction. In fact, the legislator does not recognise in this regard a general permission of a tacit non-authorisation, clearly stating that only «for certain specific [both elements must be present] activities a tacit non-authorisation scheme may be established, if it is justified by overriding reasons of public interest, particularly the legitimate interests of third parties».

In our view, this means that the scope of the tacit authorisation principle will increase significantly. For us, the administrative courts are bound to read the reference to "special laws" in Article 108 of the Code of Administrative Procedure as including services covered by DL 92/2010. The principle of full effectiveness of EU law and Article 8 (4) of the Portuguese Constitution will both command such an interpretation.

2.8.5 Formal and Substantive Effects of Tacit Authorisation

A tacit authorisation has both formal and substantive effects. The tacit authorisation under Article 108 (3) of the Code of Administrative Procedure and in some urbanistic legislation is considered, for all legal purposes, an administrative authorisation act with all the legal and practical effects.

2.8.6 Rules of Formally Granted Authorisations Applicable to Tacit Authorisation

The same rules apply to tacit (fictitious) authorisations which apply to formally granted administrative authorisations.

2.9 Articles 14, 15, 16 SD

The national legislator identified a need to adapt national law to implement these articles. An *omnibus law* covering all the activities that ought to be subject to modifications due to the principles and rules laid down in the SD is being prepared.

As regards the self-screening of the Member States some concern was expressed by civil society in a conference held in Lisbon on 10 November 2009 and promoted by the Directorate-General for Economic Activities.

2.10 Articles 14–19 SD and Articles 22–27 SD

There are no relevant issues in this context, since Portugal has long engaged in the modern regulation tradition and the state model is assumed, in general, to be that of the state regulator instead of the state provider.

2.11 Articles 28 ff. SD: Administrative Cooperation

2.11.1 Transnational Administrative Cooperation Prior to the Implementation of the Services Directive

There were no provisions on transnational administrative assistance in Portugal prior to the transposition of the SD. There are provisions generally applicable to domestic administrative assistance under the Code of Administrative Procedure and in several specific areas (e.g., medicines, competition, etc.).

2.11.2 Re-Arrangement with National Rules on Administrative Cooperation

The SD did not give a cause to (re)arrange the provisions for administrative assistance in a general or uniform way. The Draft SDIL (even in the perspective of the individuals concerned) would have had an impact on the scope and contents of administrative assistance obligations. The matter is regulated in a broader way in Articles 21 and 22 of DL 92/2010.

2.11.3 Provisions on Financial Compensation for Transnational Administrative Cooperation

As far as we are aware of, there are no provisions on financial compensation.

2.11.4 Adaption of Rules on Data Protection and Professional Secrets

No specific change was introduced in the data protection legislation. The SD on professional secrets may be directly invoked before the Administration, beginning on the 29 December 2009.

2.12 Article 29 SD and Chapter VI in General

There have been no further discussions and discourses in this context.

2.13 Convergence Programme (Chapter VII of the Services Directive)

We are aware that there are doubts on whether some service activities are included, for instance, those covered by Directive 96/96/EC, which seem to be formally included in the exception of services covered by acts adopted under the former Title V of the EC Treaty (Article 2 (2) (d) SD).

3 Assessment of the Impact of the Services Directive

3.1 Extent of the Impact

The impact of the SD on administrative procedure law, administrative law for business activities, and even beyond can be assessed as severe in Portugal, too. But the discussion has yet to be developed. Some authors have already expressed this same perspective, since the SD will have a significant impact on the need for the Administration to adapt to tacit authorisation principles. The academy has long been discussing the SD and will certainly consider it in a thorough way after publication of the implementing legislation.

3.2 Assessment on the Transposing Legislation

So far, no implementation has been carried out, except, probably, the presentation of the screening reports on the 28 December 2009. The Draft SDIL divulged by the Directorate-General for Economic Activities seems to transpose the SD in a general way, and this judgement is confirmed to a significant extent when we analyse first hand DL 92/2010. This may lead to some legal uncertainty regarding the implications of the SDIL (as *lex generalis*) in the specific authorisation regimens (*lex specialis*) still in force.

3.3 Most Important and Profound Changes Induced by the Services Directive

The adaptation of the Administration to the principle of tacit authorisation and the simplification of administrative procedures (suppressing a significant number of authorisation procedures), contravening historical Portuguese administrative tradition.

References

For legislation, jurisprudence and websites please refer to 1.1 of the report and footnotes directly.

Commission Handbook on the Implementation of the Services Directive (2007) Available at http://ec.europa.eu/internal_market/services/docs/services-dir/guides/handbook_pt.pdf

Esteves de Oliveira M, Gonçalves P, Pacheco de Amorim J (1998) Código de Procedimento Administrativo—comentado, 2.ª Edição, Almedina, Coimbra, pp 476–484

Freitas do Amaral D, Torgal L (2001) Curso de Direito Administrativo, vol. II, Almedina, Coimbra, pp 256 et seq

Ferreira Malaquias P (2008) Portuguese Report. In: Koeck HF, Karollus MM (eds) The New Services Directive of the European Union—Hopes and Expectations from the Angle of a (Further) Completion of the Internal Market, FIDE XXIII Congress Linz 2008, vol 3. Congress Publications, Nomos, Vienna, pp 299–307

The Implementation of the Services Directive in Romania

Dacian C. Dragos and Bogdana Neamtu

1 General Remarks on the Transposition Strategy and General Understanding of the Implementation

1.1 Main References Used in this Research

The main references used for this study are transposition laws and regulations and interviews with officials involved in the implementation process. We also interviewed practitioners from public administration in order to test the level of awareness regarding the existence and the implementation effects of the Directive.

The main legislative sources for this research are the Emergency Government Ordinance (hereafter EGO) no. 49/20.05/2009 (umbrella law)[1] and Governmental Decision no. 922/1.09/2010 regarding the creation of the Point of Single Contact (POSC).[2] The legal acts are available online in Romanian at www.cdep.ro (the official website of the lower Chamber of Parliament).

A list with the sector specific legislation that was amended is not publicly available; it was obtained from the Department for European Affairs with a great

Dr. Dacian C. Dragos and Dr. Bogdana Neamtu, both Babes Bolyai University, Cluj Napoca.

[1] Published in the Official Monitor of Romania no. 366 from 1.06.2009, approved by the Parliament through Law no. 68/16.04/2010.
[2] Published in the Official Monitor of Romania no. 644 from 15.09.2010.

D. C. Dragos (✉) · B. Neamtu
Babes Bolyai University, Cluj Napoca, Romania
e-mail: daciandragos@yahoo.com

B. Neamtu
e-mail: bogdananeamtu@apubb.ro

U. Stelkens et al. (eds.), *The Implementation of the EU Services Directive*,
DOI: 10.1007/978-90-6704-840-8_22,

deal of difficulty.[3] In-depth analysis of all these laws was necessary in order to assess the impact of the Directive.

Other sources include the websites of several institutions: National Center 'Digital Romania',[4] The Ministry of Communication and Information Society[5]; The front-desk of the national POSC (current form).[6]

In addition, several interviews were carried out with senior officials who were actively involved in the transposition process, mostly during screening. These officials were from the Department of European Affairs, the General Secretariat of the Government and the Ministry of Internal Affairs and Administration.

We also looked at the Policy reports regarding the status of the Services Directive in the Member States: (1) Council of the European Union, State of Implementation of the Services Directive, Information Note from the Commission Services, May 2010,[7] and (2) EUROCHAMBERS, Policy Survey: Mapping the Implementation of the Services Directive in EU Member States, February 2010.[8]

1.2 Impact of the Services Directive

1.2.1 Profound Cause of Changes to National Law?

The transposition of European Directives in general needs to be assessed in the Romanian context characterised by limited administrative capacity. Regarding transposition, this limited capacity is mainly due to a very small number of trained professionals in this respect. This situation is even more dramatic when it comes to local public authorities. In this context, transposition of Directives is usually done by adopting legal provisions that mirror the Directive. The national umbrella law adopted for transposing the Services Directive is no exception (EGO 49/2009). For several years Romania has been trying to codify administrative procedural rules (not the substantive provisions) but the process is advancing at a snail's pace. It has faced opposition from several interest groups and can be described as highly

[3] As an anecdotic parenthesis, our request based on the Freedom of Information Law was disregarded by the DEA, as were our insistent messages that we needed the information quickly. Due to the tight deadline for drafting the study we didn't have the time to go to court over this matter. So we decided to ask for the help of a journalist, whose inquiry has to be answered within 24 h (FOIA law). It worked.

[4] Online at http://www.cnrd.ro/ (only in Romanian).

[5] Online at http://www.mcsi.ro/.

[6] Online at http://www.e-guvernare.ro/.

[7] Online at http://register.consilium.europa.eu/pdf/en/10/st09/st09475.en10.pdf.

[8] Online at http://ec.europa.eu/internal_market/services/docs/services-dir/studies/euro chambers-report_en.pdf .

politicised and controversial. Given this, any radical modification of administrative laws in general and/or the codification of substantive procedures is out of the question for the time being.

As will be detailed in a subsequent section, in numerous of the amended sector specific laws, there is mention that the provisions of these laws are to be read together with those of the umbrella law, even if this law is very general and does not provide concrete and operational provisions for each sector.

With regard to the broader impact, at the level of public administration, the outlook is more encouraging. During the interviews we were told that the general perception with regard to the effect of the Directive mostly concerns the process of administrative simplification. During the process of altering the sector specific laws the Department of European Affairs carried out negotiations with the relevant line ministries regarding the elimination of redundant requirements for economic operators, the elimination of reauthorisation every two or three years, the elimination of authorisation for branch offices within Romania, and requiring simple copies for authorisation rather than original documents. Also, hope was expressed that the Services Directive will help Romanian economic operators and individuals who will either provide transnational services or will become established in other Member States.

1.2.2 Involvement in the Transposition Process

For the transposition of Directive 2006/123/CE, at a meeting on 31.10.2007 the Romanian government approved Memorandum no. 3047/AC/25.09.2007 regarding the adoption of necessary measures for speeding up the transposition and implementation process of Directive 2006/123/CE on services in the internal market, also known as Services Directive. The institution responsible at the national level for the transposition of the directive was the Department for European Affairs (hereafter DEA, the central authority whose main role is to coordinate European affairs at the national level; it is directly subordinated to the Prime Minister).

In this context the objectives of the Services Directive were split into five working dossiers: (a) the drafting of the framework legislative act for the transposition of the Services Directive; (b) the establishment of a programme for administrative simplification, which will include the creation of Points of Single Contact for services providers as well as the necessary electronic infrastructure; (c) the screening of existing legislation in order to identify and eliminate provisions which act as barriers to the free movement of services and of establishment; (d) the implementation of the mechanism for administrative cooperation among the competent authorities from the Member States in order to monitor the services providers and the provided services; and (e) the development of the system for electronic procedures for information exchanges and mutual assistance among the Member States.

For the implementation of these dossiers, based on the provisions of the Memorandum, four special inter-ministerial working groups were established (among their members were also representatives of the Ministry for SMEs, Commerce, and Business Environment, appointed through Decision no. 1451/ 07.12.2007. The Directorate for Business Environment and Liberal Professions within the Minister for SMEs appointed representatives to all four special working groups, given the economic reasoning that constitutes the foundation of the Services Directive). The groups were:

(a) Special working group on 'Legislation Monitoring and Administrative Cooperation', coordinated by the Ministry of Economy and Finance together with the Ministry of Interior and Administrative Reform;
(b) Special working group on the 'Normative Implementation Framework', coordinated by the Ministry for Small and Medium-Sized Enterprises, Trade, Tourism and Liberal Professions;
(c) Special working group on 'Electronic Procedures', coordinated by the Ministry of Communications and Information Technology (MCIT);
(d) Special working group on 'the Single Point of Contact', for which DEA proposed the Agency for the Information Society Services as coordinator.

The participation of other actors was limited. According to a policy survey from 2010 that was conducted among the National Chambers of Commerce, in Romania the Chambers' participation was limited to the framework of the social partnership discussions. Cooperation among the different tiers of government was also limited. In most cases central government authorities are responsible for the authorisation of services and of liberal professions. In Romania local and/or regional authorities might be involved in this process with regard to the POSC. However, since it was decided that there is only one national POSC, their involvement is limited to getting their websites interconnected with the POSC.

1.3 (National) Scope of Application

There has not been any public discussion in Romania with regard to the scope of the Services Directive. The umbrella law adopted states in Article 4 that its provisions concern both the services provided by operators established in Romania and the services provided in Romania by operators that are established in another Member State (transnational). This seems to suggest that there is equal treatment for both transnational services and purely domestic ones.

In practice, however, the sector specific laws amended as a result of the Services Directive tell a completely different story. A distinction needs to be made between regulations adopted prior to the transposition of the Directive by the national umbrella law and those drafted after this moment (late 2009 and ongoing). The existing regulations (amended in order to comply with the Directive) seem to favour the providers from other Member States that apply for authorisation in

Romania. The requirements for them seem to be in some cases more favourable than those for Romanian providers applying for the same authorisation. The same view was expressed during the interviews, when we were told that the philosophy of the government was to put transnational providers as well as operators from other Member States established in Romania in a better position. The reason for doing this has to do with the complexity of the process for altering existing legislation. It was easier to just add several articles stating the requirements for non-national providers than to change the entire regulation. Beginning with the newly adopted laws in the field of services (mostly in 2010), a more equal treatment is provided for, which includes both national and non-national applicants.

One interesting fact refers to the transnational provision of services. Some regulations make no reference to such possibility. They only refer to getting an authorisation, which implicitly could mean that transnational provision of services, in the absence of establishment, is not possible (tourism[9]). Another interpretation is taking into consideration that all field laws amended as a result of implementing the Directive specify that their provisions shall be read together with those of the transposing (umbrella) law, which among other things states that transnational providers may provide services in Romania freely or based on registration into a register, if this requirement follows from the transposing (umbrella) law. One of these two opposing interpretations will be confirmed by practice, when providers established in another Member State and having an authorisation there seek to provide the service in Romania.

Summarising, based on the screening of the implementing special laws, we identified three types of approaches towards service provision in Romania:

(a) Nationals are always subjected to authorisation; some of the schemes adopted in 2010, thus while in the process of implementing the Directive, have been simplified when compared with the old ones.
(b) Nationals of other Member States applying for authorisation in Romania in the context of the right of establishment are subjected to the same rules as Romanian nationals and in some cases to special rules regarding the documents to be presented or conditions to be fulfilled.
(c) Transnational providers (authorised in another Member State) may provide the service in Romania based on that authorisation, which has to be recognised by a competent authority, but are sometimes subjected to registration into a professional register. However, many special laws do not mention transnational providers, leading to the conclusion that they are either subjected to reauthorisation or covered by the Directive and transposing law and are thus free to provide services in Romania without the need to register.

[9] Order no. 1866/2010 of the Minister of regional development and tourism for the approval of methodological norms regarding the criteria and the methodology for granting the tourism license and brevet, published in the Official Journal no. 544 from 04.08. 2010.

1.4 Incorporation of Transposing Legislation

As mentioned before, since codification is a very complex and complicated process, the Services Directive was transposed by adopting an umbrella law which mirrors the general principles of the Directive (EGO no. 49/2009) and by altering sector specific laws. In addition to the umbrella law, there is another Governmental Decision regarding the creation of the POSC. While the umbrella law mirrors the provisions of the Directive, problems arose with regard to sector specific laws. According to a document from February 2010 of the Council of the European Union, in nine of the Member States, including Romania, the drafting of the required changes to sector specific legislation has been significantly delayed (the other countries are Austria, Cyprus, Finland, Greece, Ireland, Luxembourg, Portugal, Romania and Slovenia). To date, 52 sector specific laws have been modified. However, Romania has informed the Commission that other legislative acts are in the process of being adopted.

We can thus argue that there has been both a horizontal approach to transposition as well as a vertical one. The umbrella law has seven chapters—Chap. I general provisions, Chap. II administrative simplification, Chap. III freedom of establishment for service providers, Chap. IV free movement of services, Chap. V the quality of services, Chap. VI administrative cooperation, and Chap. VII final provisions. Generally it could be stated that there are no additional requirements in this law compared with the Services Directive. Most of the provisions are rather general and act as guidelines for the alteration of sector specific legislation.
For the purpose of this study, each of the 52 sector specific laws was analysed and assessed from the perspective of the following criteria: equal treatment, administrative simplification (deadlines, types of acts required, remedies etc.), and departure from the requirements of the Services Directive. Several of the conclusions are listed below:

- Most of the sector specific legislation modified in order to implement the Directive makes reference to the fact that its provisions shall be read together with the transposing law, EGO no. 49/2009. This leads to a type of circular reasoning, since the purpose of altering the sector specific laws was to incorporate the more general principles of Ordinance no. 49/2009. In many cases the specifics of how these provisions will operate in certain fields are not clear.
- As already mentioned, some of the newly adopted acts after the passing of EGO no. 49/2009 are more 'in the spirit' of the Directive, mainly providing for the equal treatment of all providers who want to be authorised in Romania.
- In certain cases the laws provide for the automatic recognition of transnational providers, who only need to make a request to be registered into a national registry. There are, however, cases when this recognition is conditional: there is the possibility to verify that requirements from the national law are met and if they are not then the likely result is refusal. For example, in the field of cadastre, geodesy and cartography, the recognition is conditioned upon the completion of an internship or applied study period ranging from one to six months and the

completion of practical work similar to the one for which the authorisation is required.[10] There are cases when there is no reference to the possibility to provide a service transnationally. In these cases there is equal treatment for establishment but no formal conditions for recognition.[11] The question here, as mentioned before, is whether this means that operators can provide the service-based directly on the provisions of EGO no. 49/2009 (umbrella law) and, if not, what requirements apply to these situations? In other situations, registration of transnational providers is required only if they provide the service on a regularly basis. If the service is provided temporarily or occasionally, no registration is required (translators).[12] A final situation that occurs is the requirement of notification imposed on transnational providers. They need to notify the Romanian Government by becoming registered into the National Commerce Registry. This, however, is equivalent with establishment.[13]

- Administrative simplification implied that limited authorisations will be eliminated from the sector specific laws. This happened in many cases. There are, however, situations where authorisation is said to be unlimited in duration but which still requires an 'application for continuation' every 4 years, which includes the verification of the fulfilment of the conditions for the granting the initial authorisation.[14] Thus, we actually have a system of limited authorisation, subjected to renewal. There are other cases when authorisation is clearly for a

---

[10] Order no. 107/2010 of the Director of the National Agency for Cadastre and Real Estate Publicity for the approval of regulation regarding the authorisation and the recognition of authorisation for Romanian natural and legal persons, for those belonging to other Member States or to the European Economic Space in order to carry out and evaluate works in the field of cadastre, geodesy, and cartography, published in the Official Journal no. 231 from 13.04.2010.

[11] Governmental Emergency Ordinance no. 25/2010 regarding the modification of Governmental Ordinance no. 58/1998 regarding the organisation and functioning of tourist activity in Romania published in the Official Journal no. 211 from 6.04.2010; Order no. 1204/2010 of the Minister of regional development and tourism for the authorisation of beaches for tourist activities, published in the Official Journal no. 239 from 15.04.2010; Order no. 1296/2010 of the minister of regional development and tourism for the approval of the methodological norms regarding the classification of tourist accommodation structures, published in the Official Journal no. 312 from 10.05.2010.

[12] Law no. 128/2010 for the approval of Governmental Ordinance no. 13/2010 for modification of regulations in the field of justice in order to transpose the Directive 2006/123/CE of the European Parliament and of the Council from 12.12.2006 regarding services within the internal market, published in the Official Journal no. 453 from 02.07.2010; Law no. 85/2010 for the modification of Governmental Emergency Ordinance no. 86/2006 regarding the organisation of the activity of practitioners in insolvency, published in the Official Journal no. 327 from 18.05.2010.

[13] Order no. 87/2010 of the Minister of the interior and public administration for the approval of the authorisation methodology for the persons who carry out works in the field of fire protection, published in the Official Journal no. 238 from 14.04.2010.

[14] Order no. 153/2010 of the State Inspector General in construction for the approval of procedures for the evaluation of laboratories and trials in the construction activity in order to get an authorisation, published in the Official Journal no. 187 from 24.03.2010.

limited period of time (3 years, for instance).[15] These cases can be considered to be an infringement of the Directive, as no reasons of public interest were invoked to support the decision to keep them. There are cases when the authorisation dossier differs for national and other Member State providers.[16] There are instances when both certified[17] and non-certified translation[18] of documents is required; also there are instances when a simple declaration of the provider is accepted as opposed to a declaration in front of a legal notary.[19]

In conclusion, it can be argued that the provisions of the umbrella law have not been implemented in a unitary and consistent manner. It is clear that the codification of administrative provisions would have led to better consistency. Steps are being made towards a unitary approach—for example the deadlines for responding to a request for authorisation have been harmonised with the Directive and national law. Currently authorities need to respond in 30 days with a possible prolongation of 15 in some cases. However, there are still cases when different deadlines apply, ranging from 60 days to 3 months.[20] It is also clear that in some cases the Romanian authorities tried to comply only 'for the record'. For example, there is only a general legal reference in the sector specific laws with regard to contestation and possible remedies available to economic operators. This is the general law which applies in cases of litigation between private parties and public authorities (Law no.554/2004 on judicial review). More specific requirements in this sense are not included. Also, the authorisation schemes have not substantially

---

[15] Order no. 391/2010 of the Minister of economy commerce, business environment regarding the approval of the procedure for technical-professional certification of specialists for the activity of closing down and reconstructing mines/quarries, published in the Official Journal no. 188 from 24.03.2010; Law no. 40/2010 for the modification of Law no. 333/2003 regarding the protection of objectives, goods, values and the safety of persons, published in the Official Journal no. 153 from 09.03.2010.

[16] Order no. 14/2010 of the president of the National Regulatory Authority in the field of energy for the modification of the regulation for the certification of economic operators who design, implement, and verify electrical works, approved through the Order of the president of the National Regulatory Authority in the field of energy no. 24/2007, published in the Official Journal no. 288 from 03.05.2010.

[17] Order no. 154/2010 of the State General Inspector in construction for the approval of the procedure for the authorisation of construction sites supervisors, published in the Official Journal no. 184 from 23.03.2010.

[18] Order 306/299/4253 of the Minister of labour, family and social protection, of the president of the National authority for disabled persons, of the Minister of education, youth and sports, for the modification of Order 671/1640/61/2007 regarding the approval of the methodology of certification of interprets for sight-impaired and hearing-impaired persons, published in the Official Journal no. 466 from 10.07.2010.

[19] Law no. 40/2010 for the modification of Law no. 333/2003 regarding the protection of objectives, goods, values and the safety of persons, published in the Official Journal no. 153 from 09.03.2010.

[20] Order no. 1083/2010 of the minister of regional development and housing modifying Order no. 777/2003 regarding the certification of specialists for activities in construction, published in the Official Journal no. 8 from 06.01.2010.

changed. There were minimal amendments regarding the acceptance of copies or of documents issued in other states and no requirements or incentives for authorities to use other languages, not even when the dossier of the transnational provider is different.

As already mentioned, codification of administrative rules could have solved many of these problems providing in the same time a more unitary perspective on how things in this field should be handled.

1.5 The Relationship of the Services Directive to Primary EU Law

There are no debates in the Romanian legal literature on this issue. We argue that in this case of divergence between the case law of the ECJ referred to by Article 4 (8) SD and the express wording of the Directive in Article 16 (1) (b), the overriding reasons established by case law should prevail, for two reasons: (a) they are referred to at some point in the Directive, so they do not just stem from the case law of the ECJ but have been included in legislation; and (b) if the Directive is addressed to Member States, these reasons should be treated as 'rights' of the Member States, to be used when transposing the Directive into national law. The restricted range of justifications shall be treated as only 'guiding', as in another part of the same piece of legislation there is a definition of the concept, which encompasses a wide range of justifications.

It appears that the reading together of the Article 16 (1) para 3 and Article 16 (3) of the Directive is confusing, as they are mostly overlapping. A simpler solution would have been to just add requirements arising from employment conditions (including collective agreements) to the definition of 'necessity'. The 'faithful' transposition of the Services Directive into EGO no. 49/2009[21] has, consequently, transposed provisions that are equally puzzling, only this time in Romanian.

1.6 Screening

The main actor involved in the screening process was the DEA, whose main role consisted of coordinating the process. In order to carry out the screening a task force comprising legal staff from the Ministry of Justice was created. Working sessions were organised with representatives of public authorities with competences in the field of services as well as with representatives of professional bodies whose role was to provide the competent regulatory agencies with data about their field and how services are operated within their field. The screening process was carried out

[21] Article 16 (3) and (4) of the EGO 49/2009.

based on a document called 'Methodology for the evaluation of legislation' approved by the Inter-ministry Committee for the coordination and monitoring of the implementation of EGO no. 49/2009. The declared goal of the screening process was to simplify the existing authorisation schemes and to terminate the requirements that were incompatible with the Directive or the ones which could not be justified. As mentioned above, the Commerce Chamber was not involved. This institution was considered less relevant, as the transposing legislation 'was a task of the Government'. Instead, they worked closely with the National Office of the Commerce Registry. Thus far, 52 sector specific acts have been amended.

2 Individual Articles of the Services Directive

2.1 Article 6 SD: Point of Single Contact (POSC)

2.1.1 Establishment of the POSC

The Romanian POSC is still under construction and not yet functioning (last checked December 6th, 2010). The umbrella law states that it should be fully operational by December 1st. A short background regarding its creation is provided below.

In the early stages of the transposition process of the Services Directive, the Agency for the Services of the Information Society was in charge of establishing the POSC (the Agency was created in 2007, it is subordinated to the Ministry of Communication and Information Technologies and has as its main goal the implementation and operation of the IT systems which provide services for e-government at the national level). Thus, ASIS was designated by a Memorandum of the Government to be the institution responsible for the conceptualisation and implementation of the POSC as well as for the coordination of the activities regarding the electronic procedures included in it. It was said at that time that an institution would be appointed for the operation of the POSC concomitant with the transposition of the Services Directive into the national legislation. In 2009, the Government adopted EGO no. 49/2009 which in Article 6 stated that ASIS was responsible for the creation of the POSC, which was meant to fulfil all the functions required by the Services Directive.

In 2009 the Ministry of Communication and Information Technology reorganized ASIS and created the National Centre 'Digital Romania' (NCDR), which became responsible for the creation, operation and administration of the POSC.[22]

[22] Law no. 329/09.11.2009 regarding the reorganisation of public institutions and authorities, the rationalisation of public expenditures, the support of business sector, and the fulfilment of the framework-agreements with the European Commission and the IMF, and Government Decision no. 1439/18.11.2009 regarding the creation of the National Management Centre for the Information Society and the National Centre 'Digital Romania'.

In 2009 NCDR started running the project entitled 'Platform for the integration of the e-Government services in the National Electronic System (NES)' whose purpose is to ensure the necessary conditions for promoting foreign investment in Romania. The project is co-financed by the European Regional Development Fund for a total of RON 20.6 million [approx. €4.8 million], of which RON 16.6 million (VAT excluded) [approx. €3.9 million, VAT excluded] will be in the form of a grant. The project will be implemented in Bucharest for 23 months. Its overall objective is to improve the quality of the central government's services for citizens, businesses and public institutions.

Following the completion of the public procurement procedure, the winning consortium of three private companies will provide the NCDR with all the products and services relating to project management, information and advertising, development, implementation, delivery, installation and system integration, thus making the platform a turnkey system. The amount of the contract signed between the NCDR and the consortium is RON 16,383,542 (approx. €3.8 million). A major part of the project is the operationalisation of the electronic Point of Single Contact.

In order for the Romanian e-Government portal's front-office (www.e-guvernare.ro) to be a single point of access to e-Government services, the National Electronic System (NES) has been developed in parallel to serve as the infrastructure of the portal. NES routes requests to a back-end system using XML-based Web services. All Romanian institutions are legally required to provide access to their online services through the portal and NES. NES works as a data interchange hub that ensures interoperability with back-end systems across government.

For the time being, there are nine forms that can be downloaded and submitted online. They regard contributions to the pension funds, to the health care system, income tax, etc. Transport licenses can also be processed online. The interconnection of the web site with the web sites of the public authorities is limited at best. Less than 1% of all authorities listed have uploaded some type of form or information. Though the website has a menu for visualising certain information in English, this is of limited value. The forms available online are just in Romanian. The Language issue will represent a problem once the POSC is launched. The Romanian umbrella law states in Article 7 (6) that public authorities may take measures to make the information available in other languages. As long as this is not a firm obligation, given the limited administrative capacity in Romania, very few authorities will act on their own initiative in this respect.

The law does not explicitly state how the functioning of the POSC will be financed. Since NCDR is a public agency subordinated to the Ministry of Communication we can assume that it will be financed from the state budget. Until now the money used to finance its creation has come from European structural funds.

A no fee system will be applicable—the legislation in place does not even mention the possibility of fees. According to Law no. 161/19.04.2003, individuals and public institutions who want to become registered in NES do not have to pay any fee. No mention is made with regard to companies.

2.1.2 Subjective Understanding and Competence Structure

The Government Decision regulating the POSC in Romania establishes a single national POSC. In light of the provisions of the law, there is no room for a subjective interpretation of the POSC. In addition to the 'general' POSC, the law makes reference to a distinct POSC for justice (e-justice), which was developed by the European Commission in collaboration with the Member States of the EU. On the website of the 'general' POSC a link to the justice POSC is to be posted.

There are, however, several already existing projects which could count as a POSC. For example, there is a portal called 'the National Portal for Public Administration' online at www.administratie.ro. The portal compiles and posts online information about the most important individuals and institutions within the Romanian public administration. It offers the possibility for public institutions to showcase their activities and to disseminate information widely and free of charge. The information is sent on a daily basis to 8000 individuals working in public institutions at both the local and national level. The summary of the informational influx also includes links to media articles relevant for public administration. Aside from the already mentioned functions, there is a section on the portal called 'forms', which refers to various documents and forms that individuals and businesses need to fill out. That section of the portal is in fact linked with www.e-guvernare.ro.

The Government also recently launched the so-called National Strategy 'e-Romania' (approved through Government Decision no. 195/09.03.2010). The strategy will result in the creation of an e-Romania portal, a friendly and transparent interface between the government on the one hand, and citizens and businesses on the other hand. The project received mixed reactions in Romania, mainly because of the huge costs involved (approximately €500 million). It is not clear how this portal will be connected to the already existing one(s).

The creation of POSC did not generate reallocations of administrative competences. Reallocation of competences in general was not a result of the transposition of the Services Directive in Romania. This is due to the fact that numerous authorisations for providing services are granted by central authorities rather than local ones. Therefore there was no need to shift administrative competences in order to facilitate the creation of the POSC.

2.1.3 Authorities with POSC-Function

As described above, the authority responsible for the POSC (ASIS, currently NCDR) was reorganized during the implementation process. The mission of ASIS went beyond the creation and implementation of the POSC. It included the implementation and the operation of IT systems which provide services necessary for e-government and the regulation of activities that are specific to e-government. ASIS also used to operate the desk for e-payments (it is part of www.e-guvernare.ro) and the site for public procurements (www.e-licitatie.ro). Based on Governmental

Decision no. 1439/18.11.2009, the activity and responsibilities of ASIS were split between the National Centre for the Management of the Information Society and the National Centre 'Digital Romania'. It is, therefore, hard to say whether or not it is a new institution.

2.1.4 Involvement of Private Partners

For the time being, private companies (a consortium of three companies) have been involved only in the technical aspects of the creation of the POSC. This consortium won a public procurement bid to manage the creation of the POSC.

2.1.5 Liability

Article 7 (4) of the umbrella law states that the NCDR is responsible for the good functioning of the POSC from a technical standpoint. The competent authorities are responsible for the informational content and the documents gathered, processed and transmitted through the POSC. We can argue that there is a joint liability of the NCDR and competent authority, depending on the problem that occurs with the POSC.

Governmental Decision no. 922/10.09.2010 regarding the creation of the POSC makes reference to other obligations (and thus potential liabilities) of the NCDR and/or the competent authorities.

- In Article 1 (4) the law states the joint responsibility of the NCDR and of the other competent authorities with regard to the protection of persons when personal data and its free circulation are involved.
- Article 4 (3) refers to the obligation of the competent authorities (who hold or manage the necessary information for the operation of procedures or forms necessary to gain access to the services implemented in the POSC) to draft internal procedures that will ensure the good functioning of the electronic public service from the POSC. They need to do this within 60 days from the moment the POSC becomes operational. The failure of public authorities to register with the POSC within 60 days from the date it becomes functional is subject to a fine of between (approx.) 1000 Euros and 10000 Euros.[23] The competence for issuing fines falls to the National Centre "Digital Romania", subordinated to the Ministry of Communications and IT. The problem is that the subject of the fine is not the head of the institution, but the institution as such, which is not very effective, as the fine will be paid from the institution's budget. We argue that a fine applied to the head of the institution would be more effective based on the fact that similar fines for non-compliance with a court decision (Law on judicial review no. 554/2004) have proved to be very effective in breaking the resistance of public authorities.

---

[23] Article 22 of the EGO no. 49/2009.

- Article 6 (3) refers to the full responsibility of each competent authority to solve the requests coming from economic operators.

Since the POSC is not yet operational, we can discuss its role only based on the provisions of the existing laws. Thus, Article 7 of the national umbrella law states that service providers can get direct access through the POSC to the following information/services:

- The legal requirements concerning the economic operators established in Romania, especially those regarding the procedures and the forms which have to be fulfilled in order to have access to the services activities and to provide them.
- The contact information of the competent authorities so that they may be contacted directly.
- The means and the conditions for access to public registers regarding services providers and services.
- The means of redress available in the case of a litigation between the competent authorities and the services provider/beneficiary, between a services operator and the beneficiary, or between services providers.
- Contact information for entities other than the competent authorities from which services providers can obtain practical assistance.

Through the POSC services providers can receive assistance from the competent authorities regarding the interpretation of the general requirements concerning establishment in Romania. This obligation of the competent authorities should not be understood as an obligation implying legal counselling for individual situations but rather as a general obligation to provide general information about certain national legal provisions and their interpretation/application in practice.

Thus, the role of the POSC is expected to be relatively complex, a front desk or electronic means of communication between service provider/applicant and the competent authorities, which also performs administrative functions on its own, for example by assisting service providers in filling out forms and answering questions as regards any requirements established by law.

2.2 Article 7 SD: Right to Information

The set of information that has to be made available through the POSC was transposed properly into national legislation (Article 7 of the EGO no. 49/2009). Nevertheless, as the POSC is still not active there is no evidence regarding the extent of the information put at the disposal of service providers through electronic means.

The rights of information provided for by the Directive are clearly higher than what national legislation requires from public authorities for the benefit of service providers. The transposition of the rights to information was made in the main legislative instrument, EGO no. 49/2009.

One area where Member States had the possibility to go beyond what is offered to national providers regards information in other Community languages. The directive states that Member States and the Commission shall take measures to encourage POSCs to make the information available in other Community languages. In Romania this provision was transposed in a slightly different manner, somewhat altering its sense. Thus, the transposing legislation transfers to the competent authorities the decision to make such information available in other Community languages. However, it is not an obligation but rather a possibility that competent authority has.[24] In our opinion, this is a transposition that does not follow the wording of the Directive, as no accompanying measure was taken by the Romanian state in this regard and the provision as transposed does not in any way 'encourage' the competent authorities to make such an administrative effort. This conclusion has to be taken into consideration within the Romanian legal culture, where any 'possibility' is ignored much more than an 'obligation' to do something, especially when such obligation is not endorsed by legal sanctions. The research that we conducted on the websites of all major municipalities in Romania may be relevant for this matter, in order to see how many of them provide public information in languages other than Romanian. We found only one website that has some (but very little) information in English. The situation in smaller municipalities (towns, communes) is worse, because even basic information in Romanian is sometimes hard to find. Against this background it can be stated that transposition of Article 7 (5) will generate additional challenges in Romania during implementation and the fact that it was done improperly will add more difficulties. The issue is of particular importance in our country because not knowing the Romanian language is more likely to be a problem for service providers from other Member States than is the case in other Member States, which often have the advantage of more 'international' languages (English, German and French, for instance).

According to Article 7 (4) of the Directive, the information and assistance shall be provided as quickly as possible. This provision was transposed by imposing a 5 working days deadline on the competent authorities for answering requests and a 3 working days deadline for informing an applicant if its request is erroneous or not grounded.[25]

The responsibility for the administration of the POSC is shared between the Ministry of Communications, which is in charge only of its technical functionality, and the competent authorities, which are responsible for the content of the information provided through the POSC. The Ministry can ask competent authority to provide information necessary for the POSC within a maximum of 15 days. Nevertheless, the Ministry has no real powers to control the compliance of competent authorities with the requirements of the transposing legislation or to impose sanctions, so it is not clear who will monitor the effective functioning of the POSC. The risk of 'throwing' the responsibility from one authority to another

[24] Article 7 (6) of the EGO no. 49/2010.

[25] Article 7 (3) of EGO no. 49/2010.

is very likely. This may also be in contradiction with the provisions of the Directive, which requires that Member States make sure that the information referred to in Article 7 is provided by the competent authorities. This, in our opinion, would imply clearer rules about accountability are necessary.

2.3 Article 8 SD: Procedures by Electronic Means

Electronic procedures cannot be evaluated in concreto because the portal is not yet functional. In the initial version of EGO no. 49/2009 the POSC was intended to become operational starting on November 28th, 2009. The deadline, as mentioned before, was extended to December 1st, 2010. During the interviews with public officials involved in transposition and implementation we were told that it is possible that there will be further delays (several months).

Before the implementation of the Services Directive there were attempts, mostly at a programmatic level (strategies, policy papers, etc.), to have an integrated system of e-government, one which would provide users with the means to pay taxes on-line, to access documentation for authorisations, etc. The system, finally set up in 2003 and accessible at www.e-guvernare.ro, is only partially functional, as many public authorities have not registered there and have not made access to the relevant documents possible. Thus, the research conducted for the purpose of this study revealed that out of (approx.) 4200 public authorities listed on the web page, less than 1% have put any kind of documents online for download by interested parties. Furthermore, not all fields of interest are covered.

Looking retrospectively, and having in mind the ambitions of the Directive, it can be argued that Romanian government has had similar ambitions before, but their implementation failed. This conclusion leads to great uncertainty about the implementation capacity required by the Directive, as the transposing legislation does not provide for clear procedures of control or for penalties in case of non-compliance. Without these necessary features, the obligations imposed by EGO no. 49/2009 lack the enforcing tools. Moreover, the obligations arising from the Directive to establish electronic procedures for all formalities relating to access to a service activity and the exercise thereof promise to be problematic to implement, as the previous (failed) attempts addressed only a portion of the formalities and never the whole procedure of setting up a service.

The secondary legislation adopted for the implementation of the Directive (Governmental Decision no. 922/2010 on the functioning of POSC) requires public authorities to digitally sign the responses given to providers through the POSC. This requirement poses an extra difficulty for the process of operationalisation of the POSC, as the procedures for authorising digital signatures are slow and inefficient. The Law on digital signature was adopted in 2001 and obligates all public authorities to have the capability to sign and receive documents signed digitally. The fact that to date the obligation has not been put into practice is relevant for our argument that this requirement is a further obstacle to the effective operationalisation of the POSC.

2.4 Article 9 SD: Authorisation Schemes

Article 9 (1) (c) of the Services Directive encourages Member States to renounce authorisation schemes when possible in favour of a more 'loose' arrangement based on 'a posteriori' control. This evolution represents a big change for our country. In addition to authorisation schemes, most economic operators had to go through reauthorisation, a bureaucratic activity which very often did nothing but increase the amount of red tape. In most cases authorisation schemes were maintained, but there are also cases when notification is sufficient for providing services (see more in Sect. 1.4).

However, it has to be stated that there exists one scheme that requires effective a posteriori control, namely the 'silent authorisation' scheme. Tacit authorisation is not a new, post-Directive feature in Romanian administrative law, as it has existed from 2003. However, the effectiveness of such schemes is expected to increase as a result of the Directive.

In the Romanian legal system there are several types of authorisations schemes.[26] The authorisations that are relevant to our study are those which relate to the production of goods, service delivery or to the establishment of an undertaking in Romania.

Among the activities covered by an authorisation scheme for the production of goods we can mention: production of food, pharmaceutical production, production of measurement and control devices, growing genetically modified cultures, etc.

In principle, commercial activities do not require authorisation except in some fields such as commerce with metals and gems, transport services, tourism services, translation services, craftsmanship, etc.

Some authorisations are required in order to benefit from a certain provision of the law (for instance, tax incentives for those who hire disabled persons).

Authorisations can also be classified into final authorisations (based on which the activity can be carried out) versus intermediary authorisations (which serves to issue a final authorisation).

The usual scheme for granting authorisations includes several aspects:

- The competent authority has the obligation to make publicly available the authorisation forms, the list of additional required supporting documents, and the procedure for applying for the authorisation;
- The deadline for granting the authorisation is usually 30 days, with an extension of 15 days in cases of complex authorisations;
- The silence of the administration means approval (EGO no. 27/2003) except for some sensitive fields like guns and ammunition, drugs, nuclear activities, and national security. However, the public authorities have had few occurrences in this respect, as the procedure of tacit (silent) authorisation has not been effective.

[26] Ghencea (2009), pp. 7–22.

The procedure of silent authorisation was extensively altered as a result of the implementation of the Services Directive. This is because the existing provisions regarding the effect of silent authorisation ('silent approval' in Romanian[27]) were interpreted ineffectively in practice, in the sense that the beneficiary of the silent approval had yet to get a confirmation of that occurrence from the public authority, in order to actually exercise the service or perform the activity. According to provisions introduced in 2010, the public authority has the obligation to issue—within 5 days upon the request of the beneficiary—a document that holds the place for the authorisation, in all cases when the authorisation does not have a standardised form. The refusal to grant an authorisation following this procedure can be sanctioned by disciplinary penalties, which is not a new provision in Romanian law. When a standardised form is necessary, or when the public authority refuses to release the confirmation, the interested person can go to court, which supposedly shall decide the matter after an accelerated proceeding (30 days). The provisions about the speediness of court proceedings are, in practice, without much effect, due to a backlog in court cases. They can only have as result disciplinary measures against the judge.

Public authorities have the obligation to publish at their premises or on their websites the list of authorisations in their field of competence for which the tacit approval procedure is applicable. Also, public authorities have to make available information related to the application forms and instructions for their completion, as well as list any other documents necessary for issuing the authorisation and competent authorities.

The simple/qualified notifications are not specific to the Romanian legal system, which is characterised by the prevalence of authorisations. However, as mentioned before, this is currently regulated in several instances by sector specific legislation for the benefit of transnational providers. This situation is even more interesting when no mention is made of any kind of notification. As already discussed, we are not sure if in this case the service provider can go ahead and provide the service or not. The question remains as to how 'a posteriori control' is going to take place.

2.5 *Article 10 SD: Conditions for the Granting of Authorisation*

The majority of regulations altered as a result of the implementation of the Directive give preeminence to authorisations granted in other Member States, in the sense that there is no need to apply for a new authorisation in Romania. The procedures for recognising such authorisations are usually brief and include a registration of the service provider in a national register, based on the verifications conducted through the Internal Market Information System (IMI).

[27] EGO no. 27/2003 on silent (tacit) approval, as amended in July 2010.

As an effect of Article 10 (3) of the Directive, duplication of controls on undertakings from other Member States or from Romania that apply for authorisation in Romania is precluded; the provision was transposed in exact wording of the Directive by EGO no. 49/2009 [Article 9 (3) and (4)]. The effectiveness of such preclusion is yet to be seen in practice, as many authorisation schemes established by field specific legislation apply to both nationals and providers from other Member States. It would take a vigilant provider to invoke this provision in order to escape the double controls and requirements.

Romania is a unitary state, so authorisations issued by central government are effective on the whole territory. For instance, licences for tourism issued by the Ministry of Tourism. Sometimes local branches of central agencies grant the authorisation. The transposing legislation makes the authorisations effective on the whole territory (Article 9 (5) of EGO no. 49/2009). However, in the next paragraph, there is a provision which gives the special legislator the duty to appreciate when there is an "overriding reasons relating to the public interest" to have territorial effective authorisations. Such approach is not in contradiction with the directive, according to the Handbook (6.1.5.), but in our opinion a reevaluation of existing procedures and the subsequent removal of those that are not justified by an overriding public interest should have been performed.

The definition of an authorisation in Romanian law implies that the applicant has the right to be granted the authorisation once all the conditions laid down by the supporting legislation are met. Of course there is a margin of discretion when assessing in concreto the fulfilment of certain requirements for authorisation, but generally there is no discretion in granting the authorisations when the conditions are met. For instance, when an authorisation scheme involves testing the applicant, the test has sometimes elements of discretion with regard to the way in which it is organised. Nevertheless, as the authorisation scheme becomes 'mature', in the sense that it is applied year after year, guidelines and rules are often established by the authorising agency in order to standardise the process. In this respect, the Services Directive did not bring anything new to the field, as no perceived change in approach is detectable in the specific legislation. As to the judicial review of authorisations by the courts, the situation is complex, as doctrine is not unitary on the issue of the review on merits/discretion and the jurisprudence is affected by this indecision. For a better understanding of the scope of judicial review in Romanian administrative law, within the context of the relation between merits/discretion, a short incursion into the general administrative law should be made here.

> Though doctrine has always discussed the issue of bound competence and discretion,[28] until as recently as 2004, when a new Law on judicial review was adopted, the general laws on judicial review allowed only for a legality control by the courts. Ever since the establishment of administrative justice in Romania (1864), the control exercised by the courts over administrative decisions was one of legality and only exceptionally, one over discretion.[29]

---

[28] Tarangul (1936/XI), pp. 56–72; Negulescu (1934), pp. 25–34; Gruia (1934), pp. 45–58.

[29] Dragoş (2001); Dragoş (2004/2008), pp. 108–117.

The 2004 Law on Judicial review intended to change this approach by promoting a review of the 'abuse of discretion', following the French model of 'détournement de pouvoir'. Thus, 'abuse of discretion' is defined as being 'the public authorities' exercise of discretion in breach of the limits of competence established by law or which infringes on the rights and liberties of citizens. It can be observed that this definition is basically enfolded in that of illegality/unlawfulness. So, even though the law tries to establish a review for excessive/abuse of discretion, because of an incorrect definition it only succeeds in reaffirming legality as the only scope for judicial review.

The courts have tried to use the concept of 'abuse of discretion' in several cases, though without proper argumentation. The decisions at issue could have been annulled as easily by just resorting to the concept of legality. Thus, the decision to revoke a building permit issued without observing the conditions stated in the law has been considered as 'abuse of discretion'; in our opinion this is evidently a blunt violation of the law, which under that circumstance gives no discretion to the issuer.[30] The same reasoning applies in the case of a decision issued outside the competence expressly stated in the law.[31] In these examples the review was one concerning legality, thus the recourse to the concept of 'abuse of discretion' was not really necessary, given the absence of any discretion.

It has to be mentioned here that the Romanian doctrine, the specific legislation and the judicial case law have always made a rather basic and underdeveloped distinction between legality (lawfulness) and discretion/merits. A generic notion of discretion is used by courts. The necessary distinction between policy discretion (weighting the public and private interest), discretion in evaluating complex factual situations and discretion in interpreting legal rules is not used in practice.[32] In other words, all matters left to the decision of the issuer are called 'discretion', and all that is exercised within bound competence is covered by the concept of'legality'. So in an instance when a public authority has room for choosing a more expedient policy measure/action to be taken in a given circumstance (French bilan coûts-avantages), it is incorporated in the concept of 'discretion'. The decision becomes unlawful only when it contradicts legal rules, even if these rules are stemming from different pieces of legislation or from administrative regulations.

Along this line of development, there is no case law on striking down manifestly irrational policy decisions. A more straightforward approach is occasionally adopted by some appeal courts regarding a 'manifest error of appreciation' in adjudicating procedures, which is considered 'abuse of discretion' and thus subject to review.[33] In one such isolated case, a teacher was refused a legal promotion because he was graded below the threshold of 50 points by an evaluation commission. The court found that the commission did not grade some aspects of the teacher's activity because allegedly no evidence was presented in his application file; such evidence was in fact enclosed in the file, but the commission did not grant any points for it. Consequently, the court considered that it was a case of a 'manifest error of appreciation' which is assigned to illegality. It has to be mentioned that such approach is not common to all the courts; it is a rather 'revolutionary' stand, as it actually disregards the uninspired definition given by the Law on judicial review to the 'abuse of discretion' in order to apply what constitutes the 'roots' of this provision, the French model of détournement de pouvoir.

30 High Court of Cassation and Justice, Decision no. 3319/2007.

31 High Court of Cassation and Justice, Decision no. 3799/2006.

32 Caranta (2008), p. 195.

33 Decision no. 3010/2008, Cluj Appellate Court, Commercial, Fiscal and Administrative Law Section.

> It should also be noted that, in the absence of an Administrative Procedure Code,[34] courts are rather shy about applying in practice the principles of administrative procedure such as weighting the conflicting interests of the parties, cost-benefit testing, hearing the parties during the procedure, full motivation of the decision, proportionality, etc., just on the basis of legal writings (doctrine). Those principles would be natural limits for exercising discretion, but the legal culture in Romania traditionally leans towards legal grounds that are expressly laid down by the law.

The transposition of the Directive (Article 10) will not influence the current situation regarding the extent of judicial review, as there are no express requirements to extend the review on discretion. The review on merits, though, could be applicable in cases regarding authorisations or refusal to grant thereof.

The transposing (umbrella) act leaves the reasoning of decisions issued within authorisation schemes at the discretion of the issuer. The provision [Article 9 (8)] requires in a general manner that the reasoning should be done 'properly', which is slightly different than the 'fully' specified in the Directive. Romanian legislation (Governmental Ordinance no. 27/2002 on petitions) provides only minimum rules on the reasoning of decisions (reasons in law), so the term 'properly' remains indefinite. In our opinion, the transposing legislation should have made reference to the detailed reasoning proposed in the Handbook (6.1.7.): reasons in fact and law, supplemented by a reference to the availability of review (competent authority/court and term limit). The fact that the possibility to review the decision exists in law does not suffice for those interested in the deadlines and the competent authority, so a full reasoning should enclose this type of information as well. Admittedly, this is more than the Directive requires, but it would be more effective for the protection of the rights of service providers.

The intention of the Services Directive not to alter the allocation of competences within the national legal system was fully respected by the transposing legislation in Romania. There are no cases in which the competences were re-allocated as a result of the implementation of the Directive.

2.6 Article 11 SD: Duration of Authorisation

The principle of unlimited validity of authorisations and its exceptions were transposed using the wording of the Directive. In the existing legal setting that accommodates both unlimited authorisations and time-limited ones. As already mentioned, in the sector specific laws for many authorisation schemes,

---

[34] A draft version of the Romanian Administrative Procedure Code is currently under consideration by the Government and will provide for a definition of the concept of discretion. Article 10: 'The discretion is the possibility granted by law to public authorities to choose between possible options when applying the law, considering also the scope of the law. The exercise of discretion shall not lead to arbitrary measures'. The draft is accessible (in Romanian) at http://www.mai.gov.ro/Documente/Transparenta%20decizionala/Proiect%20COD%20procedura%20administrativa.pdf.

reauthorisation was necessary. Currently, as a general rule, authorisation has unlimited validity. In those cases where in the past deadlines had existed, once they expired the new authorisation were unlimited. There are, however, still exceptions. In these cases we are not sure if the legislator intentionally kept them or if it is a matter of faulty transposition or altering of existing requirements.

2.7 Article 12 SD: Selection from Among Several Candidates

The transposition of Article 12 SD was done with observance of the wording of the Directive. There were, however, a few minor adjustments, such as the inclusion of the overriding reasons of 'keeping the financial equilibrium of the security system' and 'the loyalty of commercial transactions' as enumerated in par. 3 of the EGO no. 49/2009. However, other overriding reasons can be established by special legislation.

The general principle introduced by Article 12 is new to the Romanian system if we look at it as a general principle for drafting special legislation and as a practice of dealing with 'scarce rights'. Nevertheless, legislation still in force regarding some scarce rights has different solutions. As an illustrative example, in the case of taxi authorisations the authorisation is granted for an unlimited time, subject to verification of fulfilment of conditions every 5 years. New authorisations can be granted only when an existing authorisation is withdrawn or if the maximum number of authorisations is increased.[35]

2.8 Article 13 SD: Authorisation Procedures

2.8.1 A Priori Determination of the Duration of Administrative Procedures

The duration of an administrative procedure is determined by law (specific or general). The law on petitions (GO no. 27/2002) provides for a general deadline of 30 days, with the possibility to extend it for another 15 days, for all requests, notifications, complaints and proposals addressed to public authorities. This applies to all administrative procedures in the absence of specific provisions.

There is also another general regulation (GO no. 27/2003, amended in 2010) on granting authorisations tacitly and which applies only to those procedures not covered by a specific provision. The general deadline is again 30 days, with a possibility to prolong it for an extra 10 days if the matter is difficult to resolve. The petitioner has to be informed about any prolongation of the deadline.

Finally, the 'umbrella law' EGO no. 49/2009 provides for the same deadline of 30 (calendar) days, with an extension of 15 days if necessary. The problem is the effect

---

[35] Article 14 of the Law no. 38/2003 on taxi and car rentals.

of this legislative dynamic, as both GO no. 27/2003 and EGO no. 49/2009 were modified, the former case, or adopted, in the latter case, in order to transpose the Services Directive. It has to be noted that the deadlines are not exactly the same. Specifically we are referring to the extension of 10 in the former and 15 days in the latter. The question is which one applies, as EGO no. 49/2009 was adopted before the amendment of GO no. 27/2003, which occurred in 2010 and which left the deadline untouched. Our interpretation takes into consideration the fact that the deadline was not affected by the amendments introduced in 2010, so the 'most recent' deadline, in terms of conflicts of laws, is the one set up by the umbrella law EGO no. 49/2009, which is 30 days with the possibility to be extended for another 15 days.

In conclusion, the legislator determines the length of the procedure and no discretion is left to the public authorities on this matter. Nevertheless, the interpretation of the legal norms is sometimes difficult and we can say that in the instance discussed above the efforts to transpose the Directive have complicated the situation instead of contributing to a simplification of the procedure.

2.8.2 General Rule for the Duration and Exceptions

The transposing (umbrella) law established a general deadline of 30 days (plus 15 in complex cases) for all authorisation schemes. The deadline has its inspiration in a previously existing law on tacit authorisations. So it is not new to Romanian law. It should be respected by all competent authorities when granting authorisations. The deadline is applicable only to authorisation schemes and does not cover other applications. However, the law on petitions (GO no. 27/2002) provides for a similar deadline for any request, application, notification and complaint addressed to public authorities. So aside from their different legal source, the general deadline for administrative procedures and the deadline for authorisation procedures are basically the same.

The law does not allow for derogations from the deadline by specific legislation. Thus, most of the field legislation has imposed the same deadline as part of the implementation process of the Directive. However, several field regulations (6 out of 52) still provide for different deadlines—3 months, 60 days, etc.

In principle, the nonobservance of the deadline means rejection, except in case of authorisations, where it means approval.

2.8.3 Tacit Authorisation in the National Legal Order So Far

Tacit authorisation was introduced into the Romanian legal system 7 years ago by Governmental Ordinance no. 27/2003 and the outcome was an increased percentage of answers (positive or negative) within the deadline. Over time, counties and cities have developed electronic procedures which send an automatic notice to the issuer when the deadline is approaching, so that tacit authorisation would not materialise. The result for the applicant though is not much of an improvement, as the public authority does not feel a pressure to grant authorisations within the deadline, but to instead send a request for completion of additional documentation or other kinds of requests. This prolongs the procedure and prevents tacit authorisation from becoming effective. The interviews conducted with applicants and with public employees for the purpose of this study confirm that the procedure of tacit authorisation has not had a significant effect on the length of administrative procedures. There are only isolated cases when tacit authorisation has occurred, and even in these cases the courts have been reluctant to give full effect to the procedure.

2.8.4 Formal and Substantive Effects of Tacit Authorisation

Tacit authorisation means that the activity, service or profession tacitly authorised can be exercised/performed by the applicant after the deadline has passed. However, a document is needed in order to state a tacit authorisation has occurred, which can be issued either by the competent public authority or by court. The applicant has to perform a 'forum shopping' and choose among the two procedures; administrative, in front of the competent authority, or judicial, in front of the court. If the administrative procedure is preferred the law states that the document shall be released within 5 days of the request and that it shall state the fact that no response was given to the applicant within the legal deadline. The statement is equivalent to an authorisation in front of every controlling authority or other persons. Evidently, the beneficiary will have to present also the application which was tacitly granted, in order to reveal the 'content' of the authorisation.

2.8.5 Rules of Formally Granted Authorisations Applicable to Tacit Authorisation

In principle, the same conditions regarding revocation, amendment and nullity that apply to regular administrative acts shall apply also to tacit authorisations, as there is no specific provision in the law stating otherwise. In fact, this is considered the 'safety net' for public authorities that have granted authorisations tacitly, in the sense that they use the opportunity to make life harder for those who benefit from the tacit authorisation. Consequently, the competent authority can revoke the authorisation until it has 'entered the civil circuit', which means that the authorisation was followed by another legal act or put into practice.

A more complex situation arises when the authorisation is confirmed by a court decision. In this case, the competent public authority who should have issued the authorisation cannot revoke or modify it. It can only challenge it in a superior court and seek an annulment. In this context, the question is whether the court, when assessing the tacit authorisation or reviewing its legality, should analyse the application against the legal requirements for granting an authorisation or should just acknowledge the fact that nonobservance of the deadline has had as an effect a valid authorisation. In fact, the courts do perform a test of the lawfulness of the tacit authorisation, arguing that this procedure was not intended to be used passively by the administration in order to allow unlawful applications through, but to speed up the administrative proceedings for the benefit of those who follow the rules.

2.8.6 Further Information on Tacit Authorisation

Following the transposition of the Directive, public authorities that grant authorisations had an obligation to publish on their website a list of the information needed for granting said authorisations (list of documents, forms to be completed and how, other public authorities that have to issue documents for the authorisation to be granted) by mid September 2010.[36] Based on the research we conducted of the websites of several big municipalities, we found that partial information can be found there, but during the interviews with legal experts it surfaced that this was done under previous legislation and not as a result of implementing the Directive. Looking at web sites of central agencies, we found that only a few of them have made efforts in implementing this provision. For instance, we found only 'traces' of electronic procedures for authorisation on the websites of the Ministry of Environment, Ministry of Culture and National Patrimony, Ministry of Administration and Internal Affairs (National Agency for Cadastre and Real Estate Publicity). A more critical situation is to be found at the level of rural administration (communes), which are still behind on meeting the requirements of the previous legislation that required making some application forms and information available online.

2.9 Articles 14, 15, 16 SD

Articles 14, 15, and 16 of the Services Directive (prohibited requirements, requirements to be evaluated and freedom to provide services) were transposed in the exact same wording into Articles 13–16 of the EGO no. 49/2009. From the interviews conducted with officials involved in the coordination of the screening process it surfaced that the challenge was to convince all field ministries to join the effort in equal manner. Some ministries—Tourism, Administration and Internal Affairs and Public Constructions—reacted quicker and thus legislation in these fields was the first to be adapted.

Self screening by the Member State maybe the only option at the moment, but it will reveal its shortcomings when put in practice, as the screening process is bound to be incomplete due to the unequal participation of the field ministries in the

[36] Article 4 (1) of the GO 27/2003 on tacit authorisations, as amended in 2010.

process. Thus, in the years to come, service providers will identify themselves the restrictions that are still in place or legislation that has yet to be amended in order to comply with the directive. The Romanian legal system suffers more that those in other countries from excessive legislation and contradictory norms, as well as from a lack of codification of administrative proceedings. It is worth mentioning in this context that the Draft Code of Administrative Procedure, which should bring many disparate procedures now in place under the same umbrella, has sat on the desks of the Ministry of Administration and Internal Affairs for more than 3 years now.

Against this background, one can imagine the difficulty of the screening process and the accuracy of what has been done until now.

2.10 Articles 14–19 SD

There are no scholarly papers on the scope of Articles 14 and 15 of the Services Directive in the Romanian legal literature. However, our opinion is that the provisions cover both freedom of establishment and freedom to provide services. We arrived at this opinion based on the fact that the provision makes clear reference to the services offered by providers from another Member State, while on the other hand it is obvious that providers established in a Member State can easily provide services there.

The question that arises from corroborating Recital 17 and Article 17 of the Directive is whether services of general economic interest are covered by it or not. Although exceptions provided for in Article 17 are limited, the term 'inter alia' suggests that all services of general economic interest are exempted.[37] Member States seem to have an obligation, however, to review all the services of general economic interest, in order to see if the requirements necessary for the fulfilment of special tasks should be maintained as being proportionate. At least this is what can be concluded from reading together Article 15 (4) of the Directive and the corresponding guidelines from the Handbook.[38] There are, on the other hand, opinions that this interpretation of the Commission cannot be upheld.[39] In the context of this legal dispute, we note that the Romanian Government has not yet considered the issue, as no review was performed on services of general economic interest. They seem to be considered as exempt from the Directive altogether and this is held to be reason enough for not reviewing them. This leaves open the possibility (or danger) of circumventing the restrictions specified in Article 16 of the Directive by declaring all kinds of services as services of general economic interest.

[37] See Van de Gronden (2009), p. 249.

[38] European Commission (2007), p. 78.

[39] See Van de Gronden (2009), p. 243.

2.11 Articles 22–27 SD

Article 22 of the Services Directive (information on providers and their services) has been transposed in Article 26 of the EGO no. 49/2009; on top of just listing the information that has to be provided to beneficiaries, the law also imposes fines of between approx. 250 and 2500 Euros for noncompliance. Article 27 of the Directive (settlement of disputes) was transposed in the same Article 22 of the EGO no. 49/2009, again with fines of between 250 and 1500 Euros for noncompliance. The deadline for answering complaints was set at a maximum of 30 calendar days.

The competent authority for applying the fines for non-compliance is the National Authority for Consumers' Protection. An interesting choice is the provision that allows the fines to be applied only when the noncompliance leads to or has the capacity to lead to the interest of consumers being affected. We should ask ourselves, are not all the cases of noncompliance affecting the interests of consumers?; as they were established from the beginning with this purpose in mind. The question is thus whether this condition can be interpreted as giving the Agency manoeuvring room for exercising discretion when deciding in which cases a fine is necessary. It looks that this was the intention of the national legislator.

Article 26 of the Directive (policy on quality of services) was transposed in Article 25 of the EGO no. 49/2009. The National Authority for Consumers' Protection is the competent agency to assist providers in drafting codes of conduct in this field. The rest of the article follows the wording of the Directive (the Member States shall take measures..., shall ensure..., etc.), but without putting in place concrete arrangements for implementation of the Directive.

2.12 Articles 28 *ff.* SD: Administrative Cooperation

Romanian legislation has only disparate provisions regarding national administrative cooperation, while transnational cooperation is mainly regulated by sectoral EU legislation or by the national legislation implementing it.

One instance where national cooperation among public authorities should function for the benefit of service providers and citizens in general is laid down in Article 6 (1) of Governmental Ordinance no. 27/2002 on procedures for answering petitions. It requires public authorities receiving petitions that do not fall within their competence to redirect them to the competent authority, thus sparing the petitioners from the hurdle of doing it themselves. It is a form of administrative cooperation that has a general nature and was intended to change the practice of sending the petition back to the applicant on the ground that it does not fall under the competence of the public authority referred to. Based on research conducted in several counties, municipalities and deconcentrated agencies for the purpose of this study, we found that the provision has had an impact on administrative practice and that in the majority of cases (except difficult ones, where even the public authority contest each other's competence) the cooperation is effective.

Based on this experience, national cooperation among public authorities within the context of service provision should be effective. The transposing legislation maintains the same principle, requiring that public authorities that are not competent to resolve a request for assistance shall transfer the request to the competent authority (Article 33 of the EGO no. 49/2009). On the other hand, the capacity to interact with service providers and with public authorities from other Member States is limited, as in rural areas access to authorisation schemes is not granted via electronic means.

The main liaison point for the purpose of transnational cooperation/assistance is the Department for European Affairs, which can also delegate the task of acting as secondary liaison points to other units.

Upon transposition of the Directive administrative cooperation should be more active and involved in assuring a unitary approach, at least regarding authorisation schemes for service provision. However, from the interviews conducted with public officials from the central and local administrations, it seems that there are no indications of a perceived change in the way public administrations cooperate even after the (partial) implementation.

Although the Directive allows for some financial compensation for efforts to cooperate within IMI, there are no provisions for financial compensation in the Romanian transposing law. The cooperation is assumed to be on a mutual basis and thus free of charge.

The rules on data protection and professional secrets remained unaltered by the transposition of the Directive. Providing information required by the Directive is to be done with observance of the national legislation regarding protection of data and classified information.[40] It is possible that conflicts may arise between the requirements of the Directive and the provisions of the national legislation in place, but until this occurs no changes to the existing rules on privacy and state official secrets were considered necessary.

2.13 *Article 29 SD: Mutual Assistance—General Obligations for the Member State of Establishment*

There were no debates in Romania regarding the meaning of Article 29 on the conformation of unlawful business conduct. We do not think this will be problematic in practice, except regarding the quality of information gathered by the Romanian authorities, which is difficult to estimate.

[40] Article 17 of the EGO no. 49/2009 and Article 1 (4) of the Governmental Decision no. 922/ 2010 on the Point of Single Contact.

2.14 Problems and Discourses on Administrative Cooperation

In the legal literature and in administrative practice there is no interest (papers, seminars or training courses) in administrative cooperation within the context of the implementation of the Services Directive. Based on interviews conducted with public officials from all levels of administration, there is not enough awareness about the Directive and its implications in administrative practice.

2.15 Convergence Programme (Chapter VII of the Services Directive)

Chapter VII of the Services Directive brings about a rather new role for the Member States: that of initiators of private regulation. In Romania this role has recently been played by the Government, at the request of private actors in retail business.

Thus, the Government decided to draw up and put into practice a code of good practice in retail trade, thus addressing the divergences between farmers, producers and hypermarket networks. The hypermarket networks managed to bring all agricultural producers to the point of bankruptcy in a matter of a couple of years, forcing them to sell their merchandise at lower prices than the necessary costs. The practices of retailers also affect the consumers, with the prices being increased by numerous taxes applied to the products, such as the store entry tax, the shelf tax and the protection tax. Taxes were written down in confidential contracts imposed on producers, with the main retailers stealing some of the money, which was introduced in the sale price but not passed onto the producers. Answering to these accusations, the Association of Big Retail Networks in Romania argued that the super and hypermarket networks make profits of under 5 percent of turnover and that the causes of food price increases must be looked at in the production chain. The Association agreed with the introduction of a Code of good practices, as long as negotiation freedom is not limited and the producers' profit rate does not increase, which would increase the final price.

As a first stage, under the patronage and mediation of the Ministry of Agriculture, the retailers and producers agreed on a Code of good practices in 2008.[41] The Code was supposed to be enforced as such by the signatories, after the

[41] Codul de bune practici între furnizori şi supermarketuri a fost semnat şi va intra în vigoare dupa aprobarea Consiliului Concurenţei [The code for good practices between providers and supermarkets was signed and shall enter into force after its approval by the Council of Competition] by Anne-Marie Blăjan, online at http://economie.hotnews.ro/stiri-companii-3406676-update-codul-bune-practici-intre-furnizori-supermarketuri-fost-semnat-intra-vigoare-dupa-aprobarea-consiliului-concurentei.htm, Wednesday, July 2nd, 2008.

Competition Council checked its conformity with the competition rules. In the second stage the minimum involvement of the State in this agreement was considered insufficient. After both parties showed distrust in the effectiveness of such an approach, the Government was asked to intervene and transform the code into a written law. The Minister of Agriculture at the time[42] argued that such an agreement should remain a private regulation, a 'gentlemen's agreement', and that the prestige of the signatories would ensure its enforcement in practice. Interestingly enough, the two parties insisted on a written legislative instrument that would guarantee its enforcement in the absence of a developed culture of business ethics. Consequently, the Code was transposed into several provisions of Law no. 321/2009 on commercialisation of alimentary products.[43]

Against this background, we can state that the Romanian Government is encouraging private regulation when possible and intervenes only when required to do so. As for taking the initiative in private regulation, that has also been experienced recently, so it should pose no problems in implementation. Nevertheless, previous experiences show that this initiative occurs only when there is a certain kind of pressure from conflicting groups in the economy (like producers/ customers and retailers, for instance). It is highly unlikely that the initiative for private regulation would come exclusively from the Government.

Aside from the previous initiatives on private regulation, there are no real debates on this topic in the Romanian legal literature.

3 Assessment of the Impact of the Services Directive

3.1 Extent of the Impact

As long as there is no serious discussion about administrative codification, there are few expectations for a severe impact of the Directive. It is true that in certain areas significant changes occurred—for example recognition of transnational providers upon a simple notification—but because they are embedded in individual pieces of legislation the impact is smaller. In our opinion it would be more significant to have a principle in administrative law stating this recognition upon notification by transnational service providers. It remains to be seen in practice what will happen when providers challenge the noncompliance of the domestic sector specific legislation with the Directive.

---

[42] Mr. Dacian Cioloş (currently the European Commissioner for Agriculture in the second Baroso Commission).

[43] Official Journal of Romania no. 705 from 20.10.2009.

3.2 *Assessment of the Transposing Legislation*

Outside governmental circles the Services Directive is virtually unknown. Several interviews conducted at the local level proved that even legal advisers are unaware of this law. Given the fact that the EU Commission is threatening Romania with an infringement procedure due to limited amendments to the sector specific legislation, we consider that only a minimum transposition took place.

3.3 *Most Important and Profound Changes Induced by the Services Directive*

We consider that there are two main spill-over effects of the Services Directive. The first one refers to e-government. The Romanian government has been trying for several years to implement various components of e-government—online taxes, online licences (transportation), electronic signature, etc. The degree of success has varied but in general the process is still under way in most fields. Following the Services Directive, the Romanian government was forced to create a POSC. As already discussed, the obstacles have been numerous and it is not clear how the scheme will function. The most problematic aspect currently seems to be that there are no clear liabilities and sanctions established. However, the government is forced to act in order to implement this system to the fullest extent. Even with the delays, the system will become functional, eventually.

The second benefit refers to administrative simplification. Romanian public administration is often described as highly bureaucratic, valuing more the paperwork than the outcomes. While most modern administrations try to employ regulations only when necessary (green tape) the Romanian one generates only red tape. For example, authorisation has become less complicated by eliminating some redundant papers/documents and reauthorisations. One cannot understand the full extent of this benefit unless examples from other fields are considered (for example, disabled people with permanent disabilities (missing limbs) need to undergo a medical examination annually in order to qualify for governmental funds).

One can expect much from the imperative stated in the Directive of making the tacit authorisations procedure effective, regardless of the previous experiences we had with such regulations. As we already described above, the effect of the existing scheme of tacit authorisation was only to make public authorities more aware that they have to prevent the expiration of the deadline by asking for a new document or by rejecting one already deposited; so it did not advance the goal of simplification too much. This practice could be altered now by the pressure coming from transnational service providers and by the European Commission, as the Directive expressly prohibits such practices, and as a result it has a better chance of advancing simplification efforts.

However, in the majority of the transposing field legislation, the issue of tacit authorisation is not mentioned at all, which means that the provision of the umbrella law is in principle applicable to all fields. This also shows, in our opinion, a certain lack of commitment on the Government's part to make it a central piece of the simplification process, as other provisions of the umbrella law were replicated in the field legislation to give them more weight. Moreover, when the tacit authorisation effect is finally mentioned (in fields related to court proceedings—interpreters and translators for courts, mediators, and experts for courts), it is only to make sure that these fields are expressly excluded from application of tacit authorisation and thus exempt from the principle stated in the umbrella law.[44] In the above context, it is hard to assess the impact that the reaffirmation in the umbrella law of the effect of tacit authorisation will have in practice. This, however, entails further research.

References

For legislation, jurisprudence and websites please refer to 1.1 of the report and footnotes directly.

Caranta R (2008) On Discretion. In: Prechal S, van Roermund B (eds) The Coherence of EU Law: The Search for Unity in Divergent Concepts. Oxford University Press, Oxford, 195

Dragoş DC (2001) Recursul administrativ şi contenciosul administrativ. All Beck, Bucureşti

Dragoş DC (2004/2008) Discuţii privind posibilitatea anulării unui act administrativ pe motiv de inoportunitate. Dreptul, 108–117

European Commission (2007) Handbook on the Implementation of the Services Directive. Available at http://ec.europa.eu/internal_market/services/docs/services-dir/guides/handbook_en.pdf

Ghencea F (2009) Notiunea de autorizatie administrativa si fundamentarea sa in dreptul contemporan, [The notion of administrative authorisation and its fundamentals in contemporary law], Revista de drept public (Public Law Review) 1:7–22

Gruia IV (1934) Puterea discreţionară în funcţiunile statului, Pandectele săptămânale, 45–58

Negulescu P (1934) Puterea de apreciere a executivului în înfăptuirea actelor de putere publică, Pandectele săptămânale, 25–34

Tarangul ED (1936/XI) Puterea discreţionară a administraţiei, Revista de drept public, pp 56–72

Van de Gronden J (2009) The Services Directive and SGEI. In: Krajewski M, Neergaard U, Van de Gronden J (eds) The Changing Legal Framework for Services of General Interest in Europe. Between Competition and Solidarity. TMC Asser Press, The Hague

[44] Ordinance no.13/2010 for amending some normative acts in the justice domain in order to transpose Directive 2006/123/CE, published in the Official Journal no. 70/30.01.2010.

The Implementation of the Services Directive in Slovakia

Silvia Ručinská and Miroslav Fečko

1 General Remarks on the Transposition Strategy and General Understanding of the Implementation

1.1 Main References Used in This Research

The main references used in the research were the following:

- The Services Directive 2006/123/EC (SD);
- *Návrh zákona o službách na vnútornom trhu* (Proposal of the Internal Market Services Act), https://lt.justice.gov.sk/Document/DocumentDetails.aspx?instEID=-1&matEID=1610&docEID=64283&docFormEID=-1&docTypeEID=1&langEID=1;
- *Zákon č. 136/2010 Z. z. o službách na vnútornom trhu a o zmene a doplnení niektorých zákonov* (Internal Market Services Act 136/2010);
- http://www.zbierka.sk/Default.aspx?sid=15&PredpisID=209600&FileName=zz2010-00136-0209600&Rocnik=2010&AspxAutoDetectCookieSupport=1;

doc. Ing. Silvia Ručinská, PhD (silvia.rucinska@upjs.sk) and PhDr. Miroslav Fečko (miroslav.fecko@upjs.sk), Pavol Jozef Šafárik University in Košice, Faculty of Public Administration.

S. Ručinská (✉) · M. Fečko
Faculty of Public Administration,
Pavol Jozef Šafárik University, Kosice, Slovakia
e-mail: silvia.rucinska@upjs.sk

M. Fečko
e-mail: miroslav.fecko@upjs.sk

U. Stelkens et al. (eds.), *The Implementation of the EU Services Directive*,
DOI: 10.1007/978-90-6704-840-8_23,

- *Uznesenie vlády Slovenskej republiky č. 294 z 28. marca 2007* (Government Decree 294/2007), http://www.rokovania.sk/File.aspx/ViewDocumentHtml/Uznesenie-1571?prefixFile=u_;
- *Zákon č. 455/1991 Zb. o živnostenskom podnikaní (živnostenský zákon)* (Trades Licensing Act 455/1991);
- *Zákon č. 275/2006 Z. z. o informačných systémoch verejnej správy a o zmene a doplnení niektorých zákonov* (Information System in Public Administration Act 275/2006);
- *Zákon č. 71/1967 Zb. o správnom konaní (správny poriadok)* (Administrative Procedure Act 71/1967);
- *Zákon č. 514/2003 Z. z. o zodpovednosti za škodu spôsobenú pri výkone verejnej moci a o zmene niektorých zákonov* (Public Authority Responsibility Act 514/2003);
- *Dopady implementovania smernice č. 2006/123/ES o službách na vnútornom trhu v Slovenskej republike* (the SD Impact Study), http://www.economy.gov.sk/dopady-implementovania-smernice-europskeho-parlamentu-a-rady-c-2006-123-es-o-sluzbach-na-vnutornom-trhu-v-slovenskej-republike-6937/128622s;
- Self-Assessment Slovakia, Ing. Richard Paule, Ministry of Economy of the Slovak Republic; and
- Statements and documents published on the website of the Ministry of Economy of the Slovak Republic, http://www.economy.gov.sk/smernica-o-sluzbach-na-vnutornom-trhu-6141/127826s.

1.2 Impact of the Services Directive

1.2.1 Profound Cause of Changes to National Law?

The transposition of the SD was not a profound reason for the national legislator to alter administrative laws in general. The Ministry of Economy identified 25 particular laws that had to be changed (liberalised). By the end of the transposition process, 37 particular laws were changed. It was decided that the optimal form of the transposition was to pass a general services act (the Internal Market Services Act).

1.2.2 Involvement in the Transposition Process

Government Decree 294/2007 identified the Ministry of Economy of the Slovak Republic as a leading authority in the transposition process. Other partners involved in this process were the Ministry of Interior, the Ministry of Justice, the Ministry of Finance, the Ministry of Agriculture, the Ministry of Construction and Regional Development, the Ministry of Labour, Social Affairs, and Family, and the Geodesy, Cartography, and Cadastre Authority. After the SD was passed, the

Ministry of Economy created its own work team and also an interdepartmental work team. They had a total of about 20 members. In addition, cooperation and coordination between several levels of the administration was essential.

1.3 (National) Scope of Application

1.3.1 Scope of the Services Directive

According to the prevailing opinion, the directive's scope of application is to achieve the elimination of discrimination in the business field for national and international businessman in all Member States (MSs), and the simplification of the access to and realisation of services. The requirements of the SD are perceived as binding for transnational as well as domestic services.

1.3.2 Application of Transposing Legislation to Domestic Service Providers

The Internal Market Services Act specifies the rights and duties for domestic service providers in the Slovak Republic, as well as for transnational service providers.

The implementing laws/regulations are applicable to all service providers from all European Union (EU) MSs, and also to service providers from European Economic Area MSs.

Transnational and domestic service providers were treated equally. Some of the SD requirements were transposed directly, without any changes, to ensure no differences between domestic and transnational providers (rights of recipients of services, supply of information to recipients of services). On the other hand, some SD requirements had to be adapted to national relations, also to achieve the equal treatment of transnational and domestic service providers.[1]

1.4 Incorporation of Transposing Legislation

In relation to administrative proceedings, which are regulated by the Administrative Procedure Act is the new codification in position *lex specialis–lex generalis.*

To incorporate the new rules/regulations a new codification was passed, *in concreto,* the Internal Market Services Act 136/2010. This act was published on 8 April 2010 in the law collection and will step in force from 6 June 2010.

---

[1] Ministry of Economy of the Slovak Republic statement about the transposition of the SD 2006/123/ES, 12.06.2007, http://www.economy.gov.sk/transpozicia-smernice-ep-a-rady-c–2006-123-es-o-sluzbach-na-vnutornom-trhu-6219/127904s.

1.5 The Relationship of the Services Directive to Primary EU Law

No information or discussions regarding the relation of the Services Directive and primary EU law can be identified in the Slovak Republic.

1.6 Screening

The screening process was realised by cooperation between the Ministry of Economy and other interested organisations. *In concreto,* the Ministry of Economy contacted all the other ministries, state government offices, and service-related chambers (tax consultants, surveyors and cartographers, advocates, translators and interpreters, etc.). The organisations contacted had to list all their remarks to prepared legislation amendments, which are important from their point of view.

The results of the screening were published in a study of the Ministry of Economy, written by Ing. Richard Paule. The study identified a need to adopt new regulation (Internal Market Services Act) to change the Trades Licensing Act and 36 other acts, to simplify some procedures and requirements for the provision of services, to accept alternative forms of education or qualification, to remove some charges for providers who use the points of single contact (POSCs) to get certain certificates, and to remove fixed time periods for licences in certain cases.[2]

2 Individual Articles of the Services Directive

2.1 Article 6 SD: Point of Single Contact (POSC)

2.1.1 Establishment of the POSC

The Internal Market Services Act deals with POSCs only from the process point of view. The actual responsibilities and venues of POSCs are covered in already existing act, the Trades Licensing Act, which was also changed because of the transposition of the SD. The Trades Licensing Act codifies that district bureaus that are Trade Licensing Offices will also be the POSCs.[3]

---

[2] Self-assessment Slovakia, Ing Richard Paule, Ministry of Economy of the Slovak republic, see Sect. 1.1.

[3] § 66b, ods. 2 zákona č. 455/1991 Zb. o živnostenskom podnikaní (živnostenský zákon) (Article 66b (2) The Trades Licensing Act 455/1991).

2.1.2 Subjective Understanding

The Slovak Republic has 50 district bureaus (POSCs). Each one of these 50 district bureaus can also establish another office, of which there are currently 64. Consequently, there are 114 POSCs, which are a single type of authority, but with offices all over the Slovak Republic. The venues of the POSCs are the 50 (64) district bureaus for Slovak citizens, and the eight district bureaus for EU citizens who reside in each region.[4]

2.1.3 Authorities with POSC-Function

In the Slovak Republic, the tasks of the POSCs were attributed to already existing authorities, so they will be no new and independent authorities/offices in this case.

2.1.4 Involvement of Private Partners

In the Slovak Republic no private partners were involved in the introduction of POSCs, which are state government authorities.

2.1.5 Liability

Within the context of mistakes made by the POSCs (in fact, all state authorities), a specific codification was passed, the Public Authority Mistakes Responsibility Act. With regard to this act, POSCs are responsible for mistakes initiated by unlawful decisions or incorrect official proceedings.[5]

2.2 Article 7 SD: Right to Information

'Rights to information' are included in the Trade Licensing Act. *In concreto,* Article 66b (a) deals with this issue.

Rights to information were implemented only within the SD's scope of application.

---

[4] § 66b zákona č. 455/1991 Zb. o živnostenskom podnikaní (živnostenský zákon) (Article 66b The Trades Licensing Act 455/1991).

[5] Zákon č. 514/2003 Z. z. o zodpovednosti za škodu spôsobenú pri výkone verejnej moci a o zmene niektorých zákonov (The public authority responsibility act 514/2003).

2.3 Article 8 SD: Procedures by Electronic Means

Article 8 of the SD will be realised by the application of a particular act, the Information System in Public Administration Act. The Internal Market Services Act codifies the need for functioning electronic procedures on 1 January 2012 (at the latest).

The Slovak Republic's electronic procedures agenda has been important already for several years. In some areas it is fully functional, and in others it will be in the next few years.

Electronic procedures will be supplementary, which means that traditional administrative proceedings will not be replaced or removed.

2.4 Article 9 SD: Authorisation Schemes

The most common authorisation scheme is a trade license for services in the scope of the Trades Licensing Act, which applies for around 90% of all services in the scope of the SD. The services are divided into four groups, but after adoption of the implementing legislation, there will only be the three following groups:

Type 1, general qualification (age minimum 18 years, no criminal record, and legal competence),
Type 2, general qualification and specific qualification obtained by professional education,
Type 3, general qualification and another specific qualification, and
Type 4, general qualification and another specific qualification (mainly related to weapons).

By adopting the implementing legislation, types 3 and 4 will be merged.[6]

2.5 Article 10 SD: Conditions for the Granting of Authorisation

2.5.1 Recognition of Requirements

The Internal Market Services Act deals with the recognition of authorisations in Article 3. The Slovak Republic recognises documents from other MSs. Service providers who will have to submit documents in an MS language with a translation into the Slovak language. Unattested documents and translation into Slovak will be verified through the Internal Market Information (IMI) System.[7]

---

[6] Self assessment Slovakia, Ing. Richard Paule, Ministry of Economy of the Slovak republic, see Sect. 1.1.

[7] § 3 zákona č. 136/2010 Z. z. o službách na vnútornom trhu a o zmene a doplnení niektorých zákonov (Article 3 of The Internal Market Services Act 136/2010).

2.5.2 Granting Authorisation Throughout the Whole National Territory and Exceptions

The Slovak Republic has not identified problems in this context and does not use regional authorisations.

2.5.3 Court Review of Administrative Decisions

Particular laws include reviewing the decisions of the courts and reviewing the use of discretion by the authorities. There was no need to alter related articles because of the SD transposition.

2.5.4 Reasoning of Administrative Decisions

According to Article 10 (6) of the SD, there was no need to change national law because the Administrative Procedure Act includes decision reviews of the authority by a court or another appellate authority.

2.5.5 Allocation of Competences

The Slovak Republic did not change the allocation of competences in the context of Article 10 of the SD.

2.6 Article 11 SD: Duration of Authorisation

The validity of the limitation of authorisations is regulated in Slovak Republic by the Trade Licensing Act. It specifies the unlimited validity of authorisations, except in cases where services providers request limited validity.[8]

2.7 Article 12 SD: Selection from Among Several Candidates

In the Slovak Republic, Article 12 of the SD was not an issue, because services, which are covered by the SD, are not limited in the sense of that article. If all conditions are fulfiled, the SD provider can provide services (covered by the SD) without the limitation mentioned.

---

[8] § 45, ods. 2 písm. g) zákona č. 455/1991 Zb. o živnostenskom podnikaní (živnostenský zákon) (Article 45 (2) (g) The Trades Licensing Act 455/1991).

2.8 Article 13 SD: Authorisation Procedures

2.8.1 Duration of Administrative Procedures

The duration of an administrative procedure is regulated by law, generally by the Administrative Procedure Act or any other specific law.

The Administrative Procedure Act generally codifies the duration of an administrative procedure for all kinds of administrative procedures. The competent authority in simple cases should make a decision immediately, in other cases within 30 days, and in especially difficult cases within 60 days.[9]

Specified terms of an administrative procedure can be extended by appeal authority, and the person filing the application must be informed about this extension.

2.8.2 Tacit Authorisation

The Administrative Procedure Act does not codify tacit authorisation. It is usual in specific administrative laws.

A specific situation within the context of tacit authorisation is in the Internal Market Services Act, which transposes the SD. Proposal of the Internal Market Services Act codifies tacit authorisation in Article 5. Regarding this article, when the competent authority in this legal term does not make a decision, then the authorisation is granted on the day after the last day of the term. So a tacit authorisation has only formal effects. Subsequently, certification from a competent authority is needed. Instead of the certification, a competent authority can make a decision about the authorisation at any time. If a tacit authorisation was given and a competent authority finds that the requirements were not satisfied, this authority can decide not to grant the authorisation. Such a decision is possible within three years after the day following the last day of the term.[10]

The Internal Market Services Act does not codify the tacit authorisation at all. The requirements of Article 13 of the SD, however, are fulfiled. The changes of the Trades Licensing Act, initiated due the Internal Market Services Act, ensured that the authorisation procedure was not needed. In the Slovak Republic there were two types of trades: notification trades and concession trades. Concession trades, which needed an authorisation, no longer exist. To carry on a trade requires only a notification and to accomplish general conditions and special conditions (if available). General conditions are to be aged above 18 years, competence to perform legal acts, and irreproachability. Specific conditions depend on the trade

---

[9] § 49 zákona č. 71/1967 o správnom konaní (správny poriadok) (Article 49 The Administrative Procedure Act 71/1967).

[10] § 5 návrhu zákona o službách na vnútornom trhu (Article 5 Proposal of the internal market services act).

type and are, for example, educational attainment, required work experience, and specific chamber membership.[11]

Elimination of an authorisation in the Slovak Republic means that a tacit authorisation is not needed.

2.9 *Articles 14, 15, 16 SD*

All requirements included in Articles 14–16 of the SD were implemented without any serious problems.

The Slovak Republic cannot identify any special or public discussions regarding MS self-screening. There are no further problems or discourses regarding these articles that are worth mentioning.

2.10 *Articles 14–19 SD*

All remarks and comments with regard to these articles were presented in the general position to the SD proposal. There were no serious problems with the implementation of these articles.

2.11 *Articles 22–27 SD*

There was no relevant discussion regarding the transposition of Articles 22–27 of the SD. There was no need to alter administrative law or administrative procedure law because of the SD transposition.

2.12 *Articles 28 ff. SD: Administrative Cooperation*

Provisions on transnational administrative assistance are not contained, as a general rule, in the Administrative Procedure Act. The Administrative Procedure Act regulates administrative assistance, but only from the domestic view point.

Requirements of the SD related to the administrative assistance did not lead to general changes in the Administrative Procedure Act. Mentioned requirements were accomplished through the new regulation, the Internal Market Services Act.

---

[11] Zákon č. 455/1991 Zb. o živnostenskom podnikaní (živnostenský zákon) (The Trades Licensing Act 455/1991).

There are no provisions on financial compensation with regard to administrative assistance.

There was no need to change the rules on data protection. Personal Data Protection Act 428/2002 codifies this sphere, and this regulation is adequate in cases mentioned.

2.13 Article 29 SD: Mutual Assistance—General Obligations for the Member State of Establishment

No serious problems were identified regarding the implementation of Article 29 of the SD.

2.14 Problems and Discourses on Administrative Cooperation

There were no specific serious problems regarding Chapter VI of the SD.

2.15 Convergence Programme (Chapter VII of the Services Directive)

Chambers and self-government associations generally are not a part of state government, so the state is not in the position of initiator of private regulations in Article 37. It is fully the responsibility of each chamber to create its own codes of conduct by following all legislative acts.

3 Assessment of the Impact of the Services Directive

3.1 Extent of the Impact

The impacts of the SD in the Slovak Republic were published in The SD Impact Study. No impacts on the administration were identified, and the passed Internal Market Services Act did not include a need to change the Administrative Procedure Act. The SD Impact Study, available online but only in Slovak, identified impacts of the SD in several spheres, such as public finance, population, business management, employment, and the business environment. For example, it was noted that in 2012 the positive impacts of the SD transposition will exceed transposition expenses. By 2012 the number of services providers (from the Slovak

Republic) in the internal market will increase by about 15,000–20,000. The SD transposition will also lead to services providing the simplification of conditions, which will create a cost saving for every businessman. From the population perspective it will bring about the expansion of services and also an increase in the quality service provision, and so forth.[12]

3.2 Assessment of the Transposing Legislation

The transposition of the SD is, from the Slovak Republic point of view, very welcome. The SD Impact Study identified several documents and legislative acts that form the economic policy of the Slovak republic. The SD's scope of application corresponds with these documents, and the intentions of the SD are similar to those of the documents mentioned.

3.3 Most Important and Profound Changes Induced by the Services Directive

The Slovak Republic welcomes the transposition of the SD because it is another step towards the real internal market. Elimination of legal and administrative barriers is one of the Slovak Republic's policy's priorities.

[12] Dopady implementovania smernice č. 2006/123/ES o službách na vnútornom trhu v Slovenskej republike (The SD Impact Study), http://www.economy.gov.sk/dopady-implementovania-smernice-europskeho-parlamentu-a-rady-c–2006-123-es-o-sluzbach-na-vnutornom-trhu-v-slovenskej-republike-6937/128622s.

The Implementation of the Services Directive in Slovenia

Rajko Knez

1 General Remarks on the Transposition Strategy and General Understanding of the Implementation

1.1 Main References Used in this Research

In the case of Slovenia, the general transposition strategy of the implementation was the responsibility of the Ministry for Economy, which holds the competence for the transposition of the Services Directive (hereinafter SD). The Ministry of Economy followed the transposition strategy as described and proposed by the EC Commission (hereinafter the Commission) in the Handbook on the Services Directive.[1] In addition, other documents were closely taken into account, whether directly or indirectly linked to the SD, such as the following:

- The Council Common Position on the SD,[2]
- Decisions regarding the Internal Market Information System (IMI),[3]

Prof. Dr. Rajko Knez, Faculty of Law, University of Maribor, Jean Monnet Chair—Legal Studies, (rajko.knez@uni-mb.si).

[1] Handbook on implementation of the Services Directive, European Communities, 2007, available at http://ec.europa.eu/internal_market/services/services-dir/proposal_en.htm.
[2] Available at http://register.consilium.europa.eu/pdf/en/06/st10/st10003.en06.pdf.
[3] Available at http://ec.europa.eu/internal_market/imi-net/index_en.html.

R. Knez (✉)
Faculty of Law, University of Maribor, Maribor, Slovenia
e-mail: rajko.knez@uni-mb.si

U. Stelkens et al. (eds.), *The Implementation of the EU Services Directive*,
DOI: 10.1007/978-90-6704-840-8_24,

- Materials regarding the recognition of professional qualifications,[4]
- Case law on services and establishments,[5] and
- Different literatures on the free provision of services and the freedom of establishment.

A conference addressing different questions on the SD and its implementation was organised in cooperation with the Faculty of Law of the University of Maribor,[6] and a collection of papers was issued to facilitate the needs of those engaged with the SD and its consequences. It is, namely, estimated that quite some special rules on different services need to be aligned with the SD, not only the horizontal general law, which shall implement the SD, but also quite a number of *lex specialis* rules, defining the rules for services and establishments. The horizontal general law deals only with partial implementation, leaving aside a number of SD rules for implementation by special laws and statutes, as well as documents in the form of executive acts adopted by the Government of the Republic of Slovenia (hereafter RS), that is, not only legislative acts. Provisions on the subject of the implementation of sector-specific legislation are mainly provisions on the freedom of services and the freedom of establishment. These provisions are drafted in the form of negative harmonisation (i.e., prescribing what is forbidden or which national measures are prohibited but can be justified). According to the Slovene Governmental Office for Legislation, these provisions have to be drafted in a form of a positive harmonisation and included in all *lex specialis* laws dealing with the establishment of and services with cross-border elements. Therefore internal screening is of great importance, since it defines the national provisions which are to be subject to changes.

Hence, the horizontal law is mostly relevant for administrative simplification, authorisation procedures of a general nature (such as tacit authorisation), the quality of services, and administrative cooperation.

1.2 Impact of the Services Directive

The SD and its scope of application have been taken into account verbatim, meaning that the Slovene legislator, in the case of the horizontal law, took into account only those areas and scope of application defined in the SD. In addition, with respect to the sector-specific legislations defined by the internal screening, the SD will be applicable mostly to laws falling into the SD's scope of application.

During the drafting of the horizontal law and within the procedure of the internal screening, different types of cooperation took place, with the Slovene Chamber of

---

[4] Available at http://ec.europa.eu/internal_market/qualifications/index_en.htm.

[5] Some of the case law is included in the handbooks on case law on establishment and services (indeed not up to date) available at: http://ec.europa.eu/internal_market/services/docs/infringements/art43_en.pdf (for establishment) and http://ec.europa.eu/internal_market/services/docs/infringements/art49_en.pdf (for services).

[6] 15-16 June 2008.

Commerce, the Trade Chamber, and all ministries within the Slovene Government. In case of internal screening, all ministries were checked the provisions of services and freedom of establishment in sector-specific areas in light of the SD. The draft proposal of the horizontal law was open to the public for three months, with the aim of obtaining remarks and suggestions. Replies were received from different organisations, such as driving schools associations, tourist offices, and alternative medical services, etc.

1.3 (National) Scope of Application

The prevailing opinion in Slovenia is that the directive's scope of application is limited to transnational cases when dealing with services and associated rules (such as points of single contact, hereafter referred to as POSCs). In the case of establishment, however, the rules cover also purely domestic cases, since no distinction is made in cases of a foreign person (legal or natural) establishing himself or herself in Slovenia or where a legal person establishes a new legal person (daughter company, etc.) in Slovenia. As such, only transnational service providers can refer to the implementing rules of the SD. However, the rules implementing the SD are fully applicable in relation to everybody, that is, to all citizens and all economic stakeholders. Unequal treatment of domestic and foreign service providers was subject to debate, especially from a constitutional point of view, since the Slovene Constitution demands equal treatment of all persons (guarantee of equality before the law). Hence, in the legal literature one can find legal arguments for broadening the scope of the SD to domestic service providers. It is true that rules of the free provision of services that are included in the special laws will treat domestic and foreign service providers equally, and that certain rules in the general horizontal law are to be applied regardless of whether the service provider is from other Member State or not (such as for POSCs, and all rules regarding administrative procedures and their simplifications).

1.4 Incorporation of Transposing Legislation

The requirements of the SD relating to administrative proceedings were implemented in the general implementing law. Most of the provisions deal with the tacit approval by state authorities or by any other administrative authorities being competent to issue the authorisations or approvals necessary to be established in Slovenia. Rules on tacit approvals are the red line and heart of the administrative provisions being implemented due to the SD. Other rules follow this implementation but are mainly ancillary in nature. It is worth stressing that general law on administrative procedures has not been changed due to the SD, and that all changes are included in the general implementation law on services in the internal market.

1.5 *The Relationship of the Services Directive to Primary EU Law*

The relation of the SD to Articles 43, 48, and 49 of the EC Treaty (now Articles 49, 54, and 56 of the Treaty on the Functioning of the EU, hereinafter TFEU, respectively) has been extensively discussed. The discussion was twofold: First, it questioned which areas fall outside the scope of the SD and, second, is it correct that these areas are subject of the direct applications of Articles 43, 48, and 40 of the EC Treaty (now Articles 49, 54, and 56 of the TFEU). The horizontal law uses the same exceptions as the SD, and the direct application of the said articles is expressly mentioned in the law itself to disseminate awareness of the TFEU framework, which is still at hand.

Where certain situation falls within the scope of EC law, all services that are not excluded by the SD itself will be within its scope. At the same time, they will remain within the scope of Articles 49 and 56 of the TFEU, the conclusion following from the general relations with primary and secondary community law, but also from Article 3 (3) of the SD, which specifies that Member States (MSs) have an obligation to apply the Directive in accordance with Treaty provisions on the free movement of services and the freedom of establishment.

In other words, if service providers established in an MS provide a certain service, it will fall within the scope of the SD, except where specifically exempted by the Directive. Such services will be subject to either the general provisions of the TFEU or to specific sector-based directives.[7]

1.6 *Screening*

So-called internal screening, which shall be accomplished for all laws and regulations, regulating services activities and a right of establishment, has been carried out under the auspices of the Ministry of Economy. The same ministry is responsible for the proper implementation of the SD and for the appropriate proposal of the law to the Slovene Parliament. The Ministry of Economy summoned all the other ministries to check the existing legislation and to prepare appropriate proposals for changes. Some of the laws and regulations are in the legislative procedure to be changed, and, to some extent, the internal screening is done. The overall assessment of the screening is that Slovene legislation does not contain direct discrimination in light of the free provision of services or the freedom of establishment but, rather, some indirect discrimination.

---

[7] See more about this issue in Rodin (2009), p. 9–25.

2 Individual Articles of the Services Directive

2.1 Article 6 SD: Point of Single Contact (POSC)

Ministry of Economy together with the Ministry for Public Administration have long discussed POSCs. These POSCs are seen as a follow-up obligation, which can be an upgrade of the one-stop-shop POSCs (in Slovene, *vse na enem mestu*, that is, VEM, a system known in other MSs as company dockets). The crucial difference between both systems is that POSCs encompass all kinds of businesses, and not only start-ups, service recipients, and all types of procedures. The POSCs have been seen as a system that can upgrade the one-stop shop, which in Slovenia is well developed and accepted by individuals. The POSCs are therefore established only as an Internet site, which runs under the auspices of the Ministry for Public Administration,[8] but it is linked to all competent public authorities. This means that POSCs are an intermediate between public authorities and the individual. A public authority shall act not only as an authority or a body, which shall bring about a decision, but also as a service provider to the individual seeking information. This way the national legislator did not re-allocate administrative competences with the introduction of POSCs, and the tasks of the POSCs were attributed to already existing authorities.

For the possible liability that might arise from POSC services, national rules on administrative liability apply. Those rules mainly follow private law rules on liability, as well as liability for third parties and employed persons. Liability is basically not strict but, rather, fault based. Only in cases of liability for employed persons is the liability strict. In other words, the Ministry for Public Administration is liable for possible damages that may arise from the POSCs' activities.

2.2 Article 7 SD: Right to Information

Article 7 and 'rights to information' have been implemented verbatim, meaning that the substance of the article, that is, the individual's rights have been, as a list, included in the implemented text. The list of rights, therefore, is not extended by the national legislator, nor is this done by sector-specific laws. Rights to information have been implemented for the scope of application of the SD only.

2.3 Article 8 SD: Procedures by Electronic Means

Article 8, as implemented in the national legislation, is, at the moment, mainly transposed. It is hard to define how it will work *in concreto*. Mostly, it will be

[8] No private partners were involved in setting up POSCs.

combined with the POSCs as implemented in Slovenia. Public authorities, who will obtain certain demands or applications from individuals, will also reply electronically—as a service or as an authority. This way the demands regarding the electronic procedure will be respected. To some extent, Slovenia has already been using electronic procedures, mainly introduced by the one-stop-shop system. The transposition in this context has no great innovative impact. However, administrative procedures can be performed in the old-fashioned way—with the physical appearance of the individual at the administrative authorities, using paper form applications, postal services, and so forth. Procedures by electronic means are only an additional procedure to already existing procedures.

2.4 Article 9 SD: Authorisation Schemes

The implementation of Article 9 in the horizontal general law has not been carried out, since this rule will be the subject of special laws and regulations. In general, an authorisation procedure is necessary in cases where the law foresees so. If no authorisation is provided for a certain service, one is free to start the activity. Conditions relating to specific forms of legal persons or branches offices are included in the Slovene legislation. They are rare but they exist. Some authorisation schemes exist in the tourism sector, for instance, for tourist guides, tour operators, and travel agencies. In addition, in the construction sector building companies and supervisors of building works need to be registered in the general company register and must comply with certain other requirements. Certain authorisation schemes are also held in other sectors, including for real estate agents, several expert/certification/testing services, detectives, waste collection, court-related services (translators, expert witnesses, etc.), postal services, and collecting societies.

In general, these are two types of authorisation procedures. There is also a third type, which demands only simple notification (e.g., for foreign lawyers to perform services in Slovenia). These three types are not changed in the substance. The SD basically influences only previous authorisation procedures. The proposed horizontal implementation law does not totally abandon the simple authorisation procedure, but it introduces the tacit authorisation procedure. The tacit authorisation procedure is rather new in Slovenia. Apart from some possible tacit authorisations in the case of prolongations of authorisation in the field of environmental law, the tacit authorisation procedure was not in force in Slovenia prior to the implementation act. In case of inactivity of the public authority for more than two months (a general time limit for issuing an authorisation), it is up to the applicant to file an appeal.[9] Namely, in case of non-activity of the public

[9] Article 255 of the Administrative Procedure Act (Official Journal of the RS, Nr. 80/1999 with later changes).

authorities it is deemed that the application was rejected. The same option is possible in the second instance of the administrative procedure; however, in such a case a lawsuit should be filed at the administrative court. Inactivity by the administrative authority at the second level is deemed as a rejection of the application or the appeal. This general framework of the Slovene administrative rules is now affected by the SD and the implementation act. However, the Slovene legislator has not implemented the SD by using the *gold-plating method,* and therefore the tacit authorisation as defined in Para 4 of Article 13 of the SD has an effect only within the ambit of its application. The tacit authorisation is therefore only applicable for the purposes of the implementation act and in cases where *lex specialis* will refer to it.[10] In other words, *lex silencio positivo* is to be applied only in cases where service providers seek authorisation and the Law on Services in the Internal Market applies or where special rules will refer to the mentioned law.

Internal screening, which shall embrace all laws and regulations, regulating services and establishment, was carried out under the auspices of the Ministry of Economy. The purpose of the screening was to check all existing provisions regarding services and establishment conditions and to check their consistency with the SD and Article 56 of the TFEU. The screening embraces all ministries of the Slovene government and their respective fields of competences. Ministries had to submit screening tables with provisions defined that needed to be adjusted with the SD requirements, or which had to be evaluated. Screening tables were then the subject of internal meetings of the Ministry of Economy and respected ministries. For some of those provisions, the ministries proposed changes by themselves and started the legislative procedures. For others, consultation with the Ministry of Economy was necessary. The process is still ongoing and changes in several special laws are anticipated. Obstacles to the free provision of services and inconsistencies with the SD have been found; however, not in a substantial number of cases.

2.5 Article 10 SD: Conditions for the Granting of Authorisation

Article 10 of the SD is, in general, although the heart of the freedom of establishment rules and a codification of the existing European Court of Justice practice, not implemented in the general implementation law, but remains to be respected by sector-specific laws and regulations. Some aspects of it are nevertheless part of the implementation law, which is the case for its fifth paragraph.

Sector-specific legislation, so far, has not taken into account conditions for the granting of authorisation verbatim. It remains to be seen whether those conditions, as listed in para 2, will be transposed at all. According to the opinion of the

[10] Article 9 of the Law on Services on the Internal Market (Official Journal of the RS, Nr. 21/2010).

Slovene Governmental Office for Legislation, which excluded the list from the original draft proposal of the implementation law, the list should only be taken into account and not transposed verbatim. In the latter case, the law would become a superior law, although general in nature. Although this is not the case, which would be legally unacceptable, the transposition of Article 10 was not accepted by the Slovene Governmental Office for Legislation.

Under Article 10 also, 'reasons of an overriding interest' are mentioned for the first time in the SD. This term, well developed by the European Court of Justice and also explained in point 40 of the preamble of the SD, is not defined in any other way. For all cases where this rule applies, the horizontal implementation law included a definition as developed by the European Court of Justice and listed all existing reasons (so far).

The obligation of giving access and granting authorisations to service activities throughout the entire national territory, as demanded by the SD, was not transposed or implemented. Since the Slovene territory is not divided into any kind of territorial units responsible or competent to grant authorisations (that would be run by local or provincial authorities), this rule has no practical application in Slovenia, even before the implementation of the SD authorisations granted on the state level were applicable to the whole territory. Since municipalities are not competent to grant authorisations to perform services and since the whole competence is given to authorities on the state level,[11] the applicability of authorisations is not limited to one or some parts of the state's territory. However, there are possible exemptions due to state security measures (such as military objects and their surroundings) or environmental protection (such as special protected areas or territories).

Para 5 of Article 10, demanding a grant of authorisation once all conditions for the authorisations have been met, was transposed to the SD verbatim, not specifying this obligation in the details. Basically, this will not change the existing rules and administrative practices in Slovenia. Public authorities usually grant authorisations as soon as it is possible. It is up to their workload whether the time used is close to the limit of two months (general time limit in administrative procedures) or any special time limit. Within these time limits, public authorities have the discretion of when exactly to grant the authorisation, but this discretion is in practice not an arbitrary one. To maintain good relations with the public and the users of administrative public services, time limits are usually respected and authorisations granted as soon as possible. A decision granting the authorisation becomes final in the administrative procedure. Whoever would like to challenge the decision needs to start the judicial review. The administrative court is competent to judge on the issue, being also able to change it in substance. This is a case of a so-called *full jurisdiction*. It is possible under certain conditions,[12] but rarely

---

[11] Transposition and implementation of the SD did not affect competences of the state authorities. They remain untouched. Only the procedural rules used by state authorities change the way the authorities' approach to decision making.

[12] Conditions are listed under Article 65 of the Administrative Dispute Act.

used. More often the courts review the procedural requirements and leave the administrative authorities to decide on substance. However, court procedures do not suspend the effect of a decision under review. The finality of the decision allows the party to start the activity. If any other party challenges the start of the activity, it shall request the court not only for the review but also for the interim measure.

A decision granting or declining the authorisation needs to be fully reasoned. This obligation arises from the principle of the *duty to state reasons*. Notwithstanding whether the decision is in favour or not to the applicant, it must be fully reasoned. If not, the authority erred in law; i.e., an essential procedural mistake. This is a reason for an appeal of any kind of legal remedy.

2.6 Article 11 SD: Duration of Authorisation

The principle of unlimited validity of authorisations has been a part of Slovene law even before the SD. This general rule has certain exceptions, some of which the implementation of the SD took into account. The general rule on unlimited validity is not applicable if

- The authorisation is automatically renewed,
- The applicant has to continuously fulfil certain conditions (such as knowledge exams or licence renewals), and
- Prevailing public interests are at stake that justifies timely limited authorisations.

2.7 Article 12 SD: Selection from Among Several Candidates

Selection among several candidates as regulated under Article 12 of the SD was not, as such, part of the Slovene legal system before the SD, apart from the rules on public procurements. The rule is therefore transposed in the horizontal law. Requirements regarding the selection among several applicants are transposed as defined in the SD. The rule is structured in abstract terms and shall be widely applicable in case of the scarcity of available natural resources or technical capacity. What exactly is meant by scarcity is not defined in the horizontal law. It is up to the administrative practice to define this term and circumstances that shall be taken into account. Helpful in this respect is an application of the Environmental Protection Law and, especially, the Nature Conservation Act, which defines when natural resources shall be preserved. Therefore the scope of Article 12 as implemented in the horizontal law shall be interpreted in light of the provision of protection of nature and the environment.

2.8 *Article 13 SD: Authorisation Procedures*

Article 13 of the SD has been implemented in the horizontal law with special care, since it introduces into Slovene law a new set of rules regarding authorisation procedures. This set of rules differs from those in the general Law of Administrative Procedures. Horizontal law is *lex specialis* in relation to the Law of Administrative Procedures.

One of the demands of Article 13 is also the a priori duration of an administrative procedure. This is carried out by the horizontal law and is not subject to the authorities' decision. The time limit is set at three months and is one month longer than in the Law of Administrative Procedures. The difference is due to tacit approval, which is not the case in the Law of Administrative Procedures. Hence, a priori time limit of three months is only applicable within the scope of application of the SD. This time limit can be extended in certain well-justified cases (such as the complexity of the case or special evidence procedures). The extension cannot last more than six months.

In case the authority does not respond to the filed application within the prescribed time, the authorisation is 'deemed to have been granted to the provider'. The tacit (fictitious) authorisation had not been used in the Slovene legal system before. There were few exceptions in the case of prolonging an authorisation within the area of environmental legislation. However, these were cases on prolongation and not on first authorisation. This is why the tacit authorisation is among the most important rules of the SD and it demands far more than just verbatim transposition. The rules on administrative procedures in force in Slovenia are not familiar with the fictitious authorisation; the same holds true for the system of legal remedies. The tacit authorisation does not have only formal but also substantive effects. This is why the system of legal remedies has been drafted in the new way for cases of tacit authorisation.

Exception to the tacit authorisations are made by the horizontal law; some are in line with the SD and some are added due to particularities in the general administrative procedural rules, such as the participation of third parties in the procedure and procedures that demand public participation (such as an environmental impact assessment). Reasons of prevailing public interest can also justify exceptions to tacit authorisation. These reasons are the same as defined by the case law and specified in point 40 of the preamble.

In case of tacit authorisation, an application is deemed to be a decision.

2.9 *Articles 14, 15, 16 SD*

Prohibited requirements in the case of establishment and requirements subject to evaluation under Articles 14 and 15 and requirements subject to the freedom of services (Article 16) are limited and partially implemented in the horizontal law.

Articles 14 and 15 are not implemented and are subject to sector-specific sector legislation. There are some requirements in sector-specific legislation that must be taken into account and evaluated, such as legal form requirements in a number of areas, including for collecting societies, higher education services, and veterinary services. Tariffs are also regulated for several service activities, for example, for lawyers, certain court-related services (translators, expert witnesses, etc.), and laboratory services.

On the other hand, Article 16 has been transposed in the horizontal law. Prohibited requirements regarding the freedom of establishment are also part of the screening and will affect sector-specific laws and regulations, as well as general law on commercial companies, since it deals also with foreign undertakings and sets out conditions for their business activities in Slovenia. A general rule is that a service provider form other Member State can undertake activities in Slovenia only once the branch office is registered in Slovenia, which is not in line with Article 14 and the court's case law. The Ministry of Economy underwent self-screening and warned the competent authorities to align the rules under their competences with the requirements of the SD.

2.10 Articles 14–19 SD

Prohibited requirements and restrictions under Articles 14–16 and 19 of the SD are not all part of the horizontal implementation act. This is true also for further exemptions (Articles 16 (3), 17, and 18 SD). There were discussions on whether to implement them by way of negative harmonisation, as done by the Directive itself, but the Slovene Governmental Office for Legislation decided not to use the negative harmonisation approach, and those requirements and restriction shall be taken fully into consideration by drafting and changing special Slovene legislation for the individual service in question.

Article 16 with general rules on the free provision of services and possible justifications and Article 18 with possible case-by-case derogations are implemented in the horizontal implementation act. This is important from two aspects: First, the free provision of services would be undermined if an act on services on the internal market would not also comprehend rules on the free provision of services. Second, the general rule is subject to exceptions (overriding reasons relating to public interests) and justification tests. Here, the SD is no longer in line with the well-established case law of the European Court of Justice. The shift to only four overriding reasons relating to public interests (i.e., public policy, public security, public health, and protection of the environment) is of great importance; therefore such a change shall not be avoided with the horizontal implementation act and left to sector-specific legislation. The latter, when defining the services' requirement, will be limited. Requirements to perform services cannot be the same as those in cases of establishment. For instance, due to consumer protection, a service provider, established in the host MS (Slovenia), may be subject to certain national requirements, but a foreign service provider (not established in Slovenia) will not. Consumer protection is not the overriding reason of public interest in the case of the free provision of services, but only in case of an establishment. Sector-specific legislation that defines requirements and authorisation conditions must, due to the above-explained difference adopted in the SD, divide the requirements into two groups: one for services and one for establishment.

Article 16 was widely discussed during the implementation, since it derogates from the existing case law and some well-accepted overriding reasons are left behind, only to be taken into account in the area of freedom of establishment and not in the area of the free movement of services. On this basis, it can be ascertained that the case law regarding the exceptions justified by overriding reasons relating to the public interest is not changed with respect to the freedom of establishment. The SD follows the rules drawn up by the case law. However, in the area of all four types of freedom to provide services (i.e., when it is not about the freedom of establishment for service providers), the SD has enacted the country of origin principle, which is indeed restricted and weakened. Together with Article 18 (case-by-case derogations), the SD and consequently the Slovene horizontal implementation law follow the additional reason (safety of services) as possible justification of state measures, which makes foreign service providers less attractive to service recipients.

2.11 Articles 22–27 SD

The chapter on quality of services was, from the very beginning, seen as a part of the horizontal implementation act, and not subject to sector-specific legislation or rules on consumer protection.

By the same token, it must be stressed that the Ministry for Economy saw this chapter as a substitute for prohibited requirements under the chapter on freedom of services. The negative effect of the missing reasons of overriding public interest can be diminished by rules on the quality of services. However, the same effect can hardly be achieved. Nevertheless, the chapter on quality of services is seen as an important one and part of the horizontal implementation act. Even though one can see this as a shift of responsibility from the public to the private sector, it is the only possible way for the SD to influence the quality of services. Nevertheless, the act has tried to be, as much as possible, in line with the Consumer Protection Law, which already imposes some of such conditions for merchants in general (not only for service providers). To make substantial differences among merchants in general and service providers under the horizontal act, the latter has, within the allowed implementation of the SD, taken into account the Consumer Protection Law. Therefore the requirements about information and penalties for breach of the rules regarding the quality of services use language and terminology already used by the consumer protection rules. This is without prejudice of the relation between both acts: The Act on Consumer Protection is *lex specialis* in relation to the horizontal implementation act.

The Slovene proposal for the horizontal implementation act has not foreseen the role of the RS as an initiator of private regulation (Article 26 SD recertification schemes, quality charters). So far this possibility, in cooperation with the Commission, has not been taken into account and no implementation rules are to be implemented in this regard.

2.12 Articles 28 ff. SD: Administrative Cooperation

Provisions on transnational administrative assistance are implemented into the horizontal implementation act and are subject to profound adjustments to the rules on market supervision already in force in Slovenia. The SD brings, in this respect, a new set of rules to the Slovene legal system. Never before, in the field of services, was such international cooperation established. *Rapex* in the field of the free movement of goods is something at least comparable to administrative cooperation in the field of services. The chapter was therefore treated as an important one and included in the horizontal implementation act. Inspectors competent to supervise the Slovene market of services were asked to review the implemented rules and its effects. The requirements of the SD led to newly drafting the provisions for administrative assistance.

Slovene market inspection, which is defined as a central body responsible for the administrative assistance of bodies from other MSs, shall ensure the supervision of service providers and the services they provide, even if they are established in another MS. The market inspection can request information, carry out checks and inspections, and so forth, as in the case of domestic service providers. In the event of receiving a request for assistance from competent authorities in another MS, the Slovene market inspection shall ensure that providers established in Slovenia will supply information necessary for the supervision of their activities and so forth. Such information will then be transmitted to the foreign competent authorities. Slovene market inspection shall, for the purposes of the SD and the implementation act, communicate with authorities in the other MSs in the way they regularly communicate with other authorities within the Slovene organisation of executive and administrative authority.

However, no new administrative authorities are established for this reason. The tasks of international cooperation are part of the competences of the market inspection. Since this is part of their competences and since they are financed by the state's budget, financial compensation for the quite wide range of assistance is not provided for in the horizontal law.

Administrative cooperation is also quite sensitive in aspects of data protection. Therefore the horizontal implementation act lists in detail which data can be exchanged and gives authorisation to the Slovene government to adopt special rules on the exchange of information. In any case, acts on personal data protection must be respected by authorities when exchanging information.

2.13 Article 29 SD: Mutual Assistance—General Obligations for the Member State of Establishment

Article 29, which sets forth general obligations for the MSs of establishment in mutual assistance, was not seen as problematic during the work on the draft proposal of the horizontal implementation act. To our understanding, this is a logical consequence of administrative cooperation. The entire chapter was accepted by the market inspection as work added to already overloaded programs of work and the day-to-day management of inspection services. However, it is a common position that only for administrative cooperation is it not, presumably, necessary to establish a new authority.

3 Assessment of the Impact of the Services Directive

The impact of the SD on administrative procedure law, administrative law for business activities, and even beyond is assessed as a new, additional and substantive task. One of the biggest changes is seen in tacit authorisation, which brings about a totally new approach to authorities. For the first time the state and other public authorities will be burdened with time limits. Until now the burden for non-activity of the public authorities had been overtaken by the parties. The so-called negative effect of disrespecting the time limits (if the authority did not decide on a case, it was deemed that the request for authorisation was denied and the appellant was left to legal remedies, i.e., a legal suit at the administrative court) is now changed to a positive effect and tacit authorisation. Although this is not a novelty in other MSs, it brings a certain uncertainty to how it will work in the practice.

One of the uncertainties is also the establishment and follow-up obligation of POSCs. It is not clear whether the Internet site as such will fully respect the SD requirements in this regard. The idea to link POSCs with the competent authorities may well work. It will require authorities to work, on the one hand, as a service for those requesting information, and, on the other hand, as an authority with the power of decision making (under the pressure of tacit authorisation).

The horizontal implementation act was not adopted in the implementation period, but on 5 March 2010, and published in the *Official Journal of the Republic of Slovenia* (No. 21) on 15 March 2010. It came into force on 30 March 2010. It was the clear and genuine intention of the Ministry for Economy to respect the implementation time limit; however, due to numerous remarks obtained from different stakeholders, ministries, the Slovene Governmental Office for Legislation, and numerous meetings for shaping the text for the draft horizontal law on a different level, implementation of the time limit was not respected.

Some stakeholders expressed the view that the draft law was difficult to read. Although the Ministry for Economy and outside experts tried to word the text in an as user friendly way as possible, this was not fully achieved. The main reason is the complexity of the text in the SD itself and numerous references to other acts, areas falling outside the scope of the SD, and so forth.

Nevertheless, the horizontal law can be assessed as proper, but it indeed presents only a partial implementation. It does not implement the very substance of the SD, that is, codified parts of the case law. This is especially true for the rules governing the freedom of establishment. Therefore the draft horizontal act is left with more formal provisions on POSCs, administrative cooperation, and a bit more substantiality on the freedom and quality of services. What is left is to be implemented by sector-specific legislation for all the individual services in question.

The idea to transform legal rules from case law into the positive legislation as also proposed by the Handbook was not achieved in Slovenia. Personally, I think this is one of the main disadvantages of the proposed draft law. It cannot be argued that specific legislation will not achieve the same aim, but it would be pragmatic to include basic rules on both freedoms in only one act.

References

For legislation, jurisprudence and websites please refer to 1.1 of the report and footnotes directly.

Commission Handbook on the Implementation of the Services Directive (2007) Available at: http://ec.europa.eu/internal_market/services/docs/services-dir/guides/handbook_en.pdf

Council of the European Union (2006) Common Position adopted by the Council with a view to the adoption of a Directive of the European Parliament and of the Council on services in the internal market, July 2006. Available at: http://register.consilium.europa.eu/pdf/en/06/st10/st10003.en06.pdf

Rodin S (2009) Scope of the Services Directive 123/2006. In: Knez R (ed) Internal Market for Services. Pravna fakulteta Univerze v Mariboru, pp 9–25

The Implementation of the Services Directive in Spain

Marta Franch and Joan Torrelles

1 General Remarks on the Transposition Strategy and General Understanding of the Implementation

1.1 Main References Used in this Research

(i) Law 17/2009, of November 23, 2009, on Free Access to, and Pursuit of, Service Activities (the "Umbrella Law"), published in the Official State Gazette, November 24, 2009. http://www.boe.es/boe/dias/2009/11/24/pdfs/BOE-A-2009-18731.pdf

(ii) Law 25/2009, of December 22, 2009, Amending Various Laws to Adapt Them to the Law on Free Access to, and Pursuit of Service Activities (the "Omnibus Law"), published in the Official State Gazette, December 23, 2009. http://www.boe.es/boe/dias/2009/12/23/pdfs/BOE-A-2009-20725.pdf

(iii) Decision of the Council of Ministers of June 12, 2009, on the adaptation of Royal Decrees and Ministerial Orders not covered by (i) and (ii).

Prof. Dr. Marta Franch, Universitat Autonoma de Barcelona (marta.franch@uab.cat) and Joan Torrelles, Garrigues Advocats i Assessors Tributaris, Departament de Dret Públic (jtorrellestorrelles@fordham.edu).

M. Franch (✉)
Universitat Autonoma de Barcelona, Bellaterra, Spain
e-mail: marta.franch@uab.cat

J. Torrelles
Garrigues Advocats i Assessors Tributaris, Barcelona, Spain
e-mail: jtorrellestorrelles@fordham.edu

U. Stelkens et al. (eds.), *The Implementation of the EU Services Directive*,
DOI: 10.1007/978-90-6704-840-8_25,

1.2 Impact of the Services Directive

In Spain, the transposition of Directive 2006/123/EC of the European Parliament and of the Council of 12 December 2006 on services in the internal market (the "SD") was fashioned as an ambitious reform that would bring about profound change in legislation governing the State. The intention behind this reform is to achieve gains in terms of efficiency, productivity and employment in sectors affected by the SD, and to increase the variety and quality of services available to citizens and companies. Thus, the transposition of the SD into Spanish law means and, more importantly, will continue to mean a major change in the process of simplifying, modernizing and accelerating administrative procedures, which in Spain are particularly slow and inefficient.

Furthermore, the transposition of the SD will bring with it amendment of a great many provisions in national law—both those relating to general administrative procedure and those regulating the various sectors of activity falling within the scope of application of the SD. This is a particularly complex process in Spain, as it affects numerous spheres of legislation whose administrative responsibilities are distributed among various levels and institutions of government.

Under the principle of institutional neutrality, the power to include the SD in the Spanish legal system is held by the level of government that actually possesses the specific power to implement legislation in that area. Thus, in Spain, the transposition process of the SD requires introducing new legislation and amending existing legislation at the levels of (i) central government, (ii) autonomous communities and (iii) local government.

Unlike in other Member States, in Spain the inclusion of the SD in national law at the central government level was carried out principally by approving two new laws. First, the contents of the SD were transposed into Spanish law via an "Umbrella Law", which transposed almost all of the provisions of the SD, and set forth its general principles, which are to act as a guiding framework for all legislation on the services industry. Next, prior to the end of the transposition term, a second law, known as the "Omnibus Law", was approved. The aim of this law was to amend a total of 47 central government laws; this involved legislative reform in the sectors concerned in order to adapt them to the provisions of the SD. The advantage of the mechanism chosen by the Spanish government to transpose the Directive lies in the convenience of having the entire contents of the SD in a single legal instrument, the Umbrella Law, and the specific amendments that it causes in a separate law, the Omnibus Law.

Furthermore, a Decision of the Council of Ministers passed on June 12, 2009 determined the Royal Decrees to be amended as a result of the adaptation of the SD, which implies the reform of at least 117 pieces of legislation with regulation status.

It must also be taken into account that the adaptation of the SD to national law involves the need to add a parallel reform process in the various autonomous communities and in local government institutions; this process is still at a very early stage. A considerable proportion of the adaptation to the principles of the SD is to be carried out by local government institutions because a large part of the authorisations affected by the transposition of the SD fall within the powers of the municipal councils. In addition, the transposition mandate is also going to have an effect on professional associations, which are directly affected by the scope of application of the SD.

The transposition of the SD has required and will continue to require the participation of all authorities with powers in those sectors regulated by the SD: the central government, autonomous communities and local government institutions. To coordinate the work carried out at these different levels, an Inter-ministerial Task Force for the Transposition of the Services Directive was set up, in which members of the central government, the autonomous communities and local government institutions took part. The participants in the Task Force were: (i) at the central government level, the 14 ministries with powers in this area, (ii) at the autonomous community level, the various autonomous communities also took part and (iii) at the local government level, local government institutions, basically through the Spanish Federation of Municipal Councils and Provinces (Federación Española de Municipios y Provincias, or "FEMP").

1.3 (National) Scope of Application

The Umbrella Law defines its scope of application on the same terms as are used by the SD, and establishes as a general rule the principle of freedom to access and pursue service activities. In this regard, the principles in the SD transposed into Spanish law will apply to the services that are offered or provided in Spain by both Spanish service providers and service providers from any other Member State.

The provisions derived from the SD apply in the same manner and can be relied upon by Spanish service providers and by service providers from any other Member State, which are given equal treatment.

1.4 Incorporation of Transposing Legislation

In Spain, the principles established in the SD were incorporated into the Spanish legal system, primarily through the two new laws mentioned above: the Umbrella Law, which transfers practically all elements of the SD, and the Omnibus Law, which amends specific articles of pieces of central government legislation that have the rank of law in those spheres to which the respective provisions of the SD and the Umbrella Law apply.

The Umbrella Law reproduces the provisions of the SD practically verbatim, whereas the Omnibus Law extends the principles contained in the SD and in the Umbrella Law to sectors not affected by the SD.

Moreover, to ensure a transparent and efficient regulatory framework, the government has started a process of adaptation of central government regulations below the rank of law to conform with the provisions of the SD, the Umbrella Law and the Omnibus Law.

In addition, at the level of autonomous communities and of local government institutions, the transposition of the SD entails the amendment of numerous existing rules in sectors affected by the SD.

1.5 The Relationship of the Services Directive to Primary EU Law

In Spain, the SD is perceived as a way of further specifying the general principles of freedom of establishment and freedom to provide services as established in Articles 43 and 49 of the EC Treaty (now: Articles 49 and 56 TFEU); no major problems have been identified in this context.

The SD and its transposition are accepted as a necessity derived from the Community freedoms established under the EC Treaty. Despite the difficulties and the change of mentality that will be associated with the bringing into operation of the SD and of the rules transposing it, the public authorities have taken on board changes to legislation and must adopt a change of position and procedures in their dealings with citizens.

1.6 Screening

The process of adapting the general principles contained in the SD to the Spanish legal system was structured in three phases: (i) identification of the legislation that is potentially affected; (ii) evaluation of its compatibility with the SD; and (iii) amendment of the industry-specific legislation, which must be performed by the level of government invested with such power, whether the central, autonomous community or local government.

The Umbrella Law provides for the creation of a multilateral cooperation committee, formed by the central government, the autonomous communities and representatives of local government, aimed at facilitating an improvement in the regulation of service activities and, in particular, monitoring and coordinating initiatives carried out in the various levels of government for the purpose of correct transposition of the SD.

Further, to assist local government institutions with incorporation of the SD into the scope of their powers, a practical evaluation manual has been published for local government institutions. A specific collaboration line has also been set up with municipal councils that bring greater technical capacity, especially in areas where, by population or weight in economic activity, the adaptation of the legislation has a greater impact and can serve as a model for other local government institutions.

To control how the SD provisions are applied, the autonomous communities and local government institutions will notify the central government of the legal provisions and regulations that have been amended to adapt them to the provisions of the SD and the Umbrella Law.

The application and control mechanisms have been set in motion but it is too early to evaluate results, as the Umbrella and Omnibus Laws are still quite new, and the various government entities, especially local and autonomous community governments, have waited for these laws to be enacted before bringing the legislative changes under their responsibility into operation.

2 Individual Articles of the Services Directive

2.1 Article 6 SD: Point of Single Contact (POSC)

The point of single contact system was incorporated in Spanish law in Article 18 of the Umbrella Law. Under this article, services providers can gain access electronically and remotely through a point of single contact to both the information on the procedures needed to access and pursue a service activity, and to completing the formalities required to do so, including all declarations, notifications or applications needed to obtain an authorisation, in addition to applications for inclusion on a register, a roll, or for registration with associations, professional bodies and general and autonomous boards of professional bodies.

In addition, Law 11/2007, of June 22, 2007 on Electronic Access for Citizens to Public Services also contains the principles established in Articles 6, 7 and 8 of the SD, and lays the basis for establishing a point of single contact system.

In conformity with the above, in Spain an official point of single contact has been established, is now in operation, and contains the procedures and formalities affected by the SD, including the data relating to the different levels of government mentioned above. This point of single contact is in operation at the following address: www.eugo.es

This point of single contact enables citizens to obtain information and to complete, electronically, the procedures required to set in motion a service activity; it excludes only those formalities which, by their nature, require verification in person.

In particular, the point of single contact contents the following three lines of action:

(i) The Website and Information System, to respond to any questions put by providers and citizens regarding information on the formalities to be completed to exercise a service activity in Spain, regardless of whether an establishment from within the country is used. The website provides information on the steps required to establish a business, the relevant competent authority, forms of service provision, legal forms for enterprises, and complaints procedures open to providers and recipients, etc. The website also offers downloadable help guides in PDF format for each activity to be undertaken.

(ii) Electronic processing system, allowing for the electronic completion of procedures and formalities, allocating them among the various competent authorities and/or redirecting users to the electronic procedures put in place by each competent authority. Each formality is actually completed by the relevant competent authority itself.

(iii) Point of single contact content management system. Each competent authority is responsible for both the information offered about its procedures and formalities and the requirements involved, and is accordingly answerable for the quality of information furnished to providers.

The introduction of the point of single contact system was conferred on the Ministry of the Head of the Spanish Government (*Ministerio de la Presidencia del Gobierno de España*), and its aim is to supply service providers with information on the available options in connection with accessing and pursuing their business activities. The aim of the point of single contact system in Spain is to give service providers a single contact person who supplies them with complete and guided information.

The establishment of the point of single contact must in all cases observe the existing distribution of powers in Spain, and the powers of the authority responsible for performing the formality or procedure cannot be altered under any circumstances. Irrespective of the authority responsible for each formality, each such authority must adopt the necessary measures and embrace in their respective spheres the technology required to ensure that the service is provided from a unique point of contact.

The bringing into operation of this system for carrying out dealings between the citizen and the government, regardless of the authority that is handling or deciding, is underpinned by two premises which have not necessarily been achieved in Spain: the first is proper communication and coordination between public authorities, and the second is for such authorities to have the technical means to be automatically connected to each other. The introduction of the point of single contact system was implemented by the government with private parties playing no part. Moreover, no specific liability system has been determined for operating errors in the system, it being understood that the general administrative liability system would apply in any such case.

2.2 *Article 7 SD: Right to Information*

Article 19 of the Umbrella Law contains the rights established in Articles 7 and 21 of the SD, and no additions were made to them in the Spanish transposition legislation. These rights were later included in Law 11/2007, of June 22, 2007, on Electronic Access for Citizens to Public Services.

Protection is also assured in the legislation; it will now be necessary for each level of government to observe and specify in its procedures a set of rights that complies with the SD and in the Umbrella Law.

2.3 Article 8 SD: Procedures by Electronic Means

Electronic administrative procedures were already regulated in Spain prior to the transposition of the SD, having been provided for generally in the Public Authorities and Common Administrative Procedures Law 30/1992 of November 26, 1992, and later more extensively in Law 11/2007, of June 22, 2007, on Electronic Access for Citizens to Public Services.

Despite the existence of the regulations described above, not all administrative procedures are available electronically at present. One main reason behind the delay in completion of the electronic access to public services system is the absence of a specific deadline for autonomous communities and local governments for electronic implementation of their procedures and formalities.

In this sense, it must be pointed out that final provision number three of Law 11/2007, of June 22, 2007, sets December 31, 2009, as the deadline for citizens to be able to fully exercise their rights with respect to any procedure or activity that is the government's responsibility. On the contrary, at the autonomous community and local government levels, according to the same final provision, procedures and formalities must be available in electronic version only in accordance with such entities' budgetary means.

Due to the recent transposition of the SD in Spain, it is still too early to evaluate the impact of the SD on electronic procedures. As a result of provisions in the Umbrella Law and in the Omnibus Law, it is foreseeable that electronic administrative procedures will spread to all procedures and formalities required for access to a service activity or its pursuit.

The implementation of electronic procedures does not imply abolition of the traditional system for carrying out administrative procedures, since the use of electronic administrative procedures is intended as a right for citizens, who may nevertheless choose another kind of administrative procedure.

2.4 Article 9 SD: Authorisation Schemes

Transposition of the SD has reaffirmed the principle of freedom of access to and pursuit of service activities. Thus, the legislation governing a service activity or its pursuit cannot impose authorisation procedures on providers, except in certain exceptional cases meeting the following conditions, for which sufficient reasons must be provided, founded on the respective law establishing those procedures:

(i) Non-discrimination: The authorisation procedures must not be discriminatory or directly or indirectly determined according to nationality or whether the establishment is in the territory of the responsible authority or, in the case of companies, by reason of the place where the registered office is located;

(ii) Need: The authorisation procedures must be justified by an overriding reason of public interest; and

(iii) Proportionality: The authorisation procedure must be the most appropriate instrument to achieve the sought aim in that there are no other less restrictive measures that would obtain the same result, in particular, where an a posteriori inspection would be too late to have any real effect. Specifically, no authorisation procedures will be required for access to a service activity or its pursuit under any circumstances where it is sufficient for the provider to submit a notification or responsible declaration stating that it is in compliance with the requirements laid down, if any, and to provide the necessary information to the responsible authority for the pursuit of the activity.

The standard authorisation procedure in Spain is the prior administrative authorisation procedure. The transposition of the SD into Spanish law will cause the elimination of any prior administrative authorisations that are not justified by reasons of public interest or that are a disproportionate means of achieving these aims. The prior authorisation procedure will be replaced with the provision of a notification or responsible declaration to the government.

Responsible declarations and prior notifications generally mean that a right can be exercised or an activity commenced from their submission date, subject to government audit, monitoring and inspection powers.

The quality of the service will be assured by strengthening the *a posteriori* inspection and monitoring services.

This is a very important change, as alluded to above, with respect to both the way in which the Spanish government conducts itself towards its citizens and the way citizens conduct themselves towards the government. An "authoritarian" mentality has placed the government in a particular position of superiority conferred on it by the very possession of governmental power and has placed the citizen in a position of submission to this power (long waits, discretionary decisions, etc.). This is why legislative changes are not the only changes that the implementation of the Directive has brought about in the administrative procedures of Spain.

2.5 Article 10 SD: Conditions for the Granting of Authorisation

The recognition of authorisations granted by other Member States has been implemented by adding a reference to Article 9 of the Umbrella Law that public authorities cannot ask for evidence of fulfilment of any requirements, controls or guarantees that have an equivalent aim to any that the provider is required to fulfil in Spain or in another Member State. Despite the inclusion of this condition, there has been some discussion in Spain as to the difficulty of applying this principle in practice, although due to its recent introduction, it is still premature to determine the full scope of the issues surrounding application of this condition.

Further, the Umbrella Law expressly states that an authorisation, communication or responsible declaration will allow the provider to access the service activity and to pursue it fully throughout Spain, including through the establishment of branches. The Umbrella Law, however, provides that the public authorities can grant authorisations and request communications or responsible declarations which are valid only in a portion of the territory, where justified by reasons of overriding public interest based on public policy, public safety, public health or the protection of the environment, provided that such decision is proportionate, not discriminatory and sufficiently founded.

In any event, to obtain an authorisation, prior compliance with the conditions established in the legislation governing the concerned procedure is necessary. In this sense, in Spain there are two types of authorisation: regulated authorisations and the discretionary authorisations. With respect to regulated authorisations, the relevant authorities have no discretion to decide whether to grant a license, because the legislation itself establishes when to grant it and when to deny it. On the contrary, in cases of discretionary authorisations, the relevant authorities have broad decision-making powers.

Notwithstanding the above, the problem that arises from regulated authorisations is that the requirements established in the legislation contain only general concepts or need more technical precision (known as technical discretionality).

Thus, in both types of authorisation, although the legislation establishes the requirements to obtain them, in practice these requirements are subject to interpretation by the competent authority. Therefore, public authorities retain the power to decide whether to grant an authorisation, taking an interpretative role not anticipated by the law.

Implementation of the SD implies that the discretion of the relevant authorities is considerably reduced. This is because, on the one hand, in the SD all the requirements demanded to pursue the service activity in question are explicitly stated and, on the other hand, the SD limits the authority's capacity to establish additional requirements apart from those set by the SD. However, in any case, the role of interpreting the concepts established in the legislation will continue granting decision-making power to public authorities.

This same problem persists when the competent body checks compliance to the stated requirements once the responsible declaration has been completed and the activity begun.

In relation to review by the courts separately from review by governmental authorities (administrative appeals) of authorisations granted by the government, it must be understood that, under Spanish law, every administrative act may be reviewed by the courts after the requirements set out in the law are fulfilled, and accordingly, interested parties may apply for a review of the grant or denial of the authorisation; the government may also review a null and void authorisation in an *ex officio* review procedure.

Spanish law already stipulates an obligation to furnish reasons behind all administrative acts; therefore, it is not necessary to amend the legislation in relation to this issue. Thus, Article 54 of the Public Authorities and Common Administrative Procedures Law provides that:

> "1. Reasons shall be provided, with a brief reference to the facts and legal grounds, for:
> a) Acts that limit personal rights or lawful interests.
> b) Acts that decide upon ex officio review procedures of administrative provisions or acts, administrative appeals, claims prior to court proceedings and arbitration proceedings.
> c) Those that depart from the view held in previous proceedings or from the opinion of consultative bodies.
> d) Decisions to stay acts, regardless of the reason for the stay, in addition to the adoption of provisional measures under article 72 and article *136 of this Law.*
> e) Decisions to use the fast-track procedure or extend terms.
> f) Those that are performed by exercising discretional powers, and those that are required to be so under an express regulation or legal provision.
> 2. The reasons for acts that bring selection or competitive processes to an end shall be provided in conformity with the provisions in the rules governing those processes, and the grounds for the decision adopted shall be evidenced in all cases."

Lastly, as mentioned above, transposition of the SD has entailed no amendments to the powers conferred on the various public authorities.

2.6 Article 11 SD: Duration of Authorisation

The Umbrella Law expressly establishes that, generally, the submission of a communication or responsible declaration, or the grant of an authorisation, will give access to a service activity and allow it to be pursued indefinitely. The restrictions placed on this right are exactly the same as those of Article 11 (1) of the SD, and no specific reasons of public interest are given other than those mentioned in the section on definitions, which is included in the Umbrella Law in the same way as in the SD.

The authorisation system for an indefinite term already existed in particular sectors in Spain prior to transposition of the SD, subject only to compliance with the obligations related to it. In some cases, the authorities can establish a term for the activity that is directly related to the nature of the activity, or where the applicant has requested authorisation for a given term.

2.7 Article 12 SD: Selection from Among Several Candidates

The Umbrella Law transposed the requirements established in Article 10 of the SD identically in relation to the selection processes among several candidates.

It could be said in this respect, although with some exceptions, that such a system has certain similarities to the legislation on games of chance.

2.8 Article 13 SD: Authorisation Procedures

Generally, the maximum length of a procedure will be as set in the legislation governing the procedure concerned. Having said that, in the Spanish legal system, the Public Authorities and Common Administrative Procedures Law contains general legislation applicable to all administrative procedures; this law states that an administrative procedure cannot have duration longer than six months, unless legislation with the rank of law establishes a longer term or a longer term is provided for in European Community law.

This law also provides that in those cases in which the legislation governing the procedures does not set a maximum length, the duration of such procedures will be three months.

If the responsible authority does not issue a decision within the established term, the Public Authorities and Common Administrative Procedures Law states that the application for authorisation must be deemed to be approved under the principle of tacit authorisation that prevails in these cases. Approval by tacit authorisation is treated for all purposes as an administrative act bringing the procedure to an end, and is valid against the government and any individual or legal entity, whether public or private.

Even if the tacit authorisation existed in Spain prior to implementation of the SD, it was only applicable in those cases in which a regulation with the rank of law did not establish otherwise. Consequently, despite the fact that the general rule was approval by means of tacit authorisation, in practice, due to the extensive regulation of denial by administrative silence established in sectoral legislation, approval by tacit authorisation was the real exception.

One of the consequences of the transposition of the SD into the Spanish legal system was an amendment to the law on the common administrative procedure to guarantee general application of approval by tacit authorisation and that denial by administrative silence shall occur really only in exceptional cases. According to this amendment, denial by administrative silence can be established only for reasons of public interest or by the disposition of Community law. As a result, the wording of Article 43 of the Public Authorities and Common Administrative Procedures Law is as follows:

> "1. In procedures commenced at the request of the interested party, without prejudice to the decision that the government must render in the manner envisaged in point 3 of this article, should an express lawful decision not have been notified to the interested party or interested parties that made the pleadings in the request upon expiry of the maximum term it shall be deemed to be approved by administrative silence, except in cases where a piece of legislation ranking with the rank of law or overriding reasons of public interest or a piece of Community legislation dictate otherwise.

> Furthermore, silence shall have the effect of denial in procedures relating to exercising the right to petition, mentioned in article 29 of the Constitution, procedures which if approved would result in powers relating to the public domain or to public service being transferred to the applicant or to third parties, in addition to procedures to challenge acts and provisions. Where, however, an administrative appeal to a higher body has been filed against the denial by administrative silence of an application due to the elapse of the term, it shall be deemed to be approved if, within the time limit for a decision, the competent administrative body should not have issued an express decision on it.
>
> 2. Approval by administrative silence is for all purposes deemed to be an administrative act bringing the procedure to an end. The only effect of denial by administrative silence is to allow the interested parties to file the administrative appeal or appeal for judicial review to which they are entitled."

2.9 Articles 14, 15, 16 SD

The implementation of the requirements in Articles 14, 15 and 16 of the SD required a substantial change in national administrative law, and accordingly their transposition has implied proposed amendments to numerous national laws.

The principles contained in the above articles were included in the Umbrella Law, and were also used to amend various laws, which were carried out through the Omnibus Law. It must be borne in mind, however, that implementation of those articles in national law will largely affect autonomous communities and local legislation, and will require amendment of a large number of provisions pertaining to these government entities to adapt them to the contents of the SD.

2.10 Articles 14–19 SD

With the exception of certain nuances relating to Article 17 of the SD, almost the whole of the requirements, exemptions and restrictions in Articles 14, 15, 16, 17, 18 and 19 of the SD have been transposed into national law in Spain.

In relation to the provisions on additional derogations to the free provision of services in Article 17 of the SD, Spain prefers not to make any explicit reference in the Umbrella Law to the expression "services of general economic interest", due to the absence of a Community-wide definition of this concept. Spain considers that the inclusion of this concept could give rise to an ambiguous and open-ended exemption which, aside from causing an excessive reduction in the scope of application of the principle of freedom to provide services, would create uncertainty. Therefore it is proposed that the derogation be confined to those specific sectors in which it was identified from the start that problems could arise for the application of the principle of freedom to provide services in particular sectors: postal services, electricity, natural gas, water and waste services.

Similarly, the Umbrella Law does not transpose all of the exemptions made in the SD. It does not mention those relating to data protection, travel by nationals to other countries, the requirement for involvement of a notary or intellectual property rights. Nor is it deemed necessary to transpose references to activities not carried on in Spain, such as activity relating to "judicial recovery of debts".

2.11 Articles 22–27 SD

The legislation transposing the SD into the Spanish legal system attempts to transfer responsibility for the quality of the services provided to the private sector, either by establishing obligations for the provider or by encouraging private monitoring organisations authorised by the government. Upon transposing these articles, the Spanish government has shown a desire to strengthen these resources, as they are an attractive option to secure compliance with the SD without requiring a disproportionate increase in the government's workload to achieve such compliance.

2.12 Articles 28 ff. SD: Administrative Cooperation

Cooperation between governments at various levels is very important for implementing Community law. On numerous occasions, governments have had to collaborate with each other to satisfy claims from private parties which are protected and recognised by Community law (in the recognition of social security benefits, for example).

Despite the existence of these channels of communication between the Spanish government and the governments of other Member States, there can be no doubt at all that the application of the provisions of the SD will require a huge effort by the Spanish government to fulfil the requirements for administrative assistance between States.

Lastly, transposition of the SD has not given rise to any amendment to the Personal Data Protection Law (Organic Law 15/1999, of December 13, 1999).

2.13 Article 29 SD: Mutual Assistance—General Obligations for the Member State of Establishment

No particular issues were identified in relation to obligations of mutual assistance. It must be borne in mind, however, that transposition of the SD into the Spanish legal system occurred only very recently.

2.14 Problems or Discourses on Administrative Cooperation

See the above Sect. 2.12.

2.15 Convergence Programme (Chapter VII of the Services Directive)

Regarding codes of conduct, the Umbrella Law confines itself to establishing a general provision of encouragement for public authorities for the participation of professional bodies and, as the case may be, the general and autonomous boards of bodies, professional organisations and chambers of commerce in the preparation on a Community scale of codes of conduct aimed at facilitating the freedom to provide services or the establishment of a provider from another Member State, with observance in all cases of competition law, without explaining what means this participation will take.

3 Assessment of the Impact of the Services Directive

3.1 Extent of the Impact

In Spain, transposition of the SD was taken on as an ambitious project with the aim of driving a profound reform of the services sector by intensifying the application of the principles established in the SD. Although the inclusion of the SD in the Spanish legal system is still to be completed due to the fact that the transposition of the SD into the legal system was completed only very recently, the application of the SD will have a considerable impact on the Spanish legal system. In this regard, around 7,000 procedures and laws potentially affected by the SD have been identified which have been classified into 22 areas of activity which are being evaluated.

3.2 Assessment of the Transposing Legislation

As well as an obligation, the transposition into national law of the SD is perceived in Spain as an opportunity to carry out profound reform of the services industry (the largest sector of the Spanish economy in terms of GDP and employment). It is hoped that the SD transposition process will reap rewards in terms of efficiency, productivity and employment, in the sectors concerned, together with an increase in the variety and quality of services available to citizens and companies.

3.3 Most Important and Profound Changes Induced by the Services Directive

Although the transposition of the SD into national law will give rise to numerous amendments to the Spanish legal system, it could be said that the biggest change is simplification of administrative procedures, by making them more expedient, efficient, competitive and transparent, and replacing the conventional Spanish *a priori* system with a system based on a *posteriori* inspection.

As already mentioned, this change has brought about an important change of mentality in both the government and among persons dealing with the government. For the government, because private parties' activities will no longer depend on the administrative procedure and on the time that the government takes to complete such procedures, the government's activities will be based on checking that the communication or declaration is in conformity with the law before or after the interested party has started the activity. Therefore, for parties dealing with the government, their communications or declarations must be made in accordance with the legislation and such parties must meet the requirements laid down in the legislation.

The Implementation of the Services Directive in Sweden

Gunilla Edelstam

Introduction

The cooperation between the Member States (MSs) within the European Union (EU) is based on a common market with free movement for goods, people, services, and capital. Article 49 of the Treaty establishes the right to provide services within the Community and, in accordance with Article 43 of the Treaty, the freedom of establishment is ensured. However, it has been far more difficult to obtain the free movement for services than it has been to obtain the free movement of goods. Directive 2006/123/EC of the European Parliament and of the Council of 12 December 2006 on services in the internal market has been stipulated to achieve better penetrating power for the principles in Articles 43 and 49 of the European Community (EC) Treaty (now Articles 49 and 56, respectively, of the consolidated Lisbon version). The development of service activities is considered to be of great importance to the Community and its MSs with regard to the economy and employment. Elimination of barriers is needed to improve the service sector in the EU. A direct application of the articles in the EC treaty and case law from the EC court is not considered to be enough to accomplish this.

Obstacles that exist on a national level are the need for authorisations, and these can be complicated and time-consuming to obtain. The Services Directive (SD) aims at improving the service sector with regard to the option of providing services in an MS other than that of the origin. The SD is applicable to the provision of services in, for example, regulated professions such as lawyers, authorised interpreters, estate agents, electricians, and veterinarians. Other examples are building

Dr. Gunilla Edelstam—Associate Professor at Sodertorn University, Sweden

G. Edelstam (✉)
Sodertorn University, Huddinge, Sweden
e-mail: edelstam@yahoo.se

U. Stelkens et al. (eds.), *The Implementation of the EU Services Directive*,
DOI: 10.1007/978-90-6704-840-8_26,

and construction services, consulting and the coaching of businesses, tourism services such as travel agencies, services within the pleasure industry such as circuses and sport arenas, services by craftsmen such as plumbers, information services such as web portals, news channels, distribution and publishing, hotel and restaurant services, privately financed education (e.g., for driving licences), rentals and leasing (e.g., car rentals), as well as certification and testing activities.

Greater freedom for services shall, if possible, be achieved through the following changes in the legislation:

- There shall be no authorisation procedure, and so forth, for service providers established in other MSs that provide their services temporarily.
- There shall be removed authorisations etc. where, for example, notification and posteriori inspection can replace them.

The MSs can, according to Article 9 (1) of the SD, only keep their authorisation procedure for service providers that are established in Sweden if the authorisation scheme does not discriminate against the provider, the need for an authorisation scheme is justified by an overriding reason in relation to the public interest, and the objective pursued cannot be attained by means of a less restrictive measure such as, for example, an *a posteriori* inspection. For service providers that temporarily work in Sweden and are not established here, the access to or exercise of a service activity may only be restricted if it is necessary because of public policy, public security, public health, or protection of the environment.

The MSs shall, in addition,

- Remove discriminatory requirements for authorisation if the authorisation is necessary,
- Change procedures in cases where authorisations are necessary, with time limits for the procedure,
- Create electronic contacts with administrative authorities through so-called Points of Single Contact (POSCs),
- Cooperate with administrative authorities in other MSs with regard to information on service providers,
- Fulfil their duty according to the SD to regulate the information that shall be given to service consumers.

The basic idea in accordance with the EC Treaty (now the TEU and TFEU) is to simplify the procedure for service providers and thus promote the development of providing services on a transnational level. To simplify is also to modernise. Old structures can be replaced by new ones that are simpler for the citizens but which involve a new culture for the national authorities. The SD offers several possibilities of modernising the administration.

The time limits are important, as is the abolishment of authorisations, but the SD indicates several alternatives or additional ways that can be used to modernise the administration.

This paper deals with the how Sweden implemented the provisions of the SD, with the intention of assessing the implementation. Was the implementation done on a minimum level or was the ambition higher? Has a modernisation of the administration taken place?

In Sect. 1 some remarks will be made on the transposition strategy used. Section 2 deals with how different articles of the SD were implemented in the Swedish legal system. Section 3 assesses the implementation accomplished thus far.

1 General Remarks on the Transposition Strategy and General Understanding of the Implementation

1.1 Main References Used in this Research

In Sweden the foreign department was responsible for the implementation process. A special secretariat was established that coordinated the work and was the contacting organisation in relation to the ministries. It took care of the legal work, the development of the administrative system, communications, and international contacts. It also wrote the report Ds 2008:75[Ds; Preparatory legal work from the secretariat of the Foreign Ministry, first report, *Genomförande av tjänstedirektivet* (Implementation of the SD)] that preceded the government's proposal for new legislation. All of the ministries screened the regulations within their fields of law. They had to identify regulations that needed to be changed as a consequence of the SD and the results were presented by the secretariat in Ds 2008:75. This preparatory legislative work included consultations with some of the other MSs and participation in expert group meetings arranged by the EU Commission. Consultations and meetings also took place with representatives of trade and industry, labour unions, and other interest groups, as well as with different operators such as chambers of commerce, local governments, and Verva, a board for administrative development.[1]

This report has since been considered by more than 150 operators of different kinds, including municipalities and state regional authorities, courts, chambers of commerce, and central administrative agencies such as the tax authority, the customs authority, and the migration authority. In addition, universities and representatives of interest groups on the labour market and trade and industry, as well as other interest groups, took part. The report was thereafter partly changed due to remarks by the mentioned operators and the Legal Council,[2] and a proposal for legislation has been made in Reg. Prop. 2008/09:187 [Reg. Prop.; Proposal for new legislation from the government, 2008/09:187 *Genomförande av tjänstedirektivet*

[1] Reg. Prop. 2008/09:187 p. 29.

[2] A body—within the parliament—consisting of judges from the Supreme Court that review proposals for new legislation. Its suggestions for changes are not binding.

(Implementation of the SD)]. The Swedish Parliament accepted this proposal from the government in November 2009. The law and the changes in existing legislation have been valid since 28 December 2009.

Sweden has, on the national level, implemented one act of Parliament, *Lag om tjänster på den inre marknaden*, the Law on Services on the Common Market, here called the Swedish Law on Services [SSA; Swedish Services Act with regard to the Common Market (Lag *(2009:1077) om tjänster på den inre marknaden*)], which went into force 28 December 2009, and one governmental regulation, *Förordning om tjänster på den inre marknaden*[3] (the governmental ordinance in the following refers to this ordinance). The SSA law is horizontal, that is, it concerns the whole service sector. However, it explicitly states that changes with regard to time limits and to acceptance of foreign documents are stipulated in sector regulations (from the parliament, government, or central administrative agencies). Some specific laws, mainly specific administrative laws, were changed in connection with the stipulation of the SSA as a result of the screening.

Legislative work is also done by the local governments (i.e., the municipalities) in connection with the SD. They handle not only local government legislation but also make so-called recommendations that have an influence on service providers. Every municipality must decide on their legislation, and some local governmental legislation needed to be changed in accordance with the SSA. A total of 290 municipalities needed to impose the SD in their legislation. Swedish municipalities have very limited means of making binding laws, but in the area of the SD, there are a few. Municipalities in Sweden had to screen their provisions. Rather few changes have been made in such provisions.[4]

After implementation of the SD, a new legislative investigation [SOU 2010:46; foreign business activities in Sweden. An overhaul of the legislation on foreign branches in an EU perspective (*Utländsk näringsverksamhet I Sverige. En översyn av lagstiftningen om utländska filialer i ett EU perspektiv*), a preparatory legal document from a special committee appointed by the government.] proposed changes in the Foreign Branches Office Act with regard to the registration of a branch and methods of getting in contact with the service provider.

1.2 Impact of the Services Directive

The SD concerns transnational matters, that is, service activities from business persons from MSs other than the one that implement the SD in its legislation. However, parts of the SD can also apply to domestic services. In Sweden, this holds true for the POSC and for sector provisions.

---

[3] Förordning (2010:1078) om tjänster på den inre marknaden (Swedish Service Ordinance).

[4] As far made as far as can be seen from the website of the cooperative agency of the local governments, www.skl.se.

The new law on services on the Common Market, the SSA, consists of rules on services within the scope of the SD. Its title is the "Law on Services on the Common Market" and, according to Article 1 of the SSA, the law contains regulations concerning services that are covered by Directive 2006/123/EC.

The SSA has 20 articles. It is considered to be a horizontal law and has the following content.

Article 1: An introductory rule that stipulates that the law contains provisions with regard to services covered by 2006/123/EG and provisions are also to be found in specific legislation. There is also a stipulation that says that the competent authorities shall 'promote' the principles of the Directive.

Articles 2 and 3: Application area (Article 2 stipulates the application area in accordance with Article 2 SD and Article 3 stipulates that the SSA is secondary to other EU legislation).

Article 4: Definitions partly in accordance with Article 4 of the SD. Some of the provisions in the SD were not necessary to impose.

Articles 5 and 6: Provisions on POSCs, that there shall be a POSC, that the government shall institute further regulations, and that a service provider that has applied for an authorisation through the POSC shall receive the communications thereafter through the POSC.

Articles 7 and 9: Procedural rules. In § 8 there is a stipulation with regard to the content of the acknowledgement of the application. § 7 states that time limits can be found in other legislation, and § 9 states that the duty for the competent authority to accept documents is to be found in other regulations.

Articles 10–15: Provisions with regard to cooperation with administrative authorities in other EU countries via the Internal Market Information System (IMI), including obligations to help foreign administrative authorities and in some cases report to the Commission.

Articles 16–20: Information from service providers, as well as how they shall handle complaints and that they may not discriminate against the receivers of services.

Some of the provisions in the SSA thus only stipulate that the provisions are to be found in other regulations. The time limits are to be found in other provisions, according to § 7 SSA. The duty for the authorities to accept documents from other states is to be found in other provisions, according to § 9 SSA. The consequences of not complying with these time limits are also stipulated in sector legislation. Such stipulations are made in regulations at lower governmental levels,[5] from administrative authorities[6] or local governments.

Cooperation between the POSC and the IMI, as well as notifications to the Commission according to Articles 15 (7) and 39 of the SD are further dealt with in the ordinance from the government with regard to the practical accomplishment.

---

[5] Reg. Prop. 2008/09:187 p. 89.

[6] The board of Agriculture has stipulated such rules in connection to the protection of animals. Reg. Prop. 2008/09:187 p. 98.

The transposition was carried out on a minimal level. Parts of the requirements already existed in Swedish law, but others potentially implied great changes in general administrative law, such as the time limit and the tacit authorisation, were thus implemented through specific administrative laws, and few changes have been made in such laws.

In addition, legislation concerning providers from other MSs offering their services on a temporary basis in Sweden is stipulated in specific laws—about 20 on the national level—within the sectors concerned. Discriminatory requirements were taken away, time limits for the procedure introduced, and exceptions for foreign providers offering temporary services in Sweden (but who are established in another MS) were made. Further examples of new legislation are those involving unlimited authorisations and notification procedures.

1.3 (National) Scope of Application

What is the scope of application of the SD? How has it been perceived by the Swedish legislator? There was considered to be no need to implement all the provisions of the SD. Several provisions in the SD (such as Articles 10 (2) (f) and (g), 10 (5), (6), 11 (3), 12, 13 (1), 13 (2), 13 (6) and (7) SD) were considered compatible with existing Swedish legislation and there was no need for more regulation.

To whom is the SSA applicable? In the preparatory works, there were no discussions on whether the SD was applicable to domestic providers of services. However, in the SSA it is stated that this so-called horizontal Law Concerning Services on the Common Market contains regulation concerning services that are covered by 2006/123/EG and that aim to implement the directive. With such a starting point, it could be expected that the law should only be applied in cases covered by the power of the EU, that is, the transnational provision of services. In addition, with the starting point that the SD is based on case law from the EC court as a consequence of Articles 43 and 49 in the EC Treaty (now: Articles 49 and 56 TFEU), some discussion could be expected as to whether the SD and the SSA cover the domestic provision of services. Such case law covers transnational issues.

It is, however, clear that parts of the SSA have consequences for national providers as well. These providers have access to online applications at the Swedish POSC (www.verksamt.se). In addition, the specific administrative laws that are applicable to providers from other EU MSs that are established in Sweden are also applicable to national service providers. Regulations of relevance to all service providers are, above all, the POSC and time limits. The Swedish POSC (www.verksamt.se) can be used by domestic as well as transnational providers. Before implementation of the SD, a website already existed with information on how to start a company, and so forth, and to this website has been added online application and procedure options. In addition, business persons can use the POSC.

Since the time limits are stipulated in specific administrative legislation, it can apply on all providers of services and other business persons as well, if the law concerns them. The scope of the SSA is therefore, with regard to the POSC, such that anybody can use it for contacting the administrative authorities.

The duty of providers to provide certain information to service consumers has particular relevance for temporary providers of services established in another MS. The scope of the SSA is therefore, in practice, limited to non-established providers with regard to their duty to inform the receivers of services.

With regard to time limits (and tacit authorisation), such regulations shall, according to the SSA, be made in specific regulations. Such a regulation is applicable to domestic providers of services, as well as others applying for the permit, and so forth. In case a time limit is noted in specific administrative law, the relevant administrative authority shall, according to the SSA, inform the applicant of the time limit, tacit authorisation, and the legal remedies. Since this is a part of the SSA, one could presume that only transnational (established and non-established) providers should be informed. This is not, however, the case. Since the time limits are applicable to anybody applying for the relevant authorisation, the relevant/competent authorities will have to inform anyone applying for authorisation through the POSC.

A dividing line between the purely domestic provision of services and the transnational provision of services with regard to the application of Swedish law, the SSA, does not seem to exist thus far with regard to the POSC and time limits (including tacit authorisation and information on time limits, etc.). However, it is possible to find contradictory declarations in the preparatory work with regard to other parts of the SD: The demand in Article 10 (6) of the SD that a decision shall be fully motivated is not in accordance with Swedish general administrative law. There are options to exclude some information from the reason of a decision (necessarily due to the security of the realm, the protection of personal and economical circumstances or similar circumstances, or when it is urgent[7]) in general administrative law, and it is therefore declared in the preparatory work[8] that the administrative authorities shall observe that there is a further-reaching demand for reason in the SD and that the reason shall be written in such a way that sensible information is not revealed and that there must be a reason, also, in cases when the decision is urgent. It is also stated that the Swedish tradition to use standard reasons shall be used carefully in decisions covered by the SD. Shall this apply also to domestic providers? Probably not. There is no discussion with regard to the dividing line between domestic and transnational EU service providers, and whether or not there is a difference between them. It seems to depend on the issues. However, the Administrative Procedure Act (APA; *Förvaltningslagen*) and its stipulation on motivation are supposed to apply to all administrative cases, but an

7 Administrative Procedure Act Article 20 (3), (4).

8 Reg. Prop. 2008/09:187 p. 82.

exception exists in preparatory legislative work (and the SD) that is supposed to apply to transnational service matters ('services on the Common Market').

Extension to other fields of national administrative law has hardly occurred. There has been no change in general administrative law. However, the preparatory work states that the general APA shall be applied differently in transnational service matters. The regulation of major importance in the horizontal Swedish law on services, the SSA, is the POSC. This is of importance to business persons in general, including domestic providers and other business persons.

As regards time limits, information from the administrative agency with regard to time limits and consequences will be applied in all cases, to domestic as well as non-domestic providers. The few time limits that exist are stipulated in specific administrative law. The information on time limits in the SSA will therefore have to apply to anybody who applies for an authorisation where time limits exist.

In addition, the information for the receivers is mainly for the non-established providers of services. There is other national legislation that applies to established providers and national businesses. However, the SSA applies to "services on the Common Market", according to the title of the act, and therefore the regulation on information from providers is also inconsequential. The necessary definitions and application area are stipulated in the SSA, but these provisions are not of much importance if they are not connected to horizontal rights or duties.

1.4 Incorporation of Transposing Legislation

The SD was implemented through a new so-called horizontal law, the SSA. However, several stipulations in this law only establish that there are further provisions in other legislation.[9] The new procedural rules are the time limits, the duty of the authorities to inform about the time limits, and the right of the individual as well as the duty of the authority to continue the procedure on the POSC once the application is submitted through the POSC. In addition, the duty of the authorities to accept documents can be seen as a procedural rule in connection with the evaluation of proofs, as can the duty of the authorities to cooperate through the IMI. Cooperation is part of the control that shall be implemented during the procedure. The right to continue the procedure on the POSC and the duty of the authority to inform about time limits, as well as the duty to cooperate, are stipulated in the SSA.

---

[9] This in its turn means that the government and its central administrative authorities or the local governments keep the possibilities to change the regulation in the specific administrative area. It will at least be possible for the government etc. to change a regulation more quickly than it would have been for the parliament to change an act of parliament.

1.5 The Relationship of the Services Directive to Primary EU Law

The SD is a consequence of Articles 43 and 49 in the EC Treaty (now Articles 49 and 56 TFEU) and the court decisions in connection with these articles. One argument raised about the Swedish legislation was that the freedom to provide services should not be included in the new law, since the EU law had not changed (i.e., case law according to Article 49 EC Treaty, now: Article 56 TFEU).[10] The directive codifies the practice of the EU court with regard to the general principles on freedom, such as the freedom of establishment, non-discrimination, necessity, and proportionality. Such principles can be derived from the Treaties and the case law from the European Court of Justice.

However, it was found that Article 16 of the SD and the temporary provision of services is more restrictive regarding possible exceptions than earlier case law according to Article 49 EC Treaty (now: Article 56 TFEU). It was considered necessary to screen existing regulations with regard to their accordance with the SD.[11] Changes with regard to the freedom to provide services were therefore considered necessary. The word "services" was, however, considered unclear but necessary to use.[12]

Separation of the established from the non-established provision of services is difficult, since primary EU law is not clear on this issue. The Treaties and the case law must be used when such matters are to be resolved.[13] However, Sweden has found it necessary to stipulate a presumption with regard to this separation. In a report with regard to a new Foreign Branches Act and Ordinance, it has been suggested that the provision of services that is supposed to continue for less than a year shall be presumed to be non-established, and if it is supposed to continue for more than a year it shall thus be presumed to be an established provider of services. This presumption is suggested to be stipulated in the Foreign Branches Ordinance, and it shall be applied when § 2 Foreign Branches Act is applied. According to this § 2 a foreign business must have a branch (or subsidiary enterprise or agency) if it is established in Sweden. According to the act, it shall be mandatory to notify the National Company Board if the business plans to continue for more than six months or if it employs staff in Sweden. It is thereafter the National Company Board that can decide—with the help of the presumption—whether the provision of services can be considered to be an established provider. It is possible to appeal such a decision to an administrative court of first instance.

When the SSA was prepared, a remark was made that the SD shall not have influence on labour law and the labour environment. Therefore it was stressed that the government intended to return to the issue of registering foreign branches.

---

10 Reg. Prop. 2008/09:187 p. 45.

11 Reg. Prop. 2008/09:187 p. 36.

12 Reg. Prop. 2008/09:187 pp. 36 f.

13 SOU 2010:46 p. 14 compare Reg. Prop. 2008/09:187 p. 109.

1.6 Screening

During autumn of 2007, a comprehensive screening was conducted by the ministries. All the ministries were asked to identify and account for national regulations that needed to be changed within their fields as a consequence of the SD, and to give suggestions on how to change them. In 2008 an investigator was appointed, and five administrative officials and an assistant helped him with the work.[14] This SD secretariat was set up as a temporary unit within the Foreign Ministry and all the staff was appointed by March 2008. The task of this secretariat was to[15]:

- Elucidate and analyse the economic, legal, and practical consequences of the SD,
- Bring forward proposals on how to ensure the correct implementation into Swedish law and administration,
- Pay special attention to the administrative system—including the POSC—that was to be constructed,
- Represent Sweden in the expert group of the Commission,
- Guard and analyse the implementation in other MSs as well as EEA states, and
- Be responsible for internal and external information and consider how to direct efforts on larger information drives.

The results of the screening as well as considerations made with regard to the horizontal law and the necessary changes in other laws were presented by the aforementioned investigator in a report (Ds 2008:75) on the implementation of the SD. This report later resulted in the proposal for new legislation from the government to Parliament, Reg. Prop. 2008/09:187.

All laws were screened at the national level. It was found that the SD exerted an influence on 90 acts of Parliament and 75 ordinances from the government.[16] Most of these were found to be in accordance with the SD. All of those that were not were accounted for in the report. With regard to about 50 of these, there are explanations in the report as to why changes were not needed. Changes were made in about 20 specific laws on the national level (from Parliament, the government, and the national administrative authorities), and a so-called horizontal law plus an ordinance from the government were stipulated. The APA was, however, not changed.

The few provisions that the municipalities stipulated were screened by them, and few of the provisions were changed.[17]

---

[14] Ds 2008:75 p. 65.

[15] Ds 2008:75 pp. 62 f.

[16] Statement by the minister of trade in DN (daily newspaper) 090408 (Lättare väg ut i Europa, Ekonomi p. 8).

[17] Compare www.skl.se pilotprojekt Haninge kommun.

2 Individual Articles of the Services Directive

2.1 Article 6 SD: Point of Single Contact (POSC)

According to Article 6 of the SD, the MS shall ensure that it is possible for providers to complete procedures and formalities through POSCs. There is a single Swedish POSC and it can be found at www.verksamt.se. This website existed before the notion of POSC was introduced, under the name *Företagsguiden* (Guide for Enterprises). The POSC has been added to this site and there is thus an online option to apply for permits, and so forth, since 28 December 2009. The website www.verksamt.se gives advice in Swedish and in English on how to start a company, run it, and develop it, as well as how to close it down. The site has a connection, EUGO, to the POSCs of other EU MSs.

According to the § 1 SSA this law (e.g., with regard to application through the POSC) shall be applied to services covered by the 2006/123/EG and, according to www.verksamt.se, online applications and notifications can be implemented by companies, and other entities, covered by 2006/123/EG. However, online applications can also be used by others. This website is open to anybody who wants to run a business in Sweden, irrespective of whether it concerns the provision of services or other activities (or in another EU Member State). It is possible to apply online for permits, and so forth, in Sweden, not only for foreign business persons and enterprises, but also for domestic enterprises and business persons operating only in Sweden. In other words, the options that are provided on www.verksamt.se can be used by anybody.

The SSA stipulates that one or several points of contacts shall be established (§ 5 SSA). If a service provider has applied for an authorisation through a contact point, all communication shall thereafter be made through that contact point (§ 6 SSA), the POSC. The government has stated that there shall be only one[18] POSC by way of introduction, which opens up the path for more POSCs in the future. This POSC was introduced in December 2009. It was developed by three state agencies, the Chamber of Commerce, the Agency for Economic and Regional Growth, and the Consumers Board. The tasks of the POSC were thus attributed to pre-existing authorities in Sweden. Private partners were not involved but may be in the future. The POSC consists of an interactive web portal and a help desk in accordance with the directive.[19] Through the help desk function, suppliers and receivers of services are able to access information and practical advice in matters that concern services. The POSC is a middleman between service providers and administrative agencies.

---

[18] The Swedish Chamber of Commerce together with the Agency for Economic and Regional Growth and the Consumers Board have the responsibility to develop this contact point (Reg. Prop. 2008/09:187 p. 57).

[19] Reg. Prop. 2008/2009:187 p. 57.

Electronic documents will also be sent through the POSC, and the procedure for granting or not granting permits will be handled through the POSC. In the future,[20] signatures will also be handled electronically. The electronic signature still cannot be used on the transnational level.[21] The development of the POSC's functions involves several core areas of the existing national action plan for e-government. The POSC should be consistent with this plan.[22] This action plan concerns the contacts between citizens and the administration, cooperation between administrative agencies, and the necessary technical infrastructure. A so-called "E-delegation" has been appointed to coordinate the implementation of the action plan.[23] The starting point is that the action plan shall establish a user-friendly and resource-efficient integration of the functions of the POSC and e-services for service providers.[24] There is an e-governance action plan for Internet-based activities of the public sector that mentions the POSC as an important part of the increased options for citizens to have access to public authorities. The action plan intends it to be important in many other areas, such as applications for driver's licences, studies at universities, and taxes. The action plan was established in January 2008 and its overall goal is to make it as easy as possible for as many people as possible to have contacts with the public administration.[25] However, this has still not happened. It is easy to find application forms on the Internet in Sweden. Many administrative authorities have websites with such information. The complete online procedure, however, is only accessible through the POSC at www.verksamt.se, a website for businesses.

The role as a middleman leads to questions on the separation between when a service is given through information and when an authorisation case begins when documents are sent through the middleman, the POSC. The document has reached the administrative authority when it has reached the POSC. Whether there can be any control by the POSC with regard to the application without the exercise of POSC authority is unclear.[26] Whether this unclear point with regard to exercise of power will influence the distribution of functions and competences between administrative agencies is therefore unclear.

There is only one POSC and it can be found at www.verksamt.se. It is handled by the state through three of its administrative authorities. All administrative agencies concerned, including local governments (i.e., municipalities) must connect to this POSC. More POSCs may be introduced in the future, if needed.[27] The

---

[20] The EU-project Stork is developing a solution over border.

[21] The so-called Stork-project on EU-level is supposed to find solutions.

[22] Reg. Prop. 2008/09:187 p. 60.

[23] Dir 2009:19.

[24] Reg. Prop. 2008/09:187 p. 60.

[25] See Handlings plan för e–Förvaltning (Action plan for e-government) p. 16.

[26] Ds 2008:75 p. 122.

[27] Reg. Prop. 2008/09:187 p. 60.

reason why there is only one POSC handled by the state is[28] that many measures had to be adopted within a limited time (by 28 December 2010), and it was convenient to have only one handled by the state to start with. Private partners were not involved in the introduction of the POSC.

The tasks of the POSC were attributed to pre-existing authorities. The Agency for Economic and Regional Growth has the operative responsibility for the POSC. The Chamber of Commerce takes care of the help desk function and, in addition, it coordinates cooperation between Swedish administrative authorities. The Consumers Board, together with the Chamber of Commerce, is responsible for information and advice to the receivers of services.

Who is liable for mistakes made by the POSC? There is a risk that the POSC will spread and distribute information that is misleading or out-of-date. This can harm providers and the receivers of services. There is no regulation on liability in the SSA, but, according to the law on damages (*Skadeståndslagen*), the state is responsible for economic losses that have been caused by an administrative agency. The precondition for this responsibility[29] is that the agency, through fault (*fel*) or negligence (*försummelse*) provides erroneous information or advice. Compensation for damages can only be guaranteed if, in view of the circumstances, there are special reasons. Compensation for economic loss can be requested at the Legal Chancellor's Office. The Legal Chancellor (JK; *justitiekanslern*) acts as the representative and advocate of the state in such matters.[30] The Legal Chancellor's decisions cannot be appealed, but it is possible to sue the state for damages in a private law court. It is, in general, rather difficult to receive compensation from the state.

To ensure that the information to be distributed is correct, the government has found[31] that there must be a distinct division of responsibility between the administrative agencies responsible for the POSC and those connected to it. This division of responsibility has been established in the governmental ordinance[32] with regard to the three administrative authorities that are responsible for the POSC, namely, the Chamber of Commerce, the Agency for Economic and Regional Growth, and the Consumers Board. How the tasks are divided between the authorities is described above.

2.2 Article 7 SD: Right to Information

According to Article 7 of the SD, MSs shall ensure that information is accessible through the POSC and that assistance can be received from the competent authorities with regard to interpretation and application.

---

[28] Ds 2008:75 p. 118.

[29] Skadeståndslagen (1972:207) 3:3. (law on compensation for damages).

[30] See www.jk.se.

[31] Reg. Prop. 2008/09:187 p. 62.

[32] Ordinance (2009:1078) on services on the common market, SSO (Swedish Service Ordinance).

A great deal of information must be made easily accessible through the POSC according to Article 7 of the SD. This right to information has not been stipulated in the new SSA, which only stipulates[33] that the government or an administrative agency shall institute further regulations on the POSC. The ordinance from the government stipulates the duty for the three aforementioned authorities to provide electronic information through the POSC, the intermediary role of the POSC, and the provision of a help desk. In addition, there shall be a link to the portal of the Commission. This was accomplished through www.verksamt.se.

With regard to the content of the information through the POSC, there are, however, no stipulations. It has been considered that such legislation is unnecessary, because Swedish administrative procedure law already stipulates that the administrative agencies are obliged to provide guidance.[34] The preparatory work behind the SSA states that the need for support according to Article 7 of the SD is not further reaching than the stipulation on guidance that already exists in Swedish law. Thus there is no need for any new legislation on the information for service providers. This is a part of general administrative law, according to the preparatory work. The content of the information on the Swedish POSC may go beyond the SD, but there is no regulation on the content. The administrative authority must decide the need for guidance, and may go beyond the SD.

Information according to Article 7 of the SD is rather comprehensive. According to the preparatory work, the APA is a good basis for the service to providers.[35] However, the APA does not say much in regard to this, and the preparatory work does not go further into the problem of what support should be given to providers. The APA stipulates that guidance shall be given. The APA, as it is normally interpreted by the textbooks, is not a 'good basis', but it is possible that through the SD and future case law we have—in a roundabout—an explanation to the duty to guide that may be of interest to Swedish administrative procedure in general. Without a clearance of this, the interpretation might be very different from one authority to another. Since the authorities behind the POSC are responsible for mistakes, there may be a reluctance to provide certain information.

This information concerns permits, and so forth, of different kinds. Anybody can apply for such permits, and so forth. It is thus not necessary to be a service provider and the option is also open for domestic businesses of other kinds. The Swedish POSC can therefore, in fact, be considered as going beyond the scope of the SD with regard to its users, and it is also possible to find information that goes beyond that needed according to Article 7 of the SD. The website existed previously—under the name *företagsguiden*—and it was not specifically for service providers but, rather, for all businesses (*företag*).

33 § 5 SSA.

34 § 4 Administrative Procedure Act.

35 Reg. Prop. 2008/09:187 p. 61.

2.3 Article 8 SD: Procedures by Electronic Means

According to Article 8 of the SD, MSs shall ensure that procedures and formalities relating to access to a service activity can be completed by electronic means through the POSC.

The web portal is www.verksamt.se and Article 8 of the SD has been interpreted as the duty to make use of an electronic procedure with regard to the different steps involved in a procedure concerning an authorisation.[36] The Swedish legislator has found[37] that the term *electronic procedure* in the SD refers to all steps during the procedure in which a service provider has contact with the POSC (i.e., the online function on www.verksamt.se) or competent administrative agency. The legislator also found that this meant that electronic procedures should be available through a common communication network such as the Internet. The terms "completed" and "electronic means" are not clear enough in Article 8 of the SD, and therefore the government found it necessary to make this statement.

Since a transnational e-signature or e-legitimisation is necessary to fully implement the SD, it can be difficult to "complete" the procedure by electronic means without this, and e-legitimisation still does not exist on the transnational level.

The Agency for Economic and Regional Growth has, as mentioned above, the operative responsibility to develop the web portal of the Swedish POSC. This portal allows the use of an electronic proceeding. This electronic procedure is new and hence does not exist to a comparable extent in the Swedish system, but it was introduced on a pre-existing site (*Företagsguiden*) with advice and guidance for businesses. The online option for applications was added as a consequence of the SD. In connection with this on-line option and guidance and information, there is also a help desk. It is possible to mail questions or to phone and ask. Somebody is always supposed to be there to answer the questions during office hours.

It is still too early to make statements on the impact of the online options. There was no comparable electronic procedure before the online option of www.verksamt.se, but there are plans for more according to the aforementioned action plan for e-government.

Other means of administrative proceedings have not been removed. It is possible for service providers to apply for a permit or notify the authorities through the electronic system, but this method does not have to be used. The service provider can still use ordinary ways of communicating with the administrative agency; however, once a provider has communicated through the POSC, all communication thereafter shall be made through the POSC. The new SSA stipulates (§ 6) that if a service provider makes an application or gives notification to a competent administrative agency, that agency must continue the procedure through the POSC. The filing of an application, through the POSC is thus enough

[36] Reg. Prop. 2008/09:187 p. 63.

[37] Reg. Prop. 2008/09:187 p. 63.

to entitle to an electronic procedure on condition that the competent agency has been addressed. This means that the administrative procedure between the applicant and the competent administrative agency must be electronic thereafter.

2.4 Article 9 SD: Authorisation Schemes

Article 9 of the SD establishes that the MSs shall not make access to a service activity subject to an authorisation unless the authorisation scheme does not discriminate or there are overriding reasons with regard to the public interest or the objective cannot be obtained with a less restrictive measure.

In the comprehensive screening that was carried out, which included all the relevant legislation and where every ministry was asked to identify and give an account of national regulations that needed to be changed due to the SD, the laws were found to be in accordance with the SD. The regulations on the national level that were identified within the SD area were thus considered to be consistent with the SD, and the authorisation scheme was maintained.

Only one authorisation on the national level was replaced with a notification: For an authorisation concerning insemination activities and activities with eggs and embryos on animals, a business person who already has an authorisation from another EU-country only needs to notify the Swedish authorities. An a posteriori inspection has thus not been seen as sufficient in the other screened regulations.

In the Swedish administrative legal system, there are naturally many regulations that require prior authorisation and where it is thus forbidden to start activities without an authorisation or a permit. Posterior inspections can, in such cases, be made to control the activity if the inspection has support in the law. The individual party would always stand the risk that the authorisation will be recalled, but this can, of course, only be done in accordance with the law.

There are also regulations according to which a notification is sufficient and there is no need for any decision on authorisation. The enterprise or the person can then start the activity after notification. The supervising agency can, in general, make inspections in such cases and start a case *ex officio* on whether the activity can continue. Whether a 'good cause' is needed to make a material inspection depends, of course, on stipulations in the relevant law, and so do the possibilities for prohibiting the activity. To separate notifications from qualified notifications does not seem quite accurate in this context (i.e., the provision of services).

According to the preparatory work from the government,[38] Article 9 of the SD is understood to cover all procedures where a decision is needed directly or indirectly to make it possible for a service provider to run his or her business. Notifications are not further dealt with in the preparatory work from the government. However, notifications have been included in the screening that were made,

[38] Reg. Prop. 2008/09:187 p. 68.

and notification requirements were thus considered to be included in Article 9 of the SD; for example, notifications with regard to preventing serious chemical accidents and on the sale of tobacco were included in the screening.[39]

The preparatory legislative work[40] stresses that the European Court of Justice will have to decide whether a permit is in accordance with the SD or not, and there is thus probably a belief that it is possible that the changes made might not be considered sufficient by the Commission and the Court.

The account given above concerns national provisions. It is, however, possible that there are regulations from local governments that make demands on service providers which are not in accordance with the SD.[41] In addition to this, there is a stipulation in Swedish law on services on the Common Market (§ 1 SSA) according to which the relevant authorities shall promote the principles of the SD, and this is considered to be enough to guarantee the observance of the principles in Articles 9, 14, and 15 of the SD.[42]

2.5 Article 10 SD: Conditions for the Granting of Authorisation

Article 10 establishes conditions that must be fulfilled when granting an authorisation. There shall be no discrimination and the criteria shall be justified by an overriding reason relating to the public interest, proportionate to the public interest objective, clear and unambiguous, objective, and be made public in advance. It shall also be transparent and accessible. The article furthermore implies the recognition of authorisations granted by other MSs. Conditions that are given when granting an authorisation may not overlap controls and conditions that exist in the other MS.

According to Article 10 (3), the conditions shall not duplicate the requirements and controls in another MS. This stipulation is mentioned in the preparatory work, but no comments were made. Problems in connection with this are not discussed in the preparatory works. However, the stipulation was included in the screening, and changes were suggested and made in specific existing provisions.

The screening identified a few authorisations where it was necessary to take into account the authorisation in another MS. A governmental ordinance[43] on the control of ecological production where the controlling (private) agency must be accepted by an administrative authority had to be changed. It is now established that the competent authority in another EU MS can accredit it. With regard to insemination, and so forth, on animals, an authorisation from another MS will be

---

[39] See for ex. Ds 2008:75 pp. 425, 434, 439.

[40] Reg. Prop. 2008/09:187 p. 69.

[41] Reg. Prop. 2008/09:187 pp. 71 ff.

[42] Reg. Prop. 2008/09:187 p. 77.

[43] § 5 Förordningen om EG:s förordning om ekologiskt framställda produkter Ds 2008:75 p. 156.

accepted, but the Swedish authorities must be notified. This is also established in provisions on lower levels.[44] Changes were also made with regard to the building of houses and the demand for experts and persons responsible for the quality of the houses to comply with the SD.[45]

The recognition of authorisations from other MSs has been seen as an issue of material law, where the material law must be in accordance with the SD. The SSA contains information that the duty of an administrative authority to accept documents from administrative authorities in other countries is stipulated in other legislation, that is, in specific administrative law. In this way, the foreign document in question can be referred to as a prerequisite for a special authorisation. However, it can also be seen as a procedural matter, implying that the investigating authority, that is granting the authorisation, shall include and evaluate all information of relevance, including such information from other countries, during its investigation. Article 10 (3) of the SD indicates that this is a procedural issue. It stipulates that the liaison point (mentioned in Article 28) and the provider shall assist the competent authority by providing any necessary information in this regard.

There are difficulties in granting authorisations throughout the entire national territory with regard to authorisations from local governments. In fact, the issue has not been dealt with. The local governments handle approximately 15 authorisations.[46] The legislation that gives the local governments the competence to grant those permits is created through acts of Parliament.[47] The local governments cannot, in general, legislate in such matters. The local governments have, however, in accordance with some acts of Parliament, been delegated the right to stipulate conditions.[48] There are furthermore areas (concerning sewage systems and heat pumps) where a municipality can have some legislative function in accordance with its self-government. Such regulations established by the local governments (municipalities) have not been covered in the preparatory legislative work but are, instead, taken care of by the municipalities.

---

[44] Ds 2008:75 p. 157.

[45] Ds 2008:75 p. 160.

[46] Reg. Prop. 2008/09:187 p. 63.

[47] The notifications and permits that the local governments handle according to acts of parliament concern. Handling of inflammable goods. Permit to clean combustion construction. Notification on the sale of nicotine pharmaceutical. Notification on sale of tobaccos or beer or serving of beer. Permit to serve vine and spirits and strong beer. Notification on establishing of a heat pump. Notification on hygienic treatments and swimming-poles. Notification on certain environment dangerous activities. Permit to install a sewage system. Notification on manures. Buildings permits. Registration and acceptance of food enterprises including restaurants. Notification on the start of a building project.

[48] For example on: Public cleansing and refuse collection. Temporary prohibitions for cars within certain areas. Enlarged building permit (PBL 5:7). Prohibition concerning lighting of fires and conditions for chimney-sweeping. Conditions for sewage systems heat pumps. Keeping of animals that are not pets. Spreading of manure.

Local governments, that is, municipalities,[49] can only decide on authorisations within the municipality, irrespective of whether the authorisation is given according to an act of Parliament, according to delegated legislation, or through pure local government provision. Article 10 (3) of the SD stipulates that service providers shall have access to the territory of the entire country. A municipality cannot give such an authorisation. The eventual problem in connection with this was not considered in the preparatory work.[50] The preparatory legal works stress that the local governments must also implement the SD. However, the question of whether it will be possible to exercise the activity throughout the whole national territory has not been resolved in the existing legislation. In addition, the issue must consider different solutions, depending on whether the authorisation is based on an act of Parliament or local self-government. Rules of recognition were not discussed. It is possible that Article 10 (7) of the SD implies the option of a local authorisation with regard to self-government in purely local issues. There may be overriding reasons in accordance with Article 10 (4) of the SD due to self-government. However, this can hardly be the case in issues where local governments are obliged to make decisions according to acts of Parliament. Such authorisations shall be applied in the same way all over the country, and therefore there should be no overriding reason to grant the authorisation for only one municipality. Article 10 (4) has not been discussed and has not been transposed.[51]

The applicant is entitled to an authorisation once all its conditions have been met. It is, in general, possible to appeal to an administrative court and the court can also review the use of discretion by authorities and change decisions. According to Swedish legislation (APA § 22a, § 3), this is possible if the legislation, that is, the authorisation is stipulated in legislation from Parliament. However, if the regulation was stipulated by a local government in accordance with their self-government, the administrative court can only declare the decision valid or invalid, which means that the application of the local government stipulation cannot be reviewed. Discretion would hardly change the right to obtain an authorisation (Article 10 (5) SD) in cases where the decision is made in accordance with national legislation. However, if the decision is taken in accordance with municipality regulations that the municipality stipulates in accordance with its self-government, discretion could imply that the applicant is not entitled to the authorisation. This issue was not discussed in the preparatory legislative work.

Negative decisions have to be reasoned, according to the APA. It is a basic principle in Swedish administrative law. However, the Swedish APA mentions some exceptions to this principle. Only decisions that involve the exercise of power must be reasoned. This should, in general, involve no obstacles, since authorisations are considered as exercise of power, but there may be some

---

[49] There are 290 municipalities and 20 county councils. The municipalities take care of most of the local issues but the county councils are responsible for the hospitals and the medical care.

[50] Compare Reg. Prop. 2008/09:187 p. 279.

[51] Compare Reg. Prop. 2008/09:187 p. 279.

exceptions. Hunting licences are not considered to involve the exercise of power and the SD is thus further reaching in this regard than Swedish administrative law. The Swedish APA furthermore makes exceptions for decisions on employment, admission to educational institutions, and certificates from such institutions. It makes exceptions for what is necessary with regard to the security of the country or the protection of the personal or economic circumstances of individuals. In addition, urgent decisions are excluded.

With regard to urgent decisions, the preparatory work stresses that the administrative authorities shall be aware of the further-reaching demand in the SD. However, no change was made in the law. This implies that—in the absence of transposition—the SD shall be applied and the administrative authority shall be aware of this direct effect. The exception for protection with regard to the security of the country, as well as of individuals, is furthermore not in accordance with Article 10 (6) of the SD. According to the preparatory legislative work, the administrative authorities shall therefore reason their decisions in such a way that secret information is not revealed.[52]

There has been no reallocation of competences with regard to the granting of authorisations, in accordance with Article 10 (7) of the SD. On the other hand, the stipulation in Article 10 (4) of the SD involving a duty to grant authorisation throughout the entire national territory was not been transposed with regard to authorisations granted by municipalities. One way to fulfil this stipulation would be to reallocate competences.

Several of the provisions in Article 10 (2) of the SD are such that the criteria shall be "(d) clear and unambiguous", "(f) made public in advance", and "(g) transparent and accessible". That is considered to already be the case in the Swedish legislation. However, legislation on the arranging of certain automatic gambling machines had to be changed.[53] According to this law, a person who violates the provisions stipulated by the administrative authority can be punished with a penal fine or prison. The provisions that can be stipulated by the administrative authority concern "regulations that is needed in order to counteract that the gambling cause disorder". In connection with the implementation of the SD, the penalty for acting against such provisions from the administrative authority was removed. The reason for this was that the preconditions were not clear in the act of Parliament, which it had to be.[54]

The EU established the SD to increase the free movement of services on the Common Market, and regulations should be clear. This is an expression of legitimacy. The earlier regulation existed to counteract disorder and to protect children. To do this, the power of the administrative authority to act according to a framework law instead of a clear law was needed. It was obviously seen as important to have an unclear stipulation to provide the necessary protection. This

52 Reg. Prop. 2008/09:187 p. 82.

53 § 9 Lagen om anordnande av visst automatspel (Law on automatic gambling).

54 Services Directive (2006/123/EG) Articles 1 (5) and 10.

protection was seen as a pressing public interest. However, with the SD, it was stressed that the relevant laws had to be clear enough to create legal security. Now the legal security of the service providers is more important. The act of Parliament that existed before was not clear enough. Parliament thus cannot hand over such issues to the administrative authorities. The change is therefore, in addition, an expression of the need for legitimacy in administrative law.

2.6 Article 11 SD: Duration of Authorisation

According to Article 11 of the SD, an authorisation to a provider shall as a main rule be granted for an unlimited period of time. There is no prohibition against time-limited authorisations and there are thus options to limit the duration of an authorisation in the Swedish administrative legal system.

The principle of unlimited validity of authorisations in Article 11 of the SD has not been implemented in a generally applicable regulation. Instead, it is dealt with in specific administrative provisions by central national administrative authorities. One regulation on the authorisation of animal parks was changed. There used to be a limit of 10 years on authorisations for the keeping of animals in parks, and this was abolished.[55] Another regulation concerning authorisation with regard to activities with eggs and embryos used to be time limited. This regulation was abolished and the authorisation is now unlimited.[56,57]

2.7 Article 12 SD: Selection from Among Several Candidates

Article 12 of the SD stipulates that where the numbers of authorisations available are limited, MSs shall apply a procedure that is impartial and transparent information on the procedure shall be given. This article was found to be compatible with Swedish law.[58] Regulations with regard to impartiality and equal treatment exist in the Swedish Constitution and are, furthermore, the starting point of the administrative procedure law. With regard to administrative procedure law, it is stressed that its purpose is to guarantee legal certainty, impartiality, and due care.[59] The law contains stipulations on impartiality. An official may not deal with a case in which he or she has some personal interest, for example. There are stipulations in the APA concerning guarantees for legal certainty, such as the right to be heard.

---

55 DFS 2004:19 provision from the National authority for Animal Protection.

56 SVJFS 2002:66 provision from the National Authority for Agriculture.

57 Ds 2008:75 pp. 151 f. and 157 f.

58 Reg. Prop. 2008/09:187 pp. 79, 279.

59 Reg. Prop 2008/09:187 p. 81.

The principle of due care should imply at least guidance with regard to the investigation. As a consequence, the selection among several applicants must also be done in such a way that impartiality and openness are guaranteed according to the preparatory legislative work.

In connection to purchases, there is the law on public procurement. The selections among several applicants shall be made in accordance with this law with regard to purchases. The law on public procurement cannot be applied on authorisations. Provisions for the administrative procedure must be used, but there can be some stipulations in special legislation on selection among several applicants. With regard to postal services and telecommunications, there are some stipulations on such procedures.[60]

2.8 *Article 13 SD: Authorisation Procedures and Tacit Authorisation*

According to Article 13 of the SD, the authorisation procedure shall be clear, objective, impartial, easily accessible, and fast, with reasonable charges. The time limit for the procedure shall be fixed, and if the time limit is not respected, the authorisation shall be deemed to have been granted. The administrative authority must inform the applicant of the time limit.

The authorisation procedure is considered to be clear and public in advance. There are also guarantees that the issues are dealt with in an impartial and objective way. Article 13 (1) is therefore considered to be in accordance with Swedish law. Furthermore, the duty to inform the applicant of the need to supply additional documentation (Article 13 (6) SD) or to inform the applicant quickly if the application is rejected (Article 13 (7) SD) is considered in accordance with existing Swedish law and principles. Articles 13 (4) and 13 (5) are stipulated in the § 8 SSA. It states that acknowledgement of the application shall state the time limit and the consequences if the time limit is not respected, as well as available means of address.

Time limits are, however, something new to the Swedish administrative legal system. The time limit is mentioned in the horizontal SSA (§ 7) but the stipulations are made in specific administrative law. The SSA establishes (§ 7) that provisions can be found in other regulations. This article in the SSA thus only states that time limits may exist. The SSA contains what one might call an "information-rule". It gives the information that regulations concerning time limits are stipulated elsewhere. How long a time limit shall be is not mentioned in the horizontal law, and

---

[60] Such selections are rare but it was for example the case with the authorisations that board for post and telecommunication gave to a few companies that took care of the building of the net-capacity for mobile phones in accordance with a so called UMTS/IMT 200 standard, also called 3G. In some other countries this possibilities were sold by the state to the highest bidders but in Sweden authorisations were given to a few companies.

there is no mention of the possibility of prolonging it. There has thus not been any general rule established on the duration of procedures. It is, however, clear in the SSA that time limits that are to be stipulated in specific administrative legislation shall start when a complete application has been received by the administrative agency.[61]

However, the SD stipulates that the period shall start only after all the documentation has been submitted. It is not necessarily only the documentation that supports the application that the EU had in mind. An administrative procedure concerning an application implies that the applicant shall provide the required documents that support the application, but the administrative authority must control the documents, and to do so they may need additional information. Sometimes the applicant is asked to supply the administrative authority with such information; sometimes the authority requests it from somebody else or finds it themselves through an inspection, for example. The interpretation is important, because it changes the preconditions for the time limit. If no more documents are needed, only the evaluation of the documents and the decision still need to be done. The administrative authority decides when all the documents have been submitted. It should be possible for the administrative authority to tell what information is still missing and to give a time limit when all the documents have been received, even in cases involving strong public interests.

Time limits have been stipulated in specific administrative law. The few tacit authorisations stipulated on the state level are all stipulated in provisions from the central administrative authorities. With regard to stipulations on the state level (from Parliament, the government, and the central administrative authorities), some changes were made in provisions within the area of agriculture, where authorisations for animal parks and circuses have been subject to time limits. Furthermore, some authorisations in connection to the handling of food (e.g., ecological production) are subject to time limits, and there are also stipulations with regard to authorisations in connection with car rentals. In addition, this stipulation is from a national administration. In nine cases, however, existing regulations were kept and the keeping of these regulations was in accordance with the SD.[62] The public interest was the overriding reason for this.

This means that the time limits that exist are in legislation from lower agencies, meaning that the highest national administrative agency within the specific administrative fields, such as the National Agriculture Administration or the National Food Administration, stipulates the time limits. The legislator is the administration. Time limits may, in addition, exist on the local government level, where municipalities stipulate the time limits in municipal legislation.

There is thus no general rule on the duration of procedures and the time limits that do exist in specific administrative law are only applied in specific cases. The

61 Reg. Prop. 2008/09:187 p. 82.

62 Ds 2008:75 pp. 186 ff.

general rules that do exist in the horizontal SSA (§ 7) only inform that there can be stipulations on time limits.

The time limit stipulated in, for example, legislation from the National Agriculture Administration is three months, and if there is a need to prolong this period, it can be done according to the same specific administrative legislation. In such cases the period of time is not fixed in the stipulations from the National Agriculture Administration.

Tacit authorisations are unknown in Swedish administrative law. This is a completely new procedural invention and there is obviously reluctance to accept the idea. Tacit authorisations have been stipulated in very few specific administrative laws, and there is nothing on a general level except for the information rule in the SSA (§ 7).

What does a tacit authorisation imply? It has been stated by the Swedish Legal Council (a parliamentary body that controls the lawfulness of the proposed legislation before it is decided by Parliament) that tacit authorisation is not possible in the way it is stipulated in the SD.[63] The mere fact that tacit authorisations are granted due to the passivity of the administrative agency cannot imply that there are no conditions to such authorisations. The preparatory legislative work does not deal further with this issue. Instead, it says that such issues shall be considered in specific administrative legislation. Nullity and revocability will thus also have to be considered in specific administrative legislation or in praxis from the courts and administrative agencies.

2.9 Articles 14, 15, 16 SD

Article 14 of the SD stipulates the prohibited requirements in connection with the freedom of establishment for providers, and Article 15, in addition, stipulates requirements in that context to be evaluated and eventually changed by the MSs. Article 16 stipulates the freedom to provide services in a MS other than that in which the provider is established and the requirements that are put forth must respect the principles of non-discrimination, necessity, and proportionality. Necessity means that the requirement must be justified for reasons of public policy, public security, public health, or the protection of the environment. There has been a need to adapt national law to implement these articles.

With regard to Article 14 of the SD, changes were made in specific sector legislation. With regard to Article 15 (2), changes were also made in specific sector legislation. With regard to Article 15 (7), provisions were stipulated in the SSA and in the ordinance from the government. Changes have also been made in specific sector legislation as regards Article 15 (7). In addition, it has also been stipulated in § 1 of the SSA that the competent agencies shall promote the

[63] Reg. Prop. 2008/09:187 p. 273.

principles mentioned in Articles 14 and 15. With regard to Article 16 of the SD, changes were made in specific sector legislation.

With regard to Articles 14 and 15 of the SD, the specific laws that stipulate conditions for establishment were changed in two cases. One case concerns the customs law, where it was found not to be in accordance with Articles 15 (2) (b) and 15 (3) SD, that, except for customs authorities, only legal persons can receive and mediate information of importance to customs. This has been changed and now also natural persons can work with such services. The other concerns foreign branches. There was a stipulation that a manager of a foreign branch had to be a Swedish resident if the business person in charge was not a resident in Sweden. This was changed, since it was not in accordance with Article 14 (1) (b) and there was no longer such a need if the business person was a resident in the EU. Two laws were thus changed on the state level as a consequence of Articles 14 and 15.

Problems may exist with regard to the requirements in Articles 14 and 15 concerning the possibilities for local governments to issue local government instructions and guidelines. Some of the possibilities for issuing instructions exist due to delegated legislative power from Parliament, and some of the possibilities exist due to self-government for local governments. It is necessary to consider whether such instructions are in accordance with the SD, since the SD concerns the entire state of Sweden.[64] The guidelines from the local governments are not binding instructions, but they may cause a warped competition and are also included in the regulations that must be looked over with regard to their accordance with the SD, since the European Court of Justice also regards non-binding measures as a possible obstacle to trade.[65,66] There are examples where the delegated option—delegated from Parliament—has been removed as a consequence of the SD. Local governments (municipalities) may no longer authorise a person as a controller of ventilation systems.[67]

With regard to Article 15 (7), according to which the MSs shall notify the Commission of new provisions, it has been stipulated in the ordinance from the government that the government and its administrative agencies shall report proposals for new regulations to the Chamber of Commerce and that the Chamber of Commerce, in its turn, shall notify the Commission.

With regard to the freedom to provide services in Article 16 of the SD, the following changes were made in specific national legislation concerning demands that will not be put on businesses or business persons established in another EU MS and that temporarily provide services:

64 On local government level there are county councils and there are municipalities. The county council mainly takes care of hospitals and their activities are not included in the directive. The reference to local governments thus concerns the 290 municipalities in Sweden.

65 Reg. Prop. 2008/09:187 p. 72.

66 Commission against Ireland 249/81.

67 Ds 2008:75 p. 231.

- *Resegarantilagen* (Law on Guarantees in connection with travels). The demand that the business person must give security will only be made on all-inclusive tours.
- *Lagen om avtalsvillkor mellan näringsidkare* (conditions in contracts between business persons). The law contains stipulations against undue conditions in contracts and the business person can be prohibited from using the undue condition. This is not possible any longer in relation to business persons established in another MS.
- *Bostadsrättslagen och lagen om kooperativ hyresrätt* (Laws on co-operative flats). Before the sale of flats can start, a certificate concerning the seller's economic plan must be granted. Such certificates can now also be granted by a person from another MS.
- *Produktssäkerhetslagen* (security of goods). Goods and services may not cause harm to consumers, which is regulated by law, but the law will not be applied in relation to business persons who only provide services temporarily.
- *Lag om paketresor och distans och hemförsäljningslagen* (law on all-inclusive travels and door-to-door and distance sales acts). Some of the obligations (to provide information on one's address, etc.) according to these laws will not be punished with regard to business persons that temporarily provide services in Sweden.
- *Marknadsföringslagen* (law on marketing). According to this law, information shall be given on existing guarantees. Since Swedish regulation is more comprehensive than the SD, the Swedish legislation cannot be applied in relation to business persons who provide services temporarily.

In addition, some changes were made in national legislation on a lower legislative level,[68] and changes were made in the law on planning and building with regard to the controlling person and that person's qualifications and authorisations.

2.10 Articles 14–19 SD

Article 14 of the SD concerns prohibited requirements with regard to the access to service activities in the territory of the MS, Article 15 concerns requirements to be evaluated, Article 16 concerns the freedom to provide services for providers that are established in another MS, Articles 17 and 18 concern derogations (for postal services, electricity, and gas in Article 17 and measures against a provider in exceptional cases in Article 18) from the freedom, and Article 19 concerns prohibited restrictions with regard to the use of services.

With regard to the prohibited requirements in Articles 14 and 15, it was stressed[69] that Sweden must show that an authorisation procedure is not

[68] See Ds 2008:75 p. 231.

[69] Reg. Prop. 2008/09:187 p. 68.

discrimination, that it is reasoned with regard to an overriding public interest, that the aim cannot be accomplished in a less intrusive way, and that Sweden had to screen every authorisation it wanted to keep or implement. It was found during the screening[70] that most Swedish regulations are in accordance with the SD. Only the two mentioned[71] were found not to be in accordance with the SD on the national level. In the customs law, there was a stipulation according to which only a private legal person could handle certain information. This was not in accordance with Article 15 (2) SD and the stipulation was changed so that a natural person can now also handle the information. The change that caused the most discussions, however, is the Foreign Branches Office Act.[72] It contains regulations on the registration of foreign companies or persons living abroad wanting to carry on trade and other business activities in Sweden. These entities shall be registered. The act also has a stipulation according to which there had to be a manager residing in Sweden for a business person or manufacturer living abroad. This later stipulation was removed, since it was considered not to be in accordance with Article 14 (1) (b) of the SD, according to which the requirement that somebody associated with the provider shall be a Swedish resident is discriminatory. There may not be any stipulations according to which personnel shall reside in Sweden.

The change concerning the foreign branches met a lot of opposition from the labour unions, who find that this will undermine their possibilities to work in the way they are used to. According to the so-called "Swedish model" of the labour market, agreements with employers are the basis for the work of the labour unions, and if there is no manager resident in Sweden, the fear is that the labour unions will not be able to negotiate the way they used to. They want someone to negotiate with. With the changed regulation, it will become difficult for the labour unions to conclude a collective agreement and find a representative to sue. They fear that the system of how they work (i.e., negotiations and collective agreements) will lose its importance. "The Swedish model" will not function and the labour union will lose influence under such circumstances. However, previous regulation was considered to be discriminatory, according to Article 14 (1) (b) of the SD, which stipulates that there may not be any stipulations according to which personnel shall live in Sweden, which is considered to be discrimination.

The changed regulation on foreign branches is also considered dangerous in combination with the EU directive 96/71/EC concerning the posting of workers

---

[70] Reg. Prop. 2008/09:187 p. 71.

[71] Customs law and law on foreign branches.

[72] Sweden had comprehensive obstacles against foreign establishments before it became a member of the EU. It had to be wound up when Sweden entered the EU. The Foreign Branches Office act is a result of this. It was introduced in 1992. The need for an authorisation for all foreign businesses in Sweden was replaces with registering trough this act. Any foreign businessman that supplied the Swedish authorities with the required information was allowed to make businesses in Sweden. The company etc. could choose to have either a branch in Sweden or a subsidiary company. The purpose of the Act is to make it possible to supervise the activity and to get in contact with the businessmen. SOU 2010:46 pp. 101 ff.

in the framework of the provision of services. According to this directive, foreign workers can work in Sweden for six of months with minimum wages and without paying taxes in Sweden. The fear is that Swedish workers will lose their jobs or will have to work for lower salaries if workers from other countries compete under such conditions. Instead, Swedish collective agreements shall cover also workers from other countries.

This is in fact the most debated issue, and there was (in 2010) an attempt to change the law. Whether there is a possibility according to the directive to stipulate that a manager shall be a Swedish resident[73] is being considered. The overview of Swedish law on branches is being carried out partly as a result of communications from the EU Commission (28 November 2008 and 29 October 2009), according to which the law is not in accordance with Articles 49 and 56 of the TFEU (former Articles 43 and 49 EC Treaty). The Foreign Branches Office Act and the Foreign Branches Office Ordinance have also been criticised by the EU,[74] and the Commission has started a procedure against Sweden in accordance with Article 258 (and Article 260) of the TFEU. The criticism concerns, among other things, the need to appoint a representative. This may stop the provider from offering services in the country, since there are costs connected to it. The overview is, in addition, being done as a result of protests from the labour unions, and it was stated already in the preparatory legislative work that preceded the SSA[75] that the government would more closely scrutinise this matter.

It is therefore considered whether it might be in accordance with EU legislation to stipulate that a representative—with an address in Sweden—of the provider is reported to the registering authority when the manager, or other head, of the company resides abroad. The representative shall have the necessary legal rights. The opinions of the labour unions in connection to this were taken into consideration.[76] In the first legislative report[77] it was found that a notification obligation should be introduced in certain cases for foreign businesses operating in Sweden to enable independent control with the aim of ensuring that the business operation qualifies as an establishment when appropriate, and not incorrectly as a service, and to contribute to the correct implementation of the directive 96/71/EG concerning the posting of workers. A simple notification process shall suffice, and it should be possible for this to be Internet based.

It is proposed that business operations run in Sweden by foreign enterprises established outside Sweden and by business operators who are not residents of Sweden are to be reported to the Swedish Companies Registration Office. Exceptions from the notification obligation will exist for operations that are not intended to last

[73] Dir 2009:120, Dir 2010:40.

[74] Commission 2007/4800 (SG-Greffel (2009) D/8277). See also Commission 2008/10568 Markt/E1/CH/dl D (2008) 59124.

[75] Reg. Prop. 2008/09:187 p. 76.

[76] Dir. 2009:120 översyn av lagstiftningen om utländska filialer p. 43.

[77] SOU 2010:46.

for more than six months and which do not employ staff. If staff is employed in Sweden, there is to be a contact person with an address in Sweden in the event that the operation lasts longer than eight days. The contact person must also be reported to the Swedish Companies Registration Office.[78] The proposal of the duty of notification is considered necessary to avoid negative consequences within certain areas, such as economic crimes, supervision with regard to the work environment, and possibilities for the labour unions to get in contact with foreign employees.

Another point that has been stressed in connection with the requirements in Articles 14 and 15 is the need for screening local government regulations. Many of the activities of local governments are based on acts of Parliament, according to which the local governments are obliged to fulfil certain tasks. They have, according to some of these laws, a delegated power to also stipulate provisions with regard to requirements. The need to screen such regulations has been stressed by several agencies that made comments on the proposed new legislation.[79] Since the provisions of the SD have the same validity irrespective of whether authorisations are made on the state or local government level, the same kind of screening should be carried out at the local government level. In addition, local governments (i.e., municipalities) have some options according to their self-governance to issue provisions. They also issue guidelines for some activities that are not considered to be binding regulations but which may anyhow be against the SD. The government, however, left all such discussions to the local governments.[80] This was done irrespective of the fact that Parliament must have the main responsibility for giving the provider access throughout the whole territory, according to Article 10 (4) on delegated legislative power. The organisation of the local governments has taken care of some screening, but few pieces of municipal legislation have been changed.

Most Swedish legislation was considered to be in accordance with Article 16 of the SD. Seven laws (mentioned in Sect. 2.9) were changed to make it possible for temporary providers of services to work in Sweden. The difference between the establishment and freedom of services as well as the scope of the freedom of services was discussed in the preparatory work. The separation was, however, not clear; however, it is more or less resolved later in the report concerning proposed changes in the Foreign Branches Offices Act and the Foreign Branches Ordinance. In this investigation, guidelines were designed determining what should be referred to as a service or as a business establishment. This was done "in order to meet the justified demand for legal certainty and predictability in the application of the legislation on branch offices in Sweden".[81] A "presumption" rule was formulated in the proposal for changes of the ordinance. The Swedish Companies Registration Office shall make the decision according to this presumption, and this decision will be possible to appeal according to the proposal. Important assessment

[78] SOU 2010:46 p. 20.

[79] Reg. Prop. 2008/09:187 p. 71.

[80] Reg. Prop. 2008/09:187 p. 72.

[81] SOU 2010:46 p. 19.

factors besides the time during which the business operations are conducted are their continuity, regularity, and frequency, assessed with regard to the circumstances of each individual case. To define this in concrete form, a standard model has been proposed. A business operation that is intended to last for a maximum of one year is not to be regarded as permanent unless there are special supporting grounds. This shall be the presumption, and the Swedish Companies Registration Office shall be given the opportunity to determine on a case-by-case basis whether a business operation that lasts for longer than one year is to be regarded as the temporary provision of a service. The opposite—that an operation that lasts for less than a year may be regarded as an establishment—may also be the case.

With regard to options to intervene and take measures against a service provider established in another MS according to Article 18 of the SD, measures relating to the safety of services in an existing Swedish law on product security (*lag om produktsäkerhet*) were used. There is no right to appeal a decision to intervene. The administrative court of first instance questioned this, but the government responded that the option to appeal the main decision and the duty of the Commission in accordance with Article 35 of the SD to examine compatibility with Community law was sufficient.

Article 19 was found to be in accordance with existing Swedish legislation.

2.11 Articles 22–27 SD

These articles concern information on providers and their services (Article 22) for the receivers of services, the need for professional liability insurance (Article 23), commercial communications by the regulated professions (Article 24), multidisciplinary activities (Article 25), policies on the quality of services (Article 26) and provisions for the settlement of disputes (Article 27).

Article 22 is stipulated in the SSA (§§ 16 and 17). § 16 stipulates that the providers must give the information on their own initiative and § 17 contains the provisions that the service provider shall give when a receiver of services requests it. Non-compliance with these rules can be subject to administrative actions (prohibition or an injunction to act combined with a fine) and private law actions (payment of damages) according to the law on marketing (*Marknadsföringslagen*). Some providers are subject to a code of good conduct in relation to their customers, and the SSA refers to such codes. Disobedience of such codes can therefore be subject to injunctions, and so forth, according the law on marketing. The stipulations in the SSA are not different from those that already exist in the law on marketing. However, they can only be applied to the provision of services.[82] In addition, established service providers must also observe rules on information duties in other laws than the SSA.[83] Such rules partly overlap the rules

[82] Reg. Prop. 2008/09:187 p. 155.

[83] Reg. Prop. 2008/09:187 p. 155.

in the SSA. If there is a conflict, the SSA shall have priority. The MSs can stipulate further provisions, but such further reaching rules on information duties cannot be applied on non-established providers. This implies that rules on information duties in the SSA are relevant to non-established providers, but established service providers must follow also other regulations that go further. In this area, the SSA is not so horizontal, and it does not contain any simplifications for established providers, since they must keep a record of two regulations concerning similar matters.

Breaking these rules (in §§ 16 and 17 SSA) will, according to the marketing law, be supervised by the consumers ombudsman, who may give an injunction (e.g., a prohibition) in combination with a threat of a fine. It is also possible for the individual party to sue for damages. There is thus a public law part and a private law part with regard to the options to act against misconduct by the service provider, and the public law provisions can be seen as a substitute for administrative control that would have been possible with an authorisation for non-established providers. However, established service providers that have the necessary authorisations are also obliged to provide the same information to the receivers. This implies that the information duties in Article 22 are complements to the authorisation and they are not a substitute for it. But for non-established providers, they can be seen as a substitute for authorisations and an option for Swedish national administrative authorities to supervise such providers in spite of the fact that such non-established providers are to be controlled by their state of establishment.

With regard to the need for professional liability insurance and guarantees in Article 23 of the SD, there is often an obligation to have insurance to cover the responsibility. The need for such insurance is a common condition for receiving authorisation. It is common in connection with memberships in associations, where it can be included in the membership fee. It is also quite common in connection with purchasing. The government has therefore found that there is no need to stipulate such a condition. The prevailing use of professional liability insurance and guarantees in Sweden eliminates the need for further legislation on this topic.[84] However, no survey has been carried out in this regard, and the preparatory legislative work stressed that there may be a need for additional regulations when the EU presents its list of services (Article 23 (4) SD). This list can then replace a national survey on the topic and a national standpoint.

The SD provides the MS the option to introduce such a provision, but in the Swedish preparatory legislative work there is no discussion on whether professional liability insurance could be an alternative to national administrative control through authorisations, and so forth. Rather, liability insurance is seen as a complement to administrative control. The issue is thus not connected to the possibility of modernising the administration by transferring portions of administrative matters to private law and regulated mandatory professional liability insurance.

[84] Ds 2008:75 p. 277.

The eventual lacks in handling complaints is regulated through the law on marketing, which provides the possibility of penalty with an administrative sanction. In connection with this administrative penalty, damages may also be paid to the consumer/receiver of services.

The Swedish administrative authorities may have to accept documents, including insurance (Article 23 (2)) from other countries. § 9 of the SSA contains information that such obligations (to accept documents as proof in connection with authorisations) may exist in other legislation, that is, in specific administrative law.

With regard to the resolution of disputes (Article 27), it has been found that there is no need to establish the burden of proof for information, for there is practice from the EU court and an EU directive (97/55/EC and 84/450/EEC) with regard to this issue. There are stipulations in the SSA (§ 19) with regard to the need to give answers to complaints ("answer quickly and find a satisfying solution"), but there is no stipulation on any penalty in connection with this. In Sweden there are also possibilities—besides a dispute in court—to resolve the dispute in a special board for complaints, *Allmänna reklamationsnämnden*[85] (ARN). This is a national public authority and its task is to solve disputes between consumers and business persons after a complaint from the consumer. The board gives recommendations on how to solve the dispute. It takes about six months to get such a decision. There are, in addition, several similar but private boards for special issues.[86] Systematic lacks in the handling of complaints are, however, considered to be possible to punish according to the law on marketing.

Stipulations on commercial communication by regulated professions and on multidisciplinary activities (Articles 24 and 25 SD) were found to be in accordance with Swedish law. There is no "total prohibition" with regard to regulated professions in Sweden.[87] With regard to multidisciplinary activities, there are only justified requirements.[88] There are about 30 regulated professions in Sweden. With regard to "market communication" it is up to the professional organisations to provide codes of conducts and see to it that these codes are followed.[89] Cases of multidisciplinary activities have been identified. An auditor may not be involved in activities that can shake confidence in his or her abilities. There is a similar rule for real estate brokers. However, these demands are considered to be justified.

It has not been found appropriate to make any changes due to Article 26 of the SD. Instead, a long-term action plan should be developed to increase the possibilities of comparing the quality of services, and the government finds that such a plan should be developed in cooperation between trade and industry, the Commission, and other MSs.[90] The information should be available through the POSC.

---

85 In English the name would be something like "The Public Board for Complaints".

86 Ds 2008:75 p. 302.

87 Reg. Prop. 2008/09:187 p. 161.

88 Reg. Prop. 2008/09:187 p. 167.

89 Ds 2008:75 p. 286.

90 Reg. Prop. 2008/09:187 pp. 169 f.

The development of authoritative quality systems according to Article 26 shall thus take place without the interference of the regulator, but information on voluntary quality rules shall be provided through the POSC.[91]

Can the requirements in Articles 22–27 SD be seen as a substitute for prohibited requirements for granting authorisations? Requirements are then replaced by obligations on the service providers whose fulfilment is supervised by public authorities. Responsibility is transposed away from the authorities to the private sector. Articles 23 and 26 could, in combination with the sanctions and settlements of disputes in accordance with Article 27, be a substitute to administrative prohibitions. The SD expresses that the MSs may ensure that providers subscribe to liability insurance and shall encourage providers to take action on a voluntary basis. They do not have to. It can be seen as an option to choose another way instead of administrative procedure; however, it has not been seen like that or discussed like that in Sweden.

The need for professional liability insurance could be one way to substitute for prohibited requirements in the SD, but first of all there are not so many changes that have been made due to prohibited requirements, and second insurances are already common.

There are other national regulations on duties to inform and it is possible for the MS in which a service provider is established to place further claims on established providers. However, it is not possible to place further claims on service providers that are not established. This is a consequence of the free movement according to EC law. Instead, the regulations in their state of establishment are to be applied in such cases, and there may be a need for cooperation via the IMI in such cases.[92] The option to dispense administrative sanctions in connection to lacks regarding information from a non-established provider can, however, be seen as a substitute for other forms of national control.

2.12 Articles 28 ff. SD: Administrative Cooperation

Article 28 of the SD stipulates that MSs shall give each other mutual assistance. The electronic system IMI is used for this purpose. There has not been any Swedish regulation on transnational assistance with administrative agencies in other MSs, and the agencies in other MSs thus have not had any legal right to assistance.[93] The Consumers Protection Cooperation (CPC) was instituted according to regulation 2006/3004/EC with regard to transnational assistance concerning consumer protection. The customs authority is also developing a system for transnational cooperation between customs authorities in accordance

91 Reg. Prop. 2008/09:187 p. 169.

92 Reg. Prop. 2008/09:187 p. 155.

93 Reg. Prop. 2008/09:187 p. 143.

with 70/2008/EC.[94] Electronic customs systems will be installed in the future.[95] There has been administrative cooperation with regard to directive 2005/36/EC on professional qualifications.

Article 28 has been implemented in the new horizontal law, §§ 10-13 of the SSA.[96]

The SSA stipulates that the relevant administrative authority shall provide the needed support to the foreign authority and that the IMI shall be used. The Chamber of Commerce is the coordinating authority and there is a stipulation that if it is not possible to meet a request on information, the Commission as well as the other MS shall be informed.

The Swedish authorities have a duty to investigate cases in which they shall take a unilateral decision, and this duty also implies that they shall ask for the necessary assistance from other authorities. This duty can thus be also applied to transnational cases.[97] With regard to the rights of foreign authorities, there was, however, a need to stipulate a provision on their right to assistance.

There may be fees in order to gain access to certain information. Many registers are public and the foreign authorities shall have access to them. In general, access is without charges; however, there are fees for certain information. Provisions on financial compensation are, of course, the same for Swedish and foreign authorities, and therefore foreign authorities may have to pay for some of the information they want.

2.13 Article 29 SD: Mutual Assistance—General Obligations for the Member State of Establishment

Article 29 contains stipulations with regard to obligations for the MSs of establishment to supply information and undertake requested inspections and investigations. Article 29 was implemented in § 12 and § 15 SSA and in the ordinance from the government with regard to Articles 29 (1) and (2). It was implemented in § 14 SSA with regard to Article 29 (3). According to the stipulations that were made in the SSA, a competent administrative authority in Sweden shall—upon request—give the necessary assistance to the agency in the other MS and a competent administrative authority in Sweden shall inform the competent agencies in the other MS, as well as

[94] EU OJ L 23, 26.1.2008 p. 21.

[95] The customs authority finds that this system shall be used instead of the IMI as regards customs matters Reg. Prop. 2008/09:187 p. 137.

[96] Article 28 (1) has been implemented in § 12 SSA and in the governmental ordinance. Article 28 (2) has been implemented in § 10 SSA and in the governmental ordinance. Article 28 (3) has been implemented in the governmental ordinance. With regard to Article 28 (4) there is no need for any regulation. Article 28 (5) has been implemented in § 13 SSA and in the governmental ordinance. Article 28 (6) has been implemented in the § 11 SSA and in the governmental ordinance.

[97] Reg. Prop. 2008/09:187 p. 143.

the Commission, if the service activity can involve serious damage to health, security, or the environment. The power to stipulate further regulation on the exchange of information in accordance with the SD has been delegated to the government.

Cooperation is one way of improving the supervision of foreign providers. It is, however, considered as not being used enough.[98] If the MS has not used existing means, it cannot take measures against providers, and it is thus important that the MS use all possibilities to cooperate to fulfil its duties.

2.14 Administrative Cooperation and Secrecy

There may be some problems with regard to secrecy when the authorities from other MSs ask for information. A question on how to handle secret information in relation to foreign authorities was raised in the preparatory work, but it was found that to give such information to supervising authorities from other MSs is in accordance with the Swedish act on secrecy.[99] There was thus no need to rearrange the provisions for administrative assistance in a general, uniform way, since the necessary provisions already existed in the Swedish legislation. The provision that allows handing over information on a service provider is Article 3 of Chapter 8 in the Swedish Publicity and Secrecy Act according to which secret information may be given to a foreign authority if the information could have been given to a Swedish authority in a similar case and if it is clear that the transfer is in accordance with Swedish interests.

What is Sweden's interest in this context? This was not discussed, but it may have to be in the future. Besides, there are duties for the authority that receives the secret information. Secrecy shall, for example, apply to a supervising authority that receives such information. However, Swedish law cannot apply to foreign authorities. How shall this dilemma be resolved? Such problems were not discussed in the preparatory work.[100]

The mentioned regulation on the duty to help administrative authorities in other MSs was considered to be necessary to stipulate in the SSA.

2.15 Convergence Programme (Chapter VII of the Services Directive)

The convergence programme in Chapter VII, according to which the MSs and the Commission shall take measures to encourage the drawing up of codes of conduct, does not need and does not bring about any legislation on the national level.

---

[98] SOU 2010:46 p. 160.

[99] Reg. Prop. 2008/09:187 p. 145.

[100] Compare Reg. Prop. 2008/09:187 p. 145.

Professional bodies, organisations, and associations are supposed to do this. The MSs can initiate private regulations, and finding other ways to encourage good behaviour is still a way to simplify administrative law. However, it is too early to say whether this approach will be used to improve the freedom of establishing and providing services.

3 Assessment of the Impact of the Services Directive

3.1 Option to Modernise

Overly burdensome procedures and formalities hindering the freedom of establishment and the provision of services shall be removed. The SD focuses on a modernised administration and simplified procedures with the aim of improving freedoms. The SD is directed towards a different administrative culture than we are used to in Sweden. It aims at improving the situation for foreign service providers in the MSs. A modernisation of the administration could also benefit domestic businesses. The removal of obstacles can be positive for domestic service providers as well. In general, when EU establishes regulations and directives, these concern material administrative law. Procedural law is, in general, left to the MSs to decide on.

The SD describes conditions that must be fulfilled with regard to material law (e.g., forbidden requirements in Article 14), but a central part of the SD focuses on procedural law, such as time limits and information from authorities in connection with these time limits. For established providers, either there shall be no authorisation procedure at all or, if there is a procedure, it shall be carried out within a specified time. The time limit shall not start until all the documents have been submitted. In addition, the national regulator decides on the time limit. However, the time limit puts pressure on the administrative authorities to be active. They must be active in quite different ways than they are used to with authorisation procedures, where they used to receive an application and scrutinise it, making a decision in due time. The initiative is then mainly on the applicant, and the administrative authority can take the time it needs. With time limits or notifications instead of authorisations, the administrative authority must be more active and take the initiative to supervise or speed up the procedure. Authorisations with an appeal and scrutiny of the fulfilment of needed requirements can be replaced with supervision and an a posteriori inspection after a notification. The authority can start investigations *ex officio* and impose administrative penalties when needed.

The SD also provides the option to place a duty on providers to have insurance, which can imply a private law solution instead of an administrative law solution. The duty for the providers to inform the receivers of services can be another way to find private law solutions. The SD indicates a modernisation of administrative law, especially with the notifications and time limits, but also with the options of finding private law solutions through, for example, insurance and the payment of damages in connection with wrongful information. An alternative is administrative control through, for example, sanctions for not informing the receivers of services. The new administrative culture that such changes represent could improve possibilities for foreigners from other MSs to provide services and establish themselves in Sweden. It could, in addition, be of importance to domestic companies. The administrative legal system has grown rapidly during the twentieth century as industry and trade developed. A comprehensive overview of the system may be useful. With the screening that was carried out by all the ministries and the public investigation that thereafter prepared the new legislation an option to modernise by changing the administrative culture opened up.

3.2 Implementation of the Services Directive

Was the SD imposed at a minimal level or beyond? Is the Swedish law on services, the SSA, horizontal? Does this law imply simplifications for service providers in general? Whom do the changes and new regulations affect? They shall have an effect on foreign providers in Sweden. The aim of the SD is to improve the conditions for foreign providers from other MSs. Does it also have an effect on domestic providers and other business persons? Furthermore, do the Swedish changes improve conditions for foreign providers to the same extent that changed conditions in other MSs improve conditions for Swedish services providers over there?

Seven persons worked full-time during more than a year to prepare the implementation of the directive. All ministries screened the legislation within their fields. A total of 165 pieces of legislation were found during the screening to have relevance in providing services in accordance with the SD.[101] Of those, about 20 were changed, in general, with regard only to one stipulation in each of these laws. A discriminatory requirement was taken away, a time limit was introduced, and the possibility was given for non-established providers to offer their services. Most of the screened legislations were found to be in accordance with the SD.[102] In about 90 pieces of legislation, it is explained why they are in accordance with the SD. The others that had relevance were found to be in accordance without closer discussion in the preparatory work. A new so-called horizontal law was introduced. An ordinance from the government with further regulations in connection to this horizontal law was stipulated. Except for these changes on the national level, there are also changes made by the 290 municipalities. However, from what can be seen from the cooperative organ of the local governments, there are few changes on that level as well.

[101] DN (daily newspaper) 090408 Lättare väg ut i Europa.

[102] Ds 2008:75 pp. 375 ff.

The SSA is called a "horizontal law". The idea with a horizontal law is to cover the whole administration, or at least large parts of it, in this case the whole administration that deals with administrative matters regarding the provision of services. The APA is a horizontal law. Provisions in this law on, for example, the right to be heard and the duty to motivate a decision covers the entire administration. A starting point for a horizontal law is that it should be neutral with regard to specific administrative law and special regulations for specific administrative areas should be avoided.

The SSA first contains articles with pure information, that there are other rules in specific laws. There is information on the administrative authorities according to "other legislation" that may have to accept documents. There is information that time limits may exist in other legislation. Second, the SSA contains rules that introduce the POSC and cooperation through the IMI. The SSA is horizontal with regard to the POSC. Application through the POSC and international cooperation through the IMI are introduced in this law as two means of handling authorisations and investigations. These rules, however, must be completed through other rules, which are accomplished through a government ordinance. Third, there are rules that are directly applicable to individuals. Such are the rules on what information providers must give to the receivers of services, and these rules are directly applicable in individual cases with regard to rights and duties. However, these rules are mainly applicable to the provision of services by non-established providers. For established providers, there may be further-ranging regulations according to the law on marketing. Fourth, there is an article with the general principles of the SD. This article states that the relevant authorities in their activities shall promote the principles behind the SD. The article states an aim, the principles are not directly applicable however. Fifth, there are no general rules for the procedure in the SSA except for the duty of the competent administrative authority to send an acknowledgement of the application if there is a time limit. However, there are few time limits, and therefore this stipulation is not important as a horizontal provision; it covers too few time limits to have "general" importance. There is also the stipulation that the provider has the right and the administrative authority the duty to continue the procedure through the POSC once it has been started online.

The answer to the question on how horizontal the SSA is depends on what one means by *horizontal*. A horizontal law can be expected to contain provisions directly applicable to all service providers covered by the law either with regard to the procedure (as the general administrative regulations, such as the Swedish administrative procedure law) or with regard to material law. The application through the POSC and the cooperation through the IMI provide options to use electronic means for the procedure and the control of information, but they do not change the procedure as such. There is, for example, still, in general, a need for authorisation, and the procedural rules for an authorisation shall be used. The authorisation cannot be given until the administrative authority finds that it has enough information to make a decision and has evaluated this information. The procedure does not change through the SSA. There is, in addition, nothing with regard to material law in the SSA. The aim of the SD is to improve the freedom to establish and provide services, but such freedoms do not exist in any of the articles of the SSA. The invitation to the authorities to promote its principles is not a rule. The information from the authority that there is a time limit is a procedural rule that is horizontal, but it is not very horizontal, since it can be used in so few cases. The right to continue the procedure online through the POSC is horizontal.

The SSA introduces the POSC as a mean of simplifying the contact between the provider and the administrative authority, and it also introduces a way to control foreign providers by contacting administrative authorities in another MS through the IMI electronic system, except for the fact that the horizontal law contains rather few provisions on administrative law. Some changes were made in existing specific legislation through acts of Parliament or on a lower national level, after screening. In most cases, it was found that there was no need for change.[103] The SD was introduced on a minimal level in the SSA, and not many of the provisions in the SD have been introduced in other specific legislation either. Few time limits were introduced and few authorisations abolished for established providers.

The option to use codes of conduct, liability insurance, and information duties instead of authorisations was not focused as a means of control to avoid or to simplify administrative procedures in the preparatory legislative work. The administrative simplification discussed in the preparatory work[104] is the POSC and the acceptance of documents from other MSs. It is stressed that the administrative authorities themselves must simplify their administrative routines, such as the application forms, and that they have to consider how to diminish the costs for businesses when stipulating new administrative provisions.[105] This is not a horizontal approach to simplification, and the SD was not discussed in the preparatory works as a way to introduce a new administrative culture.

Criticisms were raised about such an approach to implement the SD. The risk of not changing the culture is mentioned in some comments on the legislative work.[106] For example, a remark was made that the culture might instead be changed in a roundabout way if Swedish legislation concerning the administrative culture, for instance, with regard to objectivity, equality, reasoning, motivation, and guidance with regard to the needed documents, were interpreted in light of the SD. This might happen in future case law. According to Article 249 of the EC Treaty (now Article 288 TFEU), a directive shall be binding as to the result to be achieved, but shall leave to the national authorities the choice of form and methods. The goal is to strengthen the integration through harmonised legislation. It is the MS that decides how to impose it. This does not have to be done in an act of Parliament; it can be accomplished through specific legislation on a lower level. It can be carried out at a minimal level or it can be more ambitious. However, the directive has a direct effect, implying that service providers can refer to it in national court, and the EU Court of Justice can adjudicate in another

---

103 Ds 2008:75 bilaga 1 p. 381 ff.

104 Ds 2008:75 Chapter 8.

105 Ds 2008:75 pp. 110 ff.

106 See e.g., Sieps in Reg. Prop. 2008/09:187 p. 80.

way than the national court and find that Swedish law is not in accordance with the directive. This way the culture may instead be changed in a roundabout way.

For whom is the SSA stipulated? The full name of the SSA is the Law on Services on the Common Market, and services that are not covered by the SSA are mentioned (§ 2), as well as definitions of what a service provider is, and so forth. This gives the impression that the law contains provisions for services with regard to the rights and duties of foreign providers of services. The SSA introduces the POSC as a way for contacting the administrative authority, but this online procedure is open to anyone, including foreign providers, domestic providers, and others who want some authorisation, and so forth, available on the POSC. Service providers have a duty to inform the receivers of services (§§ 16–18); however, this applies mainly to non-established providers. There are no special rights or duties for services providers. The only simplifications that exist, the POSC and the right to continue a procedure on the POSC, are for everybody, without special restrictions. In addition, the duty of the administrative authorities to inform the applicant on existing time limits can be a simplification, but, first, few time limits are introduced and, second, these will probably in practice apply to anybody that applies for authorisation, just like the POSC, and the time limit can therefore not be seen as something particularly for service providers.

The SSA is not so much a law on services on the Common Market[107] as it is a law on the POSC, IMI cooperation, and information duties for non-established providers. Service providers will find the necessary changes with regard to requirements and time limits in other specific legislation, and such specific legislation—except for the regulations for non-established providers—pertains to anybody who applies.

The SSA is not very horizontal, and it does not contain many of the simplifications with regard to procedure or the material law; it is not a law on services on the Common Market. Simplification with regard to procedure is to take place via the administrative authorities themselves, according to the preparatory legislative work,[108] or through specific laws (time limits, notifications instead of authorisations, acceptable documents).

Only minimal transposition has taken place in Sweden with regard to procedural rules and authorisations for established providers. It was established in the preparatory work[109] that Swedish law was already in accordance with the SD, and therefore few provisions needed to be changed. This can be true on a minimal level. However, a minimal level of transposition does not change the administrative culture much, and one can therefore not speak of any great success or improvement for administrative law in general. The POSC is, of course, an excellent new means for applications and for contact during the procedure, and the IMI can be an excellent tool as well for cooperation, but the procedural rules have not changed in such a way that one can talk of any renewal of the administration.

---

[107] An example of this is in addition that an investigation (SOU 2010:46) on the Foreign Branches Act proposes that that the Foreign Branches Act shall contain a stipulation on how to separate an established provider of services from a non-established provider of services.

[108] Ds 2008:75 pp. 110 ff.

[109] Reg. Prop. 2008/09:187 p. 287.

3.3 Simplification for Small Enterprises

The SD involves simplification, which is one of the basic ideas behind it. Simplification should be accomplished to increase the transnational provision of services. The administrative simplification would be modernisation, and such a modernisation could—if the culture would change—have importance also for domestic providers and others. It is important to stress that the way to handle matters with authorisations and without time limits is hardly a problem for large domestic companies. If ASEA, Volvo, and IKEA were service providers, they would hardly have any difficulties with the procedures. They have other means to quickly obtain what they want from the administrative agencies and the state. First, they have lawyers to help them with legal issues to obtain authorisations. Second, their activities can mean a lot of new jobs, and this means that it is not just a legal matter but also a political one, and the authorities of the state become more attentive for this reason. The handling of authorisations, often with long processing times for the procedure, means problems for smaller enterprises that provide services. Providers of services are often smaller enterprises or individuals, but they are numerous. A horizontal modernised procedure could be important for them, as well as for the country.

It could have been important not only to providers from other MSs, but also to Swedish service providers if the culture had been changed on a horizontal level with regard to the bureaucracy. Time limits and tacit authorisations as well as notifications and a posteriori inspections could have been good ways to improve the administration, strengthen the position of citizens in relation to the authorities, and pronounce that the administration has duties when it exercised its power. A new culture could have been achieved.

The reluctance towards change is interesting in light of recurrent demands for simplification of the legal system, especially for smaller enterprises. It is quite common that politicians in Sweden pronounce the need for less bureaucracy and simpler legislation, especially before an election to Parliament. For many years, it has been stressed that there is an overload of regulation, as well as a need for simplification, especially with regard to small and medium-sized businesses. Improvements in this area have been hard to achieve. Several Swedish governments, including the present, have made this a priority, without success.

The aim is to reduce this overload and simplify matters for smaller businesses. A special council, the Swedish Better Regulation Council, has been appointed.[110] The council does not have any decision-making power and can only indicate problems. It examines the formulation of proposals for new and amended regulations that may

---

110 Advisory boards for the regulators have been established in Sweden and in some other MS of the European Union. In Sweden: The Swedish better regulation council (swe. Regelrådet), in Germany: Nationaler Normenkontrollrat, in UK: Regulatory policy Committee, in The Netherlands: Adviescollege Toetsing Administratieve Lasten, and there is also an action programme to reduce administrative burdens in the European Union.

have effects on the working conditions of enterprises, their competitiveness, or other conditions. The council forms a view of whether regulators have carried out statutory impact assessments and assesses whether new and amended regulations have been formulated to achieve their purpose in a simple way and at a relatively low administrative cost to enterprises. There is considered to be a need for simplification measures, and the business community in Sweden is calling for regulations that are efficient, cost effective, and easy to understand and comply with. Complying with regulations is perceived as more time-consuming and costly than it should be, and therefore a strain on company resources. Existing regulation must thus be simplified and new regulation must be efficient, cost effective, and as business friendly as possible. Though it is a priority of the government, there are no or very few improvements to be found in the reports from the Better Regulation Council. With this starting point, the SD could be an interesting way to try to improve legislation with regard to procedures, by introducing time limits, for example. Other countries, such as Sweden's most important trading partner, Germany, have transposed the SD beyond the minimum.

3.4 European Loyalty

In Germany, the implementation of the SD and the changes made in national law are considered a success. This success, however, does not concern the number of new providers from other MSs offering their services in Germany, where it is too early to say much. Instead, Germany's success involves the new administrative culture. This culture was achieved while the German implementation went beyond the minimum requirements, and this means advantages to German businesses in general. In Germany, legal and administrative experts and politicians broadly discussed the SD, due to the expectation that the SD has a strong impact on the administration in Germany. The implementation in Germany goes beyond the minimum requirements and has triggered further impulses for the modernisation, simplification, and acceleration of administrative proceedings.

Simplification, deregulation, less bureaucracy, and more obligations for the administrative authorities in relation to the citizens create a changed administration. Considering the importance that even Swedish politicians give to the need for changed conditions for enterprises, it is a pity that this opportunity was not taken. Instead, the SD was implemented on a minimal level. The necessary regulation was said to have existed before the transposition. The fact that for at least two decades politicians have stressed that there is an overload of regulation for businesses—without which they would have been able to improve the situation—and a need for simplification was not taken into account.

When the SSA was introduced, the responsible minister said[111] that the SD was a big step towards the free movement of goods and services, and that it would now be easier for Swedish service providers to establish themselves in other EU MSs without complicated authorisation rules or supervisory procedures. It would, according to the minister, be easier for Swedish enterprises to enter a market with 500 million consumers of services. The minister also stressed the importance for the Swedish economy to export services.

The SD might provide opportunities to increase the Swedish export of goods. The market for services in Sweden occupies 3,200,000 persons, and, of these, 1,800,000 persons work for the private sector.[112,113] Only 20–25% of the trade that takes place within the EU is estimated to take place on a transnational level.[114] Thus a smaller part of the Swedish provision of services is exported, and it is expected to be possible to increase this amount considerably. Important in this context is also that it is the smaller companies and individuals that can benefit from changed regulations and can increase this export. They do not have lawyers to help them and it does not become a political issue of whether a small company can establish and create new jobs in the country. It is more difficult for small companies and individuals to handle contacts with administrative authorities.

The SD might provide opportunities to increase the Swedish export of services. However, the Swedish SSA and changes in specific Swedish legislation on higher and lower levels have nothing to do with the possibilities for Swedish providers to export their services. Whether Swedish enterprises can increase the export of services depends on how the SD was implemented in other countries. Some other MSs, such as Germany, implemented the SD on a more ambitious level. This may be important for the Swedish export of services, but what is our duty in relation to countries that deregulate, simplify, and modernise more than we do? Our service providers can profit from Germany's modernisation, but German service providers may not be able to profit to the same degree if our system is less modernised.

According to Article 10 of the EC Treaty (now Article 4 EUT), the MS shall take all appropriate measures to ensure the fulfilment of obligations arising from the treaty. They shall facilitate the achievement of the Community's task, which involves a positive duty to take on legislative measures needed to ensure the impact of the Community law. This is the principle of loyalty and cooperation. The MS shall do what is needed to give full impact to the EU legislation. It is possible to implement a directive on a minimal level so that it is loyal enough. However, in the context of the SD, it may mean that we should implement the SD above the minimum. In relation to our most important trading partner, Germany, this would

[111] DN (daily newspaper) 090408 Lättare väg ut i Europa (Easier way to Europe), Sydsvenska Dagbladet (daily newspaper) 091228 Öppnare tjänstemarknad ger ökad tillväxt (An open market for services gives increased Growths).

[112] 52% of the Swedish export of services goes to other EU Member States.

[113] Reg. Prop. 2008/09:187 pp. 31 ff.

[114] Eurostat Yearbook 2008.

be important. Why should it be easier for Swedish service providers to provide services in Germany than for German service providers to provide services in Sweden?

The basic idea behind the SD is to give providers from other countries access to the Swedish market. It is all about abolishing legislation to make it easier for service providers to act transnational. This must be the aim for Swedish legislation. This can, however, be a threat to national interests in several ways. One is that the administrative authorities are used to one way of working. Authorisations with a preceding procedure where all risks are assessed before the authorisation is given are one way of working, and it implies that the provider/business/company must be active. Other structures in the society can also be threatened. Labour unions and their options for collective agreements with employers, and thus the basis for their existence, are threatened.

A directive such as the SD implies a need for loyalty from the MSs. Balancing loyalty in relation to the domestic interests of control can be a delicate matter. A problem in this context is that the assessment cannot be made in relation to the benefits for Swedish providers that provide services in other MSs. However, that is what the loyalty should concern. If Swedish providers are subject to simplified procedures in other countries, more simplified than the Swedish procedures, it would not be loyal to have further reaching controls and less simplification. Loyalty is therefore not just a question of implementing the minimum necessary. It also involves not taking advantage of the possibilities for Swedish providers in other countries without offering the same possibilities in Sweden to providers from other MSs.

The Implementation of the Services Directive in the United Kingdom

Martin Trybus and Almuth Berger

1 General Remarks on the Transposition Strategy and General Understanding of the Implementation

In the United Kingdom the Services Directive (SD) was mainly transposed in the Provision of Services Regulations 2009 SI 2009/2999. However, as explained below many existing Acts of Parliament and regulations had to be adapted to comply with the requirements of the SD.

1.1 Main References Used in this Research

The main references for this country report on the transposition of the SD in the United Kingdom were:

- Guidance for Business on the Provision of Services Regulations 2009 (BERR), http://www.berr.gov.uk/files/file53100.pdf[1]

Martin Trybus, LL.M, Ph.D., is Professor of European Law and Policy and Director of the Institute of European Law at the University of Birmingham (m.trybus@bham.ac.uk); Almuth Berger, LL.M. is Rechtsreferendarin at the Landgericht Duisburg, Germany (almuth.berger@ruhr-uni-bochum.de).

[1] Hereinafter: 'Guidance'.

M. Trybus (✉)
Institute of European Law, University of Birmingham, Birmingham, UK
e-mail: m.trybus@bham.ac.uk

A. Berger
Rechtsreferendarin at the Landgericht Duisburg, Duisburg, Germany
e-mail: almuth.berger@ruhr-uni-bochum.de

U. Stelkens et al. (eds.), *The Implementation of the EU Services Directive*,
DOI: 10.1007/978-90-6704-840-8_27,

- Provision of Services Regulations 2009, http://www.opsi.gov.uk/si/si2009/uksi_20092999_en_1
- Explanatory Memorandum regarding the Provision of Services Regulations 2009, including 'Transposition Note', http://www.opsi.gov.uk/si/si2009/em/uksiem_20092999_en.pdf
- Consultation Document on Implementing the EU Services Directive in the UK, http://www.bis.gov.uk/files/file42207.pdf[2]
- The Government's official response to Consultation on implementing the EU Services Directive in the UK, http://www.berr.gov.uk/files/file46592.pdf[3]
- http://www.opsi.gov.uk
- http://www.berr.gov.uk/policies/europe/eu-services-directive

1.2 Impact of the Services Directive

The transposition of the SD did not give a profound cause to the United Kingdom legislator to alter administrative laws in general.

The Department for Business Innovation and Skills within the then Department of Business Entrepreneurship and Regulatory Reform (BERR) coordinated the implementation process of the SD in close cooperation with other relevant United Kingdom government departments and the departments of the devolved governments in Scotland, Wales, and Northern Ireland. After the elections of May 2010 the new Coalition government disbanded BERR and created the new Department of Business, Innovation and Skills (BIS) by merging the functions of BERR with those of the Department of Innovation, Universities, and Skills. BIS is now responsible for transposition of the SD.

1.3 (National) Scope of Application

The Provision of Services Regulations 2009 SI 2009/2999 apply to service providers offering or providing services in the United Kingdom, both providers of United Kingdom origin and those from other European Economic Area (EEA) States. The Regulations apply whether the provider has a United Kingdom establishment from which the service is provided (as in Part 3 of the Regulations) or is established in another EEA State and comes to the United Kingdom temporarily or operates remotely (as in Part 4). Part 2, *Duties on service providers*, applies to all service providers offering or providing relevant services in the United Kingdom, regardless of where they are established (i.e., they can be based

---

[2] Hereinafter: 'Consultation Document'.

[3] Hereinafter: 'Government's response'.

anywhere in the world). One does not have to be doing business outside the United Kingdom to fall within the remit of the Regulations, or to benefit from them.

The Provision of Services Regulations 2009 contains a separate Part 3:

Part 3: Duties of Competent Authorities in Relation to Provision of Services in United Kingdom

Introductory

13. Application of this Part
Authorisations
14. Authorisation schemes
15. Conditions for the granting of authorisation
16. Duration of authorisation
17. Selection from among several candidates
18. Authorisation schemes: general requirements
19. Authorisation procedures: time for dealing with application
20. Authorisation procedures: other requirements
Requirements which are prohibited or subject to evaluation
21. Prohibited requirements
22. Requirements subject to evaluation

In addition to a separate Part 4:

Part 4: Duties of Competent Authorities in Relation to Providers of Services Provided from Another EEA State

23. Application of this Part
24. Freedom to provide services
25. Derogations from the freedom to provide services
26. Derogation relating to the safety of a service
27. Procedure relating to derogation under regulation 26
28. Duty to notify Secretary of State of new requirements

It is submitted as this shows that the United Kingdom legislator perceived the SD as binding also with regard to purely domestic services.

The Regulations implementing the SD are applicable to service providers and recipients only. They are not applicable also in relation to everybody, i.e., they do not engender general and universal standards for the way authorities deal with all citizens or with all economic stakeholders, so that they could be claimed by every-body.

The 2009 Regulations contain rules relating to the provision of services by both "permanent" and "temporary" providers. Permanent providers are those (whether individuals or companies) who are "established" or based at premises in the United Kingdom, while "temporary" providers are those operating here but based at premises in other EEA States, or vice versa. The main difference arises in the considerations that competent authorities must take into account in authorising service providers. Part 2 of the Regulations on information obligations applies to all service providers operating within the United Kingdom, wherever they are based.

1.4 Incorporation of Transposing Legislation

As mentioned above, there is, first, a new set of Regulations transposing the SD, the Provision of Services Regulations 2009 SI 2009/2999, which entered into force on 28 December 2009.[4] General details regarding the transposition of the SD by the Provision of Services Regulations 2009 are provided in the relevant 'Explanatory Memorandum',[5] including a transposition table.

Moreover, many existing specialised laws in the respective jurisdictions of the United Kingdom had to be adapted to the requirements of the Services Directive and the Provisions of Services Regulation 2009.[6] The following overview over the amendment for the most important specialised laws and regulations will be subdivided into separate sections on the United Kingdom as a whole and England and Wales, Scotland, and Northern Ireland.

For the United Kingdom as a whole and for England and Wales the following laws and regulations had to be amended:

- Administration of Justice Act 1982/Legal Services Act 2007

The Administration of Justice Act 1982 is one of several laws with the same name regulating fundamental procedural questions regarding the powers and administration of the courts of law in England and Wales. The Legal Services Act 2007 established a new framework for the regulation of legal services in England and Wales.

The former act is to be amended by secondary legislation through the extended powers of the Law Society, especially the Solicitors Regulation Authority (SRA) which is the independent regulatory body of the Law Society of England and Wales, introduced by the Legal Services Act 2007. In particular, changes were introduced to the SRA's fee structure, including a reference to Article 13 (2) SD regarding the regulator's application fees.[7] However, this does not appear to be the sole reason for amendments in this case.

---

[4] http://www.opsi.gov.uk/si/si2009/uksi_20092999_en_1.

[5] Explanatory Memorandum, http://www.opsi.gov.uk/si/si2009/em/uksiem_20092999_en.pdf,' Transposition Note' begins at p. 106.

[6] Existing national legislation and administrative practices that will be changed because of the Provision of Service Regulations 2009 or the Directive, available at http://old.berr.gov.uk/files/file54349.pdf cf. also http://www.berr.gov.uk/policies/europe/eu-services-directive/legislation-and-implementation/implementation/services-directive-implementation-updates.

[7] http://www.sra.org.uk/sra/consultations/fee-policy-second-december-2009.page.

Furthermore, Article 13 (4) SD was mentioned as a possible cause for amendments in this case with respect to the Legal Services Act 2007, especially with regard to provide for "a judicial appeal in relation to the failure to determine an alternative business structure licensing application within the fixed time, which operated as if the application had been refused."[8] This was felt to "be necessary in order to provide an alternative to the application being "deemed to have been granted"[9] under Article 13 (4) SD. It was considered "that such an alternative by way of the appeal would be justified by an overriding reason relating to the public interest, because "deemed approval" could put the public at serious risk."[10] However, until now, this amendment appears not to have been made, as the Government stated the necessity of further information and also appears to have been reluctant with respect to an amendment of the Legal Services Act 2007 in this regard.[11]

- Care Standards Act 2000

The Care Standards Act 2000 deals with the registration of children's homes, residential family centres, fostering agencies, voluntary adoption agencies, adoption support agencies, and the registration of social workers.

This act and relevant secondary legislation will be repealed by the Health and Social Care Act 2008 in October 2010. In particular, there will be administrative changes to ensure that the registration processes for adult placement schemes, care homes, and domiciliary care are compliant with the SD and the 2009 Regulations, which will be carried forward to the new system under the Health and Social Care Act 2008.[12] As reference is made to registration, Articles 16 (2) (b) [16 (1) and (3)] SD appear to be the relevant provisions creating the need for amendment.

- County Courts Act 1984

The "Act to consolidate certain enactments relating to county courts" (full name) 1984 establishes the rules relating to the jurisdiction of and the procedure before County Courts, which are a type of lower court in the court system of England and Wales.

The definition of 'legal representative' was amended in the related Legal Services Act 2007, particularly referring to 'authorised person' in relation to the Legal Services Act 2007. This may be due to Articles 9–13 SD; however, concrete provisions are nowhere explicitly stated.

---

8 Government's response, p. 49.

9 Ibid.

10 Government's response, p. 49.

11 Ibid.

12 Existing national legislation and administrative practices that will be changed because of the Provision of Service Regulations 2009 or the Directive, available at http://old.berr.gov.uk/files/file54349.pdf.

- Companies Act 2006

The Companies Act 2006 is the main act regulating company law for the entire territory of the United Kingdom. The Act was "amended so that if an individual or partnership has a place of business in the United Kingdom it must state an address in the United Kingdom. However, if the individual or partnership does not have a place of business in the United Kingdom it must state an address where documents be served by physical delivery and where the delivery of documents is capable of being acknowledged".[13] This amendment appears to be in response to particularly the requirement of Article 16 (2) (a) SD, possibly also Article 14 (1) (b) SD.

- Courts and Legal Services Act 1990

The Courts and Legal Services Act 1990 regulates the legal professions and the courts in England and Wales. It mainly deals with the procedure in the High Court and other courts as well as the allocation of business between those courts and contains rules on certain legal services.

The Legal Services Act 2007 amended provisions relating to registered foreign lawyers in order to achieve consistency with other existing provisions (which in turn may have been already influenced by the SD). No information about specifically relevant articles of the SD could be found.

- Education Act 2002

The Education Act 2002 makes provision about school education, training, and childcare. Amendments were necessary to realise a fixed period of six months regarding the procedure of independent (private) school applications. This may have been considered to be necessary due to Articles 13 (3) and 13 (5) SD.

- Insolvency Act 1986 and Insolvency, Insolvency Account (Fees) Order 2003, and Insolvency Practitioners Regulations 2005

The Insolvency Act 1986, Insolvency and Insolvency Account (Fees) Order 2003 and Insolvency Practitioners Regulations 2005, dealing with company insolvency and winding up, insolvency and bankruptcy of individuals and the regulation of insolvency practitioners were amended by the Provision of Services (Insolvency Practitioners) Regulations 2009, which entered into force on 28 December 2009. Detailed information about the impact of the SD on these amendments is provided in the relevant 'Explanatory Memorandum'.[14] This memorandum especially states the relevant amendments which were considered necessary to comply with the SD: "The policy aim is to amend non-compliant legislation so as to comply with the Services Directive by:

---

[13] Ibid.

[14] Explanatory Memorandum on the Provision of Services (Insolvency Practitioners) Regulations 2009, available at http://www.opsi.gov.uk/si/si2009/em/uksiem_20093081_en.pdf.

- permitting a person authorised by the competent authority in one jurisdiction to hold office in the other without the requirement to obtain an authorisation from the competent authority in the other, thereby enabling a person to be authorised by one competent authority to act as an insolvency practitioner throughout the [United Kingdom]; and making provision having corresponding effect in respect of authorised persons.
- replacing the requirement for three-yearly applications to the competent authority for authorisation to act as an insolvency practitioner with one application for authorisation for a period of one year which, if granted, will be authorised for further periods of one year without a further application subject to the insolvency practitioner continuing to fulfil conditions.
- permitting professional liability insurance or a guarantee already obtained for cover in another EEA State to meet the security or caution requirements where the insurance or guarantee provides equivalent or essentially comparable cover to that provided by a bond approved for that purpose by the Secretary of State.
- replacing the requirement for insolvency practitioners to send the original bond to their authorising body with option to send a copy of the bond, insurance or guarantee providing security or caution and to send it electronically.
- reducing the insolvency experience required by persons applying to the Secretary of State for authorisation as an insolvency practitioner (and who have never previously been authorised to act as an insolvency practitioner) from 7,000 to 2,000 hours in order to remove what is considered to be an unnecessary barrier to authorisation.
- making the fee structure for applications for authorisations transparent by separating the application element from the maintenance element."[15]

The relevant 'Transposition Note' clarifies in how far certain articles of the SD concretely influenced these amendments.[16]

• Licensing Act 2003

The Licensing Act 2003 created a single scheme for the licensing though local authorities of premises supplying and selling alcohol or providing entertainment on a permanent basis applicable to England and Wales. "Regulation 49 of the Provision of Services Regulation 2009 also amends the Licensing Act 2003 to ensure that applications and notices submitted to local authorities through the electronic assistance facility referred to in regulation 38 or electronic facilities maintained by local authorities do not need to be notified separately to other public authorities by the persons submitting them."[17] No specific article of the SD is mentioned; however, this may be in response to the requirements of Articles 5 (1) and 13 (2) SD.

---

[15] Ibid.

[16] Included in ibid.

[17] http://www.opsi.gov.uk/si/si2009/uksi_20092999_en_9.

• Local Government Act (Miscellaneous Provisions) 1982

The Local Government Act (Miscellaneous Provisions) 1982 regulates the licensing of certain public entertainments, the control of sex establishments, refreshment premises, theatrical employers, street trading, and other activities.

"Regulation 47 of the Provision of Services Regulation 2009 (see above) amends the Local Government (Miscellaneous Provisions) Act 1982. Under para 10 of Schedule 3, where an application is made in relation to a sex establishment licence, a copy must be sent to the chief officer of police. Regulation 47 makes provision as to how that copy is sent in cases where the application is made through the electronic assistance facility referred to in Regulation 38 or an electronic facility maintained by a local authority,"[18] so that this copy does not have to be sent twice. "Regulation 47 also allows EEA residents or corporate bodies incorporated in other EEA States to obtain sex establishment licences,"[19] as the requirement of a six month residence in the United Kingdom immediately prior the application date is abolished. "In addition, local authorities will be required to provide reasons for refusing to grant, transfer or renew a licence, whether or not requested by the applicant."[20] Especially, Articles 5 (1), 13 (2), 14 (1) (b) and 10 (6) SD appear to be relevant in this case.

• Pedlars Act 1871

The Pedlars Act 1871 regulates the activities of pedlars including their certification.[21] Regulation 45 of the Provision of Services Regulation 2009 (s. above) amends the Pedlars Act 1871. Services are now removed from the scope of this Act. It now merely applies to the sale of goods and is no longer covered by the scope of the SD. The pedlar certification scheme was considered as an authorisation scheme, which was difficult to justify regarding the criteria set out in the SD. Therefore, it was decided to remove pedlars who provide only services from the scope of the Pedlars Act 1871. The implementing legislation entered into force on 28 December 2009. "After that date, pedlars of services only will no longer

---

18 Ibid.

19 Ibid.

20 Ibid.

21 Section 3 of the Act provides the following definition: "The term "pedlar" means any hawker, pedlar, petty chapman, tinker, caster of metals, mender of chairs, or other person who, without any horse or other beast bearing or drawing burden, travels and trades on foot and goes from town to town or to other men's houses, carrying to sell or exposing for sale any goods, wares, or merchandise, or procuring orders for goods, wares, or merchandise immediately to be delivered, or selling or offering for sale his skill in handicraft; [...]".

need a pedlar's certificate".[22] Therefore, Article 9 and 10 SD seem to be the relevant provisions which led to this amendment.

- Transmissible Spongiform Encephalopathy (TSE, England) Regs. 2008

The Transmissible Spongiform Encephalopathy (TSE, England) Regulations 2008 regulate the various ways of control of BSE with regard to establishments keeping cattle, including approvals, authorisations, licences, registrations, testing, and removal. This act contains rules on measures in the veterinary and phytosanitary fields for the protection of public health also with regard to Regulation (EC) No 178/2002 of the European Parliament and of the Council laying down the general principles and requirements of food law, establishing the European Food Safety Authority and laying down procedures in matters of food safety.

Amendments were necessary to enable laboratories outside the UK but within the EEA to be approved for the United Kingdom's TSE testing programme. This appears to be caused by the several non-discrimination requirements of the SD, especially Article 16 (1) (a) SD. The new Transmissible Spongiform Encephalopathy (England) Regulations 2010 entered into force on 6 April 2010. These Regulations apply to England only. Wales, Scotland, and Northern Ireland have their respective Regulations which had to be amended in a similar fashion.

- Enterprise Act 2002

The Enterprise Act 2002 mainly establishes the Office of Fair Trading, the Competition Appeal Tribunal and the Competition Service as well as dealing with mergers, market structures and conduct. "Regulation 48 of the Provision of Services Regulation 2009 amends the Enterprise Act 2002 so that the duties imposed on service providers in regulations 7 to 12 and 30 of the Provision of Services Regulation 2009 can be enforced under Part 8 of that Act."[23] This appears to be necessary to comply with Article 27 SD.

- Employment Agencies Act 1973

The Employment Agencies Act 1973 deals with the regulation of recruitment activities in particular conducted by so-called employment agencies and employment businesses.[24] "Regulation 46 of the Provision of Services Regulation 2009 (s. above) amends the Employment Agencies Act 1973 so as to allow information obtained during inspections of business premises under section 9 of

---

[22] Overall: Street Trading and Pedlar Laws—A joint consultation on modernising Street Trading and Pedlar Legislation, and on draft guidance on the current regime, available at http://berr.gov.uk/assets/biscore/corporate/docs/migrated-consultations/street%20trading%20and%20pedlar%20laws%20a%20joint%20consultation%20on%20modernising%20street%20trading%20and%20pedlar%20legislation%20and%20on%20draft%20guidance%20on%20the%20current%20regime.pdf.

[23] http://www.opsi.gov.uk/si/si2009/uksi_20092999_en_9.

[24] For detailed information see: http://webarchive.nationalarchives.gov.uk/tna/+/http:/www.berr.gov.uk/files/file23765.pdf/.

that Act to be disclosed for the purposes of Part 9 to competent authorities in other EEA States."[25] In this regard, Articles 28 and 29 SD seem to be the relevant provisions.

For Scotland the following laws and regulations had and have to be amended:

- Civic Government (Scotland) Act 1982

Amendments to the Civic Government (Scotland) Act 1982 were necessary for similar reasons as those described with respect to the Local Government Act (Miscellaneous Provisions) 1982 above for England and Wales. Particularly, abolition of discrimination against non-UK corporate bodies regarding sex shop licences is planned, thereby ensuring compliance with the non-discrimination requirements of the SD.

- Housing (Scotland) Act 2001

The Housing (Scotland) Act 2001 mainly contains rules on housing, including provision about homelessness and the allocation of housing by social landlords, the tenants of social landlords, and the regulation of social landlords. "A requirement to meet registration criteria that specifies bodies with a legal status only recognised in the United Kingdom would prevent providers of social housing from other EU Member States from registering as registered social landlords (RSLs) in Scotland",[26] so that this requirement is planned to be substituted by the requirement that "eligibility for registration [will be] no longer dependent on the structure and status of the body but [will be] based on what the body is established to do."[27] Therefore, the several non-discrimination provisions of the SD appear to be the relevant provisions causing the need for amendments.

- Licencing (Scotland) Act 2005

The Licencing (Sotland) Act 2005 act regulates the sale of alcohol, licenced premises and other premises on which alcohol is sold. There are possible changes to ensure that the application process is compliant with the SD.

For Northern Ireland the following laws and regulations needed and need amendment:

- Insolvency (Northern Ireland) Order 1989, Insolvency Practitioners Regulations (Northern Ireland) 2006, and Insolvency Practitioners and Insolvency Account (Fees) Order (Northern Ireland) 2006

The Insolvency (Northern Ireland) Order 1989, the Insolvency Practitioners Regulations (Northern Ireland) 2006, and Insolvency Practitioners and the Insolvency Account (Fees) Order (Northern Ireland) 2006 (equal functions as their

[25] http://www.opsi.gov.uk/si/si2009/uksi_20092999_en_9.

[26] http://www.scottish.parliament.uk/s3/bills/36-Housing/b36s3-introd-pm.pdf.

[27] Ibid.

English counterpart) were amended. Especially, a requirement of being established in the United Kingdom is abolished. Amendments were made through the Provision of Services (Insolvency Practitioners) Regulations 2009 (Northern Ireland), which entered into force on 28th December 2009. The relevant 'Transposition Note' included in the 'Explanatory Memorandum'[28] highlights the most relevant articles of the SD and provides a 'Transposition Table':

"Article 5 of the Directive prohibits a requirement for original documentation or certified copies to be provided. Article 8 establishes an obligation for Member States to ensure that all procedures and formalities relating to access to or the exercise of a service activity may be easily completed, at a distance and by electronic means. These Regulations amend the 1989 Order to make provision for insolvency documentation to be received, stored and transmitted by electronic means

- In relation to the authorisation of insolvency practitioners (IPs), Article 10 of the Directive requires that they can practise throughout the territory of a Member State unless a particular jurisdiction is justified by an overriding reason relating to the public interest in requiring a separate authorisation. Since insolvency legislation in [Northern Ireland] mirrors that of [England and Wales], there is no justifiable reason relating to the public interest to require IPs to make separate applications for authorisation in both jurisdictions.
- IPs are authorised by Recognised Professional Bodies (RPBs) or by DETI in Northern Ireland and by RPBs or the Secretary of State (SoS) in [the United Kingdom]. Authorisations by DETI and the SoS do not entitle the IP to practise in both jurisdictions since these procedures only have effect under the law of each jurisdiction. These Regulations make provision to enable IPs authorised in [England and Wales] to act legally in that capacity in [Northern Ireland] and to enable bodies having established places of business outside the [United Kingdom] to be accredited RPBs in [Northern Ireland].
- Article 11 of the Directive requires that the granting of an authorisation to provide a service must be for an indefinite period, except where the authorisation (a) is automatically renewed, or (b) is subject only to the continued fulfilment of requirements. Article 352 of the 1989 Order and Regulation 10 of the IP Regs had fixed a maximum period of three years for each authorisation granted by the Department. These Regulations make amendments to the 1989 Order and to the IP Regs to remove this restriction to comply with the Directive.
- Article 13(2) of the Directive requires Member States to ensure that authorisation procedures are neither dissuasive, nor unduly complicate or delay the provision of the service. Regulation 7 of the IP Regs requires that someone applying to DETI to be an Insolvency Practitioner (IP) for the first time must have 7,000 hours of experience. Given that the applicant must have passed the Joint Insolvency Examination Board exam and therefore has

[28] http://www.opsi.gov.uk/sr/sr2009/em/nisrem_20090401_en.pdf.

already demonstrated the academic knowledge to be an IP, it is considered that the current requirement is an unjustifiable barrier to service provision. This requirement is being reduced from 7,000 to 2,000 hours, which brings it into line with what is currently required by the Insolvency Service in [England and Wales].

- Article 14 of the Directive requires that access to a service activity in a Member State must not be made subject to criteria such as place of establishment, residence, domicile or principal provision of the service activity. Article 350 of the 1989 Order required that professional bodies had to have an established address in the UK or have members who were residents of Northern Ireland. These Regulations amend Article 350 to remove these restrictions.Article 23(2) of the Directive concerns service providers already established in one Member State who want to establish in another State. The Member State where a service provider wants to establish must take into account insurance or guarantee requirements to which the provider is already subject in the first State, and may not require the provider to take out any additional insurance or guarantee if the existing insurance or guarantee can be considered equivalent or essentially comparable."[29]

• Local Government (Northern Ireland) Order 1985

Amendments to the Local Government (Northern Ireland) Order 1985 were necessary for similar reasons as described with respect to the Local Government Act (Miscellaneous Provisions) 1982 for England and Wales above. Particularly, abolition of discrimination against non-United Kingdom corporate bodies regarding sex shop licences is planned, ensuring compliance with the non-discrimination requirements of the SD. Especially, Articles 5 (1), 13 (2), 14 (1) (b) and 10 (6) SD appear to be relevant in this case.

1.5 The Relationship of the Services Directive to Primary EU Law

The relation of the SD to Articles 49 and 56 of the Treaty on the Functioning of the European Union (formerly Articles 43 and 49 EC Treaty) is not considered a problem in the United Kingdom. The SD was transposed into the Regulations almost verbatim:

"Freedom to provide services

24.—(1) A competent authority must not make access to, or the exercise of, a service activity subject to compliance with any requirement that does not respect the following principles—[...]

[29] Ibid.

(b) necessity, that is, that the requirement must be justified for reasons of public policy, public security, public health or the protection of the environment; [...]

(3) Paragraph (2) does not prevent a competent authority from—

(a) imposing requirements that are justified for reasons of public policy, public security, public health or the protection of the environment (and which comply with Paragraph (1)),"

1.6 Screening

BIS (BERR) leads on implementation in the United Kingdom and is working closely with other government departments, the devolved administrations, local authorities, regulators and others in tasks such as screening legislation for compliance with the Directive. The screening was very extensive and appears to have included all relevant acts.

Legislation was classified under the following headings:

- Not in scope and raises no requirements under the Directive (most cases).
- In scope, provisions are justified and will be retained. A report is being prepared for the Commission.
- In scope and some amendments are needed.
- Still under consideration.
- This Act was repealed.
- In scope and further assessment is being undertaken (very rare).
- In scope [department] are examining the extent of the changes which may need to be made to the application process.

The current state of the screening process can be viewed in the following files:

United Kingdom and England & Wales:
http://www.berr.gov.uk/files/file53514.pdf

Current information:
http://www.bis.gov.uk/policies/europe/eu-services-directive/legislation-and-implementation/implementation/services-directive-implementation-updates

Scotland:
http://www.berr.gov.uk/files/file53515.pdf

Northern Ireland:
http://www.berr.gov.uk/files/file53516.pdf

There are also lists of formalities (authorisations/licences/certificates/registrations) in England, Wales, Northern Ireland, and Scotland that are within the scope of the SD and BIS believes are managed by local authorities. The list of Acts being screened for compliance with the Directive shows whether the Government has justified the relevant legislation or plans to amend it. Both of these documents together with the screening flowcharts for England will help guiding local authorities through the steps involved in screening. Devolved authorities should have received screening flowcharts and reporting forms from the relevant devolved administration.[30]

There are a very small number of formalities in these tables that were initially viewed to be in scope of the SD but further analysis by the lead Government department revealed them to be out of scope of the Directive.

2 Individual Articles of the Services Directive

2.1 Article 6 SD: Point of Single Contact (POSC)

Article 6 SD provides for "points of single contact" (POSCs). This section of the report discusses how this POSC has been introduced in concreto in the United Kingdom. First of all, research was undertaken "to get an idea of what potential users might want from the [POSC], seeking views on a range of issues including scope, cost and content and the range of delivery vehicles. These views have contributed to the policy assessment and the proposed approach to the UK [POSC…]."[31] Regarding the implementation of the SD in general, the Government conducted a public consultation on its approach for implementing the SD[32] and published its official response to that consultation in June 2008.[33] This also included detailed discussions regarding the implementation of the POSC.

As one result, Regulation 38 of the Provision of Services Regulations 2009 sets out the obligation on the Secretary of State (BERR) and Her Majesty's Revenue and Customs (HMRC), the United Kingdom Tax Authority, to provide an electronic assistance facility, Businesslink.gov.uk, which is managed by HMRC, will host the United Kingdom's POSC[34] and is available under http://www.ukwelcomes.businesslink.gov.uk. Previously, it was discussed whether a completely new website should be established or whether already existent portals (UKInvest.gov or businesslink.gov.uk) should be extended to additionally cover the POSC. With respect to the costs and risks associated with the building of a new portal, it was finally agreed to extend the service of businesslink.gov.uk, which already provided the necessary functions, although "the volume of content on the Business Link site [was considered to make] it challenging to negotiate it if

[30] http://www.bis.gov.uk/policies/europe/eu-services-directive/legislation-and-implementation/information-for-local-authorities

[31] Consultation Document, p. 25; User Requirements study, available at http://www.berr.gov.uk/files/file40401.pdf.

[32] Consultation Document.

[33] Governments's response.

[34] Guidance, at 43.

English was the second language, and [...] its performance and layout was not altogether [considered to be] satisfactory."[35] Furthermore it was also criticised that "the Business Link name may be relatively unknown outside the United Kingdom".[36] The services of the POSC will be free of charge.[37]

Although the United Kingdom Government is of the opinion that the SD allows Member States to have more than one POSC, there will be only one electronic POSC for the entire United Kingdom. While it was understood that there "may well be differences in how rules are applied in different parts of the United Kingdom, [it was not thought that] this necessitated the creation of separate POSCs".[38] Especially it was assumed that "if there were to be several POSCs, there would need to be links between them, maybe through a central [United Kingdom POSC] entry point. This would be necessary so that information on providing a service in different parts of the United Kingdom was available through all [POSCs] and to cope with service providers operating in more than one area."[39] Furthermore, "the User Requirements Study [see above] noted that regional and sectoral differences would need to be catered for but that there were benefits from having just one POSC in the [United Kingdom]".[40] In particular the devolved administrations in Scotland, Wales, and Northern Ireland confirmed that they were content with the proposal for a single POSC covering the entire United Kingdom, although details and financial implications had to be worked out further.[41]

There appears to be no relocation of administrative competences. This may be due to the agreed concept of the POSC as 'Pro-active Signposting'. It was discussed whether the POSC should only constitute a 'point of information' or a 'point of decision' or something in between the two. In this regard, the Government explained its understanding that a "fully encapsulated service (point of decision) would see the POSC authorising the provision of a very wide range of services. This sort of 'one-stop-shop' would enable users of the POSC to access all necessary information and monitor the progress of authorisation requests until the POSC takes a decision on them. As a result service providers would only need to interact with the POSC, which would undertake the complete authorisation process. However, it would also require the POSC to take on responsibilities currently performed by the competent authorities, thereby either replacing them or providing duplicate procedures. This would make high demands on staff and resources for the POSC, greatly increasing the cost of delivery."[42] "At the other extreme the POSC could [have been established to] simply provide a 'list of links' (point of information) to the relevant

35 Consultation Document, p. 11.

36 Ibid.

37 Guidance, at 52.

38 Consultation Document, p. 33.

39 Ibid.

40 Consultation Document, p. 33.

41 Ibid.

42 Consultation Document, p. 27.

competent authority websites. Whilst relatively cheap and easy to establish, it was assumed that such a system would not meet the SD's requirements, as it would mean the user would have to establish what the relevant requirements were him or herself."[43] Therefore a pure 'point of information' was considered not to comply with the SD. However, the idea of the establishment of a complete 'point of decision' was rejected with respect to costs and complexity as well as it was considered that a system of this nature is not necessary to comply with the SD and therefore such an approach was considered to be "overly ambitious at this stage".[44] Thus, a way in the middle was chosen. The 'Pro-active Signposting' approach "constitutes more than just a list of links, but not incorporating all the functionality into one system. Under this approach, the POSC will help the user [1] to identify what licences and permissions were needed, [2] to identify the information required by the relevant competent authorities, and then [3] to apply to the appropriate authorities. In effect, the POSC will facilitate a seamless electronic journey from information gathering through to completion of requests for authorisations. It will also be possible to monitor progress of applications with competent authorities through such a POSC. This will achieve some of the benefits of a "point of decision" without the duplication of responsibilities."[45]

Therefore, the POSC will work in a way presented in the flowcharts published on the BIS website regarding 'Competent Authorities'[46] as well as 'Local Authorities.'[47] These flowcharts show that the POSC is only one possible starting point of the electronic procedure. In this regard it is relevant to clarify that here 'POSC' mcans the newly designed part of businesslink.gov.uk under www.ukwelcomes.businesslink.gov.uk, which is available using the general EU portal. It is "designed specifically with the international service provider in mind" and "comes with a "UK Welcomes Business" header."[48] The businesslink.gov.uk starting point is directly accessed without using the EU portal and the "UK Welcomes Business" part and therefore not considered the 'real' POSC.

Her Majesty's Revenue and Customs (already existing) will mange the POSC on behalf of the Government.[49]

However, the flowcharts mentioned above show that 'Competent Authorities' and 'Local Authorities' responsible for the certain procedures remain responsible for conducting the administrative procedures. They also have to provide the relevant information and forms, either through their own online frontend or through the POSC:

---

[43] Ibid.

[44] Consultation Document, p. 27.

[45] Ibid, p. 28.

[46] http://www.bis.gov.uk/files/file51631.doc.

[47] http://www.bis.gov.uk/files/file51630.doc.

[48] Guidance, at 49.

[49] Guidance, at 56.

"The UK's P[O]SC is set up to have two 'sides'. The business facing side, where service providers can access information and apply for authorisations and the competent authority facing side where authorities are able to access [and manage] applications made by business on businesslink.gov.uk. The competent authority side is called the Electronic Licence Management System (ELMS). [The] ELMS contains detailed guidance on what competent authorities need to do to link up to businesslink.gov.uk (and to set up and manage applications). ELMS can be found on: http://elmsportal.businesslink.gov.uk/."[50]

Competent authorities must put the relevant authorisation online through businesslink.gov.uk. On the website there are two solutions available to them. First, they can choose to incorporate an electronic form on their own website enabling a service provider to apply and pay for an authorisation. The POSC on businesslink.gov.uk will link directly to that form. The website and electronic form will need to comply with all the relevant requirements of the Provision of Service Regulations 2009 and they will need to provide the correct deep links. Second, the competent authorities can also choose not to put the electronic form(s) on their own website. If this solution is chosen, a form can be incorporated on businesslink.gov.uk. Competent authorities will be able to include information on fees, timescales, whether tacit authorisation applies and contact details. They will also be able to access and manage any application received through this route.[51]

It is the competent authority's responsibility to ensure that their own website continues to meet the information requirements set out in the Provision of Services Regulations 2009. They have to ensure that their "authority's own information, for example, any changes to fees, the time limits to process an application, tacit authorisation and contact details, is kept up to date"[52] on their website and via ELMS if they are using the forms held on businesslink.gov.uk. Furthermore, "[they] should also ensure that [their] 'web portal officer' maintains [their] web links to businesslink.gov.uk via updates to LocalDirectGov."[53]

'Local Authorities' "need to ensure that service providers can obtain all licences, authorisation schemes, approvals etc., that they require to operate their service, through the P[O]SC and ensure that the information is accurate and kept current."[54] Regarding the existence of their own online frontend, local authorities "will be required to supply 'deep links' to their sites, so that anyone requiring information on a particular regime is sent directly to the relevant web page and does not have to navigate the Local Authority site."[55] However, "the P[O]SC is

---

[50] Guidance for Departments and Competent Authorities on the Provision of Services Regulations 2009, http://www.bis.gov.uk/assets/biscore/europe/docs/10-568-what-to-do-if-your-work-affects-service-businesses.pdf, at 54.

[51] Ibid, at 56.

[52] Guidance, supra, note 50, at 67.

[53] Ibid.

[54] EU Services Directive Guidance to Local Authorities, http://www.bis.gov.uk/files/file50026.pdf, at 12e.

[55] Ibid.

not a replacement for a Local Authority's back office technology."[56] "BIS (ex-BERR) is committed to offering an open, published interface to Local Authorities and their IT suppliers, so that data can be automatically transferred between the POSC and back office systems. [...] For any one regime, Local Authorities must elect to either supply their own online service or use the BIS service; however, they can readily swap between the two and use a combination of both channels to serve all their regimes."[57]

Private partners, especially certain business representative organisations and trade bodies were generally included in the consultation process. Furthermore, the government plans to consider, "whether the inclusion of access to private sector business advisors would bring added value to potential P[O]SC users and if so how and when to incorporate this. The Government does not rule out the possibility of the private sector being involved in the delivery of some support services within the P[O]SC."[58] However, it is not clear in how far this was actually implemented at the time of launching the POSC.

BERR and HMRC are responsible under the Crown Proceedings Act 1947 according to the general principles. The Regulations contain no provision on liability. However, the Government's response to the consultation procedure states that: "The situation is complicated because the P[O]SC is likely to rely on information from a range of sources both public and private. We will do our utmost to ensure information is as accurate as possible. However, we also do not wish to exclude third party information that may be of benefit to new service providers, but over the content of which the Government has limited control. In view of the responses, the Government will investigate further options (including alternatives suggested for disclaimer wording) for dealing with the situation where information obtained through the P[O]SC proves to be inaccurate or incomplete. In doing so, it will be important to bear in mind existing legal constraints as well as developments being considered as part of the Enterprise Review led by the Better Regulation Executive. Existing arrangements in relation to the Mutual Recognition of Professional Qualifications area will also need to be considered in this context."[59]

2.2 Article 7 SD: Right to Information

On the question whether the "rights to information" were extended in United Kingdom legislation during the transposition process the 'Transposition Note'

[56] EU Services Directive Guidance to Local Autorities, supra, note 54.

[57] Ibid.

[58] Government's response, p. 11.

[59] Ibid, p. 18.

regarding the Provision of Services Regulations 2009[60] provides that generally, "[t]hese Regulations do more than is necessary to implement the Directive only in the following areas:

- Regulation 5(4) limits the definition of 'provider' in regulation 4 to those established in an EEA state, in accordance with Article 4.2 of the Directive, but this limitation does not apply to Part 2 of the Regulations (Duties of Service Providers). This means that anyone providing a service in the UK is subject to Part 2 of the Regulations, regardless of whether they are established in an EEA state. The purpose is to ensure that recipients in the UK will benefit uniformly from the provisions in Part 2.
- Part 3 of the Regulations (Duties of Competent Authorities in relation to Provision of Services in United Kingdom) transposes Chapter III, which contains provisions on the freedom of establishment for providers from another Member State. Although Chapter III only applies to situations where there is a cross-border element, we have extended the provisions in Part 3 to cover a provider of UK origin supplying services to a recipient of UK origin. Therefore Part 3 applies even where there is no cross-border element.
- Regulation 33 transposes Article 23.2, which requires Member States to recognise equivalent or essentially comparable professional liability insurance or guarantees held by a provider in another Member State where the provider is established. The duty in Article 23.2 benefits only providers establishing in the UK, not those operating temporarily. In contrast, regulation 33 extends the duty to both these categories of provider. The purpose is to ensure that providers operating temporarily enjoy the benefit of having their existing insurance recognised, as those establishing in the UK will do.
- Regulations 31(2) and 31(3), which transpose Article 5.3, apply where a competent authority requires a provider or recipient to supply a certificate, attestation or any other document proving that a requirement has been satisfied.

The first sentence of Article 5.3 requires the competent authority to accept any document from another Member State which serves an equivalent purpose or from which it is clear that the requirement has been satisfied. Regulation 31 (2), which transposes this provision, requires the competent authority to accept any such document, regardless of whether it is from another Member State or not. This takes into account that the documents which prove that particular requirements have been satisfied may differ between England, Wales, Scotland and Northern Ireland. In these circumstances, the relevant competent authority would be required to accept the document under Regulation 31 (2).

The second sentence of Article 5.3 prohibits the competent authority from requiring a document from another Member State to be produced in its original

[60] Transposition Note available at: http://www.berr.gov.uk/policies/europe/eu-services-directive/legislation-and-implementation; also included in the previously mentioned 'Explanatory Memorandum', n. 5.

form (subject to the derogations in regulation 31 (3)(a) and (b). Regulation 31 (3), which transposes this provision, prohibits the competent authority from requiring such a document to be produced in its original form (subject to the derogations), regardless of whether it is from another Member State or not. This means that it would be open to a competent authority to require a document from the United Kingdom to be produced in its original form in circumstances where the derogations in regulation 31 (3)(a) or (b) apply.

Otherwise, these Regulations do what is necessary to implement the Directive, including making consequential changes to some domestic legislation to ensure its coherence in the area to which they apply. Further consequential changes will be included in other instruments or as a result of administrative changes."[61]

Article 7 SD is implemented by Regulations 36, 37, 38 (1), and 38 (2) of the Provision of Services Regulations 2009. Regulation 36 requires competent authorities to provide the stipulated information, which should be clear and unambiguous and kept up to date, while Regulation 38 (1) provides for its inclusion in the electronic assistance facility which will comprise the United Kingdom's POSC. Regulation 37 sets out an obligation to respond to requests for information. Regulation 38 (2) provides for a support facility within the POSC.[62]

2.3 Article 8 SD: Procedures by Electronic Means

Information entered onto the site by service providers (applicants) will only be used in accordance with the law, including data protection legislation and legislation regulating HMRC functions, for example, to further an application made through the site or as agreed on registering with the service.[63] Businesslink.gov.uk will provide a range of support services, which will primarily focus on enabling service providers to resolve any issues themselves. This will be done via an extensive set of FAQs and by providing contact details of trade bodies and other organisations that have expertise in particular services and sectors available on the site.[64] If users have technical issues using busninesslink.gov.uk or have any queries that fall outside the areas covered by the "self-serve" help service, they will be able to request further advice and guidance online.[65] Competent authorities are legally obliged to keep information provided through businesslink.gov.uk accurate and up-to-date.[66] In addition, competent authorities will provide through businesslink.gov.uk details of their complaints mechanisms and the options for

[61] Ibid.

[62] Transposition Note, supra, note 60.

[63] Guidance, at 56.

[64] Guidance, at 58.

[65] Guidance, at 61.

[66] Guidance, at 61.

redress available to users.[67] The use of the site is subject to businesslink.gov.uk's terms and conditions.[68]

Before the transposition of the SD the use of electronic procedures varied within the United Kingdom. However, it appears that the use of electronic procedures had been already well developed, especially with regard to the central government.

Service providers will be able to choose whether to apply online or use existing non-electronic means of applying. There is no requirement to use businesslink.gov.uk to apply online. The businesslink.co.uk web site will simply provide an alternative that will enable service providers to apply remotely if they wish to do so.[69] They may decide on the method that suits them best.[70]

2.4 Article 9 SD: Authorisation Schemes

Part 3 of the Provision of Services Regulations 2009 sets out the conditions under which a United Kingdom competent authority can make access to, or carry out a service activity in scope, subject to an authorisation scheme. Any requirement obliging service providers to hold a licence or to obtain some sort of approval before providing their service must meet these conditions. An authorisation scheme can only be imposed if, broadly speaking: the scheme is nondiscriminatory; it can be justified by overriding reasons relating to the public interest, such as public policy, public security, or public health; and the objective of the authorisation cannot be attained by less restrictive means.[71] This principle is set out in more detail in Regulation 14. It applies to the United Kingdom businesses and businesses seeking to establish themselves in the United Kingdom.[72]

There are many different forms of formalities including authorisations, licences, certificates, and registrations in England, Wales, Northern Ireland, and Scotland. Some of these are within the scope of the Directive and BIS believes are managed by local authorities. The list of acts being screened for compliance with the Directive shows whether the government has justified the relevant legislation or plans to amend it (see above 1.6.). There is no German style Administrative Procedures Act in any of the jurisdictions of the United Kingdom. The authorisation regime is provided in the specific act or regulation or local standing order regulating a particular service activity (for example provision of care homes, architectural services, etc.). This would mean that the relevant rules are spread over 6,000 items of national

[67] Guidance, at 62.
[68] Guidance, at 63.
[69] Guidance, at 55.
[70] Guidance, at 44.
[71] Guidance, at 66.
[72] Guidance, at 67.

legislation.[73] Some of these authorisation schemes, especially those at the level of the Whitehall and the devolved governments, are purely bureaucratic; civil servants checking the requirements of the specific act and then granting the authorisation or rejecting the application. Other procedures on activities with a local impact in particular involve decisions of licence committees, which form part of the council of local authorities. According to the government, "relatively few requirements [...] need to be amended to make them compatible with the Directive."[74] There are lists of legislation that needed to be changed.[75]

Additionally, some details regarding certain amendments of legislation above may be relevant in this case.

Regarding the definition of 'authorisation scheme', Regulation 4 of the Provision of Services Regulations 2009 indeed appears to include also mere notification requirements, which may be qualified as being broader than the definition in the SD, which expressly requires a formal or implied decision. However, this may be dependent on the understanding of the notion 'decision'. A notification may also be qualified as followed by the 'decision' of whether a certain notification contains the complete and satisfying information or simply the 'decision' to allow the provision of the service because of the notification, so that there does need not to be an assessment before the relevant decision is taken. However, there is no information about how the term 'decision' is understood. Nevertheless, the above-mentioned Transposition Note does not mention a deviation from the SD in this case, despite the fact that it claims to completely list the deviations. This may support the understanding that no difference in relation to the SD was intended.

The Provision of Services Regulations 2009 appears to include mere notification requirements; however, it is not clear whether a deviation from Articles 9 et seq. SD was intended (see above).

2.5 Article 10 SD: Conditions for the Granting of Authorisation

Article 10 (3) SD implies the recognition of authorisations granted by other Member States. Regulation 15 Provision of Services Regulations 2009 provides that, in general, service providers should not have to satisfy criteria when applying for a licence when they already met equivalent or essentially comparable requirements or controls in the United Kingdom or another EEA State.[76] Service providers may be asked to assist a competent authority in determining whether this is the case by providing necessary information that the authority may ask the service provider to provide. Regulation 15 (4) provides that the service provider

[73] Guidance, at 100.

[74] Ibid.

[75] Thanks to Dr. Adrian Hunt (University of Birmingham) for discussing this question with us.

[76] Guidance, at 68.

must provide the requested information within a reasonable time limit of being asked to do so; otherwise the competent authority may subject the service provider to duplicate requirements.[77] If a United Kingdom competent authority does authorise the access to or carrying out of a service activity, certain requirements, a list of which is set out in full in Regulation 21, are now prohibited.[78] Requirements now prohibited according to this list include: "specifying that a business's registered office or main establishment must be in the UK or a particular area of the UK", "requiring that a business's staff, shareholders, management members or supervisory bodies are British or are resident in the UK", "preventing a business from being established in the UK if it is also established in another EEA state" and "prohibiting a business from being entered on the registers or enrolled with professional bodies or associations of the UK if it already is in another EEA state". In addition, Regulation 22 provides that United Kingdom competent authorities can only impose certain other requirements if these are nondiscriminatory, necessary, and proportionate.[79]

The requirement of granting authorisations which give access to the service activity, or to exercise that activity, throughout the whole of the national territory, was a potential problem because of the devolved governments in Scotland, Wales, and Northern Ireland. Moreover, local authorities will normally only be able to grant authorisation for their local territory. However, Regulation 15 (5) Provision of Services Regulations 2009 requires that "[a]n authorisation granted by a competent authority under an authorisation scheme must enable the provider of the service to have access to the service activity, or to exercise that activity, throughout the United Kingdom, including by means of setting up agencies, subsidiaries, branches or offices, except where an authorisation for each individual establishment or a limitation of the authorisation to a particular part or area of the United Kingdom is justified by an overriding reason relating to the public interest." Moreover, Regulation 15 (6) states that "[i]n the case of a competent authority whose functions relate only to part of the United Kingdom, references in paragraph (5) to the United Kingdom are to that part of the United Kingdom." Therefore this problem appears to have been solved simply by avoiding any problems through the recognition of limitations of competences. The fact that 'overriding reason relating to the public interest' is already mentioned in Regulation 15 (5), but not referred to in Regulation 15 (6), may lead to the conclusion that the exemption in Regulation 15 (6) is not based on this approach. However, in comparison to the clear wording of Article 10 (4) SD the territorial limitations of competences of the relevant authorities nevertheless appear to have been regarded as 'overriding reason relating to the public interest' as no other exemption is mentioned. There is, however, no information regarding a discussion of this aspect, especially the documents regarding the consultation procedure do not address this problem.

---

77 Guidance, at 69.

78 Guidance, at 70 and 71.

79 Guidance, at 72.

According to Article 10 (5) SD the applicant is entitled to get an authorisation once all conditions for the authorisations have been met. The questions of (1) a difference to existing administrative laws, (2) the extent to which courts will review the decisions by the granting of authorisation, and (3) whether courts will also review the use of discretion by authorities, depend on the specific regime. However, this entitlement already existed before the implementation of the SD in the United Kingdom. Depending on the regime of the specific Act or Regulation, there is often a right of appeal which is different from judicial review, which can be sought once the appeal was not successful. The appeal also allows the revisiting of the merits of the case. The specific statutory basis of the authorisation regime might limit the grounds for appeal but will normally be wider than those for judicial review. For example, for an alcohol licence, there is a right to appeal to a Crown Court.[80] Once this right to appeal is exhausted the applicant can seek judicial review in the High Court.[81] Some regimes do not include a right to appeal. A more recent development is that private bodies exercising a public function, for example dealing with certain authorisations, will be subject to judicial review. The focus is on the (public) nature of the function they are exercising.[82]

There is an obligation to fully reason the decision of the authority in Article 10 (6) SD. Administrative law in the jurisdictions of the United Kingdom is mainly common law-based, based on case law. There is no overall and absolute obligation to fully reason decisions. However, many of the specific statutory regimes regulating individual authorisation regimes, but not all, contain a duty to give full reasons. This has increasingly been becoming the norm in recently created or amended statutes. The consequence of not giving full reasons is that it constitutes a ground for judicial review.[83]

The SD did not alter the allocation of administrative competences with regard to granting of authorisations either; see Article 10 (7), like Article 6 (2) SD on the POSC. It appears that there has been no reallocation of competences through the introduction of the POSC, which is intended as an assistance facility not as the 'competent authority'.

2.6 Article 11 SD: Duration of Authorisation

The principle of unlimited validity of authorisations is implemented in a generally applicable rule in Regulation 16 Provision of Services Regulations 2009 which closely follows the wording of Article 11 (1) SD, including the exceptions:

[80] Formerly the Magistrate's Court.

[81] The High Court is present in many larger cities of England and Wales and Northern Ireland.

[82] Thanks to Dr. Adrian Hunt (University of Birmingham) for discussing this question with us.

[83] Thanks to Dr. Adrian Hunt (University of Birmingham) for discussing this question with us.

"**Duration of authorisation**

16.—(1) An authorisation granted to the provider of a service by a competent authority under an authorisation scheme must be for an indefinite period, except where—

(a) the authorisation—
(i) is automatically renewed, or
(ii) is subject only to the continued fulfilment of requirements,
(b) the number of available authorisations is limited by an overriding reason relating to the public interest, or
(c) a limited authorisation period can be justified by an overriding reason relating to the public interest."

2.7 Article 12 SD: Selection from Among Several Candidates

Article 12 SD, regarding the selection from among several applicants, was implemented in Regulation 17 Provision of Services Regulations 2009 which partly follows the wording of the Directive:

"**Selection from among several candidates**

17.—(1)This regulation applies where the number of authorisations available from a competent authority under an authorisation scheme for a given service activity is limited because of the scarcity of available natural resources or technical capacity.
(2) The selection procedure established by the competent authority must fully secure impartiality and transparency, including, in particular, adequate publicity about the launch, conduct and completion of the procedure.
(3) Authorisation granted by the competent authority—
(a) must be granted for an appropriate limited period, and
(b) may not—
(i) be open to automatic renewal, or
(ii) confer any other advantage on a previously authorised candidate or on a person having any particular links with such a candidate.
(4) Subject to paragraph (2) and to regulations 14 and 15, a competent authority may, in establishing the rules for the selection procedure, take into account—
(a) considerations of public health,
(b) social policy objectives,
(c) the health and safety of employees or self-employed persons,
(d) the protection of the environment,
(e) the preservation of cultural heritage, and
(f) other overriding reasons relating to the public interest, in conformity with Community law."

2.8 Article 13 SD: Authorisation Procedures and Tacit Authorisation

Regulation 19 (1) Provision of Services Regulations 2009 provides that applications for authorisation must be processed as quickly as possible and, in any event within a reasonable time period from the time when all documentation has been submitted. Moreover, according to Regulation 19 (2) that time period must be made public in advance. These are the requirements of the legislator. The precise duration of the procedure is then determined by the responsible authority within these parameters set by the legislator. In the context of a number of specialised laws the time periods are prescribed by the legislator. However, this is the exception.

The national legislator did not establish a general rule on the duration of the procedures. The rule is that of Regulation 19 outlined above. It is applicable within the scope of application of the SD. There is no fixed duration.

Although there is no prescribed duration, according to Regulation 19 (3), (4) Provision of Services Regulations 2009 the duration (period) can be extended once for a limited time if this is justified by the complexity of the issue.

The SD contains the principle of a 'tacit (fictitious) authorisation'. This concept, called 'authorisation by default' is not unknown but not common in the jurisdictions of the United Kingdom. Hence it is felt that the introduction in the Regulation will lead to a major change in the system, if used by applicants in practice. A major problem might be for applicants obtaining the necessary insurances with only an 'authorisation by default'.[84]

According to Regulation 19 (5) Provision of Services Regulations 2009, in case the authority does not respond to the filed application within the prescribed time, the authorisation is "deemed to have been granted to the provider."[85] It appears the tacit authorisation has formal as well as substantive effects.

The same rules apply to tacit (fictitious) authorisations which apply to formally granted administrative authorisations (e.g., nullity, revocability, or as regards imposing collateral/additional conditions later-on, etc.).

2.9 Articles 14, 15, 16 SD

The following rules where included in the Provision of Services Regulations 2009 to transpose Articles 14, 15, 16 and SD:

[84] Thanks to Dr. Adrian Hunt (University of Birmingham) for discussing this question with us.

[85] Guidance, at 89.

"Part 5 Recipients of Services

Restrictions on use of service supplied by provider established in another EEA state

29.—(1) A competent authority may not impose on the recipient of a service any requirements which restrict the use of the service as supplied from another EEA state by a provider established in that state.

(2) The requirements referred to in paragraph (1) include in particular—

(a) an authorisation scheme;

(b) a discriminatory limit on the grant of financial assistance to a recipient by reason of the fact that the provider is established in another EEA state or by reason of the location of the place at which the service is provided.

Requirements based on nationality or place of residence

30.—(1) A competent authority may not subject recipients of a service who are individuals to discriminatory requirements based on their nationality or place of residence.

(2) The provider of a service may not, in the general conditions of access to a service which the provider makes available to the public at large, include discriminatory provisions relating to the place of residence of recipients who are individuals.

(3) Paragraph (2) does not apply to differences in conditions of access which are directly justified by objective criteria."

The Government has screened over 6,000 items of national legislation to check whether any requirements which are prohibited by the Directive exist and, where they do, to justify or abolish them.[86] As a result of regulatory simplification work in recent years, the Government has indentified relatively few requirements that need to be amended to make them compatible with the Directive. Annex B to the Provision of Services Regulations 2009 sets out the legislation that will be changed. In conjunction with this, the devolved administrations in Scotland, Wales, and Northern Ireland have been screening their legislation on devolved matters. Details of any requirements that need to be changed can also be found in Annex B to the Provision of Services Regulations 2009. Local authorities throughout the United Kingdom have also been reviewing their locally used acts, bylaws, procedural rules and other requirements that they place on business to ensure that they are allowed by the Directive. Any amendment that they are making to their requirements will be communicated by the local authorities to the business community.

Any new requirement or legislation that is introduced or amended and affects the access to or exercise of a service activity will need to be screened by the relevant Government department or competent authority and the outcome reported to the European Commission. Requirements that are prohibited under the Directive will be abolished, those that are not will be adopted.[87]

[86] Guidance, at 100.

[87] Guidance, at 103.

2.10 Articles 14–19 SD

The rules on prohibited requirements regarding the establishment of service providers (Articles 14, 15 SD) were implemented in Regulations 21 and 22 Provision of Services Regulations 2009. Regulation 14 implements the rules on authorisation schemes regarding the freedom of establishment laid down in Article 9 SD. Regulation 24 implements the rules laid down in Article 16 SD, Regulation 25 implements Article 17 SD. Regulations 26 and 44 contain measures allowing competent authorities to take action in spite of the rules in Regulation 24 in exceptional circumstances, if necessary to ensure the safety of services and therefore implement Article 18 SD. Article 19 SD is implemented by Regulation 29.[88]

2.11 Articles 22–27 SD

Article 22 SD regarding information requirements is implemented in Regulations 7–11 Provision of Services Regulations 2009, Article 23 SD regarding professional liability is implemented in Regulation 33, Article 24 SD regarding commercial communications is implemented in Regulation 34, Article 25 SD on multidisciplinary services is implemented in Regulation 35 and the rules of Article 27 SD on the settlement of disputes are implemented in Regulations 10 and 12. Regarding Article 26 (2) SD the Transposition Note states that "specific provision to implement is not necessary as information on certain labels and quality marks is already easily accessible on consumer websites."[89]

2.12 Articles 28 *ff.* SD: Administrative Cooperation

As far as general provisions on transnational administrative assistance are concerned, no previous national regime does appear to have existed in the United Kingdom. There were only certain areas where authorities were already obliged to perform transnational administrative assistance due to the implementation of Directives concerning specialised fields of administration. For example, certain changes were required with respect to the implementation of the Mutual Recognition of Professional Qualifications Directive.[90]

The Provision of Services Regulations 2009 introduced a general regime of transnational administrative assistance (see exact implementation below); however, these provisions do not appear to have a clear impact on domestic administrative

[88] 'Transposition Note', n 5 and 60.

[89] Ibid.

[90] Government's response, p. 23.

assistance, as this seems not to be regulated in a general regime but only in certain specialised areas, where this is regarded to be necessary. Generally, it is assumed that competent authorities only have to act within their already existing statutory powers.[91]

No provisions regarding a financial compensation of cross-border assistance were introduced. This may be due to the fact that the Government does not expect "any great increase in workload, especially as mutual assistance already occurs to some degree cross-border and within the [United Kingdom]. Furthermore, given the already significant degree of liberalisation in the [United Kingdom] services market and the fact that the [country] already attracts many incoming service providers, [they] do not anticipate a sudden surge in workload caused by a disproportionate increase in the number of incoming service providers applying to competent authorities at the moment when the Directive is implemented."[92] Furthermore, the Government emphasises the mutual character of this assistance and expects an increase in effectiveness and efficiency regarding the cooperation between competent authorities because of the SD.[93]

No new rules were adopted and no changes took place regarding provisions on data protection. This may have been caused by the fact that by reference to Article 43 SD it was assumed that the United Kingdom's rules on the protection of personal data (Data Protection Act 1998) can be respected when implementing the SD. It was especially emphasised that "[i]n meeting the mutual assistance obligations of the Services Directive, competent authorities may be acting as data processors or data controllers. Any bodies which are United Kingdom data controllers, or data processors acting on behalf of United Kingdom data controllers, will need to comply with the Data Protection Act 1998 and other relevant UK and EU legislation."[94] This was considered to result in the practice that "[c]ompetent authorities will need to ensure that in the communication of any personal data to other competent authorities, they do so with regard to the seventh principle of data protection, 'that appropriate technical and organisational measures shall be taken against unauthorised or unlawful processing of personal data and against accidental loss or destruction of, or damage to, personal data.' Security of data communication [...] need[s] to be appropriate to the data being transferred, and have regards to the state of technological development and the cost of implementing measures."[95] In this regard, the establishment of the IMI portal was considered to be intended to comply with these requirements.[96]

---

[91] Ibid, p. 22.

[92] Government 's response, p. 21.

[93] Ibid.

[94] Consultation Document, p. 39.

[95] Ibid.

[96] Consultation Document, p. 39.

2.13 *Article 29 SD: Mutual Assistance—General Obligations for the Member State of Establishment*

Article 29 SD was implemented in Regulation 40 Provision of Service Regulations 2009 which provides:

"Provision of information where provider established in UK

40.—(1) This regulation applies in relation to a provider of a service who is established in the United Kingdom and is providing the service in another EEA state.

(2) The competent authority must, when requested to do so by a relevant authority in another EEA state, supply information about the provider to that authority.

(3) The information referred to in paragraph (2) includes in particular—

(a) confirmation that the provider is established in the United Kingdom;

(b) whether, to the competent authority's knowledge, the provider is authorised to provide the service.

(4) The competent authority must, when requested to do so by a relevant authority in another EEA state—

(a) carry out checks, inspections or investigations in relation to the provider,

(b) inform the requesting authority of the results, and

(c) if it thinks it appropriate to take any measures in relation to the provider, inform the requesting authority of those measures.

(5) Nothing in paragraph (4) permits or requires a competent authority to do anything which it could not otherwise lawfully do."

There is no information on any part of this provision being seen as problematic. However, it is submitted as paragraph (5) "Nothing in paragraph (4) permits or requires a competent authority to do anything which it could not otherwise lawfully do" represents a safeguard clause for any provision of national law that might prevent the competent authority from carrying out activities under paragraph (4).

2.14 *Problems and Discourses on Administrative Cooperation*

Chapter VI of the SD on administrative cooperation was transposed in the United Kingdom in Regulations 39–44 Provision of Services Regulations 2009. Some of the relevant provisions of the SD were regarded as not requiring implementation by the Provision of Services Regulations 2009. Where Regulation 29 (1) implements Article 28 (1) SD, Article 28 (2) SD is not implemented in the Regulations due to the fact that "the United Kingdom's national liaison point will be located in the Department for Business, Innovation and Skills." Article 28 (3) SD is implemented by Regulation 39 (2) and (3), but Article 28 (4) was considered not to require implementation as a "specific provision is not necessary as Member States are required to act in compliance with their existing national laws [and] [competent authorities] can exercise existing powers to obtain information from providers." Article 28 (5) SD is implemented by Regulation 39 (3), Article 28 (6) SD by Regulation 39 (4), Article 28 (7) SD by Regulation 39 (5), Article 29 (1) SD by Regulation 40 (1)-(3), Article 29 (2) SD by Regulation 40 (4)-(5) and Article 29 (3) SD by Regulation 42. However, Articles 30 (1) and (3) SD were not implemented as a specific provision was not regarded to be necessary and equally Article 30 (2) was not implemented as "Clause 127 of the Coroners and Justice Bill disapplies the limitations on penalties that can be imposed in regulations implementing the Directive via the European Communities Act 1972. There is therefore power to make regulations so that [competent authorities] can take action against UK-based providers on an equal footing whether offences are committed in the UK or elsewhere in the EEA." Article 31 SD is implemented by Regulation 41, Article 32 SD by Regulation 42, Article 33 by Regulation 43, and Article 35 by Regulation 27 and 44.[97]

During the consultation process the Government stated further that it intended to look "at the statutory regimes of the United Kingdom's competent authorities to identify where, if at all, any changes [needed] to be made."[98] However, when compared to the above (1.4) changes regarded necessary to implement the SD, it appears that apart from an amendment of the Employment Agencies Act 1973 no further amendments of existing legislation were assumed necessary. Nevertheless, it needs to be emphasised that any disclosure of information is regarded as having to comply with data protection rules.[99] Furthermore, in some cases the changes already made under the Mutual Recognition of Professional Qualifications Directive were considered to be sufficient and therefore no further changes were regarded necessary under the SD.[100]

Regarding the Internal Market Information system (IMI), required to be established by the Commission under Article 34 SD, the following four options were discussed as to how competent authorities should register on the IMI system:

> "**Option 1:** all competent authorities are legally obliged to register with IMI. This would ensure full coverage of competent authorities and reduce central costs which would be faced by a national liaison point forwarding on mutual assistance requests to non-registered competent authorities".
>
> **Option 2:** only large, national regulators are obliged to register with IMI. This could mean competent authorities who might only respond to mutual assistance requests infrequently, would not need to retain knowledge as to how to use IMI. However some competent authorities, while only local in scope, might still face reasonably frequent mutual assistance requests.
>
> **Option 3:** individual competent authorities are given the option as to whether to register with IMI. The requirement to respond to mutual assistance requests from other competent authorities will be a legal obligation, and as IMI should be the simplest way to do so, those

97 'Transposition Note', n 5 and 60.

98 Consultation Document, p. 38.

99 Government's response, p. 23.

100 Ibid.

> competent authorities who face a reasonable level of mutual assistance requests could be expected to seek to register on IMI themselves. This should mean that only those competent authorities for whom access to IMI would be an advantage, would be registered on IMI.
> **Option 4:** no competent authorities are registered with IMI. This would mean that all queries requiring use of the IMI system would have to be directed through the national liaison point. This would be a costly approach for the national liaison point, slow down the communication process, and reduce the advantages to business of implementing the Services Directive. This option is strongly discouraged."[101]

Option 3 appears to be the chosen approach to the registration of competent authorities on IMI, as this is assumed to "give IMI the most appropriate coverage of competent authorities"[102] and it is recognised that some competent authorities "already have their own fully operational mutual assistance systems, and therefore should have the choice of whether to use IMI or not".[103] Therefore "helping competent authorities to locate their 'opposite number'", "ensuring that training is available" and "encouraging competent authorities to make use of it" will be the policy in this regard.[104] Nevertheless, the Government emphasised that "it is not proposed that the use of IMI will be made legally obligatory".[105]

2.15 Convergence Programme (Chapter VII of the Services Directive)

There was no discussion with regard to Chapter VII SD on convergence in the United Kingdom.

3 Assessment of the Impact of the Services Directive

Generally only a few changes of existing legislation were necessary in the process of transposing the SD in the United Kingdom. No relocation of competences was required to establish the POSC, the POSC could be introduced by using an already existent platform. Moreover, no legal procedural rules had to be amended in order to introduce an electronic procedure. The impact of the SD does not appear as severe as it is regarded in Germany, for example. However, great efforts with respect to the screening of legislation have been made.

The changes introduced by the implementation of the SD appear to be welcomed when looking at the official statements of the Government. Furthermore, a recent study estimated that the implementation of the SD by all Member States

[101] Consultation Document, p. 44.
[102] Ibid, p. 45.
[103] Government's response, p. 26.
[104] Ibid, p. 27.
[105] Government's response, p. 26.

will bring considerable benefits to the United Kingdom.[106] The effort made when transposing the SD, most notably the serious screening efforts from the central Government level down to the local authorities, public consultation procedures in order to enact the Provision of Services Regulation 2009 including private parties, extensive information policy regarding practice guides for competent authorities, local authorities and businesses, and regularly implementation updates, leads to the conclusion that more than a minimum transposition has taken place in the United Kingdom and that so far this transposition is generally welcomed. However, due to the implementation deadline and costs, some options were not taken on board (e.g., regarding the POSC). Nevertheless, it cannot be taken for granted that these options would have resulted in a substantially different transposition.

The most important aspect appears to be the complete screening of legislation and other formalities in order to comply with EU law, although only a few changes were considered to be necessary. Furthermore, the establishment of a general obligation to provide electronic procedures in conjunction with the introduction of the POSC is important. However, given the already widespread use of electronic procedures by the United Kingdom authorities, this may not have or does not need to have the same knock-on effect on public administration as this obligation hopefully will have in Germany.

References

For legislation, jurisprudence and websites please refer to 1.1 of the report and footnotes directly.

Department for Business, Innovation and Skills (BIS) Guidance for Business on the Provision of Services Regulations 2009. Available at: http://www.berr.gov.uk/files/file53100.pdf

Department for Business, Enterprise and Regulatory Reform (BERR) Implementing the Services Directive—Consultation Document on Implementing the EU Services Directive in the UK. Available at: http://www.bis.gov.uk/files/file42207.pdf

Department for Business, Enterprise and Regulatory Reform (BERR) Implementing the Services Directive—The Government's official response to Consultation on implementing the EU Services Directive in the UK. Available at: http://www.berr.gov.uk/files/file46592.pdf

Department for Business, Enterprise and Regulatory Reform (BERR) User Requirements study. Available at: http://www.berr.gov.uk/files/file40401.pdf

Department for Business, Innovation and Skills (BIS) What to do if your work affects service businesses—Guidance for Departments and Competent Authorities on the Provision of Services Regulations 2009. Available at: http://www.bis.gov.uk/assets/biscore/europe/docs/10-568-what-to-do-if-your-work-affects-service-businesses.pdf

Department for Business, Innovation and Skills (BIS) EU Services Directive Guidance to Local Authorities. Available at: http://www.bis.gov.uk/files/file50026.pdf

Explanatory Memorandum regarding the Provision of Services Regulations 2009, including 'Transposition Note'. Available at: http://www.opsi.gov.uk/si/si2009/em/uksiem_20092999_en.pdf

[106] http://webarchive.nationalarchives.gov.uk/+/http://www.bis.gov.uk/files/file53109.pdf.

The manu
Nature Cu
Germany.
contact Pr

Printed ar